T0188903

Outsourcing and Offshoring Business Services

Leslie P. Willcocks • Mary C. Lacity • Chris Sauer
Editors

Outsourcing and Offshoring Business Services

palgrave
macmillan

Editors
Leslie P. Willcocks
Department of Management
London School of Economics
London, United Kingdom

Mary C. Lacity
College of Business Administration
University of Missouri
Saint Louis, Missouri, USA

Chris Sauer
University of Oxford
Oxford, United Kingdom

ISBN 978-3-319-84953-9
DOI 10.1007/978-3-319-52651-5

ISBN 978-3-319-52651-5 (eBook)

Printed on acid-free paper

This Palgrave Macmillan imprint is published by Springer Nature
The registered company is Springer International Publishing AG
The registered company address is: Gewerbestrasse 11, 6330 Cham, Switzerland

Contents

List of Figures

List of Tables

1

Introduction

Leslie P. Willcocks, Mary C. Lacity and Chris Sauer

Overview

Modern organizations and their IT functions are increasingly choosing to rely on external service providers for IT hardware, software, telecommunications, cloud computing resources, and automation tools, a practice known as information technology outsourcing (ITO). Meanwhile

L.P. Willcocks (✉)
Department of Management, London School of Economics, London,
United Kingdom
e-mail: l.p.willcocks@lse.ac.uk

M.C. Lacity
University of Missouri, College of Business Administration, Saint Louis,
Missouri, USA
e-mail: mary.lacity@umsl.edu

C. Sauer
University of Oxford, Oxford, United Kingdom
e-mail: Chris.Sauer@sbs.ox.ac.uk

© The Author(s) 2017   1
L.P. Willcocks et al. (eds.), *Outsourcing and Offshoring Business
Services*, DOI 10.1007/978-3-319-52651-5_1

especially since 1999 and several landmark human resource outsourcing deals, business process outsourcing (BPO), has also increasingly spread across fundamental back office functions like finance and accounting, procurement, legal, real estate, human resources, insurance claims and general administration. By early 2014, global outsourcing contracts for ITO and BPO services exceeded US$648 billion (ITO $344 billion; BPO $304 billion), according to HFS Research. By the beginning of 2015 the combined total exceeded US $700 billion (Fersht and Snowden 2014). By the end of 2016, the global ITO and BPO services market was estimated to be US$1,007 billion (ITO $657 billion; BPO $322 billion) (Snowden and Fersht 2016). There are many, often wildly diverging, estimates on market growth. Much depends on the assumptions made. However, taking a conservative route through many estimates, we follow Snowden and Fersht (2016) in seeing the market experiencing a 2.2% ITO and a 4.0% BPO compound annual growth through 2016 to end of 2020, reflecting more activities being outsourced, and new service lines and delivery locations added.

Within these overall figures sits an offshore outsourcing market in which 2013 revenues exceeded US$100 billion in revenues. Estimates based on evidence from a variety of research analyst reports suggest this market will grow by 8–12% per year in the 2013–2018 period (Cullen et al. 2014). Offshore outsourcing revenues were estimated to exceed US$140 billion by end of 2016. Interestingly, despite the steady growth of outsourcing to become a globally recognized practice, satisfaction levels from these types of services remain quite mixed, and have done so across the evolution of the ITO, BPO and offshore markets (Lacity and Willcocks 2015).

Outsourcing has many definitions, but perhaps the simplest is: 'The handing over to a third party of the management of activities, assets and/ or people to achieve required outcomes' (Cullen et al. 2014). Outsourcing does not exhaust the ways of using external service suppliers. An alternative is to buy in resources which we define as 'employing external third party-resources to work under your management and control to achieve outcomes.' (Cullen et al. 2014). There has also been increasing use over the last twenty-five years of software packages, while cloud computing has also added 'rent' as-a-service options to the more traditional make-or-buy choices (see Willcocks et al. 2014.) Then, of course, there is always the in-house sourcing option. Indeed, recent years has seen a rise in captive centers – increasingly called global in house centers (GICs) – spread across the many now viable international locations (a history of captive center evolution appears in this collection).

In this volume, we as editors draw upon compelling papers selected from the *Journal of Information Technology* to address two major questions. The first is: what theoretical perspectives can be most effectively used for the study of sourcing practices? The second question will be especially interesting to practitioners: how does an organization leverage the ever-growing external services market to gain operational, business, and strategic advantage? But before we present the rich papers that seek to address these questions, a little history is in order. We need to frame and locate the studies within the evolution of the external service provider market that has grown from US$10 billion a year revenues in 1989 to what by 2016 has become nearly a US$1 trillion a year global industry.

Origins of the Modern ITO and BPO Services Industry

The landmark 1989 Eastman Kodak large-scale outsourcing arrangement with suppliers is usually pinpointed as marking the beginning of modern IT and business service outsourcing. From that date ITO accelerated. It reached $50 billion revenues in 1994, over US$152 billion in 2000, and over $344 billion by 2014. The early 1990s debate about the core competence of the corporation provided a context in which organizations increasingly sought to outsource 'commodity' IT, the main objectives then being to reduce costs, access expertise, and, if possible, catalyze performance.

The period 1989–1997 is often mistakenly characterized as a period of large-scale, long-term, single supplier, IT outsourcing deals. While there were several examples of these which all gained high profile, e.g., Commonwealth Bank, General Dynamics, Xerox, and UK Inland Revenue – in fact most deals were not like this, and few were single supplier – even at Eastman Kodak there were in fact three suppliers. By 2000 there were just over 120 so called IT outsourcing 'strategic alliances,' but the dominant practice (as it has continued to be) was multiple supplier outsourcing that used mid-term length (3–7 years) contracts (Lacity and Willcocks 2001). Such deals tended to focus on outsourcing stable, discrete activities that were well understood, and for which detailed contracts could be written. While this mitigated many of the risks that went with outsourcing, this did not mean that clients and suppliers had yet learned how to manage outsourcing arrangements effectively. Managing outsourcing remains a problem for many to this day, with the difficulty heightened by increasingly volatile business contexts and fast changing technologies and services.

The IT outsourcing market grew apace in the 2000s. As suppliers matured their ability to deliver IT services, more global locations became viable. At the same time clients built their confidence and competence. From around 2005 a more strategic interest in multi-sourcing also developed. Here ABN Amro set a new landmark. After cancelling prematurely a single supplier deal with EDS, the bank's deal with four suppliers in 2005 was portrayed as the dominant future pattern for strategic sourcing to follow. At the same time the period 2005–2016 saw more, smaller, shorter term contracts driving market growth. With the economic downturn from 2008, an interest in consolidating supplier numbers took place. As a result of this, the management and economic advantages of 'bundled' outsourcing – going with one supplier for several different IT and also business process services – grew. Another reason for this interest lay in the administrative and management costs of multi-sourcing models and the pressure to develop integrated technology platforms more closely aligned with business needs (Cullen et al. 2014).

So far we describe a largely IT outsourcing trajectory. Business process outsourcing (BPO) and offshoring/offshore outsourcing have been late-comers within the outsourcing phenomenon. The 1990s saw pioneering developments in both areas. As one example, in 1991 BP Exploration, the oil major, outsourced all European accounting operations to one supplier, Andersen Consulting. Accounting processes were consolidated in a single site at Aberdeen, Scotland. In 1996 BP did the same thing with its upstream, downstream and chemical businesses in the US, then moved to two outsourcing suppliers in 1999. The Aberdeen shared services center was interesting in that it attracted other oil industry clients, including Britannia Operator and Conoco. With offshoring, the 1990s saw several American and West European firms develop 'captive centers,' while others outsourced some IT activities offshore to India and elsewhere. Early examples included Baan and GE. Meanwhile Indian suppliers began to develop their capabilities and markets, examples being TCS, Infosys and Wipro. But the turning point came with the Y2K problem that materialized from 1996 onwards. To prepare for Y2K, companies needed low cost, trained resources for its resolution up against a 'drop dead' deadline. North American and European companies increasingly and successfully used Indian suppliers and locations to handle the Y2K problem, and this really did begin to put offshore models on the map from around 2000 (see Lacity and Rottman 2008; Willcocks and Lacity 2006). Offshoring remains a growing phenomenon to this day, and several chapters in this volume focus on offshoring practices, reflecting the considerable interest in academic research on this subject over the last 15 years.

Both BPO and offshoring opened up the global outsourcing market in the first decade of the new century, offering new and genuine routes to cost savings, and greater value from outsourcing. BP pioneered human resource outsourcing in 1999 in a deal with newly founded technology provider Exult. Its subsequent history suggests that this BPO arrangement went through a number of difficult challenges from which later BPO suppliers and clients learned a great deal. Another new BPO 'pure play' – Xchanging – signed similar deals, though on a joint venture basis, with The London Insurance Market and Lloyds of London (insurance administration) and BAE Systems (previously British Aerospace) (HR and indirect procurement) in 2001. Meanwhile Bank of America outsourced multiple HR activities to Accenture. From 2000 the BPO market picked up considerably. The key BPO issue was whether clients had enough confidence to outsource, even transform, their back offices against a background of a global supplier market still developing its BPO capabilities. By 2010 there had been rapid BPO expansion – the market was exceeding US$135 billion in revenues by end of that year – but there still remained massive untapped potential growth for the BPO market (Willcocks et al. 2011).

Of all the outsourcing variants offshore outsourcing saw much the fastest growth in the 2000–2010 period. India had a head start; it had developed scale and a group of major suppliers, and by 2010 dominated the global offshore market. At the same time many other countries have been actively offering services, and developing their outsourcing services industries, often most successfully with local government backing. By 2016 one could count viable offshore locations in over 120 countries worldwide, with India earning over 65% of the revenues, and the Philippines having the second largest industry, with both countries offering multiple ITO and BPO services.

One small market that began in 1997 – that of Application Service Provision (ASP) – is also worth commenting on here. This market grew during the e-business bubble of 1995–2001 and at one stage had over 300 suppliers serving mainly small and medium sized enterprises. Concerned with delivering applications, infrastructure and services on a rental basis over the Internet, this phenomenon was dubbed 'netsourcing,' (Kern et al. 2002). It grew rapidly across the 1997–2001 period, but then fell away with the bursting of the Internet bubble. However, it began to be resurrected from 2008, now with the nomenclature of 'cloud computing.' Cloud sourcing by 2016 had become a potentially massive market for as-a-service external service provision. Potentially cloud sourcing is also enormously disruptive of more traditional outsourcing models that had developed over its brief 26-year history as an industry). One reason for this is that cloud computing enables and amplifies the effects of other emerging technologies, and in particular Blockchain, social media, analytics, the internet of things, digital fabrication, robotics and the automation of knowledge work. Such developments raise fundamental questions for researchers and practitioners alike about the future shape and trajectory of the global sourcing phenomenon, and for client and service provider strategies.

The years 2015–2016 also saw the development of service automation – estimated to be a small market of less than US$5 billion in revenues to service providers by the end of 2016. However, as Willcocks and Lacity (2016) discuss, robotic process automation and cognitive automation has the potential to be very disruptive of the more conventional people-centric outsourcing model that offshore outsourcing vendors and captive centers were based on. Looking across these technological developments in cloud computing and service automation, it is probable that the speed with which they will eat into traditional ITO and BPO models and markets has been over estimated. As Snowden and Fersht (2016) suggest, it is likely that there will be a huge amount of legacy enterprise ITO and BPO business in play for a decade or more, not least to enable organizations to move increasingly in the direction of more digital operations.

On the Global Sourcing Learning Curve

When we review this rapid growth, we see that it has had several major impacts. The first is that clients and suppliers have all had to run very fast to stay up with the latest market twists, players, technologies, and potential new sources of competition and of value. Looking over this history, senior executives in both client companies and service providers have been, on the whole, short on time to think through long-term issues and requirements. The effort in getting deals done, and running them, has focused attention primarily on operations, and the day-to-day issues. This has left little energy and time for strategizing and innovation even though that is precisely what sourcing strategy and innovation require.

Secondly and relatedly, finding out what works and what does not has been, perhaps too often, a 'hard learning' experience. 'Suck-it-and-see' is not necessarily the optimal way to proceed, especially if committing to large-scale, possibly 10-year contracts, and potentially transformational activities. As a third point, much has been achieved, but the creation of a body of knowledge about outsourcing, covering such issues as strategizing, governance, contracting, pricing, relationships, measurement, process optimization, is still very much work in progress. As we said, this is not helped by dynamic business contexts, rapid changes in the supply industry and the speed with which new technologies emerge.

Fourthly, even by 2017 the outsourcing industry was still at the early stages of professionalizing itself. Professionalization brings with it the benefits of such things as codes of conduct, minimum standards of competence, standardized practices, a coherent career structure and an understanding of key roles required and what it takes to fill them. While client retained capabilities have become, generally, more mature, and more relevant to the tasks in hand in recent years, the benefits of global sourcing becoming a profession on both client and service provider sides are not with us yet.

Throughout this relatively brief history there has been much learning and evolution by clients and suppliers alike. The voyage of discovery that client organizations have been through is captured in a four-phase model into which one can also read developments on the supply side. The model was devised from research by Lacity and Rottman (2008) (Fig 1.1).

Phase 1 – An organization looking at its first-generation outsourcing contract(s) tends to fall on one side of a hype-fear divide. Our research shows that clients at this stage believe too much in suppliers' marketing promises, and the power of outsourcing, or, conversely, are very dubious about what outsourcing can deliver. If the client proceeds to outsource, invariably it is with insufficient managerial competence, not realizing that outsourcing tends to require different management capabilities and

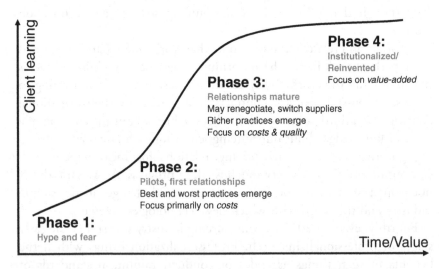

Fig. 1.1 Outsourcing learning curve (Lacity and Rottman 2008)

ethos from managing in-house resources. Neither approach adds up to a resilient way of trying to leverage outsourcing.

Phase 2 – After some hard learning through their first-generation outsourcing experiences, clients then tend to focus primarily on cost, becoming skeptical about how much can be really achieved, though often still insisting on benefits beyond cost and service improvements. The outsourcing literature sees phrases like 'your mess for less' as clients focus on the cost-service trade-off in their discussions and disputes with their suppliers.

While this sounds a limited set of objectives, nevertheless we have found a surprising number of outsourcing deals have been quietly successful at this relatively low level of ambition. Their characteristics included: cost and service objectives, retaining a lot of in-house capability; outsourcing 20–30% of activities; and outsourcing stable, and discrete activities they understood and could write detailed contracts for. They chose multiple suppliers and tended to use relatively short-term contracts of between 3–5 years in length. This approach tended to work and reflected that clients were 'smart in their ignorance,' that is did not try to step beyond their capabilities, but instead evolved their knowledge incrementally through the actual experience of outsourcing, while mitigating the risks of learning from experience (Lacity and Willcocks 2001, 2009).

Throughout the 2000s many clients were on their second or even third generation outsourcing deals. Often there was a transfer of learning into the new deals, but often also clients could react adversely to poor experiences and try to do something quite different the second or third time, thus pushing them down the learning curve as to these new arrangements, suppliers, and ways of operating. Our research shows most clients staying with existing suppliers – by the mid-2000s about 65% of deals went with incumbent service providers, though on changed contracts and scope; 30% were switching suppliers, and under 10% were bringing activities back in-house (Willcocks et al. 2011). Our research showed that many Phase 2 clients were getting smarter on contracts, including seeing the need to work with suppliers rather than having 'at-a-distance' relationships, building up more retained capability, and getting more realistic about what could be achieved through using the global external services market. Interestingly, we found quite often that the earlier learning on ITO arrangements did not always pass on into newer deals involving business process outsourcing or offshore outsourcing, raising question marks on whether client organizations place enough emphasis on organizational learning and its transfer (Willcocks and Lacity 2009).

Phase 3 – We have found many clients make it through to Phase 3 usually in their third or fourth generation outsourcing deals. These clients tend to look for value-added rather than just cost savings, and are searching for multiple business benefits from closer relationships with their service providers. At the same time they frequently look to reduce the number of their suppliers, and control them more closely on outcomes. Such clients have learned a great deal from previous outsourcing experiences, have built strong retained management capabilities, and are able to get the balance of contract and relationship management right. They have focused on leveraging the relationship with their suppliers for mutual business benefit.

Phase 4 – Few organizations have reached Phase 4 of their journey. In research into high performance in outsourcing, Lacity and Willcocks have found some 20% of BPO arrangements putting in 'world class' performance as at 2015. These achieve significant cost savings and service improvements on an ongoing basis, achieve multiple business benefits and innovation, and record high client satisfaction. They have inculcated management practices distinctively different from the 25% 'Good' outsourcing arrangements, and the 40% 'Doing OK' ones. Meanwhile as at this date 15% of arrangements still have to be classified as 'Poor' (no cost savings; costs could even increase; poor service performance; low client satisfaction). Briefly these management practice attributes were multiple: they included leadership pairings across client and supplier; a primary focus on business and strategic benefits; strong transition change management and transformation capabilities; a partnering approach; the retained organization aligned to business goals and its supplier; issues and conflicts resolved collaboratively with the provider; the use of technology as an enabler, deployment of domain expertise and business analytics; and prioritization of and incentives innovation (Lacity and Willcocks 2015).

Looking across these four phases, outsourcing performance is invariably better in Phases 3 and 4. While this is down to requisite client management capabilities, this also reflects maturing in service provider learning and capabilities over the years. Nevertheless one has to ask: why have so many organizations progressed quite slowly, often painfully, up their learning curves? One truth is mundane, which is that key people learn, then leave, in order to practice their learning elsewhere, at a higher price. But we find that while service providers frequently try to institutionalize their learning on managing outsourcing and on sector specific know-how, clients all too frequently have not. Moreover, as we pointed out above, learning on one type of outsourcing e.g., ITO, multi-supplier sourcing is not routinely transferred and applied to another e.g., BPO multi-supplier sourcing. Objectives change quite quickly in modern business environments, and new contract forms, new sourcing arrangements and new suppliers bring new unknowns into the picture requiring ever new learning, as do new technology innovations like cloud computing, business analytics and service automation. Global sourcing has become a fast-moving, dynamic high profile and impactful set of activities that remain difficult to deliver on. More reason, then, for even more studies of the kind we find in this volume.

The Papers in This Volume

This brief review of the first twenty-six years of the modern global sourcing industry sets the context in which the papers in this volume have been developed. There seems to be a fundamental practical question embedded in all these studies and that is: under what conditions can outsourcing, or other forms of sourcing contribute to organizational objectives? The answer will need a theoretical lens and, indeed, several papers provide detailed examples of attempts to develop and use different theoretical perspectives. The answer also needs to be evidence-based, and a range of papers show that academics continue to be very good at providing robust, rigorous, independent empirical research that is increasingly needed in such subject areas where so much information is being made available that does not have these qualities.

Having, as it were, 'framed' the volume, let us now look at the content. The volume includes interesting and compelling articles from the *Journal of Information Technology* pertaining to theoretical perspectives and studies of IT Outsourcing, Offshoring and BPO.

Introduction to Section 1: Theoretical Perspectives

Nearly twenty-five years of research on outsourcing has been framed and guided by many theoretical perspectives. Lacity and Willcocks (2009) examined 20 such theories from economics, strategy, sociology, and systems science. They showed that each theoretical tradition has explicit and implicit assumptions about the nature of human agency. Theories from economics, most notably Transaction Cost Economics (TCE) and Agency Theory (AT), assume that human agents make rational outsourcing decisions and engage in contracts to minimize total costs and to mitigate risks, such as the risk that an agent will behave opportunistically by hiding data, lying, or even threatening other agents. Theories from strategy, such as the Resource-Based View (RBV), Resource Dependency Theory (RDT), Game Theory, and Auction Theory, assume that human agents build or acquire resources to execute strategies that lead to 'winning'. Theories from sociology, including Social Exchange Theory (SET), Relational Exchange Theory (RET), Social Capital Theory, Institutionalism, Power Theories, and Innovation Diffusion focus on the *relationships* among human agents involved in sourcing, including levels of trust and power and the influence of social norms to elicit desired behaviors. Systems sciences have had as yet a minor influence, but this tradition views organizations as organisms that exchange resources across organizational boundaries and that learn through feedback.

For this volume, we sought to select papers that represent the breadth and depth of theoretical perspectives (see Table 1.1). Chapter 2, 'Theoretical perspectives on the outsourcing of information systems,' by Myun J. Cheon, Varun Grover, and James Teng initially appeared in the first *Journal of Information Technology* special issue on IT outsourcing published in 1995. These authors quite early on recognized the limitations of any one theory to make sense of the rich and nuanced reality of outsourcing. These authors integrated four theories, namely

RBV, RDT, TCE, and AT into a coherent framework of outsourcing decisions. Over twenty years later, this paper's influence is evidenced by over 400 citations by 2016.

Chapter 3, 'The information technology outsourcing risk: a transaction cost and agency-theory based perspective,' by Bouchaib Bahli and Suzanne Rivard applied two theories from economics (TCE and AT) to deeply assess the risks associated with outsourcing and to identify risk mitigation strategies suggested by the theories. Specifically, the authors examined how ten risk factors lead to supplier lock-in, costly contractual amendments, unexpected transaction costs, disputes and litigation. They identified nine specific risk mitigation strategies, including mutual hostaging, dual sourcing, sequential contracting, contract flexibility, clan mechanisms, use of external expertise, and alternative methods of dispute resolution such as arbitration.

Chapter 4, 'Moments of governance in IS outsourcing: conceptualizing effects of contracts on value capture and creation,' by Shaila Miranda and C Bruce Kavan used the theoretical lenses of promissory contracts, psychological contracts, and inter-organizational rents to ascertain appropriate governance structures for each outsourcing phase. During the contract negotiation phase, the authors posited that promissory contracting theory informs how structures give rise to commitment among parties. During the contract execution phase, psychological contracting theory suggests how structures build social capital to coordinate work and to resolve conflicts. Finally, inter-organizational rents theory suggests how the structures of intellectual and economic capital lead to value among partners.

Introduction to Section 2: From IT Outsourcing to Offshoring and BPO

The papers in Section 2 capture the breadth of coverage from empirical outsourcing research spanning ITO, offshoring, and BPO. These studies draw from and extend the theoretical perspectives covered in the first three chapters and several chapters build bespoke models on supplier management practices, structures, processes, and capabilities (see Table 1.1). Chapters 5 through 11 empirically examine the context of the outsourcing of information technology services, either to domestic or offshore suppliers or both. Chapters 12, 13, and 14 extend the empirical reach from exclusive ITO to include captive centers and BPO services.

Chapter 5, 'Norm development in outsourcing relationships,' by Thomas Kern and Keith Blois, is a detailed case study of BP Exploration's outsourcing of IT. Using the theoretical lens of social norms to diagnose the case, the authors asserted that BP's initial attempt to structure its multi-provider environment using a consortium failed because parties could not establish behavioral norms. Consequently, BP decided to dismantle the consortium in favor of a more traditional command and control structure.

Chapter 6, 'Organizational design of IT supplier relationship management: a multiple case study of five client companies,' by Jasmin Kaiser and Peter Buxmann, applied a strategic framework on organizational design to analyze the strategies, structures, and processes for managing relationships with suppliers in client firms. The authors examined IT outsourcing strategy in terms of degree of outsourcing and number of IT suppliers, the latter of which ranged from one supplier to several hundred suppliers. The authors compared the centralized, decentralized and hybrid structures across the cases and examined the mechanisms for involvement and collaboration.

Chapter 7, 'How do IT outsourcing vendors respond to shocks in client demand? A resource dependence perspective,' by Fang Sui, Ji-Ye Mao, and Sirrka Jarvenpaa, focused on IT outsourcing from the supplier perspective. The authors were interesting in understanding how ITO suppliers react to major drops in client demand, a significant issue after the global financial crisis of 2008. Based on five supplier-client relationships between Chinese ITO suppliers and Japanese clients, the authors found that the power of each explained the supplier's strategy for dealing with demand shocks. When the client was powerful, both weak and powerful suppliers adopted a bridging strategy to strengthen the current relationship. When the supplier was powerful but the client was not, the supplier adopted an 'exploitative buffering' strategy to attract new clients in new markets.

Table 1.1 Chapter overviews

Chapter	Theoretical contribution	Context	Empirical base	Client/Provider location
1	Overview of range of theories, development of practice, and learning over 26 years	ITO, Offshoring and BPO	n/a	n/a
2	Developed a conceptual model of outsourcing decisions based on RBV, RDT, TCE, and AT	ITO	n/a	n/a
3	Developed a risk mitigation framework based on TCE and AT	ITO	n/a	n/a
4	Developed a model of outsourcing governance based on promissory contracts, psychological contracts, and inter-organizational rents	ITO	n/a	n/a
5	Diagnosed supplier management structures and processes using social norms	ITO	One case study	UK
6	Developed an outsourcing framework based on strategic organizational design theory	ITO	Five case studies	Europe
7	Developed four propositions that related power to supplier strategies for absorbing shocks in client demand	ITO/ Offshoring	Five supplier-client relationships	Chinese providers, Japanese clients
8	Developed a process model for building provider capabilities.	ITO/ Offshoring	Four supplier case studies	Chinese providers, Japanese clients
9		ITO/ Offshoring	Five client case studies	

(continued)

Table 1.1 (continued)

Chapter	Theoretical contribution	Context	Empirical base	Client/Provider location
	Developed a dynamic model of offshoring, drawing on modular systems theory, knowledge based view, and TCE			American clients, providers based in several countries
10	Identified two types of inter-organizational trust, drawing on theories of modernity and self-identity	ITO/ Offshoring	One case study	Irish client, Indian supplier
11	Applied conversation analysis to understand client and provider interactions	ITO/ Offshoring	One case study	Client employees in UK & US; Indian supplier
12	Developed 14 propositions to examine call center outsourcing decisions and outcomes, drawing from TCE, RDT, institutional theory, industry value system, and a BPO provider capability framework	BPO	Three case studies	Australia
13	Examined four types of captive centers and their evolution over 25 years	Offshoring of IT and BP services	Primary and Secondary data	Global
14	Developed models of sourcing decisions and outcomes derived from empirical studies	ITO, Offshoring and BPO	Literature view of 174 empirical studies	Global; Clients based in 23 countries; providers based in 34 countries

Chapter 8, 'Operational capabilities development in mediated off-shore software services model,' by Sirkka L Jarvenpaa and Ji-Ye Mao, is another look at Chinese ITO suppliers, but this paper questioned the process by which ITO providers build human resource, process and client-specific capabilities. The authors studied four small Chinese ITO suppliers that service Japanese clients indirectly through a 'mediated model' via a Japanese IT supplier. The IT personnel career development capability was the most difficult for Chinese providers to develop, yet it was the main determinant of the other two capabilities. Chinese suppliers operated at the low end of the value-chain (coding and testing) and therefore opportunities to build client-specific relationships were restricted to the more senior people in Chinese firms.

Chapter 9, 'A dynamic model of offshore software development,' by Jason Dedrick, Erran Carmel, and Kenneth L Kraemer is an important theoretical and empirical contribution to the explanation of ITO decisions and outcomes. The authors criticized static theories of sourcing and instead developed a dynamic model based on their case studies. The authors identified five feedback loops (scramble, snowball, balancing, fundamental, and environmental) among economic factors, activity attributes, and management practices that affected an organization's sourcing mix through time.

Chapter 10, 'Anxiety and psychological security in offshoring relationships: the role and development of trust as emotional commitment,' by Seamas Kelly and Camilla Noonan brought a completely new perspective to the study of offshore outsourcing relationships. The authors applied Anthony Giddens' work on modernity and self-identity to examine how clients adjust to alien work arrangements like offshoring. The authors found two different modes of client-supplier trust that were built during the stages of courtship and cohabitation. The trust established during the courtship phase helped the relationship survive a crisis during the cohabitation phase.

Chapter 11, 'Cross-cultural (mis)communication in IS offshoring: understanding through conversation analysis,' by David Avison and Peter Banks, appropriated from anthropology the method of conversation analysis to study interactions between clients and offshore suppliers. The authors found that American and British client employees dominated the conversations with Indian supplier employees. Degrees of participation were explained by the lack of shared understanding, perceived hierarchical differences and the lack of cues or responses, all of which prompted US/UK employees to 'hyper-explain'.

Chapter 12, 'Applying multiple perspectives to the BPO decision: a case study of call centres in Australia,' by Mark Borman, is the first chapter in this volume to examine the outsourcing of call centers. The author drew on TCE, RDT, institutional theory, industry value system, and a BPO provider capability framework to develop 14 propositions. Each proposition was assessed using three client-supplier relationships. The author concluded that the multi-theoretical perspective was indeed needed to explain the richness of the cases.

Chapter 13, 'A historical review of the information technology and business process captive centre sector,' by Ilan Oshri and Bob van Uhm is the only paper that examined a special type of *insourcing* model, called a captive center. A captive center is an offshore delivery center owned by the client organization. The authors examined four types of captive center models (basic, hybrid, shared, and divested). Using primary and secondary data, they looked at the evolution of these models over time from 1985 to 2010. Similar to other chapters in this volume, the authors found that insourcing decisions are dynamic, changing with both internal and external influences.

Chapter 14, 'Review of the empirical business services sourcing literature: an update and future directions,' by Mary Lacity, Shaji Khan, and Aihua Yan, aimed to summarize 174 empirical studies on all ITO and BPO studies published in 78 academic journals between 2010 and 2014, thus bringing two prior literatures reviews published in JIT up to date (Lacity et al. 2010, 2011). Compared with the earlier literature reviews, this review found a deeper exploration of the direct effects of transaction attributes, sourcing motivations, client and provider capabilities, and governance on sourcing decisions and outcomes. The authors also assessed the research progress that has been made on ten previously identified gaps in knowledge. The authors proposed a future research agenda that included continued, incremental progress on 'normal science' research questions, as well as novel and ambitious research studies.

Conclusion

By 2017 one of the interesting speculations was: are we witnessing the death throes of outsourcing? Many have claimed transformative powers for cloud computing (rent as a service over the internet), digitization (especially of sourcing and the supply chain), robotic process and cognitive automation (move from a labor-centric to a machine centric model), and the rise of global in-house centers (eliminating external service providers).

If true, it would follow that the accumulated knowledge of the subject, as partly evidenced in this volume, would increasingly become irrelevant. However, all informed predictions suggest continued outsourcing growth globally, albeit at an overall slower pace than before. To reinforce this, some 60% of IT and 80% of back office business process work is still done in-house so there is still plenty of room for the market to grow. Moreover, we are not seeing a marked swing back to in-house options – this has always been a minority practice, and usually takes the form of adjustments rather than total 'backsourcing.' Outsourcing will continue to grow, and the imbeddedness of existing contracts signed for anything between three to ten years will slow down the impacts of new trends and new technologies.

That said, however, there are real disrupters in this overall growth pattern. Outsourcing will increasingly change its character, as providers themselves adopt new technologies, and build and offer services based on them. We will see a number of disruptors impact the traditional outsourcing scene more forcefully. Cloud vendors like Amazon, Google, and cloud platform providers like IBM and Microsoft have enough market clout to move on from impacting on SMEs to move up the value chain with larger corporations. Software-as-a-service could seriously impact on outsourcing as an option in many important back office functions like accounts payable, indirect procurement, payroll, and benefit administration. Using software over the internet, companies may spend much more time serving themselves through their own managed services. 'Everything-as-a-service' looks like a major, if long-term trend – not just data storage, applications, but infrastructure, business processes, and global human and virtual workforces, as well, just to name some existing developments. Robotics-driven vendors began operating at the bottom of the BPO stack, and in IT help desk and IT support. But 2016 saw dramatic increases in the take-up of robotic process automation (RPA) in back offices and shared service operations, and amongst BPO service providers themselves. If the multiple business benefits continue to materialize like the ones we found in our studies (Willcocks and Lacity 2016), then RPA will find bigger markets, and could be followed by widespread adoption of cognitive automation, eating further into outsourcing's dominant labor-centric economics and contracting modes.

All these trends presage dramatic changes in the character of outsourcing, of which clients and providers themselves are very aware and to which they are always seeking to respond. Undoubtedly in each round of contract renewals across 2017–2020 we will see clients make new demands – on cloud computing, robotic process automation, as-a-service, and adoption of new technologies and business analytics, and we will see providers adjusting their services to reflect these developments. All this makes the body of knowledge built over the last 27 years more, not less valuable. Sourcing theory, managing the sourcing life-cycle, relationships between parties, effective practices, the dynamics of offshore service delivery remain central to organizations driving themselves up the sourcing learning curve. As Nietzsche suggested, invariably you need to go back *'like anyone who wants to make a great leap forward.'* Academic studies, such as in this volume, form the rich foundation, for further research designed to explore the dynamic field of outsourcing and offshoring of business services.

References

Cullen, S., Lacity, M., & Willcocks, L. (2014) *Outsourcing – All You Need To Know*. White Plume, Melbourne.

Fersht, P., & Snowden, J. (2014) *The HFS Market Index – IT Services and BPO Market Size and Forecast 2014–2018*. HFS Research, Boston.

Kern, T., Lacity, M., & Willcocks, L. (2002) *Netsourcing: Renting Applications, Services and Infrastructure over Networks*. Prentice Hall, New York.

Lacity, M., & Rottman, J. (2008) *The Offshore Outsourcing of IT Work*. Palgrave, London.

Lacity, M., & Willcocks, L. (2001) *Global IT Outsourcing: In Search of Business Advantage*. Wiley, Chichester.

Lacity, M., & Willcocks, L. (2009) *Information Systems and Outsourcing: Studies in Theory and Practice*. Palgrave, London.

Lacity, M., & Willcocks, L. (2015) *Nine Keys To World Class BPO*. Bloomsbury, London.

Lacity, M., Khan, S., Yan, A., & Willcocks, L. (2010) 'A Review of the IT Outsourcing Empirical Literature and Future Research Directions.' *Journal of Information Technology*, 25 (4): 395–433.

Lacity, M., Solomon, S., Yan, A., & Willcocks, L. (2011) 'Business Process Outsourcing Studies: A Critical Review and Research Directions.' *Journal of Information Technology*, 26 (4): 221–258.

Snowden, J., & Fersht, P. (2016) *The HFS Market Index – IT Services and BPO Market Size and Forecast 2016–2020*. HFS Research, Boston.

Willcocks, L., & Lacity, M. (2006) *Global Sourcing of Business and IT Services*. Palgrave, London.

Willcocks, L., & Lacity, M. (2009) *The Practice of Outsourcing: From Information Systems to BPO and Offshoring*. Palgrave, London.

Willcocks, L., & Lacity, M. (2016) *Service Automation, Robots and The Future of Work*. SB Publishing, Stratford.

Willcocks, L., Cullen, S., & Craig, A. (2011) *The Outsourcing Enterprise: From Cost Management To Collaborative Innovation*. Palgrave, London.

Willcocks, L., Venters, W., & Whitley, E. (2014) *Moving To The Cloud Corporation*. Palgrave, London.

Leslie P. Willcocks is Professor in Technology Work and Globalization at the Department of Management at London School of Economics and Political Science. He heads the LSE's Outsourcing Unit research centre and is Editor-in-Chief of the *Journal of Information Technology*. Previously he taught at Oxford University for nine years. His doctorate is from University of Cambridge.

Leslie has a global reputation for his work in robotic process automation, AI, cognitive automation and the future of work, outsourcing, global strategy, organizational change, and managing digital business. He is co-author of 54 books, and has published over 230 refereed papers in journals such as *Harvard*

Business Review, Sloan Management Review, California Management Review, MIS Quarterly, Journal of Management Studies.

Dr. Mary Lacity is a curators' professor of Information Systems and an International Business Fellow at the University of Missouri-St. Louis. She is a Senior Editor at *MIS Quarterly Executive*, coeditor of the *Palgrave Series: Work, Technology, and Globalization*, and on the Editorial Boards for *Journal of Information Technology, MIS Quarterly Executive, IEEE Transactions on Engineering Management, Journal of Strategic Information Systems, and Strategic Outsourcing: An International Journal.* She was inducted into the IAOP's Outsourcing Hall of Fame in 2014, one of only three academics to ever be inducted. She has published 24 books, including *Nine Keys to Worldclass Business Process Outsourcing* (Bloomsbury Publishing, London, 2015; coauthor Leslie Willcocks) and *The Rise of Legal Services Outsourcing* (Bloomsbury Publishing, London, 2014; coauthors Leslie Willcocks and Andrew Burgess). Her publications have appeared in the *Harvard Business Review, Sloan Management Review, MIS Quarterly, IEEE Computer, Communications of the ACM*, and many other academic and practitioner outlets. She was Program Cochair for ICIS, 2010.

Chris Sauer is Senior Tutor of Green Templeton College at Oxford University. He is Joint Editor-in-Chief of the *Journal of Information Technology*. His research interests have focused on the management of information systems projects and software quality processes.

Part I

Theoretical Perspectives

2

Theoretical Perspectives on the Outsourcing of Information Systems

Myun J. Creon, Varun Grover and James T. C. Teng

Introduction

In recent years there has been an increasing amount of attention paid to outsourcing of information systems (IS) functions in organizations. A recent survey of IS senior executives highlights outside services management as one of the six strategic management issues confronting organizations in their management of corporate systems (Clark, 1992). Another recent study by the Yankee Group indicates that by 1994 every Fortune 500 company would have considered IS outsourcing. The changing and more strategic role of outsourcing in business firms

M.J. Creon
College of Business Administration, University of Ulsan, Ulsan, Korea

V. Grover (✉) · J.T.C. Teng
Management Science Department, University of South Carolina, Columbia, USA
e-mail: vgrover@darla.badm.scarolina.edu

© The Author(s) 2017
L.P. Willcocks et al. (eds.), *Outsourcing and Offshoring Business Services*, DOI 10.1007/978-3-319-52651-5_2

has been given much coverage in trade publications like *Computerworld, Datamation, Network World,* and *MIS Week.*

This area of study has produced a number of conceptual and practitioner-oriented articles proposing the particular outsourcing practices that would be associated with various business strategies. In addition, recent research has begun to examine the determinants of outsourcing practices from a strategic perspective. However, there has been little in the way of strong theoretical models to aid in understanding both the role of outsourcing in organizations and the determinants of various outsourcing practices. This deficiency in the literature needs to be addressed before significant progress can he made.

The purpose of this paper is to provide a foundation to guide future outsourcing research and practice by reviewing alternative theoretical models that have and can be applied to explain the role of outsourcing in an organization's IS management. In order to accomplish this task, we will first review the general background of outsourcing and offer a definition of outsourcing. In the context of outsourcing, we review the components of theory construction and its importance to the outsourcing research process. We will then present four specific theoretical perspectives and evaluate them for their potential in enhancing our prescriptive understanding of the determinants of outsourcing practices. Finally, these perspectives are put together towards a contingency model of outsourcing that can be used to guide future empirical studies.

General Background on Outsourcing

In this paper we define broadly outsourcing of IS functions as the organizational decision to turn over part or all of an organization's IS functions to external service provider(s) in order for an organization to be able to achieve its goals. This definition includes the following external services: applications development and maintenance, systems operation, networks/telecommunications management, end-user computing support, systems planning and management, and purchase of application software, but excludes business consulting services, after-sale vendor services, and the lease of telephone lines. An organization can obtain these services through complete outsourcing, facilities management, systems integration, time-sharing, and other contracts (including rental, installation and procurement, and maintenance and programming).

The IS functions involve technological resources or the entire infrastructure including hardware, software and communications systems deployed, and human resources with managers, programmers, systems administrators, maintenance and related personnel involved in the design, maintenance and operation of the overall IT infrastructure (Loh and Venkatraman, 1992). A rational perspective on outsourcing presumes that organizations attempt to make these decisions in their best interests.

It is important to note however, that IS outsourcing is neither a new phenomenon nor is it homogeneous. There are various kinds of outsourcing arrangements, some of which are depicted in Fig. 2.1 (Loh and Venkatraman, 1991). Facilities management which involves high externalization (or low internalization) of human resources, and time sharing which involves externalization of technical resources, have been around for decades. However, the nature of outsourcing has evolved. Compared with the 1970s, current outsourcing practices differ in the following key ways (Aucoin, 1991; Schiffman and Loftin, 1991):

(1) Larger companies are outsourcing although there is evidence that in the current environment size does not affect the outsourcing decision (Grover *et al.,* 1994b).
(2) A greater range and depth of services are being outsourced.
(3) Service providers are accepting more responsibility and risk.
(4) The nature of the relationship with the service provider is evolving and in many cases is a partnership.
(5) Information technology intensity and complexity is higher, giving more companies the option of outsourcing in a competitive provider market.

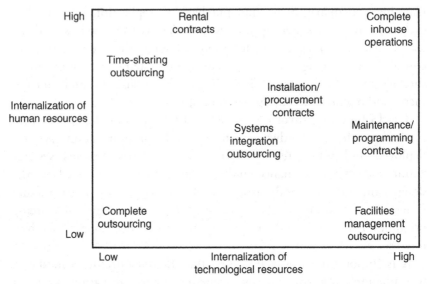

Fig. 2.1 Alternative types of IS outsourcing (Adapted from Loh and Venkatraman, 1991)

The rapid changes in the technological base and the increasingly competitive environment have caused some companies to shift the focus of their outsourcing strategy from technology to information utilization and management. From this perspective, organizations can spend less time and resources building an internal computing infrastructure while concentrating their efforts on the effective use of information and the creation of new analytical data with which they can improve management's responsiveness to organizational needs (Grover and Teng, 1993). Others can choose their outsourcing strategy based on their current deficiencies and the nature of the outsourcing marketplace. Such flexibility offered to corporations in today's outsourcing environment provides the impetus for the need to develop a contingent model that facilitates evaluation and eventually prescriptions on IT outsourcing. Guidance for such a model can be obtained through theoretical perspectives in other fields.

The Role of Theory in Outsourcing Research and Practice

Rudner (1966, p. 10) defines a theory as 'a systematically related set of statements, including some law like generalizations, that is empirically testable'. The purpose of theory is to increase scientific understanding through a systematized structure capable of both explaining and predicting phenomena (Rudner, 1966). In more detailed terms, Bacharach (1989, p. 498) views a theory as 'a system of constructs and variables in which the constructs are related to each other by propositions and variables are related to each other by hypotheses'. The whole system, presented in Fig. 2.2, is bounded by the theorist's assumptions. Dubin (1969) maintains that the notion of specific critical bounding assumptions is important because it sets the limitations in applying the theory.

The function of a theory', then, is to fulfil the objectives of prediction (knowledge of the outcome) and understanding (knowledge of the process) regarding the relationships among the variables of interest (Dubin, 1976). Thus, a good theory enables one both to predict what will happen given a set of values for certain variables, and to understand why this predicted value should result. Further, a good theory enables one to determine whether the theory is constructed such that empirical refutation is possible (Bacharach, 1989).

Although the primary goals between theorist researchers and practitioners may differ (Dubin, 1976), a strong theoretical model has great value to both. Practitioners are primarily concerned with the accuracy of prediction of a theoretical model in order to guide their decision-making when outsourcing: thus, an accurate theoretical model is 'practical precisely because it advances knowledge in a scientific discipline, guides research toward critical questions, and enlightens the profession of management' (Van de Ven, 1989, p. 486). On the other hand, theorist researchers have greater concern for understanding the 'why' behind the prediction. For them, a well-developed theoretical model allows for testing of the model and) based on these tests, revision of the model to increase its accuracy.

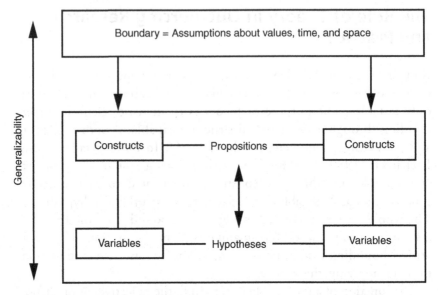

Fig. 2.2 Components of a theory (Adapted from Bacharach, 1989)

Outsourcing research and practice can benefit from various theoretical notions developed in the fields of strategic management and economics. The next section will discuss the basic theoretical models in order to describe each approach and its implications for outsourcing research and practice.

Theoretical Models of Outsourcing

Strategic management as a discipline is concerned with how firms formulate and implement strategies in order to accomplish a desired performance goal (Schendel and Hofer, 1979). Economic theories examine the coordination and governance of economic agents in their transactions with one another. In the context of this paper, resource-based theory (RBT), resource dependence theory (RDT) from strategic management, transaction cost theory (TCT), and agent cost theory (ACT) from economics are reviewed in order to understand the growing trend towards outsourcing of IS functions.

Resource-Based Theory

Resource-based theory views a firm as a collection of productive resources. The growth of the firm depends upon a desire to utilize slack resources (Penrose, 1959). Rubin (1973, p. 937) further defines a resource as a 'fixed input which enables a firm to perform a particular task'. A variety of authors have generated a list of firm resources which may enable a firm to conceive of and implement strategies that improve its efficiency and effectiveness (Thompson and Strickland, 1983; Hitt and Ireland, 1986; Barney, 1991). These possible firm resources can be conveniently classified into three categories: physical capital resources, human capital resources and organizational capital resources (Barney, 1991).

According to the resource-based theory, competitive advantage can only occur in situations of firm resource heterogeneity and firm resource immobility. Firm resource heterogeneity refers to the resources of a firm (physical, human and organizational capital) and how different these resources are across firms. Firm resource immobility refers to the inability of competing firms to obtain resources from other firms (Barney, 1991; Williams, 1992).

In order for a firm's resource to provide sustained competitive advantage, four criteria must be attributable to the resources: value (the resource must be valuable to the firm), rareness (the resource must be unique or rare among a firm's current and potential competition), imperfect immutability (the resource must be imperfectly imitable) and nonsubstitutability (the resource cannot be substituted with another resource by competing firms) (Barney, 1991).

Thus, the essence of the resource-based theory is that given resource heterogeneity and immobility and satisfaction of the requirements of value, rareness, imperfect immutability and non-substitutability, firm's resources can be a source of sustained competitive advantage. The role of resources in firm growth and (sustained) competitive advantage has been developed by Rumelt (1974), Barney (1991), Grant (1991) and Wernerfelt (1984). In other words, according to the resource-based approach to strategic management, a firm's competitive position (above normal returns) depends on its ability to gain and defend advantageous positions concerning resources important to production and distribution (Rumelt, 1974; Wernerfelt, 1984; Barney, 1986; Conner, 1991).

Thus, the critical problem faced by the firm is how to maintain the distinctiveness of its product – or for identical products, its low-cost position – while not investing so much in obtaining this difference as to destroy above normal returns. Distinctiveness in the product or low costs are tied directly to distinctiveness in the inputs (resources) used to produce the product (Conner, 1991). Grant (1991) provides in his five-stage procedure a practical framework for a resource-based approach to strategy formulation: analysing the firm's resource base; appraising the firm's capabilities; analysing the profit-earning potential of the firm's resources and capabilities; selecting a strategy; and extending and upgrading the firm's pool of resources and capabilities.

Further, Grant (1991) argues that a resource-based approach to strategy is concerned not only with the deployment of existing resources and capabilities, but also with the development of the firm's resources and capabilities. In order both to fully exploit a firm's existing stock of resources and capabilities, and to develop competitive advantage, the external acquisition of complementary resources and capabilities may be necessary (Grant, 1991). This external acquisition (i.e., outsourcing) is known as filling gaps of resources and capabilities in the strategic management literature (Stevensen, 1976).

Filling gaps of resources and capabilities through an outsourcing strategy not only maintains the firm's stock of resources and capabilities, but also augments resources and capabilities in order to buttress and extend positions of competitive advantage as well as broaden the firm's strategic opportunity set (Grant, 1991). Figure 2.3 indicates the relationships

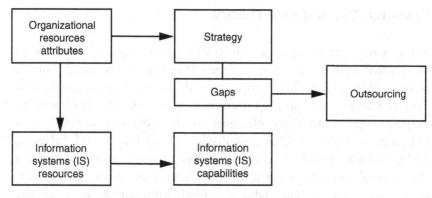

Fig. 2.3 A resource-based perspective of outsourcing

among firm's strategy, organizational resources, IS resources, IS capabilities and outsourcing. This resource-based perspective for outsourcing provides a framework for examining the pool of IS resources and capabilities (i.e., financial condition, people, machinery, facilities) that may or may not be able to carry out a given strategy during the formulation phase. Thus, the resource-based theory may demonstrate the fact that strategies are not universally implementable, but are contingent on having the necessary IS resource and capability base.

According to the resource-based perspective, outsourcing is a strategic decision which can be used to fill gaps (i.e., the difference between desired capabilities and actual capabilities) in the firm's IS resources and capabilities (e.g., information quality, IS support quality, staff quality, cost effectiveness and financial condition). The firm's IS resources and capabilities may vary depending both upon the firm's resource attributes (value, rareness, imperfect imitability and non-substitutability) and upon the amount of the firm's resources allocated for IS. Thus, the outsourcing decision can be formulated as the following linear relationship:

Outsourcing = f(gaps in IS capabilities)
Gaps = f(resource attributes, resource allocation)

Resource-Dependence Theory

While a resource-based approach to strategic management focuses on an internal analysis of a firm in terms of resources and capabilities, a resource dependence theory focuses on the external environment of a firm and argues that all organizations find themselves dependent, to varying degrees, on some elements in their external environments (Thompson, 1967; Aldrich and Pfeffer, 1976; Pfeffer and Salancik, 1978; Aldrich, 1976). This external dependence is usually based on the external elements' control of some resources which an organization needs, such as land, labour, capital, information, or a specific product or service (Kotter, 1979). Aldrich states that 'environments affect organizations through the process of making available or withholding resources, and organizational forms can be ranked in terms of their efficacy in obtaining resources'. Thus, a resource-dependence theory stresses the organizational necessity of adapting to environmental uncertainty, coping with problematic interdependence, and actively managing or controlling resource flows (Pfeffer and Salancik, 1978).

According to the source and nature of the interdependence between the environment and the organization, Emery and Trist (1965) describe four types of environments: first, placid-randomized, in which the necessary resources are randomly distributed, with a constant probability of uncovering them; second, placid-clustered, in which the pattern of resources are sequentially predictable; third, disturbed-reactive, in which the distributions and probabilities of resources are created by the actions of the organizations themselves; and fourth, turbulent, in which many groups of organizations are closely interconnected and interdependent. Based upon this work, Pfeffer and Salancik (1978) provide three dimensions of organizational task environments: concentration, munificence and interconnectedness. Each dimension differs according to 'the nature and the distribution of resources in environments, with different values on each dimension implying differences in appropriate structures and activities' (Aldrich, 1976, p. 54). Concentration refers to the extent to which power and authority in the environment is widely dispersed.

Munificence refers to the availability or scarcity of critical resources. Interconnectedness refers to the number and pattern of linkages among organizations.

In the context of these dimensions of organizational task environments, a resource-dependence approach to strategic management argues that organizations adopt strategies to secure access to critical resources, to stabilize relations with the environment, and to enable survival (Pfeffer and Salancik, 1978; Zeithaml and Zeithaml, 1984). These strategies depend on the task environment and might involve alignment with powerful units in the environment, outsourcing or control of weaker units. Yuchtman and Seashore (1967) have defined organizational effectiveness in terms of the organization's success in obtaining scarce and valued resources from the environment. That is, resource dependence theory maintains that organizational survival is dependent on the acquisition of necessary resources from the environment.

To obtain externally resources that cannot be generated internally organizations might enter into exchange relationships with other organizations in the environment. That is, organizations alter their structures and behaviours to acquire and maintain needed resources (Ulrich and Barney, 1984). The organization is likely to attempt to form a mutually beneficial coalition. 'For example, a firm can minimize its uncertainty in supply relationships by engaging in coalition activities such as forming links with influential individuals in supplier firms, becoming partners with such firms in joint ventures, or acquiring key supplier firms' (Ulrich and Barney, 1984, p.472). Thus, resource dependence theory (Pfeffer and Salancik, 1978), which emphasizes the dependence of organizations on their external environment, provides a useful perspective from which to examine the relationship between an organization's decision to outsource IS functions and that organization's effectiveness.

Further, Pfeffer and Salancik (1978) argue that three factors are critical in determining the external dependence of one organization on another.

First, there is the importance of the resource – the extent to which the organization requires it for continued operation and survival. The second is the extent to which the interest group has discretion over the resource allocation and use. And third, the extent to which there are few alternatives, or the extent of control over the resource by the interest group, is an important factor determining the dependence of the organization (pp. 45–46).

Pfeffer and Salancik (1978) then define the term 'environmental dependence' as 'the product of the importance of a given input or output to the organization and the extent to which it is controlled by relatively few organizations (p. 51). Thus, the organization's dependence on any other organization (outsourcing) is determined by the importance of the resource to the organization, the number of potential suppliers, and the cost of switching suppliers.

Figure 2.4 shows the relationships among dimensions of organizational task environments, dimensions of resources, firm's strategy, and resource acquisition (outsourcing). The resource-dependence perspective for outsourcing provides a framework for examining those dimensions of task environments that may determine the firm's dimensions of resources. These dimensions of resources then determine an organization's decision to outsource IS functions. Further, a firm's strategy may affect the decision to outsource IS functions, since an organization may need to obtain critical resources from external sources in order to implement its strategy. Thus, outsourcing strategy is composed of different degrees of dependence of one organization on another in order to obtain critical resources which are not available internally. Thus, out-

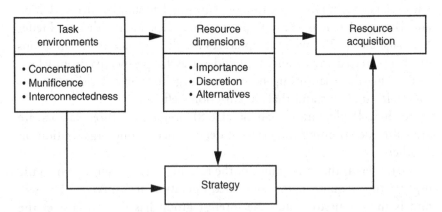

Fig. 2.4 A resource dependence perspective of outsourcing

sourcing as a strategic option can be formulated as the following linear relationship:

Outsourcing = f(dimensions of resources, strategy)
Dimensions of resources = f(task environments)

Transaction Cost Theory

The transaction cost theory, introduced by Coase (1937) and developed principally by Williamson (1975, 1979, 1981, 1985), maintains that the organization of economic activity depends on balancing production economics, such as scale, against the cost of transacting. Transactions are here the exchanges of goods or services between economic actors, who are technologically separate units, inside and/or outside the organization (Williamson, 1981). The analysis of transactions focuses on achieving efficiency in their administration. In this perspective, organizational success depends on managing transactions efficiently. Organizations exist to mediate the economic transactions among members inside and/or outside the organization (Ulrich and Barney, 1984).

The transaction cost approach offers a method of evaluating the relative advantages of the different internal and external organization forms for handling transactions. This theory also provides an excellent framework for analysing the outsourcing option, since the essential choice here is between using an outsourcing service provider (a market mechanism) and providing in-house services (an organizational hierarchy) (Elam, 1988; Clemons and Row, 1989; Apte, 1990; Lacity and Hirschheim, 1993b). First, the theory seems to be very useful for investigating the outsourcing option as an economic reorganization of *IS* departments. Second, the theory appears to be useful for formulating an action plan that reduces transaction cost and thereby improves the benefit one can realize through outsourcing.

Transaction cost theory identifies two costs to be considered in determining whether the appropriate governance structure for a transaction is a market or a hierarchy: production costs and transactions costs. Outsourcing leads to smaller production cost (i.e., the cost of delivering

IS functions) primarily due to the economies of scale that a service provider enjoys in providing IS functions such as data centre and communication operations and systems development (Apte, 1990) and generally leads to higher transaction costs arising from negotiating, monitoring and enforcing contracts. Therefore, the outsourcing option can be evaluated with respect to the increase in transaction costs through a framework that examines factors which influence the magnitude of transaction costs.

Transaction costs increase as a result of three factors: asset specificity or the degree to which the transaction will produce an asset that is dedicated to a special purpose with poor alternative uses; the degree of uncertainty in the environment as it impacts the contract and its fulfilment; and infrequency of contracting, or the infrequency with which the two parties contract together (Williamson, 1985).

Asset specificity in the context of outsourcing refers to the uniqueness of the firm's hardware and/or software architectures and the skill set of IS employees. Such idiosyncratic investments would serve to increase the costs of any transactional relationship with a vendor. Uncertainty is another factor that influences transaction costs. Conditions of high uncertainty in this relationship may be a result of unpredictable market, technological, economic trends, contractual complexity and quality of outputs. These might be mitigated through a complex control structure instigated by the firm or the adoption of standards. Such mechanisms can be used to reduce opportunism but may increase costs of enforcing the transactional relationship. Also, the infrequency of contracting might increase associated transaction costs due to initial 'relationship building' during contract negotiation. Consistency of goals between the contracting parties is critical to promote this relationship. It should be recognized however, that certain IS functions tend to be inherently more 'commoditized' and can benefit from market relationships (i.e., lower asset specificity, uncertainty and higher frequency of contracting) such as transaction processing while others such as specialized application development might benefit from hierarchical relationships.

Figure 2.5 indicates the relationships among transaction costs, their determinants and outsourcing. Each of these factors raises the effort and cost of structuring an agreement between service receiver and provider

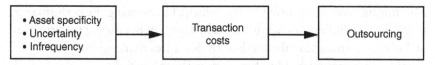

Fig. 2.5 A transaction costs perspective of outsourcing

that will assure the successful completion of the contract and its future enforcement. Based upon the factors determining the magnitude of transaction costs (or the relative trade-off between transaction and production costs), the decision to outsource can be expressed as the following linear relationship:

Outsourcing = f(transaction costs)
Transaction costs = f(asset specificity, uncertainty, infrequency)

Agency Cost Theory

The agency cost theory, developed by Ross (1973), Mitnick (1975, 1986) and Jensen and Meckling (1976), examines the reasons for principal-agent relationships and the problems inherent in them. Jensen and Meckling (1976, p. 308) define an agency relationship 'a contract under which one or more persons (principal(s)) engage another person (the agent) to perform some service on their behalf which involves delegating some decision making authority to the agent'.

The focus of the agency theory is on determining the most efficient contract (behaviour-oriented versus outcome-oriented) that governs the relationship between a principal and an agent (Eisenhardt, 1988). The choice between a behaviour-based contract (e.g., hierarchy governance, insourcing) and outcome-based contract (e.g., market governance, outsourcing) depends on the agency costs, which are the costs incurred as a result of discrepancies between the objectives of the principal and those of agents. That is, the agency costs are the sum of the monitoring costs by the principal, the bonding costs by the agent, and the residual loss of the principal.

Monitoring costs are incurred by the principal in assessing the performance of the agent, bonding costs are incurred by the agent in assuring the principal of 'his' commitment and the residual loss is the loss resulting from having an agent (with a parochial utility function) perform the task.

The agency cost theory provides an excellent framework for evaluating the relative advantages of the different internal and external organization forms for handling contracts between an outsourcing service receiver and a provider. An agency cost perspective of outsourcing offers a method of examining factors which influence the magnitude of agency costs. The presumption is that organizations will base their outsourcing decisions on factors that influence agency costs. Agency costs are determined by five factors: outcome uncertainty due to government policies, economic climate, technological change, competitor actions and so on; risk aversion of the outsourcing receiver (or provider); programmability or the degree to which appropriate behaviour by the outsourcing provider can be specified in advance; outcome measurability or the extent to which outcomes can be easily measured; and the length of the agency relationship (Eisenhardt, 1989). Agency costs (monitoring, bonding and residual loss) increase in outsourcing relationships with high uncertainty, high risk aversion, low programmability, low outcome measurability and greater length of relationship.

Based upon the factors determining the magnitude of agency cost, the decision to outsource may be expressed as the following linear relationship (see Fig. 2.6):

Outsourcing = f(agency costs)
Agency costs = f(uncertainty, risk aversion, programmability, measurability, length)

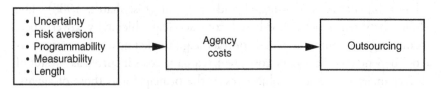

Fig. 2.6 An agency costs perspective of outsourcing

The following section integrates the theoretical perspectives discussed into a framework to guide empirical work in this area.

Towards a Contingency Model for IS Outsourcing

Structural contingency theory has dominated the study of organizational design and performance during the past twenty years (Hofer, 1975; Miles and Snow, 1978; Miller and Freisen, 1978; Drazin and Van de Ven, 1985; Ginsberg and Venkatraman, 1985). It is the perspective underlying the prescribed dual approach to strategic analysis (Grant and King, 1982): environmental threats and opportunities analysis, and organizational strengths and weaknesses.

Contingency perspectives on business strategy indicate that the appropriateness of different strategies depends on the competitive setting of business (Hambrick and Lei, 1985). Further, the perspectives rest on the belief that 'no universal set of strategic choices exists that is optimal for all businesses, irrespective of their resource positions and environmental context' (Ginsberg and Venkatraman, 1985, p. 421). Thus, effective strategies are those which achieve a fit or congruence between environmental conditions and organizational factors (Drazin Van de Yen, 1985; Venkatraman and Camillus, 1985). Fahey and Christensen (1986) present a strategy research paradigm which indicates that the central research question of strategy content is typically some variant of the following: what results arise from following strategies under different conditions? In the case of IS outsourcing, the question becomes: what results arise from following IS outsourcing strategies under different conditions? Therefore, the basic premise of contingency theory is that outsourcing strategy is only one of several types of economic restructuring by which an organization adapts to the environment (Child, 1987; Clemons and Row, 1989). Therefore, there are situations under which outsourcing mayor may not be appropriate. These situations include discrepancies in IS factors, dimensions of IS resources and firm's costs that are perceived by decision-makers as they seek to formulate the outsourcing strategy.

Figure 2.7 puts together the variety of contingency variables discussed earlier (in resource-based theory, resource-dependence theory, transaction costs theory and agency theory) into a conceptual model for studying outsourcing. We believe that such a framework can provide guidance in examining the various aspects of the outsourcing phenomenon in a consistent and cumulative manner.

Integrative Aspects of the Model

It should be emphasized that the various theoretical concepts depicted in the model are interrelated. For instance, based on perspectives of resource-based theory and transaction costs theory, Clemons and Row (1989) examine economic reorganization and the role IT plays in it. Economic restructuring is viewed in terms of changes in the allocation

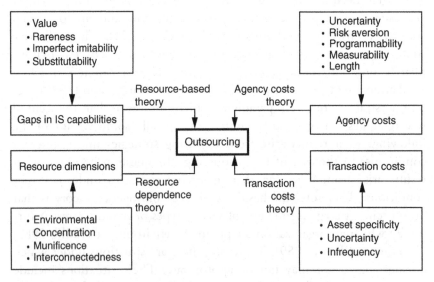

Fig. 2.7 A conceptual model for studying outsourcing

and integration of strategic resources. They suggest that change in competitive position comes from leveraging an advantage or mitigating a disadvantage in critical resources. Changes in economic structure are classified by the basic ways firms can alter or redeploy their resources:

Horizontal Integration of Resources within a Market

Firms can expand or contract within a particular market, relative to the total market size. IT contributes to increasing scale economies both as a resource by itself and as a mechanism for coordinating other resources. Due to these scale economies, there could be pressure for increased concentration of the IT resource, depending on the importance of IT to the business and its cost relative to other costs. The firm concentration takes ownership consolidation, outsourcing and cooperative supply – depends on the potential economies of integration, the initial resource positions, and the transaction costs in transferring the services of the resource.

Outsourcing strategy is adopted where the transaction costs of accessing the resources are low relative to the savings from scale economies, and where the risks of dependence are low. Smaller competitors may outsource the services of the resources from third parties who are larger players within the industry or from industries with significant overlap in the key resources.

Horizontal Integration of Resources between Markets

Firms can expand into, or withdraw from, different markets and industries. Economic benefits may be creating scale advantages in resources that are similar in multiple markets, reducing average unit costs. However, this type of economic restructuring can also create scope economies where the value of the integration is greater than the parts independently. This integration between markets can take on any form: ownership consolidation, outsourcing or cooperative agreement. Outsourcing between markets is very common in financial services due to the high overlap in the resources required in the different markets.

Vertical Integration of Resources

Firms can expand into, or withdraw from, activities that are vertically related within a single value chain. Vertical resource integration refers to the transfer of goods and services along a single value chain. Unlike the horizontal integration case, vertical integration indicates that decreased transaction costs or increased production economies leads more to resource disintegration. IT can lead to vertical disintegration (outsourcing) in access to strategic resources when a firm (compared to larger competitors or other service providers) is at a scale disadvantage in operating those resources, and it is prohibitive to acquire the resources necessary to be competitive.

While resource dependence theory, though emphasizing that much organizational action is determined by environmental conditions, recognizes the possibility of intentional adaptation to environmental conditions through management actions, resource-based theory emphasizes the necessity of critical IS resources and capabilities. Thus, an organizational decision to outsource IS functions depends both on a firm's pool of IS resources and capabilities and on environmental conditions. Pfeffer and Salancik (1978) derive three roles for management – symbolic, responsive and discretionary to explain how organizations may act upon the environment. The degree to which the organizations outsource their IS functions can be classified by the different roles for management actions:

Symbolic Approach to Outsourcing

In the symbolic role, actions of an organization are unrelated to constraints. Organizational performance is determined primarily by the firm's existing IS resources and capabilities. Thus, the outsourcing strategy involves low levels of dependence on external environment.

Responsive Approach to Outsourcing

In the responsive role, organizational actions are developed in response to the demands of the environment. The organization acts according to the interdependencies it confronts. Here constraints and actions are directly related. It is expected here that the outsourcing option involves medium levels of dependence on external environment.

Discretionary Approach to Outsourcing

In the discretionary role, constraints and environments are managed to suit the interests of the organization. Management's function is to direct the organization towards more favourable environments and to manage and establish negotiated environments favourable to the organization. Unlike other approaches, this approach to outsourcing involves high levels of dependence on environment.

Thus, the decision to outsource IS functions is the result of the complex interplay of two factors: the organization's dynamic environmental conditions and the extent to which the organization needs to fill gaps in IS resources and capabilities.

Empirical Study Based on the Model

The model depicted provides insight, albeit preliminary, into the nature and structure of outsourcing concepts and variables. These can be used to direct inquiry into the phenomenon. For instance, propositions based on resource-based theory would suggest that organizations that have deficiencies in their information resources would seek outsourcing alternatives. These propositions could relate to a homogeneous monolithic outsourcing or to discretionary introspection of specific IS functions (i.e., applications development may be retained in-house but operations and end user computing outsourced). Similar introspection could facilitate assessment of the value, rareness, imitability and substitutability of IS resources. Based on resource-based theory, corporations that perceive these assessments in favour of there is resources would tend to outsource. It could also be proposed that firms that follow aggressive strategies in fulfilling resource gaps tend to outsource more and have a higher risk profile of outsourcing arrangements.

Similarly, propositions based on resource dependence theory seek to examine the nature of environmental resources (i.e., vendor market) and their ability to enter into contractual or partnership arrangements with powerful vendors. Propositions examining the vendor market, vendor versus firm power (concentration of resources) and uniqueness of IT skill desired (munificence) as related to degree and nature of outsourcing would facilitate understanding from this perspective. Integrated studies that look at both firm, environment and their interaction through strategy (e.g., symbolic, responsive and discretionary approaches) can provide greater explanatory power.

Transaction cost theory examines outsourcing from an economic perspective, trading off transaction costs and production costs. Propositions based on this perspective would suggest that, since vendors possess inherent economies of scale due to production efficiency and labour specialization, outsourcing IS functions with low asset specificity (e.g., network management, operations, transaction processing) would be desirable while unique IS products such as application development and planning should be insourced. There is preliminary evidence that supports and questions these notions (e.g., Lacity and Hirschheim, 1993a; McFarlan and Nolan, 1995). Also, transaction costs increase with asset specificity, uncertainty and infrequency in the didactic relationship, thereby making outsourcing difficult.

Agency cost theory suggests that agency costs increase based on various factors. The costs of enforcing 'tight contracts' based on uncertainty, measurability, length, programmability, etc., would inhibit outsourcing. These effects would be compounded if there was a lack of goal congruence between the contracting parties.

There has been some early empirical work on some of the factors suggested. For instance, Fitzgerald and Willcocks (1994) have examined the degree of uncertainty in contractual definition. Loh and Venkatraman (1992) have studied financial determinants of outsourcing. Grover et al. (1994a) and Teng et al. (1995) have evaluated the role of strategy in pursuing a resource gap model of the outsourcing of IS functions. Based on a market approach for meeting information processing requirements, Elam (1988) proposed the use of cooperative arrangements (e.g., outsourcing) for future IS organizations in the following areas: in developing back office and support applications, the IS organization will seek cooperative arrangements (external to the organization) that result in the divestment of skills, knowledge, and technology; in developing strategic applications, the IS organization will seek cooperative arrangements (external to the organization) that result in the acquisition of new skills, knowledge, and technology.

Conclusion

The increasing pervasiveness of IS outsourcing, the competitiveness and diversity of the vendor market and the growing interest among IS researchers systematically to examine this phenomenon, provide the impetus for this paper. The framework presented and the theoretical perspectives reviewed, both strategic and economic, provide insight into the complexity of variables that need to be studied. While making no pretensions of comprehensiveness, the framework, its concepts and interactions can guide future empirical research. While studies based on one theoretical perspective have been reported, opportunities exist to study the phenomenon in a more integrative manner, thereby facilitating a robust understanding. Future work should expand this model, identify specific and testable constructs, and propose and test hypotheses. Doing so will contribute to understanding current research and to improving future research and practice while establishing a cumulative tradition for this work.

References

Aldrich, H. (1976) Resource dependence and interorganizational relations: relations between local employment service office and social services sector organizations. *Administration and Society*, 7, 419–455.

Alrich, H. and Pfeffer, J. (1976) Environments of organizations. *Annual Review of Sociology*, 2, 79–105.

Apte, U. (1990) Global outsourcing of information systems and processing services. *The Information Society*, 7, 287–303.

Aucoin, P. (1991) Internalizing the vendor's resources: outsourcing in the 1990s, Critical Technology Report No. C–6–1 (Carrollton, TX: Chantico Publishing Co., Inc.).

Bacharach, S.B. (1989) Organizational theories; some criteria for evaluation. *Academy of Management Review*, **14**, 496–515.

Barney, J. (1986) Strategic factor markets: expectations, luck, and business strategy. *Management Science*, **32**, 1231–1241.

Barney, J. (1991) Firm resources and sustained competitive advantage. *Journal of Management*, **17**, 99–120.

Child, J. (1987) Information technology, organization, and the response to strategic challenges. *California Management Review*, **30**, 33–50.

Clark Jr., T.D (1992) Corporate systems management: an overview and research perspective. *Communications of the ACM*, **35**, 61–75.

Clemons, E.K. and Row, M.C. (1989) Information technology and economic reorganization, in *Proceedings of the Tenth International Conference on Information Systems*, DeGross, J., Henderson, J. and Konsynski, B., eds, Boston, MA, pp. 341–351.

Coase, R.H. (1937) The nature of the firm. *Economica*, **4**, 13–16, 386–405.

Conner, K.R. (1991) A historical comparison of resource-based theory and five schools of thought within industrial organization economics: do we have a new theory of the firm?. *Journal of Management*, **17**, 121–154.

Drazin, R. and Van De Ven, A.H. (1985) Alternative forms of fit in contingency theory. *Administrative Science Quarterly*, **30**, 514–539.

Dubin, R. (1969) *Theory building* (The Free Press: New York).

Dubin, R. (1976) Theory building in applied area, *Handbook of Industrial and Organizational Psychology*, Dunnette, M., ed. (Rand McNally: Chicago), pp. 17–40.

Eisenhardt, K.M. (1988) Agency- and institutional-theory explanations: the case of retail sales compensation. *Academy of Management Journal*, **31**, 488–511.

Eisenhart, K.M. (1989) Agency theory: an assessment and review. *Academy of Management Review*, **14**, 57–74.

Elam, J.J. (1988) Establishing cooperative external relationships, *Transforming the IS Organization*, Elam, J., Ginzberg, M., Keen, P. and Zmud, R., eds. (ICIT Press: Washington, DC), pp. 83–98.

Emery, F.E. and Trist, E.L. (1965) The causal texture of organizational environments. *Human Relations*, **18**, 21–33.

Fahey, L. and Christensen, H.K. (1986) Evaluating the research on strategy content. *Journal of Management*, **12**, 167–183.

Fitzgerald, G. and Willcocks, L. (1994) Contracts and partnerships in the outsourcing of IT, in *Proceedings of the International Conference on Information Systems*, Vancouver, BC, pp. 91–98.

Ginsberg, A. and Venkatraman., N. (1985) Contingency perspectives of organizational strategy: a critical review of empirical research. *Academy of Management Review*, **10**, 421–434.

Grant, J. and King, W.R. (1982) *The Logic of Strategic Planning*. (Little, Brown and Company: Boston).

Grant, R.M. (1991) The resource-based theory of competitive advantage: implications for strategy formulation. *California Management Review*, **33**, 114–135.

Grover, V., Teng, J. and Cheon, M. (1994a) The impact of corporate strategy and role of information technology on a discrepancy model of IS functional outsourcing. *European Journal of Information Systems*, **3**, 179–190.

Grover, V., Teng, J. and Cheon, M. (1994b) A descriptive study on the outsourcing of IS functions. *Information and Management*, **27**, 3–44.

Grover, V. and Teng, J. (1993) The decision to outsource information systems functions. *Journal of Systems Management*, **44**, 34–39.

Hambrick, D.C. and Lei, D. (1985) Toward an empirical priorization of contingency variables for business strategy. *Academy of Management Journal*, **28**, 763–788.

Hitt, M. and Ireland, D. (1986) Relationships among corporate level distinctive competencies, diversification strategy, corporate strategy and performance. *Journal of Management Studies*, **23**, 401–416.

Hofer, C.W. (1975) Toward a contingency theory of business strategy. *Academy of Management Journal*, **18**, 784–809.

Jensen, M.C and Meckling, W.R. (1976) Theory of the firm: managerial behavior, agency costs and ownership structure. *Journal of Financial Economics*, **3**, 305–360.

Kotter, J.P. (1979) Managing external dependence. *Academy of Management Review*, **4**, 87–92.

Lacity, M.C. and Hirschheim, R. (1993a) The information systems outsourcing bandwagon. *Sloan Management Review*, **34**, 73–86.

Lacity, H.C. and Hirschheim, R. (1993b) *Information Systems Outsourcing: Myths, Metaphors, and Realities*. (John Wiley and Sons: Chichester).

Loh, L. and Venkatraman, N. (1991) 'Outsourcing' as a mechanism of information technology governance: a cross-sectional analysis of its determinants,

Working Paper No. BPS 3272–91, Massachusetts Institute of Technology, Alfred P. Sloan School of Management, Cambridge.

Loh, L. and Venkatraman, N. (1992) Determinants of information technology outsourcing. *Journal of Management Information Systems*, **9**, 7–24.

McFarlan, P.W. and Nolan, R.L. (1995) How to manage an outsourcing alliance. *Sloan Management Review*, **36**, 9–23.

Miles, R. and Snow, C. (1978) *Organizational Strategy, Structure and Process.* (McGraw-Hill: New York).

Miller, D. and Freisen, P.H. (1978) Archetypes of strategy formulation. *Management Science*, **24**, 921–933.

Mitnick, B. (1975) The theory of agency: the policing 'paradox' and regulatory behavior. *Public Choice*, **24**, 27–42.

Mitnick, B. (1986) The theory of agency and organizational analysis. Paper presented at annual meeting of American Political Science Association, Washington.

Penrose, E.T. (1959) *Theory of the Growth of the Firm.* (Blackwell: Oxford).

Pfeffer, J. and Salancik, G.R. (1978) *The External Control of Organizations.* (Pittman: Baston).

Ross, S. (1973) Economic theory of agency: the principal problem. *American Economic Review*, **63**, 134–139.

Rubin, P.R. (1973) The expansion of firms. *Journal of Political Economy*, **81**, 936–949.

Rudner, R.S. (1966) *Philosophy of Social Science.* (Prentice-Hall: Englewood Cliffs).

Rumelt, R. (1974) *Strategy, Structure, and Economic Performance.* (Harvard University Press: Cambridge).

Schendel, D. and Hofer, C.W. (eds) (1979) *Strategic Management: A New View of Business Policy and Planning.* (Little, Brown & Company: Boston).

Schiffman, S. and Loftin, R. (1991) Outsourcing of information systems services, in *Proceedings of 1991 Decision Sciences Institute Annual Meeting*, Melnyk, S. ed, Miami Beach, FL, pp. 922–925

Stevensen, H.H. (1976) Defining corporate strengths and weaknesses. *Sloan Management Review*, **17**, 51–68.

Teng, J., Cheon, M. and Grover, V. (1995) The information system outsourcing decision: empirical test of a strategy-theoretic discrepancy model. *Decision Sciences*, **26**, 75–103.

Thompson, A.A. and Strickland, A.J. (1983) *Strategy Formulation and Implementation.* (Business Publications: Dallas).

Thompson, J.D. (1967) *Organizations in Action.* (McGraw-Hill: New York).

Ulrich, D. and Barney, J.B. (1984) Perspectives in organizations: resource dependence, efficiency, and population. *Academy of Management Review*, **9**, 471–481.

Van De Ven, A.H. (1989) Nothing is quite so practical as a good theory. *Academy of Management Review*, **14**, 486–489.

Venkatraman, N. and Camillus, J.C. (1985) Exploring the concept of 'fit' in strategy management. *Academy of Management Review*, **9**, 513–525.

Wernerfelt, B. (1984) A resource-based view of the firm. *Strategic Management Review*, **5**, 171–180.

Williams, J.R. (1992) How sustainable is your competitive advantage?. *California Management Review*, **34**, 29–51.

Williamson, O.E. (1975) *Markets and Hierarchies: Analysis and Antitrust Implications*. (Free Press: New York).

Williamson, O.E. (1979) Transaction-cost economics: the governance of contractual relations. *Journal of Law and Economics*, **22**, 233–261.

Williamson, O.E. (1981) The economics of organization: the transaction cost approach. *American Journal of Sociology*, **87**, 548–577.

Williamson, O.E. (1985) *The Economic Institutions of Capitalism*. (Free Press: New York).

Yuchtman, E. and Seashore, S.E. (1967) A system resource approach to organizational effectiveness. *American Sociological Review*, **32**, 891–903.

Zeithaml, C.P. and Zeithaml, V.A. (1984) Environmental management: revising the marketing perspective. *Journal of Marketing*, **48**, 46–53.

Varun Grover was an Associate Professor of MIS in the Management Science Department at the University of South Carolina. He holds a BTech. in Electrical Engineering from the Indian Institute of Technology, an MBA from SIUC and a PhD degree in MIS from the University of Pittsburgh. Dr Grover has over 60 refereed articles published on outsourcing, reengineering, strategic information systems, the management of information systems and telecommunications. He coedited a book *Business Process Change*. He received an Outstanding Achievement Award from the Decision Sciences Institute and is a member of AIS, TIMS and DSI.

Myun J. Cheon has a PhD in MIS from the College of Business Administration at the University of South Carolina. He holds an MBA from Indiana State University and a BBA from Keimyung University in Korea. His primary areas of interest include outsourcing of IS functions and IS security.

James T.C. Teng was an Associate Professor at the College of Business Administration, University of South Carolina. He holds an MS in Mathematics from the University of Illinois and a PhD in MIS from the University of Minnesota. His research interests are in the areas of IS outsourcing, data resource management, DSS and business process redesign. He received an Outstanding Achievement Award from the Decision Sciences Institute in 1992. He has published over 40 research papers in leading IS journals.

3

The Information Technology Outsourcing Risk: A Transaction Cost and Agency Theory-Based Perspective

Bouchaib Bahli and Suzanne Rivard

Introduction

The reliance on outsourcing as a means of providing information technology (IT) services has been growing steadily over the past decade. It was recently estimated that IT outsourcing would reach US$156 billion in 2004 (Lacity and Willcocks 2000). The fact that firms are increasingly turning to external suppliers in order to meet their IT needs does not mean that outsourcing is a panacea or that it is without problems. While it may help clients achieve major benefits such as cost savings, increased flexibility, higher quality services and access to new technology (McFarlan and Nolan 1995), unsuccessful outsourcing experiences are often reported in which suppliers have failed to meet expected service levels and deliver the expected cost savings (Earl 1996;

B. Bahli (✉)
Concordia University, Montreal, QC, Canada

S. Rivard
HEC Montréal, Montreal, QC, Canada

© The Author(s) 2017   **53**
L.P. Willcocks et al. (eds.), *Outsourcing and Offshoring Business Services*, DOI 10.1007/978-3-319-52651-5_3

Willcocks et al. 1999). A number of studies published on the risks associated with IT outsourcing have provided useful insights into the phenomenon (Earl 1996; Aubert et al. 1998; Willcocks et al. 1999). Notwithstanding their contribution, systematic efforts at refining the conceptualization and measurement of IT outsourcing risks are required (Willcocks et al. 1999). This has been the primary goal of this study.

This paper addresses the issue of risk assessment by proposing a conceptual definition of the IT outsourcing risk. Adapting and extending a risk definition used in engineering and proposed by Kaplan and Garrick (1981), it defines risk as a quadruplet composed of possible scenarios, the likelihood of their occurrence, their associated consequences and the risk mitigation mechanisms that can prevent them or attenuate their impact. The proposed definition of risk is then applied to IT outsourcing drawing on previous work on IT outsourcing in general and the IT outsourcing risk in particular (Earl 1996; Aubert et al. 1998; Lacity and Willcocks 2001; Kern et al. 2002b) and using transaction cost theory (Williamson 1985) and agency theory (Eisenhardt 1989) as theoretical foundations.

Risk Defined

'Risk' is probably one of the most frequently used words today. It is heard every day, under extremely different circumstances, with respect to the variability of investments, predispositions for cardiovascular disease or the dangers of air travel. These various uses have different underlying meanings, such as the probability of occurrence of an undesirable event, the severity of its consequences or the variability of returns on assets. In a comprehensive paper on risk March and Shapira (1987) proposed two perspectives for defining and studying risk: the economic perspective and the managerial perspective. In the economic perspective risk is the variance of a probability distribution of possible gains and losses associated with a given alternative. In the managerial perspective uncertainty about positive outcomes is not considered important (as they constitute the attractiveness of a given alternative). Rather, risk is associated with negative outcomes. Risk is therefore perceived as a 'danger or hazard'.

Kaplan and Garrick (1981) adopted such a managerial perspective in their widely-cited paper from the engineering discipline titled 'On the Quantitative Definition of Risk' and argued that a complete risk assessment requires that three questions be addressed. These questions are as follows.

(1) What can happen?
(2) How likely is this outcome?
(3) If it does occur, what are the consequences?

They proceeded by proposing a general definition of risk as a complete set of triplets involving scenarios, the likelihood of each scenario and the consequences or an evaluation measure of each scenario (that is a measure of the damages). Hence, in assessing the risk of a given situation, one would make a list of outcomes or 'scenarios', as suggested in Table 3.1 [deleted in this reprint],[1] where the ith line is a triplet $<s_i, p_i, x_i>$, where s_i is the scenario, p_i is the probability of occurrence of scenario s_i and x_i is the consequence of the occurrence of scenario s_i.

In IT outsourcing the scenarios suggested by transaction costs and agency theory are not 'acts of God': they are within the client's 'feasible' limits of control. They can therefore be acted upon using risk mitigation mechanisms that reduce their likelihood of occurring or help prevent them altogether (Lacity and Willcocks 2001; Kern et al. 2002a). In other words, if a risk mitigation mechanism m_i were introduced the corresponding scenario might not occur. Hence, risk measurement requires that these mechanisms be taken into account. Kaplan and Garrick's (1981) definition of risk is therefore extended with a fourth component and risk is defined as a set of quadruplets including scenarios, the likelihood and consequences of each scenario and the corresponding risk mitigation mechanisms.

Formally, risk is defined as $<s_i, p_i, x_i, m_i>$, where s_i is the scenario, p_i is the likelihood of that scenario, x_i is the consequence and m_i is the risk mitigation mechanism.

---

[1] Table 3.1 deleted in this reprint for copyright reasons.

While in some instances it is possible to estimate the likelihood of a given scenario on the basis of past performance of the object under study, it is not feasible to do so in several areas (Barki et al. 1993). Consequently, several risk assessment methods adopt the approach of approximating the probability of undesirable outcomes by identifying and assessing the factors that influence their occurrence (Barki et al. 1993). The degree to which each factor is present in an endeavour will contribute to the increased likelihood of a given scenario. Once this list is drawn, risk management methods will consist of devising and using mechanisms that will either diminish the loss related to the scenario itself or decrease the likelihood of its occurrence by reducing the level of the risk factors (Aubert et al. 2002).

Information Technology Outsourcing Risk

Kaplan and Garrick (1981) extended definition was applied to IT outsourcing risk. Potential scenarios in an IT outsourcing project and their associated consequences were identified, the likelihood of each scenario was determined through the risk factors leading to them and risk mitigation mechanisms that could help avoid or attenuate their likelihood were identified. Table 3.2 presents the resulting risk assessment framework. Following on and extending the work of Aubert et al. (1998), the linkages shown in Table 3.2 are anchored in transaction cost theory (Williamson 1985) and agency theory (Eisenhardt 1989). In that Table 3.2 is not exhaustive, since it is limited to the suggestions of two closely related theories. It is recognized that it would be possible to study IT outsourcing risk from other theoretical and empirical perspectives, such as contract theory and law. For instance, following Crocker and Reynolds (1993), Aubert et al. (2003a) examined the costs and benefits of contract completeness as a risk-reducing mechanism. The perspective of law could also be adopted. Collins (1999) and Vincent-Jones (2000) discussed the use of private law for protecting consumers within the context of the market and the role and limitations of the law of contract as a form of regulation. In addition, counter-posing discrete and relational contracts each associated with their own distinctive modes

Table 3.2 The IT outsourcing risk assessment framework

Scenarios	Risk factors	Consequences	Mitigation mechanisms
Lock-in	Asset specificity Small number of suppliers Client's degree of expertise in outsourcing contracts	Cost escalation and service debasement	Mutual hostaging Dual sourcing
Costly contractual amendments	Uncertainty	Cost escalation and service debasement	Sequential contracting Contract flexibility
Unexpected transition and management costs	Uncertainty Client's degree of expertise in IT operations Client's degree of expertise in outsourcing contracts Relatedness	Cost escalation and service debasement	Clan mechanisms Use of external expertise
Disputes and litigation	Measurement problems Supplier's degree of expertise in IT operations Supplier's degree of expertise in outsourcing contracts	Cost escalation and service debasement	Alternative methods of dispute resolution Clan mechanisms Use of external expertise

of legal reasoning, MacNeil (1983) developed a comprehensive analysis of the sources of 'bindingness' in contractual relations. While it is recognized that IT outsourcing risk could be studied from these and other stances, this paper limits the analysis to the perspective of transaction cost and agency theory.

Transaction cost theory provides much of the theoretical background for research on IT outsourcing (Lacity and Hirschheim 1993; Aubert et al. 1996, 1998). This theory is centred on governance structures, suggesting that the most efficient structure for governing a transaction – either the market or the firm – depends on transaction costs, which are related to some key characteristics of the transaction themselves.

Transactions differ in a variety of ways by the degree to which relationship-specific assets are involved, the amount of uncertainty about the future and the actions of other parties, measurement problems, the relatedness of IT operations and the number of suppliers in the market.

Transaction cost theory is based on two behavioural assumptions (Williamson 1985). First, it operates on the assumption of bounded rationality, which refers to how the cognitive limitations of the human mind rule out a complete evaluation of the consequences of all possible decisions. In an outsourcing context, the impact of bounded rationality depends in part on the knowledge and skills the client can draw on in specifying requirements, selecting appropriate suppliers and managing and controlling the relationship. Second, the theory operates under the assumption of opportunism, which posits that people do not only act in self-interest, but that they also act with guile. For instance, IT suppliers may lie about – or exaggerate – their capabilities or use their knowledge advantage in order to sell IT resources to clients who have little experience and/or knowledge about their needs or market prices. They may also do so because they want to enter a new market, to dominate a market segment or to lock out competitors (Kern et al. 2002b). Research has shown that these two behavioural assumptions are indeed relevant in the context of IT outsourcing. For instance, Aubert et al. (2003b) analysed the case of an insurance company – Emptor – the unfortunate decisions of which regarding supplier selection, asset transfer, performance measures and arbitration mechanisms led to excessive costs for both partners, unrealistic deliverables and deadlines, poor service quality and, ultimately, contract failure. While the analysis emphasized the role played by the supplier's opportunism, bounded rationality, in terms of the client's lack of expertise with outsourcing, also played an important role in this case.

The second economic theory of interest is agency theory (Eisenhardt 1989). The major issue in agency relationships is ensuring that the agent acts in the interests of the principal. The theory would assume, in the case of IT outsourcing, that each party in the relationship has their own profit motive, because the parties' goals are not congruent. The principal cannot monitor the actions of the agent perfectly and without cost (Sappington 1991).

Risk Scenarios and their Associated Risk Factors

Agency theory and transaction cost theory suggest four main risk scenarios that can be associated with outsourcing: (1) lock-in, (2) contractual amendments, (3) unexpected transition and management costs and (4) disputes and litigation. These correspond to those identified in the literature on the IT outsourcing risk (Aubert et al. 1998). Since the probability of occurrence of a given scenario is estimated on the basis of risk factors, the presence of which would be likely to increase this probability, each scenario is presented here along with the associated risk factors (see Table 3.2).

The term lock-in refers to a situation where a client cannot get out of a relationship except by incurring a loss or sacrificing part or all of its assets to the supplier (Aubert et al. 1998).

Three main risk factors are conducive to a lock-in situation. The first is asset specificity, which concerns investments made specifically because of a given contract and which have a much higher value because of the contractual relationship. If one party were to breach the contract, the value of the relationship-specific investments would fall. This is the so-called lock-in effect, where much can be lost to one or both parties if the relationship dissolves (Williamson 1985; Kern et al. 2002b). The very nature of the outsourced activity may contribute to increasing the degree of asset specificity. The client's idiosyncrasies may be such that, even for a supplier with much experience, it constitutes a new environment (Kern et al. 2002b). Having invested a great deal of time and effort in getting the initial supplier fully operational, the client itself may be reluctant to do so with a new supplier. Since some clients do not retain in-house competencies with the outsourced activity, they may even be unable to do so (Aubert et al. 2003b). The second risk factor often associated with lock-in is a restricted number of suppliers, since the bargaining power of suppliers increases as their number decreases (Porter 1985). Often a lack of alternative sources of supply is the primary cause of a client's dependency on its supplier (Williamson 1985). Transaction costs can arise when the presence of competitors does not constrain the supplier from behaving opportunistically (Walker and Poppo 1991). Finally, the client's lack of expertise with outsourcing contracts may also lead to a lock-in (Aubert et al. 1998). The term expertise is used here to refer to a combination of skill level with a given activity and length of time the activity has been performed (Thompson et al. 1994). A client with little expertise may make decisions that will directly lead to a lock-in situation. Such is the case of allowing a long initial term (5–10 years) without adequate termination for poor performance or termination for convenience clauses or not having asset buy-back or employment offer provisions, no disengagement and handover obligations, no intellectual property clauses governing the supplier modifications in event of termination, thus rendering the removal system inoperable or no usable source code in escrow.

The second risk scenario, costly contractual amendments, refers to any alterations, redrafting or changes made at any time during the contract to part or all of its clauses whenever a contractual party (the client and/or IT supplier) deems it necessary. Contracting parties are rationally bounded and cannot foresee all eventualities, so writing and enforcing complete contracts is impossible. As a consequence both parties must rely on incomplete contracting and any amendment will be made at a cost (Williamson 1985). Amendment costs include the direct costs of communicating new information, renegotiating agreements or coordinating operations in order to reflect new circumstances (Walker and Weber 1984).

Contractual amendments are mainly due to the uncertainty about future events and the other party's actions. Three types of uncertainty exist. The first is environmental volatility or the rapidity of market and demand changes. Environmental uncertainty coupled with bounded rationality diminishes the ability of partners for planning effectively and, therefore, increases the transaction costs surrounding contractual amendments (Pilling et al. 1994). In the second case uncertainty is tied to technological discontinuity (technological changes and breakthroughs that may render the technology of the original contract obsolete). Such changes may force the parties to amend their contract, at a certain cost (Earl 1996; Aubert et al. 1998). The third type of uncertainty is related to the nature of the outsourced activities. An activity will be said to have a high level of uncertainty when it is difficult to describe with exactitude the outputs it should produce (Aubert et al. 1998). Research in IT on the determination of user requirements has demonstrated how difficult such an activity is in the context of system development. Hence, any increase in uncertainty provides an incentive for opportunistic behaviour when contract clauses need to be amended (Williamson 1985).

Unexpected transition and management costs are hidden and/or underestimated costs (Lacity and Hirschheim 1993). Transition costs include set-up, redeployment or relocation costs, sales tax on equipment purchases, equipment transfers, leasing costs, etc. Management costs include the human resources devoted to managing an outsourcing contract, termination, handover and reimplementation costs of the next generation contract – these can certainly be significant switching barriers where there is a lock-in (Klepper and Jones 1998).

The literature suggests three factors as antecedents to the occurrence of unexpected transition and management costs: (1) the client's lack of expertise with the outsourced activity, (2) the client's lack of expertise with outsourcing and (3) the degree of relatedness of the outsourced activity. As suggested by Aubert et al. (1998), a client's lack of expertise with the outsourced activity may lead to hidden costs and, therefore, cause a loss of control over costs. Authors also suggest that a client's lack of expertise in contract management may lead to increased costs of service (Lacity and Willcocks 2001). According to Klepper and Jones (1998), a client without relevant expertise in outsourcing may expect to incur more costs transferring and relocating people and transferring equipment, leases and software licences. This results in unexpected transition and management costs (Klepper and Jones 1998).

Relatedness, which is also called interdependence or connectedness, refers to the interconnections between tasks, business units or functions, such as the performance of one discrete piece of work that depends on the completion of other discrete pieces of work (Wybo and Goodhue 1995; Van Der Vliert 1998). Some consequences of relatedness may have a negative impact on business performance through inflexibilities and poor responsiveness to market changes. The greater the interdependence, the greater the need for coordination, joint problem solving and mutual adjustment and this may impede cost control (Milgrom and Roberts 1992). Such obvious costs may be small compared to hidden costs and constraints such as the time managers must spend explaining decisions to top management or the time spent in committees and on task forces coordinating with sister units (Porter 1985).

There are two types of relatedness in IT outsourcing. First, an outsourced IT operation may have a direct (or indirect) link to an in-house IT operation. Second, an outsourced IT operation may have a direct (or indirect) link to another outsourced IT operation. When IT operations are interdependent, the outsourcing of one may subtly weaken the ability of the other in order to perform successfully (Earl 1996). For instance, interfaces between systems provided by the supplier and those provided in-house can be difficult and complex to build, maintain and operate. If an outsourced shareholder system batch processes mutual fund buy–sell transactions that are then fed into an in-house trust accounting system, the timeliness and accuracy of the system output will depend on the timeliness and accuracy of the output from the mutual fund system. Coordinating the interface, timing and data structures will become difficult due to the separation of facilities and the companies' different agendas (Lowel, 1992). The client's ability for delivering its own products will therefore depend on the supplier delivering the required data processing services.

The fourth risk scenario, disputes and litigation, refers to any controversy concerning the association or representation of the contracting parties in negotiating, fixing, maintaining, changing or seeking to arrange the terms or conditions of a contract and the process of bringing and pursuing a lawsuit (Klepper and Jones 1998).

Three risk factors are particularly apt to cause disputes and litigation: the supplier's degree of expertise (the term expertise is used here as defined in the case of client expertise) in handling the outsourced operation, its degree of expertise in outsourcing and measurement problems.

It has been suggested that a lack of supplier expertise with the outsourced activity may lead to disputes and litigation (Aubert et al. 1998). A supplier may not be able to respond to a rapid change in business conditions or may not have a firm grasp of the client's business and objectives or the necessary range of expertise to fulfil its needs (Clark et al. 1995; Lacity and Willcocks 2001), thereby causing disputes between the parties over the services rendered. The supplier may over-estimate its capabilities and/or be unable to handle the operation as technology changes (Aubert et al. 1998). If the supplier's skills do not improve, service quality will most probably decline, the potential for cost reduction will be compromised and target setting will be suboptimal (Earl 1996). Therefore, a failure to meet performance requirements will affect the quality of the service received. If the supplier lacks expertise with the business aspect of the activity, the client is exposed to business risk, which may affect profitability. Since the supplier does not possess comparable knowledge of both internal and industry requirements, the client has to train the supplier's personnel and explain user require-ments, thereby incurring additional costs.

Because of its awareness of the impact of contractual clauses, a supplier with much expertise with outsourcing contracts may very well haggle more than an inexperienced one during the process of reaching an agreement. On the other hand, while a supplier with less expertise will often not haggle much during contract negotiation, they may end up signing clauses that will, in the future, give rise to disputes and litigations (Aubert et al. 1998). Examples of such clauses are (1) unlimited liability including consequential damages, (2) an obligation for back-to-back contracts with subcontractors even though the level of insurances, liabilities and financial guarantees are disproportioned to the work the subcontractor(s) is doing, (3) allow-ing a termination for convenience right without compensation before capital assets are fully amortized within the pricing regime, (4) agreeing to match benchmarked costs conducted by an independent organization without the right to agree the benchmarking methodology, source data and sample selection and without the right to disaggregate the unique contractual economic variants (i.e. forced to acquire more client staff than required, insurance levels, financial guarantees, etc.) between the sample and the contract, etc. (The authors are particularly grateful to one of the anonymous reviewers for suggesting this particular nuance, along with the exam-ples of clauses.)

Disputes and litigation are also associated with measurement problems. Alchian and Demsetz (1972) identified measurement problems where it was impossible to evaluate the individual contributions of each party and measure their fair value. The market can be 'inefficient' when performance cannot be easily assessed, because it is not known what to reward or how (Williamson 1985). The accuracy with which buyers measure the quality of the products or services determines the efficiency of market exchanges. In the absence of an accurate measure, buyers must engage in a costly process of monitoring or suppliers must engage in a costly process of signalling (Barzel 1982): the ability to measure outcomes easily is therefore critical to the overall performance of markets. Genus (1997) examined aspects of the contractual relationship between the principal actors in a construction project. Differences about how to interpret the supplier's performance led to disputes between the parties. The conflict focused on how to interpret contractual clauses concerning 'optimization' or the achievement of the best balance between capital and operating costs. The case of Emptor cited earlier (Aubert et al. 2003b) is another illustration of the disputes that may result from measurement problems. A few months into the contract with its supplier, the volume of Emptor activities increased and batch window problems began to appear. Since there was not enough time at night to process the jobs and have the systems available in the morning, the supplier decided to skip some jobs and process them over the weekend. This resulted in major problems for Emptor and haggling over the definition of service level started. The supplier was arguing that its commitment was to have the system available 97% of the time and that if a batch run was skipped and the system was still on-line at 07.00 h the 97% target was met. Emptor's management obviously did not agree with that interpretation.

Consequences

Two main consequences are associated with the four risk scenarios: service debasement and cost escalation (Lacity and Hirschheim 1993; De Looff 1995; Earl 1996; Aubert et al. 1998; Kern et al. 2002a).

Service debasement refers to any reduction in the quality of services received by a client (Aubert et al. 1998). Service quality may decline throughout the contract or may just fall below agreed-upon levels. Cost escalation refers to all costs incurred in the completion of the outsourced activity that overrun originally contracted costs and occur throughout the period covered by the contract. It is not limited to the cost of actually performing the IT activity: it covers a broad range of costs that are not present when an activity is performed in-house, including the development and maintenance of an exchange relationship, monitoring exchange behaviour and guarding against opportunism in an exchange situation (Williamson 1985).

All four scenarios may lead to either or both consequences. For instance, in a lock-in situation the supplier may very well be tempted to increase its costs unduly. Aubert *et al.* (forthcoming) gave the example of a large public corporation, whose supplier, at contract renewal time, proposed a contract where the costs were 50% higher than the second bidder's proposal. The supplier was convinced that its client was locked-in: the corporation had not retained any in-house expertise with the activity and relatively few suppliers were large enough to offer the breadth and depth of service required. In some instances the termination costs, along with handover and reimplementation costs of the next generation contract, can be such that they themselves constitute significant switching barriers. Because the client cannot easily turn towards another service supplier, a lock-in situation may also lead the supplier to renege on service levels.

Contractual amendments and contract renegotiation can indeed be very costly. As an extreme example, when renegotiation goes as far as contract cancellation the costs can become prohibitive. Transition and management costs can represent an important proportion of the total costs of an outsourcing agreement. According to some sources, percentages of between 5 and 7% of the value of an outsourcing contract may have to be devoted to these costs (Scheier 1996). In some instances, these additional costs make the benefits a firm expected to gain from outsourcing its IT activities vanish altogether.

The extremely publicized lawsuit between EDS and Xerox (Wall Street Journal 2001) illustrates how costly disputes and litigations can become.

EDS brought suit against its client alleging that it breached its contract by bringing back some activities in-house that were part of the outsourcing contract. Not all disputes and litigations are as publicized, but they are indeed costly. Apart from the direct costs of lawyers' and experts' fees the costs of the in-house resources whose time is spent working on the litigation, indirect costs, associated with reputation effects, may also be incurred. Even when disagreements do not lead to open disputes and litigations, they can be costly. Kern et al. (2002b) gave the example of Clientco, a firm affiliated with a large petroleum company, where disagreements between the client's and the supplier's operation managers in charge of managing the relationships became ongoing confrontations, up to a point where both managers had to be replaced. According to Kern et al. (2002b) this was very costly for both the client and the supplier. Disputes can also lead to service debasement. For instance, because of its dissatisfaction with its supplier's performance, Detroit Medical Center recently sued to dissolve a 10-year $300 million contract with Provider HealthNet Services. According to the client, Provider HealthNet Services failed to achieve timely completion of medical records and to deliver a plan for training employees and for organizing the department for computerized records. Yet the supplier argued that it was the uncooperative and obstructive action by Detroit Medical Center officials that caused the performance problems (Morrissey 2003).

The two consequences, service debasement and cost escalation, are closely related and one can lead to the other. For instance it may happen that, because of service debasement, the client has to step-in in a 'fire-fighting' mode and perform some of the operations that should normally be conducted by the supplier, hence incurring direct costs. On the other hand, faced with increasing costs, the decision may be made to decrease the service level.

Risk Mitigation Mechanisms

The four scenarios described above are not 'acts of God': rather they are within the limits of what can 'feasibly' be controlled by the client. They can therefore be affected by the use of risk mitigation mechanisms that would influence their likelihood of occurring or help prevent them altogether. Hence, risk assessment can only be meaningful if a scenario is less likely to occur because of a would-be effective mitigation intervention. In other words, the measurement of risk implies taking these mechanisms into account. A review of the literature on IT outsourcing as well as transaction cost and agency theory led to the identification of seven mitigation mechanisms that can influence the likelihood of the occurrence of a scenario or decrease the severity of the consequence, should the scenario take place.

These risk mitigation mechanisms are listed in Table 3.2 and are limited to the suggestions of the two theories used in this study. Since the design, negotiation, implementation and monitoring of any given risk management mechanism can be costly, decision makers will have to compromise between the levels of risk they are assuming and the extent of use of each mechanism (Aubert et al. 2003a). It is not possible to generalize with respect to the cost-effectiveness of a given mechanism: each situation ought to be analysed with respect to its particular cost/risk reduction situation.

Risk Mitigation Mechanisms Associated with Lock-in

Clients may be exposed to a lock-in scenario if specific investments involve a small number of suppliers and a single source of services (Klein et al. 1978). Two mechanisms may be used for influencing the likelihood of this scenario. The first is reciprocal exposure to specific assets, that is mutual hostaging (Koss and Eaton 1997). A credible commitment to mutually advantageous exchange may be achieved, however, if both parties have symmetric exposure to specific investments through partial redistribution of specific investment costs to the potentially opportunistic party. For instance, the client may invest in the supplier's learning of the company's processes, tools and methods and the supplier may also invest in physical equipment, site relocation, human resources learning, etc. The second mechanism is dual sourcing (Richardson 1993; Kern et al. 2002b). This multiple vendor strategy can be traced to Porter's (1985) recommendation for using several competing vendors in order to ensure low-cost, high-performance levels and acceptable service quality. The argument posits that the ever-present threat of losing business to the other supplier will induce each vendor to provide a higher level of performance and quality (Ngwenyama and Bryson 1999). Dual sourcing is often seen as a mechanism for mitigating the effects of a lock-in scenario in that it protects clients from complacency on the part of the single source (Aubert et al. 1998; Currie and Willcocks 1998). The well-documented example of dual sourcing at BPX is an example of the risk reduction role of this mechanism (Cross 1995; Lacity and Willcocks 2001). Having an agreement with three suppliers BPX could deflect the impact of a service slowdown by spreading services between the suppliers and by keeping suppliers conscious of the company's ability to switch to another supplier (Aubert et al. 2001). Aubert et al. (2003b) gave the example of Publix, a large public corporation that also opted for dual sourcing as a means of preventing lock-in.

Risk Mitigation Mechanisms Associated with Contractual Amendments

Under highly volatile conditions and in order to avoid costly contractual amendments parties can develop sequential relationships and agree to flexible contracts (Harris et al. 1998; Kern et al. 2002b). An essential aspect of cooperation in the face of unanticipated change is that the parties to a contract forgo short-term, unilateral advantages. Such forbearance is easier when the firm is confident that bilateral expectations of continuity provide the capacity for retaliating against opportunism and reciprocating forbearance. Uncertainty requires procedures for sequential decision making within an ongoing relationship, thereby simplifying the adaptation process (Williamson 1985). The second mitigation mechanism is flexible contracting, which consists of flexibility in price adjustment, contract provisions for renegotiation, termination of the contract and shortening the contract period. Harris et al. (1998) asserted that the prime rationale for creating flexible outsourcing contracts is to recognize that uncontrollable external factors may intervene. This leaves parts of a contract open for renegotiation because of the parties' changing circumstances or the change mechanisms built into the contract for protecting both the client and the supplier.

Risk Mitigation Mechanisms Associated with Unexpected Transition and Management Costs, Disputes and Litigation

When bounded rationality and opportunism are combined with asymmetries in information, perceptions of inequity may arise (Ouchi 1980). Sometimes the measurement of behaviour, outcome or both may be impossible (Eisenhardt 1989). This leads to unexpected transition and management costs as well as disputes and haggling over who is right. The literature proposes three risk mitigation mechanisms that can potentially prevent these scenarios from occurring or attenuate their severity: the hiring of external technical and legal expertise (Lacity and Hirschheim 1993), clan mechanisms through socialization and shared organizational norms and values (Ouchi 1980) and the use of alternative means for dispute resolution (Klepper and Jones 1998).

External Expertise Procurement

Outsourcing technically immature operations may engender disastrous outcomes because the client organization is not in a position to negotiate sound contracts with its supplier (Lacity et al. 1995). The authors recommend buying expertise, but also integrating external resources into an internally managed team. According to Johnson (1997), appointing a contract or relationship manager who has the responsibility for making it all work can also be helpful. This manager should be knowledgeable about both overall company business as well as the outsourced activity. Any outsourcing agreement of substance will require consistent and robust management if its objectives and benefits are to be achieved. Hence, an expert is needed who understands the core contract management processes (White and James 1996). An outsourcing evaluation and negotiation requires technical, legal, management, negotiation and outsourcing expertise (Lacity and Hirschheim 1993). The right consultants and lawyers can greatly simplify an outsourcing transaction for both parties (Klepper and Jones 1998). In addition, Key (1995) suggested establishing a team of experts for serving as watchdogs and advisers. They should be familiar with service details and capable of scrutinizing the vendor's performance. Ashton (1998) examined health care services using transaction cost analysis and found a negotiator who was also contracted to negotiate on behalf of the primary care groups.

Clan Mechanisms

Clan mechanisms rely on normative considerations for influencing behaviour. Clan mechanisms are means to induce desirable behaviour through soft measures: they are associated with terms such as 'informal control', 'normative control' and 'clan control', as opposed to formal control (Leifer and Mills 1996). Influence comes in the form of shared goals, values and norms. Since there is no explicit restriction on behaviour, clan mechanisms imply more interpersonal respect and less mistrust than are found in formal control mechanisms. Clan mechanisms often provide a supportive environment in which partner firms come to understand the processes and objectives of alliance management, which are often initially unclear (Doz 1996). Where it is difficult to measure outcomes and/or supplier behaviour, clan mechanisms can be used if the parties share a vision, goals and norms.

Alternative Dispute Resolution

Alternative dispute resolution refers to a variety of techniques for resolving disputes without litigation. Two of the better-known alternative dispute resolution methods are mediation (in which parties voluntarily settle a dispute with the help of a skilled facilitator) and arbitration (in which a disinterested, neutral party is chosen to hear the case and give a legally binding ruling). In arbitration a dispute is submitted to one or more impartial persons for a final and binding decision (Auer 1999). Arbitration is an adversarial process that resembles litigation but is less formal: it is therefore generally less costly and time-consuming. Mediation, however, involves an attempt to resolve a dispute with the assistance of a neutral third party: the parties must voluntarily and cooperatively resolve the case. The mediator plays an advisory role. Mediation facilitates the bargaining process by convincing the parties that they will be better off with a settlement than in continued litigation. The parties do not appear on a public court record or in the press: this strict confidentiality can be an important consideration on both sides.

Arbitration can be beneficial for outsourcing contracts dealing with very technical matters if it uses knowledgeable people from the industry as arbitrators (Klepper and Jones 1998). The agreement should also contain sensible complaints and dispute resolution procedures in order to minimize the risk of future litigation and provide resolution procedures for matters that are best resolved by means other than litigation. Two measures should be considered.

(1) A simple procedure for enabling the parties to notify one another of a complaint and then (if necessary) participate in a simple negotiation or mediation process.
(2) An 'expert clause' that enables disputes about particular matters to be resolved by an appropriate, nominated expert. Matters for resolution by an expert include disputes about the achievement of agreed levels of performance and availability and whether proposed variations in workload are beyond pre-agreed bounds or should be provided free of charge. Furthermore, in the absence of registered mediators and arbitrators skilled in the specific nature of the dispute, both parties need to negotiate the expert determination option.

Conclusions, Limitations and Research Avenues

This paper has proposed a framework for the conceptualization and measurement of the risk construct and has applied this framework to IT outsourcing. The main underlying idea is that treating risk as a probability or an expected value of undesirable consequences is of limited usefulness. Rather, risk should instead be viewed as a set of quadruplets composed of scenarios (what can happen?), the likelihood of each scenario or risk factor occurring (how likely is this outcome?), risk mitigation mechanisms (what may prevent this scenario from occurring?) and the consequences of each scenario (if it does happen, what are the undesirable consequences?).

The conceptualization of IT outsourcing risks presented here allows for the systematic capture of four risk dimensions: risk factors, scenarios, their consequences and risk mitigation mechanisms. It describes and establishes a comprehensive theoretical framework for assessing IT outsourcing risks that identifies the interrelationships between these dimensions. The proposed definition provides interesting avenues for future investigation and applications. Managers are also provided with a formal tool for assessing IT outsourcing risks and our understating of this ill-defined construct has been improved.

The main limitation of the proposed framework is closely related to its strength. Indeed, the authors purposefully made the decision to base the analysis on strong theoretical groundings and chose transaction cost theory and agency theory for doing so. Notwithstanding the soundness and usefulness of this theoretical background, it is recognized that other theoretical frameworks are most relevant for the analysis and the understanding of IT outsourcing. For instance, the mitigation mechanisms proposed are limited to those suggested by agency theory and transaction cost theory. In reality, other mechanisms exist. For instance, by ensuring that the option of repatriating the activity is viable and cost-effective lock-in can be mitigated. Furthermore, even with a small number of suppliers, explicit legal power (disengagement, buy-back and handover) coupled with clear obligations and procedures to handover to another supplier on an agreed cost basis can mitigate lock-in against the incumbent supplier. Lastly, one of the greatest mitigation factors is the way the relationship is managed (Kern and Willcocks 2002). The paper has already referred to contract completeness and to law as possible domains. It is recognized that other domains, such as political theory (Lacity and Hirschheim 1993), would also be relevant. A first avenue for research would be to complete the framework developed here with insights from these areas.

Future research also needs to address issues related to the dynamic nature of risk over time. For instance, the degree of a risk factor before signing a contract may change upwards or downwards throughout the contract period. In addition, legal issues regarding the complexity of contract behaviour should be included in the framework developed in this paper in order to have a more comprehensive view of the IT outsourcing risk. Finally, a rigorous empirical validation of the constructs developed in this study is needed in order to have a sound measure of the IT outsourcing risk.

Acknowledgements The authors would like to thank the anonymous reviewers and the senior editors for their judicious comments and useful suggestions.

References

Alchian, A.A., and Demsetz, H. (1972) Production, information cost and economic organization. *American Economic Review*, **62**, 777–792.

Ashton, T. (1998) Contracting for health services in New Zealand: a transaction cost analysis. *Social Science Medicine*, **46**(3), 357–367.

Aubert, B.A., Rivard, S., and Patry, M. (1996) A transaction costs approach to outsourcing: some empirical evidence. *Information and Management*, **30**, 51–64.

Aubert, B.A., Patry, M., and Rivard, S. (1998) Assessing IT outsourcing risk. In *Proceedings of the 31st Hawaii International Conference on System Sciences*, H. Watson. (ed.) IEEE, Hawaii.

Aubert, B.A., Patry, M., Rivard, S., and Smith, H. (2001) IT outsourcing risk management at British Petroleum. In *Proceedings of the 34th Hawaii International Conference on Systems Sciences*, H. Watson. (ed.) IEEE, Hawaii, January.

Aubert, B.A., Patry, M., and Rivard, S. (2002) Managing IT outsourcing risk: lessons learned. In *Information Systems Outsourcing: Enduring Themes, Emergent Patterns and Future Directions*, R.A. Hirschheim, A. Heinzl, and J. Dibbern. (eds.) (Springer-Verlag, New York), pp. 155–176.

Aubert, B.A., Houde, J.F., Patry, M., and Rivard, S. (2003a) Characteristics of IT outsourcing contracts. In *Proceedings of the 36th Hawaii International Conference on System Sciences*, R. Sprague. (ed.) IEEE, Hawaii.

Aubert, B.A., Patry, M., and Rivard, S. (2003b) A tale of two outsourcing contracts: an agency-theoretical perspective. *Wirtschaftsinformatik*, **45**(2), 181–190.

Auer, J. (1999) Arbitration could be better alternative in IT contracts disputes. *Computerworld*, **33**(9), 58–59.

Barki, H., Rivard, S., and Talbot, J. (1993) Toward an assessment of software development risk. *Journal of Management Information Systems*, **10**(2), 203–225.

Barzel, Y. (1982) Measurement cost and the organisation of markets. *Journal of Law and Economics*, **25**(1), 27–48.

Clark, T.D., Zmud, R.W., and McGray, G.E. (1995) The outsourcing of information services: transforming the nature of business in the information industry. *Journal of Information Technology*, **10**(4), 221–237.

Collins, H. (1999) *Regulating Contracts* (Oxford University Press, Oxford).

Crocker, K.J., and Reynolds, K.J. (1993) The efficiency of incomplete contracts: an empirical analysis of air force engine procurement. *Rand Journal of Economics*, **24**, 126–146.

Cross, J. (1995) IT outsourcing: British Petroleum's competitive approach. *Harvard Business Review*, **73**(3), 95–102.

Currie, W., and Willcocks, L. (1998) Analyzing four types of IT outsourcing decisions in the context of size, client/supplier interdependency and risk mitigation. *Information Systems Journal*, **8**, 119–143.

De Looff, A.L. (1995) Information systems outsourcing decision-making: a framework, organizational theories and case studies. *Journal of Information Technology*, **10**(4), 281–297.

Doz, L. (1996) The evolution of co-operation in strategic alliances: initial conditions or learning processes?. *Strategic Management Journal*, **17**, 55–79.

Earl, M.J. (1996) The risks of outsourcing IT. *Sloan Management Review*, **37**(3), 26–32.

Eisenhardt, K.M. (1989) Agency theory: an assessment and review. *Academy of Management Review*, **14**(1), 57–74.

Genus, A. (1997) Unstructuring incompetence: problems of contracting, rust and the development of the Channel Tunnel. *Technology Analysis and Strategic Management*, **9**(4), 419–436.

Harris, A., Giunpero, C.L., and Hult, M.T. (1998) Impact of organisational and contract flexibility on outsourcing contracts. *Industrial Marketing Management*, **27**(5), 373–384.

Johnson, M (1997) *Outsourcing in Brief* (Butterworth-Heinemann, Oxford).

Kaplan, S., and Garrick, B.J. (1981) On the quantitative definition of risk. *Risk Analysis*, **1**(1), 11–27.

Kern, T., Willcocks, L., and Lacity, M.C. (2002a) Application service provision: risk assessment and mitigation. *MIS Quarterly Executive*, 1(2), 47–69.

Kern, T., Willcocks, L., and Van Heck, E. (2002b) The winner's curse in IT outsourcing: strategies for avoiding relational trauma. *California Management Review*, 44(2), 47–69.

Kern, T., and Willcocks, L (2002) Exploring relationships in information technology outsourcing: the interaction approach. *European Journal of Information Systems*, 11, 3–19.

Key, R. (1995) Outsourcing: how to contract with third party vendors. *ABA Bank Compliance*, 16(4), 5–12.

Klein, B., Crawford, G., and Alchian, A. (1978) Vertical integration, appropriable rents, and the competitive contracting process. *The Journal of Law and Economics*, 1, 297–326.

Klepper, R., and Jones, O.W. (1998) *Outsourcing Information Technology, Systems & Services* (Prentice-Hall, Upper Saddle River, NJ).

Koss, A.P., and Eaton, C.B. (1997) Co-specific investments, hold-up and self-enforcing contracts. *Journal of Economic Behaviour & Organisation*, 32(3), 457–470.

Lacity, M.C., Willcocks, L.P., and Feeny, D.F. (1995) IT outsourcing: maximize flexibility and control. *Harvard Business Review*, 73(3), 85–93.

Lacity, M.C., and Hirschheim, R. (1993) *Information Systems Outsourcing: Myths, Metaphors and Realities* (John Wiley & Sons, Chichester).

Lacity, M.C., and Willcocks, L.P. (2000) *Inside IT Outsourcing: A State-of-Art Report* (Templeton College, Oxford).

Lacity, M.C., and Willcocks, L.P. (2001) *Global Information Technology Outsourcing: Search for Business Advantage* (John Wiley & Sons, Chichester).

Leifer, R., and Mills, K. (1996) An information processing approach for deciding upon control strategies and reducing control loss in emerging organizations. *Journal of Management*, 22(1), 113–138.

Lowell, M. (1992) Managing your outsourcing vendor in the financial services. *Journal of Systems Management*, 43(5), 23–33.

MacNeil, I. (1983) Values in contract: internal and external. *Southern California Law Review*, 78, 340–349.

March, J., and Shapira, Z. (1987) Managerial perspectives on risk and risk taking. *Management Science*, 33, 1404–1418.

McFarlan, W., and Nolan, L. (1995) How to manage an IT outsourcing alliance. *Sloan Management Review*, 36(2), 9–23.

Milgrom, P., and Roberts, J. (1992) *Economics, Organisation, and Management* (Prentice-Hall, Englewood Cliffs, NJ).

Morrissey, J. (2003) Not paying off. *Modern Healthcare*, **33**(19), 3.

Ngwenyama, K.O., and Bryson, N. (1999) Making the information systems outsourcing decision: a transaction cost approach to analyzing outsourcing decision problems. *European Journal of Operational Research*, **115**(2), 351–367.

Ouchi, W. (1980) Markets, bureaucracies and clans. *Administrative Science Quarterly*, **25**(1), 129–147.

Pilling, B.K., Crosby, L.A., and Jackson, D.W. (1994) Relational bonds in industrial exchange: an experimental test of the transaction cost economic framework. *Journal of Business Research*, **30**, 237–251.

Porter, M. (1985) *Competitive Advantage Creating and Sustaining Superior Performance* (The Free Press, New York).

Richardson, J. (1993) Parallel sourcing and supplier performance in the Japanese automobile industry. *Strategic Management Journal*, **14**(5), 339–350.

Sappington, D. (1991) Incentives in principal–agent relationships. *Journal of Economic Perspectives*, **3**(2), 45–66.

Scheier, R.L. (1996) Outsourcing's fine print. *Computerworld*, **30**(34), 70.

Thompson, L.R., Higgins, A.C., and Howell, M.J. (1994) Influence of experience on personal computer utilization: testing a conceptual model. *Journal of Management Information Systems*, **11**(1), 167–187.

Van Der Vliert, E. (1998) Motivating effects of task and outcome interdependence in work teams. *Group and Organisation Management*, **23**(2), 124–143.

Vincent-Jones, P. (2000) Contractual governance: institutional and organizational analysis. *Oxford Journal of Legal Studies*, **20**(3), 317–351.

Walker, G., and Poppo, R. (1991) Profit centers, single-source suppliers, and transaction costs. *Administrative Science Quarterly*, **36**, 66–87.

Walker, G., and Weber, D.A. (1984) Transaction cost approach to make-or-buy decisions. *Administrative Science Quarterly*, **29**(3), 373–391.

Wall Street Journal (2001) EDS wins contract extension for Xerox project. 29 November, B8.

White, R., and James, B. (1996) *The Outsourcing Manual* (Gower Publishing Limited, Hampshire, England).

Willcocks, L., Lacity, M., and Kern, T. (1999) Risk mitigation in IT outsourcing strategy revisited: longitudinal case research at LISA. *Journal of Strategic Information Systems*, **8**, 285–314.

Williamson, O.E. (1985) *The Economic Institutions of Capitalism* (Sage Free Press, New York).

Wybo, D.M., and Goodhue, L.D. (1995) Using interdependence as a predictor of data standards: theoretical and measurement issues. *Information and Management*, **29**(6), 317–329.

Bouchaib Bahli was Assistant Professor of Management Information Systems in the John Molson School of Business at Concordia University. His research interests include risk management of software development projects, information technology outsourcing and e-business security systems. Dr Bahli's publications appear in Communications of AIS, the *International Conference on Information Systems*, and *the Hawaii International Conference on System Sciences*, among others. He is an experienced systems developer.

Suzanne Rivard is Professor of Information Technology and holder of the Chair of Strategic Management of Information Technology at HEC Montréal. She received a Ph.D. from the Ivey School of Business, the University of Western Ontario. Dr Rivard's research interests are in the areas of outsourcing of information systems services, software project risk management, strategic alignment of information technology, and the adoption of information technology.

4

Moments of Governance in IS Outsourcing: Conceptualizing Effects of Contracts on Value Capture and Creation

Shaila M. Miranda and C. Bruce Kavan

Introduction

Early research on IS outsourcing focused largely on the role of the contract and service level agreements in structuring and governing the client–provider relationship (e.g., Lacity and Willcocks 1998). More recently, researchers have begun to consider the role of non-contractual mechanisms such as trust and psychological contracts, which may be implemented at different moments during the inter-organizational relationship (e.g., Koh et al. 2004; Sabherwal 1999; Willcocks and Kern 1998; Davis 1996). Research has also begun to consider alternate forms of governance, that is, arm's-length *vs* embedded, that may be implemented via each mechanism (e.g., Lee et al. 2004). With these research

S.M. Miranda (✉)
University of Oklahoma, Norman, OK, USA
e-mail: shailamiranda@ou.edu

C.B. Kavan
University of North Florida, Jacksonville, FL, USA

© The Author(s) 2017   **79**
L.P. Willcocks et al. (eds.), *Outsourcing and Offshoring Business Services*, DOI 10.1007/978-3-319-52651-5_4

streams has been a growing realization that different forms of governance invoked at different times during a relationship have different impacts on the nature of the rents that accrue to the client. The objective of this paper is to synthesize our understandings of the different forms of governance that may be exercised at different moments in the client–provider relationship and the manner in which governance choices at one moment constrain those at another, and subsequently the nature of rents mobilized. We draw upon the organizational literature on inter-organizational relationships to extend and sharpen our understanding of governance in the IS outsourcing relationship.

IS outsourcing is a boundary-spanning inter-organizational relationship, in which functions traditionally performed in-house are performed by another organization. In the IT discipline, governance has been defined as 'specifying the decision rights and accountability framework to encourage desirable behavior in the use of IT' (Weill and Ross 2004: 8). As a strategy though, we consider governance not just in terms of pre-specified frameworks, but also those frameworks that emerge in interactions between client and provider (Mintzberg 1978). Three forms of governance are widely recognized: the *market* is an institutionally derived and transaction- or contract-based governance form; the *hierarchy* is an institutionally derived authority-based form; the *network* is a socially-derived informal form (Williamson 1994; Shapiro 1987)[1].

The following sections develop a model of IS outsourcing as a series of governance choices that constrain or promote certain outcomes. The model addresses the question of how governance choices affect outcomes of IS outsourcing in terms of (1) value capture and (2) value creation. The focus of the MoG model is on post-adoption governance choices, that is, after the decision has been made to outsource an IS function. The model identifies three outsourcing phases: the promissory contract, the psychological contract, and elicitation of inter-organizational rents.

---

[1] These parallel the price-, authority-, and trust-based governance forms identified by Davis (1996). However, the governance forms identified by Davis have a more limited meaning that those appearing in organizational theory (OT) literatures. For example, trust is only one aspect of network governance (e.g., Nahapiet and Ghoshal 1998). We therefore adopt the governance typology provided by the OT literatures.

In each of these three phases, the building blocks derived from Ring and Van De Ven (1994) and Nahapiet and Ghoshal (1998) delineate specific processes undertaken and structures that emerge. We view the promissory contract and the psychological contract as two moments of governance following adoption.[2] The promissory contract represents formally stipulated 'paid for promises' (Rousseau and Parks 1994: 4). Psychological contracts refer to 'an individual's beliefs regarding terms and conditions of a reciprocal exchange agreement between that person and another party' (Rousseau and Parks 1994: 19). We focus on psychological contracts rather than social contracts as a counterpoint to promissory contracts because social contracts are based on 'shared, collective beliefs regarding appropriate behavior' (Rousseau and Parks 1994: 3). While it is hoped that such shared, collective beliefs will emerge at this governance moment, they cannot be assumed. Furthermore, social contracts are believed to be automatically 'inherited at birth or acquired by membership' (Rousseau and Parks 1994: 4). In contrast, psychological contracts emerge in the course fulfillment of the terms of the promissory contract. Clients' capture and creation of value is enabled and constrained by these two governance moments.

At each governance moment, firms govern the outsourcing relationship via market, hierarchy, or network arrangements (Adler 2001). Note that our reference to governance specifically entails governance of the inter-organizational relationship, not the governance of the participant organizations. In the following section, we describe governance choices at each moment, how the choices are constrained and acquire specific meaning within the IS arena, and how choices at one moment affect later options.

Overview of the Theoretical Model

Researchers on organizational strategy have noted two mechanisms whereby organizations attain rents – via the capture of value via efficiency-seeking or the creation of value through innovation (e.g., Dutta

---

[2] This distinction is consistent with Macneil's (1985) legal *vs* behavioral contracts.

et al. 2003). Research on inter-organizational relationships, and, more recently, on IS outsourcing, has recognized the existence of arm's-length *vs* embedded governance structures in inter-organizational relationships (e.g., Uzzi 1997, 1999; Jarillo 1988; Lee et al. 2004). Arms-length relationships are those that are exclusively economic and rely solely on formal means of governance. Embedded relationships are those in which the economic and social content of the relationship overlap and the social relationship is tapped for regulating the relationship. These studies have recognized that the different governance structures tend to elicit different types of rents in inter-organizational relationships. Thus, while arms-length relationships facilitate the efficient deployment of economic and intellectual capital, embedded relationships lead to the creation and growth of these inter-organizational resources. The different rent-mobilizing governance pathways elucidated in this paper are summarized in Fig. 4.1. This model highlights two 'moments' of governance in inter-organizational relationships – the moment of the promissory contract

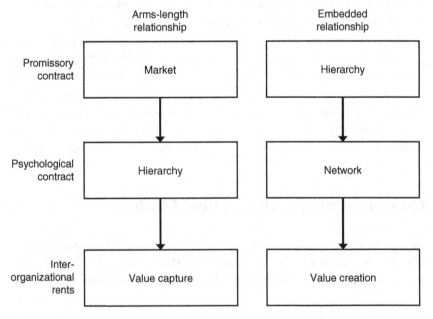

Fig. 4.1 Alternate governance patterns in IS outsourcing relationships

and the moment of the psychological contract. At each moment, one of two viable governance choices is available – market *vs* hierarchy at the moment of the promissory contract and hierarchy *vs* network at the moment of the psychological contract (Adler 2001). As depicted in Fig. 4.1, path-dependencies are engendered by the initial governance choice at the moment of the promissory contract, culminating in the acquisition of rents through either the capture of value or the creation of value. Alternatively, at the moment of the psychological contract, the terms of the promissory contract may be re-negotiated, commencing a new arrangement and re-starting the governance cycle.

In order to understand *how* these path-dependencies emerge, we consider the nature of the promissory and psychological contracts. We delineate the choices entailed in each of these moments, which, along with rent-mobilization choices, aggregate into arms-length *vs* embedded strategies. In doing so, we develop the MoG model summarized in Fig. 4.2. This model considers the process and emergent structure at

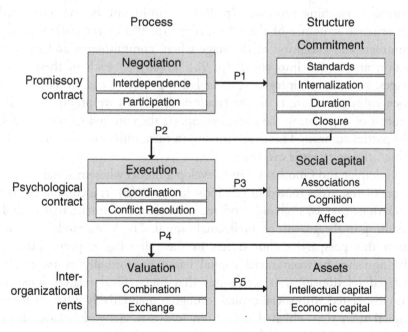

Fig. 4.2 A moments of governance (MoG) model of IS outsourcing

each governance moment and in the mobilization of inter-organizational rents. Here, structure is defined as rules and resources (Giddens 1979) or as assets that can be utilized by the organization (Stewart 1999). Such an approach enables a more comprehensive picture of the outsourcing relationship.

The building blocks for the MoG model are derived from Ring and Van de Ven's (1994) developmental framework of cooperative inter-organizational relationships and Nahapiet and Ghoshal's (1998) theory of intellectual capital creation via social capital. Ring and Van de Ven identify three stages in the development of inter-organizational relationships: negotiation, commitment, and execution. While these authors view the development of the explicit, formal contract and the implicit, informal contract as concurrent, based on the outsourcing literature (e. g., Willcocks and Kern 1998), we model them as consecutive moments. Furthermore, we explicitly model negotiation and execution as processes and commitment as the structure of the formal contract. This is consistent with Ring and Van De Ven (1994) who view negotiation as 'formal bargaining processes' (p. 97), commitment as 'the terms and governance structure of the relationship' (p. 98) or the *content* of the contract, and execution as the stage when 'commitments and rules of action are carried into effect' (p. 98). Finally, at each of these three stages, we contrast integrative *vs* isolative processes and structures and their subsequent effects on the relationship. Thus, we propose that the process of negotiating the contract impacts the contract terms to which the parties commit. This commitment, in turn, influences the manner in which the contract is executed.

Nahapiet and Ghoshal (1998) develop a model wherein social capital, 'a set of resources rooted in relationships' (p. 243), is a conduit for the valuation, that is, exchange and recombination, of intellectual capital, resulting in the growth of intellectual capital. The MoG model borrows from this perspective, but differs in the following respects. First, it distinguishes between social capital based on formally or informally derived relationships. It recognizes that hierarchical relationships are also associated with social capital, though a qualitatively different social capital than that which derives from informal, network relationships. Second, the MoG model views economic capital as a structure that parallels intellectual capital in its diffusion through social networks. Third, based on Moran and Ghoshal (1999), the model distinguishes between types of combination and exchange. Finally, we model alternate outcomes in regard to intellectual and economic capital, that is, value capture *vs* value creation. Specifically, we propose that the manner in which the contract is executed defines the social capital as formal and hierarchical or as informal and network-based. This social capital, in turn, influences the manner in which the valuation of resources takes place, ultimately determining the extent to which resources are developed or simply protected.

Promissory Contract Choices

The promissory contract is an important element of any complex business relationship. It facilitates communication of expectations and needs (Macaulay 1963). The promissory contract has been legitimized as an initiation point for IS outsourcing (e.g., Willcocks and Kern 1998; Hu et al. 1997; Lacity and Hirschheim 1993). It is a formal mechanism. As such, it precludes governance via the network and limits governance at the moment of the promissory contract to formal mechanisms, that is, market or hierarchy governance (Williamson 1996).

There can be considerable variation in the construction and language of contracts. Researchers have distinguished among types of promissory contracts as transactional *vs* relational (Rousseau and Parks 1994) and market *vs* hierarchy (Ang and Beath 1993; Stinchcombe 1985). We synthesize these earlier perspectives and identify processes and structures as constitutive of a market or hierarchy form of governance at the stage of the contract. The MoG model focuses exclusively on those contract terms that are entirely discretionary *vs* those constrained by task or technological requirements. For example, Rousseau and Parks (1994) distinguish between transactional and relational contracts in terms of Thompson's (1967) notion of interdependence and based on the dedication of resources to the relationship. Pooled *vs* reciprocal interdependence represents a task constraint (Thompson 1967), while resource allocations are a function of requirements. We therefore exclude such distinctions from our model. Table 4.1 delineates and defines the elements of the promissory contract that are the focus of the MoG model. The source of the element in the literature is indicated. The next two columns of Table 4.1 indicate what market and hierarchy forms of governance mean vis-à-vis each of the promissory contract elements identified.

'Alliance negotiations set the tone for the relationship' (Hutt et al. 2000: 59). We model the contract negotiation process as entailing varying levels interdependence and participation during the negotiation of the contract.

Unilateral contracts and limited participation are indicative of market-type relationships. In such relationships, the abilities, needs, and constraints of one partner are viewed as interchangeable with those of others, making pro-forma contracts seem viable. In other words, the provider views the needs of one client as identical to another or the client views providers' abilities and constraints as identical. Rather than attempting to involve multiple constituents in the relationship, the relationship is restricted to those immediately contracting for services. This sets up a classic buyer-seller relationship in which the 'identity [of the buyer and seller] is unimportant' (Williamson 1994: 102). In contrast, bilateral negotiation with extensive participation by both constituencies sets up an integrated relationship, which may then be hierarchically structured.

The content of a contract specifies the commitments or obligations of each party to the relationship. These commitments set up alternate governance structures. We explore the following contract terms: standards, internalization, duration, and closure. Behavior-based benchmarks and incentives, and cost-recovery approaches are viewed as hierarchical structures, while outcome-based benchmarks and incentives and market-pricing are viewed as market structures (Ang and Beath 1993; Stinchcombe 1985). Internalized and integrative authority structures and dispute resolution are also characteristics of conventional hierarchical structures (Ang and Beath 1993). Note that a unilateral authority and dispute resolution structure is not truly internalized in that it would offer no internal recourse to the excluded party: 'A one-sided holding of hostages, a one-sided monopoly, a one-sided transfer of control over

Table 4.1 Alternative forms of the promissory contract

Elements of promissory contract			Governance alternatives	
Element	Definition	Source	Market	Hierarchy
Promissory contract processes: negotiation				
Interdependence	Bilateral negotiation of the contract	Hutt et al. (2000)	Use of pro-forma contract	Bilateral negotiation of contract
Participation	Extent to which individuals from different organizational levels and functional areas are involved in the contracting process	Hutt et al. (2000)	Limited	Extended
Promissory contract structures: content/commitment				
Standards	Benchmarks for performance and compensation, including incentive and pricing systems	Ang and Beath (1993); Stinchcombe (1985)	Outcome-based benchmarks and incentives; outcome-pricing: specification of what should be accomplished	Behavior-based benchmarks and incentives; rule-based input-pricing: specification of what should be done
Internalization	Specifications of authority systems, that is, 'contractual terms that certify given orders or communications as authoritative', and mechanisms for internal resolution of disagreements	Ang and Beath (1993); Stinchcombe (1985)	Authority relationships not specified or are unilateral; Dispute resolution is externalized in the legal system	Authority relationships and dispute resolution are internalized and integrated (bilateral)
Duration	Time frame of the contract	Rousseau and Parks (1994); Stinchcombe (1985)	Brief, close-ended, specific duration	Open-ended, evergreen
Closure	Scope of contract and ability to switch providers	Rousseau and Parks (1994)	Narrow scope of relationship; ability to negotiate new contracts with alternate providers	Pervasive and comprehensive relationship

one's resources, all lead to slavery' (Stinchcombe 1985: 133). Such a relationship would necessitate the externalization in the resolution of inequities or problems experienced by the excluded party. Such externalization of dispute resolution characterizes market relationships.

Given the extended nature of hierarchies and the transitory nature of pure market relationships (Williamson 1994), evergreen or open-ended contracts are indicative of a hierarchical structure: 'A chief feature of the hierarchical incentive system would be the continuity of exchanges' (Stinchcombe 1985: 131–132). Similarly, pure market transactions are characterized by easily soluble relationships with multiple others (Williamson 1994), whereas hierarchies are characterized by relatively durable relationships with a few (Weber 1978). Large hierarchies translate to wider spans of control or additional hierarchical levels. A wider span of control generates higher informational and monitoring costs (Eisenhardt 1988). Additional hierarchical levels create information losses during communication, which also adds to monitoring costs (Williamson 1985). Thus, as a hierarchy grows in size, 'the effects of control loss eventually exceed the gains' of the hierarchy over market transactions (Williamson 1985: 134).

The four elements of contract content or commitments tend to be inter-related. For example, relationships that emphasize 'long-term membership largely focus on behaviorally oriented assessments' (Rousseau 1995: 77). Similarly, contracts with 'endogenous safeguards', that is, internalized authority and dispute resolution systems, tend to be associated with extended and committed relationships (Ring and Van De Ven 1994).

Psychological Contract Choices

The promissory contract alone has proved inadequate in governing IS outsourcing (Koh et al. 2004). While it is useful in communicating initial expectations, no contract can fully cover exigencies that emerge during fulfillment (Macaulay 1963; Ring and Van De Ven 1994). Furthermore, if parties to a formal contract need to reference it during fulfillment, the ensuing discord breaks down the relationship (e.g., Willcocks and Kern 1998). Researchers therefore recognize that additional governance is required after signing a promissory contract. The objective of such governance is to facilitate cooperative work (Sabherwal 1999; Willcocks and Kern 1998). We term this governance stage the psychological contract. In IS outsourcing research, psychological contracts have been considered in terms of vendors' and clients' expectations of each other's obligations (Koh et al. 2004). Here, however, the psychological contract is considered in terms of shared or mutual understandings about parties' obligations.

At this stage in the IS outsourcing process, the market ceases to be a viable governance option, at least for the duration specified by the promissory contract and frequently for a period that extends beyond that specified by the contract. Unlike supply-chain relationships, for example, a client cannot shop around for an alternate provider at the first signs of provider non-performance or malfeasance. Once a provider assumes responsibility for a client's telecommunications or application development, the client and provider are both locked into the relationship – minimally for the duration specified within the contract. However, the prohibitively high costs of changing a provider may extend the relationship even beyond the specifications of the contract (Lacity and Willcocks 1998). For example, application service providers (a specialized type of outsourcing arrangement in which client applications are hosted by the provider) that provide ERP services may charge to transport data that they have hitherto hosted. Thus, once a promissory contract has been signed, the only viable governance choices are hierarchy and network.

At this moment of governance, a hierarchy form of governance implies the extension of firms' internal bureaucratic structures to incorporate the other firm: 'The easy way to get flexible continuous performance over time is a hierarchy isolated from direct market processes' (Stinchcombe 1985: 122). In contrast, the network form of governance relies on less formalized inter-organizational structures to govern the relationship. Elements of the psychological contract that distinguish between hierarchy and network forms of governance are summarized in Table 4.2.

The psychological contract emerges during the process of executing the promissory contract. The psychological contract facilitates

Table 4.2 Alternative forms of the psychological contract

Elements of psychological contract			Governance alternatives	
Element	Definition	Source	Hierarchy	Network
Psychological contract processes: execution				
Coordination	'Integrating or linking together different parts...to accomplish a collective set of tasks'	Van de Ven, Delbecq, and Koenig (1976)	Document-based (standards and schedules/ plans)	Interaction-based (mutual adjustment and teams)
Conflict resolution	Addressing disputes regarding expectations	Kale et al. (2000)	Distributive	Integrative
Psychological contract structures: social capital				
Associations	Nature of the linkages across the inter -organizational relationship	Nahapiet and Ghoshal (1998)	Few, formal	Extensive, informal
Affect	Presumed opportunism or trust within the relationship	Williamson (1985); Nahapiet and Ghoshal (1998)	Presumed opportunism	Presumed trust
Cognition	Extent to which the relationship has common knowledge and a shared identity	Nahapiet and Ghoshal (1998)	Discrete identities, codes, and understandings	Shared identity and common knowledge

adjustment or alignment across the boundaries of client and provider firms. Based on the literature on alignment across inter-departmental and inter-organizational boundaries, we identify two processes – routine alignment via coordination and non-routine alignment via conflict resolution (e.g., Adler 1995; Kale et al. 2000). These have been identified as key processes in eliciting cooperation from disparate constituencies such as global virtual teams (Montoya-Weiss et al. 2001) and supply-chain collaboration (Spekman 1988).

Coordination in hierarchical or bureaucratic governance 'is based upon written documents' (Weber 1978: 957). Bureaucracies rely on the impersonal application of pre-specified rules (Weber 1978). This impersonal application of rules to conflict situations is likely to preclude the exploratory behaviors necessary for integrative conflict resolution. In contrast, network governance that derives from social interaction and a focus on the common good (Uzzi 1997; Powell 1996) translate into interaction-based coordination mechanisms and integrative conflict resolution.

The inter-organizational structures that emerge during execution are referred to as social capital. Social capital has been defined in terms of the patterns of associations and the resources that may potentially be accessed through those associations (Nahapiet and Ghoshal 1998: 243). While social capital is typically viewed as derived from informal network relationships (e.g., Burt 1992; Granovetter 1985), we apply the term social capital also to formally constituted hierarchical relationships. However, the nature of this social capital is qualitatively different.

The literature on social capital and the structure of socio-economic relationships has identified three elements: the associations among socio-economic actors, their feelings of toward one another, and shared language and cognitive resources (e.g., Nahapiet and Ghoshal 1998; Kogut and Zander 1996). Based on these we delineate three structural elements of control: associations, affect, and cognition.

Extensive associations are necessary for network governance. Whereas sparse ties in a socio-economic domain make for tenuous relationships and enable self-interested behavior (e.g., Burt 1992; Padgett and Ansell 1993), a dense network creates a social structure through which the behavior of individuals may be informally regulated (Granovetter 1985). Trust is critical to informal regulation (Granovetter 1985). Finally, common knowledge, that is, shared identity, beliefs, expectations, and understandings, are also invaluable in informally regulating the relationship. They provide a basis for mutual understanding in inter-organizational relationships (Sabel 1993) and the rules for interaction (Grant 1996). Thus, extensive, informal ties, common knowledge, and trust will characterize network governance at the stage of the psychological contract. In contrast, hierarchical governance will be marked by sparse, formal ties, and presumed opportunism. To the extent that clients and outsourcing providers operate in different industries, their identities and knowledge-bases will differ. Whereas an internal bureaucratic structure facilitates a common identity and shared understandings, the underlying plurality of an inter-organizational bureaucratic structure will make such a shared identity and knowledge-base more difficult to achieve. Therefore, hierarchical governance will manifest discrete identities and lower levels of overlap in knowledge bases. In contrast, network structures that are based on informal, interaction-based identities will facilitate a shared identity that is independent of the formal identity of the individual firms. Thus, hierarchical and network inter-organizational structures mark different types of social capital with regard to interpersonal associations, affect, and cognition.

Inter-organizational Rents

Alternate forms of governance mobilize inter-organizational rents differently. We consider organizational rents in terms of value capture and value creation (Dutta et al. 2003; Priem 2001). We see two disparate orientations toward the mobilization of rents in inter-organizational relationships: allocative efficiency or efforts at value capture and adaptive efficiency or efforts at value creation (Priem 2001; Moran and Ghoshal 1999; North 1990). These distinctions between value creation and value capture map also to firms' efforts to balance 'trying to learn and trying to protect' (Kale et al. 2000: 217) and are summarized in Table 4.3. Allocative efficiency or value capture focuses on efficient, Pareto-optimal deployment of resources. This orientation focuses on hoarding or guarding capital, so as to protect ones' core competencies or positions. In contrast, adaptive efficiency or value capture is oriented 'to acquire knowledge and learning, to induce innovation, to undertake risk and creative activity of all sorts, as well as to resolve problems and bottlenecks of the society through time' (North 1990: 80). This orientation focuses on learning from partners and building or increasing capability.

Table 4.3 Alternative mobilizations of inter-organizational rents

	Elements of inter-organizational rents			Alternate mobilizations	
Element	Definition	Source		Value capture	Value creation
Inter-organizational rent processes: valuation					
Exchange	Process of trading resources, thereby making them available to those who can put them to better use	Moran and Ghoshal (1999)		Planned, impersonal, formal, immediate compensation	Impromptu, personal, informal, deferred compensation
Combination	Deployment of resources, except deployments entailing exchange; process by which 'resources are pressed into service'	Moran and Ghoshal (1999: 392)		Routine, known ends, deterministic relationship between inputs and process and outcome	Novel, unknown ends, probabilistic relationship between inputs and processes and outcomes
Inter-organizational rent structures: assets					
Intellectual Capital	'The knowledge and knowing capability' accessible to parties to the outsourcing relationship	Nahapiet and Ghoshal (1998: 245)		Retention of core competencies	New knowledge, inimitable capabilities, and sustainable future advantage
Economic Capital	Financial and material assets	Nahapiet and Ghoshal (1998); Dyer and Singh (1998)		Independent and non-specific assets	Relationship-specific and complementary assets

'Allocative efficiency and adaptive efficiency may not always be consistent. Allocatively efficient rules would make today's firms and decisions secure – but frequently at the expense of the creative destruction process that Schumpeter had in mind' (North 1990: 81–82). Limiting the relationship to independent and non-specific assets can ensure the protection of firms' assets or value capture by permitting the client to easily transfer the outsourced operations to an alternate provider or allowing the provider to not suffer undue losses in the event of termination of the relationship. The development of relationship-specific and complementary assets, in contrast, yields sustainable advantage to the relationship (Dyer and Singh 1998). Inter-organizational relationships therefore need to address this 'tradeoff between current profitability and investing in future capability' for long-term survival (Kogut and Zander 1992: 393).

Rents – either value capture or value creation – accrue via processes of exchange and combination (Moran and Ghoshal 1999). Combinations refer to the appropriation of resources (Moran and Ghoshal 1999). Processes of exchange serve to make resources available were toward productive use; they also stimulate innovation by increasing the possibility for the perception of creative combinations (Moran and Ghoshal 1999).

The attainment of rents may be noted in the accumulation of different types of capital. Consistent with prior business literature, we focus on two forms of capital in addition to social capital, that is, economic and intellectual capital (Nahapiet and Ghoshal 1998). While other forms of capital have been identified, e.g., cultural capital (Bourdieu 1983), economic capital and intellectual capital are of interest as rents that accrue from economic action (Nahapiet and Ghoshal 1998).

Illustration of the Proposed Model

Before we develop the proposed MoG model, we consider the Xerox-EDS outsourcing arrangement as a preliminary anecdotal validation of the model. To initiate the outsourcing arrangement, Xerox constituted a 'very small Core Outsourcing Team', which included two

lawyers (Davis 1996: 163). The Xerox team tended to dictate promissory contract terms, and Davis observes that statements by team
members appeared inadequately informed and lacking in concern for
EDS' processes or cost of providing service. This led to a commitment that was unilaterally structured and price-driven. Consider the
following statement by a member of the Xerox outsourcing team:
'We believe that we are developing a contract that will guarantee us
a competitive price throughout the period. We are going to build
into the contract productivity guarantees [and] price performance
guarantees...' (Davis 1996: 162). Final authority in regard to contract changes and dispute resolution lay with Xerox. Thus, the
standards defined for performance and rewards and the manner in
which authority structures and dispute resolution were set up represented market governance. However, the scope and duration of the
contract were representative of hierarchical governance. The Xerox–
EDS relationship was extensive in nature, with EDS assuming all
functions that 'did not qualify as core competencies', that is, 'the
majority of Xerox's IT function' (Davis 1996: 149). The contract
was an evergreen contract, indicating Xerox's anticipation that its
relationship with EDS would be long-term (Kern and Willcocks
2001; Applegate et al. 1999). The contract was 'formulated to
encourage partnering, and both EDS and Xerox's senior managers
had committed to this notion' (Kern and Willcocks 2001: 100).

It is clear from Davis' account that the promissory contract initially impaired the type of psychological contract needed and desired
by Xerox and EDS. In the process of executing the contract, 'both
sides realized that the relationship required an integration of efforts,
which could only be achieved through a high degree of cooperation'.
However, 'the very existence of 'price' based control clauses within
the contract ensured that price controls would be operative', which
created a 'disconnect between the contract and the need for cooperative controls' (Davis 1996: 171). The interorganizational structure
represented a hierarchical form in which Xerox occupied a position of
supremacy: 'Clearly the customer has received an elevated position'
(Davis 1996: 176). While both parties came to believe that 'trust was
an important part of the relationship' (p. 179), Xerox and EDS

initially believed the other to be exclusively self-interested and that the relationship 'was no different than our relationship with anyone else who supplies us with parts' (Davis 1996: 162).

The promissory contract had set up a psychological contract that was at odds with the value generation that Xerox hoped for. Among a variety of objectives, 'Xerox managers were relying on EDS' environmental scanning expertise' to help Xerox transition to a client–server architecture as well as stay current with other IT developments in the field. In other words, Xerox anticipated novel technical knowledge to assist in the development of new architectures and solutions and the possible development of relationship-specific assets.

Only after deliberate efforts to overcome the limitations of the initial contract through bilateral negotiation were Xerox and EDS able to establish a cooperative relationship. This cooperative relationship was predicated on Xerox's realization that 'some of the stuff that we wrote in [the contract] isn't the right way of working' (Davis 1996: 181). Interventions that focused on team-based coordination and joint problem-solving helped Xerox and EDS develop the atmosphere of trust necessary for the achievement of its desired outcomes (Davis 1996). Central to these interventions were joint social activities and EDS' conscious efforts to leverage the personnel transferred from Xerox to EDS following the outsourcing to facilitate a trust-based relationship (Kern and Willcocks 2001). Then, 'authority control was replaced with a greater reliance on trust', at which point 'Xerox and EDS [began] to explicitly deemphasize the contract' (Davis 1996: 180). Critical to this transition was also the shared identity – the 'perceived similarity in the organizations' strategic intents' (Kern and Willcocks 2001: 100).

In addition to Xerox's learning objectives, though, efficiency was also important. 'The intention was to reduce costs by cutting the headcount, by diminishing IT spent on legacy systems including applications, and by changing the cost structure from fixed to variable' (Kern and Willcocks 2001: 97). That the embedded relationship is antithetical to value capture or allocative efficiency is apparent in the Xerox–EDS relationship, in which 'unanticipated cost increases' were noted to occur (Kern and Willcocks 2001: 87). Problems with allocative efficiency were also evident in EDS' inability to 'manage the migration and integration, while handling in parallel the day-to-day problems and requests... As a result, frustrated [Xerox] managers began to micro-manage' (Kern and Willcocks 2001: 107–108). Such micro-management resulted in a downward relational spiral and in the renegotiation of the contract. At this time, detailed service levels and compensations were specified in the contract.

Thus, the embedded relationship initially structured by Xerox and EDS was inconsistent with Xerox's value capture objectives. 'The conditions underlying Xerox's outsourcing initiative were essentially... a drive for operational efficiency and a refocus on core competence' (Kern and Willcocks 2001: 122). To attain these objectives, the appropriate pathway was an arm's-length, not an embedded, relationship. The application of a hierarchical contract and efforts at a networked psychological contract, while conducive to adaptive efficiency – as manifest in Xerox's migration to the new client–server architecture, thus frustrated the achievement of the desired allocative efficiency.

Causal Relationships in the Moments of Governance

Having delineated the building blocks of the MoG model, we now explore the causal relationships among them that are depicted in Fig. 4.2. We examine how processes produce structures and how these structures constrain and enable subsequent processes.

From Promissory Contract to Psychological Contract

Promissory contract structures, or the terms to which parties commit, emerge from contract processes. A bilaterally negotiated contract, that is, interdependence in the promissory contract process, fosters a mutual understanding of firms' objectives and processes. Behavior-based standards address how people do their jobs (Rousseau 1995). *A priori* specification of such standards in an outsourcing relationship requires that the parties to the contract understand how jobs are done across client–provider boundaries. Similarly, the specification of internal authority systems and dispute resolution mechanisms requires an understanding of how the other organization works and a shared understanding of how the inter-organizational relationship will function. Interdependence in contract negotiations provides such an understanding. Thus, interdependence during the negotiation of the promissory contract will promote the utilization of behavior-based standards and internal authority systems.

Different functional areas have different perspectives to contribute to the contract (Macaulay 1963). The involvement of business personnel, in addition to technical and legal experts, assists in identifying how the provider may add value (Kavan et al. 1999). Extensive and multi-level organizational participation thus provides the information necessary for informed contracting (Rousseau 1995). Information supplied by individuals in the functional area being outsourced can be invaluable in specifying behavior-based standards. Participation of top management signals higher level of involvement and the 'direct interpersonal contact between the two senior executives at the partnering firms created the opportunity for cooperation' (Hutt et al. 2000: 53). Top management participation is necessary for agreement on internalized authority systems and dispute resolution mechanisms. Top management participation also provides the commitment necessary for undertaking riskier relationships, that is, relationships that are long-term and relatively exclusive or closed. In sum, increased interaction via participation and interdependence will provide the information and enable the sense-making necessary for specifying a more detailed and involved relationship (Nahapiet and Ghoshal 1998; Ring and Van De Ven 1994). Thus, extensive participation in the contracting process will promote internalization of control and longer-term and more exclusive relationships. In contrast, in the absence of the rich understandings fostered by interdependence and widespread participation in the negotiation process, clients will default to outcome-based standards, externalization of control, and more tentative contracts in terms of duration and exclusiveness.

Proposition 1A *Market governance processes at the time of the promissory contract, that is, low participation and pro-forma contracts, promote market structures in the promissory contract.*

Proposition 1B *Hierarchical governance processes at the time of the promissory contract, that is, extended participation and bilateral negotiation, promote hierarchical structures in the promissory contract.*

Detailed fee-for-service contracts, that is, outcome-based standards, have been found to be more successful in yielding economic benefits than more generic contracts (Lacity and Willcocks 1998). However, absent total control, a focus on outcomes *vs* behaviors 'fuels destructive behavior' (Pfeffer and Sutton 2000). It limits provider flexibility and responsiveness in the face of technological or task changes. The heightened objectivity of outcomes vis-à-vis behavior further lessens the perceived need for interaction (Rousseau and Parks 1994). Outcome-based contracts therefore reduce coordination efforts to references to outcomes specified in the contract. They preclude integrative behaviors by pre-specifying desired outcomes.

The specification of authority systems and internalization of dispute resolution helps institutionalize modes of conflict resolution before conflict occurs (Kale et al. 2000). By precluding or minimizing references to the formal institutional environment, internalization of authority systems and dispute resolution focuses attention on interaction in navigating the relationship (Ring and Van De Ven 1994). Coordination efforts, therefore, tend to be interaction-based. Since such internalized systems derive from joint sense-making across organizational boundaries, they are likely to foster integrative efforts in resolving conflict.

The time frame of the contract has been the focus of much research on IS outsourcing (Lacity and Willcocks 1998; Kavan et al. 1999). Lacity and Willcocks (1998) report that short-term contracts were more successful than long-term, and more recent contracts were more successful than older contracts. This may be because the rapid pace of technological change renders the terms of longer-term contracts obsolete. Another reason for the apparent success of shorter-term contracts may be the outsourcers' ability to cut their losses if the provider does not meet their objectives. However, this failure to meet objectives may be a result of a lack of clarity of objectives and outsourcers' focus on pre-specified transactions rather than value-added in the uncertain future environment of information technology. Kavan et al. (1999) conclude that longer-term contracts are preferable because high-setup costs can be distributed over a longer period. A short-term contract would therefore inhibit costly innovation on the part of the provider even where the innovation would provide benefit to the outsourcer.

Time introduces an element of indeterminacy or risk in relationships (Coleman 1990). However, this risk may be offset by the benefits of a prolonged relationship. Time distinguishes purely economic transactions from social relationships (Coleman 1990). In time, social interactions facilitate mutual accommodation (Ring and Van De Ven 1994). The effects of time have been noted in the attitudinal disparities between contract and permanent workers: contract workers tend to display lower in-role and extra-role behaviors than permanent workers and are perceived by supervisors as being less loyal, obedient, and trustworthy; their job scope is therefore limited, heightening the perception of them being less committed (Ang and Slaughter 2001).

Contracts may be narrow in scope, with multiple providers being utilized to complete various tasks; the contract may allow for easy dissolution of the relationship and re-negotiation of terms with alternate providers (Rousseau and Parks 1994). Alternatively, contracts may set up pervasive and comprehensive relationships with a single or few providers. These terms set up the level of closure within the client–provider relationship. Many providers are a continuous reminder that the provider is dispensable and thereby creates fear and distrust in the relationship (Nahapiet and Ghoshal 1998). Fear and distrust pre-empt open interaction and integrative problem-solving (Pfeffer and Sutton 2000). Close, exclusive relationships, on the other hand, force both parties to find solutions to difficult situations (Nahapiet and Ghoshal 1998). Furthermore, non-exclusive relationships exacerbate concerns about protecting organizational resources from 'leakage' (Kale et al. 2000). This results in efforts to minimize spontaneous, non-document-based coordination and facilitate a distributive approach to conflict resolution.

Thus, in longer-term, closed relationships, a greater sense of commitment motivates parties to accommodate each other's needs. A focus on behavior-based standards requires that parties remain cognizant of each other's efforts. Internalized authority resolution also requires ongoing communication. These requirements for ongoing interaction over time enhance the likelihood that parties will avail of interaction-based coordination. The heightened commitment and mutual understanding fostered by hierarchical contracts will foster integrative conflict management. In contrast, market-oriented contract structures will provide fewer opportunities for communication and for the development of an emergent understanding of each other's needs. The absence of a long-term, committed relationship will dissuade parties from accommodating each other's needs.

Proposition 2A *Market governance structures in the promissory contract, that is, outcome-based standards, externalized authority and dispute resolution systems, limited duration, and multiple providers, promote reliance on hierarchical governance in the process of developing the psychological contract.*

Proposition 2B *Hierarchical governance structures in the promissory contract, that is, behavior-based standards, internalized authority and dispute resolution systems, extended duration, and closure promote reliance on network governance in the process of developing the psychological contract.*

From Psychological Contract to Inter-Organizational Resources

As noted earlier, the manner in which firms coordinate and resolve conflict derives from the terms of the promissory contract and sets up the relationship's social capital or the structure of the psychological contract. This social capital, in turn, influences the manner in which inter-organizational resources are mobilized.

The objective of coordination is to facilitate integration across specialized groups (Grant 1996; Adler 1995). There are two sets of coordination mechanisms: document-based coordination via standards and schedules/plans and interaction-based coordination via teamwork and mutual adjustment (Adler 1995; Van De Ven et al. 1976). Document-based coordination is impersonal and requires minimal interaction and communication across organizational boundaries; tasks may be jointly completed by simply referencing written standards, plans, and schedules (Van De Ven et al. 1976). Interaction-based coordination necessitates communication and depends on committees and teams for the synchronization of tasks across organizational boundaries (Adler 1995).

The inherent dependencies, coupled with divergent partner goals in inter-organizational relationships, necessitate ongoing conflict resolution in managing inter-organizational relationships (Kale et al. 2000). Crises points that drive conflict and the process of conflict resolution can also provide occasions for joint sense-making (Weick 1995). How the conflict is resolved, however, determines whether the conflict has a productive or destructive effect on the relationship (Deutsch 1969). The two types of conflict resolution strategies that may be undertaken in inter-organizational relationships are integrative or distributive strategies (Kale et al. 2000). In integrative strategies, attempts are made to seek out mutually satisfying outcomes; distributive strategies entail prioritizing one's own outcomes over those of the other party (Sillars 1980). Integrative strategies are interaction-intensive and entail joint problem-solving. They are suitable on complex tasks on which there are no right answers and in circumstances in which there is not a disparate distribution of power across the conflicting parties (Rahim 1985). In distributive conflict resolution, where each party is concerned only about their own outcomes, such interaction and joint-problem solving is unnecessary.

Interactive coordination and integrative conflict resolution strategies facilitate the formation of inter-organizational linkages as people are required to interact and communicate repeatedly in order to accomplish tasks or resolve disputes and cannot simply refer to written documents or external entities (e.g., Nahapiet and Ghoshal 1998). Interaction-based coordination provides the opportunities for parties to socialize and to develop positive affect and shared understandings that are the hallmark of network structures (Adler 2001). Such interactions increase the possibility for forging new ties across organizational boundaries. Social ties emerge while individuals are involved in social activities (Feld 1981). Such informally developed ties increase the coverage of the inter-organizational network. Deep, personal relationships emerge from sympathetic interactions, rather than necessary interactions (Silver, 1990). Interaction-based coordination facilitates the development of shared cognition since it enables greater information sharing and immediate feedback (Van De Ven et al. 1976).

Integrative conflict resolution can contribute to the development of process trust. Reciprocity and a mutual concern is key to process trust. In Uzzi's study of firms in New York City's garment district, trust was found to be an important element in the relationship. Trust emerged when one party offered extra effort voluntarily and when such effort was then reciprocated (Uzzi 1997). These 'extra efforts' were not easy to value in a monetary sense, but typically involved voluntary problem-solving when the other party was faced with a crisis. In Davis' (1996) study of the Xerox–EDS and Kodak–IBM relationships, interaction-based coordination via groups and committees facilitated the development of inter-organizational trust. At Kodak, partners' training in negotiation and conflict management helped develop inter-organizational trust (Davis 1996).

The ties that develop from interactive coordination and integrative conflict resolution transcend those specified in the contract in breadth, that is, the number of ties increase over time, and in depth, that is, they develop a social content, rather than a purely economic content. Such ties are the hallmark of a network structure (Nahapiet and Ghoshal 1998). They promote a common identity and foster shared norms and trust (Coleman 1990). They dispel concerns about partner opportunism as voluntary good-faith is demonstrated.

In contrast, document-based coordination entails referencing the contract and service-level agreements in order to ensure that specialized activities across client and provider organizations are synchronized. Distributive conflict resolution focuses parties on their own interests (Rahim 1985), requiring no understanding of the emergent needs and constraints of the other party. These relationship–management strategies therefore preclude the development of close, personalized ties and a shared understanding necessary for network relationship (Adler 2001).

As such, presumptions of opportunism prevail and contentions necessitate recourse to formal channels for resolution.

> **Proposition 3A** *Hierarchical control processes, that is, document-based coordination and distributive conflict resolution, promote hierarchical control structures.*
>
> **Proposition 3B** *Network control processes, that is, interaction-based coordination and integrative conflict resolution, promote network control structures.*

The nature of the social capital that emerges in the management of the psychological contract circumscribes the rent-attainment processes available to the outsourcing relationship. Ties between boundary-spanners in inter-organizational relationships are important in cementing the relationship (Seabright et al. 1992). Direct ties facilitate knowledge-spillover benefits (Ahuja 2000). They provide privileged access to intellectual (e.g., Burt 1992; Granovetter 1978) and economic resources (e.g., Lincoln et al. 1996). A reliance on close, personal ties is evident in studies of IS outsourcing too: Speaking of his/her relationship with Kodak, an IBM manager said: 'I've gotten more direct coaching from Kodak managers than from my own boss. We play golf together, we go out to dinner together; there is a level of social interaction' (Davis 1996: 259).

The nature of inter-organizational affect, that is, presumed trust or opportunism, is critical to resource sharing too. Presumed opportunism refers to the belief that others will act in a self-interested fashion; in its ultimate sense, opportunism is seen as 'calculated efforts to mislead, deceive, obfuscate, and otherwise confuse' (Williamson 1994: 102). Presumed opportunism prompts guarded interaction with others. By contrast, trust is the assumption of risk with the expectation that another will act in a beneficial fashion (Gambetta 1988). In defining trust, we explicitly adopt the position that trust in informal governance structures parallels opportunism in formal governance structures.[3] Zucker (1986) identifies

---

[3] This is in opposition to the position sometimes implicitly adopted in the literature, that is, that trust is an informal regulatory mechanism. Trust, *per se*, has no regulatory value. Rather, it enables the reliance on shared norms and values that are informally constituted. Based on Nee and Ingram (1998), we view the regulatory potential of networks as stemming from shared norms. Thus, the

three forms of trust: characteristic-based trust, process trust, and institutional trust. Characteristic-based trust surfaces swiftly based on demographic similarities. Process trust emerges over time, in the process of interaction. Rousseau et al. (1998) refer to this type of trust as relational trust. Institutional trust refers to trust that derives from third-party regulation.

IS researchers have found trust to be important in outsourcing relationships. Trust was found to contribute to a virtuous circle marked by quality and on-time performance; distrust formed a vicious cycle of poor-quality performance and delays (Sabherwal 1999). In another study, trust was found to be a determinant of perceived partnership quality (Lee and Kim 1999).

Trust facilitates voluntary exchange (Uzzi 1997). In Davis' research, trust-based controls enabled the informal, personalized exchanges necessary for the achievement of the firms' complex goals. The commitment of resources in inter-organizational relationships is often incremental (Khanna et al. 1998). Trust facilitates the commitment of economic resources across organizations (Sabel 1993).

Similarities in cultural attributes are essential to successful alliances (e.g., Hutt et al. 2000). Shared beliefs, expectations, and understandings do not have to be all pervasive, but cover the relationship and joint operations (Sabel 1993). This facilitates the sharing of knowledge that is not common (Grant 1996). Common knowledge and a shared identity can help circumvent issues of bounded rationality in individuals' ability to acquire and process information (Grant 1996). It defines rules for interaction and processes for social learning (Kogut and Zander 1996).

As seen earlier, perceived commonalities are essential to characteristic-based trust (Zucker 1986). Characteristic-based trust is rooted in the expectation that those who are demographically and socially similar to us are more likely to act in an anticipated fashion than those who are dissimilar to us. This is supported by the mergers and acquisitions literature where cultural incompatibility has frequently been found to impede the

---

network counterpoint of the externally-and formally constituted and legitimized rules of market- and hierarchy-based regulation are internally- and informally legitimized norms and sanctions.

development of trust (Doherty 1988). Thus, organizational similarities or compatibility will tend to facilitate characteristic-based trust. Further, compatibility provides a common ground for negotiating relational or process-based trust. Sabel (1993) posits that trust can emerge even among relatively disparate organizations when they are motivated by the possibility of long-term benefits. Such studied trust arises out of a joint reframing of organizational identities resulting in shared beliefs, expectations, and understandings.

Cultural similarity across disparate organizations may be affected by identity reconstruction (Wishart et al. 1996; Sabel 1993). A shared identity fosters a belief that others will not act in an opportunistic fashion; this promotes expectations of cooperation and thereby encourages cooperative exchanges (Kogut and Zander 1996). A shared identity expedites the transfer of tacit knowledge (Grant 1996).

Formal relationships, anticipated opportunism, and disparate identities promote only impersonal, planned, and immediate exchanges. Formal relationships will offer fewer occasions for the occurrence of what Moran and Ghoshal (1999) term the 'multiple coincidence', that is, existing opportunity, perceived opportunity, and motivation for all parties. Anticipated opportunism will result in a reliance on planned exchanges alone so as to forestall the other's opportunistic behavior (e.g., Kale et al. 2000). Identity discontinuities serve as knowledge boundaries, preventing the seepage of knowledge from one identity to another (e.g., Kogut and Zander 1996).

Strong ties, trust, and a shared identity also facilitate novel combinations. Strong ties facilitate the incorporation of knowledge from an old project into a new project (Hansen 1999). This represents a novel combination. A reframed, shared inter-organizational identity enables organizations to attract resources from other public and private organizations (Sabel 1993), thereby increasing the pool of resources available, and the possibility of novel combination (Moran and Ghoshal 1999).

Again, formal relationships, anticipated opportunism, and disparate identities promote only routine combinations. Exchanges via formal relationships alone constrain the pool of resources available for combination, thus limiting the probability of novel combinations. Presumed opportunism leads to efforts to minimize uncertainty (e.g., Williamson

1985). Since uncertainty is the hallmark of novel combinations, beliefs that the other party will act opportunistically will minimize efforts at novel combination. Finally, since a shared identity is necessary the transfer of knowledge (Kogut and Zander 1996), disparate identities will hamper such knowledge transfer.

> **Proposition 4A** *Hierarchical governance structures, that is, limited, formal associations, presumed opportunism, and disparate identities, lead to imperso- nal exchange and routine combination of capital.*
> **Proposition 4B** *Network governance structures, that is, extensive, informal associations, presumed trust, and a shared identity, promote personal exchange and novel combination of capital.*

The final process in the MoG model is that of valuation, that is, the manner in which resources are exchanged and combined in the relation- ship. Personalized exchanges are informally and socially regulated, impersonal exchanges rely on formal institutional support (Moran and Ghoshal 1999). Another distinction between impersonal and personal exchanges is in the nature of reciprocation. Instantaneous reciprocation reduces a social act to an economic transaction (Simmel 1978). Therefore, reciprocity is immediate in the case of impersonal exchanges and deferred in the case of personal exchanges. Moran and Ghoshal (1999) stipulate three conditions necessary for exchange: 'the opportu- nity for exchange must exist, it must be motivated and perceived' by all parties to the exchange (p. 387). They term these three conditions a 'multiple coincidence', alluding to the relative improbability of its occurrence. Thus, in order for impersonal exchanges to occur, they need to be planned. The likelihood of personalized exchange is fairly high, though, since it is intrinsic to most voluntary social interactions and immediate repayment is unnecessary.

Routine combinations 'are more likely to replicate services that already exist' (Moran and Ghoshal 1999). They are manifested in conventional production. Novel combinations facilitate the discovery of innovative processes, products, or services, for example, 3 M's Post-It Notes (Moran and Ghoshal 1999). While the process of routine combi- nation is structured and deterministic, the process of novel combination is not. In other words, one knows what the final product will be in routine production and exactly what needs to be done in order to obtain the final product. In the case of innovation, however, the final product is not known *a priori*. In fact, it may be unintentionally derived and once a product is obtained, it may or may not be one that is commercially viable (Moran and Ghoshal 1999). Thus, the process of novel combination is fraught with uncertainty.

Impromptu exchange makes additional resources available for novel combination, which in turn facilitates innovation (Moran and Ghoshal 1999). We see considerable evidence of capital development via impromptu exchange and novel combination. For example, the success of Silicon Valley firms, in contrast to those in the Massachusetts' Route 128 area, has been attributed to the development of technological knowledge via exchange (Saxenian 1996). Rolm provides an excellent example of knowledge development through recombination. Leveraging their technical knowledge and customers' knowledge of firms' telecommunication needs and inter-organizational social ties, Rolm was able to create not only a marketable product but also a marketing infrastructure that enabled them to gain a distinctive advantage (Lane and Maxfield 1996). The joint problem-solving observed among the garment-industry firms studied by Uzzi (1997) is yet another example of growth through personalized exchange and novel combination. Research on the Sydney hotel industry found that network ties translated to a dollar-value in terms of improved hotel yield; these economic benefits were augmented by the density of network ties, that is, when one's friends were also friends (Ingram and Roberts 2000). These advantages accrued through improved collaboration, mitigated competition, and richer information exchanges.

While authors have observed that intellectual capital grows with personalized exchange and novel combination, the potential for the growth of economic capital has frequently gone unnoticed. Money has typically been viewed as a zero-sum asset, to which one no longer has access once it is given up in exchange. However, Parsons (1963) describes the non-zero-sum nature of money. He points to the vehicle of credit through which money acquires multiple simultaneous uses in collectives. Money is therefore not a static or a social resource. Those with economic resources are more likely to attract additional resources by being deemed credit- or investment-worthy. This tendency is captured in the Matthew Effect. Merton (1968) observes that real-life frequently parallels the biblical parable of the talents in that those who have the resources attract further resources, while those that do not tend to lose even what they have. Further, economic resources are convertible to other forms of capital (Bourdieu 1983). Money attracts rich social ties and can purchase knowledge. Relationships extend the credit available (Stark 1990).

Through mechanisms of credit, investment, and risk-diffusion, economic resources can be reallocated across the relationship so that they may be pressed into more effective service. Direct evidence of such combination and exchange entailing economic capital in networks is sparse. Nonetheless, we find some preliminary evidence of resource combination and exchange in diffusing economic risk and facilitating economic recovery. Research on post-socialist enterprises in Hungary notes the pervasiveness of 'recombinant property', property 'that can be justified or assessed by more than one standard of evaluation' (Stark 2001). Such recombinant property facilitates coping with uncertainties stemming from a volatile economic environment and enables heightened responsiveness to state mandates. In diffusing risks, recombinant property enables the assumption of risk (Stark 2001). Research on keiretsus demonstrates that firms with network ties were able to invest more in times of financial distress than did independent firms, and subsequently stronger sales growth (Hoshi et al. 1991). Thus, impromptu exchanges and recombination will facilitate the development of advantageous complementary and potentially relationship-specific assets.

In contrast, planned exchanges enable parties to an interorganizational relationship to identify in advance what resources will be shared and what will be 'off-limits'. This facilitates protection of indigenous resources (Kale et al. 2000) and the capture of value along pre-negotiated lines. Routine combinations will enable the organizations to preserve their existing positions or those stipulated in the contract (Moran and Ghoshal 1999). In other words, the provider will attain rents via the economies of scale and scope that they are able to leverage, less the rents they are contractually obligated to transfer to the client.

Proposition 5A *Planned exchanges and routine combinations facilitate the capture of value with regard to intellectual and economic capital.*

Proposition 5B *Impromptu exchanges and re-combinations facilitate the creation of value with regard to intellectual and economic capital.*

Power-asymmetries Associated with Governance Strategies

An organization's need for financial, physical, and informational resources makes it dependent on resource sources external to the organization; external organizations that control these resource streams enjoy heightened levels of power (Pfeffer and Salancik, 2003/1978). Initial command over resources offers firms disparate opportunities to define the relationship and outcomes that would constitute an effective relationship (Sydow and Windeler 1998). These initial disparities in dominance are then produced and reproduced in the execution of the relationship (Sydow and Windeler 1998). Conditions set up by hierarchical contracts permit provider control of decision-making within the client organization. Exclusive and long-term contracts concentrate the external control of the client's critical IS resources in the hands of a single vendor. Such concentration of control confers power over the client to the provider (Pfeffer and Salancik 2003/1978).

Proposition 6A *Clients in embedded relationships experience greater control by their provider than clients in arm's-length relationship at the moment of the promissory contract.*

Conditions of resource dependence promote the development of stronger inter-organizational relationships (Pfeffer and Salancik 2003/1978). They stimulate inter-organizational communication and, consequently, the incidence of interaction-based coordination and consensus, which, in turn, promotes heightened exchange and referrals (Van De Ven and Walker 1984). These mechanisms can serve to reduce the client's experience of dependence on and control by the vendor (Pfeffer and Salancik 2003/1978; Van De Ven and Walker 1984).

Proposition 6B *The external control experienced by clients in embedded relationships is no different than that experienced by clients in arm's-length relationship at the moment of the psychological contract.*

Situational Boundaries of the Model and Research Directions

An important aspect of theory development is circumscribing the boundaries of the theory (Whetten 1989). These situational boundaries are summarized in Fig. 4.3. From this figure, it will be apparent that we anticipate that the nature of the transaction, the resource environment, institutional conditions, and geographies of time and space serve as external constraints on the moments of governance in IS outsourcing. Below, we consider each of these conditions.

Transactions

The nature of a transaction can engender high transaction costs, that is, costs of safeguarding a transaction from performance gaps (Williamson 1994). Transactions that are asset-specific, that is, are idiosyncratic to the client, create an ex-post small-numbers condition wherein the client is dependent on the existing provider because no other provider has developed the competence to meet its needs. This renders the client vulnerable to opportunism (Williamson 1985). Transactions may also be uncertain, that is, where knowledge about 'the future state of the environment and what will be required to cope with that world' is unavailable (Pfeffer 1982: 135). On such transactions, boundedly rational decision-makers will be unable to ascertain the potential outcomes associated with alternate courses of action.

Conditions of asset-specificity and uncertainty that give rise to transaction costs therefore impose constraints on governance choices, enabling efficiencies for internalized transactions and vulnerability to hazards for externalized transactions (Williamson 1985). Under such

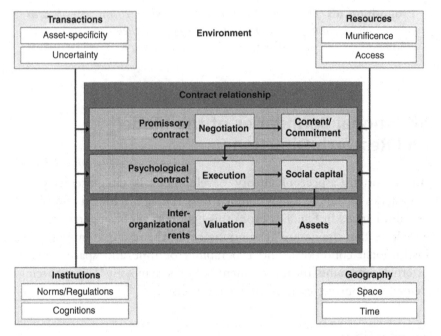

Fig. 4.3 Environmental conditions

conditions, it the promissory contract can at best be loosely structured and the psychological contract must be well-developed (Williamson 1985).

Resources

Social capital has been defined as 'the aggregate of the actual or potential *resources* which are linked to possession of a durable *network*' (Bourdieu 1983: 248–249). Two salient resource attributes are therefore munificence and access (Lin 2001). Organizational slack facilitates experimentation because slack buffers against downside risks (Reuer and Leiblein 2000; Wiseman and Bromiley 1996; Hannan and Freeman 1984). As slack reduces, organizations are more cognizant of risks and attempt to limit their downside exposure (Steensma and Corley 2001). Under such conditions, decision-makers also resort to more rational decision making, using objective and justifiable criteria (Schick 1985); low slack intensifies belt-tightening strategies (Hambrick and D'Aveni 1988).

Not all members of a social network have equal access to the resources within the network; rather, access is a function of one's position – location or status – within a network (Lin 2001). Thus, a client that is highly visible within the business community is likely to enjoy heightened resource access vis-à-vis the provider. The nature of the resources held also influences access: relationship-specific resources permit easier access, while access to organization-specific resources requires negotiation (Dyer and Singh 1998).

Key individuals or groups can determine the pool of resources available to the entire network and accessible to specific players. When such players exit the relationship, it can prove to be extremely detrimental to the network. One reason for the downfall of Japanese networks was the exit of key players such as Toyota from financial networks. As these organizations became more successful, they began to finance their own growth, no longer relying on banks. Consequently, Japanese banks were forced to seek out weaker players, without recourse to the stronger players to offset these new risky investments (Ozawa 1999).

The potential for the exit of key players is particularly problematic in complex outsourcing relationships such as application service providers. A vendor's failure or the turnover of critical employees could have a detrimental effect on the effectiveness of embedded relationships. Prior to the development of an embedded relationship, parties need to carefully investigate each player's long-term financial and managerial viability so as to ensure that critical players do not abruptly exit the relationship.

Institutional Pressures

Institutions constrain organizational choices and the viability of those choices (Meyer and Rowan 1977; North 1990). This is no less true of governance choices. The choice of an embedded strategy, for example, is susceptible to organizations' institutional environment, which may render embeddedness a liability instead of an asset. Uzzi (1997) proposes that when firms face contravening institutional pressures, embeddedness may prove to be a liability. He cites the example of the large conglomerate Federated, Inc. who acquired retailers such as Macy's and Bullocks in the 1980s, and forced a shift from a relationship orientation to transaction orientation among retailers. Besides such direct effects, contravening institutional pressures also indirectly impact the viability of a network governance choice.

We also see evidence of the constraints of institutions in Asian financial networks. In reconstructing its economy after WWII, Japan sought to also preserve the integrity of its social values. This gave rise to the distinctive Japanese management model. The Japanese Model has been characterized by embedded internal and inter-organizational relationships. Internal embeddedness is manifested in social contracts of lifelong employment. External embeddedness is evident in keiretsu arrangements. Toward the late 1980s, these embedded relationships became problematic for the Japanese economy for two reasons. First, firms in keiretsus focused exclusively on growth rather than profit. Networks facilitate asset sharing and a diffusion of risk (Stark 2001). This funded the growth of firms in keiretsus. This growth, coupled with their insulation from knowledge that the market was slowing down, led to their investment in unsustainable growth (Ozawa 1999). Second, culturally favored collectivist values precluded penalizing weak or non-performing keiretsu members. When faced with a market slow down, keiretsus were no longer able to offset the losses racked up by its weaker members (Ozawa 1999).

Thus, a normative and regulatory environment that favored the sustenance of ties irrespective of their financial viability operated as a constraint. The internal cognitive environment may also pose institutional constraints on governance choices and their success (Selznick 1957). While a shared identity facilitates learning and cooperative endeavors, it can limit exploration and encourage the misapplication of existing rules (Burgelman 2002; Kogut and Zander 1996). In embedded relationship, a shared identity may create a diminished inclination to reconstruct the identity, even when such identity reconstruction is essential to the recognition and diagnosis of major problems. Just as the successful creation of an inter-organizational relationship necessitates a cognitive reframing of identities (Sabel 1993), the diagnosis of major problems may necessitate similar reframing. Sense-making is after all inextricably linked to identity construction (Weick 1995). Consider, for instance, the Ford–Firestone relationship.

The Ford–Firestone relationship, by all accounts a close and collegial relationship until recently, goes back nearly a hundred years. The current Ford chairman, William Clay Ford, and his sisters are progeny of Ford and Firestone lineage. John Nevin, Firestone's chairman and CEO at the time of Bridgestone's acquisition of Firestone, was previously a 17-year Ford employee. The two companies' collective response to Ford's problem with its Explorer line is clearly illustrative of what Uzzi (1997) terms joint problem-solving. However, their very embeddedness and motivation to solve each other's problems resulted in their inability to recognize the catastrophic situation unfolding. As problems with the Ford–Firestone solution began to emerge, recognizing the problem could have resulted in significant dissonance between the organizations' desired identity and the identity that recognition of the problem may have necessitated. Ford and Firestone would have to construe of themselves as having settled on a fatal long-term solution to an immediate problem. An identity that encompassed either party or both parties as being the cause of customer fatalities would have represented a departure from the prevailing identity, and been untenable. Loyalty to each other and guilt for having suggested/agreed to the initial solution would also have precluded such a voluntary reconstruction of identity, necessary to recognize the problem.

Institutional pressures can also offset resource dependencies that emerge in embedded relationships (Pfeffer and Salancik 2003/1978). They thus encourage transactions that are otherwise difficult to sustain based on competitive market conditions (North 1990).

Geography of Space and Time

Research has suggested that social relationships are viable resources and governance structures in economic relationships. Such research, however, has focused exclusively on proximal, spatially bounded (e.g., Uzzi 1997; Saxenian 1996) and/or temporally continuous relationships (Kumar et al. 1998; Uzzi 1997). This raises the question: how can embeddedness be an asset in the spatially – and temporally – mobile context that represents the majority of American businesses? In the outsourcing context, this issue of geography is particularly salient given the rapid proliferation of off-shore sourcing arrangements.

In Saxenian's (1996) account of Silicon Valley, we see embeddedness as deriving from geography: 'the natural boundaries of the peninsula... ensured a density of [real estate] development that minimized physical distances between companies and facilitated intensive informal communications' (p. 30). Spatial proximity contributed relationship development in three ways: First, the local university, associations, and trade groups facilitated formal interchanges. Second, engineers' met and shared information at impromptu gatherings around local watering holes. Third, due to the dense population of high-tech firms, job mobility within the area did not necessitate a disruption of one's family. Such mobility facilitated the development of embedded relationships among engineers. Kumar et al. (1998) see embeddedness as relating to time in two ways: First, merchants at Prato had long histories of associations from school, church, trade associations, and political parties. Second, Italian culture pre-disposes a longer-term, cross-generational memory of favors and betrayals than would be typical in US culture.

Geography need not preclude embedded relationships. Saxenian (1996) reports that embeddedness also derived from ad hoc information sharing via phone conversations. Robey et al. (2000) found that while co-location facilitated practice-based learning (associated with embeddedness) in virtual teams, such learning was also possible among remote members. Future research needs to better understand the effects of space and time on embeddedness. These may prove to moderate the possibility and/or the effectiveness of embeddedness in outsourcing relationships.

Conclusions

We now consider the implications of our proposed model for practice. We then delineate research issues and directions suggested by the model.

Implications for Practice

A prescriptive implication of the model presented in Fig. 4.1 is that governance choices need to be made based on the nature of the outcomes desired. Governance choices and desired outcomes define the relationship as either arms-length or embedded. A value creation strategy is inherently uncertain. The outcomes are frequently unknown and unspecifiable at the time of the promissory contract. Therefore, the manner in which desirable outcomes might be attained is also unknown. Such inherent uncertainties call for a hierarchical promissory contract (Stinchcombe 1985). Such a contract stipulates ongoing authority relationships via which an alignment of understanding may constantly be pursued.

In contrast, the more determinable nature of the outcomes and processes underlying a value capture strategy lend themselves to initial specification via a market-type promissory contract. In such a contract, the clear specification of desired efficiencies, along with commensurate rewards and penalties, fosters clients' ability to capture value from the provider's economies of scale and scope in the outsourcing relationship.

Research Directions

This paper modeled the processes and outcomes involved in the governance of IS outsourcing. Specifically, we suggest, embeddedness as an alternative governance mechanism and chart the consequences of this alternative in contrast to arms-length outsourcing relationships. However, before our proposed research model is investigated, preliminary research is needed to confirm the feasibility of embedded relationships in the geographically- and temporally mobile environment characteristic of US firms. Research also needs to build on the existing model, specifically attending to the issue of power.

In empirically examining the model presented in Fig. 4.1, the nature of the initial contract may be assessed by a content analysis of the document or from factual information regarding a firm's outsourcing activities (e.g., Ang and Beath 1993). Literature on coordination and conflict resolution mechanisms is extensive, with an adequate supply of metrics from which to draw (e.g., Adler 1995; Kale et al. 2000). Existing measures are also available to assess associations, trust, and cognition. The nature of exchange and combination of economic and intellectual capital may be assessed via interviews or a review of archival data.

Research may also wish to investigate how promissory contract choices affect the governance cycle following the renegotiation of a promissory contract. Our position in this paper was that the renegotiated contract would simply start another governance cycle. However, it is likely that the cycle initiated by the renegotiated contract is not independent of the initial governance cycle. The nature of these potential path dependencies bears further consideration.

The proposed model may be investigated with a cross-sectional study. If such a study were to be undertaken, it is important to note that the complexity of the proposed model likely allow for only a portion of the model to be tested in a single study. However, in order to best explore the dynamics of the inter-organizational context, and provide a richer theoretical understanding of initial and emergent governance structures, a longitudinal, comparative, case study approach may be most appropriate. This approach will allow us to investigate the process of relationship development and the processes involved in moving from one governance scenario to another. It may also enable us to understand the circumstances under which embeddedness ceases to be a relational asset and becomes a liability.

At a more generic level, this paper proposed that governance choices circumscribe the capital that may accrue to relationships. Our analysis of IS outsourcing may be viewed as a case in point – an illustration of the effects of the terms of promissory and psychological contracts on capital. These effects may also pertain to other types of economic relationships – intra-organizational relationships *and* inter-organizational relationships. Future research may want to investigate the generalizability of our propositions to other organizational relationships. More attention is also required in conceptualizing and testing the boundary conditions of the model proposed in this manuscript.

Acknowledgments We are grateful for the valuable comments from Carol Saunders, Dan Robey, Rick Watson, and anonymous reviewers. We also acknowledge comments from the following practitioners – Marq Ozanne of the Outsourcing Institute, Michael Flock, a former President of Dun & Bradstreet, and Karl Nicosia, Vice President of Dun & Bradstreet Outsourcing.

References

Adler, P.S. (1995). Interdepartmental Interdependence and Coordination: The case of the design/manufacturing interface, *Organization Science* **6**(2): 147–167.

Adler, P.S. (2001). Market, Hierarchy, and Trust: The knowledge economy and the future of capitalism, *Organization Science* **12**(2): 215–233.

Ahuja, G. (2000). Collaboration Networks, Structural Holes, and Innovation: A longitudinal study, *Administrative Science Quarterly* **45**: 425–455.

Ang, S., and Beath, C.M. (1993). Hierarchical Elements in Software Contracts, *Journal of Organizational Computing* **3**(3): 329–361.

Ang, S., and Slaughter, S.A. (2001). Work Outcomes and Job Design for Contract Versus Permanent Information Systems Professionals on Software Development Teams, *MIS Quarterly* **25**(3): 321–350.

Applegate, L.M., McFarlan, W.F., and McKenney, J.L. (1999). *Corporate Information Systems Management*, Boston, MA: Irwin McGraw-Hill.

Bourdieu, P. (1983). Forms of Capital, In J.G. Richardson (ed.) *Handbook of Theory and Research for the Sociology of Education*, New York: Greenwood Press.

Burgelman, R.A. (2002). Strategy as Vector and the Inertia of Coevolutionary Lock-in, *Administrative Science Quarterly* **47**: 325–357.

Burt, R.S. (1992). *Structural Holes.*, Cambridge, MA: Harvard University Press.

Coleman, J. (1990). *Foundations of Social Theory*, Cambridge, MA: Harvard University Press.

Davis, K.J. (1996). *IT Outsourcing Relationships: An exploratory study of interorganizational control mechanisms (unpublished doctoral dissertation)*, Cambridge, MA: Harvard University.

Deutsch, M. (1969). Conflicts: Productive and destructive, In F.E. Jandt (ed.) *Conflict Resolution through Communication*, New York, NY: Harper and Row.

Doherty, T (May/June 1988). Resolving Cultural Conflicts During the Merger, *Chief Executive* Vol. **45**: 18–22.

Dutta, S., Zbaracki, M.J., and Bergen, M. (2003). Pricing Process as a Capability: A resource-based perspective, *Strategic Management Journal* **24**: 615–630.

Dyer, J., and Singh, H (1998). The Relational View: Cooperative strategy and sources of interorganizational competitive advantage, *Academy of Management Review* **23**(4): 660–679.

Eisenhardt, K.M. (1988). Agency- and Institutional-theory Explanations: The case of retail sales compensation, *Academy of Management Journal* **31**(3): 488–511.

Feld, S.L. (1981). The Focused Organization of Social Ties, *American Journal of Sociology* **86**(5): 1015–1035.

Gambetta, D. (1988). *Trust: Making and breaking Cooperative Relations*, New York: Basil Blackwell.

Giddens, A. (1979). *Central Problems in Social Theory*, Berkeley, CA: University of California Press.

Granovetter, M. (1978). The Strength of Weak Ties, *American Journal of Sociology* **78**: 1360–1380.

Granovetter, M. (1985). Economic Action and Social Structure: The problem of embeddedness, *American Journal of Sociology* **91**: 481–510.

Grant, R.M. (1996). Toward a Knowledge-based Theory of the Firm, *Strategic Management Journal* **17**: 109–122.

Hambrick, D.C., and D'Aveni, R.A. (1988). Large Corporate Failures as Downward Spirals, *Administrative Science Quarterly* **33**(1): 1–23.

Hannan, J., and Freeman, M.T (1984). Structural Inertia and Organizational Change, *American Sociological Review* **49**: 149–164.

Hansen, M.T. (1999). The Search-transfer Problem: The role of weak ties in sharing knowledge across organization subunits, *Administrative Science Quarterly* **44**: 82–111.

Hoshi, T., Kashyap, A., and Scharfstein, D. (1991). The Role of Banks in Reducing the Costs of Financial Distress in Japan, *Journal of Financial Economics* **27**: 67–88.

Hu, Q., Gebelt, M., and Saunders, C. (1997). Achieving Success in Information Systems Outsourcing, *California Management Review* **39**(2): 63–79.

Hutt, M., Stafford, E., Walker, B., and Reingen, P. (Winter 2000). Case Study: Defining the social network of a strategic alliance, *Sloan Management Review* **41**(2): 51–62.

Ingram, P., and Roberts, P. (2000). Friendships Among Competitors in the Sydney Hotel Industry, *American Journal of Sociology* **106**(2): 387–423.

Jarillo, J. (1988). On Strategic Networks, *Strategic Management Journal* **9**(1): 31–41.

Kale, P., Singh, H., and Perlmutter, H. (2000). Learning and Protection of Proprietary Assets in Strategic Alliances: Building relational capital, *Strategic Management Journal* **21**: 217–237.

Kavan, C., Saunders, C., and Nelson, R. (September–October 1999). virtual@-virtual.org, *Business Horizons* **10**(4): 73–82.

Kern, T, and Willcocks, L.P. (2001). *The Relationship Advantage: Information technologies, sourcing, and management*, Oxford, UK: Oxford University Press.

Khanna, T., Gulati, R., and Nohria, N. (1998). The Dynamics of Learning Alliances: Competition, cooperation, and relative scope, *Strategic Management Journal* **19**: 193–210.

Kogut, B., and Zander, U. (1992). Knowledge of the Firm, Combinative Capabilities, and Replication of Technology, *Organization Science* **3**(3): 383–397.

Kogut, B., and Zander, U. (1996). What Firms Do? Coordination, identity, and learning, *Organization Science* **7**(5): 502–518.

Koh, C., Ang, S., and Straub, D.W. (2004). IT Outsourcing Success: A psychological contract perspective, *Information Systems Research* **15**(4): 356–373.

Kumar, K., Van Dissel, H., and Bielli, P. (1998). The Merchant of Prato – Revisited: Toward a third rationality of information systems, *MIS Quarterly* **22**(2): 199–226.

Lacity, M., and Hirschheim, R. (Fall 1993). The Information Systems Outsourcing Bandwagon, *Sloan Management Review* **35**(1): 73–86.

Lacity, M., and Willcocks, L. (1998). An Empirical Investigation of Information Technology Sourcing Practices: Lessons from experience, *Management Information Systems Quarterly* **22**(3): 363–408.

Lane, D., and Maxfield, R. (1996). Strategy Under Complexity: Fostering generative relationships, *Long Range Planning* **29**(2): 215–231.

Lee, J.N., Miranda, S.M., and Kim, Y.M. (2004). IT Outsourcing Strategies: Universalistic, contingency, and configurational explanations of success, *Information Systems Research* **15**(2): 110–131.

Lee, J.N., and Kim, Y.G. (1999). The Effect of Partnership Quality on IS Outsourcing Success: Conceptual framework and empirical validation, *Journal of Management Information Systems* **15**(4): 29–62.

Lin, N. (2001). *Social Capital: A theory of social structure and action*, Cambridge, UK: Cambridge University Press.

Lincoln, J.R., Gerlach, M.L., and Ahmadjian, C.L. (1996). Keiretsu Networks and Corporate Performance in Japan, *American Sociological Review* **61**(1): 67–89.

Macaulay, S. (1963). Non-contractual Relations in Business: A preliminary study, *American Sociological Review* **28**: 55–67.

Merton, R. (1968). The Matthew Effect in Science, *Science* **159**: 56–63.

Meyer, J.W., and Rowan, B. (1977). Institutionalized Organizations: Formal structure as myth and ceremony, *American Journal of Sociology* **83**: 340–363.

Mintzberg, H. (1978). Patterns in Strategy Formation, *Management Science* **24** (9): 934–948.

Montoya-Weiss, M.M., Massey, A.P., and Song, M. (2001). Getting It Together: Temporal coordination and conflict management in global virtual teams, *Academy of Management Journal* **44**(6): 1251–1262.

Moran, P., and Ghoshal, S. (1999). Markets, Firms, and The Process of Economic Development, *Academy of Management Review* **24**(3): 390–412.

Nahapiet, J., and Ghoshal, S. (April 1998). Social Capital, Intellectual Capital, and the Organizational Advantage, *The Academy of Management Review* **23** (2): 242–266.

North, D.C. (1990). *Institutions, Institutional Change and Economic Performance*, Cambridge, UK: Cambridge University Press.

Ozawa, T. (June 1999). The Rise and Fall of Bank-loan Capitalism: Institutionally driven growth and crisis in Japan, *Journal of Economic Issues* **33**(2): 351–358.

Padgett, J.F., and Ansell, C.K. (1993). Robust Action and the Rise of the Medici, 1400–1434, *American Journal of Sociology* **98**(6): 1259–1319.

Parsons, T. (1963). On the Concept of Political Power, *Proceedings of the American Philosophical Society* **107**(3): 232–262.

Pfeffer, J. (1982). Organization Level Rational Action, *Organizations and Organization Theory*, Boston: Pitman, 121–177.

Pfeffer, J., and Salancik, G.R. (2003 1978). *The External Control of Organizations*, New York, NY: Harper and Row.

Pfeffer, J., and Sutton, R. (2000). *The Knowing-Doing Gap: How smart companies turn knowledge into action*, Boston, MA: Harvard Business School Press.

Powell, W.W. (1996). Trust-based Forms of Governance, In R.M. Kramer and T.R. Tyler (eds.) *Trust in Organizations: Frontiers of Theory and Research*, Thousand Oaks, CA: Sage.

Priem, R.L. (2001). The Business-level RBV: Great wall or Berlin wall, *Academy of Management Review* **26**(4): 499–501.

Rahim, A. (1985). A Strategy of Managing Conflict in Complex Organizations, *Human Relations* **38**(1): 81–89.

Reuer, J.J., and Leiblein, M.J. (2000). Downside Risk Implications of Multinationality and International Joint Ventures, *Academy of Management Journal* **43**(2): 203–214.

Ring, P., and Van De Ven, A. (1994). Developmental Processes of Cooperative Interorganizational Relationships, *Academy of Management Review* **19**(1): 90–118.

Robey, D., Khoo, H., and Powers, C. (February/March 2000). Situated Learning in Cross-functional Virtual Teams, *IEEE Transactions on Professional Communication* **43**(1): 51–66.

Rousseau, D., Sitkin, S., Burt, R., and Camerer, C. (1998). Not so Different After All: A cross-discipline view of trust, *Academy of Management Review* **23**(3): 393–404.

Rousseau, D.M. (1995). *Psychological Contracts in Organizations*, Thousand Oaks, CA: Sage.

Rousseau, D.M., and Parks, J (1994). The Contracts of Individuals and Organizations, In L.L. Cummings and B.M. Staw (eds.) *Research in Organizational Behavior*, Vol. 15, Greenwich, CT: JAI Press, pp. 1–43.

Sabel, C. (1993). Studied Trust: Building new forms of cooperation in a volatile economy, *Human Relations* **46**(9): 1133–1170.

Sabherwal, R. (1999). The Role of Trust in Outsourced is Development Projects, *Communications of the ACM* **42**(2): 80–86.

Saxenian, A (1996). *Regional Advantage: Culture and competition in Silicon Valley and route 128*, Cambridge, MA: Harvard University Press.

Schick, A.G. (1985). University Budgeting: Administrative perspective, budget structure and budget process, *Academy of Management Review* **10**(4): 794–802.

Seabright, M.A., Levinthal, D.A., and Fichman, M. (1992). Role of Individual Attachments in the Dissolution of Inter-organizational Relationships, *Academy of Management Journal* **35**(1): 122–160.

Selznick, P. (1957). *Leadership in Administration: A sociological interpretation*, Berkeley, CA: University of California Press.

Shapiro, S.P. (1987). The Social Control of Impersonal Trust, *American Journal of Sociology* **93**(3): 623–658.

Sillars, A.L. (1980). Attributions and Communication in Roommate Conflict, *Communication Monographs* **47**(3): 180–200.

Silver, A. (May 1990). Friendship in Commercial Society: Eighteenth-century social theory and modern sociology, *American Journal of Sociology* **95**(6): 1474–1504.

Simmel, G. (1978). *The Philosophy of Money*, New York, NY: Routledge.

Spekman, R.E. (1988). Strategic Supplier Selection: Understanding long-term buyer relationships, *Business Horizons* **31**(4): 75–82.

Stark, D. (November 1990). Work, Justice, and the Comparability of Worth in a Socialist Mixed Economy. published in French as: 'La valeur du travail et sa rétribution en Hongrie', *Actes de la Recherche en Sciences Sociales*, (Paris) **85**: 3–19.

Stark, D. (2001). Ambiguous Assets for Uncertain Environments: Heterarchy in postsocialist firms, In P. DiMaggio, W. Powell, D. Stark, and E. Westney (eds.) *The Future of the Firm: The Social Organization of Business*, Princeton, NJ: Princeton University Press, pp. 69–104.

Steensma, H.K., and Corley, K.G. (2001). Organizational Context as a Moderator of Theories of Firm Boundaries for Technology Sourcing, *Academy of Management Journal* **44**(2): 271–291.

Stewart, T.A. (1999). *Intellectual Capital: The New Wealth of Organizations*, New York, NY: Currency Doubleday.

Stinchcombe, A.L. (1985). Contracts as Hierarchical Documents, In A.L. Stinchcombe and C.A. Heimer (eds.) *Organizational Theory and Project Management*, Oslo, Norway: Norwegian University Press, pp. 121–171.

Sydow, J., and Windeler, A. (1998). Organizing and Evaluating Interfirm Networks: A structurationist perspective on network processes and effectiveness, *Organization Science* **9**(3): 265–284.

Thompson, J.D. (1967). *Organizations in Action: Social Science Bases in Administrative Theory*, New York, NY: McGraw-Hill.

Uzzi, B. (1997). Social Structure and Competition in Interfirm Networks: The paradox of embeddedness, *Administrative Science Quarterly* **42**: 35–67.

Uzzi, B. (1999). Embeddedness in the Making of Financial Capital: How social relations and networks benefit firms seeking financing, *American Sociological Review* **64**: 481–505.

Van De Ven, A.H., Delbecq, A.L., and Koenig, R. Jr. (1976). Determinants of Coordination Modes Within Organizations, *American Sociological Review* **41**: 322–338.

Van De Ven, A.H., and Walker, G. (1984). The Dynamics of Interorganizational Coordination, *Administrative Science Quarterly* **29**(4): 598–631.

Weber, M. (1978). *Economy and Society*, Berkeley, CA: University of California Press.

Weick, K. (1995). *Sensemaking in Organizations*, Thousand Oaks, CA: Sage.

Weill, P., and Ross, J.W. (2004). *IT Governance: How top performers manage IT decision rights for superior results*, Harvard Business School Press: Boston, MA.

Whetten, D. (1989). What Constitutes a Theoretical Contribution?, *Academy of Management Review* 14(4): 490–495.

Willcocks, L.P., and Kern, T. (1998). IT Outsourcing as Strategic Partnering: the Case of the UK Inland Revenue, *European Journal of Information Systems* 7(1): 29–45.

Williamson, O.E. (1985). *The Economic Institutions of Capitalism*, New York, NY: Free Press.

Williamson, O.E. (1994). Transaction Cost Economics and Organization Theory, In N. J. Smelser and R. Swedberg (eds.) *The Handbook of Economic Sociology*, Princeton, NJ: Princeton University Press.

Williamson, O.E. (1996). *The Mechanisms of Governance*, New York: Oxford University Press.

Wiseman, R.M., and Bromiley, P. (1996). Toward a Model of Risk in Declining Organizations: An empirical examination of risk, performance, and decline, *Organization Science* 7(5): 524–543.

Wishart, N.A., Elam, J., and Robey, D. (1996). Redrawing the Portrait of a Learning Organization: Inside Knight-Ridder, Inc, *Academy of Management Executive* 10(1): 7–20.

Zucker, L. (1986). Production of Trust: Institutional sources of economic structure, 1840–1920, In B.M. Staw and L.L. Cummings (eds.) *Research in Organizational Behavior*, Vol. 8, Greenwich, CT: JIA, pp. 53–111.

Shaila M. Miranda an Associate Professor of MIS at the University of Oklahoma. She obtained her doctorate in Management Information Systems from the University of Georgia in 1991. She also has an M.A. in Sociology from Columbia University, and a Master of Management Studies and a B.A. in Psychology from the University of Bombay. Her current research interests in information systems include electronic collaboration, outsourcing, and alternate work arrangements. She also has a strong interest in sociological theory. She is an Associate Editor of *MIS Quarterly* and has published in journals such as the *Information Systems Research, Journal of Management Information Systems*, and *Information and Management*.

C. Bruce Kavan was the Bank of America Professor of Information Technology at the University of North Florida. Prior to completing his doctorate at The University of Georgia in 1991, he held several positions with Dun & Bradstreet including vice president of Information Services for their Receivable Management Services Division. Dr. Kavan is an extremely active consultant in the strategic use of technology, system architecture, and client/server technologies. His main areas of research interest are in inter-organizational systems, the delivery of IT services, and technology adoption/ diffusion. His research has appeared in such publications as *MIS Quarterly, Information Strategy: The Executive's Journal, Journal of Strategic Performance Measurement, Journal of End User Computing, Information Resources Management Journal, Auerback's Handbook of IS Management,* and *Journal of Service Marketing.*

Part II

From IT Outsourcing to Offshoring and Business Process Outsourcing

5

Norm Development in Outsourcing Relationships

Thomas Kern and Keith Blois

Introduction

This paper describes BP Exploration's decision to outsource its information technology (IT) function, that is to contract out the organization's IT assets, people and activities to outside suppliers, which in exchange provided and managed the assets and services for monetary returns over an agreed time period (Loh and Venkatraman 1992; Lacity and Hirschheim 1993). This decision led to an initial attempt to create a consortium rather than to using a number of bilateral agreements. However, this attempt was not successful and it was subsequently reorganized using a 'hierarchical' form of organization. The paper describes the history of this process and suggests that a crucial factor

T. Kern (✉)
Department of Information and Decision Sciences, Rotterdam School of Management, Erasmus University Rotterdam, Rotterdam, The Netherlands

K. Blois
Templeton College, University of Oxford, Oxford, UK

© The Author(s) 2017   **129**
L.P. Willcocks et al. (eds.), *Outsourcing and Offshoring Business Services*, DOI 10.1007/978-3-319-52651-5_5

leading to the collapse of the consortium approach was the failure to establish norms of behaviour.

Research Approach

This paper is based on information collected through the use of an in-depth longitudinal case research method. Case research in such a context is particularly appropriate for exploratory research of this nature (Pettigrew 1990; Walsham 1993). The approach makes it possible to investigate 'sticky, practice-based problems [such as outsourcing relationship practice] where the experiences of actors are important and the context of action is critical' (Benbasat et al. 1987, p. 369).

Three issues influenced the research design. First, the BP Exploration/multiple-supplier outsourcing contract involved an innovative deal that focused on developing alliance type relationships between a group of suppliers and a customer. Second, this outsourcing relationship involved many stakeholders including users/benefactors of the outsourcing service, client relationship managers, vendors' account management teams and the vendors' technical service groups. Third, access to senior managers was possible for both customers and suppliers. This made it feasible to obtain a comprehensive view of the development of the relationship.

Data Collection and Analysis

The data collection was undertaken between December 1996 and June 1997. Interviews using open-ended questions developed from the literature on IT outsourcing, norms, interorganizational relationships, behaviour in relationships and relationship management in outsourcing were conducted with managers from BP Exploration and the vendor companies. The semi-structured interview protocol (a copy of the actual interview protocol can be obtained from the authors upon request) was designed for eliciting data about the outsourcing situation, relationship practice and relationship behaviours. The interviews were transcribed and verified with the relevant respondents. A higher level of abstraction and interpretation was achieved by applying the precepts of intentional analysis to the transcripts (Sanders 1982). In addition, by using reviews of internal documents, newspaper articles and trade press articles about BP Exploration a comprehensive case history was constructed. These procedures made it possible to develop a qualitative, interpretative approach to the construction of the case study described in the next section.

The Case

Background

BP Exploration, BP's second largest and most capital-intensive division, is responsible for exploration and production operations in 16 countries. In 1989 BP Exploration's IT infrastructure was primarily based on mainframe systems with approximately 1400 personnel. In the 1990s, BP Exploration was made more autonomous and it decided to develop a new flatter global management team (Cross et al. 1997). Key to this change was the use of IT for facilitating communications and as an essential ingredient for improving overall productivity. In addition, BP Exploration's IT function played a critical role in supporting the exploration and production operations.

By 1995 it was becoming evident that BP Exploration's IT function was not only being challenged to decrease costs and improve operational efficiency, but was expected to make an active contribution to BP Exploration's future business. BP Exploration now believed that it no longer needed to own the technologies that provided business information to employees (Cross et al. 1997) and by 1995 IT services were not viewed as being one of BP Exploration's core competencies.

The Move to Outsourcing

In November 1991 BP Exploration issued requests for information stating BP Exploration's intention to refocus its IT department and summarizing the scope of the work that would be outsourced. This was the start of a search that lasted 15 months. The potential suppliers ranged from niche providers in areas such as data centre management, applications development and telecommunications groups to every major service provider in the market.

BP Exploration's view was that outsourcing should reduce costs and also rebuild the whole of its IT function and services on a different and more effective basis. The aim was to reposition the internal IT team in order to create much more value rather than having them deliver IT services themselves. Outsourcing was also part of BP Exploration's strategy for developing a common operating environment with standard packages. Together with BP Exploration's internal restructuring efforts, management expected the outsourcing arrangements to help diminish the costs of finding new oil fields and improve productivity.

By mid-1992 a final shortlist of six suppliers had been established, but BP Exploration now realized that no single supplier could provide all their IT requirements to a best in class level (Currie and Willcocks 1997). BP Exploration's managers were aware from previous outsourcing experiences of the difficulties in maintaining a coordinated interface between individual suppliers and this convinced them that, although it needed different suppliers with differing skills for different activities, they had to have the ability to work together. BP Exploration recognized that an effective interface between suppliers was dependent on it having good relations with each of them but, because some of the suppliers were competitors, this was recognized to be a challenge. Thus, although BP Exploration had originally decided to outsource its services selectively, it now wanted a consortium of more than one and fewer than five companies for putting forward a proposal for all its IT needs through the provision of a seamless service.

The challenge to the suppliers, even though several were at least in part competitors, was to form a consortium for presenting a proposal with the best cost–performance target. The potential suppliers explored what each could do, testing their capabilities, forming alliances, dissolving them and forming new ones. In October 1992 BP Exploration accepted the proposal submitted by the Sema Group, Science Applications International Corporation (SAIC) and British Telecommunications (BT) Syncordia as these three suppliers best complemented each other's expertise and capabilities and all were capable of providing BP Exploration with services globally. (The Sema Group's 1995 turnover was in excess of £677 million with its major markets being the UK and France. SAIC, based in San Diego, had an annual turnover of $3.1 billion in 1997. BT owns Syncordia, which had revenues of £250 million in 1996 and had a £1.2 billion contract value (which implies that most of the contracts were between 3 and 5 years).)

BP Exploration established 5-year agreements with the Sema Group and SAIC and a 2-year agreement with BT Syncordia which was later renewed in 1995 for another 2 years. However, because of the high price volatility of IT services (in particular for telecommunication services) new performance contracts were to be negotiated annually for price rates, services and performance levels.

Outsourcing Scope

The Sema Group was contracted to operate BP Exploration's UK data centres in Glasgow and the computer centre in Harlow and to provide IT services for BP Exploration's offices at Stockley Park and BP Exploration's head office in London. SAIC was contracted to manage the IT facilities at BP Exploration's European headquarters and all the company's other applications. This included all the technical applications such as applications for seismic assessment. In addition, it was to manage desktop and local area network services in Aberdeen. BT Syncordia was contracted to manage BP Exploration's telecommunications and telex networks worldwide providing data, voice and video communications services.

The contracts and arrangements between BP Exploration and the three vendors took a great deal of time to finalize. European 'anti-trust' law stopped the three suppliers from formally joining in a consortium for delivering services to BP Exploration. Thus, BP Exploration was forced to contract individually with each of the suppliers, but with the implicit agreement that they had to provide the services for BP Exploration's needs conjointly. One supplier was to be the primary contractor coordinating the services the trio provided to the businesses supported by the site for each of BP Exploration's eight major business sites.

The Aston–Clinton Principles

In late 1992 senior managers from SAIC, the Sema Group, BT Syncordia and BP Exploration developed the Aston–Clinton principles, which encapsulated what these parties believed to be the characteristics of a successful partnering relationship.

> [I]n terms of the intent for the relationship, all companies signed for us what was called the Aston–Clinton principles of relationships. It was something which we all wanted to adhere to, it was not a contract but it was the spirit in which we wanted the relationship to move forward. [...] It is the characteristics of what a partnership arrangement is. So that is about long-term relationships, mutual commitment, sharing the rewards and risks, commitment to each other's success, creating win–win relationships and scenarios. Totally dependent on one another. [...] This is about working together in a way that was different (IT director, BP Exploration).

These principles formed an addendum to the contracts agreed between all parties, but were only a guiding framework and had no legal status. In essence the principles outlined the following:

(1)   Simplicity of practice.
(2)   Visibility of costs.
(3)   Trust between the parties.
(4)   Common understanding between the parties.
(5)   The creation of a win–win relationship.
(6)   Fair returns for consortium members.
(7)   A long-term relationship but no legal partnership between the parties.
(8)   Site targets, including margins, to be agreed locally.
(9)   Risk/Reward arrangements to apply to the difference between the costs included within the target and the actual costs as demonstrated via an open book policy.
(10) Principles generally to apply on a site-by-site basis as well as on a global basis.

(11)   From time to time benchmarks to be established by BP Exploration in order to validate the 'best in class' performance, not necessarily just financial performance.

(12)   Other alternative financial arrangements for *ad hoc* activities can apply where appropriate, for example fixed fee or incremental costs.

The agreement covered generic and specific services, legal provisions, general commercial principles, financial targets, margins and incentives, quality assurance and performance reviews. BP Exploration's managers at each of BP Exploration's 16 sites negotiated individual contracts with the IT suppliers, specifying the scope of services, service levels and performance targets.

Costs were very closely scrutinized.

> The three suppliers' books are open to us; they itemize all costs clearly in quarterly or annual invoices, distinguishing among direct, allocated and corporate overhead costs charged to BP Exploration [...]. Our agreement stipulates that we can audit our suppliers' accounts of services to us, if it proves necessary (IT director, BP Exploration, quoted in Currie and Willcocks (1997)).

Benchmarking provisions were also included in the framework agreements and suppliers were required to deliver best in class services for specific areas. In circumstances where another provider could supply an important service more cost-effectively, then BP Exploration could insist on the relevant supplier being subcontracted and managed by the existing vendors.

The Start-Up Period

The start-up period was more challenging than expected. Early concerns arose with the negotiation of the site-specific contracts and service level agreements where service level targets, price margins and other aspects still had to be localized. Not surprisingly in the first-year activity frequently relapsed into merely defining and finalizing agreements at each of the business sites.

Initially there was a drop in service levels as the suppliers attempted to understand the systems and requirements, which was difficult within BP Exploration's fast-changing IT strategy and structure. The suppliers found it difficult to keep up with BP Exploration's intention to lead the market in terms of technological developments. In addition, the vendors faced problems with BP Exploration's culture and operational structure. All this affected service performance negatively and damaged relationships.

By 1995 each of BP Exploration's eight (16 by 1997) key business sites globally had one member of the consortium operating as the primary contractor coordinating the services provided by the other suppliers. Each vendor in turn was appointed as the primary contractor somewhere with ultimate responsibility for a seamless service to a business site and the service levels at each site. However, although by 1994 the vendors were performing according to agreed service levels, users remained dissatisfied with the services.

Delivering services within BP Exploration's expected cost boundary was not always easy, particularly as BP Exploration's activities had spread geographically. This presented large challenges to the vendors, particularly for BT Syncordia, which had to provide the fundamental telecommunications link with parts of the world that are not as technologically advanced as others.

The New Contract

BT Syncordia was initially only contracted for 2 years. In early 1995, when BT Syncordia was asked to rebid for its area, the Sema Group and SAIC were also encouraged to submit bids. In the end BT Syncordia was re-contracted for 3 years, but the process had seriously strained relations between members of the alliance.

By early 1996 all BP Exploration sites were using outsourcing suppliers and relations in the first sites outsourced had settled down. Operationalizing the consortium approach was not easy for the vendors and relations between them had already been seriously strained by the re-bidding for BT Syncordia's business. In addition, disputes had erupted, particularly between the Sema Group and SAIC, with every placement of new business because their portfolios and offerings were so similar. However, relations between the suppliers did not break down, not least because BP Exploration required that they did not do so, but because they had also agreed to the Aston–Clinton principles.

In early 1996, the vendors' account managers were voicing concern that BP Exploration's management infrastructure required numerous regional contracts and interface responsibilities, which were becoming difficult to manage. Although BP Exploration's IT managers recognized that each account manager had to interface with up to 15 people they could not find a solution to this difficulty.

With so many relationships, managers could not keep themselves informed on BP Exploration's strategic moves. Internal reports, memorandums and newsletters were often the only source of information about BP Exploration's plans and, consequently, in a number of cases vendors faced unexpected surprises and pressures that drove them to their limits. This lack of sharing reflected BP Exploration's line managers' perspective that the IT suppliers were commodity suppliers. This contrasted with BP Exploration's senior management's expectation that the vendors would be innovators using their experiences with other clients and their expertise and knowledge of technology and processes. Yet this did not occur and the vendors mostly delivered process and commodity type services even though these suppliers considered themselves to be best in class in their areas.

BP Exploration's Re-Evaluation

In early 1997, BP Exploration began reconsidering its IT organization. As outsourcing by then represented 80% of their annual IT budget and the contracts were coming to an end in March 1998, the role of outsourcing was a critical factor. In addition, there was a need for BP Exploration to devise a corporate-wide common operating environment that required a standard platform. However, it was becoming obvious that if global IT commonality (involving 35 000 users) was to be achieved it was necessary to think about reducing the suppliers down to one and, hence, it was becoming questionable what role the consortium would then have after 1998.

BP Exploration now recognized that, as an outsourcing venture, the consortium approach had not worked as initially planned. Even though the vendors had committed themselves to providing a seamless service in many cases they found it increasingly difficult to actually work together and cooperate. In effect, the vendors had remained competitors, particularly in those instances where BP Exploration placed additional business or asked for project bids. Performance had suffered, forcing BP Exploration's managers to become involved in managing the vendors (particularly in adjudicating disputes about service provisions and responsibilities). As a result, even though one of BP Exploration's objectives had been to decrease the amount of management time spent on IT, additional managers had been allocated to the outsourcing relationships.

BP Exploration therefore decided that the consortium approach was too complicated and, although some advantages had arisen from having multiple suppliers for particular areas, it was not felt that the benefit of economies of scale were being gained or that innovation from the outsource suppliers had been obtained. So BP Exploration decided to move to another model for seamless end to end management.

By June 1997 BP Exploration had redefined their IT structure and now its outsourcing strategy was to have one global strategic partner responsible for providing the service management of their total IT infrastructure. Additional vendors such as the Sema Group, SAIC and BT Syncordia would continue to deliver commodity services such as data centre management, application support and telecommunications.

IBM and EDS as well as SAIC, the Sema Group and BT Syncordia were asked to bid against this new specification. EDS was chosen as the preferred supplier and was recommended to the BP Exploration board, which subsequently ratified the choice. In August 1998, both BP Exploration and EDS signed a 5-year renewable contract for the infrastructure part.

Interpretation

It is increasingly being recognized that investigations of alternative forms of governance that only consider the structure of the organization cannot provide a complete insight into its efficiency and effectiveness. For example, it has been shown that the costs of managing relationships differ across similarly organized dyads as a result of the different relational norms that exist in the dyads (Artz and Brush 2000). As a result, while many writers have sought to create 'a rich classificatory apparatus' (Williamson 1979) of types of governance relationships, great stress is now also placed on the role of the norms that underpin the way a relationship operates. It has been suggested that Macneil's (1983, 2000) work both provides 'a rich descriptive apparatus' (Blois, 2002, p. 547) that gives insights into the nature of those norms that determine the success of a business relationship and also shows that 'quite different relationships can exist even within the same governance structure' (Blois, p. 546). (Macneil thinking has developed over many years, but Macneil (1983) is a good summary of his current thinking, which he defended and slightly extended in Macneil (2000).) Thus, the centrality of norms in creating both the atmosphere within which relationships exist and the manner in which they operate is increasingly being recognized (e.g. Heide and John 1992; Gundlach and Achrol 1993). However, there are four fundamental questions regarding norms that are illustrated by this case.

Question 1: What Do Norms Do?

'Norms' create expectations of behaviour and 'imply a certain action and are shared by the actors' (Hakansson and Johanson 1993, p. 44). Indeed, Macneil (1983) believed that society shares a number of common norms that make it necessary for contracts to contain certain features but not necessary to include statements about others. Yet norms vary a great deal between and within societies as is illustrated by international contracts where 'a "foreigner's" requirements as to what should go into a contract will often surprise us but what we would not consider necessary to include may surprise them' (Blois 1999, p. 8).

Businesses recognize the impossibility of a contract meeting every eventuality so that there is a need for adaptability within a contract and the completion of a contract is frequently dependent upon 'workers being able to take up a lot of the uncertainty' (Stinchcombe 1990, p. 236). Indeed, 'Both the normal economic models of a market transaction and the legal model of a contract tend to obscure the degree to which large numbers of contracts are (realistically, though not legally) agreements to deliver an indefinite good or service for an indefinite price' (Stinchcombe 1990, p. 215). Without such willingness to be adaptable many business relationships would grind rapidly and regularly to a halt. Norms are in a sense the lubricants that keep relationships from being stymied by their contractual terms.

In this case three problems arose. First, the consortium's members, though competitors, were expected to work closely with each other as the senior partner on some sites and as the junior partner on others! Yet neither BP Exploration nor any member of the consortium recognized in advance that the norms that they usually applied in their relationships with their clients would not be applicable to this situation. Consequently, their staff were working with norms that were at best not appropriate to the new situation and at worst made for difficulties. For example, a company's norms do not normally encourage the acceptance of flexibility, information exchange and solidarity in contacts with competitors, all of which are needed if sound relationships are to be developed between organizations (Heide and John 1992).

Second, BP Exploration's line managers conducted their relationships with the consortium members as if they were buying a commodity service. Yet a major reason for outsourcing was BP Exploration's desire to obtain a state of the art IT service! Its behaviour towards the consortium was therefore based on norms that were inappropriate relative to its stated objectives.

The third problem was that SAIC was not familiar with European modes of operations and 'had a horrendous job trying to adapt to a non-US culture' (BP Exploration manager).

Initially the various participants in the relationship continued to apply the norms appropriate to their past experience, yet these were almost totally inappropriate for the new relationships within which they were expected to work.

It could be argued that the Aston–Clinton principles were an attempt to 'create' a set of norms. However, it is first questionable whether norms can be 'created' in this way (see below). Second, in specific situations the correct way to proceed within the spirit of the Aston–Clinton rules could only be decided within a set of norms! In other words the Aston– Clinton rules were either so vague as to be meaningless or so specific as to leave no room for doubt that the norm was that BP Exploration was in charge!

Question 2: How Are Norms Formed?

Some norms' roots can be related to cultural backgrounds, but the roots of others are more difficult to identify. However, how norms develop when new industries or, as in this case, new forms of organization evolve is far from apparent. This is particularly a problem where industries and organizational forms have evolved very rapidly and include genuinely new structures (see Bjorn-Andersen and Turner 1994). The importance of establishing norms is hinted at by Heide and John's (1992) view that, without them, 'a buyer's ability to exercise needed vertical control is limited' (p. 00), for it is a reminder that the lack of agreed norms has cost consequences for those involved in a relationship.

The work of Axelrod (1984) and Gronovetter (1985) is suggestive in this matter, but little in the way of empirical studies seems to have been carried out. In relationships such as the one described in this case, which develop in a new environment, the relative power of the parties involved is presumably a major factor. Thus, where one organization is very dominant in a new market it seems probable that their values and approaches to business will be very influential.

As the case indicates, the Aston–Clinton principles were an attempt to create norms and these encapsulated what the parties believed to be the characteristics of a successful partnering relationship. Indeed, in the first year the consortium's members tried to work together, but in this period the relationships within the consortium were so poor that the arrangement nearly collapsed, particularly as IT service levels dropped in this period. However, gradually acceptable service levels were established. Yet relationships between the individual consortium members and BP Exploration remained 'frosty' as the BP Exploration's managers' perception was that this was a commodity outsourcing deal and so treated it as a transactional exchange rather than a relationship. Throughout this period the consortium's members were learning to work with each other (i.e. developing norms) and with BP Exploration. BP Exploration then disrupted the development process by encouraging the Sema Group and SAIC to submit bids against BT Syncordia for the renewal of its contract.

Commons (1950), while accepting that they overlap, suggested that transactions are dynamic and go through three temporal stages: negotiation, agreement and execution. It is in the agreement stage that the governance structures plus the structural and procedural safeguards that will organize the deal are set up. In the execution stage, renegotiation and adaptation of these structures and safeguards may be required if those already set up prove to be inadequate. The difficulty in this case was that the members of the consortium needed to go through these stages in order to establish relationships with each other while almost simultaneously, but acting as a consortium, they went through these three stages with BP Exploration!

BP Exploration expected to implement the first outsourced arrangements 15 months after issuing the initial requests for information to potential suppliers. With a normal outsourcing arrangement this would have been a challenge but, between issuing the requests for information and letting the contract, BP Exploration changed the nature of their demands to require outsourcers to form consortia! It is therefore not entirely surprising that problems arose following such rapid changes not least because personal relationships contribute a great deal to the establishment and maintenance of agreed norms. As Ring and Van De Ven (1994) stated, 'if personal relationships do not supplement formal relationship over time, then the likelihood increases that conflicts will escalate' (p. 109) and personal relationships take time to develop.

Question 3: How Do Norms Operate within Complex Relationships?

Within business relationships the nature of exchanges that occur between the personnel involved can vary a great deal. Sometimes the relationships at a senior level are more relaxed than those at a junior level. Yet the opposite can be true with junior staff making the relationship work on a day to day level in spite of adversarial behaviour between the directors.

Sometimes staff roles also strongly influence the interactions that occur (Green 1995). Here the common language and values of professions or crafts may be more important than the organizations' view of the relationship. Indeed, it has been asserted that 'More efficacious negotiation appears to result when the counterpart architects of negotiating strategy between two organizations play the same roles (that is, manager and managers or lawyers and lawyers)' (Ring and Van De Ven 1989, p. 186).

This would suggest that, not only may there be a hierarchy of norms that apply to a relationship, but also that norms are multidimensional (Noordewier et al. 1990; Hiede and John, 1992) with an overarching set of norms within which those individuals whose job it is to operationalize the relationship have to function. However, they may consciously operate with different norms. For example, a salesperson and a buyer may work closely together freely 'bending the rules' in order to keep the relationship working smoothly at a day-to-day level, even though the norm imposed by their separate organizations is that everything should be 'done by the book'. Of course, the opposite could be the case. Both Guitot (1977) and Gabarro (1987) commented that, within a newly formed organizational relationship, individuals' relationships will at first be determined by their role. Over time though their role will not disappear; it may merely diminish in favour of the *qua persona* (Guitot 1977). However, the nature of exchange, even within a role, is strongly influenced by the personality of those involved (Zaheer et al. 1998).

The consortium's structure and its relationships with BP Exploration were complex. The outsourcing management board composed of senior managers from BP Exploration and the consortium were overseeing the outsourcing venture. The vendors' account managers ultimately controlled the relationship on behalf of the consortium both on a global and also regional level. Their responsibility was to oversee site performance, new business opportunities and resolve any major problems. However, the account managers had little impact on day-to-day interactions. The vendors' line managers or relationship managers were responsible for service performance regionally and interfaced with BP Exploration's regional partner resource manager and business information managers. Apparently, while at the higher levels relationships were good, at the operational level they were mostly adversarial. There are many possible reasons for this discrepancy of approach, but it is possible that the rapid setting up of the arrangement had left too little time for senior management in BP exploration and the consortia to communicate effectively with their operational managers.

Question 4: How Can Norms be Classified?

Many classifications of norms have been proposed, but no one is regarded as dominant. Macneil's (1983) ten norms are influential though they have been less used than might be expected. Other writers (e.g. Kaufman and Stern 1988) have produced modified versions of Macneil's (1983) norms. Heide and John (1992), working from Macneil's (1983) norms, proposed that relational norms are a higher order construct consisting of three dimensions.

(1)   Flexibility, which defines a bilateral expectation of the willingness to make adaptations as circumstances change.

(2)   Information exchange, which defines a bilateral expectation that parties will proactively provide information useful to the partner.
(3)   Solidarity, which defines a bilateral expectation that a high value is placed on the relationship. It prescribes behaviours directed specifically towards relationship maintenance.

Of these only flexibility is evident as being displayed by the members of the consortium. However, such flexibility did not seem to be reciprocated by BP Exploration. In contrast, there is evidence of BP Exploration's failure to accept that information exchange with members of the consortium was important.

As for solidarity, BP Exploration's encouragement of the Sema Group and SAIC to submit bids against BT Syncordia and implicitly against each other was guaranteed to create distrust between them. It also implied that BP Exploration had little long-term commitment to the members of the consortium and that BP Exploration would always be seeking out alternative suppliers if only as a method of keeping the consortium members on their toes.

Certainly, if the presence of flexibility, information exchange and solidarity is necessary in order for relational norms to operate then it is not surprising that this complex relationship effectively failed.

Some Implications

It is often suggested that close business to business relationships are characterized by the willingness of both parties to adapt. However, the literature often only implies that adaptation involves investment in tangible facilities. For example, 'Adaptations presume investments that may partially lead to relationship-specific assets' (Moller and Wilson 1995, p. 42). However, what was important in this case was the need for adaptation with regard to intangible features such as 'norms'.

In more typical buyer–supplier relationships (such as, for example, the relationship that BP Exploration developed with EDS in 1998) the adaptation of norms is less significant if only because competitors are not being expected to cooperate. However, when a new form of organizational inter-relationship is created it cannot be presumed that appropriate norms will evolve. Having talked 'partnership' BP Exploration effectively subcontracted a major problem to the consortium members assuming that the members of the consortium would sort out their inter-relationships. Moreover, BP Exploration made it clear that it was in charge of the overall relationship between the consortium and itself. BP Exploration seemed to have initially allocated no managerial time to assisting the members of the consortium in establishing new norms of behaviour that were appropriate to their roles as collaborators – while remaining competitors outside of this context. In addition, some of BP Exploration's managers were not clear about the objectives of the exercise and saw it only as a commodity supply arrangement rather than a partnership ensuring BP Exploration's access to leading edge developments. What is worse, just as norms were evolving, BP Exploration 'reminded' them that they were still fundamentally competitors by inviting them to bid against each other!

Selznick (1957) argued that a relationship only becomes institutionalized when norms and values have been established with enough clarity for the relationship to be able to continue beyond the immediate tenure of its founders. Such a process must take time yet BP Exploration moved to implement these new outsourcing arrangements extremely rapidly. Although commentators recognize that negotiation, agreement and execution – the three stages of a transaction – may overlap, it is not generally recommended that any two of them are conducted almost simultaneously. In fact BP Exploration's timetable left little room for anything but discussion of technical matters.

The timetable also seems to have failed to recognize 'that underlying formal contracts are a host of backstage interpersonal dynamics that mobilize and direct the formal contracting process but are seldom visible or explicitly written into the formal contract' (Ring and Van De Ven 1989, p. 179). Neither does BP Exploration seem to have understood 'the tension produced by inherently contradictory roles enacted by transacting individuals' (Ring and Van De Ven 1989, p. 172) whereby an individual needs to reconcile their personal interests with those of the organization. Such reconciliation takes time.

Finally, if the consortium was to be a success then its members would have had to show flexibility, information exchange and solidarity towards each other. However, BP Exploration's conduct made it unlikely that they would behave in this way. Particularly damaging was BP Exploration's decision to encourage them to compete against each other, but nearly as serious was BP Exploration's treatment of them as commodity suppliers. Commodity suppliers after all do not make profits by being flexible or showing solidarity towards each other or by exchanging information.

In summary the case suggests the following:

(1)   Where an unusual organizational structure is proposed manage ment must recognize the possibility that the norms dominant within the constituent organizations will not necessarily be compatible.

(2)   Where the norms are not compatible then action must be taken through changing management schemes in order to develop appropriate norms.

(3)   The development and internalization of new norms takes time.

Concluding Comments

Influenced by its experience in the 1980s with facilities management arrangements, which had highlighted the difficulties of obtaining value and true benefits, BP Exploration decided that, if it was to outsource again, it would pursue partnering-based relations that integrate risk–reward sharing arrangements in order to attain real value. In addition, the sheer size of BP Exploration's undertaking and the resulting requirements led it to consider using more than just one supplier partner and to try using a consortium-based partner arrangement (Currie and Willcocks 1997).

BP Exploration entered this outsourcing arrangement with many of the usual overheads found in large organizations already reduced. It had also gained invaluable knowledge from its prior experience of outsourcing.

The downside of the consortium outsourcing arrangement was the increase in transaction costs of handling three suppliers. BP Exploration made efforts to transfer the management responsibility to the consortium by appointing a lead contractor for each site and compelling them to deliver a seamless service for all areas contracted. Yet on many occasions the competitiveness between the vendors demanded adjudication and, hence, active BP Exploration management involvement. When such coordination problems arose the responsibility was passed between the suppliers resulting in a 'finger pointing match', with nobody in the end taking the blame for poor service performance (Currie and Willcocks 1997). The aftermath of these disputes about service competencies diminished the sharing of both resources and commercial knowledge.

Many factors led to this being a less than successful experiment in outsourcing. However, a major contributor was a failure to recognize the need for establishing norms of behaviour that were appropriate to this form of organization. As was commented in retrospect, 'You do not assemble a group of vendors and say be nice boys and go off and do good things for us' (head of the Business Information and Process International Systems Programmme, BP Exploration).

However, given that the four questions above, namely what do norms do?, how are norms formed?, how do norms operate within complex relationships? and how can norms be classified?, remain as yet at least partially unanswered, this is not a criticism of the participants but a challenge to researchers. Certainly after its experiences BP Exploration reverted to a more traditional buyer–supplier relationship leaving EDS to supply its IT by managing a group of suppliers on a hierarchical basis. Within such a traditional type of relationship all parties would understand the norms.

Finally, the norm questions are of particular interest to understanding relationship practice in outsourcing in general. We found that the four norm questions offer a lens through which the outsourcing relationship's *modus operandi* can be interpreted, discussed and explored in other outsourcing cases discussed in a particular relationship context (see Kern and Willcocks 2001). As such the four questions provide a crucial starting point for researchers in delving into the non-tangible issues of outsourcing relationship practice. Moreover, it also offers managers involved in an outsourcing venture from both the supplier and client side a useful set of questions by which to assess their practices in fostering and maintaining a successful outsourcing relationship.

References

Artz, K.W., and Brush, T.H. (2000) Asset specificity, uncertainty and relational norms: an examination of coordination costs in collaborative strategic alliances. *Journal of Economic Behavior and Organization*, **41**, 337–362.

Axelrod, R. (1984) *The Evolution of Cooperation* (Basic Books, New York).

Benbasat, I., Goldstein, D.K., and Mead, M. (1987) The case research strategy in studies in information management. *MIS Quarterly*, **11**(3) September, 369–386.

Bjorn-Andersen, N., and Turner, J.A. (1994) Creating the twenty-first century organization: the metamorphosis of Oticon. In *Transforming Organizations with Information Technology*, R. Baskerville, S. Smithson, O. Ngwenyama, and J.I. DeGross. (eds.) (North-Holland, Elsevier Science B.V. Amsterdam), 379–394.

Blois, K.J. (1999) A framework for assessing relationships. In *28th Annual Conference of the European Marketing Academy*, 11–14 May 1999 Hummboldt Universitat, Berlin.

Blois, K.J. (2002) Business to business exchanges: a rich descriptive apparatus derived from Macneil's and Menger's analyses. *Journal of Management Studies*, **39**(4), 523–551.

Commons, J.R. (1950) *The Economics of Collective Actions* (University of Wisconsin Press, Madison, WI).

Cross, J., Earl, M.J., and Sampler, J.L. (1997) The transformation of the IT function at British Petroleum. *MIS Quarterly*, **21**(4), 401–423.

Currie, W.L., and Willcocks, L. (1997) *New Strategies in IT Outsourcing* (Business Intelligence Ltd, London).

Gabarro, J.J. (1987) The development of working relationships. In *The Handbook of Organizational Behaviour*, J.W Lorsch. (ed.) (Prentice-Hall Inc, Englewood Cliffs, NJ), 172–189.

Green, R.L. (1995) Partnering and alliances: theory and practice. In *Offshore Europe Conference*, Aberdeen, 5–8 September, 54–60.

Gronovetter, M. (1985) Economic action and social structure: the problem of embeddedness. *American Sociological Review*, **91**, 481–510.

Guitot, J.M. (1977) Attribution and identity construction: some comments. *American Sociological Review*, **42**, 692–704.

Gundlach, G.T., and Achrol, R.S. (1993) Governance in exchange: contract law and its alternatives. *Journal of Public Policy and Marketing*, **12**(2), 141–156.

Hakansson, H., and Johanson, J. (1993) The network as a governance structure. In *The Embedded Firm*, G. Grabher (ed.) (Routledge, London), 35–51.

Heide, J.B., and John, G. (1992) Do norms matter in marketing relationships?. *Journal of Marketing*, **56**, 32–44.

Kaufman, P.J., and Stern, L.W. (1988) Relational conflict norms, perceptions of unfairness, and retained hostility in commercial litigation. *Journal of Conflict Resolution*, **32**, 534–552.

Kern, T., and Willcocks, L.P. (2001) *The Relationship Advantage: Sourcing, Information Technologies, and Management* (Oxford University Press, Oxford).

Lacity, M.C., and Hirschheim, R. (1993) *Information Systems Outsourcing: Myths, Metaphors and Realities* (John Wiley & Sons Ltd, Chichester).

Loh, L., and Venkatraman, N. (1992) Diffusion of information technology outsourcing: influence sources and the Kodak effect. *Information Systems Research*, **4**(3), 334–358.

Macneil, I.R. (1983) Values in contract: internal and external. *Northwestern University Law Review*, **78**(2), 340–418.

Macneil, I.R. (2000) Relational contract theory: challenges and queries. *Northwestern University Law Review*, **94**(3), 877–907.

Moller, K., and Wilson, D. (1995) Business relationships – inve. In *Business Marketing: An Interaction and Network Perspective*, K. Moller and D. Wilson. (eds.) (Kluwer Academic Publishers, Boston), 23–52.

Noordewier, T.G., George, J., and Nevin, J.R. (1990) Performance outcomes of purchasing arrangements in industrial buyer–vendor relationships. *Journal of Marketing*, **54**, 80–93.

Pettigrew, A.M. (1990) Context and action in the transformation of the firm. *Journal of Management Studies*, **24**(6), 649–670.

Ring, P.S., and Van De Ven, A.H. (1989) Formal and informal dimensions of transactions. In *Research on the Management of Innovation*, A.H. Van De Ven, H.L. Angle, and M.S. Poole. (eds.) (Harper & Row Inc, New York), 171–192.

Ring, P.S., and Van De Ven, A.H. (1994) Developmental processes of cooperative interorganizational relationships. *Academy of Management Review*, **19** (1), 90–118.

Sanders, P. (1982) Phenomenology: a new way of viewing organizational research. *Academy of Management Review*, **7**(3), 63–79.

Selznick, P. (1957) *Leadership in Administration* (Harper & Row, New York).

Stinchcombe, A.L. (1990) *Information and Organizations* (University of California Press, Berkeley, CA).

Walsham, G. (1993) *Interpreting Information Systems in Organizations* (John Wiley & Sons, Chichester).

Williamson, O.E. (1979) Transaction-cost economics: the governance of contractual relations. *Journal of Law and Economics*, **22**(2), 233–261.

Zaheer, A., McEvily, B., and Peronne, V. (1998) Does trust matter? Exploring the effects of interorganizational and interpersonal trust on performance. *Organizational Science*, **9**(2), 141–159.

Thomas Kern was in the Department of Information and Decision Sciences, Rotterdam School of Management, Erasmus University Rotterdam, Rotterdam, The Netherlands.

Keith Blois was Fellow at Templeton College, University of Oxford, Oxford, UK.

6

Organizational Design of IT Supplier Relationship Management: A Multiple Case Study of Five Client Companies

Jasmin Kaiser and Peter Buxmann

Introduction

IT organizations face enduring demands to drive down cost and increase efficiency. As a preferred strategic option, many rely on outsourcing arrangements with specialized IT suppliers, which fulfill a substantial part of their IT services. The management of these outsourcing relationships has become one of the key issues, which mostly plays a crucial role in IS/IT outsourcing.

A thorough exploration of successful client-supplier relationships has also become a newer focused theme in IS/IT outsourcing literature, which has shifted research away from the exploration of initial steps in a sourcing process, for instance outsourcing decision making (see e.g., Hirschheim et al. 2008: 9–10). However, management of external suppliers is not solely an issue in IS/IT outsourcing. The general importance of supplier relationship management (SRM) was already stated in 1991 by Cusumano and Takeishi, when presenting results from a survey

J. Kaiser (✉) · P. Buxmann
Technische Universität Darmstadt, Darmstadt, Germany

© The Author(s) 2017   **153**
L.P. Willcocks et al. (eds.), *Outsourcing and Offshoring Business Services*, DOI 10.1007/978-3-319-52651-5_6

of automobile plants in Japan and the US: 'Supplier relations and management are crucial areas for any firm that subcontracts portions of components design and production because of the dependence this creates on the skills of outside organizations' (Cusumano and Takeishi 1991: 563). As the example shows, the concept of SRM has also evolved in other fields of research, such as supply chain management (SCM), highlighting its cross-industry wide importance.

In this paper, we adopt a client perspective regarding the management of supplier relationships. In this context, IT SRM covers a variety of activities, ranging from identifying potential IT suppliers through developing and monitoring supplier relationships, to terminating an underlying outsourcing contract. Thus, IT SRM has many facets and researchers have tried to address them. A wide range of contributions has appeared in the respective subphases, covering, for example, important elements of contract negotiations (Lacity and Hirschheim 1993) or contract design (Fitzgerald and Willcocks 1994), as well as factors that influence the duration of an outsourcing arrangement (Goo et al. 2007). To further manage outsourcing relationships, it has been argued that firms need sourcing competencies and capabilities to succeed (Feeny and Willcocks 1998; Cohen and Young 2006: 12; Willcocks et al. 2006). Furthermore, the role of two modes of governance – formal control (e. g., written contracts) and relational governance (e.g., unwritten, practice-based mechanism) – have been studied in research (e.g., Poppo and Zenger 2002; Goo 2009). Further work was done by McFarlan and Nolan (1995) who identified areas within a company that are crucial for managing external suppliers. Another contribution in this context explored formal *vs* informal approaches to the management of supplier relationships (Heckman 1999). An overview of relevant articles published from 1988 through 2000 is provided by Dibbern et al. (2004). Recent work to the implementation phase of outsourcing is revealed in follow-up literature reviews (Gonzales et al. 2006; Alsudairi and Dwivedi 2010; Lacity et al. 2010).

The purpose of the paper at hand is to explore IT SRM from a more holistic perspective, extending prior research that primarily focused on single subphases, for example, supplier selection or relationship building. More precisely, we pay attention to the client's organizational design to manage outsourcing relationships. It is widely believed that organizational design can positively impact corporate performance, as long as organizational design decisions fit to certain contingency or context factors, such as a company's strategy (Drazin and Van De Ven 1985; Galbraith et al. 2002). In IS/IT outsourcing, the role of organizational design at the 'client-supplier interface' (Willcocks and Lacity 2006) is, however, an under-researched topic. One exception is the work of Jimmy et al. (2011), which recently examined the organizational design of the 'customer interface' on the supplier side. This paper contributes to IS outsourcing relationship literature by addressing a client's organizational design choices on the interface to its suppliers. Filling this gap in research helps to pave the way to a better understanding about how to 'fit' organizational design to a given company's context, thereby contributing to IT SRM effectiveness and, ultimately, IS/IT outsourcing success.

Literature on organizational design was used to guide the study on organizational design of IT SRM. The following research question guided the research process and analysis: 'how can IT supplier relationship management be efficiently organized on the client side?'

To answer the research question, the remainder of the paper is organized as follows: The next section reviews literature on organization design in general and provides the conceptual background of this study. With a description of our empirical study design, we illustrate our chosen research approach. Third, the results of a multiple case study, conducted in the IT organizations of five large-scale enterprises, are presented along our research framework. The article closes with a discussion of findings, limitations and possible directions for future research.

Conceptual Framework

Organization design is often simplifying thought of organizational structure, but it goes far beyond the step of drawing boxes and lines in organizational charts (Champoux 2000). There is a long tradition on organization research that gave rise to several theories and frameworks in the past 60 years (Snow et al. 2005). For example, Galbraith (1977) proposed his star model, a framework composed of strategy, structure, processes, human resources, and reward systems. A similar model was offered by Peters and Waterman (1982) called the 7-S model, which contained seven major organizational components. Miles and Snow (1978) empirically examined relationships among organizational strategy, structure and process, and they identified three commonly occurring configurations called the prospector, defender and analyzer. Despite some differences in the frameworks, scholars stress the importance of an alignment of the components (Drazin and Van De Ven 1985). In this paper, we guided our study on the star model offered by Galbraith et al. (2002) (see Fig. 6.1).

Strategy encompasses the company's vision as well as short- and long-term goals and depicts the 'cornerstone' in the organization design process. Consequently, design decisions should be in accordance with strategy.

The second component of the star model addresses organizational *structure*. Organizational structure determines the location of formal

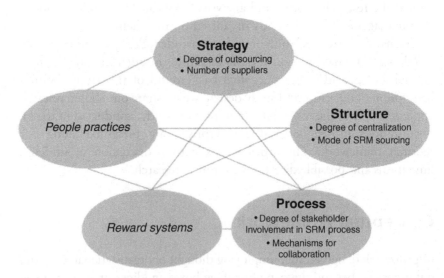

Fig. 6.1 Conceptual framework of organizational design (adapted from Galbraith et al. 2002)

power and authority within an organization. Designing an organization's structure determines organizational components and defines their relationship and hierarchical structure.

After strategy and organizational structure have been defined, the framework continues with *process* design. According to Galbraith et al. (2002), each organizational structure creates 'silos' that might in turn be harmful when collaboration across organizational units is needed. Defined processes and lateral connections (e.g., informal networks, cross-boundary teams) present mechanisms to create collaboration of structurally separated organizational units.

The last two components are *reward systems* and *people practices*. Reward systems 'define expected behaviors and influence the likelihood that people will demonstrate those behaviors' (Galbraith et al. 2002). The following four components were deemed essential for a successful reward system: performance metrics, desired values and behaviors, monetary and non-monetary rewards. The final point on the star model comprises people practices that include human resources systems and policies within an organization. As typical elements, selection and staffing, performance feedback mechanisms, training, and career development are included.

In this paper, we investigate three aspects of organization design that also occurred frequently in other evolved frameworks: strategy, structure and process. Although organizational design is often primarily thought of as being relevant for the customer interface, a company is also challenged to build organizational design on the procurement and supply side (Trent 2004). Given the focus on IT SRM in this article, we discuss these three components from an IT organization's perspective. Therefore, we focused on several constructs, for example, degree of outsourcing, required to assess appropriately the respective organizational components in the context of IT SRM (see Fig. 6.1).

Strategy

A company's IS/IT sourcing strategy is ideally derived from corporate strategy (Lasch and Janker 2005) and basically covers decisions on what to outsource and what to insource. Furthermore, a sourcing strategy may determine preferred suppliers and guidelines on how they should be contracted (Feeny and Willcocks 1998). Therefore, ideally, a company's IT SRM activities, for example, supplier selection and contract negotiation, are in accordance with the overall sourcing strategy. Two crucial determinants of a firm's sourcing strategy are the aspired degree of outsourcing and the number of external sources or suppliers involved in the provision of IT services and products, often also discussed as single *vs* multi-sourcing.

The degree of outsourcing has been an element of various empirical studies (e.g., Lacity and Willcocks 1998; Lee et al. 2004) and is often measured as the proportion of outsourced services of a company's IT budget (Lacity and Willcocks 1998). Researchers have introduced several theories to explain outsourcing and decision making, for example, resource-based theory, transaction cost theory or agency theory (e.g., Dibbern et al. 2004).

From a transaction cost economics view (Coase 1937; Williamson 1981, 1985), a sourcing or 'make *vs* buy' decision can be seen as a 'tradeoff between production costs and coordination or transaction costs' (Malone et al. 1987: 485). This idea is based on two fundamental observations. First, competition and economies of scale typically lead to lower production costs in markets ('buy') than in hierarchies ('make'). Contrarily, transaction costs are, in general, higher in markets than in hierarchical arrangements (Williamson 1981, 1985; referring to Coase 1937). Transaction costs encompass a variety of costs, such as costs for searching for an adequate supplier, negotiating a contract and controlling and monitoring a supplier's performance. Precisely, these costs limit the number of suppliers that can be managed by a customer; in other words, it may be assumed that when adding a supplier to an organization's supplier base, the sum of transaction costs increases (Bakos and Brynjolfsson 1993: 39). However, transaction cost theory is only one perspective that has been adopted to study 'the optimal number of suppliers.' When reviewing literature, many statements can be found that address differing strategic benefits by either decreasing or even increasing the number of suppliers. Table 6.1 lists a short selection that was adopted from a literature review of Levina and Su (2008).

Table 6.1 Selected literature of supplier base strategies (adapted from Levina and Su 2008)

Author (year)	Recommendation and implications
Rottman and Lacity (2006)	Firms should employ a relatively small number of suppliers (but at least two) to reduce strategic and operational risk and increase competition.
Cousins (1999)	Focusing on fewer suppliers helps build high-dependency relationships, shares technological advantages, and allows time to build relationships, which improves resource utilization and reduces costs. Focusing on a few suppliers risks missing critical changes in supplier markets, reduces flexibility, and increases dependency.
Lacity and Willcocks (1998)	Employing multiple providers and fostering competition among them can help firms maximize flexibility and control.
Richardson and Roumasset (1995)	Single sourcing supplier policy creates lock-in and increases costs due to the lack of supplier competition.
Bakos and Brynjolfsson (1993)	Firms should limit the number of employed suppliers to induce suppliers' investments in 'noncontractibles' such as quality, responsiveness, and innovation.

A related research area worth mentioning is the development of theoretical models at the beginning of the 1990s that investigated the impact of an increased use of information technology on the extent of a supplier base. Early research predicted that the use of IT may reduce client's coordination costs with suppliers (Malone et al. 1987), their search costs (Bakos 1991) and costs for supplier performance monitoring (Clemons et al. 1993: 14). In consequence, an extensive use of IT would tend to increase the optimal number of IT suppliers (Bakos and Brynjolfsson 1993: 39). However, it was hard to find empirical evidence for these early assumptions. Driven notably by studies of the automobile industry that reported a move to fewer suppliers (e.g., Cusumano and Takeishi 1991), further theoretical considerations were made. Bakos and Brynjolfsson (1993) showed that when suppliers' commitment is needed, such as certain investments in innovation or quality, it can be optimal to rely on a small number of suppliers in order to increase their incentives to make such noncontractible relationship-specific investments. Clemons et al. (1993) argue that an increased use of IT will lead to a higher degree of outsourcing. They argue that IT decreases not only coordination costs, but additionally the risks associated with an outsourcing endeavor. On the basis of these considerations, they advanced their 'move to the middle' hypothesis: In light of the favorable effects of information technology, firms will increase their outsourcing degree but will rely on fewer suppliers, taking advantage of long-term relationships that allow for steeper learning curves and economies of scale.

The discussion shows that strategies are generally not static and are subject to alter over time due to changes in markets, external environment factors or dissatisfaction with current performance (Markides 1999; Johnson and Leenders 2001). However, dynamic studies of changes in IT sourcing strategies are scarce. One exception is the study of Aral et al. (2010), which examined companies' IT sourcing decisions over a 5-year period, revealing that companies globally prefer to rely on long-term relationships with known IT suppliers. In this study, sourcing strategy was also assessed dynamically to better understand the 'cornerstone' of the remaining organizational dimensions, structure and processes.

Structure

As the famous statement 'structure follows strategy' (Chandler 1962) stipulates, ideally, the organizational structure of IT SRM should be in line with the IS/IT sourcing strategy. In general, five common ways of structuring an organization exist, namely, grouping by function, by geography, by product, by customer/markets, or by workflow processes (Galbraith et al. 2002). While doing so, it has to be determined where decision-making authority and power is located (Galbraith et al. 2002). This task refers to the classic issue of centralization *vs* decentralization (Pugh et al. 1968; Monczka et al. 2010). Organizations position themselves on a continuum with complete centralization at one end and complete decentralization on the other, choosing thereby a specific *degree of centralization*. With our study's focus on IT SRM, a centralized unit that has the authority for the majority of SRM activities can be envisioned on one extreme. Similarly, we might encounter more decentralized organizations where the majority of SRM responsibilities have been assigned to divisional sub-units within the IT or purchasing departments. There may be organizations that do not lie at these extremes, but rather rely on a combination of a centralized and decentralized approach, called *hybrid* (Monczka et al. 2010). Given that IT SRM is a boundary-spanning activity in the sense that interaction with suppliers from the company's external environment is needed, it appears to additionally be a challenging task to determine which activities should be centrally led and which should be assigned to operating units. The challenge arises because each fundamental structure, centralized or decentralized, has advantages and disadvantages. For example, centralized structures can often more easily obtain cost savings, efficiencies, and decisions with increased clout, while decentralized structures are known for an increased speed of response, easier coordination, and a better opportunity of reacting to unique requirements.

In the context of IT SRM, the approach of a centralized or hybrid structure is related to the organizational concept of a 'Vendor Management Office' (VMO), a term primarily discussed in publications for IT professionals, such as CIO Magazine or Computerworld. According to Guth (2007), the first VMOs appeared in 2000 and were first adopted by IT departments of large companies, like Cisco Systems. According to a study by Forrester Research, centralized SRM models have been widely implemented in companies, either in the IT or purchasing department (Connaughton 2011). However, profound literature about VMOs is lacking. Functions that a VMO should ideally fulfill, their potential added value and organizational structure have to the best of our knowledge not yet been addressed by academic studies.

One might now be reminded of a related organizational entity seen in many companies, the Project Management Office (PMO). The Project Management Institute (2008) defines a PMO as 'an organizational body or entity assigned various responsibilities related to the centralized and coordinated management of those projects under its domain. The responsibilities of the PMO can range from providing project management support functions to actually being responsible for the direct management of a project.' The definition is broad and empirical cases show that in practice structure, function and roles of a PMO vary to a high degree (Arttoa et al. 2011), similar to what one might expect in the case of a centralized unit (CU) for IT SRM.

However, organizations need not solely rely on resources within an organization to carry out their SRM (pure in-house model). Theoretically, companies have various 'sourcing alternatives' for IT SRM (mode of SRM sourcing). As in initial IS/IT outsourcing of, for example, IS development or operations, it might also be conceivable here to outsource the subsequent management of IT suppliers completely (or more likely to a certain degree) to a specialized third party. In case of an outsourced IT SRM, four different structural types can be differentiated. First, SRM may be assigned to either (I) an internal provider, for example, a subsidiary company, or (II) to a provider external to the company. Second, we can distinguish whether (a) the focal company has still direct contractual relationships with its suppliers or (b) whether the provider acts primarily as a prime contractor for the focal company and has a number of subcontractors further down the supply chain.

While the case of contracting a prime contractor (type b, internal or external) is already a well-known outsourcing configuration in IS/IT outsourcing literature (e.g., Cullen et al. 2005), especially the approach of contracting a 'specialized' provider for the management of the company's remaining IT suppliers opens up various opportunities for future research (type a). One central question that arises here is: To which degree it is advisable to outsource the management of IT suppliers to a third party? Accordingly, this model can be combined with a retained internal organization (centralized, decentralized or hybrid) to fit a company's needs and strategy.

Figure 6.2 aggregates the aforementioned organizational structures for IT SRM, varying upon degree of centralization and mode of SRM

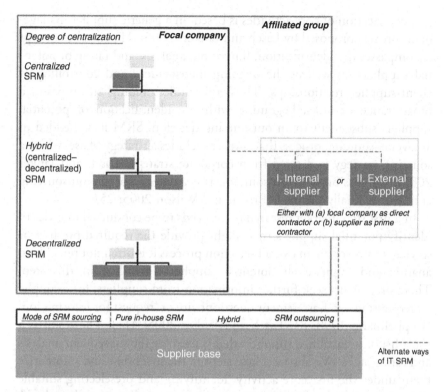

Fig. 6.2 Organizational structure models of IT supplier relationship management

sourcing. The results of our multiple case study give further insights into the shape of these models in practice.

Process

As a third dimension of organization design, the process layer of IT SRM is now examined (see Fig. 6.1). At the beginning, we introduced IT SRM, ranging from selecting potential IT suppliers through developing and monitoring supplier relationships to terminating an underlying outsourcing contract. This section takes up this idea and outlines nine core activities that were deemed to be central to IT SRM.

This selection of core activities is based on a generic supplier management process proposed by Lasch and Janker (2005). Herein, the concept encompasses the identification, limitation, analysis, and rating of potential suppliers, as well as the ongoing management and controlling of client-supplier relationships. Thus, this understanding encompasses a broad range of tasks, beginning with the identification of potential suppliers subsequent to an outsourcing decision. SRM is embedded in an overall sourcing process that further includes a strategy phase, where a sourcing strategy is derived from corporate strategy (Lasch and Janker 2005), the feasibility of outsourcing is evaluated, and the outsourcing endeavor is finally planned (Brown and Wilson 2005: 25).

In a first step, market research often needs to be conducted in order to identify potential suppliers that might provide the required product or service. However, in an overall selection process it is often not possible to analyze and evaluate all potential suppliers identified in this step. Therefore, clients seek further information from suppliers, for example, by requesting a self-assessment questionnaire or 'request for information' (Koppelmann 1998: 81; Lasch and Janker 2005: 411). The result is a short list of prequalified suppliers that is used for the subsequent analysis and rating steps. We abstract these steps in the first phase and summarize them under the first core activity 'identifying and preselecting suitable IT suppliers.' In supplier analysis, results from market research and self-information, and if necessary from additional audits, are collected and processed to the following rating or evaluation step ('analyzing and evaluating the performance of potential IT suppliers'). Evaluation should be conducted systematically and be based on key factors relevant to supplier choice. Many methods for evaluating and supporting decision making are discussed in literature (e.g., Lasch and Janker 2005: 411). A typical tool is the supplier scorecard that lists the selection criteria, assigns weightings and is filled out with quantitative and/or qualitative data gained from supplier analysis (Monczka et al. 2010: 175). The evaluation process is normally followed by a contract negotiation phase ('conducting contract negotiations') with one or more short-listed suppliers, where the design of a contract itself is seen as a very critical issue (Van Weele 2009: 171). The future outsourcing parties need to agree upon, for example, the type and scope of contract, terms of agreement, and pricing and fee structure (Van Weele 2009: 172). With the final supplier selection and the signing of an outsourcing contract ('selecting IT supplier for service provision'), the pre-contractual and contractual phase are completed.

Once a contract has been signed and the supplier has started contract fulfillment, monitoring and controlling of supplier performance need to be carried out ('monitoring and controlling contractually agreed IT services'). In order to encourage suppliers to improve their service, companies can take corrective measures such as incentives or sanctions ('taking measures (incentives, sanctions) to manage external service provision') (Sparrow 2003: 109; Lasch and Janker 2005). In SCM literature, additional concepts, for example, supplier advancement, supplier development or supplier integration, are often discussed (Monczka 2000: 47 f.; Lasch and Janker 2005). We did not go into depth on this point. However, we see opportunities for future studies to explore, for example, relevance and shape of these concepts in the IS/IT outsourcing context. The next step covers 'maintaining IT supplier relationships' in terms of relationship building and care.

So far, we have derived seven core activities of IT SRM from SCM literature. In a second step, we compared our activities with the 'supplier management process' introduced in ITIL (IT Infrastructure Library), a recognized framework of best practices for IT Service Management worldwide (Office of Government Commerce 2010: 3). Inherently, the process steps explained therein were already 'IT-related.' However, the described ITIL process is quite similar to our process, derived from 'generic' SCM literature and encompassing four core activities ranging from evaluation of new suppliers/contracts up to contract renewal and termination (Office of Government Commerce 2007: 151). Since it seemed reasonable to include the step 'contract renewal or termination' as well, we extended our process with 'renewing/terminating active contracts.' Furthermore, ITIL recommends the establishment of a supplier/contract database to increase consistency and effectiveness in the implementation of overall supplier strategy and policies. Therefore, we included a more 'administrative,' ongoing task with 'maintaining an IT supplier and/or contract database.' Based on literature, we finally derived nine major activities of IT SRM (see Fig. 6.3).

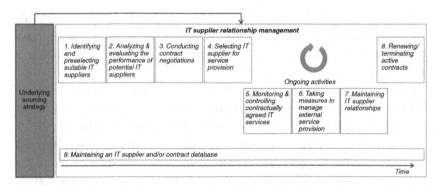

Fig. 6.3 Core activities of IT supplier relationship management process

The process described is by its nature 'cross-functional' and involves several people with different competencies and skills, who are typically active in different organizational entities throughout an organization. On a department level, the following five entities are conceivable as relevant stakeholders in IT SRM within large-scale client firms (Heckman 1999: 61; Office of Government Commerce 2007: 150): (1) A business department demanding a specific IT product or service, (2) the IT department fulfilling the IT needs of their internal customers (typically with the support of IT suppliers), and (3) the purchasing department with its traditional tasks, like the identification of potential sources of supply, bid and contract preparation, negotiations, and supplier performance evaluation. (4) Legal departments might also be involved in the SRM process, since they typically handle a company's legal issues and act as advisers, for example, in drafting contracts with suppliers. And finally, (5) the financial department in charge of organizing financial and accounting information necessary to make sound business decisions.

In order to achieve the involvement of these usually separated departments, at least two ways exist to bridge boundaries established by an organization's structure, here referred to as mechanisms for collaboration (Galbraith et al. 2002). First, a company can formalize its processes, that is, documenting activities and clearly defining and articulating roles and responsibilities. In addition to process formalization, lateral connections can be used to bridge barriers. Informal networks, as well as cross-business teams, can help to foster work collaboration. Especially when selecting an appropriate supplier, a temporary, cross-functional purchasing team may be assembled to combine skills of different stakeholders (Johnson et al. 2001: 127; Sparrow 2003: 70–71).

Research Approach

Research Design

Relating to our main research question 'how' IT SRM is organized with regard to strategy, structure and process, the case study approach was deemed particularly appropriate (Yin 2003: 13). Despite traditional criticism, for example its lack of generalizability, the case study method has seen extensive application in the IS field (Dubé and Paré 2003; Gonzales et al. 2006). Since IT SRM has not yet been studied from an organizational research perspective, the case study approach was deemed especially appropriate because it allows researchers to thoroughly study the phenomenon of interest from different sources of evidence.

Given that multiple cases usually yield more general results, a multiple-case design was chosen (Yin 2003). Relying on multiple individual cases ensures that 'the events and processes in one well-described setting are not wholly idiosyncratic. At a deeper level, the aim of multiple case study is to see processes and outcomes across many cases, to understand how they are qualified by local conditions, and thus to develop more sophisticated descriptions and more powerful explanations' (Miles and Huberman 1994: 172). According to this rationale, five cases were selected for this study, which allow us to deepen our understanding of organizational design in relation to IT SRM. The investigation of five cases complies with the evaluation of Eisenhardt (1989), who considers a number between

4 and 10 cases appropriate for most purposes. Furthermore, by the end of the fifth case, little new knowledge about the research object was acquired and we deemed the number sufficient with regard to 'theoretical saturation' (Eisenhardt 1989).

This utilization of case study research methodology follows a widely recognized positivist research approach, which assumes that the researcher plays a passive, neutral role and does not intervene in the phenomenon under study (Dubé and Paré 2003). According to Yin (2003), case studies can further be of exploratory, explanatory and descriptive nature. The objective of this case study approach is to compare each individual case with the a priori developed organizational design framework. Although the theoretical background of the framework has been discussed, it is not the primary aim of this case study to establish or to test causal relationships. Thus, our case study approach is best described as a descriptive one. Within our five cases, IT organizations of large-scale client companies form the units of analysis. The sample of enterprises covers different industry sectors, such as automotive, finance, transport, travel, and logistics. Apart from this sectoral variation, we tried to raise homogeneity in our selection and focused on companies with headquarters in Germany. Furthermore, our selection was driven by criteria that point to similar challenges with regard to IT sourcing and SRM. In addition to a comparable size and complexity (the cases had IT budgets in the region of three-digit million euro in 2010), all investigated IT organizations have outsourced activities such as the development and/or operation of their information systems to a substantial part to IT suppliers, leading to a degree of outsourcing ranging from 60 to 80%. To justify this limitation in our selection, it can be argued that the proportion of in-house production is inherently interrelated with the number and types of contracted IT suppliers, as well as the role that IT SRM might play in the respective organization. With this in mind, the selection of cases follows theoretical and literal replication (Yin 2003: 47). Basically, we ensured that the basic conditions just explained were similar in each case (literal replication). Apart from that, cases were selected to predict contrasting results due to differing case conditions, for example, whether or not a large in-house provider was in place (theoretical replication).

Data Collection

The whole study was conducted in a time period of three months, starting in January 2011. For data collection, we relied on multiple sources, because data triangulation is highly recommended in case study research (Eisenhardt 1989: 534; Yin 2003: 97–101). Altogether, a questionnaire, five in-depth interviews and company documentation were used to raise confidence in our findings (Yin 2003: 86). Qualitative data were interlinked with quantitative data to elaborate our analysis later on (Miles and Huberman 1994: 40–43).

The questionnaire consisted of seven pages, comprising qualitative and quantitative questions. The structure was related to our research questions and divided into four sections. In the first section (two pages), we queried general information about size, core activities, and organizational structure of the IT organizations under study. The second section (one page) contained questions about the past and current developments in IS/IT sourcing strategy. The process activities of IT SRM and the involvement of different stakeholders was the subject of the next section (two pages). The last section covered questions with regard to the organizational structure of SRM (two pages). A pretest of the questionnaire with three respondents was initially conducted, discussing reactions to the form, wording, and order of the questions.

The key-informant method was then used to obtain knowledge on organizational design in our case study companies (e.g., Campbell 1955; Bagozzi et al. 1991). The key informants were staff members of the respective IT organization, relatively high in hierarchy (most of them with direct reporting to the CIO) or entrusted by their CIO to conduct the study with us. The experts had several years of experience in the company/within the IT organization and were suitable contact persons for our study subject. In a first step of data collection, the key informants were asked to send us a completed version of the questionnaire. An early analysis of responses proved that using a standardized questionnaire was fruitful in revealing first similarities and irregularities between the five cases. In a subsequent step of data collection, the contact persons were available for semi-structured face-to-face interviews. Here, we used the completed questionnaire as a guideline for more detailed questions. In one case, due to time and availability constraints, the questionnaire had to be filled out during the in-depth interview. In almost all cases, we were able to collect additional information material encompassing, for example, organizational charts and process descriptions. In this way, potential errors and biases resulting from our key informants' judgments were reduced.

During data collection, a case study protocol and database supported our research and helped to raise the reliability of our study (Yin 2003). The protocol was established prior to data collection and recorded the objectives of our study, procedures, as well as the questionnaire design. Therefore, it was easier to ensure that data collection followed the same guidelines in each case. Our case study database kept all relevant data in one place. It contained raw material, including completed question-naires, interview transcripts and company documentation, as well as data displays and analysis results.

Data Analysis

After transcription of the audio-taped interviews, the data gained from the three collection techniques were interlinked and analyzed. In a first step, each case was analyzed separately along our conceptual framework. Data from the three sources were brought together and checked for consistency. Case analysis meetings with two research assistants, priorly involved in data collection, were frequently held, discussing the data and interpretations to create a common under-standing of the respective cases (Miles and Huberman 1994). Various data displays (Miles and Huberman 1994) of the qualitative and quantitative data were created and assigned to the conceptual organizational design framework, also allowing for the identification of patterns from cross-case analysis.

During the different phases of research, we attempted to increase validity in several ways, as recommended by Yin (2003) among others. As already mentioned, we relied on multiple information sources during data collection to enhance construct validity. For the same purpose, we sent a result report in anonymized form to all companies participating in the study and discussed it specially with experts from one case company in depth. To enhance external validity, we used replication logic in our multiple-case design. Furthermore, our underlying framework was built upon existing literature and theories, raising both the conceptual level and comprehensibility of our work (Eisenhardt 1989: 544 f.) (Appendix table A1).

Empirical Findings

In the following, the findings that emerged during case study analysis are presented along the conceptual framework of organizational design. Thus, the findings on our research question, how IT SRM is organized across the five cases, as well as the observable reasons that lead to a specific organizational design, are discussed in the following three sections.

Strategy

To assess strategy as the first component of organizational design of IT SRM, the study examines the degree of outsourcing and the number of contracted IT suppliers as two major determinants of an IT department's strategy that have naturally a high impact on the shape of IT SRM.

Degree of Outsourcing

The current degree of outsourcing was measured as the proportion of IT budget in 2010 spent on outsourcing (see Table 6.2). In three of the five companies, the degree was measured exactly with the reported numbers of total IT budget and purchasing volume. For the remaining two

Table 6.2 Overview of IT SRM findings on strategy, structure and process

	A: Automotive	B: Travel	C: Logistic	D: Transport	E: Finance
Strategy					
Degree of outsourcing					
Current (2010) Percentage of total IT budget	69 %	76%	63%	80%	60%
Significant increase in the last 5 years?	no	no	no	no	yes
Future development	Slight increase	Rather constant	Rather constant	(provider:) increase	/
Number of IT suppliers					
Total (2010)	'several hundred' (group-level)	182	60	basically 1 in-house provider	5-10 large & 50-100 smaller suppliers
Significant reduction in the last 5 years?	yes	no	yes	no	yes
Expected change in the next years?	further reduction	reduction/consolidation	rather constant	Rather constant	similar strategy as before
Structure					
Degree of centralization	Hybrid (one central unit)	De-centralized (planning to establish a central unit)	Hybrid (two central units)	Rather	decentralized

Mode of SRM sourcing	Hybrid (several central units)	Hybrid (In-house SRM & Outsourced SRM, type IIb)	Hybrid (In-house SRM & Outsourced SRM, type Ib)	Hybrid (In-house SRM & Outsourced SRM, type Ib and IIb)	Pre-dominantly Outsourced SRM (type Ib)	Pre-dominantly Pure In-house SRM
Process						
Degree of involvement[a]						
IT Dep.		2.8	1.9	2.4	1.1	2.4
Purchasing Dep.		1.8	1.6	2.1	2.7	1.1
Legal Dep.		0.4	0.6	0.7	0.2	1.4
Financial Dep.		0.0	0.4	0.0	0.4	0.0
Business Dep.		0.6	1.1	1.0	0.6	0.3
Mechanisms for collaboration		Process formalization, cross-functional teams	Process formalization, cross-functional teams	Process formalization, workflow management system, cross-functional teams	Process formalization, cross-functional teams	Process formalization, cross-functional teams

[a] Data for activity 'maintaining an IT supplier and/or contract database' was not available in case E. Scale: 0 'not at all' to 3 'very intensive.'

companies (cases D and E), the degree of outsourcing in relation to the IT budget was estimated by our key informants or calculated by themselves. The current degree of outsourcing was relatively high in all five companies, ranging from 60 to 80%. As described earlier, a high outsourcing degree was a selection criterion in our study, since it seems reasonable that companies with a high outsourcing degree are particularly challenged to set up an efficient SRM.

Since strategies, and hence the degree of outsourcing, are subject to change, an attempt was made to capture a dynamic view of the underlying sourcing strategy. While analyzing the responses towards past and future trends in the degree of outsourcing, it was striking that except for *company E*, no one reported an increased outsourcing within the last five years. During interviews, however, we gained the impression that the general degree of IT outsourcing has already been on a high level for more than five years in all five companies. A further significant increase of outsourcing was not expected in the next years. Companies *B, C,* and *E* in particular started to reduce their in-house activities approximately 10 years ago, shifting the provision of IT services and products towards external sources. *Case A* reported that the degree of in-house activities was increased during the financial crisis in the last years. However, now, they again pursue an opposite strategy and are increasing outsourcing. Furthermore, *company D* reported that its in-house IT supplier would increase outsourcing with regard to coding and testing activities.

Number of Suppliers

To assess the current status of companies' IT supplier bases, the number of active IT suppliers (based on purchase orders in 2010) was queried. Four of five companies have implemented a 'multi-sourcing' model and purchased from a multitude of IT suppliers, ranging from 60 up to 'several hundred' in 2010. *Case A* had difficulties in indicating the exact number of its suppliers. Whereas the number of external IT suppliers operating their information systems was well known with 7, the number of IT suppliers supporting IS development was not exactly determinable.

The total number here was estimated to reach several hundred IT suppliers, whereby the key informant adopted a group perspective. *Case B* was able to exactly indicate the number of IT suppliers in their division, mainly because the number was 'manually' determined by the company with great effort prior to this study. The number includes one in-house provider that accounts for a substantial part of total IT spending. *Case C* reported that they contracted about five large outsourcing partners and about 35 medium-sized businesses. A large number of smaller IT suppliers are purchased through a general contractor, resulting in a total of 60 suppliers. Compared with the other cases, *case D* was particular. A subsidiary company receives 90–95% of the total IT spending yearly, that is, a 'single sourcing' model was basically adopted here. Finally, our key informant of *case E* indicated that they basically relied on 5-10 large IT suppliers on a group level. Although the informant was not able to indicate the exact total, the number of smaller IT suppliers was estimated to range between 50 and 100.

Three of our five companies surveyed indicated that they had decreased their number of IT suppliers noticeably in the last five years. Among these was *company A* that significantly reduced the number of suppliers contracted for operating their information systems: the number decreased here from 270 to 7 in 2008. In the domain of information systems development, a comparable reduction was not yet achieved. Owing to an increased 'level of complexity' resulting basically from the process-oriented structuring of the IT organization, a significant decrease is therefore considered more difficult. However, first approaches were made: One large IT supplier was contracted to act like a prime contractor. This prime contractor then contracted further suppliers that had previously had direct contractual relationships with *company A*. Thus, the number of 'direct suppliers' was decreased in this case by a form of 'subcontracting' from *company's A* perspective. Similar changes were reported in *case C*. The logistics company reduced their numbers from 250 in 2003 to 60 in 2010. Again, a substantial part of this reduction was achieved by 'subcontracting,' also known as 'tiering' in SCM literature: the 'tiering approach reduces the number of suppliers that the organization deals with directly, but does not necessarily reduce the total number of suppliers in the supply chain' (Ogden and Carter

2008: 9). The third company (*case E*), which has streamlined its supplier base, explained its strategy as follows:

> We have strategically concentrated our purchasing to a few suppliers. In the bidding procedure we have guidelines of preferred suppliers. When you have niche products or projects then we might involve smaller suppliers. But we have followed the overall strategy to a few larger suppliers within the last years. (case E)

With regard to future changes in the supplier bases, several forward-looking statements were gained. Whereas *case A* expects a further decline in their supplier base in the next years, *C's* supplier base is expected to remain rather stable. Our key informant in *company E* was more unsure on how to predict an outcome for his company and commented cautiously that the future number would depend on changes in markets and project volumes. However, for the coming years he expects that the desired trend towards a few strategic partners would continue. Although the *companies B* and *D* have not significantly reduced their supplier bases in the last years, *case B* at least expects a move to fewer outsourcing relationships in the upcoming years. *Company D* sees no imminent shift in strategy and expects to continue contracting almost exclusively through its subsidiary company.

Taken all together, we observed that many companies still deal with a large number of IT suppliers. However, when trying to interpret these numbers we have to keep in mind that our cases were based on large-scale companies, where IT needs cannot be compared with mid- or small-sized companies. Whether the large number of suppliers was a strategic decision or whether the supplier bases had grown uncontrolled was not subject to our study. Nevertheless, we found evidence that some IT organizations have realized a substantial reduction of their supplier bases (*cases A, C,* and *E*) or have planned to do so in the next years (*case B*). In addition, as described earlier, all companies had a high degree of outsourcing at the time of the survey. Although we have not explored the favoring role of increased use of IT, we might notice that some companies have started a 'move to the middle' approach (increase of outsourcing but to fewer suppliers) expected by Clemons et al. (1993). However, the two parts of the approach – increased outsourcing and reduction of supplier numbers – do not seem to occur in parallel. The findings suggest that strategic decisions that can be dated back to more than five years ago lead to today's high outsourcing degree in the investigated companies, and have seemingly reached a 'steady state' now. In contrast, significant reductions in the IT supplier bases appear to have taken place in the last five years and/ or to be taking place in the next few years. From a cost perspective, it might be argued that in the past few years the case study companies have turned their attention towards potential cost savings that reside in supplier base reductions, instead of relying solely on 'optimal' outsourcing decisions.

Structure

With regard to the second organizational design element, structure, the case study companies have implemented various models for the management of their IT suppliers. In the following, the findings on degree of centralization and implemented mode of SRM sourcing are presented.

Degree of Centralization

The majority of the five companies surveyed have implemented a centralized unit for SRM, pursuing a hybrid approach (*cases A, C, E*). *Case B* still has a 'decentralized' structure in place, but is also considering implementing a central unit within the next years. The internal structure of *case D* to carry out the management of its large in-house provider also follows rather a 'decentralized' approach. The three companies that have implemented a centralized SRM point to a high heterogeneity regarding organizational position, structure and the responsibilities of a centralized unit (see Fig. 6.4). The central units were established in a time period from 2000 to 2009 and encompass at least 10 people today.

Beginning with *case C*, the company decided to even implement two separated units for SRM, one dealing with 'build'-suppliers, that is,

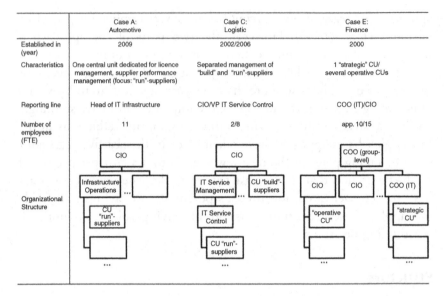

	Case A: Automotive	Case C: Logistic	Case E: Finance
Established in (year)	2009	2002/2006	2000
Characteristics	One central unit dedicated for licence management, supplier performance management (focus: "run"-suppliers)	Separated management of "build" and "run"-suppliers	1 "strategic" CU/ several operative CUs
Reporting line	Head of IT infrastructure	CIO/VP IT Service Control	COO (IT)/CIO
Number of employees (FTE)	11	2/8	app. 10/15
Organizational Structure			

Fig. 6.4 Characteristics of central units in hybrid supplier relationship management models

suppliers contracted for IS development, and one addressing 'run'-suppliers, responsible for IS operations. The separation was explained as follows:

> We separated the tasks into two units. One is dealing with a large number of development suppliers and one is dealing with a small number of IS operations suppliers. [. . .] Furthermore, we have different levels of service depths in each unit. In the first unit, staff members of the purchasing department and business departments are more involved than in the second unit. (case C)

The organizational unit that manages suppliers for IS development has a specific 'controlling function' and therefore involves stakeholders central to the SRM process:

> They [staff members of the unit] ensure that the purchasing department concludes an appropriate contract. Besides, they involve the business departments' ideas and call the legal department in legal matters. (case C)

The second organizational entity focuses on the management of contracts/licenses in the domain of IS operating and is orientated towards ITIL's service agenda for 'supplier management.'

Company A established a centralized unit within its IT department two years ago and takes a similar approach to that followed by *company C*. Again, a unit, reporting to the head of IT infrastructure, was established to fulfill the management of suppliers providing IT operations. Alongside carrying out license and contract management, the unit is responsible for monitoring supplier performance. However, a similar unit for the management of suppliers for IT development has not been established yet.

Company E established one unit with a direct line reporting relationship to the Chief Organizational Officer of IT and assigned 'strategic tasks,' for example, development of sourcing strategy and maintaining relationships to strategic outsourcing partners. In addition, a central unit was established within each of several CIO divisions, carrying out more 'operative' tasks, for example, monitoring suppliers' performances and conducting contract negotiations.

Across all three cases, perceived benefits that resulted from the implementation of one or more central units for IT SRM were reported to be the following:

- Facilitating the development and enforceability of guidelines and standards for IT sourcing/SRM, for example, procedure models or security guidelines, and their check of compliance;
- Raising transparency of a company's contractual relations with one supplier across different divisional units;
- Helping leveraging synergy potentials and cost savings by bundling activities and optimal utilization of resources.

Mode of SRM Sourcing

With regard to our second structure variable, mode of SRM sourcing, our case companies relied on different alternatives previously discussed theoretically. As described earlier, we found that during supplier base reduction, a 'tiering' approach was often chosen (*cases A* and *C*): multiple contractual relationships to smaller IT suppliers were terminated and they were now serving as subcontractors to one general company contractor. From a SRM perspective, we might expect that a substantial part, if not all, of the management of these 'second tier' suppliers was assigned to the prime contractor in this way (type IIb – external provider, focal company has no direct contractual relationships with suppliers). Subsidiary companies, internal to the group, are in place in *cases B, C,* and *D* (type Ib – internal provider, focal company has no direct contractual relationships with suppliers). In the latter case, the in-house provider is considered to be primarily responsible for IT SRM for the group. Except for the management of this in-house provider and a small number of direct commissioned external suppliers, the IT organization is significantly relieved from the management of IT suppliers.

To a lesser extent, cases *B* and *C* have an in-house provider in place, whereby the directly commissioned suppliers are still managed in-house. *Case E* follows a pure in-house model, in which the SRM of external IT suppliers is predominantly fulfilled by client staff.

The theoretical consideration that companies may still have contracts in place with various IT suppliers (types Ia and IIa), but have delegated their management to an internal or external party, was not predominantly observed in our case companies. However, this scenario is not unrealistic. To increase professionalism or realize cost savings, companies might choose to contract a specialized third partner for supplier selection or performance monitoring. We see at least specialized suppliers in the market, offering a broad range of SRM activities. As mentioned above, further research is specifically needed here to understand the shape, benefits, and limitations of this model from a theoretical and empirical point of view.

Process

The whole process of IT SRM described above was expected to be cross-functional and involve resources, skills, and competencies that are located most likely in different organizational entities, such as the purchasing or IT department.

Degree of Involvement

A dedicated section in our questionnaire tried to capture the relevance of the derived nine core activities, as well as the involvement of the five stakeholder departments within the organization. To achieve this, the case study respondents were asked to rate the intensity of stakeholder involvement throughout the process. The five departments included were IT, purchasing, legal and financial departments, as well as the respective business departments representing internal customers. For each activity and stakeholder department, a four-point intensity scale, ranging from 'not at all' to 'very intensive,' was provided to indicate the degree of involvement. Table 6.2 shows the average involvement of the five departments in IT SRM across the five cases. Here, we coded the response options with integers, ranging from 0 ('not at all') to 3 ('very intensive') and calculated the arithmetic mean across all nine activities.

Beginning with *case D*, due to its 'unique conditions' in our case selection, the involvement of the purchasing department (2.7) was in average rated here much higher than the involvement of the retained internal IT department (1.1). An essential reason is that the internal IT department of *case D* has transferred a substantial part of SRM to its in-house provider. In other words, the in-house provider is basically in charge of selecting and contracting new suppliers, as well as managing the ongoing contractual relationship. Nevertheless, the in-house provider's activities are controlled by the remaining IT organization of the group. The interplay between D and its subsidiary company was exemplarily explained regarding strategy development as follows:

> Our in-house provider is in charge of further developing our IT sourcing strategy. Of course, it needs to be accepted by our CIO, but the provider is the driving force here. (case D)

Apart from a variance in the absolute degree of involvement, the results in the remaining four cases, which fulfill still significantly SRM activities in-house, show a similar distribution: the IT department (arithmetic mean 2.3) and purchasing department (arithmetic mean 1.6) are the departments being most involved in the management of a company's IT suppliers. A predominant role in IT SRM was often attributed to the IT department. Legal and business departments play a supporting role. In particular, financial departments seem to play a minor role in IT SRM.

Looking more closely at the average involvement in the nine core activities of IT SRM within these four cases, the findings suggest the following (see Table 6.3):

- The role of an IT department is predominant regarding the following tasks: identification and pre-selection of suitable IT suppliers, monitoring and controlling suppliers' performance, as well as taking measures to improve service provision.
- The steps of analyzing and evaluating the performance of potential IT suppliers, conducting contract negotiations, as well as the final selection of an IT supplier are jointly fulfilled by an IT and purchasing department.

However, these results must be interpreted carefully. The rating was solely done from an IT organization's perspective, that is to say: for example, a purchasing manager might have rated the involvement of his department differently (see limitations of our study).

Mechanisms for Collaboration

The star model of Galbraith et al. (2002) suggests that organizations need to find ways to bridge structural boundaries that might especially exist between IT and purchasing departments in this context. The IT organization of *case B* shows a good example of how formalization and the use of teams, as a more lateral connection, facilitates the collaboration across structurally separated departments. Similar to the remaining cases, *B* has developed guidelines for the whole sourcing process, ranging from development of a sourcing strategy through selection of suppliers to the termination of a contract. A formal process description governs the sequence of steps and the involvement of the purchasing department. In addition, it

Table 6.3 Average rating in all nine core activities of IT supplier relationship management (scale 0 'not at all' to 3 'very intensive')

Department	1. Identifying & preselecting suitable IT suppliers	2. Analyzing & evaluating the performance of potential IT suppliers	3. Conducting contract negotiations	4. Selecting IT supplier for service provision	5. Monitoring & controlling contractually agreed IT services	6. Taking measures to manage external service provision	7. Maintaining IT supplier relationships	8. Renewing/ terminating active contracts	9. Maintaining an IT supplier and/or contract database	Overall average degree of involvement
IT	2.5	2.3	2.8	2.8	2.5	2.3	2.0	2.8	1.3	2.3
Purchasing	1.3	2.0	2.5	2.5	0.3	1.0	1.0	2.3	2.3	1.7
Legal	1.3	0.8	2.0	1.0	0.0	0.3	0.0	1.3	0.0	0.7
Financial	0.3	0.3	0.3	0.3	0.0	0.0	0.0	0.0	0.0	0.1
Business	1.5	0.8	0.5	1.5	1.0	0.5	0.3	0.5	0.0	0.7

defines when a temporary purchasing team with representatives from, for example, the purchasing and financial department needs to be established. In *case C*, it was reported that their SRM process was even supported technologically by a workflow management system, facilitating an active control of the process steps across organizational boundaries. Thus, in the five case companies, process formalization and the use of cross-functional teams were the observed predominant means of guaranteeing the exchange of information in the context of IT SRM. While not focused in our study, we expect informal networks to be additionally in place within the companies, favoring also cross-functional collaboration in IT SRM.

Conclusion

This paper can be classified as a research paper paying attention to an emerging issue in IS research: the management of outsourcing relationships. Organizational design decisions on the client side were selected as the focus of this study to provide better insights into effective ways to manage IT supplier relationships. Three core elements of organization design, strategy, structure, and process, were examined in five IT organizations of large-scale enterprises. The findings suggest that IT SRM is widely perceived as an important aspect in IS/IT outsourcing leading to various changes in IT organizations' design.

Discussion of Key Findings

As the star model of Galbraith et al. (2002) suggests, companies' underlying sourcing strategies that have an essential influence on IT SRM, were first explored. Here, we focused on two aspects: outsourcing degree and number of suppliers. In general, all companies surveyed have a relatively high outsourcing degree and have outsourced a substantial portion of their IS development/operating to third parties. Except for one company, which contracts almost exclusively to its subsidiary company, the number of IT suppliers was from 60 up to 'several hundred' IT suppliers across all remaining cases large.

However, we partially observed a sharp reduction in the supplier bases within the last few years. While the automotive industry is the classic example where a significant reduction of the number of suppliers has been observed (Cusumano and Takeishi 1991; Clemons et al. 1993; Lemke et al. 2000), similar investigations of a company's reaction to a very large number of contracted IT suppliers are very scarce in today's academic research. One exception is a recent study of Willcocks et al. (2010), which also indicated that some client companies have started working on a reduction and consolidation of their supplier bases. Here we have brought the 'move to the middle' hypothesis to mind, which predicted a move to more outsourcing but with fewer suppliers (Clemons et al. 1993). A dynamic view on companies' sourcing strategies suggests that the investigated IT organizations have recently aimed much effort at an efficient management of their contractual relationships instead of relying solely on 'optimal' sourcing decisions.

This shift of emphasis does not only affect sourcing strategies, but leads to changes in organizational structure as well. Our conceptual framework distinguished between different organizational models of IT SRM, varying upon the degree of centralization and mode of SRM sourcing. The two extremes on a continuum, 'decentralized supplier relationship management' and 'centralized supplier relationship management,' present ways to structure SRM intra-organizationally. The outsourced SRM model covers an alternative where a company decides to outsource (a part of) its SRM to a third party. Our case studies covered these structural models and showed examples of their practical implementation. The predominant in-house model was a hybrid (centralized-decentralized) structure, where IT organizations have established one or more centralized units for a part of the related activities, stressing the importance of IT SRM. Although a great variety of design and responsibilities of these centralized units appear to be in place in practice, two ways to efficiently structure the units emerged from our case companies: Separating either strategic and more operative tasks, or separating units, dealing with suppliers contracted for IS development or IS operations.

The last section addressed the process layer of organization design and studied the core activities and stakeholders involved in IT SRM. Conceptually, we derived nine core activities from a generic process gained from SCM literature and the best-practice framework ITIL.

These activities basically constitute a process, ranging from identification of potential suppliers through building relationships and performance monitoring to the termination of contractual relations. Owing to the process' wide scope, several competencies and skills need to be involved. Therefore, companies usually need to involve staff members from IT, purchasing, and legal departments etc. throughout the process. We shed some light on the distribution of IT SRM tasks, showing that IT and purchasing departments play the major role (from IT perspective) here. Formalizing SRM processes and relying on lateral connections, for example, purchasing teams, presented two predominant ways to bridge barriers between different organizational entities, that is, departments central to IT SRM (Galbraith et al. 2002).

Not reported so far, our study tried additionally to provide the total number of people (full time equivalents, FTE) involved in the described SRM process within the IT organizations. However, our case companies had great difficulties to provide such a number. Since we do not want the reader to be deprived of the 'lessons learned,' we try to briefly summarize the reasons, why our attempt did not prove successful. First of all, as already mentioned, companies that followed a hybrid approach and established central units were able to provide us the number of people devoted to SRM centrally (10 people and more). When trying to get the number of people also involved in SRM, but active in more decentralized organizational entities, the key informants could only give us relatively little information. Even the attempt to estimate the number of people involved in SRM turned out to be difficult, but revealed some further characteristics of today's SRM implementation in practice. First, there still seems to be a large extent of people across the IT organization involved in the SRM process only part-time and temporary, which itself shows that the extent of people needed for SRM changes dynamically. Therefore, the need of people for SRM does not depend only on a given contract size, but seems also to be depending on, for example, the type of contract (fixed-price, etc.), the subject of the contract and the activities that are retained in-house (IS operations, development, etc.), as well as the delivered quality and know-how level of the commissioned suppliers. Given the lack of transparency and the partially dynamic involvement in SRM activities, it is likely that there is a further great potential for companies to streamline their SRM activities to reach a more mature IT SRM. Bundling and centralization of further SRM activities might be one way to do this, but we expect companies thereby facing a major challenge in finding their optimal degree.

Limitations and Future Work

To advance research in the field of IT SRM, we conducted a multiple case study into the IT organizations of five large-scale German enterprises, attempting to understand how IT SRM has been implemented from an organizational design perspective. The multiple case study pointed out the barely examined issues in research and we will now briefly discuss promising directions for future research in the field.

Although we did not conduct a single case study but studied a total of five cases, there is still a need for other studies to discuss, argue or confirm our findings. One major limitation arises from the fact that we applied the single key informant method. Despite our attempt to compensate this limitation by relying on, for example, data triangulation, future studies could extend research by adopting additionally a purchasing or legal perspective. Second, a larger empirical basis is needed to gain a representative picture of current shape and trends in IT SRM. Owing to our relatively small case number, we were, for example, not able to explore cultural or sectoral differences. Determining whether there is a remarkable trend towards a significant reduction in IT supplier bases, as well as studying the spread of centralized units, appears to be worthwhile research areas. Future studies are needed to study, for example, conditions, success factors, risks and benefits of these concepts to support companies planning to implement them.

Further research efforts should be made to additionally consider the remaining two organizational elements of the star model, reward systems and people practices, along with the potential benefits companies might reap from an alignment of these organizational design facets. At this point, one should remember contingency theory, which suggests that there is no universal best way of organizing, but that the optimal organization design is rather contingent upon various internal and external constraints (Galbraith 1973; Donaldson 2001). In this context, our case organizations suggest the following conclusions: Centralized units seem to 'fit' especially well into organizations with a certain size and favoring strategic conditions, such as a high outsourcing degree and/or a large supplier base. The most straightforward reasons might be the eventually increased ability to handle the complexity that arises out of these aforementioned contingency factors. And secondly, given the variety of activities necessary for IT SRM and the number of different organizational entities needed to carry them out, they call for a clear regulation of responsibilities, or in other words, process formalization. To further generalize, these initial and other assumptions, additional empirical studies are needed, elaborating on the applicability of organizational contingency theory in the context of IT SRM, and its influence on IS/IT outsourcing success.

Another field that is deemed to valuably contribute to IS outsourcing research is a thorough investigation of the organizational model of 'outsourced supplier relationship management,' that is, outsourcing (a part) of SRM activities to specialized third-party providers. Many pros and cons can be named for both alternatives, pure in-house *vs* outsourced SRM. That is, for example, independency and control keeping on one side and the further leverage of economies of scale and concentration of business core competencies on the other. In our opinion, it would be worthwhile to view this model through different theoretical lenses and studying it in empirical studies, verifying its potential to succeed in the IS/IT outsourcing market.

In the beginning, we pointed to the fact that SRM has already been well studied in SCM literature, albeit not with a focus on IT suppliers. Some principles known in SCM, for example, 'supplier base reduction' or 'tiering' were observed in our cases. Another interesting direction for future study would be to evaluate whether further SRM concepts from 'mature' industries, such as the automobile industry, can be applied to the IT/software industry. Furthermore, an additional look at differences between the industries, for example the fact that spatial proximity is less important in the software industry, could further point to particularities in the management of IT suppliers.

Acknowledgments This study and paper was extensively discussed in a series of meetings and extensive exchanges over a period of a year. The authors want to thank Heiko Russow, Dr. Christoph Klingenberg and Dr. Michael Frank for their valuable comments and support during this time. The authors are also grateful to Prof. Mary Lacity, Prof. Leslie Willcocks and anonymous reviewers for providing their valuable comments and suggestions, which have greatly improved the paper. Without the efforts and openness of our interview partners, whose names cannot be mentioned here without violating the anonymity of the case companies, this study would not have been possible – we are very grateful for the time each of them spent on this work.

Appendix

Table A1 Framework to assess descriptive case studies (Adapted from Dubé and Paré 2003)

Research design	
Clear research questions	Yes, 'how'
Multiple-case design	Yes, five cases
Nature of single-case design	Not relevant, due to multiple-case design
Replication logic in multiple-case design	Both theoretical and literal replication logic
Unit of analysis	Companies' IT organizations with special focus on IT supplier relationship management
Pilot case	Not conducted, since it is recommended for studies with highly exploratory nature
Context of the case study	Research was conducted both off-site (questionnaire) and on-site (face-to-face interviews). The two data collection periods were well-described and the period of investigation was reported (January to March 2011). Nature of data was retrospective and ongoing.
Team-based research	Yes
Different roles for multiple investigators	Author 1 and two research assistants in data collection
	Author 1, 2 and two research assistants in data analysis
Data collection	

(*continued*)

Table A1 (continued)

Elucidation of the data collection process	Yes
Multiple data collection methods	Yes, questionnaires, interviews and documents
Mix of qualitative and quantitative data	Yes, both qualitative and quantitative data
Data triangulation	Yes, for different sources
Case study protocol	Yes
Case study database	Yes
Data analysis	
Elucidation of the data analysis process	Yes, see section 'Data Analysis'
Field notes	Yes
Coding and reliability check	Reliability of study findings was tried to reach in several ways. First, evaluation of questionnaires and interview data were checked by research assistants to minimize errors and biases. Furthermore, interpretations were discussed in case analysis meetings. The use of a case study protocol and database present herein important prerequisites for ensuring reliability (Yin 2003).
Data displays	Yes
Flexible & opportunistic process	Yes. Since our data collection process overlapped with an initial data analysis, process flexibility was guaranteed. An initial analysis of the completed questionnaire data helped to make adjustments in the interview guide and to ask supplementary questions.
Logical chain of evidence	Yes. Our research questions lead to the conceptual framework of organizational design. Then the framework guided data collection and analysis that provided finally evidence to our initial research questions.
Searching for cross-case patterns	Yes
Quotes (evidence)	Yes
Project reviews	Yes, in form of case analysis meetings

References

Alsudairi, M, and Dwivedi, Y.K (2010). A Multi-disciplinary Profile of IS/IT Outsourcing Research, *Journal of Enterprise Information Management* **23**(2): 215–258.

Aral, S, Bakos, J.Y, and Brynjolfsson, E. (2010). How Trust, Incentives and IT Shape Global Supplier Networks: Theory and evidence from IT services procurement [www document] http://ssrn.com/abstract=1635891 (accessed 16th August 2011).

Arttoa, K, Kulvika, I, Poskelab, J, and Turkulainen, V (2011). The Integrative Role of the Project Management Office in the Front End of Innovation, *International Journal of Project Management* **29**(4): 408–421.

Bagozzi, R.P, Yi, Y, and Philips, L.W (1991). Assessing Construct Validity in Organizational Research, *Administrative Science Quarterly* **36**(3): 421–458.

Bakos, J.Y (1991). A Strategic Analysis of Electronic Marketplaces, *MIS Quarterly* **15**(3): 295–310.

Bakos, J.Y, and Brynjolfsson, E (1993). Information Technology, Incentives, and the Optimal Number of Suppliers, *Journal of Management Information Systems* **10**(2): 37–53.

Brown, D, and Wilson, S (2005). *The Black Book of Outsourcing: How to manage the changes, challenges, and opportunities*, Hoboken, NJ: John Wiley & Sons.

Campbell, D.T (1955). The Informant in Quantitative Research, *American Journal of Sociology* **60**(4): 339–342.

Champoux, J.E (2000). *Organization Behavior – Essential tenets for a new millennium*, Cincinnati: South-Western College Publishing.

Chandler, A.D (1962). *Strategy and Structure*, New York: Wiley.

Clemons, E.K, Reddi, S.P, and Row, M.C (1993). The Impact of Information Technology on the Organization of Economic Activity: The 'move to the middle' hypothesis, *Journal of Management Information Systems* **10**(2): 9–35.

Coase, R (1937). The Nature of the Firm, *Economica* **4**(16): 386–405.

Cohen, L, and Young, A (2006). *Multisourcing: Moving beyond outsourcing to achieve growth and agility*, Boston, MA: Harvard Business School Press.

Connaughton, P.M. (2011). Inside the Next Generation Vendor Management Office [www document] http://www.cio.com/article/678325/Inside_The_Next_Generation_Vendor_Management_Office (accessed 16th August 2011).

Cousins, P.D. (1999). Supply Base Rationalisation: Myth or reality?, *European Journal of Purchasing & Supply Management* **5**(3): 143–155.

Cullen, S, Seddon, P.B, and Willcocks, L.P (2005). IT Outsourcing Configuration: Research into defining and designing outsourcing arrangements, *Journal of Strategic Information Systems* **14**(4): 357–387.

Cusumano, M.A, and Takeishi, A (1991). Supplier Relations and Management: A survey of Japanese, Japanese-transplant, and U.S. auto plants, *Strategic Management Journal* **12**(8): 563–588.

Dibbern, J, Goles, T, Hirschheim, R, and Jayatilaka, B (2004). Information Systems Outsourcing: A survey and analysis of the literature, *ACM SIGMIS Database* **35**(4): 6–102.

Donaldson, L (2001). *The Contingency Theory of Organizations*, Thousand Oaks, CA: Sage Publications.

Drazin, R, and Van De Ven, A.H (1985). Alternative Forms of Fit in Contingency Theory, *Administrative Science Quarterly* **30**(4): 514–539.

Dubé, L, and Paré, G (2003). Rigor in Information Systems Positivist Case Research: Current practices, trends, and recommendations, *MIS Quarterly* **27**(4): 597–635.

Eisenhardt, K.M (1989). Building Theories from Case Study Research, *The Academy of Management Review* **14**(4): 532–550.

Feeny, D.F, and Willcocks, L.P (1998). Re-designing the IS Function Around Core Capabilities, *Long Range Planning* **31**(3): 354–367.

Fitzgerald, G, and Willcocks, L.P. (1994). Contracts and Partnerships in the Outsourcing of IT, in International Conference on Information Systems (Vancouver, Canada, 1994), [www document] http://aisel.aisnet.org/icis1994/8/ (accessed 16th August 2011).

Galbraith, J (1973). *Designing Complex Organizations*, Reading: Addison Wesley.

Galbraith, J (1977). *Organization Design*, Reading: Addison-Wesley.

Galbraith, J.R, Downey, D, and Kates, A (2002). *Designing Dynamic Organizations: A hands-on guide for leaders at all levels*, New York: Amacon.

Gonzales, R, Gasco, J, and Llopis, J (2006). Information Systems Outsourcing: A literature analysis, *Information and Management* **43**(7): 821–834.

Goo, J, Kishore, R, Nam, K, Rao, H.R, and Song, Y (2007). An Investigation of Factors that Influence the Duration of IT Outsourcing Relationships, *Decision Support Systems* **42**(2): 2107–2125.

Goo, J (2009). Promoting Trust and Relationship Commitment through Service Level Agreements in IT Outsourcing Relationship, In R. Hirschheim, A. Heinzl, and J. Dibbern (eds.) *Information Systems Outsourcing: Enduring themes, global challenges, and process opportunities*, Berlin: Springer-Verlag, pp. 27–54.

Guth, S.R (2007). *The Vendor Management Office: Unleashing the power of strategic sourcing*, Breiningsville: Lulu Press.

Heckman, R (1999). Managing the IT Procurement Process, *Information Systems Management* 16(1): 61–71.

Hirschheim, R, Dibbern, J, and Heinzl, A (2008). Foreword to the Special Issue on IS Sourcing, *Information Systems Frontiers* 10(2): 125–127.

Jimmy, J., Seddon, P.B, and Reynolds, P. (2011). Exploring the Organizational Structure and Coordination of Multi-national IT Outsourcing Vendors, in European Conference on Information Systems, (Helsinki, Finland, 2011), [www document] http://aisel.aisnet.org/ecis2011/66/ (accessed 16th August 2011).

Johnson, P.F, Leenders, M.R, Klassen, R.D, and Fearon, H.E (2001). A Cross-sector Comparison of Purchasing Team Use, In A. Erridge, R. Fee, and J. McIlroy (eds.) *Best Practice Procurement: Public and private sector perspectives*, Hampshire: J. Gower Publishing.

Johnson, P.F, and Leenders, M.R (2001). The Supply Organizational Structure Dilemma, *Journal of Supply Chain Management* 37(3): 4–11.

Koppelmann, U (1998). *Procurement Marketing: A strategic concept*, Berlin: Springer-Verlag.

Lacity, M.C, Khan, S, Yan, A, and Willcocks, L.P (2010). A Review of the IT Outsourcing Empirical Literature and Future Research Directions, *Journal of Information Technology* 25(4): 395–433.

Lacity, M.C, and Hirschheim, R.A (1993). The Information Systems Outsourcing Bandwagon, *Sloan Management Review* 35(1): 73–86.

Lacity, M.C, and Willcocks, L.P (1998). An Empirical Investigation of Information Technology Sourcing Practices: Lessons from experience, *MIS Quarterly* 22(3): 363–408.

Lasch, R, and Janker, C.G (2005). Supplier Selection and Controlling Using Multivariate Analysis, *International Journal of Physical Distribution & Logistics Management* 35(6): 409–425.

Lee, J.-N., Miranda, S.M, and Kim, Y.-M (2004). IT Outsourcing Strategies: Universalistic, contingency, and configurational explanations of success, *Information Systems Research* 15(2): 110–131.

Lemke, F, Goffin, K, Szwejczewski, M, Pfeiffer, R, and Lohmüller, B (2000). Supplier Base Management: Experiences from the UK and Germany, *International Journal of Logistics Management* 11(2): 45–58.

Levina, N, and Su, N (2008). Global Multisourcing Strategy: The emergence of a supplier portfolio in services offshoring, *Decision Sciences* 39(3): 541–570.

Malone, T.W, Yates, J, and Benjamin, R.I (1987). Electronic Markets and Electronic Hierarchies, *Communications of the ACM* **30**(6): 484–497.

Markides, C.C (1999). A Dynamic View of Strategy, *Sloan Management Review* **40**(3): 55–63.

McFarlan, F.W, and Nolan, R.L (1995). How to Manage an IT Outsourcing Alliance, *Sloan Management Review* **36**(2): 9–23.

Miles, M.B, and Huberman, M. (1994). *Qualitative Data Analysis: A sourcebook of new methods*, Beverly Hills: Sage Publications.

Miles, R.E, and Snow, C.C (1978). *Organizational Strategy, Structure, and Process*, New York: McGraw-Hill.

Monczka, R.M. (2000). *New Product Development: Strategies for supplier integration*, Milwaukee: ASQ Quality Press.

Monczka, R.M, Handfield, R.B, Guinipero, L.C, Patterson, J.L, and Walters, D (2010). *Purchasing and Supply Chain Management*, Hampshire: Cengage Learning EMEA.

Office of Government Commerce (2007). *Service Design*, Volume2 of ITIL Series, UK: The Stationary Office.

Office of Government Commerce (2010). *Introduction to the ITIL Service Lifecycle*, UK: The Stationary Office.

Ogden, J.A, and Carter, P.L (2008). The Supply Base Reduction Process: An empirical investigation, *International Journal of Logistics Management* **19**(1): 5–28.

Peters, T.J, and Waterman, R.H. Jr. (1982). *In Search of Excellence: Lessons from America's Best-Run Companies*,New York: Harper and Row.

Poppo, L, and Zenger, T (2002). Do Formal Contracts and Relational Governance Function as Substitutes or Complements, *Strategic Management Journal* **23**(8): 707–725.

Project Management Institute (2008). *A Guide to the Project Management Body of Knowledge*, Newton Square: PMI.

Pugh, D.S, Hickson, D.J, Hinings, C.R, and Turner, C (1968). Dimensions of Organization Structure, *Administrative Science Quarterly* **13**(1): 65–105.

Richardson, J, and Roumasset, J (1995). Sole Sourcing, Competitive Sourcing, Parallel Sourcing: Mechanisms for supplier performance, *Managerial and Decision Economics* **16**(1): 71–84.

Rottman, J.W, and Lacity, M.C (2006). Proven Practices for Effectively Offshoring IT Work, *MIT Sloan Management Review* **47**(3): 56–64.

Snow, C.C, Miles, R.E, and Miles, G (2005). A Configurational Approach to the Integration of Strategy and Organization Research, *Strategic Organization* **3**(4): 431–439.

Sparrow, E (2003). *Successful IT Outsourcing: From choosing a provider to managing the project*, London: Springer-Verlag.

Trent, R.J (2004). The Use of Organizational Design Features in Purchasing and Supply Management, *Journal of Supply Chain Management* **40**(3): 4–18.

Van Weele, A.J (2009). *Purchasing and Supply Chain Management: Analysis, strategy, planning and practice*, Hampshire: Cengage Learning EMEA.

Willcocks, L, Feeny, D, and Olson, N (2006). Implementing Core IS Capabilities: Feeny–Willcocks IT governance and management framework revisited, *European Management Journal* **24**(1): 28–37.

Willcocks, L, Oshri, I, and Hindle, J. (2010). *To Bundle or Not To Bundle? Effective Decision-making for Business and IT Services*, London: The Outsourcing Unit/Accenture.

Willcocks, L, and Lacity, M.C (2006). *Global Sourcing of Business and IT Services*, New York: Palgrave Macmillan.

Williamson, O.E (1981). The Economics of Organization: The transaction cost approach, *The American Journal of Sociology* **87**(3): 548–575.

Williamson, O.E (1985). *The Economic Institutions of Capitalism: Firms, markets, relational contracting*, New York: The Free Press.

Yin, R.K (2003). *Case Study Research, Design and Methods*, Thousand Oaks: Sage Publications.

Jasmin Kaiser was a Ph.D. student and research member at the Chair of Information Systems at Darmstadt University of Technology in Germany. She holds a diploma in information systems with focus on software engineering, marketing and human resources. Her research fields include information systems sourcing, supplier relationship management and outsourcing relationships. Further, Jasmin Kaiser is scholarship holder of the Foundation of German Business (Stiftung der Deutschen Wirtschaft).

Peter Buxmann was Full Professor for Information Systems at Darmstadt University of Technology. His research fields include Software Business, Information Management, Standardization of Information Systems, and Future Internet Economics. Moreover, he serves as a Department Editor of the Journal *Wirtschaftsinformatik* resp. Business & Information Systems Engineering. Peter Buxmann is member of the Executive Board and Research Director of the House of IT.

7

How Do IT Outsourcing Vendors Respond to Shocks in Client Demand? A Resource Dependence Perspective

Fang Su, Ji-Ye Mao and Sirkka L Jarvenpaa

Introduction

IT outsourcing vendors rely on client orders as they grow toward a steadily increasing number and variety of client projects (Levina and Ross 2003). However, there are numerous factors that can threaten the demand certainty of clients. For example, clients might choose to sign sequential and short-term contracts (Lacity and Willcocks 1998; Bahli and Rivard 2003), or divide orders and create competition among multiple vendors (Currie 1998; Rottman and Lacity 2006), to mitigate their exposure to risks. Such practices not only have a negative effect on long-term collaboration between a vendor and its

J.-Y. Mao (✉) · F. Su
School of Business, Renmin University of China, Beijing, China
e-mail: jiyemao@yahoo.com; jymao@ruc.edu.cn

S.L. Jarvenpaa
Center for Business, Technology and Law, University of Texas at Austin, Austin, TX, USA

© The Author(s) 2017
L.P. Willcocks et al. (eds.), *Outsourcing and Offshoring Business Services*, DOI 10.1007/978-3-319-52651-5_7

client but also make it hard for the vendor to forecast future demand and manage its resources. Moreover, in a globally competitive environment, relationships between clients and vendors become vulnerable to sudden and unexpected environmental jolts (Grewal et al. 2007; Lavie et al. 2010), such as terrorist attacks (Nolan et al. 2004) and financial crises (Grewal et al. 2007). Such environmental jolts further exacerbate IT vendors' demand uncertainty (Grewal and Tansuhaj 2001) and can lead to a rapid decline in client orders, or what we call demand shocks.

It is therefore important for vendors to identify effective response strategies to reduce the inimical effect of environmental jolts (Aubert et al. 2002). However, prior studies have primarily focused on risk sources, risk factors, and risk mitigation from the clients' point of view, paying far less attention to risks faced by vendors (Aundhe and Mathew 2009). Furthermore, whereas the extant research has explored several measures for vendors to mitigate risks that threaten the success of IT projects (e.g., Taylor 2007), not much is known about how vendors respond to shocks in client demand, which have a direct and serious effect on vendors' business (Grewal et al. 2007). For example, building collaborative partnerships with clients is helpful for reducing the probability and potential impact of risks before their occurrence (Taylor 2007; Aundhe and Mathew 2009), but how vendors rebuild and reinforce collaborative relationships, *ex post* to drastic decline in client orders, is not well understood. Therefore, this research aims to address the following questions: How do IT vendors mitigate the effect of demand shocks, and why?

The transaction cost economics theory and agency theory are among the most commonly adopted theoretical foundations in IT outsourcing risk research (Bahli and Rivard 2003; Mathew 2011). These theories are helpful for understanding mechanisms for mitigating risks through contract design (Taylor 2007; Mathew 2011), but they are not useful for understanding exogenous risks that are caused by sources independent of vendor and client actions.

This research adopts resource dependence theory (RDT) (Pfeffer and Salancik 1978; Hillman et al. 2009) as its theoretical lens. 'Organizations must transact with other elements in their environment to acquire needed resources' (Pfeffer and Salancik 1978: 234), and they rely upon their cooperation with partners to achieve business objectives (Emerson 1962; Anderson et al. 1994). RDT helps explain how organizations stabilize external resource provision after environmental jolts such as demand shocks (Bode et al. 2011). In fact, RDT also suggests 'ways to reduce or overcome environment uncertainty' (Carroll 1993: 243) that disturbs a firm's external resource provision (Bode et al. 2011), such as a merger, joint venture, and co-optation (Pfeffer and Salancik 1978; Carroll 1993). Central to these actions is the concept of power (Hillman et al. 2009). RDT argues that power relations with the exchange partner have an effect on the focal firm's action (Casciaro and Piskorski 2005). For example, an IT vendor in a disadvantageous power relationship can obtain stability by seeking reciprocal dependence between itself and its client. Hence, our secondary research question is: How do power relations with the client influence an IT vendor's response strategies to demand shocks?

Chinese IT vendors' experience during the financial crisis of 2008 provided a valuable opportunity to extend the IT outsourcing literature. Previously, offshore IT outsourcing from Japan experienced rapid growth from 2003 to 2008 at an annual rate of 30% (Beijing Association of Sourcing Service 2010), with highs of 42.8% in 2005 and more than 50% in 2006. However, the industry suffered a major blow from the global financial crisis of 2008. The volume of Japanese offshore outsourcing business declined 10% in 2009 and further declined 15% in 2011 (Beijing Association of Sourcing Service 2011). The effect on Chinese vendors, which collectively made up the largest share of Japanese offshore IT outsourcing, was exacerbated by rapid appreciation of the Chinese currency and rising labor costs. Some vendors were wiped out completely, whereas most of them downsized significantly. Shocks in demand not only decreased vendors' profits and increased operation costs (Nolan et al. 2004; Bahli and Rivard 2005) but also threatened their survival (Huang et al. 2004; Grewal et al. 2007).

This research examines strategies used by Chinese IT vendors to mitigate the effect of demand shocks. A multiple case study was conducted involving five pairs of vendor–client relationships involving two Chinese vendors, both of which experienced sudden and drastic declines in business and cancellation of orders as a result of the financial crisis of 2008. The unit of analysis was a single vendor–client relationship, as each vendor took different response strategies on a client-by-client basis. This research advances theory development by explaining the differences in IT vendors' response strategies to demand shocks.

Theoretical Background

RDT and IT Outsourcing

RDT focuses on a firm's external environment (Javalgi et al. 2009). It considers the firm as an open system that needs to exchange resources with the environment (Pfeffer and Salancik 1978) to achieve its business objectives (Anderson et al. 1994), and thus the firm is constrained by its context (Pfeffer 1981). The scarcity of key external resources creates a firm's dependence on its exchange partners (Bode et al. 2011). This dependence on external resources (and their exchange partners) creates a potential risk for the firm because the firm lacks control over its external resources (Pfeffer 1981, 1987). Exchange partners' actions may disrupt the flow of needed external resources (Casciaro and Piskorski 2005). Therefore, the firm must adapt to environmental uncertainty and actively manage or control external resource flows (Javalgi et al. 2009).

In IT outsourcing, clients outsource their projects to procure professional services or assets from vendors, while vendors learn domain knowledge and gain revenue from clients (Levina and Ross 2003; Jarvenpaa and Mao 2008). Both sides depend on each other to varying extents (Scott and Davis 2007; Caniëls and Roeleveld 2009). Therefore, RDT helps explain interfirm relationships between IT outsourcing clients and vendors (Huang et al. 2004). However, few prior studies have drawn significantly on RDT to examine IT outsourcing (e.g., Rao et al. 2007), and most of them are from the clients' perspective (e.g., Huang et al. 2004). For example, Huang and colleagues pointed out that a client can become strategically dependent on the vendor and be exposed to the vendor's opportunism or nonperformance, particularly when the vendor cannot be easily replaced (Aubert et al. 2002; Bahli and Rivard 2003; Huang et al. 2004; Aron et al. 2005).

Vendors depend on clients for profit and resources (Jarvenpaa and Mao 2008). In fact, a large number and variety of IT contracts drive and enable vendors to build operational capabilities and grow their resources (Levina and Ross 2003; Ethiraj et al. 2005). However, to reduce their dependence on vendors, clients might engage multiple vendors (Bahli and Rivard 2003; Huang et al. 2004), sign short-term contracts (Lacity and Willcocks 1998), break a project into segments (Rottman and Lacity 2006), and insource assets that are core to the client's business (Watjatrakul 2005). These client practices not only impair vendors' bargaining power (Lacity et al. 2009) but also create uncertainty in demand (Scott and Davis 2007). As outsourcing vendors' main expense is the cost of human resources, which stays the same despite any decline in orders and associated increase in employee idle time, demand shocks threaten the survival of vendors. Although prior research suggests that vendors could try to stabilize demand by becoming an expert in the client's IT needs (Aundhe and Mathew 2009) and sharing value with the client (Levina and Ross 2003), these measures are mitigations *ex ante* to demand attenuation. Little is known about response strategies to demand shocks that occur suddenly and have to be dealt with *ex post*.[1]

Power Relations

Power is important for understanding organizational actions (Pfeffer and Salancik 1978; Davis, and Cobb 2010), which can be traced back to Emerson's (1962) theory of power-dependence relations. Emerson defined dependence as a function of resource criticality and the availability of alternative providers of critical resources. More specifically, the dependency of actor i on actor j is determined by two factors: the strategic importance of resources provided by j for i's survival and the extent to which j controls the resource (Pfeffer and Salancik 1978). According to Emerson's exchange framework, the power of i over j is

---

[1] The term 'demand shocks' in this research primarily refers to sudden and drastic declines in client orders, without considering rapid increases.

equal to and based on the dependence of j upon i, which means the power of i over j comes from the control of resources that j values and that are not available elsewhere (Davis, and Cobb 2010).

There are two distinct theoretical dimensions of resource dependence: power imbalance and interdependence (Casciaro and Piskorski 2005; Gulati and Sytch 2007). The former refers to the power differential between two organizations, whereas the latter is determined by the sum of their mutual dependence. Both power imbalance and interdependence need to be considered simultaneously to characterize a power relation accurately (Casciaro and Piskorski 2005; Caniëls and Roeleveld 2009). The reason is that any power-imbalance relation can involve varying levels of mutual dependence, and conversely, any given level of interdependence can be associated with different levels of power imbalance in the dyad of firms.

Therefore, the effect of a power relation cannot be properly assessed by considering the dependence of one firm on the other without taking into account its reciprocal dependence (Casciaro and Piskorski 2005; Caniëls and Gelderman 2005; Gulati and Sytch 2007; Caniëls and Roeleveld 2009). On the basis of the literature, we classify power relations in a dyadic relationship (actor i and actor j) accordingly into four scenarios in terms of high-high, high-low, low-high, and low-low (see Table 7.1). In Configurations 1 and 4 (low-low and high-high), i and j have equal power over each other, and they are in a power balance. In Configuration 4, the power of both i and j is high, and hence they are in a high-interdependence situation, whereas in Configuration 1, because of the low power possessed

Table 7.1 Configurations of power relation

i's power over j			
		Low	High
j's power over i	Low	Configuration 1: Power balance low interdependence	Configuration 2: Power imbalance: i dominance medium interdependence
	High	Configuration 3: Power imbalance: j dominance medium interdependence	Configuration 4: Power balance high interdependence

Source: Caniëls and Roeleveld (2009) and Casciaro and Piskorski (2005)

by each firm, *i* and *j* are in a low-interdependence situation. Configurations 2 and 3 (low-high and high-low) represent power-imbalance situations. When *i*'s power over *j* is higher than *j*'s power over *i*, *i* is in a dominant situation, and vice versa (Emerson 1962; Caniëls and Roeleveld 2009).

Strategies to Reduce Demand Uncertainty Based on RDT

Resource dependence on business partners leaves firms vulnerable (Scott and Davis 2007); however, they can acquire and maintain external resources by increasing the dependence of other firms on them and/or decreasing their dependence on others (Ulrich and Barney 1984). RDT suggests a wide range of actions that firms can take to reduce dependence and uncertainty, such as a merger and acquisition, joint venture, and interlocking boards of directors (Pfeffer and Salancik 1978; Scott and Davis 2007; Hillman et al. 2009). These actions can help control and stabilize resource flows to varying degrees (Scott and Davis 2007; Davis, and Cobb 2010).

Many prior studies have examined the relationship between power-relation and dependence-mitigation actions. For example, interdependence was positively associated with a merger (e.g., Burt 1980) and a joint venture (e.g., Park and Mezias 2005) because of the importance of the resources provided by each firm. However, most of the prior studies focused on controlling and managing demand uncertainty and dependence (Davis, and Cobb 2010) in an attempt to reduce the probability of uncertainty and its potential impact. To our knowledge, little effort has been directed to the questions of how a firm should respond when demand shocks do occur, and how does the power relation affect the choice of a response strategy?

Bode et al. (2011) examined how firms responded to supply chain disruption. Just as supply uncertainty is a key area of supply chain management, so is demand uncertainty (Paulraj and Chen 2007). Bode and colleagues identified two types of strategies in response to resource flow disruption: buffering and bridging (Thompson 1967). Buffering works *outside* the current relationship either by reducing the importance of the valued resource, such as building up slack resources (Bode et al. 2011; Chattopadhyay et al. 2001) or by reducing the importance of the supplier, such as seeking alternative sources of supply

(Caniëls and Gelderman 2005). This strategy aims to 'gain stability by establishing safeguards that protect a firm from disturbances that an exchange relationship confers' (Bode et al. 2011: 834). In contrast, bridging works in the context of an *existing* relationship and directs resources to 'control or in some manner coordinate one's actions with those of formally independent entities' (Scott and Davis 2007: 235). This strategy tries to 'manage uncertainty through boundary-spanning and boundary-shifting actions with an exchange partner' (Bode et al. 2011: 834), for example, by investing in collaborative structures (e.g., a joint venture), modifying an existing exchange relationship, such as a merger or acquisition (Pfeffer and Salancik 1978; Carroll 1993), or offering valued resources (e.g., information) to the exchange partner (Casciaro and Piskorski 2005).

Moreover, Bode et al. (2011) examined the relationship between dependence on the exchange partner and the choice of buffering and bridging, and they found a positive association between dependence and bridging but an inverse U-shaped relationship between dependence and buffering. That is, bridging is the only option in the case of extremely high dependence on an exchange partner. For example, firm A is one of numerous small suppliers of firm B, which is big and the only client of A (i.e., A is highly dependent on B). If firm B demands a lower purchase price by threatening to cut orders from A, A can only meet B's demand (bridging). A better option for A is to form a long-term relationship with B (bridging), but B's likely resistance has to be considered because B does not want to lose its bargaining power and its advantageous exchange condition (Casciaro and Piskorski 2005). This example shows that the effect of the power relation on a firm's behavior cannot be properly assessed by considering the dependence of one firm on the other without taking into account its reciprocal (Caniëls and Gelderman 2005; Casciaro and Piskorski 2005; Caniëls and Roeleveld 2009).

Furthermore, a power relation may have different effects on the response strategies used to manage uncertainty in demand *vs* the response strategies used to manage demand shocks. The existing literature focuses largely on the management of the *ex ante* uncertainty, not on the response strategies to demand shocks, as is the focus of this research. For example, Casciaro and

Piskorski (2005) argue that the higher the dependence on a partner, the more desirable buffering is for minimizing future uncertainty and for absorbing constraints resulting from dependence. However, in case of demand shocks, the literature has found that a firm should strengthen its relationship with the exchange partner (Grewal et al. 2007; Bode et al. 2011), which is, in fact, bridging. Because of the differences in focus of the past research (demand uncertainty vs demand shocks), the literature does not provide a clear understanding of the relationship between power relations and response strategies. Hence, it is important to investigate the relationship further. Our research questions can be further specified for the IT outsourcing context – namely, how does an IT outsourcing vendor respond to a decline in orders from a client according to its power relation with the client, and why?

Research Methods

We adopt the case study method in this research for two reasons. First, this research essentially addresses the 'how' and 'why' questions, and thus the case research method is deemed appropriate (Yin 1994). Second, a case study is 'most appropriate in the early stages of research on a topic' (Eisenhardt 1989: 548). As efforts in theory building for IT outsourcing vendors' response to demand shocks have been scanty (Aundhe and Mathew 2009), we choose the case study method. Following Eisenhardt's (1989) recommendation for multiple case studies, we examine the relationships between five pairs of vendor–clients.

Research Setting and Case Selection

Case selection was based on the following considerations. First, a candidate vendor's business was primarily in the Japanese market before the financial crisis in 2008. Vendors that operated in multiple markets were excluded to make sure the sampled vendors faced the same environment. Second, the selected vendors suffered a great deal from demand shocks that ensued from the financial crisis. Third, sufficient variation was apparent both in power relations between vendors and their clients and in their response strategies. Finally, a practical factor was access to the informants (Yan and Gray 1994). It was essential for the researchers to have multiple visits and access to various levels of management. Therefore, two IT vendors satisfying these criteria, Alpha and Beta,[2] were chosen.

Both Alpha and Beta were based in Beijing, which hosted the largest cluster of offshore IT outsourcing businesses in China. The revenue of IT outsourcing from Japan had maintained an annual growth rate of 30% from 2000 to 2008. However, the volume of executed contracts suddenly declined, by double digits, in 2009 and 2010 (Beijing Association of Sourcing Service 2011). Beginning in 2009, Japan was no longer the largest source of offshored IT services for Beijing, and its market share also declined from the 2008 high of 45.7% to 30% in 2009, and to merely 18% in 2010, according to the Report on the Development of the Service Outsourcing Industry in Beijing (2010, 2011). Not until 2011 did the Japanese market rebound, and the volume of executed contracts regained its 2008 level.

Most of the local vendors were small- and medium-sized enterprises (SMEs) and vulnerable to demand turbulence. Among the 400 vendors servicing overseas clients in 2008, emerging and small ones accounted for close to three-fourths of the total, according to the Beijing Association for Offshore Outsourcing. The Association classified vendors with revenue exceeding US$100 million as large, $10–100 million as medium-sized, $2–10 million as emerging enterprises, and those under $500,000 as small. Alpha was medium-sized, with a revenue of $80 million in 2008, but it was also a top 10 IT outsourcing vendor in Beijing and publicly listed in Hong Kong Stock Exchange since 2004; meanwhile, Beta was a small vendor.

Alpha

Founded in 1995, Alpha grew by a factor of 10 in the 7 years before the crisis and had more than 3,200 employees in 2008. The Japanese

---

[2] Their real names are disguised, as are the names of their Japanese clients.

market accounted for more than 90% of Alpha's revenue, mostly in the securities brokerage and financial services industry. In fact, business from the two key clients, X and Y, accounted for more than 80% of Alpha's business. Alpha's clients were not able to escape the ripple effects of the financial crisis. As a result, many employees suddenly had no work to do, and Alpha downsized to around 2,300 employees at the end of 2010. Moreover, profit declined 21% in 2009 and another 32% in 2010. Finally, along with the rebound of the Japanese market in the first half of 2012, Alpha saw an increase in its revenue, and the size of the firm stabilized at 3,000 employees.

Since its foundation, Alpha operated on the principle of 'just following the lead of the client' and emphasized establishing a long-term client relationship. For example, top leaders of Alpha developed a close personal relationship with their counterparts in the client firms. There were social functions biannually at the top management level. In addition, Alpha also encouraged its middle managers to travel to Japan to develop friendships with clients' project managers. Furthermore, Alpha emphasized a prompt response to change requests by the client.

Beta

Beta was founded in 2003 and maintained an annual growth rate of 30–40% till 2007, and the number of staff members also increased from around 70 to more than 240. Beta had a stellar performance in 2007 and experienced its strongest growth ever. However, it was hit hard by the 2008 financial crisis, and orders disappeared suddenly in the second half of 2008. Business did not improve in 2009, with no new project in sight (except some small legacy maintenance projects). Layoffs and resignations followed in waves. The size of the firm shrank to 90 employees. Beta operated at a loss in 2009 and 2010.

Beta's business model was based on rigorous software development processes. To achieve technical excellence, it invested a great deal of resources and manpower in Capability Maturity Model Integrated certification, which was seen as important for winning client trust and securing orders. The co-founders were all from a technical background and had little contact with the senior management of clients above the division head level.

Before the crisis, over 90% of the business came from the Japanese market and the remaining 10% from a local Chinese client. However, considering the worsening long-term outlook of the Japanese market, along with the appreciation of the Chinese currency, Beta decided during the crisis to gradually shift its focus to the domestic market. While waiting for the Japanese market to rebound, Beta developed its own products for the domestic market and intensified its marketing accordingly. By the end of 2011, revenues were roughly equal between the Japanese market and the local market. The firm was transformed and able to 'walk with two legs' by adding a growing local business.

Theoretical Sampling

Because of the potential effect of the vendor–client power relation on vendor behavior, we used a vendor–client relationship as the unit of analysis, instead of just vendors. We selected five pairs of vendor–client relationships from Alpha and Beta, which covered all four scenarios (high-high, high-low, low-high, and low-low). On the basis of Caniëls and Roeleveld (2009) and Emerson (1962), the vendor's power[3] and the client's power were assessed separately, as the basis for theoretical sampling, as follows. A given client's share in the vendors' total revenue was considered an indicator of the client's power. Given that a vendor typically served multiple clients, we set 20% as the threshold for assessing the power relation. This value was also consistent with the industry norm: '[I]f a client takes up 20% of our business, it would have major clout over us,' one of our interviewees indicated.

To measure a vendor's power, we considered two factors: its importance to its suppliers and its substitutability to its suppliers. First, the importance of a vendor was determined by both the nature of tasks that it performed

---

[3] 'Vendor's power' is the short form for 'a vendor's power over its client.'

(e.g., upstream work, such as functional design and system integration tests, *vs* downstream work, such as coding and unit test) and the importance of the project to the client (e.g., whether it was an upgrade of production systems or a new application development *vs* maintenance of legacy systems). Compared with downstream projects, upstream work required business knowledge of the client and developers that had experience and advanced skills. The client's dependence on the vendor would be high if the outsourced task required specific knowledge (Caniëls and Roeleveld 2009). Similarly, the more critical the project was for the client, the more important was the vendor. The importance of a vendor was assessed based on the effect of the outsourced task to the client. If the service might enhance or disrupt the client's business operation (e.g., an upgrade or maintenance to the core transaction processing system), it would be considered important. Second, the number of alternative vendors was used as the indicator of substitutability of a vendor. Assessment of vendor power was based on both its substitutability and its importance to the client. A vendor's power would be high only if it was both important and non-substitutable. The reasoning is that a nonessential resource does not create dependence, regardless of whether it is substitutable. Similarly, as long as a resource is substitutable, it does not create dependence, regardless of its importance[4] (Pfeffer and Salancik 1978: 51).

Table 7.2 summarizes the characteristics of the five pairs of relationships. As shown in the table, the five collaborative relationships experienced decline in business during the financial crisis to varying degrees. The five clients included both end-user clients and IT outsourcers in a variety of industries. Clients ranged from small to medium to large sizes. The scale of vendor–client collaboration, measured by the number of participating employees of the vendor servicing the client, also varied across a wide range. The years of the partnership varied from under 5 years to more than 10 years. Such a diverse set of cases offered a firmer grounding of theory than more homogenous ones (Harris and Sutton 1986).

---

[4] Note that revenue from a client is a critical resource to any vendor. Therefore, if a client's share of a vendor's business exceeds 20%, the client would be considered both important and non-substitutable. If a client contributes less than 20% of a vendor's total revenue, it is important but substitutable.

Table 7.2 Profile of the five vendor–client relationships

	Case 1	Case 2	Case 3	Case 4	Case 5
Vendor	Alpha	Alpha	Alpha	Beta	Beta
Client	X	Y	Z	S	T
Nature of client	IT firm (outsourcer)	IT firm (outsourcer)	End user	IT firm (outsourcer)	End user
Client's industry	Finance	Finance	Trade and logistics	Many industries	Manufacturing
Client's size[a]	5,000+	1,500+	300+	10,000+	10,000+
Years of partnership	10+ years	10+ years	7 years	8 years	2–3 years
Scale of collaboration in 2007[b]	900	1,000	100	50	10
Scale of collaboration in 2010	600	800	60	<10	5
Scale of collaboration in 2012	855	1,100	100	30	7
Client's share of vendor business in 2007	35–40%	40–45%	5%	30%	<5%
Number of alternative vendors[c]	None	10+	None	10+	10+

Nature of tasks	Basic design, coding, and unit test	Coding, unit test, and little basic design	Coding, unit test, system integration test	Coding and unit test	Coding and unit test
Importance of project[d]	Maintenance and upgrade of core business systems	Product development and minor maintenance	Upgrade and maintenance of core products	Development of a variety of small projects	Development of PDM systems
Vendor–client power relation[e]	High-High	Low-High	High-Low	Low-High	Low-Low

PDM: Product data management

[a] Client size measured in terms of the number of employees

[b] The average number of developers servicing the client during the year, which is an estimation

[c] The number of Chinese vendors in a business relationship with the client in 2007

[d] The degree to which the outsourced project affected the operation of the client. For example, Alpha performed maintenance and upgrade of the transaction processing system for Client X's core business and provided software development and technical support for a core product of Client Z (for its most important market with the highest market share among all products). Beta undertook part of the development work for the PDM system of Client T. These projects had high importance because they would affect the client's core business and operation. In contrast, the projects undertaken in the remaining two cases had a much smaller effect on the clients

[e] Assessed based on a client's share of vendor business, in terms of the number of alternative vendors, nature of tasks, and importance of the project in this table. The client's power was deemed high when the client accounted for more than 20% of the vendor's business, which occurred in three cases: Alpha-X, Alpha-Y, and Beta-S; it was deemed low in the remaining two cases. In terms of a vendor's power, the vendor was both important for providing essential services and non-substitutable in the Alpha-X and Alpha-Z cases only, and thus its power was high. Vendor power was low in the other three cases

Data Collection

This research was part of a larger project on IT outsourcing in China. Alpha and Beta were two of the multiple vendors that the researchers followed from 2007 to 2012. The research team conducted semi-structured interviews onsite. Our questions initially centered on capability development and later shifted to the impact of the financial crisis and the firms' responses. The focus of our investigation also narrowed down from the firm level to the individual vendor–client relationship level. The interviewees held senior positions, including top managers and co-founders, and most of them were division heads and project managers (see Table 7.3). Each interview lasted about one to one-and-a-half hours.

Table 7.3 Profiles of interviews

Cases[a]	Interviewees	Number of interviews	Time of visit
Alpha-X	President, a vice president, head of planning department, head of quality assurance, a division head	5	July 2007, July 2010, January 2012
Alpha-Y	President, a vice president, director of development center, division heads, and project managers	10	July 2007, July 2010, January, February, and April 2012
Alpha-Z	Director of development center, division heads, and project managers, subleaders	9	July 2010, January, February, and April 2012
Beta-S	Co-founders, division heads, and project managers	11	July 2007, July 2010, January, February, and April. 2012
Beta-T	Co-founders, division heads, and project managers	10	July 2007, July 2010, January, February, and April 2012

[a]In Japan–China outsourcing, vendors typically maintain a division structure. Each division services one or more clients, and the divisions operate independently. In our cases, each of the five clients was serviced exclusively by one division of the corresponding vendor.

The interviews were recorded and transcribed for analysis. The research team also accumulated a large amount of archival data, consisting of industry reports, corporate annual reports of Alpha, and interviews with professional associations.

Data collection and data analysis overlapped. In addition to interviews, we made follow-up phone calls or used email to collect additional data from the interviewees, whenever it was deemed necessary. We stopped data collection when it became apparent that no new insights had emerged and when inconsistencies between our emerging theory and the data ceased to exist.

Data Analysis

We followed the approach by Santos and Eisenhardt (2009) and Martin (2011) in research design and data analysis in general. Both within-case analyses and cross-case analyses were conducted to seek patterns of relationship between the power relation and response strategies. As is typical in comparative case research, we first created individual case write-ups based on the interviews and archival data (Eisenhardt 1989). During this process, we described the evolving scale of collaboration (client engagement), task type, project type, impact of the financial crisis, and the response strategies for each pair of vendor–client relationship. Figures and tables were drawn to help understand the relationship between the power relation and the response strategies in each case (Miles and Huberman 1994). Through repeated readings of the interview transcripts, we developed an understanding of the response strategies, which were labeled as buffering or bridging based on the prior literature. We then identified the relationships between the power relation and the response strategies in each single case. In this process, we found similarities and differences among different cases but deferred further analysis until all individual case write-ups were completed in order to maintain the independence of the replication logic (Eisenhardt and Graebner 2007).

We then turned to cross-case analysis, in which insights that emerged from each case were compared with those from other cases to identify consistent patterns and themes (Eisenhardt and Graebner 2007). Cases were grouped randomly and by emerging constructs (e.g., buffering), power relations, and vendor in order to facilitate comparisons and identify patterns. Comparisons were made between varied pairs of cases. Through comparisons, some constructs were refined, such as explorative buffering and exploitative buffering; and some relationships were emerged, such as the effect of the vendor's power on response strategies. As patterns emerged, other cases were added to develop more robust causal relationships (e.g., Santos and Eisenhardt 2009). Discrepancies and agreements in the emergent theory were noted and investigated further by revisiting the data. We followed an iterative process of cycling among theory, data, and literature to refine our findings, relate them to existing theories, and clarify our contributions (e.g., Santos and Eisenhardt 2009). As with all theory building from cases, it was not an exact match, but a close one. The process yielded consistent and robust explanations for different response strategies for the four scenarios of power relation.

Results of Data Analysis

Before we discuss the relationships between power relations and response strategies, we report on the repertoire of response strategies. The analysis of the five vendor–client relationships reveals a wide range of response strategies. More importantly, the analysis suggests important variations within buffering and bridging that have not been previously identified. The added specificity on buffering and bridging develops a more nuanced understanding of them. We look at buffering first and then bridging.

Response Strategies to Demand Shocks

Buffering

Buffering is a strategy that is external to and bypasses an interfirm linkage to reduce the severity of the impact from *ex post* demand fluctuations (Bode et al. 2011). Two distinct buffering strategies emerged from our data analysis. One was to reduce the importance of orders from a specific client by improving efficiency and cutting cost based on accumulated knowledge and other resources; the other was to seek orders from alternative clients or other markets, which required expanding the knowledge base and bringing changes to the current organization. What was distinctively different between these two strategies was the focus on either existing knowledge/resources *vs* new knowledge/resources. According to March's (1991) notion of exploring new possibilities and exploiting old certainties, and Lavie et al.'s (2010) argument, exploration means pursuit of a new or novel knowledge base and resources, whereas exploitation refers to taking advantage of the existing knowledge base and resources. Accordingly, we define the two types of buffering strategies as exploitative buffering and explorative buffering. Each strategy involves multiple actions, as we discuss in detail in the following paragraphs.

Exploitative Buffering

When client orders decline drastically, cost cutting and improving efficiency can alleviate the effect to some extent (Chattopadhyay et al. 2001). Our data indicate that in each of the five cases the vendor indeed took a large array of measures to lower cost to cushion the impact of demand shocks.

The first reaction of both firms to the crisis was to cut costs. Every interviewee mentioned efforts targeting cost control, from the company level down to project teams, in response to the decline in revenue and rising costs. For example, Alpha laid off 926 employees, while Beta fired about 150, which was more than 60% of the total. For the retained employees, 'some employees were forced to take vacation on a half salary, which lasted for two to three months' (a division head of Beta), whereas others were loaned to other IT outsourcing companies during idle time to earn revenue.

Both Alpha and Beta also emphasized improving efficiency. As the head of *Y* division in Alpha (serving client *Y* exclusively)[5] described it, 'in the

---

[5] *Y* division here is the short form for the division that exclusively served client *Y*. Similarly, the unit that served clients *X*, *S*, and *T* is referred to as the *X* division, *S* division, and *T* division, respectively.

past, we might assign 120 developers to a 100 person-month project. Now we put on 110 or even 100 to try to get it done.' A co-founder of Beta also mentioned that 'our personnel utilization rate was 70–80% prior to the crisis, but is almost full capacity now. Work that was done by five developers previously is handled by three.' Moreover, when Beta realized the magnitude of the crisis, it put together a project team to develop a software development tool for productivity, despite the cost pressures resulting from disappearing orders. The tool was ready to use in 2010, after more than a year's effort, and achieved its objective for improving productivity. According to a co-founder of Beta, the tool facilitated 'the completion of a project in 50 to 60 person-months that was estimated to take 80 to 90 person-months.'

Alpha provided domain knowledge, technical training, and Japanese language training for employees during idle time, because of lack of work, to prepare for new opportunities once the Japanese market condition improved. Whereas training on technical skills and Japanese language was organized by the human resources unit, training on domain knowledge was new and occurred within project teams or work units. In contrast, Beta reduced routine training for employees to cut cost.

Reducing costs and improving efficiency are effective absorbers to environmental jolts (Meyer 1982; Chattopadhyay et al. 2001), and they produce an immediate effect. Although training to enhance employee skills is not able to absorb the consequences of a demand shock, it contributes to establishing safeguards to protect firms from future uncertainty (Scott and Davis 2007). None of these measures requires new knowledge or resources because they are refinements of current skills or processes; both reducing costs and improving efficiency are characteristic of exploitative activities (Levinthal and March 1993). Therefore, these activities constitute an execution of exploitative buffering.

Explorative Buffering

Our data revealed two kinds of explorative buffering: developing new markets and seeking alternative clients. The Beta-T and Alpha-Z cases illustrate this pattern.

During the worst time of the crisis, in 2009, the T division of Beta received only minimal work from T. Management of Beta started to realize, 'if we only do generic work (coding and unit testing) that can be done by anybody, we have no advantage.' Furthermore, 'while costs in China keep increasing, vendors' value propositions to Japanese clients keep diminishing. Life will be harder and harder. However, along with the growth in China over the past years, demand for custom-made solutions started to emerge in domestic firms ... I felt this could be an area of future growth,' reported a co-founder. After much deliberation, Beta started to invest in the exploration of new markets, under the supervision of the co-founder who used to concentrate on offshore outsourcing business. He identified specific targets in developing the domestic market and 'now spends only about one third of his effort on offshore projects and the rest on developing the new domestic market.'

Drawing from the domain knowledge gained while collaborating with the Japanese client, the T division of Beta allocated several employees to try to develop a product data management (PDM) system for domestic SMEs. Although the effort failed later, the division head and the co-founder realized that product development should be based on market requirements, and this lesson helped their next initiative.

In the Japanese market, Beta's management concentrated its attention on existing clients with large volumes of business. For example, the head of T division recalled, 'we made frequent visits to clients during the crisis, to communicate with them, by focusing our effort on key clients, such as client S. Our attention was not on T because their business was small.' The same was true in the Alpha–Z relationship. During the crisis, the executive in charge of clients Y and Z said, 'I directed my energy to collaboration with Y, doing little to strengthen our tie with Z.' The head of Z division in fact sought business from other Japanese clients and got a small project with potential to evolve into a significant one.

To develop new products and to enter a new market requires new knowledge because, in both cases, the vendor needs to be familiar with a new partner's business processes and domain knowledge, which are explorative activities (Beckman et al. 2004; He and Wong 2004). In other words, entering a new market or seeking alternative clients not only reduces the importance of the existing client but also involves learning or exploration of new knowledge. Therefore, we refer to this strategy as explorative buffering.

Bridging

Bridging refers to actions that seek to strengthen the current relationship (Bode et al. 2011). Our data show there are two distinct strategies here as well. One explores new collaborative relationships with the current client that seeks new market opportunities; the other consolidates the current relationship by more efficiently exploiting existing knowledge and resource bases. According to Lavie and Rosenkopf's (2006) argument about function exploration–exploitation, explorative activities involve acquiring and generating new knowledge, while exploitation accesses and leverages existing knowledge. Accordingly, we define these two strategies as explorative bridging and exploitative bridging, respectively.

Exploitative Bridging

Exploitative bridging involves activities that target the existing interfirm linkage by exploiting existing knowledge and resources more efficiently and effectively. Several types of vendor behaviors were found to be associated with this strategy, including offering discounts and making cost-saving proposals to clients, accepting challenging projects, and strengthening customer relationships.

During the financial crisis, Japanese clients endured significant cost pressures, and they asked their vendors to lower unit prices. However, there had been no increase in the unit price already over the previous decade, despite rapidly rising labor costs and currency appreciation, which all squeezed vendors' profit margins. Alpha and Beta responded to the requests differently. The Y division of Alpha did not compromise on unit price but decided to offer volume-based discounts to help the client. According to the division head, 'I would not negotiate with you on unit price. However, if you increase business with me by 50%, I can give you a 5% discount. The bigger the project, the deeper the discount. This offer helped seize some opportunities, which signaled our goodwill when the client was going through a difficult time. The discount was small but produced a significant result, compared to other vendors.' In contrast, Beta reluctantly agreed to a lower unit price because 'we had no choice; otherwise, there would be no business,' the division head acknowledged helplessly.

Alpha also offered cost-saving proposals to the client, based on its accumulation of experience. As the head of *Y* division in Alpha described it:

We emphasized proactively providing rationalization proposals to the client. The clients normally would not take detailed design into consideration at analysis and functional design stages; thus, their design would have a lack of discipline [and thus be hard for us to implement], although it could still be sound. However, if they used our design template, to which our people were accustomed, our development work would be faster. Moreover, the client might ask us to do many things by the end of the month. If it was not possible, I'd tell them which ones should have higher priorities, which ones should be postponed, which ones needed to go through testing first, and which ones could be put into use without testing. Recently, in some projects, we prepared design templates for our client and told them, 'If you document your design this way, my development work would be expedited.' They agreed. The client was happy with this arrangement and adopted our templates. Our profit decreased for certain [because of the reduced number of contracted man-months], but if I could not make the delivery schedule, a higher profit would be meaningless.

The head of *Y* division in Alpha commented, 'since the financial crisis, we traveled to Japan again and again, visiting each client that we had dealt with before. There was always some information, or potential projects. If nothing materialized immediately, we built goodwill for the long term. When they have the business, they'd remember us first.' A co-founder who was in charge of *S* division in Beta also took similar actions to strengthen customer relationships: 'We worked hard proactively to increase our contact with *S*. Because of its size, there might be benefits associated with routinely visiting clients.'

The vendors also made concessions by taking on challenging projects that they might not have taken otherwise. For example, during the financial crisis, new projects from S were 'mostly complex, challenging short-term projects, because easy projects went to subsidiaries of S. . . . Although the profit margin was low, requiring hard effort and overtime work, we had no choice and had to take them. Otherwise, we would have nothing to eat,' described a project manager of S division in Beta.

Providing discounts and cost-saving proposals helped the client lower its costs, which is consistent with the literature suggesting that vendors aim to acquire more orders by sharing with clients gains from collaborative relationship (Levina and Ross 2003). Taking on challenging projects expanded the scope of collaboration with existing clients, while trying to increase the business volume. Customer relationships were brought closer through frequent client visits. In sum, all of these responses involved an existing relationship and the intent to strengthen the ties (Beckman et al. 2004). The responses leveraged the vendor's internal resources and capabilities, such as human resources and operational know-how.

Explorative Bridging

This strategy seeks to strengthen the relationship with a current partner by expanding the relationship through new forms of collaboration. To develop a closer relationship with X, top leaders of Alpha engaged in a marathon negotiation with their counterparts in X regarding the formation of a joint venture. Confronted by the sudden environmental jolt, Alpha sought to strengthen its ties with X and to regain its business. Alpha leaders also sensed that X eagerly wanted to reduce costs. Therefore, Alpha's President saw 'a new opportunity' and proposed an alignment to X: 'You are pushed to the corner [by the crisis]. Only I can help you move forward. You'd better work with me, and cut out ties with others. Forget about turning back. . . . Let's align our organization structures.' The joint venture was officially set up in early 2011. As a result, X eliminated its

IT department in Japan and relocated its much reduced IT staff to the joint venture on Alpha's site in China.

Besides cutting costs, a more important objective of the joint venture was to explore the Chinese market together. The President of Alpha mentioned that 'the domestic market is growing bigger, but we are not able to overcome the entrance barriers by ourselves. Our basic strategy is to collaborate with our major Japanese partners, which are more experienced with the market. We leverage their strengths by setting up a joint venture, aiming to enter a particular industry.' The Japanese client also 'wanted their products to be adopted by more Chinese firms, and they needed our market research, and participation in the entire product development [process]. They wanted our support in marketing this product to the Chinese market,' said the head of X division.

Such a new form of collaboration with a client constitutes function exploration (Lavie and Rosenkopf 2006), for jointly developing a new product or new market. On the one hand, it strengthens customer relationships. On the other hand, by collaborating with clients, the vendor can acquire new knowledge and resources to enter a new market. Therefore, this form of response is defined as explorative bridging.

The four response strategies are juxtaposed in Table 7.4 to highlight their differences along three dimensions: target of action, goal, and means to mitigate demand shocks.

Power Relation and Response Strategies

A cross-case analysis revealed patterns of vendors' different response strategies based on varying power relations with their client (see Table 7.5). For example, in light of demand shocks, exploitative buffering was adopted in all power relations, whereas the bridging strategy was executed only when the client was in a high-power position. The effect of the power relation on vendors' response strategy is elaborated further in the following paragraphs from both the vendor's and the client's power perspectives.

Table 7.4 Four response strategies

	Exploitative buffering	Explorative buffering	Exploitative bridging	Explorative bridging
Target	The vendor internally	Other relationships	Current relationship	Current relationship
Goal	To reduce dependency on key resources	To explore new markets and clients	To strengthen the current relationship	To reform or tighten the current relationship with new forms of collaboration
Means	Lowering cost and improving efficiency	Gaining new resources from other sources	Gaining more of the same resource from the current partner	Gaining new resources from the current partner

Table 7.5 Power relations and response strategies

The client's power			
		High	Low
The vendor's power	High	Alpha-X: Explorative bridging and Exploitative buffering	Alpha-Z: Explorative buffering and Exploitative buffering
	Low	Alpha-Y; Beta-S: Exploitative bridging and Exploitative buffering	Beta-T: Explorative buffering and Exploitative buffering

Exploitative Buffering Independent of Power Relations

Our data indicate that all five cases involved exploitative buffering (Table 7.5). This strategy aims to lessen the importance of key resources by enhancing productivity, reducing resource consumption, or creating slack. It is an internally oriented strategy (Chattopadhyay et al. 2001) that does not require new resources (e.g., clients and business knowledge, in this case), takes effect more quickly and easily, and requires lower costs (March 2006). Others have argued that in the event of external crisis, cost control is always an effective measure (Suarez and Oliva 2002). In this research, both Alpha and Beta took various measures to control costs in the face of demand shocks. Therefore, we put forward the following proposition:

Proposition 1: When faced with a sudden decline in orders from a client, an IT vendor will adopt exploitative buffering, regardless of its power relation with the client.

The Effect of the Client's Power

The correspondence between power relations and the remaining three strategies is less straightforward. As described earlier, Alpha adopted the bridging strategy with X and Y, its two major clients, which had a high power over Alpha; meanwhile, it pursued the buffering strategy toward Z, with which Alpha had a high-power relation. Similarly, Beta adopted the bridging strategy in dealing with the power-advantaged client S but chose to implement the buffering strategy with client T, which had low power over Beta. In sum, when the client's power was low, the vendors adopted buffering, and when the client's power was high, the vendors chose bridging.

Why does the client's power have an effect on the vendor's response? First, firms generally tend to optimize the use of limited resources by investing in potentially important clients (Wang and Hong 2006). The client's high power implies that resources provided by the client are critical. Cancellation or reduction of orders from such a client on a massive scale imposes a serious hazard on the vendor's operation (Pfeffer and Salancik 1978; Casciaro and Piskorski 2005). Therefore, the vendor has a higher probability of regaining and stabilizing demand by strengthening its relationship with such clients (Bode et al. 2011). Second, it is difficult for a vendor to find alternative clients that contribute a high proportion of its revenue in a short time. In contrast, clients that generate a small business volume are highly substitutable because the vendor can expand its relationship with other clients to compensate for the loss of the small client's business. As the head of Y division of Alpha indicated, 'it is hard to find a major client like this [with such a high business volume], nearly impossible.' Third, it can be easier for a vendor to obtain new business from its large clients than from small clients because the large clients can offer more opportunities for new business and to scale up than small clients can. Moreover, accumulation of prior experience (e.g., familiarity with the client's management style and processes) can facilitate the execution of new projects (Levina and Ross 2003). On the basis of these arguments, we conclude:

> **Proposition 2:** When a client's power is high, the IT vendor will adopt bridging in response to a sudden decline in orders from the client.
>
> **Proposition 3:** When a client's power is low, the IT vendor will adopt buffering in response to a sudden decline in orders from the client.

The Effect of the Vendor's Power

As shown in Table 7.5, although Alpha responded to the demand shock with bridging strategies to strengthen links with both X and Y, there were major differences. Alpha was in a high-high power relation with X, and it adopted explorative bridging by negotiating a joint venture with X, thereby establishing a new and stronger link with X. However, exploitative bridging was adopted for Y, which had a power advantage over Alpha, such as providing favorable terms of service. Similarly, Beta also used an exploitative bridging strategy with S, with which it had a low-high power relation. From these observations, we found that a vendor's power influenced its choices.

In dealing with high client power, why does the vendor's power have any effect on the response strategy? First, the reason might lie in the willingness of the client to collaborate. High vendor power implies that an interruption to interfirm linkage is highly damaging to both parties, and thus the motivation to collaborate is strong and mutual (Caniëls and Gelderman 2005). The client is motivated to stabilize its resource flow, just as the vendor is, and would be willing to invest in collaboration with the vendor of high power. In such a circumstance, an explorative bridging by the vendor requires investment from both sides (Rothaermel 2001). In contrast, if the vendor with low power faces a client with low motivation to collaborate and to invest in the relationship, such a client is likely to seek other vendors. For example, *Y* had numerous IT vendors in China, 'as *Y* is always in search of what is the best for them, and they do not believe we are always the best.... They'd hire other firms if they are cheaper' (a vice president of Alpha). In comparison, Alpha was the only Chinese vendor for *X*.

Second, the power-advantaged party might prefer to maintain its superior bargaining power to squeeze more value from the less powerful side (Gargiulo 1993). Explorative bridging requires closer collaboration and knowledge integration between the two parties in search of a new market or other business opportunities (He and Wong 2004; Lavie and Rosenkopf 2006). The closer cooperation can increase both parties' dependence on each other (Jean et al. 2010). In contrast, exploitative bridging is more one sided, which likely has a smaller effect on interdependence (Casciaro and Piskorski 2005). Therefore, in a power-imbalance situation, explorative bridging might not be feasible because the power-advantaged party does not want to forgo its advantageous position. Following these arguments, we propose:

> **Proposition 4:** Bridging activities are contingent upon the vendor's power: If the vendor also has high power, it will seek explorative bridging; otherwise, it can only choose exploitative bridging.

Conclusions and Discussion

This section consists of four elements: key findings, theoretical contributions, managerial implications, and limitations and directions for future research.

Key Findings

This study addresses two research questions: How do IT outsourcing vendors respond to demand shocks, and why? Drawing on RDT, we found that a vendor adopted one or more of the following four response strategies, depending on the power relation with its client: (1) exploitative bridging to gain more repetitive orders from the current client, by leveraging existing resources; (2) explorative bridging, seeking new business from the current client through a new form of relationship; (3) explorative buffering by seeking new markets and/or clients; and (4) exploitative buffering by lowering costs, improving efficiency, or enhancing the vendor's own capabilities.

Moreover, a vendor's choice of response strategy varies from client to client, based on the power relation with the client. On the one hand, the client's power determines the vendor's options of response to demand shocks: bridging or buffering. More specifically, in the case of high client power (i.e., there exists a high dependency on the client), the vendor strives to strengthen its relationship with the client and to stabilize the supply of orders. This goal results in the vendor's adopting a bridging strategy. In contrast, when the client's power is low, the vendor might choose not to strengthen its relationship with the client. The vendor will adopt explorative buffering by directing its resources to areas of higher return, in addition to exploitative buffering. These findings are consistent with the empirical study by Bode et al. (2011), who showed that when dependence on the resource supplier is high, the pursuit of bridging strategies increases. Their study also suggests that when the dependence is low, the probability of the vendor's buffering is small because the effect of disrupted resource supply from the client is small. However, their latter finding is different from ours. In our study, characterized by a drastically contracted market, vendors could not afford to lose any client or project.

On the other hand, the vendor's power constrains the feasibility of the vendor's choice (i.e., it limits the number of feasible response strategies). If both the client and vendor are in a high-interdependence relationship, explorative bridging is likely to be acceptable to the client so that the two choose to strengthen their link through cross-investments. This result is consistent with Yan and Gray (1994), who show that alliances (joint ventures) occur when firms are mutually dependent. In contrast, in the case of high client power but low vendor power, the client lacks motivation to develop a closer relationship with the vendor, although it would not reject favors from the vendor. As a result, explorative bridging has a lower feasibility for the vendor, but exploitative bridging is nearly always welcomed by the client. This scenario is consistent with the finding of Casciaro and Piskorski (2005) that power imbalance is negatively associated with activities for absorbing the source of external constraints, but interdependence is positively associated with constraint absorption. Our study finds that explorative bridging is closely aligned with constraint absorption because it also needs the client to invest resources and knowledge.

Our research indicates that the IT vendor in a disadvantageous power relation has to reinforce its collaboration with the client (bridging) after a demand shock. This finding is different from prior work on RDT (e.g., Casciaro and Piskorski 2005; Scott and Davis 2007), which suggests that seeking another partner (explorative buffering) is also a choice for the power-disadvantaged side to reduce potential uncertainty. This discrepancy arises from the difference between demand shocks and demand uncertainty. In the former case, when a firm has suffered already after demand uncertainty became demand shrinkage, explorative buffering would not be a wise choice because it could take much more time and effort to search for new partners than to repair the link with the client.

Our data analysis also reveals that the four strategies are not mutually exclusive.[6] For example, exploitative buffering, which is an internally oriented organization strategy, is compatible with the other three externally oriented strategies. Both internal and external actions can be taken simultaneously in response to an environmental jolt (Chattopadhyay et al. 2001). In particular, explorative buffering and exploitative bridging can be pursued together. For example, in the cases of Alpha-Z and Beta-T, while managers directed their energy mainly to seeking alternative clients or developing new markets (explorative buffering), they also took actions to consolidate their

---

[6] The authors would like to thank an anonymous reviewer for the advice on discussing the compatibility among the four response strategies.

link with the existing client by, for example, increasing their routine visits to the client (exploitative bridging). Such coexistence of buffering and bridging is consistent with the prior literature (e.g., Fennell and Alexander 1987; Meznar and Nigh 1995; Bode et al. 2011).

Furthermore, we found that the effects of the three externally oriented strategies are different in the following three ways[7]: First, explorative bridging can change the vendor's power relation with a client by increasing the client's dependence on the vendor. In the Alpha-X relationship, the client's substantial investment of resources and provision of domain knowledge to Alpha increased the dependence of X on Alpha. For the establishment of the joint venture, 40% of the capital came from X. Before the financial crisis, Alpha was X's only vendor in China but nevertheless a second-tier supplier. After this crisis, the joint venture became the tier-one supplier to X and replaced the IT department of X.

Second, the effects of exploitative bridging vary. For example, the Y division of Alpha offered preferential terms of contract and volunteered cost-saving proposals to respond to Y's consolidation strategy by dealing with fewer large vendors. As a result, Alpha was able to gain more business from Y. When the Japanese market rebounded in 2011, Y's business also recovered quickly, and Alpha became the largest Chinese vendor of Y. Alpha's volume of business with Y also exceeded the historical high, which resulted in a stronger link with Y, although Alpha still faced competition from several key vendors of Y in China. In comparison, exploitative bridging did not improve Beta's collaboration with S. By 2011, the volume of business from S recovered to near pre-financial crisis levels, but projects from S became harder and harder to do, with tight delivery schedules. These projects tended to be 'hard bones to chew,' with tight schedules and without any prospect for long-term collaboration.

Third, explorative buffering can reduce the vendor's dependence on the client. In Beta's case, although T handed out 'some projects occasionally, on and off' to Beta after the financial crisis, the overall volume remained insignificant. The T division of Beta was rewarded by its efforts to develop the domestic market, to the extent that revenue from the domestic market accounted for 50% of the company's total revenue in 2012, compared with less than 10% in 2007. As a result, Beta's dependence on its Japanese clients was greatly reduced.

Theoretical Contributions

This research has made three important theoretical contributions to the IT outsourcing literature. First, whereas the extant literature focuses on how clients manage and reduce uncertainty and risks caused by vendors, we examine vendors' response strategies to mitigate the effect of demand shocks. Second, this study enriches research on vendors' risk management. None of the past studies, to our knowledge, considered IT outsourcing risks *ex post* from a vendor's perspective. We identified four types of response strategies to demand shocks and found their choice and execution were influenced by the power relation between a vendor and its client. Third, this research offers new insights into relationship management in IT outsourcing. Despite a large body of prior research (Lacity et al. 2010), including studies on the effect of relationship management on success (Lee and Kim 1999; Haried and Ramamurthy 2009) and capabilities of relationship management by a vendor or client (Willcocks et al. 2007), there is a paucity of research on the mitigation of risks through relationship management (Mathew 2011). This research shows that relationship management offers strategies for reducing the effect of environmental jolts after their occurrence, such as providing cost-saving proposals to strengthen the collaboration.

Demand uncertainty is a critical issue in supply chain management (Primo et al. 2007). This research on responses to demand shocks also contributes to research on supply chain disruption. Although much prior research exists on supply chain management, little attention has been directed to response strategies to supply chain disruption (Bode et al. 2011). The four strategies identified from this research, along with the determinants of their choice, could be potentially applicable to managing supply chain disruption. Moreover, this research provides more specificity to the bridging and buffering strategies by focusing on the firm's reciprocal power relation with its partners. These findings shed new light on the management of supply chain disruption.

Managerial Implications

This study has implications for IT outsourcing vendors managing demand shocks caused by environmental jolts. Managers need to consider power relations with their clients in selecting response strategies. More specifically, faced with a drastic reduction in business from a client, the IT vendor needs to take the following two factors into consideration: First, it must assess the importance of the partnership to the client. If the partnership is important to both parties, the vendor should strengthen the mutual interdependence with the client (e.g., via joint venture or other forms of close ties), which may result in higher mutual dependence. Otherwise, if the vendor is dependent on the client but has little effect on the client's operation and growth, the vendor in such a low-power relation should aim to provide more value for the client to improve its own power relation. Second, the vendor should be clear about what extra value it might be able to offer the client. Only by offering value-added service enhancements can the vendor secure the client's business. For example, in the context of this research, cost savings were a key motivator for the Japanese clients. When a client faces cost pressures, the vendor can help by offering more cost savings for its client than other competitors do (e.g., volunteering proposals on software development processes and enhanced productivity). In sum, although environmental jolts are beyond the control of IT outsourcing vendors, the key to containing the damage is to increase their power relation with their clients.

Limitations and Future Directions

This research has several limitations, which also represent directions for future research. First, this study has not considered vendors' business culture (e.g., market orientation), organizational strategy, and confidence in the market. A vendor's market or client orientation facilitates the attainment of high client satisfaction and loyalty (Kirca et al. 2005), which can increase the vendor's power over its client. For example, being sensitive to client requirements, Alpha was able to maintain a close collaborative relationship with its clients. In contrast, Beta's lack of deliberate effort to foster client relationship did not help improve its low-power relations with clients, despite a decade-long client engagement. Moreover, a vendor's response strategy to demand shocks can be affected by its market orientation because its choices are subject to the influence of its past actions (Teece et al. 1997; Sydow et al. 2009). To deal with demand shocks, a vendor with a strong client orientation might be more inclined to adopt bridging and thus to strengthen ties with clients, as in the case of Alpha. By comparison, as a technically oriented firm, Beta's first reaction to demand shocks was to develop a new product for a different market (buffering) and thus leverage its technical strengths. Furthermore, interpretation of the demand shock also affects response strategies. For example, a vendor's confidence in the market likely induces bridging. In contrast, a vendor without confidence might consider buffering. Therefore, future studies should take a more comprehensive approach to investigating vendor responses by considering their business culture, strategy, and interpretation of market changes. Second, as with any case study, generalizability of findings is a weakness. Propositions developed in this study are subject to empirical testing in future studies, especially surveys based on a large sample. Nevertheless, we hope the findings of this study stimulate further studies on IT vendors' responses to demand shocks, which is an important but ignored topic. Finally, some exploitative bridging activities seem to increase a client's dependence on the vendor, but others might not. Future research needs to examine response strategies more closely and their effect on power relations.

Acknowledgments This research is supported by the National Natural Science Foundation of China (Project Number: 70888001).

References

Anderson, J.C, Håkansson, H, and Johanson, J (1994). Dyadic Business Relationships within a Business Network Context, *The Journal of Marketing* **58**(4): 1–15.

Aron, R, Clemons, E.K, and Reddi, S (2005). Just Right Outsourcing: Understanding and managing risk, *Journal of Management Information Systems* **22**(2): 37–55.

Aubert, B.A, Patry, M, and Rivard, S (2002). Managing IT Outsourcing Risk: Lessons learned, In R.A. Hirschheim, A. Heinzl, and J. Dibbern. (eds.) *Information Systems Outsourcing: Enduring themes, emergent patterns and future directions*, New York: Springer-Verlag, pp. 155–176.

Aundhe, M.D, and Mathew, S.K (2009). Risks in Offshore IT Outsourcing:, A service provider perspective, *European Management Journal* 27(6): 418–428.

Bahli, B, and Rivard, S (2003). The Information Technology Outsourcing Risk: A transaction cost and agency theory-based perspective, *Journal of Information Technology* 18(3): 211–221.

Bahli, B, and Rivard, S (2005). Validating Measures of Information Technology Outsourcing Risk Factors, *Omega* 33(2): 175–187.

Beckman, C.M, Haunschild, P.R., and Phillips, D.J (2004). Friends or Strangers? Firm-Specific uncertainty, market uncertainty, and network partner selection, *Organization Science* 15(3): 259–275.

Beijing Association of Sourcing Service (2010). *Beijing Outsourcing Industry Development Report*, China: Beijing Association of Sourcing Service.

Beijing Association of Sourcing Service (2011). *Beijing Outsourcing Industry Development Report*, China: Beijing Association of Sourcing Service.

Bode, C, Wagner, S.M, Petersen, K.J, and Ellram, L.M (2011). Understanding Responses to Supply Chain Disruptions: Insights from information processing and resource dependence perspectives, *Academy of Management Journal* 54(4): 833–856.

Burt, R.S (1980). Cooptive Corporate Actor Networks: A reconsideration of interlocking directorates involving American manufacturing, *Administrative Science Quarterly* 25: 557–582.

Caniëls, M.C.J, and Gelderman, C.J (2005). Purchasing Strategies in the Kraljic Matrix – A power and dependence perspective, *Journal of Purchasing & Supply Management* 11(2): 141–155.

Caniëls, M.C.J, and Roeleveld, A (2009). Power and Dependence Perspectives on Outsourcing Decisions, *European, Management Journal* 27(6): 402–417.

Carroll, G.R (1993). A Sociological View on Why Firms Differ, *Strategic Management Journal* 14(4): 237–249.

Casciaro, T, and Piskorski, M.J (2005). Power Imbalance, Mutual Dependence, and Constraint Absorption: A closer look at resource dependence theory, *Administrative Science Quarterly* 50(2): 167–199.

Chattopadhyay, P, Glick, W.H, and Huber, G.P (2001). Organizational Actions in Response to Threats and Opportunities, *Academy of Management Journal* 44(5): 937–955.

Currie, W.L (1998). Using Multiple Suppliers to Mitigate the Risk of IT Outsourcing at ICI and Wessex Water, *Journal of Information Technology* **13**(3): 169–180.

Davis, G.F., and Cobb, J.A (2010). Resource Dependence Theory: Past and future, In C.B. Schoonhoven and F. Dobbin. (eds.) *Stanford's Organization Theory Renaissance, 1970–2000*, West Yorkshire, UK: Emerald Group Publishing, pp. 21–42.

Eisenhardt, K.M (1989). Building Theories from Case Study Research, *Academy of Management Review* **14**(4): 532–550.

Eisenhardt, K.M, and Graebner, M.E (2007). Theory Building from Cases: Opportunities and challenges, *Academy of Management Journal* **50**(1): 250–32.

Emerson, R.M (1962). Power-Dependence Relations, *American Sociological Review* **27**(1): 31–41.

Ethiraj, S.K, Kale, P, Krishnan, M.S, and Singh, J.V (2005). Where Do Capabilities Come From and How Do They Matter? A study in the software services industry, *Strategic Management Journal* **26**(1): 25–45.

Fennell, M, and Alexander, J.A (1987). Organizational Boundary Spanning in Institutionalized Environments, *Academy of Management Journal* **30**(3): 456–476.

Gargiulo, M (1993). Two-Step Leverage: Managing constraint in organizational politics, *Administrative Science Quarterly* **38**(1): 1–19.

Grewal, R, Johnson, J.L, and Sarker, S (2007). Crises in Business Markets: Implications for interfirm linkages, *Journal of the Academy of Marketing Science* **35**(3): 398–416.

Grewal, R, and Tansuhaj, P (2001). Building Organizational Capabilities for Managing Economic Crisis: The role of market orientation and strategic flexibility, *Journal of Marketing* **65**(2): 67–80.

Gulati, R, and Sytch, M (2007). Dependence Asymmetry and Joint Dependence in Interorganizational Relationships: Effects of embeddedness on a manufacturer's performance in procurement relationships, *Administrative Science Quarterly* **52**(1): 32–69.

Haried, P, and Ramamurthy, K (2009). Evaluating the Success in International Sourcing of Information Technology Projects: The need for a relational clientvendor approach, *Project Management Journal* **40**(3): 56–71.

Harris, S, and Sutton, R.I (1986). Functions of Parting Ceremonies in Dying Organizations, *Academy of Management Journal* **29**(1): 5–30.

He, Z.L, and Wong, P.K (2004). Exploration *vs* Exploitation: An empirical test of the ambidexterity hypothesis, *Organization Science* 15(4): 481–494.

Hillman, A.J, Withers, M.C, and Collins, B.J (2009). Resource Dependence Theory: A review, *Journal of Management* 35(6): 1404–1427.

Huang, R, Miranda, S, and Lee, J-N (2004).How Many Vendors Does It Take to Change a Bulb? Mitigating the risks of resource dependence in information technology outsourcing, In Proceedings of 25th International Conference on Information Systems, Washington, USA.

Jarvenpaa, S.L, and Mao, J.Y (2008). Operational Capabilities Development in Mediated Offshore Software Services Models, *Journal of Information Technology* 23(1): 3–17.

Javalgi, R.R.G, Dixit, A, and Scherer, R.F (2009). Outsourcing to Emerging Markets: Theoretical perspectives and policy implications, *Journal of International Management* 15(2): 156–168.

Jean, R.J.B, Sinkovics, R.R, and Kim, D (2010). Drivers and Performance Outcomes of Relationship Learning for Suppliers in Cross-Border Customer–Supplier Relationships: The role of communication culture, *Journal of International Marketing* 18(1): 63–85.

Kirca, A.H, Jayachandran, S, and Bearden, W.O (2005). Market Orientation: A meta-analytic review and assessment of its antecedents and impact on performance, *Journal of Marketing* 69(2): 24–41.

Lacity, M.C, Khan, S.A, and Willcocks, L.P (2009). A Review of the IT Outsourcing Literature: Insights for practice, *The Journal of Strategic Information Systems* 18(3): 130–146.

Lacity, M.C, Khan, S, Yan, A, and Willcocks, L.P (2010). A Review of the IT Outsourcing Empirical Literature and Future Research Directions, *Journal of Information Technology* 25(4): 395–433.

Lacity, M.C, and Willcocks, L.P (1998). An Empirical Investigation of Information Technology Sourcing Practices: Lessons from experience, *MIS Quarterly* 22(3): 363–408.

Lavie, D, Stettner, U, and Tushman, M.L (2010). Exploration and Exploitation Within and Across Organizations, *The Academy of Management Annals* 4(1): 109–155.

Lavie, D, and Rosenkopf, L (2006). Balancing Exploration and Exploitation in Alliance Formation, *Academy of Management Journal* 49(4): 797–818.

Lee, J.N, and Kim, Y.G. (1999). Effect of Partnership Quality on IS Outsourcing Success: Conceptual framework and empirical validation, *Journal of Management Information Systems* 15(4): 29–61.

Levina, N, and Ross, J.W (2003). From the Vendor's Perspective: Exploring the value proposition in information technology outsourcing, *MIS Quarterly* 27(3): 331–364.

Levinthal, D.A, and March, J.G (1993). The Myopia of Learning, *Strategic Management Journal* 14(S2): 95–112.

March, J.G (1991). Exploration and Exploitation in Organizational Learning, *Organization Science* 2(1): 71–87.

March, J.G (2006). Rationality, Foolishness, and Adaptive Intelligence, *Strategic Management Journal* 27(3): 201–214.

Martin, J.A (2011). Dynamic Managerial Capabilities and the Multibusiness Team: The role of episodic teams in executive leadership groups, *Organization Science* 22(1): 118–140.

Mathew, S.K (2011). Mitigation of Risks Due to Service Provider Behavior in Offshore Software Development: A relationship approach, *Strategic Outsourcing: An International Journal* 4(2): 179–200.

Meyer, A.D (1982). Adapting to Environmental Jolts, *Administrative Science Quarterly* 27(4): 515–537.

Meznar, M.B, and Nigh, D (1995). Buffer or Bridge? Environmental and organizational determinants of public affairs activities in American firms, *Academy of Management Journal* 38(4): 975–996.

Miles, M.B, and Huberman, A.M. (1994). *Qualitative Data Analysis: An expanded sourcebook*, 2nd edn, Beverly Hill, CA: Sage.

Nolan, J.F, Ritchie, P, and Rowcroft, J (2004). September 11 and the World Airline Financial Crisis, *Transport Reviews* 24(2): 239–255.

Park, N.K, and Mezias, J.M (2005). Before and After the Technology Sector Crash: The effect of environmental munificence on stock market response to alliances to E-Commerce firms, *Strategic Management Journal* 26(11): 987–1007.

Paulraj, A, and Chen, I.J (2007). Environmental Uncertainty and Strategic Supply Management: A resource dependence perspective and performance implications, *Journal of Supply Chain Management* 43(3): 29–42.

Pfeffer, J (1981). *Power in Organizations*, Marshfield, MA: Pitman.

Pfeffer, J (1987). A Resource Dependence Perspective on Interorganizational Relations, In M.S. Mizruchi and M. Schwartz (eds.) *Intercorporate Relations: The structural analysis of business*, Cambridge, UK: Cambridge University Press, pp. 22–55.

Pfeffer, J, and Salancik, G.R (1978). *The External Control of Organizations: A resource dependence perspective*, New York: Harper and Row.

Primo, M.A.M, Dooley, K, and Rungtusanatham, M.J (2007). Manufacturing Firm Reaction to Supplier Failure and Recovery, *International Journal of Operations & Production Management* **27**(3): 323–341.

Rao, M.T, Brown, C.V, and Perkins, W.C (2007). Host Country Resource Availability and Information System Control Mechanisms in Multinational Corporations: An empirical test of resource dependence theory, *Journal of Management Information Systems* **23**(4): 11–28.

Rothaermel, F.T (2001). Incumbent's Advantage Through Exploiting Complementary Assets via Interfirm Cooperation, *Strategic Management Journal* **22**(6–7): 687–699.

Rottman, J.W, and Lacity, M.C (2006). Proven Practices for Effectively Offshoring IT Work, *Sloan Management Review* **47**(3): 56–63.

Santos, F.M, and Eisenhardt, K.M. (2009). Constructing Markets and Organizing Boundaries: Entrepreneurial power in nascent fields, *Academy of Management Journal* **52**(4): 643–671.

Scott, W.R, and Davis, G.F (2007). *Organizations and Organizing: Rational, natural, and open systems perspectives*, Upper Saddle River, NJ: Pearson Prentice Hall.

Suarez, F.F, and Oliva, R (2002). Learning to Compete: Transforming firms in the face of radical environment change, *Business Strategy Review* **13**(3): 62–71.

Sydow, J, Schreyogg, G, and Koch, J (2009). Organizational Path Dependence: Opening the black box, *Academy of Management Review* **34**(4): 689–709.

Taylor, H (2007). Outsourced IT Projects from the Vendor Perspective: Different goals, different risks, *Journal of Global Information Management* **15**(2): 1–27.

Teece, D.J, Pisano, G, and Shuen, A (1997). Dynamic Capabilities and Strategic Management, *Strategic Management Journal* **18**(7): 509–533.

Thompson, J.D (1967). *Organizations in Action: Social science bases of administration*, New York: McGraw-Hill.

Ulrich, D, and Barney, J.B (1984). Perspectives in Organizations: Resource dependence, efficiency, and population, *Academy of Management Review* **9** (3): 471–481.

Wang, H-F, and Hong, W-K (2006). Managing Customer Profitability in a Competitive Market by Continuous Data Mining, *Industrial Marketing Management* **35**(6): 715–723.

Watjatrakul, B (2005). Determinants of IS Sourcing Decisions: A comparative study of transaction cost theory and the resource-based view, *Journal of Strategic Information Systems* **14**(4): 389–415.

Willcocks, L.P, Reynolds, P, and Feeny, D (2007). Evolving IS Capabilities to Leverage the External IT Services Market, *MIS Quarterly Executive* **6**(3): 127–145.

Yan, A, and Gray, B (1994). Bargaining Power, Management Control, and Performance in United States-China Joint Ventures: A comparative case study, *Academy of Management Journal* **37**(6): 1478–1517.

Yin, R.K (1994). *Case Study Research: Design and methods*, Thousand Oaks, CA: Sage.

Fang Su was a doctoral candidate in the School of Business, Renmin University of China. She got her Master's degree in Management from Renmin University of China in 2011. Her research has been published in *Journal of Information Technology Teaching Case*, Pacific Asia Conference on Information Systems (PACIS), and several Chinese journals. Her current areas of research include IT outsourcing, risk management, and organization change.

Ji-Ye Mao was a professor in the School of Business, Renmin University of China. Previously, he has taught at the University of Waterloo in Canada (1995–2001). He received his Ph.D. in MIS from the University of British Columbia (1995). His areas of research include behavioral and managerial issues related to the design and implementation of information systems, and IT outsourcing management. His research has appeared in *Journal of Management Information Systems, Journal of Information Technology, Journal of Association for Information Systems*, and various *Human-Computer Interaction journals*.

Sirkka L. Jarvenpaa is the James Bayless/Rauscher Pierce Refsnes Chair in Business Administration at the McCombs School of Business, University of Texas at Austin, where she is the director of the Center for Business,

Technology, and Law. She currently serves as the Director of Information Management Program at McCombs School of Business. She has held visiting professorships in leading business schools in the United States, Europe, and Asia. She is the coeditor in chief of the *Journal of Strategic Information Systems*. She has served as the editor-in-chief of the *Journal of Association for Information Systems* and as the senior editor of *Organization Science, Information Systems Research and MIS Quarterly*. She holds honorary doctorate degrees from the University of Jyvaskyla, Aalto University, and the University of Goteborg.

8

Operational Capabilities Development in Mediated Offshore Software Services Models

Sirkka L. Jarvenpaa and Ji-Ye Mao

Introduction

Offshore outsourcing, or offshoring, involves crossing national boundaries to purchase services. Although offshoring includes both activities contracted to independent third parties abroad and international insourcing to foreign subsidiaries, here we will only consider the former. Offshoring of services is critically dependent on a supply of providers (vendors) that have operational capabilities to offer comparative cost advantage, satisfactory quality, and on-time delivery despite the differences in distance, time zones, and culture (Carmel and Tjia 2005). Yet, the literature on information technology (IT) offshoring as well as

S.L. Jarvenpaa
Center for Business, Technology, and Law, University of Texas at Austin, Austin, TX, USA

J.-Y. Mao (✉)
School of Business, Renmin University of China, Beijing, PR, China
e-mail: jymao@ruc.edu.cn; jiyemao@yahoo.com

© The Author(s) 2017   **239**
L.P. Willcocks et al. (eds.), *Outsourcing and Offshoring Business Services*, DOI 10.1007/978-3-319-52651-5_8

outsourcing of IT services more generally has largely focused on customers (particularly in the USA and Europe) (e.g., Willcocks and Lacity 2000, 2007; Goles 2001). The vendor perspective has been much less studied (Levina and Ross 2003; Feeny et al. 2005; Borman 2006). In the context of offshoring, research is largely limited to India-based providers and the business models they use with their US customers (e.g., Rajkumar and Mani 2001; Kaiser and Hawk 2004; Vashistha and Vashistha 2006; Oshri et al. 2007).

In software services offshoring, China represents an understudied setting, yet an important one for several reasons. First, there are strong expectations of the Chinese software services industry's explosive growth in the coming years (Qu and Brocklehurst 2003). China's software services outsourcing reached RMB 2.6 billion (about US$340 million) in the first quarter of 2006. During the same time in 2007, the market increased to RMB 3.3 billion (about US$430 million) (Analysis International 2007). The development of the software industry is designated in China as a national priority with aggressive targets for export (Economic Daily, 2007). Second, the Chinese providers use business models that are different from those presented in the offshoring literature. The software export firms based in China are largely small- and medium-sized with heavy reliance on the *mediated offshoring business model* whereby a Chinese vendor delivers offshore software services to a larger foreign-based IT contractor (vendor) that interfaces with the end-client firms.

The mediated business model has both theoretical and practical implications for the development of the operational capabilities in the Chinese software services firms. To survive and grow, these firms must be able to develop operational capabilities that go beyond country-level comparative low labor costs that are shared by all the Chinese firms and by firms in many other low cost countries (Qu and Brocklehurst 2003). Yet, the development of those capabilities is impeded by the business model the firms deploy. Among the limiting factors are small-sized projects, low value-adding tasks, and limited opportunities to interface with the end client.

This paper focuses on the development of operational capabilities in the mediated business model. Operational capabilities are those involved in the provision of a service or a product. Prior literature on large vendors has found three types of operational capabilities of critical importance to IT vendor success: client-specific capabilities, process capabilities, and human resources capabilities (Rajkumar and Mani 2001; Levina and Ross 2003; Ethiraj et al. 2005). Although some capabilities cannot be deliberately created due to their rare existence or social complexities (e.g., culture), many capabilities reflect an evolutionary learning process in which an organization needs to invest financial, cognitive, and emotional resources (Zollo and Winter 2002). Deciding on what capabilities to build and how to build them are critical managerial choices for any firm, but the decision is particularly perennial for small- and middle-sized offshore software services firms with limited resource base. Capabilities development can sap critical resources without necessary returns and undermine not only firm growth but also survival (Sapienza et al. 2006). The current theories on the development of capabilities relate mainly to large firms or firms in mature economies (Zollo and Winter 2002; Zahra et al. 2006). Hence, the unique context of the current research can benefit both theory development and practice of global services offshoring.

In this paper, we advance theory by arguing that small- and medium-sized Chinese firms face major hurdles for developing their operational capabilities at least partly because of the mediated business model. Client-specific capabilities, process capabilities, and human resources capabilities are all affected by the small size of projects, low value-adding tasks, and lack of direct interaction with the end client. We also build theory of the mechanisms that Chinese firms use to overcome these challenges and develop the three sets of capabilities to accomplish profitable growth in a highly competitive industry. Our theorizing is based on interviews and interactions with industry experts and consultants as well as four case studies in Chinese firms where we conducted semi-structured in-depth interviews with knowledgeable informants including owners, senior management, project management, developers, human resources managers, and quality managers.

In this paper, we refer to the vendor as the firm supplying IT services and the client as the buyer of the IT services. The rest of the paper is organized as follows. In the next section, we present the background on the mediated model in China, operational capabilities in IT offshoring, and the learning perspective to the development of capabilities. Then, we present the research approach and methods. In the fourth section, we present the case analyzes on four vendors. Subsequently in the last section, we suggest some theoretical and practical implications from the cases followed by conclusion.

Theoretical Background: The Mediated Business Model, Operational Capabilities, and Capabilities Development

The information systems literature on offshore outsourcing is recent but rapidly increasing. Much of the literature focuses on client capabilities to manage offshore vendors (e.g., Nicholson and Sahay 2001), client decision processes of what, how, and when to offshore (Carmel and Agarwal 2002; Aron and Singh 2005; Rottman and Lacity 2006), transforming the client–vendor relationship from tactical to strategic (Kaiser and Hawk 2004), organizational form and location decisions (Aron and Singh 2005; Vestring et al. 2005), and the deployment of advanced software process approaches (Pries-Heje et al. 2005).

Although broad in issues covered, the literature is narrow in its geographic coverage. The offshore studies are mostly limited to India-based vendors (Nicholson and Sahay 2001; Rajkumar and Mani 2001; Kaiser and Hawk 2004; Aron and Singh 2005; Levina 2006; Rottman and Lacity 2006; Oshri et al. 2007). Other regions have been much less studied, such as Russia (Pries-Heje et al. 2005; Levina 2006), China[1] (Qu and Brocklehurst 2003), and Taiwan (Wu 2006).

Transaction cost economics has been the dominant theoretical paradigm in offshore sourcing (e.g., Qu and Brocklehurst 2003), although recently the theoretical frameworks have become more diverse

---

[1] The literature on offshoring to China (e.g., Kennedy and Clark 2006; Feenstra and Hanson 2005; Hsieh and Woo 2005) focuses on manufacturing and product outsourcing, not services outsourcing.

encompassing the systems dynamics approach (Dutta and Roy 2005), knowledge systems perspective (Garud and Kumaraswamy 2005), and the resource-based view of the firm (Wu 2006). The resource-based view of the firm (Penrose 1959; Barney 1991) is still debated, although largely an accepted theoretical lens in information systems research to examine how firm-specific capabilities are developed and how the capabilities contribute to firm performance (Gonzales et al. 2006).

Our focus is on capabilities development in a mediated business model. Only few empirical studies have examined offshore vendor capabilities development and largely from the vantage point of large India-based vendors that are independent players whose work is not contracted through other IT firms (e.g., Kaiser and Hawk 2004; Ethiraj et al. 2005). Hence, we break new ground by focusing on China and examining a mediated offshoring model.

Mediated Business Model in Chinese Software Services Firms: Drivers

The mediated business model is briefly mentioned in the literature (e.g., Rajkumar and Mani 2001; Ethiraj et al. 2005), but largely viewed as a transitory model during the early phases of a vendor's life. For example, Morstead and Blount (2003) associate the mediated model with Tier 2 vendors that have yet to mature to Tier 1 vendors.

The mediated model is common in the export business of Chinese software services to Japan (Qu and Brocklehurst 2003). Japan represents the largest market to Chinese firms (Hu et al. 2007). Similarly, China constitutes the main offshoring destination to Japan (OECD, 2007). According to Qu and Brocklehurst (2003: 62), 'China has at least managed to compete with India on an equal footing in the Japanese market.'

In the Chinese–Japanese offshoring services, the mediated business model developed over time. Initially, the Chinese firms provided on-site staffing to alleviate cost pressures that Japanese firms faced in early 1990s, but over time, the staff augmentation model was complemented or substituted with offshore development to deliver greater cost reduction to the Japanese firms. Expatriate Chinese who had worked in Japan started to set up offshore facilities in China.

In the mediated model, the *client* is not the end user of the software, but a Japanese IT company (see Fig. 8.1). The Japanese IT firm (client) contracts work with the Chinese software services firm (vendor) to carry out tasks such as program design, coding, and unit testing. The Japanese IT firm (client) performs the high-level functional design, and it might break the application to several different projects to be subcontracted to different Chinese vendors. It is also the client who integrates the different deliverables into a functioning system and manages the interactions with the *end client* (end user of the software such as bank) (Qu and Brocklehurst 2003).[2]

The mediated model competes primarily with country-level comparative low labor costs and less with skill or competence advantage (Carmel and Tjia 2005). Chinese firms face Japanese IT firms that maintain arguably the best quality control and most sophisticated process management in the world. Chinese process management capabilities lag behind. For example, in 2005, only 21.6% of the software services businesses in Beijing had been certified as capability maturity model (CMM)/CMMI level 3 or above, and only one of them reached CMMI level 5.

Drivers of mediated model. The drivers for the mediated model are multifold. Perhaps the primary ones are the lagging maturity in process capabilities and the fragmented market comprised of small-sized firms (Organisation for Economic Co-operation and Development (OECD) 2007). The largest Chinese vendor, Neusoft, has only 9000 employees (Neusoft 2006). The mediated model allows firms of small size and with limited process capabilities to enter the market. Indeed, the low entry barriers have triggered high levels of entry by new firms in China (Vashistha and Vashistha 2006). The growth has occurred despite the limited supply of managerial resources with experience in software industry and prior experience in client industry (Ju 2001).

The mediated model also helps to overcome the lack of robust partnership networks overseas. Chinese software firms are found to

---

[2] The material was supplemented with interviews with various experts in the industry during July 2004. The material is based on interviews with experts in the industry during July 2004.

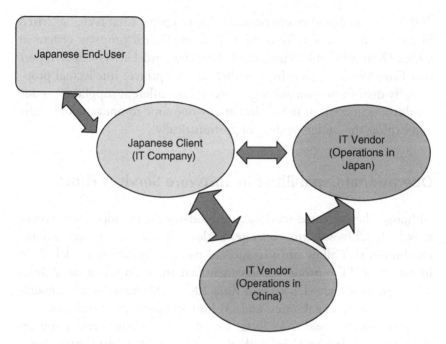

Fig. 8.1 Business models in Chinese–Japanese software services offshoring

have weak partnership networks compared to their Indian counterparts (Wu et al. 2005).

The mediated model overcomes some of the obstacles related to work culture and legal system. Although geographically, culturally, and linguistically, Chinese firms have an advantage with the Japanese clients compared to the Indian or Western firms, there are still major differences. The Chinese mentality of 'cha-bu-duo' (close enough is good enough) promotes ad hoc work practices. The mediated model lowers the client risk from ad hoc work practices. Gupta and Raval (1999) suggest that cultural issues can 'make or break an offshore project.'

Finally, the mediated model also increases the client's control over issues that pose legal risks. Chinese legal system, while improving, is an important impediment to China's growth as an offshoring destination (Organisation for Economic Co-operation and Development (OECD)

2007). The mediated model protects clients against what is characterized in the literature as a weak contract and intellectual property system in China (Kennedy and Clark 2006). Rottman and Lacity (2006) report that firms break projects into smaller ones to protect intellectual property. By distributing smaller segments among different suppliers, no one vendor sees enough of the project at any one time to understand it fully and exploit the understanding opportunistically.

Operational Capabilities in Software Services Firms

Although the mediated model accommodates the broader environment in which Chinese firms operate, little is known about operational capabilities that allow firms to succeed with the mediated model. Prior literature on IT outsourcing has identified three classes of capabilities with vendor success (Levina and Ross 2003): (1) client-specific capabilities, (2) process capabilities, and (3) human resources capabilities.

Client-specific capabilities focus on relational routines and resources that align vendor activities with the client's goals and priorities on a short- and long-term basis (Levina and Ross 2003; Ethiraj et al. 2005). The vendor must develop an understanding of the client's business and design cost-effective communication and interaction patterns (Rajkumar and Mani 2001). The vendor must have sufficient knowledge of the business (e.g., banking), functional domain (e.g., stock trading), and the specifics and idiosyncrasies of the client's operating environment. The vendor's interactions with clients must help clarify expectations and establish a sense of client trade-offs (user needs *vs* budget limits). Ongoing communication must clarify priorities, anticipate resource requirements, and report on issues and changes in project status.

Process capabilities relate to task delivery routines and resources that accomplish software design, development, and execution (Levina and Ross 2003; Ethiraj et al. 2005). The capabilities reflect technical competences, skills, and resources in systems and software development processes. The CMM developed by the Software Engineering Institute at Carnegie Mellon University is commonly used to improve software development processes. However, to improve process maturity requires substantial discipline and explicit learning investments in infrastructure, systems, and training programs (Ethiraj et al. 2005). This is likely the main reason for the relatively low percentage of Chinese vendors with higher levels of CMM/CMMI certification.

Human resources capabilities are associated with recruiting practices, training, and mentoring programs, designing jobs with a balanced mix of specialization and exposure to a variety of project tasks, and developing a performance appraisal and compensation systems (Levina and Ross 2003; Ferratt et al. 2005). Rotating employees across projects and tasks gives them opportunities to learn new skills and interact with different team members (Argote 1999). Individual career development plans, promotion from within, and alternative career hierarchies are all associated with beneficial effects on human resources capabilities (Levina and Ross 2003).

Levina and Ross (2003) found in a study of a large US vendor that the three operational capabilities had to be simultaneously present and mutually reinforcing each other. Their findings suggest that making choices among the three capabilities might be misguided, as all three capabilities must be developed in concert.

In the offshoring context, Ethiraj et al. (2005) examined client-specific and process management capabilities in the context of a large Indian offshore vendor. They found both capabilities to be associated with firm performance. The project management capabilities helped to maximize internal operational efficiencies and improve quality and profitability in rapidly maturing Indian software industry that targets offshore markets. In the software development literature more broadly, many have found that the increased levels of formalized routines in systems development improve quality and productivity (e.g., Herbsleb et al. 1997; Krishnan and Kellner 1999).

For client-specific capabilities, Ethiraj et al. (2005) note the key role of personnel used by offshore vendors at the client site (the so-called onsite personnel). A similar finding was reported by Kaiser and Hawk (2004) who examined the development of vendor and client capabilities among a large Indian vendor and US financial services clients. The onsite personnel was critical to ensure robust communication channels and develop a long-term relationship between the firms. In her study of a small Russian and

Indian provider, Levina (2006) found the boundary-spanning practices of middle managers at the client organization to be more critical for effective collaboration than the middle managers at the provider organization. Outside the offshoring and outsourcing literature, such middlemen are often labeled as relationship managers, account managers, client executives, or consultants (Iacono et al. 1995; Brown 1999).

In terms of human resources capabilities, Ethiraj et al. (2005) only mention the need to invest in training programs in new technologies and software processes for both developers and managers. Others, not specific to the offshoring literature, have noted that human resources practices are closely aligned with firm strategy (Youndt et al. 1996). Ferratt et al. (2005) review two human resources archetypes. Archetype 1 has a short-term transactional orientation that puts lower emphasis on firm-specific investments in terms of formal training and mentoring. Archetype 2 has a longer term relationship orientation that puts greater emphasis on worker participation in firm decisions, significant investment in formal training and mentoring. Following the notion of 'fit' (see Ferratt et al. 2005), firms competing primarily on comparative labor cost advantage would be expected to emphasize Archetype 1.

Development of Operational Capabilities in Mediated Offshoring Model

The mediated model has implications for the development of operational capabilities. The mediated model is associated with *small project size, low value-adding tasks*, and *limited interaction with the end client*. Qu and Brocklehurst (2003: 64) note that 'most Chinese suppliers are not even aware who the end users are.' Others have noted that Chinese firms have little contact with the end user's business except for at certain stages of project such as field support.[3] This limits the acquisition of client-specific capabilities particularly business domain knowledge and the development of robust communication routines. The high-level and high-paying work is retained by the Japanese IT firms, which leave low-level work to the Chinese vendors. The low-level work demands low technical skills from the Chinese developers. Therefore, the mediated model can also impede the development of human resources capabilities. Small-sized projects, low-valued tasks, and limited end-client interaction limit the degree of employee specialization as well as the variety of tasks that they are exposed to. In such an environment, the firms are challenged to develop meaningful career paths.

Although the mediated model can be constraining in terms of capabilities development, we counter argue that Japan–China offshore outsourcing presents an environment where Chinese vendors are able to overcome – at least partially – some of these constraints and develop their capabilities incrementally. Since the Chinese vendors work with Japanese clients (Japanese IT companies), which tend to possess strong process capabilities, it is an opportunity for the Chinese firm to learn and gain maturity. Also, the projects involve substantial knowledge transfer from the client to the vendors in terms of business knowledge and project management know-how. Japanese clients maintain a hands-on approach to project management, which allows them to assess quality, progress, and costs, and to take intervening actions if necessary, as they do in other industries (Liker and Choi 2004). The client's technical experts often remain on the vendor site for extended stay to introduce business requirements to the project team, perform design reviews, and monitor quality.

Learning mechanisms for developing capabilities. How are Chinese firms exploiting these opportunities to develop their capabilities despite the constraints of the mediated model? In the remainder of the paper, we take a learning perspective to the development of operational capabilities (Zollo and Winter 2002). Zollo and Winter (2002) distinguish between two types of learning mechanisms in capabilities development in large firms: (1) deliberate and explicit firm-specific investments and (2) implicit 'learning by doing.' The deliberate investments involve explicit knowledge articulation and knowledge codification mechanisms and require greater managerial and financial resources than the passive experiential processes of learning by doing. The explicit investments involve time and energy to engage in collective discussions, performance evaluation processes, and codification of knowledge in the form of manuals, blueprints, and project management software. The implicit learning by doing involves repeated and cumulative experiences. Both implicit and explicit categories of learning mechanisms result in improved performance, although the degree of improvement can be impacted by a variety of factors such as internal organizational processes and structures (Eisenhardt and Martin 2000).

The mix of learning mechanisms also depends on the characteristics of the capabilities to be developed (Zollo and Winter 2002). Ethiraj et al. (2005) argue specifically that implicit and tacit experience by doing is the dominant learning mechanism for client-specific capabilities, whereas improvements in process capabilities require explicit learning investments in infrastructure, systems, and training programs. By inference, Ethiraj et al. (2005) argue for explicit investments for human resources capabilities development.

Importantly, Ethiraj et al. (2005) focus on large firms. Zollo and Winter (2002) focused on large firms in mature economies and industries. We know of no study that has explicitly examined capabilities development in small- and medium-sized offshore software services firms, although studies exist on capabilities development in call centers (Pan et al. 2005) and IT hardware component sourcing (Wu 2006).

Research Method

Data collection took place in two phases. During the summer of 2004, the 2 researchers conducted 12 interviews to get a broad view of the software services industry in China. A diverse group of interviewees included developers (team and project leaders), user manager, senior managers, business consultants, senior analyst of a research firm, founders, and CEOs of software firms. The interviews were all held in Beijing and involved Americans, Chinese, and expatriate Chinese representing diverse enterprises that included a start-up, state-owned enterprise, foreign companies, and private Chinese firms. The interviewees were asked to help us understand the industry structure and macro-environment in which the Chinese software firms operate.

The second phase took place during the summer of 2005 and involved case studies in four software services firms in Beijing, China. The purpose of the case studies was to explore the capabilities development in small- and mid-sized Chinese firms. Case study research is appropriate in situations where the research question involves a 'how,' 'why,' or exploratory 'what' question, the investigator has no control over actual behavioral events, and the focus is on contemporary phenomenon (Yin 1989). The research presented in this paper fits all of these three criteria.

The four firms in Beijing were selected for three reasons. First, Beijing represents the largest base for software development and export, as well as the most rapid pace of growth in China. Second, the researchers had connections or could get referrals to the four firms in Beijing. Third, although all four firms were exporting software services, they varied in terms of backgrounds, sizes, and software services. Two of them were considered well-established services providers to Japan, whereas the other two were recent entrants to Japanese–Chinese outsourcing. One of the latter two was already established in American–European export markets. Three of them were founded by Chinese entrepreneurs and under the control of Chinese managers at the time of the study. The other one was a joint venture of the Japanese IT firm and a Chinese research institution. Although the ownership and management of this Japanese joint venture was quite different from others, we decided to keep it in the analysis to provide a contrast to the other three firms (see Tables 8.1 and 8.2).

The unit of analysis is the vendor company regarding the development of capabilities via various learning mechanisms. In each case, interviews were arranged through a senior executive of the target firm, and senior management including the CEO or President usually participated in the study (see Table 8.3). The interviews in each firm were scheduled in a top-down sequence, and this way assured open and active participation of lower-level personnel. Site visits had the duration of one or two working days. Each interview lasted from 1 to 2 hours. Both researchers participated in the interviews, and extensive notes were taken. In one of the four companies, a research assistant was also present at the interview to help transcribe the interviews. The two researchers then compared their notes and combined a consolidated version. In addition to interview data, relevant information in the public domain, such as company web sites, news releases, publicities in the media, and financial statements of public company, were all collected and used.

Table 8.1 Profile of the companies studied

Company	Primary services to Japan	No. of employees	Starting time	Ownership	Market
A – High growth publicly held firm	Testing, coding, design, architectural design	1200+ (72)[a]	1995	Listed in Hong Kong Stock Exchange, initially held by management and Japanese clients with minority interests of less than 15%	90+% to Japan
B – Slow growth small firm	Testing/Coding, some design	130 (60)	2001	Management and Japanese minorities	96% to Japan, 4% in China
C – Established firm, new to Japanese market	Staffing, some development	700+ (20)	1995	Management and strategic investors lately	90% Euro to US, 10% to Japan
D – Slow growth joint venture	Middleware software services	576 plus 100+ contractors	1994	Japanese parent – 90% Local partner – 10%	99% to Japan

[a] All numbers are based on summer 2005 data, and those in parentheses indicate the number of employees in Japan

Table 8.2 General background of the companies studied

Company	Background
A – High growth publicly held firm	Started up by two former university classmates, previously an experienced developer in Japan and a software sales representative in China for a multinational
	Publicly listed in Hong Kong Stock Exchange in 2004
	One of the largest vendors in China, with over 10 subsidiaries in China, and one in Japan, in 2006
B – Slow growth small firm	Founders previously worked in a Japanese joint venture company in China, or Japan
	Worked with many different clients and various types of projects
	Much of the initial work had been at the lower end of the value chain but increasingly moving up to higher value-adding work
C – Established firm, new to Japanese market	Ranked among the top 10 offshore vendors in China, founded by 4 former university classmates
	Outsourcing business to the Japanese market since 2003
	Initially staffing by internal people, and after some setbacks replaced them with Chinese developers with Japanese work experience
D – Slow growth joint venture	The Japanese parent IT firm and a Chinese research institution held 90% and 10% of the stakes, respectively. Ninety percent of the business was in middleware and platform software, e.g., web server, database server, directory server, and storage server
	Technological expertise spanned over 30–40 different middleware products plus mobile application software, and quality control tools
	The CEO emphasized, 'we are a technology company'

Prior to visiting the sites, an interview guide was prepared. For qualitative research, some (Eisenhardt 1989; Yin 1989) recommend predetermined research questions, themes, and data collection plans. Especially when multiple case studies are used, having predetermined data collection plans is helpful to make data collection more systematic

Table 8.3 Interviewees' job title

Company	Job titles
A	President, senior manager for training, quality assurance engineer, project manager, senior developer, developers
B	Co-founder and director, software development division; manager, quality assurance, project manager; developer, HR manager, internal training instructor
C	Chairman and CEO, VP marketing, GM Japanese business, marketing manager, Japanese business manager, PR manager
D	Chairman, president, director, systems development, project manager, group leader

and enhance comparability of results. Following these recommendations, the relevant literature in the area of capabilities management was reviewed and the interview guide developed (see Appendix).

Qualitative case analysis involved writing individual case write-ups based on the interviews and the archival data. These individual case write-ups were then 'coded' in terms of the client-specific, project management, and human resources management capabilities. The second author did the first round of the coding and the first author did the second round. The cross-case comparison of data explored the commonalities and differences in capabilities and in their development.

Results

In our analysis, we organized the case studies around the three types of capabilities identified as critical for vendor success in prior outsourcing and offshoring literature (Levina and Ross 2003; Ethiraj et al. 2005): client-specific capabilities, process capabilities, and human resources capabilities. Furthermore, we explored the learning mechanisms (Zollo and Winter 2002) in the development of those capabilities in the context of the mediated model of offshoring.

As synthesized in Table 8.4 and Fig. 8.1, all of the four firms heavily relied on tacit knowledge accumulation in building the client-specific capabilities although deliberate investments in firm-specific structures

Table 8.4 Learning mechanisms of the capabilities

Capabilities	Learning mechanisms
Client specific	Top management's overseas work experience, familiarity with the client culture, focus on long-term relationship with clients, and ability to creatively adapt client procedures to the suit the Chinese context
	Infrastructure development to cater client needs in safety and security measures, separate venues and work units, and communication channels for client
	Extensive use of onsite staffing and bridge engineers, including native Japanese, decentralized quality control (QA) function to cater to client needs
	Having client expert onsite, participating in training sponsored by clients
Process	ISO 9000:2000, CMM certification and related training; employee work report; standardized requirements documentation, templates, and design review procedures
	Adopting the client company's procedures, tools, QA systems, and philosophy ('accounting approach' to process management, 'quality first' and productivity)
	Deliberate effort in learning by doing, and then fixed as standard processes; extensive effort in 'optimizing' ISO processes based on client needs
	Learning from clients, e.g., by applying a US-based major client's sophisticated testing procedures for Japanese clients; managerial training
Human resources	Middle managers received external training, hiring fresh graduates and providing training regardless of firm sizes, and experienced expatriates; systematic career development systems
	Frequent visits by employees to the client firm; cultural blending activities; employees' self-driven learning
	'People-oriented' philosophy; flat organizational structure and friendly work environment; Japanese language training, opportunity to work overseas on client sites and raises to motivate employees
	Adopting tools and platforms in Japanese language; team-building camps and mandatory half a year's language training; employee development programs

and processes were also evident in the case data but to a lesser extent. The accumulation of learning about the client's business domain and hence the development of client-specific capabilities were strongest at middle and top management levels. The top management brought years of experience in responding to clients' needs and their business networks, or lack of thereof, in Japan. The repeated interactions had developed high levels of familiarity between the management of the vendor and the client. Lower levels of the firms had much fewer opportunities to gain customer-specific capabilities including domain knowledge.

Similar to client-specific capabilities, process capabilities were developed from both deliberate investments and experience accumulation. Although here, the explicit investments were more apparent than with the development of client-specific capabilities. Most of the firms also made proactive investments in deliberate learning of project management tools and methodologies. The firms had pursued CMM process maturity competences to varying extents, and more importantly each firm adapted the standard processes to their circumstances. The nature of the projects and the interface with the client, who possessed not only domain knowledge but also process capabilities and technical skills, appeared to be determining factors. This is a unique feature of the mediated model, influencing the mix of learning mechanisms by the Chinese vendors.

The practice to develop human resources capabilities was a response to the constraints of limited firm financial and managerial resources as well as the turnover of lower-level staff, which were common in such mediated business model. Skill development, promotional policies, encouragement, and incentives remained somewhat ad hoc except in Company C. Most visible learning and improvements took place at middle levels.

Next we discuss how the firms appeared to have overcome the constraints of the mediated model and be able to develop their capabilities. It is worth noting that one of the four companies, Company D, was a 90% Japanese subsidiary; therefore, it was not representative of the China vendors in general and better be used as a reference only for comparison.

Company A – High Growth Publicly Held Firm

Client-specific Capabilities

To a large extent, Company A's capabilities development occurred implicitly via close coupling with its clients. The bulk of the company's business came from a couple of very large Japanese IT firms that served end-user clients in the banking and securities industry (e.g., electronic trading solutions).

Initially, the President of the firm and co-founder had brought with him years of experience in responding to the clients' needs and their business networks in Japan. The repeated interactions had developed high levels of familiarity in the business domain and practices of the client. According to the President, 'trust with Japanese clients has evolved to such a stage over time that I can sign a contract without looking at the financial details. If I lose money on a particular project, they will make it up with extra in the next contract to me. If I bid 100 man-months and ended up using 80 only, we'd do more on usability and user interfaces, so that we are not too far off. If my client has to cancel a project, and asks me to share some of the loss, I'd do it because I know they'll pay me back in the next project.' The President continued, 'This is hard for the Indian companies to do, coming from a Western contract-based culture. This is in the root of east agricultural economies, which is something common between Chinese and Japanese culture.' On an ongoing basis, much of the learning of client-specific capabilities occurred implicitly at the project level through the Japanese technical experts whom the clients sent to the vendor site.

Company A had also made explicit investments to stay closely connected with the clients. But so did also their clients. Company A's divisions and departments were structured with direct correspondence to clients. In some cases, a client paid for a fixed charge to retain a department on long-term contracts for staff stability and guaranteed availability. This allowed the vendor to develop a work force with a high level of domain knowledge in a client's business. The staff for different clients were housed in different geographic locations as the way to manage security and protect customer confidentiality. In some cases, the technical development environments were physically disconnected from the company's infrastructure but connected with that of the client's. Company A had also dedicated onsite personnel, so-called bridge engineers for major projects at the client sites. Bridge engineers handled the day-to-day interaction between the client and the offshore vendor site.

Process Capabilities

Company A's process capabilities originated from the President's creative adaptation of the methodology he had learned in Japan to the local culture and client needs. The company continued to develop process capabilities via learning from the technical experts sent to the vendor site and from 'the bridge engineers.' The project teams used the client's software design and building platforms. Effort estimation was based on prior projects with the particular client.

Compared to learning from the clients via experience and adopting their sophisticated processes, it was less important for the firm to invest extensively in standard processes and quality standards beyond certain degrees. Two of the company's departments passed CMM 2 in 2002, but the company had made a conscious decision not to pursue CMM 3. One project manager remarked, 'CMM is a reference point for us, the client requirements are our guiding principles.' A developer remarked, 'we do not practice quality here as a straight-jacket.' To be responsive to client needs, the quality assurance function was decentralized. Most of the quality personnel resided within the departments serving specific clients. There was only a small central quality assurance group.

Human Resources Capabilities

Naturally, the frequent changes in requirements and rigid process adherence featured in the mediated model were not always welcome by the developers. One of them described how in one project, 90%

of the team quit because of fatigue and the lack of recognition of individual contribution. The developers also resented that their development environments were locked by the client's needs and had little opportunity to gain skills on new platforms. One described the work environment as '"blue-collar" style, equipped with basic furniture and crowded, and offices scattered in the city for cost-saving.' The developers complained about the lack of challenging projects that involved new technologies. The task features imposed a challenge for human resources capabilities development, to identify and train the people with the right skill set and attitudes. The company's strategy was focused on operational efficiency at the low-level coding and unit testing, which involved lower risks and required less capabilities. This meant low-level and low value-adding work for developers, however.

A key mechanism for human resources capabilities was recruitment. At the entry level, the company preferred to hire fresh college graduates as the main source of developers and then provided initial training for them. It was believed that people who had worked for 3–5 years become hard to train and indoctrinate with the company values. Training was conducted in a centralized intensive mode for 3 months, consisting of Japanese language training and working on prior client projects. Through this explicit process, codified knowledge is shared and transferred to new employees. Much of the task-specific and client-specific training occurred on the job later on.

Company B – Slow Growth Small Firm

Client-specific Capabilities

Similar to the case in Company A, a director of Company B attributed his firm's client-specific capabilities to 'our senior management's experience in working with Japanese clients.' The senior management had much tacit knowledge of the clients' operations and stayed in close daily contact with the client's project personnel. For middle- and lower-level personnel, developing client-specific capabilities was more challenging. Company B got disparate and relatively small projects from a diverse set of clients. A project manager described their work as 'hard bones with little meat to bite.'

Process Capabilities

Company B was still searching for the optimal mix of deliberate and experiential learning mechanisms to build its process capabilities. As the smallest and youngest company in our sample, Company B faced the biggest resource constraint. One of the examples given by a project manager was very telling of the reliance on ad hoc implicit learning. Many of his projects 'came with tight schedules and changing objectives. As a result, there were many versions to manage, a modification might affect not only just one module, but all modules need to be inspected for the rippling effect.' It was only through trial-and-error and gradual accumulation of experience that the project team figured out an approach in response. Their devised approach was to have full multi-rounds of internal discussion aimed at thorough understanding of the design. This approach was also used to deal with the client's desire for a joint discovery of requirements. As another example, an individual programmers' first reaction to technical challenges was to get on the internet or other forms of self-learning, rather than formal institutional infrastructure for support.

As the company grew and projects became larger, the increasingly complex work put pressure on the company to move away from ad hoc practices to developing a more disciplined approach. 'Initially, we had no methodological guidance for estimation and resourcing but after many setbacks we developed our own system of project management,' noted the quality manager. Some of the major clients, especially those that had developed closer relationships with the company through a history of successful past projects, had also sent their personnel to the company to train developers in process management.

To enhance its process capabilities, Company B augmented its learning from clients by investing in both standard processes and certification. The firm had achieved 1SO 9000 certification and was planning for CMM 3 at the time of our data collection. Part of the task of the central quality group was to optimize ISO processes, understand CMM requirements, and consolidate CMM and ISO into the firm's processes. This work was very hands-on. The quality manager reported, 'Right now, Q/A is involved in the full process of product development, but once the processes are mature, we [Q/A] might just follow the key points.' However, Company B struggled with finding the right balance between best-in-class processes and the client's tight delivery deadlines. A manager commented, 'indeed we have improved our competence through doing outsourcing for Japanese clients. Our clients have strict quality processes. We follow their processes as much we can and in the process, improve our own abilities.' One of the founders noted that 'our Japanese clients do not care much about the level of CMM because Japanese companies have their own procedures and processes. We are building a quality system to develop our own processes, a uniformed system to respond to all kinds of requirements from Japan. It allows a common response to all scenarios.'

Human Resources Capabilities

The strategy to develop human resources capabilities was similar to that of Company A, especially in terms of recruitment practices. The company hired entry-level developers mostly from universities in Beijing, whereas the middle tier was recruited from job fairs. New hires were asked to attend new employee training programs and redo a previously completed project in order to accumulate experience. As in Company A, Company B's human resource practices aimed to promote Japanese business customs that stressed the needs of the client company. Moreover, the company maintained a large percentage of the team onsite. The opportunity to work in Japan was used as both a reward and employee development practice.

Company C – Established Firm, New to the Japanese Market

Client-specific Capabilities

Having used to conducting business with Western clients, learning client-specific capabilities in the Japanese market had been challenging. The CEO noted that it took 2–3 years of work with Japanese customers before gaining their confidence. Technological know-how was not an entry barrier, but trusting relationships, as 'steady business comes after trust is established.' Because of the differences in business practices and customs, the firm was able to leverage little of its international reputation with European and US clients in Japan. To overcome this constraint, the firm used its human resources practices to build client-specific capabilities. The firm had hired several seasoned Chinese managers with work experience in Japan to develop client relationships.

Process Capabilities

As in the other companies, process capabilities were also built via learning from the clients as well as deliberate investments in certification. Company C heralded its superior ability to learn from clients by sending its personnel to the client's training courses. One of the founders explained, 'we send employees to our clients' project management training courses. We have adopted many procedures from our customers including their internal quality tools.' Company C passed ISO 9000 quality certification in 2004 and CMM 3 certification in December 2006, partly because its US clients valued the CMM certification. Regarding Japanese clients, a manager explained, 'Japanese have different methodologies, but still the general process thinking is the same. We can leverage our process management successes from the US and European side in our Japanese business.' In practice, this meant meeting the internal quality frameworks of Japanese clients using the CMM and ISO reference points internally.

Human Resources Capabilities

Company C had the most extensive and deliberate human resources capabilities among the four companies. The CEO's motto was 'great people come through good human resources processes,' which highlighted the central importance of human resources capabilities. The company had an extensive internal training program that focused not only on technical skills but also on cross-cultural and client management as well as process management. Such extensive training was exceptional in the software services industry in China. The company was known for its emphasis on learning and team-oriented culture. All of its senior managers had earned their EMBA degree on a part-time basis. After 3 years of service, employees were sponsored to study for a master's degree in software engineering from top software engineering schools.

Whereas the recruitment practice was similar to that of the competitors targeting fresh university graduates at the entry-level and veterans in the industry at the middle level, Company C invested more in formal training. For example, fresh graduates were given 3 months of training, conducted by two outside companies. For a project manager hired from overseas, he or she would be brought back to Beijing for at least 1 week for orientation and cultural immersion.

To complement deliberate learning mechanisms, the firm also created an environment to facilitate experiential learning. When asked for examples, the general manager of Japanese operations mentioned that despite the multimillion losses in his initial management responsibilities, he was still trusted by founders and given more opportunities. A junior employee compared his experience with his previous employer and noted how Company C went out of its way to assign work that leveraged his talents and strengths. Managers knew their employees well through social and training camps, which were exceptional among Chinese offshore firms.

Company D – Slow Growth Joint Venture Firm

Client-specific Capabilities

Because Company D was a joint venture of its client (Japanese IT firms), developing firm-specific capabilities was less of a priority. The senior management had previously worked in the client company. Members of the core team for key projects visited the parent company to experience the culture and to get to know the client. The company also invested and participated in cultural exchange visits to Japan organized by third parties for selected employees. One of the project managers told us that she had visited Japan 7 or 8 times during the last 5 years.

Process Capabilities

Compared to the other three firms, Company D invested heavily in quality certification processes and formal training curricula. The firm was the first software company in Beijing to reach CMM 5, the third or fourth in China. The strong emphasis on process capabilities and deliberate learning was consistent with the nature of project tasks, as Company D was specialized in software product development, mostly in complex middleware. According to the CEO, the reasons for CMM 5 certification included: (1) it was 'considered important to outsiders, particularly as we try to enter the Chinese market,' (2) it could serve as 'a reference point to the current quality system and help enhance the current process,' and (3) it could help improve an employee's pride in the company. Furthermore, by implementing explicit assessment of process capability, the company could gauge gaps and implement targeted improvements and become the 'No. 1 in quality and productivity in China' as a software services vendor. At the project level, the company claimed to have achieved deeper analysis and improved estimation skills. CMM 5 had led to the development of a risk management capability.

Human Resources Capabilities

The general recruitment practices of the firm not only were similar to that of competitors (e.g., targeting fresh university graduates for entry-level jobs) but also varied to some extent. For example, consistent with the nature of project tasks, the company had a high ratio of advanced degree holders (25% had a masters or Ph.D.). The company emphasized management training and preferred to promote from within. Developers interviewed by us also expressed a strong motivation and belief in continuous learning and recognized its importance.

To recap across the four cases, different firms emphasized somewhat different capabilities and employed different mechanisms to suit the mediated business model. Some of the contingences that appeared to affect capabilities development and learning mechanisms were vendor scale, project tasks, and client relationships. What also surfaced was the foundational nature of human resources capabilities.

Discussion

This study addresses an important issue for researchers and practitioners of offshoring of software services: how do offshore vendors develop their capabilities in a mediated offshoring business model? We used the three-part organizing framework for operational capabilities by the Levina and Ross (2003) study on outsourcing. The same capabilities have been studied by Ethiraj et al. (2005) in the offshoring context and found to relate to an offshore vendor's project success, but the vendor was a large established one in India providing offshoring services to the USA.

Our study focused on small- and medium-sized firms that do their business as subcontractors to Japanese IT firms to carry out tasks such as software testing and coding. To the extant literature and theoretical background, we made three important arguments. First, we suggested that the mediated model can help overcome some of the challenges that small- and medium-sized Chinese firms face including their small size, low maturity of process capabilities, and the weak legal environment, although the mediated model can also constrain the development of certain operational capabilities. Second, moving beyond the prior literature on the three types of capabilities, we further examined their relationships in the mediated model and identified the pivotal role of human resources capabilities. Third, we have integrated the three types of capabilities and the contingency factors into a synthesized model (shown in Fig. 8.3) and examined their two-way relationships between the capabilities and contingency factors. The latter is also seen as the outcome of capabilities development in a dynamic model.

The Mediated Model

All four companies studied have been in existence for several years. All of them were considered financially solvent according to the industry experts. The mediated model has also allowed considerable growth and financial success in two of the firms, and strong performance in the other two. In particular, Company A was ranked among the top five Chinese firms providing offshoring software services to Japan (in terms of revenues). Company C was ranked among the top 10 offshoring firms in China.

The more successful firms have managed to incrementally develop their capabilities following a successive path that allowed them to move beyond from coding and unit-testing work, to functional design, conceptual design, and even architectural design. Moving to larger and higher-level projects allowed the Chinese firms to deliver greater cost advantage and reap higher profitability, provided satisfactory quality, and on-time delivery could be assured.

The case studies suggest that the mediated model affects capabilities development; but rather than constraining, the mediated model shifts the development of capabilities from the vendor's organizational boundaries to the 'extended organizational forms' (Aron and Singh 2005). Long-term close relationships with clients facilitate the transfer of domain knowledge, IT technical knowledge, and process management.

Human resources capabilities appeared to be constrained by the mediated model. In some of the firms, only low-level ('blue collar') work is assigned for the vendor. In such a model (as in manufacturing), scale and operational efficiency are important for the vendors. The work can be tedious and result in low morale. Some of the Chinese developers conveyed a sentiment that they feel that they are required to act passively doing everything according to the design specifications, without any need to think on their own.

The constraint on human resources put pressure for the firms to invest in recruiting, development, and appraisal processes that fit with their strategy. Whereas firms shared common recruiting approaches, they also exhibited different human resources practice archetypes in training and employee development. For example, Company A and B followed Archetype 1: short-term orientation, reliance on recruiting rather than developing personnel, and lower emphasis on firm-specific investments on ongoing employee training. In contrast, Company C and D were more of Archetype 2: longer term orientation, promotion from within, significant investment in training and development. The finding might appear surprising given that the mediated model is seen to be primarily competing on efficiency and comparative low labor costs, which suggests Archetype 1. A closer examination of the cases reveals that the differences can be accounted for with the contingency factors such as project tasks, vendor scale, and client relationship.

Similar to the prevailing offshore models described in the literature (Kaiser and Hawk 2004; Ethiraj et al. 2005; Levina 2006; Oshri et al. 2007), the mediated model accommodated vendor personnel ('bridge engineers') at the client site. However, the bridge engineers' role was 'narrowed' compared to what has been described with the non-mediated offshore models. For example, Kaiser and Hawk (2004) describe how the on-site vendor personnel accomplished requirements determination for new applications and even conducted performance reviews for the client technical personnel. In a mediated model studied here, the bridge engineers' role seemed to be more limited in terms of functions as well as client access. Particularly early on the projects, the access was limited but widened as the project moved to testing and maintenance phases. The limited access was overcome by top management's prior experience in Japan and their ongoing close involvement in the projects.

The mediated model also required high levels of vendor flexibility and adaptive capability. With Japanese clients, requirements were specified at the high level at the start of the project. These requirements had to be further discovered and specified while the software was developed. This led to the client's sending their own technical personnel to the vendor locations to manage the discovery process. The vendor visits promoted learning, but they also could lead to cultural conflict. China and Japan have different customer service cultures. This is not unique to software services firms but prevails more generally between China and Japan. While Japanese clients tend to strive for perfection in customer services, which leads to the frequent changes in the requirements to satisfy their end clients, Chinese developers are under the influence of their 'cha-bu-duo' attitude ('close enough is good enough'). Human resources practices were needed to help employees to deal with these cultural conflicts.

Development of Operational Capabilities

As illustrated in the case analysis (e.g., see Fig. 8.2), the development of client-specific capabilities involved a variety of implicit and explicit learning mechanisms. Client-specific relationships were built on the basis of repeated interactions and contracts, investments in organizational design, and training in the client's service culture. Process capabilities were built by exploiting both implicit and explicit learning mechanisms as were human resources capabilities.

Prior literature (e.g., Levina and Ross 2003) has noted the complementary relationships among the capabilities. Our case studies extend their findings by anchoring human resources as the foundation for the development of the two other capabilities (see Fig. 8.2). In the mediated model, each company's success is tied to its capabilities development effort in recruiting various levels of talents, providing training in the client language, culture, technical skills, project management processes, and client-service mentality in the employees to cater to the clients' communication style, business requirements, and processes. The importance of human resources capabilities was stressed by all of the four companies and interviewees of all levels.

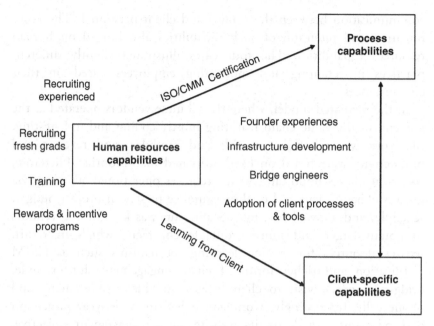

Fig. 8.2 Learning mechanisms in the four cases

Whereas the four companies exhibited varying degrees of reliance on formal process certification such as ISO and CMM/CMMI, the four companies had a nearly identical approach to recruiting at the entry level and middle level. To some extent, process capability is developed and acquired via a combination of recruiting and training.

In the mediated model, client-specific capabilities are manifested in the effective adoption of the client process, processes and procedures, communication styles, and business knowledge. As one of the managers pointed out the adoption of client processes and tools was important, and sometimes more so than ISO and CMM standards, because it could facilitate the mediating Japanese IT firm's effort to integrate the final systems, which may be developed by several parties. In addition to training, client-specific capabilities gradually developed via bridge engineers, staffing on client site (e.g., for system integration and support), client representatives' visit, and regular communication between the vendor and client personnel. The accumulation and retention of such capabilities also hinged on human resources capabilities. The four cases illustrated slightly different practices in retaining and motivating employees based on their circumstances.

In the mediated model, where the Chinese vendors operated at the low end of the value chain featuring mostly coding and unit-testing, the work was relatively portable and modular, and revenue and productivity were based on fixed estimated man-months. Therefore, cost control was important, which requires operational efficiency via process enhancement and quality assurance to stay in project budget, schedule, and allowed bug rate. Scaling up was key for the vendors to obtain larger and more profitable contracts, which in return secures resources for explicit learning mechanisms such as CMM certification and richer forms of client engagement, for example, bridge engineers, visit to client sites, and video conferencing and phone calls. Interestingly, Company B had its multi-year projection of head-count growth on its website, as a management objective. Figure 8.3 illustrates these interdependencies among the operational capabilities.

Contingent Nature of the Learning Mechanisms

We identified three factors that appeared to influence the adoption of learning mechanisms, and each of them will be elaborated below. First, the scale of the company is a factor. Larger ones possess more resources, bigger bargaining power, and internal specialization of organizational units and individuals (e.g., dedicated QA personal), which led to bigger and more profitable projects. Only after firms became larger could they afford the certification (CMM and ISO) and other forms of deliberate learning. Smaller firms such as Company B had to rely more upon experience accumulation. For example, as mentioned in the previous section, one of the teams had a lot of problems with the evolving client requirements, and it was only through trial-and-error that gradually they figured out their own way to deal with it.

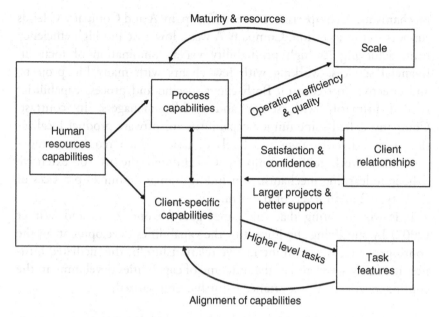

Fig. 8.3 The full model of capabilities development

Second, the strong orientation to long-term client relationship was a key factor in capabilities development in the mediated model. Through repeated interactions with two to three of its largest clients over time in supplying software services, Company A had developed not only a better understanding of the client's business requirements and customer service culture but also efficient approaches to deal with clients' style of communication and requirements specification. For example, the company had developed customer-specific development and review check lists. An interesting finding of the four case studies is that in these companies the client relationships tended to grow tighter for mutual gains, along with vendors' capabilities development and maturity. Tighter relationships might result in clients' financial investment in the vendor firm for minority interests, as in Company A and B.

Third, as predicted by Zollo and Winter (2002), a firm's task features (originating from its strategy) tend to exert influence on the learning mechanisms. A comparison between Company A and Company C lends support to this assertion. Company A was a low-cost and high efficiency firm, achieving its high profitability via a combination of focus in financial services, working with few clients with many big projects, and effective cost control. Both client-specific and process capabilities resided primarily with senior and middle managers. In contrast, Company C had some unique capabilities in software product localization and a diverse range and levels of tasks, which required a more specialized work force. Company C exhibited the use of extensive deliberate learning mechanisms including human resources practices of Archetype 2 at all levels of the firm.

It is worth noting that this paper goes beyond Zollo and Winter (2002) by specifying the impact of the capabilities development on the contingency factors in an interactive relationship for the mediated business model. Viewed also as the outcome of capabilities development, the contingency factors' importance is further emphasized.

Conclusion

Our findings contribute to the stream of research that emphasizes context-specific capabilities. The business model of the offshore vendor impacts its capabilities development. The learning mechanisms of capabilities can take on more generic mechanisms, however. Although the companies varied in the level and value of client-specific capabilities, interactions with clients were part of mechanisms to develop the capability in the different firms. Of course, some mechanisms can be specific to firms as well. For example, company A dealt with financial services firms that were particularly concerned with security and privacy. Security procedures that protected client confidentiality were a critical part of customer-specific capabilities.

Whereas this study focused on offshore vendors' perspective and has obvious implications for them, our findings have implications to clients as well, especially for overseas IT firms seeking cost-reduction. In managing relationships with vendors that lack both business domain knowledge and project management capabilities, deep relationships that embed knowledge transfer are critical. Deep relationships can evolve through escalation of project sizes via repeated interaction, to reach co-dependence to maximize mutual gains. However, at least initially, it is the client (the buyer of services) that must make implicit and explicit learning investments to help develop the vendor's capabilities.

Limitations and Future Studies

This research has several limitations. First, the sample is a convenience one, based on accessibility to vendors. All firms were headquartered in Beijing, where one of the authors is located and has industry contacts. However, our focus on Beijing-based vendors is appropriate, since Beijing is the largest base in China for software export. Second, as an exploratory study, this research is aimed at identifying issues concerning capabilities development, not to prove or test any theory. Also, our study lacked a longitudinal perspective. Our next step is to develop hypotheses and launch a survey of capabilities development by Chinese offshore software vendors. Moreover, the offshore outsourcing industry is under-going a consolidation process involving many merger and acquisition deals to create the necessary scale to compete internationally. This certainly will impact on the firms' operational capabilities and learning mechanisms and will be an interesting direction for future research. Future research also needs to attend to the financing structures and ownership that are undergoing rapid changes in China.

Appendix

Interview guide

How would you categorize your company's business?

- business model, financial structure
- products and services you offer to customers

- internal processes you use to produce and deliver those products and services
- customer, brand, and channel activities

What are your firm's core competencies? How have their changed over time?

What is your company's strategic intent? How does it differ from your closest competitors?

Where do the good ideas come from developing new capabilities or improving existing ones? Levels? Areas? Inside/Outside? Whose responsibility is it to develop capabilities?

How is 'capability improvement' and 'learning' incorporated into the incentive structure and performance review process of your employees and management? What about contracts with clients?

Describe a recent example of developing a core competency? What triggered it? Had you tried to improve it before?

How did the outsiders play a role...what made you choose this approach of developing it? Did you have some false starts? What were the risks? What have been the benefits from improving the capability?

Focus on one important project/external relationship? How has it helped you develop competencies?

What type of internal changes has the company experienced in building competences? Culture? Structure? Incentives? Technology? IP?

How would you expect the way your company managed capabilities *change* over the next 2 years? Why? Will the changes be incremental *vs* revolutionary?

Over the past 5 years, which companies in your industry have best capitalized on new capabilities? If appropriate, ask them to clarify the type of capabilities?

Does your way of managing core capabilities differ from the way that Western businesses tend to do it? Other Chinese firms? Indian firms?

References

Analysis International (2007). Analysis International Says China Offshore Software Outsourcing Market Reached RMB 3.315 in Q1 of 2007, http://english.analysys.com.cn/home/index.php, last accessed September 30, 2007

Argote, L. (1999). *Organizational Learning: Creating, retaining, and transferring knowledge*, MA: Kluwer Academic Publishers.

Aron, R, and Singh, J.V (2005). Getting Offshoring Right, *Harvard Business Review* **83**(12):135–140.

Barney, J.B. (1991). Firm Resources and Sustained Competitive Advantage, *Journal of Management* **17**(1):99–120.

Borman, M (2006). Applying Multiple Perspectives to the BPO Decision: A case study of call centres in Australia, *Journal of Information Technology* **21** (2):99–115.

Brown, C.Y (1999). Horizontal Mechanisms Under Differing IS Organization Contexts, *MIS Quarterly* **23**(3):421–454.

Carmel, E, and Agarwal, R (2002). The Maturation of Offshore Sourcing of Information Technology Work, *MIS Quarterly-Executive* **1**(2):65–77.

Carmel, E, and Tjia, P (2005). *Offshoring Information Technology: Sourcing and outsourcing to a global workforce*, Cambridge: Cambridge University Press.

Dutta, A, and Roy, R (2005). Offshore Outsourcing: A dynamic causal model of counteracting forces, *Journal of Management Information Systems* **22** (2):15–35.

Economic Daily (2007). Second Batch of Chinese Service Outsourcing Cities, 1/7/2007.

Eisenhardt, K, and Martin, J (2000). Dynamic Capabilities: What are they?, *Strategic Management Journal.* **21**: 1105–1121.

Eisenhardt, K.M (1989). Building Theories from Case Study Research, *Academy of Management Review* **14**(4):532–550.

Ethiraj, S.K, Kale, P, Krishnan, M.S., and Singh, J.V (2005). Where Do Capabilities Come From and How Do they Matter? A Study in the Software Services Industry, *Strategic Management Journal.* **26**: 25–45.

Feenstra, R.C, and Hanson, G.H (2005). Ownership and Control in Outsourcing to China: Estimating the property-rights theory of the firm, *Quarterly Journal of Economics* **120**(2):729–761.

Feeny, D, Lacity, M, and Willcocks, L.P (2005). Taking the Measure of Outsourcing Providers, *MIT Sloan Management Review* **46**(3):41–48.

Ferratt, T.W, Agarwal, R, Brown, C.V, and Moore, J.E (2005). IT Human Resource Management Configurations and IT Turnover: Theoretical synthesis and empirical analysis, *Information Systems Research* **16**(3):237–255.

Garud, R, and Kumaraswamy, A (2005). Vicious and Virtuous Circles in the Management of Knowledge: The case of Infosys technologies, *MIS Quarterly* **29**(1):9–33.

Goles, T (2001). The Impact of Client–Vendor Relationship on Outsourcing Success, Unpublished Ph.D. Dissertation, University of Houston, Houston, TX.

Gonzales, R, Gasco, J, and Llopis, J (2006). Information Systems Outsourcing: A literature analysis, *Information & Management* **43**(7):821–834.

Gupta, U, and Raval, V (1999). Critical Success Factors for Anchoring Offshore Projects, *Information Strategy* **15**(2):21–27.

Herbsleb, J, Zubrow, D., Goldenson, D., Hayes, W, and Paulk, M (1997). Software Quality and the Capability Maturity Model, *Communications of the ACM* **40**(6):30–40.

Hsieh, C.-T, and Woo, K.T (2005). The Impact of Outsourcing to China on Hong Kong's Labor Market, *The American Economic Review* **95** (5):1673–1687.

Hu, W, Chen, Y, Fan, Y, and Cao, K. (2007). Software Outsourcing in Beijing: Fundamentals, Trends, and Implications, Working Paper, Renmin University of China.

Iacono, C.S, Subramani, M, and Henderson, J.C. (1995). Entrepreneur or Intermediary: The nature of the relationship Manager's job, *Proceedings of the 16th International Conference on Information Systems*, Amsterdam, 289–3001.

Ju, D (2001). China's Budding Software Industry, *IEEE Software* **18**(3):92–95.

Kaiser, K, and Hawk, S. (2004). Evolution of Offshore Software Development: From outsourcing to co-sourcing, *MIS Quarterly Executive* **3**(2):69–81.

Kennedy, G, and Clark, G (2006). Outsourcing to China – Risks and Benefits, *The Computer Law and Security Report* **22**(3):250–253.

Krishnan, M.S, and Kellner, M.I (1999). Measuring Process Consistency: Implications for reducing software defects, *IEEE Transactions on Software Engineering* **25**(6):800–815.

Levina, N. (2006). Collaborating Across Boundaries in a Global Economy: Do Organizational Boundaries and Country Contexts Matter?, Twenty-Seventh International Conference on Information Systems (Milwaukee), pp. 627–542

Levina, N, and Ross, J.W (2003). From the Vendor's Perspective: Exploring the value proposition in information technology outsourcing, *MIS Quarterly* **27**(3):331–364.

Liker, J.K, and Choi, T.Y (2004). Building Deep Supplier Relationships, *Harvard Business Review* **82**(12):104–113.

Morstead, S, and Blount, G (2003). *Offshore Ready: Strategies to plan & profit from offshore IT-enabled services*, USA: ISANI Press.

Neusoft (2006) http://www.neusoft.com/en/news/html/20060705/ 778123936.html (last accessed on December 15, 2006).

Nicholson, B., and Sahay, S (2001). Some Political and Cultural Issues in the Globalization of Software Development: Case experience from Britain and India, *Information and Organization.* **11**: 25–43.

Organisation for Economic Co-operation and Development (OECD) (2007). Is China the New Centre for Offshoring of IT and ICT-enabled Services?, March 29 2007, JT03224696.

Oshri, I, Kotlarsky, J, and Willcocks, L. (2007). Managing Dispersed Expertise in IT Offshore Outsourcing: Lessons from Tata Consultancy Services, *MIS Quarterly Executive* **6**(2):53–65.

Pan, S, Pan, G, and Hsieh, M.J (2005). A Dual-Level Analysis of the Capability Development Process: A case study of TT&T, *Journal of the American Society for Information Science and Technology* **57**(13):1814–1829.

Penrose, E.T. (1959). *The Theory of the Growth of the Firm*, New York, Wiley.

Pries-Heje, J, Baskerville, R, and Hansen, G.I (2005). Strategy Models for Enabling Offshore Outsourcing: Russian short-cycle-time software development, *Information Technology for Development* **11**(1):5–30.

Qu, Z, and Brocklehurst, M. (2003). What will it Take for China to Become a Competitive Force in Offshore Outsourcing? An Analysis of the Role of Transaction Costs in Supplier Selection, *Journal of Information Technology* **18**(1):53–67.

Rajkumar, T.M., and Mani, R.V.S. (2001). Offshore Software Development: The view from Indian suppliers, *Information Systems Management.* **18**: 63–73.

Rottman, J.W, and Lacity, M.C (2006). Proven Practice Effectively Offshoring IT Work, *MIT Sloan Management Review* **47**(3):56–63.

Sapienza, H.J, Autio, E, George, G, and Zahra, S.A (2006). A Capabilities Perspective on the Effects of Early Internationalization of Firm Survival and Growth, *Academy of Management Review* **31**(4):914–933.

Vashistha, A, and Vashistha, A (2006). *The Offshore Nation: strategies for success in global outsourcing and offshoring*, New York: McGraw-Hill.

Vestring, T, Rouse, T, and Reinert, U (2005). Hedge Your Offshoring Bets, *MIT Sloan Management Review* **46**(3):27–29.

Willcocks, L., and Lacity, M (2007). *Global Sourcing of Business and IT Services*, London: Palgrave.

Willcocks, L, and Lacity, M.C. (2000). Relationships in IT Outsourcing: A stakeholder perspective, In R. Zmud (ed.) *Framing the Domains of IT Management*, Cincinnati, OH: Pinnaflex Inc., pp. 355–384.

Wu, L.-Y (2006). Resources, Dynamic Capabilities and Performance in a Dynamic Environment: Perceptions in Taiwanese IT enterprises, *Information and Management*. **43**: 447–454.

Wu, Q, Klincewicz, K, and Miyazaki, K. (2005). Sectoral Systems of Innovation in Asia: Partnership networks of software companies in China and India, Working paper, Graduate School of Innovation Management, Tokyo Institute of Technology, 16 December 2005

Yin, R.K (1989). *Case Study Research Design and Methods*, 5th Edition, Newbury Park, CA: Sage Publications.

Youndt, M.A, Snell, S.A, Dean, J.W, and Lepak, D.P (1996). Human Resource Management, Manufacturing Strategy, and Firm Performance, *Academy of Management Journal* **39**(4):836–866.

Zahra, S.A, Sapienza, H.J, and Davidsson, P (2006). Entrepreneurship and Dynamic Capabilities, A review, model, and research agenda, *Journal of Management Studies* **43**(4):917–955.

Zollo, M, and Winter, S.G. (2002). Deliberate Learning and the Evolution of Dynamic Capabilities, *Organization Science* **13**(3):339–351.

Sirkka L Jarvenpaa is the James Bayless/Rauscher Pierce Refsnes Chair in Business Administration at the University of Texas at Austin. She holds a Ph.D. and MBA from the University of Minnesota, and BS from the Bowling Green State University. She is the Director of the Center for Business, Technology, and Law at the McCombs School of Business, University of Texas at Austin. She is the coeditor in chief of the *Journal of Strategic Information Systems*. She has served as the editor-in-chief of the *Journal of Association for Information Systems* and as the senior editor of *Information Systems Research* and *MIS Quarterly*. Her research interests are in the area of strategy and policy of information management.

Ji-Ye Mao was a Professor in the School of Business, Renmin University of China. Prior to appointment, he taught at the University of Waterloo in

Canada (1995–2001, tenured in 2000), and the City University of Hong Kong. In addition, he was a Visiting Scientist at the IBM Toronto Lab (User-Centred Design Lab, 2000–2001). He holds a Ph.D. in MIS from the University of British Columbia (1995), MBA from McGill University, and B. Eng. from Renmin University (1985). His areas of research include user participation in the design and implementation of information systems, human–computer interaction (HCI), and IT outsourcing management. His research has appeared in *Journal of Management Information Systems, Communications of the ACM, International Journals of Human–Computer Studies*, and other leading journals of HCI.

9

A Dynamic Model of Offshore Software Development

Jason Dedrick, Erran Carmel
and Kenneth L. Kraemer

Introduction

As the offshoring of knowledge work has accelerated, theoretical models to explain the phenomenon have not kept up. Most theoretical models assume a static transactional relationship between factors that lead to a binary offshoring decision. Such models do not take into account the mix of sourcing choices at the level of a firm, nor do they consider dynamic changes over time. As a result, it is difficult to predict the extent to which the growth of offshoring will continue, and what

J. Dedrick (✉)
School of Information Studies, Syracuse University, Syracuse, NY, USA

E. Carmel
Kogod School of Business, American University, Washington, DC, USA

K.L. Kraemer
Personal Computing Industry Center, University of California, Irvine, CA, USA

© The Author(s) 2017   **281**
L.P. Willcocks et al. (eds.), *Outsourcing and Offshoring Business Services*, DOI 10.1007/978-3-319-52651-5_9

its implications might be. This paper helps to address the issue by developing a dynamic model of offshore software development.

The pace of offshoring has been striking. India's exports of software, business processes, and information technology (IT) services grew from $12.9 billion in 2004 to $31.3 billion in 2007 (Nasscom 2008), and offshoring has grown rapidly in places such as Israel, China, the Philippines, and Russia. IBM alone hired 90,000 workers in low-cost countries over 3 years ending in 2007 (Hamm and Schneyer 2008), and other IT companies such as Accenture, Oracle, and EDS hired aggressively in offshore locations. Companies in other industries moved internal IT operations offshore or outsourced to offshore IT service providers such as Infosys, TCS, and Wipro.

There has been a surge in academic research on offshoring since around 2007. For example, special issues of *MIS Quarterly*, the *Journal of Information Technology*, and the *Journal of Operations Management* have been published on offshoring. Other empirical research has looked at offshore sourcing of business processes (Tanriverdi et al. 2007) and the global disaggregation of service occupations (Mithas and Whitaker 2007).

However, there is still a need for more complete conceptual models to understand the drivers and process of offshore sourcing. We use qualitative research on the offshore migration of software services by major US companies to develop a dynamic model of sourcing. A dynamic model is useful in understanding the adoption of a practice such as offshoring that can take place over time with each company having its own trajectory.

We find that the offshore sourcing decision is driven by powerful economic forces, primarily cost pressures, access to new sources of skilled workers, and the opening of fast-growing markets outside the developed world. The sourcing decision also is influenced by the nature of the activity, including its modularity and maturity, and by the management practices and capabilities of firms making the sourcing decisions.

Yet the relationships are not unidirectional, nor static. Rather, they are iterative and dynamic, involving feedback loops, learning cycles, and cumulative effects over time. The element of time has been introduced analytically in the offshoring literature by Dutta and Roy (2005), but while Dutta and Roy study offshoring at the country level, we look at the firm level. We find an iterative process as the sourcing decision is repeated with each new project/task/process that is rolled out. As firms source activities offshore, they manage the process proactively to facilitate further offshoring. Such management practices can change the very nature of the activity, making it more amenable to offshoring. Meanwhile, future sourcing decisions are influenced by the mix of capabilities and preferences left from prior decisions.

Our dynamic model improves on static models by accounting for such changes over time. The implication of our model is that globalization of knowledge work (such as software development) may go further and faster than a static analysis would suggest. That is, firms continue to look for and find new opportunities to reduce costs and gain access to skills and markets, creating greater capabilities in offshore locations and pulling even more activities offshore in a spiral of accelerated migrations.

Background on Offshoring

Our model building in this paper is set in the domain of globalization and offshoring. Therefore, we briefly summarize key dynamics of the increase in globalization and offshoring in recent decades.

Globalization has been led by multinational corporations (MNCs) looking for new market opportunities and sources of low cost natural and human resources. Changes in the global economic environment, including trade and financial liberalization, and falling transportation and communication costs, facilitated globalization.

The first wave of globalization mostly involved manufacturing, as disaggregation of production processes enabled manufacturing to move offshore, and in many cases, to be outsourced to other firms (Sturgeon 2002). However, during this earlier era, most higher skilled work – such as R&D, engineering, administration, and marketing – remained under the firm's control and usually in its home country. The trend was toward a division of labor in which developing countries did physical production work and developed countries specialized in knowledge work.

This division of labor has changed in recent years, however, with the well-publicized trend toward offshoring of services to developing countries. Beginning with call centers and software development, and expanding to include product development, back-end financial and legal services, and even R&D, more and more knowledge work has moved offshore (Lewin and Peeters 2006).

These trends raised the questions of why offshoring was suddenly growing so fast and how far it would go. There have been several attempts to identify and quantify the number of occupations and jobs that could, or were likely to, end up offshore (ACM Job Migration Task Force 2006). Forrester research estimated that 3.3 million high tech and service jobs would move offshore from the USA by 2015 (Hilsenrath 2004), whereas Blinder (2007) found that 28–42 million service jobs in the US economy could at least potentially be moved offshore. These analyses involve identifying characteristics of an activity or occupation that make it easier or harder to move offshore, and then adding up the number of jobs that fall in the 'offshorable' category. They are not based on a well-defined conceptual model of firm behavior with regard to offshoring, nor do they incorporate factors that may accelerate or slow the process over time.

In 'Theory and foundation model' section, we review the literature on offshore drivers and present a foundational model based on the literature. In the 'Research methodology' section, we describe our fieldwork, protocol, and data sources. In the 'Factors influencing sourcing decisions' section, we report the results of our research on the key factors influencing offshore decisions. In 'A dynamic model of offshore sourcing' section, we present our complete model and map our cases back to that model. The 'Conclusion' section discusses our contributions and implications, whereas the 'Limitations and future research' section acknowledges limitations of our small number of case studies and suggests future directions for research.

Theory and Foundational Model

Literature Review

Various theories have been employed in studies of sourcing decisions. One is transaction cost economics (TCE), which is used primarily to explain the boundaries of a firm, that is, why it carries out some activities within the firm's hierarchy, even when the market offers a lower cost alternative. TCE focuses on the risk of opportunism by trading partners and other coordination costs associated with market transactions (Williamson 1979; Clemons et al. 1993). Although TCE focuses on the market *vs* hierarchy sourcing decision, it also has been used to hypothesize when firms will locate activities offshore (Tanriverdi et al. 2007). Limitations of TCE in explaining IT sourcing decisions have been identified (Willcocks and Lacity 1995) and have led to the adoption of other frameworks as alternatives or complements. For instance, Dibbern et al. (2008) apply TCE and the knowledge-based view of the firm, as well as country-specific factors, to explain extra costs faced by clients in offshore outsourcing relationships. The knowledge-based view brings firm characteristics and capabilities into the picture, along with economic and transactional factors. It also allows for dynamic effects such as feedback or learning loops, in which firm characteristics and capabilities can evolve over time in response to experience and the development of new knowledge (Jensen 2005).

Modular systems theory has been used to explain how the nature of products or processes can affect sourcing decisions (Sanchez and Mahoney 1996; Baldwin and Clark 1997; Schilling and Steensma 2001). This theory proposes that loosely coupled product or process interfaces lower coordination costs and facilitate the use of flexible organizational forms such as contract manufacturing and outsourcing. There are conceptual arguments and empirical evidence that modularity is associated with greater use of offshoring (Sargent and Meares 2006; Tanriverdi et al. 2007). So far, no dominant theory has been established, but given the complexity of the process, it is likely that any comprehensive explanation of offshoring will draw on multiple theories.

Foundational Model: Factors Influencing Offshore Sourcing Decisions

Many factors have been posited to influence the sourcing decision, for both outsourcing and offshoring. These include economic drivers, the nature of the activity, and firm-level management practices and capabilities. The relationships among these are illustrated in Fig. 9.1 and elaborated below. In the subsequent section, we will enhance this foundational model with additional factors and dynamic feedback loops based on findings from our case studies.

Sourcing Decision

The sourcing decision we are concerned with is whether software development is carried out in the home country of the parent firm (onshore) or in a foreign (offshore) location, and whether it is done by the firm

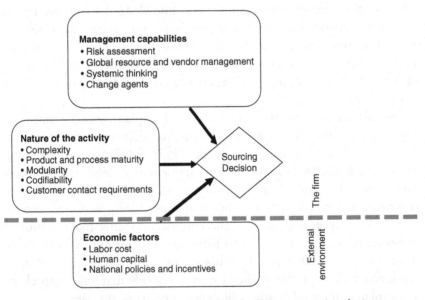

Fig. 9.1 Foundational conceptual model of offshore sourcing factors

(in-house/captive) or by an outside firm (outsourced) (Sobol and Apte 1995). The dimensions of the decision can be represented in a 2 × 2 matrix, with four potential sourcing options (Fig. 9.2) (Metters 2008). A sourcing decision is made for each development project, and sometimes for each activity/phase within a project – for example, design might be done inside the firm and onshore, whereas coding and testing are outsourced to an offshore provider.

There are three sets of independent variables in the foundational model, each of which include factors that influence the sourcing decision. Prior research on factors that influence the location of knowledge work has included economic factors, the nature of the activity being sourced, and the capabilities of client and vendor firms (Dibbern et al. 2008).

Economic Factors

Economic factors include labor cost differences across countries, availability of skilled workers, and access to foreign markets (Sobol and Apte 1995; Sargent and Meares 2006; Metters 2008). Other factors include

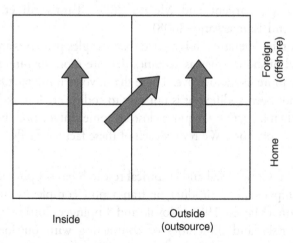

Fig. 9.2 Classic 2 × 2 sourcing decision matrix with arrows indicating the direction of the decisions of interest to this paper.

government incentives or barriers, and cost and quality of infrastructure (Porter 1990; Dutta and Roy 2005; Heeks 2007).

Related to purely economic factors are the legal, cultural, and social context of both the sending (home) and receiving (host) countries, which determine the broader environment in which offshoring occurs. These include intellectual property and other legal protections in receiving countries, privacy laws, and public pressure against offshoring in the sending country, and the compatibility of business cultures in sending and receiving countries (Kshetri 2007). Like economic factors, they are external to the firm and the activity.

Nature of the Activity

A second major group of factors involves the nature of the activity being considered for offshoring. These factors are consistent with the view that transaction costs associated with certain types of interactions can favor internalizing some activities, even when production costs are lower in market transactions (Williamson 1979; Clemons et al. 1993). The impact of the nature of an activity on sourcing decisions has been well studied in the outsourcing literature and more recently in studies of offshoring (e.g., Sargent and Meares 2006; Tanriverdi et al. 2007; Youngdahl and Ramaswamy 2008).

In the sourcing literature, it is argued that complex processes are less likely to be moved offshore, whereas activities that are more mature, stable, and modular are more likely to move. Those that involve more tacit knowledge, which has not been codified or is not easy to codify, are less likely to move offshore. When an activity requires close customer interaction, it also is less likely to move offshore. We review each of these factors briefly.

- *Complexity.* Conceptual and empirical research has supported a positive relationship between product or transaction complexity and vertical integration (Masten 1984; Novak and Eppinger 2001). It is argued that the risks and difficulties of contracting with outside suppliers become greater as complexity increases. The same logic applies to offshoring: as complexity increases, so does the need for additional coordination, thus adding to the cost and difficulty of working across distances (Sargent and Meares 2006; Hirschheim et al. 2007). However, Aron and Singh (2005) argue that even complex processes can be offshored if they can be codified.

- *Product and process maturity.* Firms will find it easier to offshore more mature products and processes, which are well known and understood and for which the development process is more predictable (Banker et al. 2006). As applications become more stable and mature, with fewer change requests, it is easier to move them offshore (Sargent and Meares 2006). When a system is unstable or there are many change requests from the customer, it is more difficult to manage offshore, and therefore less likely to be moved.

- *Codifiability.* Codification of knowledge makes it easier to transfer across firm boundaries and geographic distance (Zander and Kogut 1995; Youngdahl and Ramaswamy 2008). It is more difficult to transfer tacit knowledge. Such knowledge resides in the minds of individuals, requires experience to understand, or may be embedded within a certain social context, making it difficult to specify or communicate outside that context (Polanyi 1983). Work that involves higher degrees of tacit knowledge is thus posited to be less likely to be moved offshore.

- *Modularity.* Modular activities are defined as those which can be performed independently and then later integrated (Schilling and Steensma 2001). When modularity is low, knowledge activities are difficult to separate from each other because the performance of one element depends on integration with another or because work at one stage in the process must be done in a way that it does not cause problems at the next stage. This situation calls for close and frequent communication to iterate and solve problems and makes offshoring more difficult. By contrast, when modularity is high, it is easier to carry out separate tasks in different locations. The relationship of sourcing decisions to modularity has been argued conceptually (e.g., Sanchez and Mahoney 1996; Schilling and Steensma 2001; Langlois 2006) and modularity has been linked empirically to a greater likelihood of offshoring of knowledge work (Tanriverdi et al. 2007).

- *Customer contact requirements.* When knowledge work involves a high level of customer interaction, it is less likely to be moved offshore (unless the customer is offshore) (Youngdahl and Ramaswamy 2008). This can be the case for a number of activities, from business requirements analysis to implementation and training, all of which require close interaction with the end user (Mithas and Whitaker 2007).

Management Practices and Capabilities

We turn next to a set of factors that involve the management practices and capabilities of the offshoring firm and its potential outsourcing partners. Capabilities have been defined as 'a distinctive set of human resource-based skills, orientations, attitudes, motivations, and behaviors that have the potential... to contribute to achieving specific activities and influencing business performance' (Willcocks and Feeny 2006: 49). Feeny and Willcocks (1998: 10) identify business and IT vision, IT architecture design, and delivery of information systems (IS) services as core capabilities that enable outsourcing. Likewise, management practices and capabilities have been identified as enablers of offshoring (e.g., Aron and Singh 2005; Leonardi and Bailey 2008; Ramasubbu et al. 2008).

Some management practices and capabilities that have been posited to influence offshoring are as follows:

- *Risk assessment.* The potential benefits of offshoring can be analyzed in relatively straightforward economic terms, that is, they can be calculated using labor cost differences or the potential value of entering a new market. By contrast, the potential cost and risk of offshoring are not so easily measured and can go far beyond the direct cost of the project, especially if strategic processes are involved. As a result, risk assessment has been identified as a key capability enabling offshoring (Aron and Singh 2005).
- *Systemic thinking.* In order to go offshore successfully, firms need to be able to think strategically and develop principles to guide their offshore sourcing decisions and efforts (Aron and Singh 2005; Ranganathan and Balaji 2007). Offshoring decisions are affected by the degree to which

firms can assess their own processes, set realistic goals, and gain support within the firm for offshore options (Ranganathan and Balaji 2007). Without this capability for systemic thinking, firms are more likely to avoid offshoring due to perceived risks, or 'inshore' work to the home country after an offshoring failure (Aron and Singh 2005).

- *Global resource and vendor management.* The ability to manage a firm's own resources and that of its vendors (in the case of outsourcing) is identified as a key management capability (Ranganathan and Balaji 2007). This includes managing human resources, knowledge, and distributed work, as well as vendor selection, contracting, and governance. Firms who consider offshore outsourcing to external vendors must consider the capabilities of those vendors, whether they are US-based companies such as IBM, EDS, Accenture, or CSC, who have large offshore operations, or foreign-based companies such as Infosys, Wipro, and TCS, who do most of their development in their home countries. Vendor capabilities evolve over time (Levina and Ross 2003), and client firms must consider the match of vendor capabilities with their own needs. Equally important is the ability of the client to manage the vendor relationship to realize offshore outsourcing goals (Rottman and Lacity 2008).
- *Offshore champions.* Offshoring is often driven by so-called change agents in an organization. These 'offshore champions' (Carmel and Agarwal 2002) are individuals or groups who actively promote offshoring. Individuals with social ties to other countries have been identified as facilitating entry into foreign markets (Ellis 2000), whereas managers with experience running operations in foreign countries have played key roles in decisions to move manufacturing offshore (Dedrick and Kraemer 1998).

Research Methodology

Our research involves the study of offshore software development in large US-based multinational firms. Software development includes the full range of development activities, from requirements analysis through architecture, design, coding, testing, installation, and maintenance. The software includes applications developed for internal use, applications developed by IT services providers for clients, and software developed as part of a physical product such as a mobile phone or an integrated circuit.

Our findings are based on primary field data analyzed through an iterative process of item surfacing, refinement, and regrouping. We used a multiple case study approach to capture the experiences and context of actors directly involved in the offshoring process (Benbasat et al. 1987; Eisenhardt 1989). We interviewed multiple respondents (in most firms), including vice presidents (VPs), senior directors, business unit managers, country managers, and directors of offshore migration offices. The interviews utilized a common semi-structured protocol (see Appendix), which was structured loosely around the items in Fig. 9.1. The questions were refined over time as ongoing interviews revealed new issues to explore. These interviews were transcribed and coded to look for patterns among responses. From these patterns, a set of empirically based findings was developed. These were compared with existing literature to identify those that confirmed or extended theory and then synthesized into a new framework.

Our primary data area was divided into two source types. The first and principal source is made up of five units of four very large, influential firms in which data were collected in 2007 for purposes of the study described in this paper. While firms of all sizes have participated in offshoring, the largest US-headquartered firms have led the charge and set the example. The firms we chose include two of the three largest IT services firms ('Big 3'), the embedded software division of a top five semiconductor company, and both the internal IS department and the software products division of a top five mobile phone manufacturer. As these interviews were confidential, we use pseudonyms for each as detailed in Table 9.1. We had access to senior level leaders in each of these firms. Our interviews examined firm-wide (or division-wide) topics and generally did not discuss specific projects. Our scope is on the software development processes – whether in IT activities or in software R&D. We did

Table 9.1 Firms interviewed for this study (data were collected in 2007)

Pseudonym	Characteristics	Unit of study	Major offshore locations	Interviews conducted
IT-Mega	One of the 'Big 3' US IT services companies Revenues: >20 billion USD Employees (total company): >100,000	European division	India, China, Brazil, Russia, Eastern Europe	Managing Director, IT Business Services, Partner, Application Delivery
IT-Giant	Another of the 'Big 3' US IT services companies Revenues: >20 billion USD Employees: >100,000	Applications division in United States	India, China, Argentina, Egypt	Seven executives and high-level managers: managing director of application services (+), head of business development, manager of one of the Indian delivery centers, and others
ChipCo	One of the top five US semiconductor manufacturers Revenues: >10 billion USD Employees: >25,000	Software division in USA	India, Israel	Divisional chief technology officer (+); silicon development manager
MobComm-IT	Major US mobile communications firm Revenues: >20 billion USD Employees: >50,000	IS department in USA	China, Taiwan, Brazil, India	Senior director for business operations (+)
MobComm-SW	Same mobile communications firm – revenues and employees for software are not broken out separately	Product software division in USA	India, China, Israel, Argentina, Russia, Poland, Singapore, Malaysia	Corporate VP – software development group; General Manager – software development group

Note: (+) indicates multiples interviews with respondent

not include other knowledge activities such as BPO or services such as data centers or desktop support.

Factors Influencing Sourcing Decisions

In our analysis, we first looked to find evidence confirming or contradicting the offshore-sourcing factors identified in Fig. 9.1. We then looked for other factors identified in the interviews that were not evident in the literature-based foundational model. Those factors were defined and located within the broad categories of economic factors, nature of the activity, and management practices and capabilities. The most important set of new factors was a group of proactive management practices adopted by firms to facilitate and promote offshoring.

Beyond just identifying new factors within existing categories, we also created a new construct, which we call sourcing mix. This construct came about from seeing consistent references in the interviews to the importance of the overall mix of resources in different locations across the firm or business unit. Finally, we developed a set of feedback loops that emerged from seeing that sourcing decisions and the ensuing sourcing mix led to changes in management practices, and in some cases in the nature of the software development activity itself.

Economic Factors

Our interviews confirm the expected impact of economic factors, with particular emphasis on the cost side. The Divisional Chief at ChipCo complained about 'spreadsheet managers' driving the company offshore with little concern about a bigger view that would optimize cost, quality, timeliness, and other factors. At the other companies, we heard that cost was the initial driver but now they are increasingly motivated by access to skills not easily available at home. These motivations are what would be predicted by economic theory.

Nature of the Activity

Our interviews also confirmed the importance of activity character-istics, as posited in the literature. Specifically, interviewees stated that more complex and less codified activities were harder to move off-shore, and IT-Giant's offshore assessment process explicitly included both complexity and quality of documentation as factors in recom-mending offshoring of a development task. Likewise, the need for customer contact was identified by several interviewees as a restriction on moving an activity offshore. Since our findings on economic factors and nature of the activity primarily confirm existing theory, we turn our attention to look in detail at the new findings that have emerged from our analysis.

Management Practices and Capabilities

While many of the factors that influence offshoring are fixed in the short run, we found that most can be influenced over time by manage-ment decisions and practices. When the economic forces that motivate offshoring are strong enough, firms will make exceptional efforts to identify opportunities to offshore, and to overcome the obstacles that might discourage offshoring in the short term. Therefore, we have clustered these factors under the label 'proactive' to denote the dynamic nature of these behaviors. These are clearly *advocacy* beha-viors, which is a concept that we shall return to later.

This cluster of factors is what makes our model of sourcing decisions and impacts a dynamic one. Firms do not simply respond to conditions, they actively try to change those conditions to expand the scope of their offshore activities. To understand how this takes place and what the impacts are, we consider the institutions, policies, and people that are involved.

We introduce five factors here. The first is an institutional driver of offshoring; the next three involve policies and processes that facilitate and promote offshoring; while the last involves creation of new capabilities in offshore locations. Some of these factors are consistent with existing research on outsourcing but have specific characteristics in the offshoring context, such as the role of immigrants driving work to their home countries. Others are new, particularly No. 2, the proactive search for offshoring opportunities in every new project or engagement.

Institutional Advocacy

Firms often create mechanisms, such as special teams, organizational units, or committees, to institutionalize strategic or operational initiatives across the boundaries of the formal organization. In large firms there are examples of creating an offshoring advocacy organization to promote and facilitate offshoring throughout the company or business unit.

In IT-Giant's application division, an Assessment and Migration Office (AMO) was created to help business managers assess what work to offshore and where to locate the work, and to help manage the migration. The company was continuing to develop a suite of delivery models to standardize and improve the migration process. AMO opened in Q4 2006 and as of mid-2007, this unit was leading 34 migrations involving 1100 full-time employees. Any migration of applications that involved 10 or more people was supposed to be handled by this unit. AMO not only worked to facilitate offshoring after a contract had been signed but proactively sold offshoring to the client as part of a proposal.

IT-Mega has a 'solutioning' team that assesses offshorability and makes decisions about offshoring. At IT-Mega's German subsidiary, this team was made up of 30–40 people involved with design solutions and also involved in decisions about offshoring. MobComm's internal IT group created 'solutions' teams that coordinate work across different locations, helping to facilitate offshoring.

In each of the cases, these new institutions not only facilitate offshoring but advocate it within the firm. As a result, it is more likely that a given activity will migrate offshore than if individual project managers or business units were left to make 'neutral' sourcing decisions in the absence of such institutional advocacy.

Triage Process

Along with creating institutions to promote offshoring, firms may also give these organizations the task of developing processes to assess new projects systematically for offshoring opportunities. Smaller firms might hire outside consultants to identify opportunities but then advocate internally. We refer to this process of searching for offshoring opportunities as 'triage,' as it is similar to the analyses made by doctors and nurses in prioritizing patients for treatment.

In companies that are more aggressive in offshoring, every new project is broken into specific activities and each activity is analyzed for 'offshorability.' This is important as it is not necessary for an entire project to be done offshore, but instead it can be broken up with some parts onshore and other parts offshore.

IT-Giant used a spreadsheet that gives a score to each specific task in the development process on a number of criteria, including system stability, complexity, and documentation status. Based on these scores, each activity is rated as red, yellow, or green for offshoring, with red being unsuitable, yellow being marginal, and green being ready to move.

In making its offshore decisions, IT-Mega's solutioning team used a checklist of 30–40 items, such as how many changes are required and how many user interactions are anticipated. These factors were then translated into a score that measures suitability for offshoring.

Another part of triage is to identify internal resources that have the right skills and are available at the time a project is planned. This can take the form of knowledge management systems or other widely accessible databases. One web-based tool used by IT-Mega allowed all internal decision makers to see where resources were available around the world, including who is sitting 'on the bench' (in other words, who is not assigned at the moment).

When such triage processes are in place, we find it more likely that activities will be carried out offshore, as specific tasks can be identified as separate and move. Also, triage creates the tools and impetus to codify knowledge, standardize practices, and modularize processes to expand the scope of activities that can be done offshore, as we discuss in the next subsection.

Codification and Modularization

Firms with large offshore operations often make considerable efforts to codify and document knowledge, and to standardize processes across locations and even across organizational boundaries. IT is a key tool for codifying information and making processes more modular. ChipCo standardized on Eclipse, an open source, open architecture development platform. ChipCo's clients liked working with this platform, according to the Divisional Chief of the software group, because they were familiar with this framework and could easily plug into it. This common software platform increases modularity and facilitates the movement of work between locations and organizations.

IT-Giant used a development framework called GADQMS – Global Application Development Quality Management System. This system development lifecycle framework defines processes for different scenarios or environments and serves as a basis for standardizing development processes around the world.

The more that knowledge can be codified and documented, the easier and cheaper it is to transfer. When processes are more modular and standardized they are easier to divide across different locations, making offshoring more likely.

Knowledge Transfer

Transferring knowledge from onshore to offshore staff is one of the most vital and sensitive aspects of offshoring IT work (Chua and Pan 2008; Rottman 2008). Effective knowledge transfer is necessary for offshore locations to be able to work on ongoing projects, take over work from onshore teams, or work with current clients.

Some knowledge is well documented and can be transferred simply by sending files from one location to another. This type of knowledge usually involves routine work processes, standard rules of operations, well-defined product specifications and project plans, or customer information. Other knowledge is more tacit and must be explained, placed in context, or elaborated on, often via two-way communication. Such knowledge is usually transferred through training programs, phone calls, travel for face-to-face meetings, or other interactive means.

For instance, IT-Giant emphasized rotation of people, sending subject matter experts to India to train local people, and sending some offshore staff to the USA to meet with clients. Successful migrations involve ongoing communication between the client and the offshore location. As IT-Giant Managing Director for Application Services said, 'If you don't build relationships, the work will fail every time. Building the virtual team is the only way to make it work. In the past we tried to save money and not do the traveling, and it was a disaster.'

MobComm-IT also used travel for transferring knowledge. For instance, most of MobComm's offshore developers did not have domain experience on how American retail companies operate, so when they were assigned to develop a retail solution using radio frequency identification (RFID), Mobcomm-IT flew members of the Indian team to the USA and showed them the process by visiting electronics retailers. MobComm-IT also sought to develop management skills in China and India to handle more tasks. When they assigned expatriates to those countries they tried to assign people who were good at training as well as operations.

The ChipCo sources said that fostering communication and collaboration is 'hard.' They addressed this with ample travel and face-to-face meetings with offshore teams and managers. We were told that the benefits of doing so are significant as they can share methodologies and intellectual property across the organization.

Not all firms relied as much on face-to-face interaction for knowledge transfer, training, and collaboration. For example, IT-Mega tried to limit travel because of cost and visa issues. As a travel alternative, IT-Mega invested in video capture approaches. The firm videotaped clients interacting with systems developed by IT-Mega so that offshore personnel could understand how the system was being used. The videos were also accompanied by screen sessions, data entry, interfaces, and back end operations information. IT-Mega had several editing/production personnel to put all this together. The respondent stated that it was time-consuming in the beginning but believed that this would pay off with better work and productivity gains.

Location Upgrading and Specialization

Companies often move work offshore with the goal of reducing costs on the most routine tasks, partly because the skills to do more advanced tasks do not (yet) exist in the offshore location. However, people in offshore locations are eager to learn and take on more advanced activities to promote their own careers, whereas managers try to grow their own businesses by bringing in more work from the parent unit. In some cases, governments give incentives to firms to upgrade the firms' local operations (Poon 2004). Local outsourcing firms also work to upgrade their capabilities as they gain experience (Jarvenpaa and Mao 2008). In addition to upgrading, offshore locations may begin to specialize according to business function or technology, either as a corporate policy or as a by-product of prior work assignments.

Consistent with this thinking, IT-Giant preferred to offshore projects that involve some degree of offshore (onsite) project management or program management. Such multidimensional projects create opportunities for better career paths offshore, as junior people can get experience and work their way up to management levels. Such an approach also continuously upgrades the capabilities of offshore locations to handle more advanced work.

IT-Giant's offshore locations have begun to specialize according to industry and business function. We learned that these centers of expertise sometimes get started when personnel are located in proximity to a major client and begin to develop knowledge of the client and its industry; later, if the firm gets a contract with another company in the same industry, it can leverage this knowledge. Offshore locations can also specialize in specific technologies. Even within India, each of IT-Giant's locations has some specialized knowledge. For example, Chennai specializes in manufacturing, financial services, and government sectors, with technical skills in software testing and in Java, dot.net, and mainframes. IT-Giant's manager of application development for a major industry vertical (transportation) said that 'I have to place my bets on a few key places. It was Brazil and India before, now it's also Wuhan. I want to plant my transportation workers in a few places, not go to 98 places to get it done.'

At MobComm-SW, offshore locations were pushed to specialize in different technologies, often building on existing knowledge. For instance, Russia specializes in Java applications and Java Virtual Machine while Montreal specializes in open source software and Internet applications.

IT-Mega created centers of excellence all over the world. These are based on an intersection of sectoral knowledge and functional expertise (e.g., in strategy, customer relationship management, supply chain, or human resources).

As offshore locations upgrade their capabilities and develop deeper specialized knowledge, it is likely that more work will be moved to those locations. Specialization is important for higher cost locations, but even low cost locations are able to incrementally pull more work offshore by upgrading and specializing.

Summary of Factors Influencing Sourcing Decisions

So far, we have identified factors that explain firms' sourcing decisions, including economic drivers, the nature of the activity being sourced, and management practices. This is consistent with our foundational model, but we have expanded the model to include new factors.

We find that economic factors, particularly cost, but also access to talent and markets, are the primary drivers of offshoring of any kind of knowledge work. The nature of the work determines the ease or difficulty of moving offshore. Activities that are more mature and modular and involve knowledge that is more codified and standardized are easier to offshore. Those which are more complex or strategic, less mature, involve more tacit knowledge and are closely linked to other onshore activities are harder to move offshore.

In addition, there is a connection between the decision to move offshore and the adoption of various management practices to analyze, prioritize, and migrate processes offshore. Some of these are familiar, such as documentation, transfer of knowledge, or using IT tools. Others are newer. For instance, we identify a class of practices as 'triage' by which firms analyze all activities in a project for their potential to be offshored. We also identify two organizational drivers of offshore migration – individual change agents and formal advocacy teams.

What is most notable is the extent to which some firms consciously seek to expand the scope of activities that can be moved offshore. The economic imperatives are so strong in some cases that it is not enough just to identify good opportunities for offshoring. For example, IT services firms in the USA are not only competing with other US firms, but also with Indian firms that have become formidable competitors. These American firms needed offshore operations to allow them to compete on cost.

Firms also try to change the nature of activities so those that were marginal or even poor candidates can eventually be moved. With experience and learning in both the home and host country locations, it becomes easier to move more tasks offshore. At some point when enough activities have moved, the forces of proximity actually start to work in favor of the new location, and start to become a driver rather than an impediment that keeps tasks in the onshore locations.

A Dynamic Model of Offshore Sourcing

In this section, we enhance the foundational model of Fig. 9.1 and present a dynamic model that captures the interaction – over time – of the factors discussed above. We detail specific changes that occur as activities are moved offshore and various management practices are employed – leading to feedback loops that can accelerate offshore migration. Our model is likely the first dynamic model of offshore sourcing, though the IS literature has offered dynamic models in other

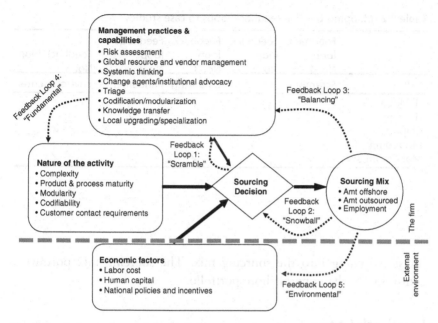

Fig. 9.3   A dynamic model of offshore sourcing factors and interactions

domains such as e-business strategy (Burn and Ash 2005), IT alignment (Burn 1996), and organizational learning (Holmqvist 2003).

Figure 9.3 presents the dynamic model of offshoring, which shows economic factors, nature of the activity, and management practices directly driving sourcing decisions, as we showed in Fig. 9.1.

Sourcing Mix

In moving from the static model to the dynamic model, we first add 'sourcing mix' as a new variable which did not appear in Fig. 9.1. This 'mix' variable can be measured as the amount of knowledge work being done, the type of activities being done, and the number of workers employed in onshore and offshore locations at a given time. This is closer to the economic concept of a 'stock' measure, while the individual sourcing decisions can be seen as a 'flow' measure, with each sourcing

Table 9.2 Mapping the five feedback loops to case studies

Firm	Feedback loop No. 1 Scramble	Feedback loop No. 2 Snowball	Feedback loop No. 3 Balancing	Feedback loop No. 4 Fundamental	Feedback loop No. 5 Environmental
IT-Mega			✓		
IT-Giant			✓	✓	
ChipCo		✓			✓
MobComm-IT		✓	✓		
MobComm-SW	✓		✓	✓	✓

decision feeding into the sourcing mix. The sourcing mix portrays a continuously changing offshore portfolio.

Feedback Loops

We next discuss the dynamic interactions represented by the five feedback loops in Fig. 9.3. In creating the dynamic model, with its five feedback loops, we used specific data from our five cases, as we document in Table 9.2. It is important to note that the absence of specific data for specific feedback loops does not mean that there is no support. We suspect that in all five data points that we would find support for most feedback loops – but we did not always have specific data from our interviews. For example, this is the case for Feedback Loop 1 because initial offshoring decisions were taken before some of our interviewees were involved, so they could not inform us about changes that occurred.

The first four feedback loops operate at the firm level and move in a continuum from short-term reaction to fundamental or structural change. In analyzing these loops, we will apply the concept of learning loops. Loop 5 is external to the firm and usually the result of actions over time by a number of firms. As we will discuss below, the first four can be seen as examples of two types of learning loops.

Feedback Loop 1: Sourcing Decisions to Proactive Management Practices

Although this appears, at first, to be counter-intuitive, the firm often makes an offshoring decision and then realizes it must begin to implement management practices to carry out a project. Hence, we label this loop 'scramble' to denote its reactionary nature. For instance, the decision to move an activity will require knowledge transfer and the firm will begin to document some of its knowledge, and also might relocate domestic personnel to set up a subsidiary offshore. Or a firm may set up an offshore site to win a contract and then invest in its local capabilities to win more work.

This has been the case with MobComm-SW where the manager said that the firm was able to win contracts with government agencies or state enterprises because it established a development center in that country, as it needed to have a certain amount of local content for government contracts, or it just made MobComm look better in the eyes of the government. As one interviewee said, 'For a $100 million contract, we'll do anything.' In one case they set up a center to win a government contract in Quebec, and in order to keep the center open after that contract, MobComm pushed the center to specialize in the technologies that MobComm-SW could use in the future. The corporate software division VP said that it is wasteful to set up centers and then close them down after one contract.

Feedback Loop 2: Sourcing Mix to Sourcing Decision

Once a project is completed in a particular location and the sourcing mix has been altered, there are resources left in place, primarily the people who did the work. As a greater share of a firm's sourcing mix goes to one location, more resources are accumulated there. We label this loop 'snowball' because this accumulation of resources is like a snowball growing over time.

As offshore capabilities develop and locations become more specialized, this influences future sourcing decisions. No longer is cost the only or even primary consideration in choosing a site for a particular activity. Instead, decisions are made on the basis of cost and capabilities. ChipCo's Divisional Chief of Technology said that allocation of tasks is based partially on expertise within locations: 'Projects are located on a design center basis more than a cost basis. This includes Israel, Japan, India, as well as US sites. Things that tend to gravitate to India with an eye more on straight cost – are things like device drivers and operating system porting.'

The Senior Director at MobComm-IT had a similar comment: 'When we began outsourcing and offshoring, maybe 5 years ago, it was for cost reasons. Now it depends more on capabilities. If you want Java programming done, sometimes you can't get it from suppliers in the US because programmers aren't available, but we can go to Wipro or Infosys and always get it.'

Once there is a critical mass of activities and capabilities in offshore locations, those locations begin to politically influence sourcing decisions and compete among themselves to attract new corporate activities, such as a software development center or a data center. Corporate country managers often work with government officials to provide incentives (tax; subsidies) to sway the sourcing decision.

Feedback Loop 3: Sourcing Mix to Proactive Management Practices

Three of our four US-headquartered firms made a dramatic shift in the sourcing mix between 2000 and 2007 (the fourth firm was already extensively offshoring). The early 2000s were a turning point for these firms that had relatively few personnel providing services from offshore. By 2007 the change was dramatic with workforces of 10,000 and more in India alone. This transformation was enabled by the institutional advocacy and triage processes. This was particularly evident at IT-Mega and IT-Giant. The workforce (in the 'Sourcing mix') was expanded, spurring changes in 'Management Practices' through the feedback loop.

A familiar refrain in the world of offshoring is specialization. Once the offshore sites become large and experienced, these sites become centers of expertise inside the giant companies. These were specializations that emerged and were not created whole-cloth. At IT-Giant the specialization is by industry vertical: 'if it is financial services then go to Chennai, if it is manufacturing then go to Cordoba.'

At that point, the company's management practices begin to change to accommodate the new circumstances. Offshore locations can manage their own projects, and sometimes even manage onshore staff. Previously, knowledge was presumed to reside onshore, and knowledge transfer was one way but now, at these firms, knowledge transfer can run in both directions. We refer to this loop as 'balancing' because there is a rebalancing of capabilities, activities, and relationships in the management structure.

Feedback Loop 4: Proactive Management Practices to Nature of the Activity

Proactive management practices can actually change the nature of an activity. We refer to this feedback loop as 'fundamental' because of this change in the underlying nature of the activity itself. Knowledge that was not codified can be codified, processes that were idiosyncratic can become standardized, activities that were closely integrated can become more modular and loosely linked. As coordination technologies (such as web 2.0, or governance tools) improve, tasks can be shared with offshore locations and even outside partners, and proximity becomes less important. The act of performing triage on every project will identify processes that are borderline cases for offshoring and target them for standardization and codification to prepare them to migrate. The knowledge transfer process not only moves specific knowledge to the offshore location, it also transfers more general business practices and corporate culture, making it easier to transfer even more tacit knowledge in the future as the receiving personnel will have an understanding of the context in which the knowledge was created.

In our interview, an IT-Giant manager said: 'Work has to be modularized to be able to be shifted to the next low-cost centers. We use consistent methodology, documentation, and processes.' He said that this changes the work fundamentally from 'yellow' to 'green' in terms of offshorability. This comment emphasizes the ongoing effort to change the nature of the work to facilitate further offshoring to other low-cost locations.

In time, most of the characteristics of an activity that make it difficult to move offshore can potentially yield to proactive management practices. The limits to offshoring in the long run may depend more on the motivation of managers to implement such practices than on obstacles inherent in the activity. In our case studies, only one firm, IT-Giant, clearly pointed to such fundamental changes as an explicit outcome. Another, MobComm, spoke of being one of the first firms to reach capability maturity model (CMM) level 5 status, an achievement that speaks of changing the nature of development activities; however, it was not clear if this was related to offshoring or just a result of management practices at the company level.

Feedback Loop 5: Sourcing Mix to Economic Factors

Over time, a firm's sourcing mix, combined with the sourcing decisions of other firms, can affect the economic factors in a particular location through externalities (both positive and negative). We refer to this loop as 'environmental,' as it involves changes to the external environment of the firm.

When an offshore location attracts enough MNCs or local firms in one industry, an industry cluster can develop. Generally, cluster effects benefit firms located there, as they have access to suppliers and specialized services such as engineering, legal and financial expertise, and potential business partners (Saxenian 1994; Porter 1998). Such industry clusters attract knowledge work even though they may be expensive compared to other locations that otherwise would look equally attractive.

In software, Bangalore was chosen initially by GE, ChipCo, and some of the leading Indian firms such as Infosys. In time, the knowledge and experience gained by programmers and others in that location attracted other firms to develop software there. Other IT clusters have emerged around the world – in Costa Rica, Tel Aviv, and elsewhere. These clusters become a magnet to firms who look for a broad and deep mix of skills and complementary assets for a particular technology or industry.

For ChipCo, India is attractive not just because of low-cost talent but also because of the cluster, or ecosystem of software subcontractors making complementary products to augment its own products. The Divisional Chief talked about an 'abundance of 3rd party software partners that can provide middleware, etc. on top of our products.'

But clusters can have their disadvantages as well. Although clusters can be considered a positive externality in economic terms, they can lead to negative externalities (e.g., traffic, housing shortages, pollution) and even erode the economic advantages of a location. Companies complain about higher wages and frequent job-hopping by developers in Bangalore to the extent that some firms (including large Indian outsourcers) are moving some development to other places (King 2008). In the words of MobComm-SW's Corporate VP, 'Wages get bid up in clusters and competitors move in next door and try to take your talent.' For US companies, the changing economics could lead to diversifying to other locations, or even keeping some work at home that might have been moved offshore.

Feedback Loops as Learning Loops

In analyzing these feedback loops, we can apply the concepts of learning loops (Fiol and Lyles 1985; Argyris and Schon 1996; Romme and Dillen 1997) to understand the process as one of organizational learning, rather than just a case of unplanned path dependence (although the evolution of offshoring in firms does appear to exhibit some element of chance). The literature distinguishes between single-loop and double-loop learning processes. Single loop refers to short-term incremental changes in a process based on repetition of past behaviors. Double-loop learning involves fundamental changes to a process, based on new rules, norms, or understanding, often involving significant organizational change

(Fiol and Lyles 1985). In our model, Feedback Loop 1 is clearly a short-term single-loop learning process, whereas Loop 2 is a transition toward a double-loop process as the sourcing mix changes and capabilities are created. Loops 3 and 4 represent more fundamental shifts in management practices and ultimately in the nature of the development process itself and thus can be seen as cases of double-loop learning. Loop 5 occurs outside the firm and is not interpreted here as a learning loop.

Conclusions

Previous research has identified a number of factors that influence sourcing decisions into the four locations of the classic 2 × 2 decision matrix (Fig. 9.2). These factors include economic factors such as labor costs, availability of skills, and coordination costs. They also include characteristics of the work being done, such as maturity, codifiability, modularity, and complexity. Our first contribution here has been to confirm the validity of those factors through intensive interviews with companies developing software both internally and for commercial products and services.

We make two principal contributions. First, we have identified a set of proactive management practices utilized by these firms to facilitate and promote offshoring. These include identification of offshoring opportunities through 'triage,' promotion by change agents and formal institutional structures, codification of knowledge, various knowledge transfer mechanisms, and upgrading and specialization of offshore locations.

Second, we developed a dynamic model of offshoring factors, management practices, and sourcing decisions. The model shows that causal relationships do not just run one way but over time go in both directions through feedback loops. Reinforcing cycles can develop between sourcing decisions, the overall sourcing mix, management practices, and the nature of an activity. Firms continue to look for and find new opportunities to reduce costs and gain access to skills and markets, creating greater capabilities in offshore locations and pulling even more activities offshore in a spiral of accelerated migrations. Learning takes place that may evolve from temporary or superficial single loops to more transformative double loops that fundamentally change the firm's management practices and even the nature of the activity. Taken together, the sourcing mixes of multiple firms can even change economic environments within localities and regions. Clusters can develop that attract further knowledge work to a location, but costs also can rise and cause a shift to other locations.

This model is useful in understanding how much software development is likely to move offshore over the long term. It is not simply a matter of relative labor costs, or even the initial level of modularity in an activity that will determine the overall scope and limits to offshoring. Just as important are the managerial practices of firms that 'go offshore,' and how prior and ongoing decisions change the environment for future sourcing choices. While prior studies have been more static in nature, considering activities or occupations to be inherently offshorable or not, this approach suggests a great deal of potential change in the factors that determine offshorability and in turn decide the actual levels of offshoring. Moreover, this approach suggests that offshoring tends to become self-reinforcing.

While software development has unique characteristics, our model and findings should generalize to other types of knowledge work. Specific factors might be different, but we would expect that offshore migration of knowledge work in general will be driven by economics, shaped by the nature of the activity, and be facilitated and even pushed by proactive management practices. It is possible that similar feedback loops will develop that might accelerate the pace and scale of offshoring, although in times of economic slowdown the feedback loops could turn negative.

This research has managerial implications as well. It identifies factors in the nature of software development that can make offshoring easier or more difficult, such as the modularity of processes and codifiability of knowledge. Managers should take these factors into consideration, along with potential cost savings, when deciding whether to offshore software development. The research also identifies a set of proactive management practices used by firms with experience in offshore software development to optimize performance of offshore teams and to facilitate greater use of offshore development to reduce costs, reach new markets, and tap new sources of skills. Managers might implement similar practices in their own offshore projects. Finally, managers should understand the dynamic nature of offshoring and realize that there are feedback effects that will affect future decisions and may reshape the global structure of their software organizations. This has implications for their own future roles and the career paths of their employees.

Limitations and Future Research

A limitation of this study is the small number of cases that are developed in depth. However, the cases were sufficient to develop new insights about offshoring that go beyond the existing IT literature while also confirming it. As indicated by Eisenhardt (1989) and Benbasat et al. (1987), fieldwork and case studies are highly appropriate for developing conceptual frameworks, especially in a dynamic and emerging context as is the situation with offshore software development.

The second limitation is that the model is not yet tested. Thus, the future research challenge is to use such a framework to develop testable propositions and then to conduct systematic empirical research on our theoretical model. Doing so may require multiple cross-sectional surveys, or even a longitudinal study of the same sample of firms. Progress toward this goal might be made by a single cross-sectional study to examine support for the static model, which might pare down the factors to be considered. The simpler model could then be studied as a whole over time, or by studying each linkage at a time. We hope that this work will stimulate others to do so.

Future research could also extend the scope of analysis to include smaller companies that lack experience offshore and could look at the role of external intermediaries as enablers of offshoring.[1] Also, we would encourage other researchers to study the generalizability of our dynamic

---

[1] The authors thank an anonymous reviewer for this suggestion

model to other types of knowledge work, other industries, and other home country environments. Finally, our data were collected a year before the onset of the global economic crisis of 2008. If offshoring goes through a backshoring phase, then our model should also be able to capture and help explain a deceleration of offshoring through successive feedback loops.

Acknowledgment This research is supported by a grant from the US National Science Foundation (SES-0527180).

Appendix

Interview protocol

1. Company/Unit overview

   a. Company size.
   b. Number of developers.
   c. What types of software development are done? How is the development process organized?

2. Economic factors:

   a. To what extent are you decisions to locate work offshore driven by cost reduction goals? What costs are taken into consideration? For example direct labor costs, cost of coordinating onshore and offshore teams, communications, travel, other?
   b. What are the key skills required for your development activities? Are they in short supply in the US? Are they more easily available in offshore locations?
   c. What risks are associated with offshoring this activity?
   d. To what extent are your onshore/offshore and location decisions influenced by access to local markets?
   e. To what extent are they influenced by government incentives or other policies?

3. Nature of activities and relational factors:
   a. Complexity: Is this activity highly complex, or relatively simple?
   b. Modularity: How much can various activities be carried out independently of other activities?
   c. Codified *vs* tacit knowledge: How well is knowledge documented and easily transferred?
   d. Proximity: Does this activity require or benefit from close proximity?
   e. Social networks: Relationships that are ethnic, geographic, professional, family, alumni, etc.

4. Management practices:
   a. What organizational structures and management processes are in place for collaborative work?
   b. How are the different processes involved in this activity coordinated within the organization or across organizational boundaries?
   c. Have your management practices changed as a result of offshoring?
   d. How does your firm manage resources and vendors on a global basis?
   e. Are you decisions made with a broad systemic view, or on a more individual basis?
   f. Was there an individual (or individuals) who championed offshoring in the company? Who? What was the basis of their enthusiasm?

5. Sourcing decisions and trends:
   a. Offshoring: How does your company divide software development geographically, that is, what is done in the US, what is done in other locations?
   b. Outsourcing: How does your company organize these processes organizationally, that is, what is done in-house and what is outsourced?
   c. Industry trends: What is the trend in your company in recent years in terms of offshoring and outsourcing? What is the trend in your industry? Are your decisions influenced by industry trends?
   d. IT provider: Chicken and Egg. Are your locational resources dictating where work is sent or is it client demand?

e. Are your offshore outsourcing contracts larger/smaller or longer/ shorter than onshore contracts?

6. Dynamics and feedback effects:
   a. How have the experiences from prior offshore sourcing decisions affected later decisions?
   b. What resources have been created in offshore locations? How do these affect sourcing decisions?
   c. Have your management practices or organizational dynamics (e.g., who makes what decisions?) changed since you've been developing offshore?
   d. Has the nature of your software development activity been affected by offshoring and your associated management practices? Is it more mature, modular, better documented, more codified?

References

ACM Job Migration Task Force (2006). *Globalization and Offshoring of Software: A report of the ACM Job Migration Task Force*, W. Aspray, F. Mayadas, and M. Y. Vari (eds.) New York: Association for Computing Machinery.

Argyris, C, and Schon, D.A (1996). *Organizational Learning II: Theory, method and practice*, Massachusetts: Addison-Wesley.

Aron, R, and Singh, J.V (2005). Getting Offshoring Right, *Harvard Business Review* **83**(12): 135–143.

Baldwin, C.Y, and Clark, K.B (1997). Managing in an Age of Modularity, *Harvard Business Review* **75**(5): 84–93.

Banker, R.D, Bardhan, I, and Asdemir, O (2006). Understanding the Impact of Collaboration Software on Product Design and Development, *Information Systems Research* **17**(4): 352–373.

Benbasat, I, Goldstein, D.K, and Mead, M (1987). The Case Research Strategy in Studies of Information Systems, *Management Information Systems, Quarterly* **11**(3): 369–386.

Blinder, A. (2007). How Many U.S. Jobs Might Be Offshoreable? CEPS Working Paper No. 142.

Burn, J.M (1996). IS Innovation and Organizational Alignment – A professional juggling act, *Journal of Information Technology* **11**: 3–12.

Burn, J.M, and Ash, C (2005). A Dynamic Model of E-business Strategies for ERP Enabled Organizations, *Industrial Management and Data Systems* **105** (8): 1084–1095.

Carmel, E, and Agarwal, R (2002). The Maturation of Offshore Sourcing of Information Technology Work, *Management Information Systems Quarterly Executive* **1**(2): 65–75.

Chua, A.L, and Pan, S.L (2008). Knowledge Transfer and Organizational Learning in IS Offshore Sourcing, *Omega* **36**(2): 267–281.

Clemons, E.K, Reddi, S.P, and Row, M.C (1993). The Impact of Information Technology on the Organization of Economic Activity: The 'move to the middle' hypothesis, *Journal of Management Information Systems* **10**(2): 9–35.

Dedrick, J, and Kraemer, K.L (1998). *Asia's Computer Challenge: Threat or opportunity for the United States and The World*, New York: Oxford University Press.

Dibbern, J, Winkler, J, and Heinzl, A (2008). Explaining Variations in Client Extra Costs between Software Projects Offshored to India, *Management, Information Systems Quarterly* **32**(2): 333–366.

Dutta, A., and Roy, R (2005). Offshore Outsourcing: A dynamic causal model of counteracting forces, *Journal of Management Information Systems* **22**(2): 15–35.

Eisenhardt, K.M (1989). Building Theories from Case Study Research, *Academy of Management Review* **14**(4): 532–550.

Ellis, P (2000). Social Ties and Foreign Market Entry, *Journal of International Business Studies* **31**(3): 443–469.

Feeny, D.F., and Willcocks, L.P (1998). Core IS Capabilities for Exploiting Information Technology, *Sloan, Management Review* **39**(3): 9–21.

Fiol, C.M, and Lyles, M.A (1985). Organizational Learning, *Academy of Management Review* **10**(4): 803–813.

Hamm, S, and Schneyer, J. (2008). International isn't just IBM's First Name, *Business Week*, Issue 4068, pp. 36–40.

Heeks, R (2007). Using Competitive Advantage Theory to Analyze IT Sectors in Developing Countries: A software industry case analysis, *Information Technologies and International Development* **3**(3): 5–34.

Hilsenrath, J.E. (2004). Forrester Revises Loss Estimates to Overseas Jobs, *The Wall Street Journal* May 17.

Hirschheim, R., Loebbecke, C, Newman, M, and Valor, J (2007). Offshoring and its Implications for the Information Systems Discipline: Where perception meets reality, *Communications of Association for Information Systems* **2007**(20): 824–835.

Holmqvist, M (2003). Dynamic Model of Intra- and Interorganizational Learning, *Organization Studies* **24**(1): 95–123.

Jarvenpaa, S, and Mao, J.Y (2008). Operational Capabilities Development in Mediated Offshore Software Services Models, *Journal of Information Technology* **23**: 3–17.

Jensen, P.E (2005). A Contextual Theory of Learning and the Learning Organization, *Knowledge and Process Management* **12**(1): 53–64.

King, R. (2008). The New Economics of Outsourcing: Efforts to send IT work anywhere but Bangalore are taking on added urgency as costs of doing work in India rise and the dollar sinks, *Business Week* [www document] http://www.businessweek.com/technology/content/apr2008/tc2008043_531737.htm?chan=top+news_top+news+index_businessweek+exclusives (accessed 7th April 2008).

Kshetri, N (2007). Institutional Factors Affecting Offshore Business Process and Information Technology Outsourcing, *Journal of International Management* **13**(1): 38–56.

Langlois, R.N (2006). The Secret Life of Mundane Transaction Costs, *Organization Studies* **27**(9): 1389–1410.

Leonardi, P.M, and Bailey, D.E (2008). Transformational Technologies and the Creation of New Work Practices: Making implicit knowledge explicit in task-based offshoring, *MIS Quarterly* **32**(2): 411–436.

Levina, N, and Ross, J.W (2003). From the Vendor's Perspective: Exploring the value proposition in information technology outsourcing, *Management Information Systems Quarterly* **27**(3): 331–364.

Lewin, A, and Peeters, C (2006). Offshoring Work: Business hype of the onset of fundamental transformation?, *Long Range Planning* **39**: 221–239.

Masten, S (1984). The Organization of Production: Evidence from the aerospace industry, *Journal of Law and Economics* **27**: 403–417.

Metters, R (2008). A Typology of Offshoring and Outsourcing in Electronically Transmitted Services, *Journal of Operations Management* **26** (2): 198–211.

Mithas, S, and Whitaker, J (2007). Is the World Flat or Spiky? Information Intensity, Skills and Global Service Disaggregation, *Information Systems Research* **18**(3): 237–259.

Nasscom (2008). Indian IT Industry, [www document] http://www.nasscom.in/upload/5216/Strategic_Review_Feb2008.pdf (accessed 15th July 2008).

Novak, S, and Eppinger, S.D (2001). Sourcing by Design: Product complexity and the supply chain, *Management Science* **47**(1): 189–204.

Polanyi, M (1983). *The Tacit Dimension*, Gloucester, MA: Peter Smith.

Poon, T. (2004). Beyond the Global Production Networks: A case of further upgrading of Taiwan's information technology industry, *International Journal of Technology and Globalization* 1(1): 130–144.

Porter, M.E (1990). *The Competitive Advantage of Nations*, London: MacMillan.

Porter, M.E (1998). Clusters and the New Economics of Competition, *Harvard Business Review* 76(6): 77–90.

Ramasubbu, N, Mithas, S, Krishnan, M.S, and Kemerer, C.F (2008). Work Dispersion, Process-based Learning and Offshore Software Development Performance, *Management Information Systems Quarterly* 32(2): 437–458.

Ranganathan, C, and Balaji, S (2007). Critical Capabilities for Offshore Outsourcing of Information Systems, *Management Information Systems Quarterly Executive* 6(3): 147–164.

Romme, G, and Dillen, R (1997). Mapping the Landscape of Organizational Learning, *European Management Journal* 15(1): 68–78.

Rottman, Jr. J.W. (2008). Successful Knowledge Transfer within Offshore Supplier Networks: A case study exploring social capital in strategic alliances, *Journal of Information Technology* 23(1): 31–43.

Rottman, J.W, and Lacity, M.C (2008). A US Client's Learning from Outsourcing IT Work Offshore, *Information Systems Frontiers* 10: 259–275.

Sanchez, R, and Mahoney, J (1996). Modularity, Flexibility, and Knowledge Management in Product and Organizational Design, *Strategic Management Journal* 17: 63–76.

Sargent, J.F, and Meares, C.A (2006). Workforce Globalization in the U.S. IT Services & Software Sector, ACM Job Migration Task Force Meeting; December, Office of Technology Policy, US Department of Commerce: Washington, DC.

Saxenian, A. (1994). *Regional Advantage: Culture and Competition in* Silicon Valley *and Route*, Vol. *128* Cambridge, MA: Harvard University Press.

Schilling, M.A, and Steensma, H.K (2001). The Use of Modular Organizational Forms: An industry-level analysis, *Academy of Management Journal* 44(6): 1149–1168.

Sobol, M.G, and Apte, U (1995). Domestic and Global Outsourcing Practices of America's Most Effective IS Users, *Journal of Information Technology* 10 (4): 269–281.

Sturgeon, T (2002). Modular Production Networks. A new American model of industrial organization, *Industrial and Corporate Change* 11(3): 451–496.

Tanriverdi, H., Konana, P, and Ge, L (2007). The Choice of Sourcing Mechanisms for Business Processes, *Information Systems Research* **18**(3): 280–299.

Willcocks, L.P, and Feeny, D (2006). IT Outsourcing and Core IS Capabilities: Challenges and lessons at DuPont, *Information Systems Management* **23**(1): 49–56.

Willcocks, L.P, and Lacity, M.C (1995). Information Systems Outsourcing in Theory and Practice, *Journal of Information Technology* **10**(4): 203–207.

Williamson, O.E (1979). Transaction-cost Economics: The governance of contractual relations, *Journal of Law and Economics* **22**(2): 233–261.

Youngdahl, W, and Ramaswamy, K. (2008). Offshoring Knowledge and Service Work: A conceptual model and research agenda, *Journal of Operations Management* **26**: 212–221.

Zander, U, and Kogut, B (1995). Knowledge and the Speed of the Transfer and Imitation of Organizational Capabilities: An empirical test, *Organization Science* **6**(1): 76–92.

Jason Dedrick was an associate professor at Syracuse University's School of Information Studies and is codirector of the Personal Computing Industry Center. His research is focused on the globalization of technology and innovation, and on the impacts of information technology at the firm, industry, and national level. He currently is studying the globalization of innovation and knowledge work and its implications for firms, countries, and workers. He is coauthor of *Asia's Computer Challenge: Threat or Opportunity for the United States and the World?* (Oxford University Press, 1998) and coeditor of *Global E-Commerce: Impacts of National Environment and Policy* (Cambridge University Press, 2006). His research has appeared in a number of edited volumes and in journals such as *Management Science, Information Systems Research, the Journal of Management Information Systems, Communications of the ACM, California Management Review*, and *IEEE Computer*.

Erran Carmel's area of expertise is globalization of technology work. He studies global software teams, offshoring of information technology, and emergence of software industries around the world. His 1999 book *Global Software Teams* is a pioneering book on the topic. His second book *Offshoring Information Technology* came out in 2005 and is used in many global sourcing courses. He has written over 80 articles, reports, and manuscripts. He consults and speaks to industry and professional groups. He has been a tenured full professor at the Information Technology Department, Kogod School of Business at American University, Washington DC. He was recently awarded the International Business Research Professor. While writing this chapter, he was the Orkand Chaired Professor at the University of Maryland, University College. He has been a Visiting Professor at the University of Haifa (Israel) and at University College Dublin (Ireland).

Kenneth L. Kraemer was a research professor in the Paul Merage School of Business, University of California, Irvine and co-director of the Personal Computing Industry Center. His research spans the social implications of information technology (IT), national IT policies (*Asia's Computer Challenge*, Oxford 1998), and the contributions of IT to productivity and economic development. His recent books are *Globalization of E-Commerce* (Cambridge University Press, 2006) and *Computerization Movements* (Info Today Press, 2009). He is engaged in new work on the offshoring of R&D and who captures the financial value and jobs in global innovation networks (http://pcic.merage. uci.edu).

10

Anxiety and Psychological Security in Offshoring Relationships: The Role and Development of Trust as Emotional Commitment

Séamas Kelly and Camilla Noonan

Introduction

This paper explores the role of anxiety and psychological security in the development and sustenance of information systems (IS) offshoring relationships. In particular, we are concerned with understanding the processes by which clients, who have little or no previous experience of offshoring, may develop and sustain adequate levels of psychological security to enable them to bracket risk and productively engage in such unfamiliar and alien work arrangements. By broadening the discussion of risk, and considering its particular salience in the context of IS offshoring initiatives, we attempt to move beyond the cognitivist perspectives that have traditionally dominated the management/organization studies literature, to rescue concerns

S. Kelly (✉) · C. Noonan
Centre for Innovation, Technology and Organisation (CITO), UCD School of Business, University College Dublin, Dublin, Ireland
e-mail: seamas.kelly@ucd.ie

© The Author(s) 2017
L.P. Willcocks et al. (eds.), *Outsourcing and Offshoring Business Services*, DOI 10.1007/978-3-319-52651-5_10

with important emotional dimensions of organizational life from the margins of scholarly discourse (cf. Ciborra 2006; Mcgrath 2006).

While the management of risk has long been seen as a central problem in software development generally (Barki et al. 1993; Willcocks and Margetts 1994; Boehm and Demarco 1997), and IT outsourcing more specifically (Earl 1996; Willcocks and Lacity 1999; Willcocks et al. 1999), work in this area has focused mainly on rational strategies for dealing with risk (e.g. its identification, assessment, and management), rather than on the manner in which it is experienced and handled at an emotional level. One notable exception[1] is Wastell's (1996) use of psychoanalytic theory to examine the unhelpful ways in which systems development methodologies may be used to combat insecurity and anxiety on the part of developers (see also Wastell 1999, 2003). Wastell draws on the work of writers such as Melanie Klein (Segal 1989) and DW Winnicott (1987) to explore the psychodynamics of organizational life. In particular, he considers how ostensibly 'rational' tools and practices (such as development methodologies) may play important roles as 'social defenses' against the acute anxieties of organizational life (cf. Hirschhorn 1988; Menzies-Lyth 1988). While this insightful analysis opened up a very promising direction for the study of systems development practice, however, it has not been built upon subsequently. Moreover, the ideas have not been applied to contemporary globalized contexts where distributed forms of development and offshoring are commonplace.

Although having much in common with Wastell's work, our theoretical point of departure in this paper is slightly different. Specifically, we draw on Anthony Giddens' ideas on the changing nature of risk, anxiety, and trust in the context of the contemporary globalization of social relations.[2] Using this work, and particularly Giddens' notion of trust as an 'emotional commitment,' we attempt to illustrate the central role

---

[1] For examples of other interesting work that places issues of anxiety and insecurity center stage, see Miller and O'Leary (1987), Knights (1990, 1992), Bloomfield and Coombs (1992), Knights and Murray (1994), Sturdy (1997), and Knights and Willmott (1999).

[2] Of course, Giddens was himself deeply influenced by the psychoanalytic tradition, in particular by the work of Sigmund Freud, Erik Erikson (1950), and RD Laing (1971).

of anxiety in shaping the contours of organizational life and to examine the mechanisms used to produce the sense of psychological security that is vital to active engagement with environments characterized by risk. Furthermore, we highlight the particular importance of such a perspective to the area of IS offshoring, by arguing that the globally distributed nature of such work alters the risk profile of systems development while simultaneously problematizing conventional mechanisms for producing psychological security. We illustrate these insights in the context of an ongoing, in-depth, longitudinal study of an Ireland–India IS offshoring relationship.

The case focuses on a crucial 18-month period in the Irish firm's (NetTrade) commercial evolution, during which a decision was made to outsource the development of a replacement for their core technology to the offshore facilities of a large Indian software vendor (IndiaSoft). We examine the ongoing implementation process as it unfolded: from NetTrade's initial decision to look for a suitable vendor, through the development of the NetTrade–IndiaSoft relationship, to the delivery of the first major component of the system. The notions of risk and anxiety had a special salience in this context due to the key strategic importance of the system and the scale of the development project in relation to the size of NetTrade (the projected cost of the system actually exceeded the Net Asset Value of the entire firm at the time). Moreover, before IndiaSoft was suggested as a possible option to NetTrade, nobody in the firm had any awareness of, let alone given any consideration to, an offshore IT sourcing model. IndiaSoft, for its part, has no other Irish client of equivalent size to NetTrade.

In our analysis of the case, we argue that the development of the offshoring relationship to this point involved two distinctive, yet overlapping and mutually reinforcing, phases (Courtship and Cohabitation) that demanded different kinds of practices and skills for their successful negotiation. From the client's point of view, two salient forms of trust were important: trust in the qualities of the vendor, and trust in the stability and predictability of the collaborative social order (i.e. trust as 'habitus'). In the Courtship phase, the emphasis was primarily on the client developing trust in the vendor's ability to deliver the system and in the latter's integrity and benevolence toward the former. This trust rested primarily on presentational (through the performances of vendor representatives at key access points) and reputational bases, although characteristic-based and institutional-based mechanisms also played a role. In the Cohabitation phase, by contrast, the emphasis shifted to a struggle to construct a stable collaborative order, where both parties had to come to mutual accommodations about key social practices (primarily communicative practices in this case). These practices contributed to the predictability of the social order and, importantly, their successful negotiation and institutionalization was dependent on the skillful balancing of 'trust, tact and power' (Giddens 1990: 82).

The paper is structured as follows. In the following section we synthesize a distinctive theoretical perspective that illuminates the relationship between the emergence of new modes of global working, risk, anxiety, and trust. In particular, we emphasize the important role of trust, as an 'emotional commitment,' for the production of a sense of psychological security that facilitates the bracketing of risk and engagement with unfamiliar practices that are distributed across time–space. We then go on to outline our research approach to the empirical fieldwork (i.e. the NetTrade–IndiaSoft case) upon which the paper is based, before describing and analyzing the case study in some detail. We conclude by reflecting on the key conclusions that might be drawn from the work and their wider implications for research and practice.

The Problematization and Production of Psychological Security in a Globalized Context – Risk, Anxiety, and Trust as 'Emotional Commitment'

In this section, we draw on the work of Anthony Giddens and others, in an attempt to synthesize a distinctive theoretical lens that illuminates some of the social/psychological challenges associated with working and living in an increasingly globalized contemporary world. The perspective presented not only underscores the renewed importance of mechanisms for containing anxiety, and establishing a robust sense of psychological security within the altered risk profile of high modernity, but it also casts light on the practical operation of such mechanisms. In short, it provides insight into the practices through which psychological security is actively produced, thus facilitating the bracketing of risk necessary for meaningful engagement in social relations that extend across time–space. Not only does this direct analytical attention to crucial, yet often neglected, aspects of software development practice, but it also sensitizes us to the difficulties that arise when these practices are stretched across tracts of time–space, as is the case in offshore development contexts.

Anthony Giddens' (1990, 1991) ideas on globalization, anxiety, and the production of trust provide the conceptual starting point for our work.[3] In what follows in this section, we introduce some of Giddens' key ideas in relation to globalization, risk, anxiety, and the production of trust, before going on to supplement this perspective by drawing on the work of a number of other important scholars in the area. This synthesized theoretical basis is then employed to make sense of the NetTrade–IndiaSoft case that is described subsequently.

Giddens on Globalization, Risk, Anxiety, and the Production of Trust

Giddens (1990) argues that the risk profile of the modern globalized world has been dramatically altered as institutional reflexivity has increased, and social relations are disembedded from local contexts and stretched over extended tracts of time–space. These new social arrangements have problematized the means by which individuals establish and maintain a sense of psychological security and coherent identity (Giddens 1991), which has resulted in the simultaneous transformation, and renewed importance, of trust relations.

According to Giddens, trust is inherently connected to *absence* (there is no need to trust what one can directly monitor) and is bound up with the organization of 'reliable' interactions across time–space. He defines trust as

---

[3] By highlighting the importance of trust, however, we do not wish to downplay that of more conventional means of control as a risk management strategy. Following Das and Teng (1998), we see trust and control as playing mutually supplementary roles in the production of an overall sense of confidence. As Hart (1988) felicitously puts it, trust exists 'at the interstices of control.'

confidence in the reliability of a person or system, regarding a given set of outcomes or events, when that confidence expresses a faith in the probity or love of another, or in the correctness of abstract principles. (Giddens 1990: 34)

Thus, he distinguishes between two types of trust relations prevalent in modern societies: *trust in abstract systems*[4] and *personal trust*. The former are based, to a large extent, on *faceless commitments* while the latter depend on *facework commitments* (trust relations that are sustained by, or expressed in, social connections established in conditions of copresence).

The investment of trust in abstract systems (especially expert systems) is a central feature of modern life. No one can completely opt out of the abstract systems involved in modern institutions; yet, due to their diversity and complexity, our knowledge of their workings is necessarily limited. Therefore, trust (or faceless commitments) becomes a very important means of generating the 'leap of faith' that practical engagement with them demands. Often, however, engagement with abstract systems involves encounters with individuals who 'represent' or are 'responsible' for them (e.g. in the case of visiting a medical doctor who represents a broader system of medical knowledge). Such contacts with experts are very consequential and take place at *access points*, which form the meeting ground of facework and faceless commitments.

In the case of some experts (e.g. a doctor) where encounters take place regularly over a period of years, these can take on the characteristics of

---

[4] Giddens uses the term 'abstract systems' to collectively refer to two distinct types of disembedding mechanism that allow social interactions/relations to be 'lifted out' of the particularities of specific locales and restructured across indefinite spans of time–space:

- *Symbolic tokens*: These refer to media of exchange that have standard value and thus are interchangeable across a plurality of contexts. Money is an important example. It can be passed around regardless of the specific characteristic of the individuals or groups that handle it at any particular juncture.
- *Expert systems*: These bracket time and space by deploying modes of technical knowledge that have validity independent of the practitioners and clients who make use of them (e.g. the system of Western medical knowledge). Thus, like symbolic tokens, they provide 'guarantees' of expectations across distanciated time–space.

trustworthiness associated with friendship and intimacy. However, in general, encounters with experts are much more irregular and transitory than this and, therefore, they have to be managed very carefully by the expert if he or she is to win or maintain trust of the laypeople involved. Drawing on the work of Erving Goffman (1956), Giddens argues that facework commitments are dependent on the demeanor of operators and, therefore, such encounters often involve displays of 'manifest trustworthiness and integrity, coupled with an attitude of "business as usual" or unflappability' (Giddens 1990: 85). Access points remind people of the fallible nature of system operators and, therefore, reassurance is called for, both in the reliability of the individuals involved and in the knowledge or skills upon which their expertise relies. Thus, experts must make a strict division between 'frontstage' and 'backstage' performance at access points, and the control of threshold between the two is the essence of professionalism. Attitudes of trust are strongly influenced by experiences at access points, as well as by updates of knowledge provided by mass communications media and other sources.

Thus, facework commitments are an important means of generating continued trustworthiness in the abstract systems of modernity with which we routinely interact. In this way, trust in impersonal abstract systems is anchored in the trustworthiness and integrity of colleagues. Of course, regular encounters and rituals are required to sustain such collegial trustworthiness: that is, trust rests on a 'presentational base.'

Crucially, in Giddens' terms, trust is not a cognitive/calculative phenomenon but, rather, is based on an *emotional* commitment to things being as we expect them to be. This marks a key distinction between his perspective and more conventional approaches to conceptualizing trust as the product of calculative, deliberative, rational decision-making processes that are common in the mainstream management literature (Mcallister 1995; Ring 1996; Rousseau et al. 1998).[5] For Giddens, then, trust should be understood as a sense of emotional

---

[5] These conventional approaches implicitly adopt a 'cognitivist' perspective (Chaiklin and Lave 1996; Dreyfus and Dreyfus 2005; Kelly 2005) that has been roundly criticized by those who would advocate a more holistic approach to understanding the human subject – that is, one that avoids a dualism between the cognitive and the emotional (cf. Ciborra 2006; Mcgrath 2006).

comfort, a device that can be used to 'bracket out' potential risks (Giddens 1990) and generate the 'leap into faith' that cooperative engagement with others demands (Gambetta 1988).

From this perspective, then, trust is a continuous state, rather than a discrete decision, and a key mode of trust production are stable institutionalized routines, what Misztal (1996: 127) terms *trust as 'habitus.'* Having stable and well-recognized rules of interaction gives a sense of predictability, reliability, and legibility to social life, thus reducing the anxiety caused by the ambiguity and openness of many social situations. The construction of a shared set of stable social practices among people who are strangers or mere acquaintances, however, can be problematic and calls for the balancing of 'trust, tact, and power' (Giddens 1990: 82). As Giddens (1990: 82–83) puts it:

> Tact and rituals of politeness are mutual protective devices, which strangers or acquaintances knowingly use (mostly at the level of practical consciousness) as a kind of implicit social contact. Differential power, particularly where it is very marked, can breach or skew norms of tact and politeness rituals.

The implications of this are twofold. First, it emphasizes the importance of a stable social order for the production of trust and reduction of anxiety.[6] Second, it emphasizes the important role of tact and rituals of

---

Indeed, a key shortcoming of the notion of 'calculative trust' is that it fails to adequately discriminate between trusting behavior and calculated risk taking.

[6] Zollo et al. (2002) have also drawn attention to the importance of stable routines in facilitating productive interorganizational relations. Specifically, they draw on evolutionary economics to argue that such routines facilitate '... information gathering, communication, decision-making, conflict resolution, and the overall governance of the collaborative process' (p. 709). Moreover, they draw an explicit distinction between the development of interorganizational routines and trust, because they view trust rather narrowly as an 'interpersonal' (p. 709) phenomenon and as the result of 'deliberative efforts to assess the likelihood of opportunistic behaviour' (p. 709). While we would agree with these authors' conclusions that interorganizational routines are extremely important, we would argue that the view of trust synthesized here is more insightful, in that it does not confine the importance of such routines to mere 'information gathering' and 'communication'. Rather, 'trust as habitus' also emphasizes the important anxiety reducing functions of such routines.

politeness, in the absence of marked differential power, in helping to bring about the mutual accommodations required to develop and sustain any stable collaborative order. In other words, attention is drawn to the micropolitics of trust production.

Overall, then, we argue that Giddens' perspective is based upon a richer conceptualization of the human subject (i.e. one that incorporates emotional concerns with anxiety and psychological security at its very core). This constitutes a refreshing departure from much of the mainstream management literature on trust, which tends to have a cognitivist orientation, focuses mainly on interpersonal (or interorganizational) forms of trust, and has little to say about the distinctive role of trust (and the means by which it might be established) in the context of increasingly globalized social relations. Three issues are especially salient in this regard: Giddens' view of trust as a matter of 'faith' or an 'emotional commitment,' his distinction between personal and impersonal forms of trust (and his theorization of the relationship between the two), and his observation that new modes of trust production (based on the interaction between personal and impersonal forms of trust) become especially important for securing a sense of emotional comfort in the context of a more globalized world. Not only does Giddens illustrate the importance of impersonal forms of trust in systems, but he also demonstrates how this is linked to, and indeed grounded in, personal forms of trust. Despite the emphasis Giddens places on personal trust, however, he does not explore its constitution in any great detail. In the next section, we draw on ideas from other scholars to supplement Giddens' work in this regard.

Supplementing Giddens' Ideas – Exploring the Nature of, and Bases for, Personal Trust

In a review of the literature, Mayer et al. (1995) identify three characteristics of a trustee that consistently appear: ability, benevolence, and integrity. Ability is defined (Mayer et al. 1995: 717) as 'the group of skills, competencies and characteristics that enable a party to have influence within some specific domain. The domain of the ability is specific because the trustee may be highly competent in some technical areas, affording that person trust on tasks related to that area. However, the trustee may have little aptitude, training or experience in another area, for instance, in interpersonal communication. . . . Thus, trust is domain specific.' Benevolence, on the other hand, is defined as the extent to which a trustee is believed to want to do good *to the trustor*, aside from an egocentric profit motive (suggesting that the trustee has some specific attachment to the trustor). Finally, the relationship between integrity and trust involves the trustor's perception that the trustee adheres to a set of principles that the trustor finds acceptable.

If the dispositions and character of a collection of people are individually well known to each other, then cooperative relations may be founded on, what Williams terms, *thick trust* (Williams 1988: 8). In other words, cooperation among a group of individuals is greatly facilitated if they have established personal bonds and know one another very well. However, where thick trust does not exist, other means of establishing or producing trust are required as a basis for cooperation. Zucker identifies three key modes of trust production in the modern world (Zucker 1986): *process-based* (information based on personal experience), *characteristic-based* (information based on ascribed characteristics), and *institutional-based* (formal protection against default).

In modes of process-based trust production 'a record of prior exchange, often obtained second hand or by imputation from outcomes of prior exchange, provides data on the exchange process' (Zucker 1986: 60). Therefore, process-based trust is based on the availability of large quantities of person- or group-specific information that can often be in the form of positive reputations.[7] Information about prior exchange histories can be obtained by engaging in repetitive exchanges with a party and, therefore, such informal trust-producing mechanisms 'require extensive interaction

---

[7] Although Zucker's emphasis on information and deliberation clearly has cognitivist leanings that would sit uncomfortably with the perspective synthesized here (i.e. we would view interaction as consisting of much more than mere information exchange), we nonetheless believe that the broad mechanisms that she identifies are a very helpful supplement.

over long periods of time and/or produce trust between a small number of individuals involved in a limited set of exchanges' (Zucker 1986: 62). Such exchange relationships are generally highly specific to the parties involved in the exchange and involve idiosyncratic understandings and rules. Thus, trusting relationships are built in successive stages, tentatively and conditionally over time (Good 1988).

A more formal mechanism for the production of process-based trust involves the use of reputation (or brand name in the case of products). As Misztal puts it:

> Reputation permits us to trust another person by providing us with some information regarding the sort of person we are dealing with, before we have had a chance to have contact with that person. (1996: 120–121)

Thus, reputation serves as a warrant for trust and can, therefore, be seen as valuable social capital (Misztal 1996: 121). The establishment of a favorable reputation requires significant investments of time and resources and is, thus, something that individuals and groups will be very careful to maintain. Therefore, a reputation not only provides information about the trustworthiness of an individual or group but also serves as a device for restricting the behavior of those who have invested in it (Misztal 1996: 98). Reputation, therefore, promotes cooperation by increasing the possibility of carrying out promises, thus helping to facilitate efficient contractual relations by allowing economic agents to reduce transaction costs and overcome limited information (Dasgupta 1988; Lorenz 1988: 198–202).

The second basis for trust, according to Zucker (1986), is individual characteristics. Such characteristics may be ascribed to individuals through labeling or stereotyping mechanisms:

> When there is scarcity of information, particularly when we have more information about the group than an individual member, there is a tendency to simplify the perception of the social environment by identifying all individuals with the groups to which they belong. (Misztal 1996: 126)

Thus, characteristics such as gender, ethnicity, family background, or age may be used as an index of trust in a transaction, as they 'serve as indicators of membership in a common cultural system, of shared background expectations. In general, the greater the number of social similarities (dissimilarities), the more interacts assume that common background expectations do (do not) exist, hence trust can (cannot) be relied upon' (Zucker 1986: 63). Furthermore, as in the case of reputations, stereotypes or preconceptions are not easily changed, even in the face of challenging evidence. New information about an individual will tend to be interpreted in accordance with existing preconceptions, thus serving to reinforce those preconceptions (Good 1988: 41).

The third basis of trust production, institutional, is more generic in its application, in that it extends beyond a specific transaction or set of exchange partners (Zucker 1986: 63). Two types of institutional-based trust are identified: person-specific (or firm-specific) and intermediary mechanisms. Person- or firm-specific trust depends on membership of a social group 'within which carefully delineated specific expectations are expected to hold, at least in some cases based on detailed prior socialization' (Zucker 1986: 63). The professionalization of occupations (see Reed 1992: 206–213) provides a very clear illustration of how this type of trust can be signaled. Thus, for example, the attainment of specific educational or professional certifications can signal one's trustworthiness within a particular social sphere. The second type of institutional trust, intermediary mechanisms, involves insuring against potential losses in the event of a transaction not being completed or failing to produce the expected results. Intermediary institutions such as courts of law or insurance companies specialize in protecting parties involved in an exchange in this way.

CODA

In summary, then, we have attempted to synthesize a distinctive theoretical perspective that emphasizes the important role of anxiety and the production of psychological security in globalized contexts. This perspective draws largely upon Anthony Giddens' ideas about the relationship between the risk profile of the contemporary globalized world, existential anxiety, and the production of trust. The value of this approach lies in the emphasis that it places on important emotional and existential aspects of organizational life that are typically marginalized in the mainstream literature. Trust is viewed as an inherently non-calculative phenomenon, an active accomplishment that is founded on emotional commitments. It is through the establishment of trust in people and systems that agents can be psychologically comfortable enough to 'bracket' risk and productively engage with an inherently insecure world, where social relations routinely span cultural and geographical boundaries.

Research Approach and Methods

The empirical research described in this paper is the result of an ongoing, in-depth, longitudinal, interpretive study of the establishment and ongoing development of the offshoring relationship between NetTrade and IndiaSoft. We followed the project since its inception in the latter part of 2005, when we were introduced to the case by John (joint CEO of NetTrade), a close friend of one of the research team. Through John we managed to secure the cooperation and involvement of IndiaSoft. We established contact with their local office in Dublin and negotiated further access to the development center (IndiaCity) in India. In this paper, we focus on the key events that shaped the project, from its instigation in late 2005 to the delivery of the first working software in January 2007.

At the outset, the data collection consisted mainly of informal chats with John, but as the project gathered pace, a more systematic approach was employed. A range of ethnographic methods was used. In addition to a number of visits to the NetTrade offices in Dublin, we spent 1 week at IndiaCity development center conducting interviews, observing activities, and reviewing various documents associated with this project. Overall, we interviewed the 14 key players involved in the project, in formal and informal settings, many of them repeatedly and for extended periods of time. This amounted to approximately 35 h of formal interviews and at least this much time again spent observing in the workplace and attending informal outings. Furthermore, key personnel at NetTrade were requested to keep a written journal, reflecting on their interactions with IndiaSoft, particularly during their early visits to India. Herein, they recorded their impressions and observations at critical junctures in the project. Obviously, our presence in the workplace, and respondents' awareness that their journals would be read by us, inevitably had a bearing on their actions and reports. This, however, was mitigated to some extent by the fact that we developed good relationships with participants over time, and by our efforts to deliberately cultivate an open, reflective, learning culture around the offshoring project. As time went on we noticed that people appeared to be much more willing to discuss more sensitive issues (such as mistakes that they might have made) with us in an open and forthright way.

Although we present a very granular discussion of the evolution of this offshoring relationship, we acknowledge that, owing to the relationship that exists between John and one of the researchers, we had much richer access to data from the NetTrade side (which constitutes the analytical focus of this paper). We fully acknowledge that interviews held at the Indian site were likely to have been colored by this relationship and we are keenly aware of this limitation. As the research progresses, however, our relationship with IndiaSoft is becoming much stronger and independent of NetTrade. Moreover, as our concern in this paper is mainly with the manner in which the key actors at NetTrade developed a sense of trust in the offshoring relationship, the quality of our access to the Irish side was of prime importance.

In line with our interpretive research approach our emphasis was on developing a rich historical, processual analysis of the relationship as it unfolded over time (Pettigrew 1990; Van de Ven and Poole, 1995, 2005), as such the aim was to produce an idiographic, as opposed to a nomothetic, explanation (Tsoukas 1989). More precisely, our analytical strategy borrowed heavily from a grounded theory research perspective (Strauss and Corbin 1990, 1997). Although we decided against explicitly coding the data, our concern was to identify key themes therein and develop them with reference to extant theoretical literatures (see Walsham 1995). We followed a hermeneutical approach (Klein and Myers 1999), iterating constantly between the data and broader theoretical constructs as we gradually synthesized and refined, in a grounded manner, the conceptual perspective described earlier. At all stages in the process we were careful to adhere to established canons of good practice for performing this kind of interpretive analysis (see, especially, Klein and Myers 1999). As the process of relationship development in the project is still at quite an early stage, however, we acknowledge that our perspective at the time of writing is necessarily partial and may be subject to some revision as the research progresses.

Distance and the Production of Psychological Security in the NetTrade–IndiaSoft Case

NetTrade, a small Irish financial services firm, was established in 2001 by joint CEOs, John and Niall. They described themselves as '*a small unknown company with the standard start-up mentality*' (John, joint CEO, NetTrade). After four very successful years in operation, they began to plan for future growth. The key strategic issue related to their IT system, which was core to their business. Up to now, NetTrade had leased the software from a small UK-based supplier but the attraction of having their own bespoke system was always apparent. In addition to the risk associated with overreliance on a supplier, two additional factors influenced their decision to develop their own bespoke system. First, as the business grew, their requirements for additional system functionality were also growing. Second, under the current arrangement, they owned the license for this system but not the code. Consequently, they felt that a bespoke trading system would '*put us [them] on a different planet entirely*' (John, joint CEO, NetTrade).

In autumn 2005, NetTrade set out to formally identify a partner to develop the system for them. As this was the key strategic system upon which future prosperity depended, the quality of the delivered product was paramount. Consequently, it was with some trepidation that NetTrade approached the development project:

> It was difficult because we didn't know what we were doing...we were shooting in the dark and did not know who would be even interested in doing business with us. (John, Joint CEO, NetTrade)

The firm was very conscious that it would be financially exposed should anything go wrong (the projected cost of the system was greater than the Net Asset Value of the entire firm at that point in time). They decided to manage this risk by insisting to potential vendors that the project be structured in stages (or '*bite-sized chunks*'). This meant that NetTrade would pay for each deliverable and would reserve the right to pull back from the other stages of the project in the event of dissatisfaction or changing financial circumstance.

After meeting with a number of '*singularly unimpressive*' local consulting firms, a personal friend of John and Niall's suggested that they might explore an offshoring model and introduced them to IndiaSoft, a major Indian software vendor with a base in Dublin. After an initial meeting with Ajit (the Indian General Manager of IndiaSoft's Irish operation) and Stephen (an Irish Business Development Manager for IndiaSoft), NetTrade were extremely impressed and, despite some significant apprehension about their unfamiliarity with this mode of development, decided that an offshoring approach was worth exploring further. Throughout their initial interactions with IndiaSoft, NetTrade were very honest about their anxieties, their inexperience, and their need for guidance through the process that lay ahead:

> We knew what we wanted but we were not 'deal' savvy. We were not through the RFP process, which was the first thing we told everybody. Don't expect us to tell you, you need to tell us. We didn't know but we knew we didn't know. We did make a big deal about that. (John, joint CEO, NetTrade)

In addition to stated concerns about their inexperience, and consequent dependence on the vendor, another major issue concerned NetTrade.

They were very conscious of the fact that in IndiaSoft's eyes, they might be viewed as a small, relatively unimportant, and insignificant Irish company in the context of the firm's overall client portfolio. They feared that this imbalance could be problematic going forward:

> That was a big deal because the first question (and one that we kept coming back to) was, what happens when Ford or GM or whoever calls, will we get screwed? ... it is engrained in us, people will value you less because you are smaller. (John, joint CEO, NetTrade)

As is evident in our discussion below, the Indian firm went to considerable lengths to address these fears, thereby laying the foundations for a successful relationship that developed over the 2005/2007 period under study. In late December 2005, and in line with the 'bite-sized chunks'

Key events over this time period include	
December 2005	First meeting with IndiaSoft and signing of the initial agreement for requirements specification
January 2006	First visit by John (joint CEO, NetTrade) and Paul (Head of Finance) to IndiaSoft's development center in IndiaCity, India to commence the requirements gathering and scoping process
March 2006	Representatives from IndiaCity visit Dublin to complete requirements gathering
April 2006	Functional specification completed and negotiations take place around the signing of the contract for the development work. Work commences
August/September 2006	John (joint CEO, NetTrade) and Deborah (Head of IT) visit IndiaCity to view prototypes Issues around live data feed requirements surface
December 2006	Paul (Head of Finance) and Deborah (Head of IT) visit IndiaCity to monitor progress NetTrade receive invoice for cost overruns
January 2007	New IndiaSoft Business Relationship Manager (BRM) (Ajay) joins the project Representatives from IndiaSoft visit Dublin to ensure smooth delivery Installation difficulties at NetTrade

philosophy of the firm, an agreement was reached that IndiaSoft would be engaged to do an initial requirement specifications and scoping exercise. NetTrade were extremely satisfied with the resulting document and decided to contract with the Indians for delivery of the system.

These events will be returned to in the subsequent analysis.

One of the notable aspects of this case is that the offshore development project, for the most part, ran relatively smoothly and was not beset by any major crises. This is not to say that frustrations and anxieties were not encountered along the way, but these were addressed and repaired in a relatively calm and mature manner. Here we argue that a key factor in understanding this smooth running of the project was the way in which trust was produced and sustained over time. The careful cultivation of a sense of psychological security, although costly and resource intensive, played a key role in the success of the project. Here, we draw on some of the theories of trust introduced earlier, in an attempt to trace some of the mechanisms by which this sense of security was produced, enhanced, undermined, and reestablished over time.

Following Giddens, we suggest that a key source of anxiety in the offshoring project was the difficulty in establishing trust in the expert systems of technical and professional knowledge upon which IndiaSoft drew (i.e. to provide 'guarantees' with respect to the 'correctness' of the technological solution that would be delivered across distanciated time–space (from India to Ireland)). Of critical importance here, then, was the manner in which this abstract system was 're-embedded' in the concrete context of the NetTrade–IndiaSoft relationship.[8]

We argue that within the timeframe outlined above, two distinctive, yet overlapping and mutually constitutive, phases are discernible. In the

---

[8] More precisely, building on the notion that any such abstract system will be interpretively flexible and may be enacted or embedded differently in different contexts, we argue that the key issue at stake is the expert *system-in-use* (i.e. the specific way in which such abstract principles are instantiated in the practices that constitute this project). The fact that systems *always* have to be reembedded underscores the importance of making the connection between forms of system trust and personal trust, between the rule and its application (Wittgenstein 1953). It is not merely trust in 'abstract principles' that needs to be reestablished at access points but, also, trust in the manner in which these principles are appropriated and applied.

Courtship phase the emphasis was on establishing a sense of trust in IndiaSoft as the suitor of choice, thus allowing NetTrade to bracket the associated risks and comfortably proceed with the project.[9] In the Cohabitation phase a new emphasis emerged, which focused on the joint construction of a stable collaborative order. In what follows, we examine and compare the social practices that underpinned these important processes.

Stage 1: Courtship – Establishing Trust in IndiaSoft

With respect to becoming comfortable with the notion of an offshoring arrangement, John identified three different components with which he and his colleagues at NetTrade needed to reconcile themselves: the generalized offshoring model, the idea of offshoring to India specifically, and IndiaSoft as the vendor of choice. The fact that John had only vaguely heard of software offshoring prior to the initial suggestion by a friend in August 2005 illustrates the distance he had to travel before committing to this route:

> To me now it seems like an easy decision. But then I knew very little about the whole outsourcing area . . . it was a real dark place that we were trying to figure out . . . I asked myself whether this made sense, how did it work? Were we just looking for a cheap option? Were we crazy? (John, Joint CEO, NetTrade)

The initial sense of security that created the impetus to explore the offshoring model and aligning with IndiaSoft specifically was based mainly on established trust relations, that is, *process-based trust*. Both

---

[9] We could, indeed, countenance a further stage immediately prior to this Courtship one. At the Dating stage, NetTrade explored a number of options and had some brief liaisons with a number of other vendors. (They had to kiss a few frogs before finding their Prince!) In fact, these encounters were very important in framing their subsequent relationship with IndiaSoft. Here, however, we believe that the anxiety-reducing mechanisms at play were essentially the same as those in the Courtship phase, and so we rejected the idea of analyzing them separately.

direct and indirect forms of such trust were apparent. Direct forms are observed in the case of recommendations of friends and friends of friends. John and Niall approached IndiaSoft in the first place on the recommendation of a close personal friend with experience of the IT industry. Furthermore, and perhaps more importantly, on approaching a very senior manager in a large global IT consulting firm, who was a friend of a fellow NetTrade board member, for advice on the subject, they received a 'big thumbs up' with respect to the offshoring model and IndiaSoft's capability in the area. A final example was seen in April 2006, when the two firms entered into negotiations around the contract. Niall talked about how reassured he was by the minimalist nature of IndiaSoft's contract:

> I am still surprised by their template contract that they had for us in terms of how short it was. I was totally taken aback that, for a company like IndiaSoft, it was not more comprehensive and did not cover more areas. Even from their point of view, I thought there would be more protections in there for themselves. Even perceiving it like that was quite reassuring – they were obviously not out to screw anybody. (Niall, Joint CEO, NetTrade)

The initial awareness of the offshoring possibility was followed by the commencement of what John described as a *'demystification process,'* where he began to notice and actively seek out articles about outsourcing in, what he considered, trusted sources such as *The Economist*. The reputational effects (indirect process-based trust) of such sources, supplemented by testimonies from IndiaSoft reference clients, contributed to a growing sense of comfort with the overall offshoring model.

A more *firm-specific, institutional basis* for establishing trust and creating a sense of security was drawn on as IndiaSoft outlined and explained their CMM Level 5 certification in their presentations to NetTrade.

The first major *access point* to the IndiaSoft offshoring model came with the initial face-to-face meeting with Ajit and Stephen in NetTrade's office in Dublin. This meeting appears to have been very consequential for the development of the relationship, as John and Niall were left feeling extremely impressed and reassured.

I remember vividly the meeting with Ajit and Stephen and I just found them incredibly impressive – very, very impressive – particularly Ajit. From a cultural point of view, I am used to Anglo-Saxon meetings; everyone is fairly machismo and everybody makes themselves heard... he was a GM and everyone around the table knew that he was very senior and he said almost nothing. And then at the end he said four or five sentences and they were so pithy and so... I personally like people like that that do not talk too much. He finished it off, summarized the meeting, and he was very impressive. (Niall, Joint CEO, NetTrade)

They wowed us in terms of their apparent ability to deliver quality and this on top of what appears to be an unbeatable proposition from a cost perspective. (John, Joint CEO, NetTrade)

Reflecting on their early meetings when representatives presented information about IndiaSoft and the offshoring models employed, John was clearly impressed by their apparent ability. He described the presentations as '*extremely slick and professional*' and he was struck by their '*systematic approach to software development.*' This professional manner and slickness was reinforced by references to IndiaSoft's CMM Level 5 certification (even though neither John nor Niall had previously heard of CMM, they were able to find out more about it subsequently). Interestingly, however, it was not the apparent professional ability of the IndiaSoft representatives that made the greatest impression; rather, it was their *general demeanor* and their *care and attentiveness*, which was to become a recurring feature of subsequent interactions.

A number of qualities seemed to set IndiaSoft apart from the other software firms that they had approached. First, there was the overall sense of *integrity* that was largely born from a sense of value congruity with NetTrade. Of crucial importance here was NetTrade's conception of their own values and sense of identity, which had been the subject of lively ongoing reflection and discussion since the inception of the company. In particular, a set of five core values had been agreed upon and, perhaps unusually for a financial services company, two of the principal ones were '*humility*' and '*basic honesty.*' The former emphasized the importance of a low-key, unfussy, and modest style, while the latter emphasized the value of integrity in dealing with people. In this respect, then, IndiaSoft were viewed as fellow travelers with whom NetTrade's guiding values were very well aligned and their humility and integrity seemed to indicate a kind of dependability:

> Bottom line – It was their humility. It is a value that we very genuinely hold and when we are selecting people to work with . . . if they don't have it and are more on the arrogant side, they are not for here. IndiaSoft definitely have it. (Niall, Joint CEO, NetTrade)

This apparent *value congruity* generated a kind of *characteristic-based trust* that both John and Niall generalized to, what they saw as, the distinct cultural affinities between Ireland and India. Memorably, John subsequently remarked how the Indian people he interacted with at the outset, and throughout the project, reminded him of Irish software engineers he had worked with on graduating with a computer science degree, nearly 20 years before. They were, he claimed, '*modest, hard working, and hungry*' before the more recent Irish economic success enjoyed on the back of the so-called 'Celtic Tiger' made them '*too complacent and brash.*' In IndiaSoft, then, John and Niall saw values that they could identify with and were trying to foster in their own company: values that they nostalgically associated with an apparently bygone 'golden' age of Irish economic development.[10]

---

[10] Whether this was an 'accurate' impression of IndiaSoft or not is, perhaps, beside the point. While we are conscious of the danger of resorting to cultural stereotypes here, the key issue is that John formed and sustained this impression of them, and acted on that basis. One point worth considering in this respect is the extent to which IndiaSoft staff were 'mirroring' (perhaps unconsciously) particular traits of their client. It would be interesting, for instance, to observe how their 'presentation of self' (Goffman 1956) would differ with a very different kind of client. On the evidence of our interaction with IndiaSoft staff, however, both in Ireland and in India, we could also clearly recognize the kind of traits to which John drew attention, and broader social values appear to be a very important feature of life in the firm. Furthermore, there are some good bases for making cultural comparisons between Ireland and India. Not only do both countries share a similar British colonial history (indeed India adopted a modified version of the Irish constitution postindependence and even a modified version of the Irish national flag!) and an emphasis on familial and community ties, but comparisons might also be drawn between recent modes of economic development based on engineering and high technology (see e.g. Foley and O'Connor 2004). Indeed, as John Stuart Mill once pointed out, '[t]hose Englishmen who know something about India, are even now those who understand Ireland best' (Cook 1993: 53).

The *care and attentiveness* that they received from IndiaSoft came as a very pleasant surprise and was greatly welcomed by NetTrade. John and Niall were both greatly impressed by IndiaSoft's thoroughness in responding to points and requests made by NetTrade:

> they responded to everything on our list – they wanted us; they loved us and we like being loved... they seemed to want our business – they showed an interest in our business in a way that others didn't.... When you meet somebody that you are impressed with, it is just a good experience and you want to proceed... we (had) a connection here and we like(d) them... we were constantly getting good vibes. (John, Joint CEO, NetTrade)
>
> IndiaSoft had such a huge capacity to listen and respond to this – it is absolutely brilliant, they are great listeners. (Niall, Joint CEO, NetTrade)

While this level of attentiveness was quite unexpected on the basis of their dealings with other agencies and companies in Ireland (*'it is engrained in us, people will value you less because you are smaller,'* John), it was instrumental in allaying one of their key fears: that of their project being so small and insignificant that it would *'get lost'* within a big organization such as IndiaSoft. This apparent *benevolence* on the part of IndiaSoft toward NetTrade was reinforced by John's relationship with Stephen who, importantly, was based in IndiaSoft's Dublin office (located only a short distance from NetTrade's office). Stephen *'did a good job initially in selling IndiaSoft as IndiaSoft Ireland'* and so reassuring John that whatever fears he might have of NetTrade *'getting lost'* in IndiaSoft, that there was no way this would happen in IndiaSoft Ireland (another relatively small, but growing, Irish company), or indeed in the IndiaCity development center (again a small, but growing, business entity). Here again we see an example of IndiaSoft 'mirroring' NetTrade and, in so doing, strengthening the sense of trust and mutual affiliation.

IndiaSoft's care and attentiveness was also manifested in the numerous ways in which they appeared to go the extra mile to accommodate NetTrade's needs, thereby making them feel valued as a client. Key events here included Stephen making a trip to the delivery center in IndiaCity to coincide with John and Paul's initial visit there; the attentiveness and personal hospitality afforded by Pratima (the head of the IndiaCity delivery center) to John and his colleagues during his visits to India (the fact that someone so senior was taking an interest in the project made a very big impression on John); the fact that IndiaSoft appeared to be very sensitive to NetTrade's anxieties about the project and did everything they could to accommodate their '*bitesize chunks*' risk management philosophy (for instance the fact that they agreed to break the total cost of the system into four manageable-staged payments was seen as a very significant gesture by NetTrade and provided some welcome relief from the financial burden that they were undertaking to develop the system); and the fact that they went to great lengths to take the unusual step of providing ongoing remote access to a working prototype of the system at John's behest.

One interesting observation about this process of security building was that the steps taken to ease NetTrade's anxiety appeared to appeal to both cognitive and emotional elements of John and Niall's personalities. The 'bite-sized chunks' approach, for example, was a very rational and sensible strategy for risk management. By contrast, however, both John and Niall spoke often about the (much less tangible) '*good vibes*' that they constantly got from IndiaSoft and the important role that this played in their decision-making. In this regard, we are reminded of Giddens' assertion that trust is always blind and that it involves an emotional, as opposed to a cognitive, commitment to a given set of outcomes. Dealing with risk in this case, then, involved both trust (an emotional commitment) and calculation (more of a cognitive sense of assurance[11]).

---

[11] Of course, we would be sympathetic to the general idea that even ostensibly rational/cognitive exercises are often enacted in ritualistic ways as a means of facilitating a more emotional type of commitment. This illustrates the difficulties associated with making a clean separation between the 'cognitive' and the 'emotional.'

Stage 2: Cohabitation – Constructing a Stable Collaborative Order

Despite the excellent and reassuring early impressions as to the ability, benevolence, and integrity of the IndiaSoft representatives, and the reliability of their software delivery systems and processes, it was clear that increasing levels of trust were developed only tentatively over time. In other words, the mechanisms for developing trust discussed above were not confined to one identifiable period of the project but extended throughout the duration of the relationship. As the project progressed, process-based trust again came to the fore as NetTrade became more comfortable with the IndiaSoft offshore development model. Key to this was the quality of the intermediary deliverables and, more importantly, the deepening personal relationships between key actors in both companies. In particular, these relationships gave the project a new robustness, which allowed issues to be dealt with in a more open and direct manner.[12]

In the Cohabitation phase, however, a new emphasis emerged: that of constructing a *stable collaborative order*. While a good basis for trust had been developed in the earlier period, both parties now had to collectively establish communal social practices to enable them to work closely together. Of critical importance here, from the point of view of producing trust, was the stability and predictability that such practices would confer on the project interactions. Once activities around the project commenced, incongruent *communication practices* quickly surfaced and presented a number of challenges. The first evidence of tension in the relationship emerged during John's initial visit to India. Together with his Head of Finance (Paul), John spent 8 days in intensive meetings meticulously explaining their requirements to the Indians. He became

---

[12] At the same time, however, the trust also had a brittle quality. In September 2006, one of the researchers met an Irish software developer who had worked with IndiaSoft in India for a short, and unhappy, period. His experience of working with IndiaSoft was not very positive and was dramatically at odds with NetTrade's impression of them. John, on hearing this story, became extremely worried about the project, and for a short time began to seriously question his own judgments.

immediately concerned that the process lacked direction and input from the Indians:

> I'm concerned that there is not a strong leader outlining the process and stepping us confidently through it. (John, Joint CEO, NetTrade)
>
> One negative aspect would be that they seem a bit too accommodating. I would prefer if they sometimes disagreed and instead gave their views as alternatives. (Paul, personal journal)

On several occasions John repeatedly asked the then project sponsor (Suran) to send him copies of the Indian team's rough notes from the requirements sessions. He wanted these to ensure that the Indians understood NetTrade's needs around the new system. This was new to IndiaSoft – they had never received such a request from a client and they were reluctant to comply, preferring instead to complete a draft of the requirements document that might then be reviewed by John:[13]

> sometimes we wanted things that were not planned for as a deliverable and I don't think their processes allow for it...and this was frustrating because they did not tell us this explicitly...we were not getting a straight answer. (John, personal journal)

At later stages, further frustrations were evident around the directness of communication:

> I remember I got into a very bitter discussion around the issue of volume testing. (...) We asked what they planned to do around volume testing (...) he would not answer the question (...) even if the answer was 'we don't know' – that would have been an honest answer – but getting the other response was annoying. (John, Joint CEO, NetTrade)

---

[13] This kind of interaction became a familiar theme in the project and might be understood as involving the negotiation of the boundary between frontstage and backstage (Goffman 1956). Such was John's anxiety that he was always trying to 'peep backstage.' In his view, however, IndiaSoft did not want to show him their *'dirty laundry'.* The fact that trust rests on a presentational base, where frontstage impression management is vital, would suggest that IndiaSoft's reluctance to accede to John's wishes was well founded.

These communication deficits were even acknowledged on the Indian side as one informant confided how sometimes '*things tend to go from green to red with no amber light*.'

Despite weekly status meetings and ongoing contact, John felt that '*there are big silences in the process*,' and these silences made him very uncomfortable.[14] A good example of this was seen toward the end of 2006 when a dispute ensued about the acquisition of the data feed to test the software. After an initial delay around selecting and reaching an agreement with a data provider that would feed the live data into Dublin, NetTrade were surprised to learn that IndiaSoft also needed a live feed link into the development site in India:

There was one deliverable from the NetTrade site – the live data feed. There was a delay on NetTrade's side as to the provider.... For us to proceed with our work, we needed this basic information. The delay had an impact. This was discussed at status meetings. 'The dash board/status report went to Dublin and there was a traffic light on the report in terms of the effort, costs, schedule etc. We communicated it explicitly enough but John thought we did not communicate it correctly. He realised that this would have a schedule impact but said that we were not explicit on the cost impact. This reflected the lack of project experience on NetTrade's side.' (Suresh, Project Sponsor, IndiaSoft)

This was later confirmed by Ajay (the new BRM, who joined the project in January 2007):

Ahmed must have mentioned it about five times on the status reports and got no response and when you get no response you tend to ignore it (...) and we should not have done this. (Ajay, BRM, IndiaSoft(Irl.))

John notes how this came as a big surprise to NetTrade:

---

[14] Cramton (2001) notes how physical separation and reliance on communications technologies can exacerbate uncertainty when trying to interpret the meaning of silence.

... it wasn't there earlier in the summer when we were setting up. I kept saying ye are the experts, tell us what you want, tell us how it works... you are supposed to have done this many times in many different ways – so guide us. (John, joint CEO, NetTrade)

John claimed that IndiaSoft had casually alluded to this in August 2006, but the issue was hardly raised again. They sent the Application Programmer Interfaces of potential data providers assuming that this would enable IndiaSoft to proceed with development. It took a few weeks for NetTrade to sign a contract with a provider and once this was secured, an additional problem arose – IndiaSoft could not read the live data at their development site and, considering it *out of scope*, were reluctant to engage directly with the provider to find a solution. John notes that this caused a lot of anguish for NetTrade's IT manager (Deborah):

They were always reluctant to do this, which is very frustrating because we have no expertise. (John, joint CEO, NetTrade)
We provided this for them – they could not read it... so we had to go back to the provider and figure it out... it was very difficult dealing with the provider. For us (i.e. Deborah), being in the middle was actually the most frustrating part of it all... and I could see the guys getting frustrated... but it was a shared problem. (John, joint CEO, NetTrade)

It resulted in significant upheaval and delays in the project and a demand was made by IndiaSoft for an additional payment of €80,000.[15] NetTrade were very aggrieved about the manner in which this communication was managed and, on this occasion, responded angrily and forcefully:

I was livid.... (John, joint CEO, NetTrade)
It was extremely disappointing from a project management point of view. We were very genuinely angry, and justifiably angry with Stephen. The

---

[15] Demonstrating their irritation over the issue, the €80,000 bill that they received was always referred to as a '*penalty*' by NetTrade but as a '*cost overrun*' by IndiaSoft.

fact that it was totally out of the blue was just crazy and we communicated it to them hundreds of times. It was bad project management on their side and this should not have got through their controls. (Niall, joint CEO, NetTrade)

This invoice was delivered at a particularly anxious and tense time in the project and served to further strain interfirm relations. However, neither firm was tempted to resort to the terms of the contract, or to refer to minutes of meetings or status reports in support of their position. Drawing attention to his emotional commitment to his relationship, John later explained the precarious nature of the situation that they found themselves in:

> (...) the contract is useless in many respects isn't it? If you are a small contract up against IndiaSoft...its almost unimaginable that we will really go down the legal path...somehow the contract is not what it's about. (...)

Ajay joined the project and insisted that the issue be pushed to one side so that full attention could be devoted to the critical task at hand. John was happy with this arrangement:

> Nobody is trying to screw anybody. We are all honourable and we will come to an agreement. (John, joint CEO, NetTrade)

This indicates the important role of the social capital, which had been so painstakingly created, and contributed to an extraordinary resilience in interfirm relations. However, despite this resolution, the project was beset by further problems throughout the month of January:

> There was an awful lot of tension around the installation. It has gone from the one day that they predicted to the three days that we allowed for...then it was 5 days and now its ten days and we are still not finished. There was a big blame game going on.... (John, Joint CEO, NetTrade) Suresh claimed that his people (though our opinion is that this was his opinion) were saying that installation and issues like this was outside scope for them...the tone was really wrong...the suggestion was that there

was no solution . . . . Or at least that he could be part of the solution . . . I got angry . . . that kinda stuff can make you really annoyed . . . and I'm goin. 'your kidding me! We need to get this thing solved, we need to come together. (John, Joint CEO, NetTrade)

John noted how Ajay seemed to be visibly perturbed by this conversation and he felt that even Suresh realized that this was not the correct approach. After this meeting another conference call took place between Stephen, Suresh, and Ajay, following which the project was judged to be back on track:

We have all hands on deck. And the team in India is delighted. They want to stop with the politics and get in there and solve problems and they are great. (John, Joint CEO, NetTrade)

Throughout this Cohabitation phase, we see ongoing negotiation of appropriate communicative practices, which proved to be most challenging as it involved difficult processes of finding mutual accommodations between Irish and Indian cultural norms. This process was complicated by the temporal/geographical separation. Moreover, the deeply embedded nature of such practices meant that attempts to alter them required significant skill, as well as the balancing of 'trust, tact and power' (Giddens 1990: 82). In what follows, we explore these *micro-political processes* in more detail, by illustrating how agents attempted to balance trust, tact, and power in the course of their strategic actions. In so doing, we introduce three concepts that emerged from our grounded analysis of the data: namely, '*tactical signaling*,' '*brokering*,' and '*the third man*.' Ironically, while NetTrade bemoaned the fact that IndiaSoft were less than direct in some of their modes of communication, the former often made use of similarly indirect modes themselves as they tried to shape the project by appropriately balancing trust, tact, and power.

The first example of tactical signaling was seen during the first visit to the delivery center. John recalls how less than impressed he was by the project manager (Sumeet) who had been assigned to the project. In contrast, he was very impressed and enthusiastic about Sunil, the younger functional requirements person. This played heavily on John's mind throughout his stay but he found it difficult to raise the point directly with IndiaSoft. In an effort to subtly deliver this unpalatable message, he opted for a different strategy:

> The other guy was the yes, yes, yes, he hadn't a clue. I made a point of praising Sunil and did not say anything about the other guy so he disappeared from the team, which was a good thing. (John, Joint CEO, NetTrade)

The message was understood, it seems, as Sumeet was promptly moved from the project. On the other hand, even though John privately admitted to being a little concerned about the extent to which he seemed to be driving the initial requirements gathering process in India, he tactfully decided against raising these issues directly with IndiaSoft at the outset, for fear of being seen to question their professionalism.

These subtle and very careful forms of signaling were also helpfully used in other contexts. On the advice of friends, John made it very clear to IndiaSoft at the outset that he was keen to inspect the résumés of all staff assigned to the project. He later confessed that, despite the fact that he found it difficult to make sense of them, his main intention was to signal to IndiaSoft that he was being very vigilant and watching things closely:

> They sent us CVs. I glanced through them... it was hard to decipher them... Indian colleges etc. I asked for them and there was a bit of posturing around wanting to get good guys etc. We couldn't really read them, but they looked grand. (John, Joint CEO NetTrade)

The symbolism associated with making regular trips to India was also seen as important:

> We went back over in December... it was really to show them that we were taking things seriously and even just to enhance the relationship... to reaffirm it. (Paul, Head of Finance, NetTrade)

'*Brokering*' was another vital means of facilitating productive communication while minimizing damage to the integrity of important relationships. The importance of brokers (or *boundary spanners*) has been highlighted in the knowledge management literature. Typically, these are described as individuals who facilitate the sharing of expertise between groups of people who are separated by location, hierarchy, or function (Allen and Cohen 1969; Tushman 1977; Wenger 1998; Pawlowski and Robey 2004; Levina 2005). Much of the emphasis is placed on the importance of translating/decoding idiosyncratic domain knowledge. The theoretical perspective that we developed earlier would suggest that a broker's role might extend beyond translating/communicating, embracing an enlarged remit of reassurance and anxiety reduction.

Stephen, who had cultivated very strong relationships with people at NetTrade (especially John) and at the IndiaCity delivery center, was a particularly good example of a broker. John described Stephen as someone who '*appeared to have a foot in both camps*' and was very receptive to, and understanding of, any issues raised by NetTrade. The fact that Stephen was Irish and of a similar age and background to John meant that both parties found it very easy to communicate with one another. As the project progressed, Stephen was replaced by Ajay, John found himself not only increasingly using Stephen (and then Ajay) to broker important issues that needed to be communicated to India but also as a vehicle through which frustrations could be vented. For example, John talked about '*regularly thrashing Suresh to Stephen (and Ajay) . . . and I (he) had a sympathetic audience.*'

Stephen appeared to align with NetTrade's perspective on various issues. This was nicely articulated by Niall when he reflected on a meeting that was held to iron out the penalty fee imposed on the firm in December 2006:

(. . .) it was very interesting from a cultural perspective watching Stephen and Ajay – both representing the same company but they were not singing from the same hymn sheet (. . .) Stephen ended up being a little more on our side and Ajay was very much protecting IndiaSoft – his heart and mind were back in IndiaCity whereas Stephen was looking at it from our perspective (...) Stephen ended up agreeing with us on almost everything and he probably should not have. (Niall, joint CEO, NetTrade)

This perception of having like-minded allies on the Indian side served to allay concerns and anxieties and uphold NetTrade's position on various issues that arose. For example, as noted earlier, John was concerned about the silences in the process at various junctures – at a later stage, he was very frustrated at how NetTrade were being blamed for delays in the project. Stephen's appreciation of NetTrade's viewpoint and position seemed to reassure John that his anxieties and frustrations with the Indian firm were well founded. In turn, this seemed to instill confidence around his judgment:

> Even Stephen would say that they need to do more to speak up.
> If you think about, what they are saying here is that their development environment is dependent on the successful setting up of the UAT and production environment in order for them to finish the development ... and I'm going ... that's just daft! ... and Stephen agreed.

As noted earlier, Ajay's introduction to the project in January 2007 immediately served to diffuse tensions and re-instill a sense of security about relations going forward. John recalled how Ajay told them that Stephen would sort the dispute out at a later stage. He told them that he would not *get into that 80,000 thing* but that he would *make it his business to flag things well in advance going forward.* Niall recalled: *When Ajay came, he said he would tell us everything (...) and (our meetings) are very frank.* Consequently, John spoke about a renewed sense of optimism around the project.

The other key broker between NetTrade and IndiaSoft was Sunil (an Indian). From the very early stages of the project Sunil and John began to form a very good relationship. As noted above, John was initially very impressed by Sunil's ability and by the extent of his domain knowledge. Moreover, he appreciated Sunil's style of interaction, which was much less diffident than some of the other IndiaSoft team members: 'Sunil was like a dog with a bone; he was constantly pursuing problems and issues and in the end he knows much more about our systems than we do ourselves!' The two months that Sunil spent in Dublin during the onsite requirements gathering phase facilitated the blossoming of this relationship with John. The two found that they had a lot in common and spent significant time together discussing the system and broader business and cultural issues.

The formation of these kinds of strong relationships, however, did not come without a cost. Sunil sometimes found that his relationship with John put him in a difficult position with respect to his loyalties within the project. For instance, while Sunil was onsite in Dublin during the deployment phase in January 2007, he was inadvertently caught in a minor dispute over the release of source code to NetTrade. John was keen to have access to the code so that his technical staff could inspect it and familiarize themselves with it. Unbeknown to him, however, Suresh (the project sponsor in India) had explicitly instructed Sunil not to release the code, without publicly making this known. At one particular tense project meeting in Dublin when John kept asking Sunil for the code, Sunil had to ask John for a private word outside of the meeting, whereupon he disclosed that Suresh had vetoed this.

John seemed very sensitive to the difficulties that Sunil faced and even described an incident where he used a combination of signaling and brokering to deliver a message to India. In the course of the dispute over the implications of the data feed delay, John had complained that Suresh was not adequately communicating problems in advance of them escalating. Following this criticism, John received an email from Suresh that went into great detail about ongoing issues. In full knowledge that Sunil was seated close by, John loudly and angrily complained about the fact that Suresh had suddenly 'gone from giving no information about what's going on to giving way too much' in the hope that his annoyance would be relayed back to India by Sunil.

A further tactic that was used by NetTrade, often inadvertently, might be termed the '*third man.*' This involved introducing a third party who did not have a close relationship with IndiaSoft and who could consequently be more ruthless in their dealings with them. Two brief examples can be cited to illustrate this. First, during the contract negotiations between John and IndiaSoft in April 2006, John made regular reference to the importance of reaching an agreement that would be acceptable to NetTrade's board. Indeed, in the end, one of the major reasons IndiaSoft reduced their price substantially was on the basis that if it exceeded a certain critical amount the board had decreed that the contract should be submitted to public tender:

> We went back to IndiaSoft that the non executive board was a weight upon which everything hung...what would board think?...it was a useful entity...we probably over played it.... (John, joint CEO, NetTrade)

Second, NetTrade hired a specialist software firm (TestCo) in September 2006 to help them develop their user acceptance testing plan. One of the TestCo consultants sat in on a user acceptance testing meeting at which we were present in January 2007 and proceeded to aggressively question Sunil about the way IndiaSoft were prioritizing problem reports in a manner that John or his colleagues would have found difficult. At the conclusion of this meeting (which was attended by one of the researchers), Sunil looked visibly upset at the tenor and tone of the questioning, despite the fact that he appeared to handle the substantive issues raised very competently. Without a '*third man*' this kind of robust interaction would have been almost impossible at this stage of the project. The imperatives of trust and tact would simply not have allowed it.

Discussion and Conclusions

In this paper we have explored the notion of anxiety and its management in the context of a model of offshore software development that is becoming increasingly common in the contemporary world. In particular, we have focused on the important question of how psychological security is produced in circumstances that may involve high risk and a very opaque development process that is inherently difficult to monitor, not least because of issues associated with geographical and cultural separation. By so doing, we draw attention to the, often invisible, 'relationship work' that is required to develop and sustain the crucial social infrastructure that underpins project relationships, lending them an important robustness.

The paper makes empirical and conceptual contributions. With respect to the former, the case study presented is particularly interesting for a number of reasons. First, the existence of strong personal relationships between members of the research team and some of the key players involved in the project facilitated an unusually high level of access to the research site. This provided a rare window on the intimate workings of key social processes as they unfolded over time, allowing us to explore the '...ebbs and flows of the evolution of relationships' (Lacity and Willcocks 2001: 290). In the context of an accepted dearth of published in-depth, idiographic accounts of the development and dynamics of offshoring relationships (Sahay et al. 2003), then, the study provides a basis for a relatively nuanced and granular understanding of such activities. A further interesting feature of the study is the Ireland–India connection. Whereas other studies have focused on global software alliances spanning such locations as USA–India (Kumar and Willcocks 1996), USA–Caribbean (Abbott 2004), Canada–India (Sahay 2003), United Kingdom–India (Nicholson and Sahay 2001, 2004), Norway–Russia (Imsland and Sahay 2005), etc., we know of no study that has specifically explored cultural aspects of an Ireland–India relationship. Finally, the study offers an unusual example of offshoring practice, in that it involves a very small and young firm that has entered into a sourcing relationship with a large and well-established vendor of IT development services (see Nicholson and Carmel 2003).

From a conceptual point of view the paper attempts to introduce a language that enables us to problematize and shed light on some crucial, yet intangible and often overlooked, aspects of offshoring practice. As such, the emphasis has not been on 'theory generation,' where this enterprise is conceived of as the development or refinement of a set of testable propositions. Rather, our aim here has been to synthesize, in a grounded manner, a sophisticated theoretical lens that illuminates important features of the dynamics of offshoring relationships (see Walsham (1995) for a discussion of this notion of theory as a 'sensitizing device') and of its importance in the context of interpretive studies in the

IS field. Specifically, we have drawn on the work of a diverse range of scholars on trust (in particular Anthony Giddens, Lynne Zucker, and Barbara Misztal) to synthesize a rich and novel conceptual lens, with a view to making sense of our experiences in the field.

This synthesized perspective provided us with the means to explore the process by which psychological security was produced within the context of, what was for NetTrade, a very risky and anxiety provoking journey into the unknown. The distinctiveness of the conceptual lens developed here offers the possibility of opening up a number of novel theoretical directions for research on software offshoring. In particular, the emphasis on anxiety and its management offers fresh perspective on the challenges associated with managing such global work arrangements. Not only does it draw attention to important mechanisms by which trust as psychological security is produced and anxiety contained, but it illustrates how these processes become especially problematic in an off-shore model where interaction routinely spans temporal–geographical and cultural distance. We argued that the development of confidence involves both cognitive/calculative (i.e. the adoption of rational strategies for reducing risk exposure) and emotional (trust) components that enabled a (partial) bracketing of risk and associated anxiety, thus facilitating productive engagement with the project at hand. Our emphasis on the emotional dimension of organizational life, inspired by Anthony Giddens' distinctive approach to understanding trust and its role in the contemporary world, constitutes a significant departure from much of the mainstream literature in the management/organization studies area, thus opening up new research vistas. Specifically, it provides an enlarged, noncognitivist, perspective on the supposed role of, *inter alia*, interorganizational routines (Zollo et al. 2002) and brokers/boundary spanners (Levina 2005), which indicates that these are more than mere mechanisms for facilitating information exchange/sharing or communication; their importance might also be due to the manner in which they offer reassurance and help produce a sense of psychological security. Furthermore, the perspective on trust developed here broadens the scope of much of the extant literature on the subject by explicitly considering impersonal forms of trust (system trust), while linking these with forms of personal trust.

We drew on the synthesized theoretical lens to explore two distinctive kinds of trust production that appeared especially important in the NetTrade–IndiaSoft case. First, there was the establishment of trust by NetTrade in IndiaSoft as a suitable offshoring partner and, second, there was trust as 'habitus' – the struggle to establish a stable, predictable, and productive collaborative order (consisting of a set of well-understood and mutually acceptable social practices, especially communicative practices).

In the course of our analysis of the case, we attempted to illustrate how these different modes of trust production operated and complemented one another. In so doing, we considered two distinctive phases of the relationship to date (Courtship and Cohabitation), where one mode appeared to take precedence over the other. While these kinds of distinctive phases have been used as analytical devices elsewhere in the outsourcing literature (e.g. Cartwright and Cooper 1993; Klepper 1995; Mcfarlan and Nolan 1995; Lacity and Willcocks 2001), the work presented here attempts to go beyond mere categorization to provide a more in-depth analysis of the key functions of each stage and the practices required to support them (cf. Ring and Van De Ven 1994; Kern 1997; Willcocks and Kern 1998). Furthermore, we were careful to point out that these were not strictly linear sequential stages. The trust generating practices that predominated in each stage were not absent in the other; it was merely a question of emphasis; both sets of concerns endure throughout the lifetime of a project and, indeed, are mutually constitutive, but at different points the emphasis tends to be on one over the other.

In the Courtship phase, in the early part of the relationship, the emphasis was primarily on 'manifest displays of trustworthiness' at key meetings/interactions (i.e. access points), on reputational effects (i.e. indirect forms of process-based trust), and on apparent value congruence between Indian and Irish graduates (characteristic-based trust). Of critical importance was the establishment of trust in the reliability of the expert system of knowledge/practices employed by IndiaSoft, which was grounded in personal interactions with IndiaSoft representatives at access points to the system. With a view to enlarging Giddens' perspective, we focused on perceptions of ability, integrity, and benevolence as constitutive features of personal trust. With respect to the latter quality specifically, a key feature appeared to be the extraordinary care and attentiveness lavished upon NetTrade by IndiaSoft.

In the Cohabitation phase, the emphasis shifted to other kinds of strategic action that involved the balancing of trust, tact, and power in the construction of a stable collaborative order (trust as 'habitus'). Here, we identified a number of micropolitical tactics that were employed in attempts to establish mutually acceptable working practices, especially communicative practices. These were essentially indirect and tactful ways of dealing with important issues so as not to cause offence, and they included 'signaling,' 'brokering,' and 'the third man.' The aim here was to draw attention to the complex micropolitics of trust, in the context of the development of secure, stable, and predictable practices that would keep anxiety at bay.

A striking feature of this analysis is the amount of effort, care, and attentiveness that was required to establish productive social relations, notwithstanding the apparent value congruity of the two firms involved. These efforts, however, contributed to the creation of important social capital that gave the project a new robustness that sustained it during difficult periods. The dispute concerning the data feed was perhaps the most significant problem that beset project relations in the process to date, but what was remarkable was the manner in which the potential damage was managed and repaired. Neither parties referred back to contracts or written records but, rather, decided to push the issue to one side, to proceed with the project, and to revisit the issue at some future point.

> Nobody is trying to screw anybody. We are all honourable and we will come to an agreement. (John, joint CEO, NetTrade)

This last quotation indicates the extent of the social capital that had been developed between these two firms in such a short period of time; John felt obligated to act honorably in relation to IndiaSoft and, perhaps more importantly, he was confident that IndiaSoft would behave honorably toward him.

Finally, and to extend this theme, there is evidence to suggest that this NetTrade–IndiaSoft relationship may run for some time yet. The current plans to extend and deepen the relationship might suggest the transition to a new more stable phase (Marriage) marked by an explicit mutual commitment to a longer term, ongoing strategic relationship (thus leveraging the social capital and mutual understanding that had been so painstakingly built). Should this come to pass, it will be interesting to compare and contrast the challenges associated with this phase to subsequent ones and to explore the practices required to sustain and enhance the relationship for mutual benefit.

We hope that practitioners may find value in the depth and richness of the case material presented. By addressing the dearth of detailed accounts of the dynamics of such relationships in the IS literature to date (Sahay et al. 2003), we aim to contribute to the formation of enhanced levels of practitioner expertise in the area of software off-shoring (Flyvbjerg 2001; Dreyfus and Dreyfus 2005). In keeping with our philosophy of the distinctive strengths of interpretive, idiographic case study research (see Flyvbjerg 2006), we have resisted the temptation to attempt to distill the richness of the empirical material presented to a small number of highly generalized prescriptions for practice. Furthermore, we hope that the theoretical perspective that has guided our analysis will provide managers with a productive way of seeing, and engaging with, the world of practice.

References

Abbott, P.Y (2004). Software-Export Strategies for Developing Countries: A Caribbean perspective, *Electronic Journal of Information Systems in Developing Countries (EJISDC)* **20**: 1–19.

Allen, T.J, and Cohen, S.I (1969). Information Flows in Research and Development Laboratories, *Administrative Science Quarterly* **14**: 12–19.

Barki, H, Rivard, S, and Talbot, J (1993). Towards an Assessment of Software Development Risk, *Journal of Management Information Systems* **10**: 203–225.

Bloomfield, B, and Coombs, R. (1992). Information Technology, Control and Power: The centralization and decentralization debate revisited, *Journal of Management Studies* **29**: 459–484.

Boehm, B.W., and Demarco, T (1997). Software Risk Management: Principles and practices, *IEEE Software* **14**: 17–19.

Cartwright, S, and Cooper, C.L (1993). The Role of Culture Compatibility in Successful Organizational Marriage, *The Academy of Management Executive* **7**: 57–70.

Chaiklin, S, and Lave, J (eds.) (1996). *Understanding Practice: Perspectives on activity and context*, Cambridge University Press: Cambridge.

Ciborra, C (2006). The Mind or the Heart? It Depends on the (Definition of) Situation, *Journal of Information Technology* **21**: 129–139.

Cook, S.B (1993). *Imperial Affinities. Nineteenth Century Analogies and Exchanges between India and Ireland*, Delhi: Sage.

Cramton, C.D (2001). The Mutual Knowledge Problem and its Consequences for Dispersed Collaboration, *Organization Science* **12**: 346–371.

Das, T.K, and Teng, B.-S (1998). Between Trust and Control: Developing confidence in partner cooperation in alliances, *Academy of Management Review* **23**: 491–512.

Dasgupta, P. (1988). Trust as a Commodity, In D. Gambetta (ed.) *Trust: Making and Breaking Cooperative Relations*, Oxford: Basil Blackwell.

Dreyfus, H.L, and Dreyfus, S.E (2005). Expertise in Real World Contexts, *Organization Studies* **26**: 779–792.

Earl, M.J (1996). The Risks of Outsourcing IT, *Sloan, Management Review* **37**: 26–32.

Erikson, E (1950). *Childhood and Society*, New York: Norton.

Flyvbjerg, B. (2001). *Making Social Science Matter: Why social inquiry fails and how it can succeed again*, Cambridge: Cambridge University Press.

Flyvbjerg, B. (2006). Five Misunderstandings about Case-Study Research, *Qualitative Inquiry* **12**: 219–245.

Foley, T, and O'Connor, M. (eds.) (2004). Ireland and India, Colonies: Culture and the Empire – Proceedings of the fourth Galway conference on colonialism, Irish Academic Press: Dublin, Ireland.

Gambetta, D. (ed.) (1988). *Trust: Making and breaking of cooperative relations*, Oxford: Blackwell.

Giddens, A (1990). *The Consequences of Modernity*, Cambridge: Polity.

Giddens, A. (1991). *Modernity and Self-Identity: Self and society in the late modern age*, Cambridge: Polity.

Goffman, E (1956). *The Presentation of Self in Everyday Life*, London: Penguin.

Good, D (1988). Individuals, Interpersonal Relations, and Trust, In D. Gambetta (ed.) *Trust: The Making and Breaking of Cooperative Relations*, Oxford: Blackwell.

Hart, K (1988). Kinship, Contract and Trust: The economic organization of migrants in an African city slum, In D. Gambetta (ed.) *Trust: The Making and Breaking of Cooperative Relations*, Oxford: Blackwell.

Hirschhorn, L (1988). *The Workplace Within: The psychodynamics of organizational life*, Cambridge, MA: MIT Press.

Imsland, V, and Sahay, S. (2005). Negotiating Knowledge': The case of a Russian–Norwegian software outsourcing project, *Scandinavian Journal of Information Systems* 17: 101–130.

Kelly, S (2005). New Frontiers in the Theorization of ICT-Mediated Interaction? Exploring the Implications of a Situated Learning Epistemology, In W.R. King and R. Torkzadeh (eds.) Proceedings of the International Conference on Information Systems (ICIS), Las Vegas: Association of Information Systems.

Kern, T (1997). The *Gestalt* of an Information Technology Outsourcing Relationship: An exploratory analysis, Eighteenth Annual International Conference on Information Systems (ICIS), Atlanta, Georgia: Association of Information Systems.

Klein, H.K, and Myers, M.D (1999). A Set of Principles for Conducting and Evaluating Interpretive Field Studies in Information Systems, *MIS Quarterly* 23: 67–88.

Klepper, R. (1995). The Management of Partnering Development in I/S Outsourcing, *Journal of Information Technology* 10: 249–258.

Knights, D (1990). Subjectivity, Power and the Labour Process, In D. Knights and H. Willmott (eds.) *Labour Process Theory*, London: Macmillan.

Knights, D. (1992). Changing Spaces: The disruptive impact of a new epistemological location for the study of management, *Academy of Management Review* 17: 514–536.

Knights, D, and Murray, F (1994). *Managers Divided: Organisation politics and information technology management*, Chichester: John Wiley.

Knights, D, and Willmott, H (1999). *Management Lives: Power and identity in work organizations*, London: Sage.

Kumar, K, and Willcocks, L.P (1996). Offshore Outsourcing: A country too far? Fourth European Conference on Information Systems (ECIS), Lisbon, Portugal: Association of Information Systems.

Lacity, M.C, and Willcocks, L.P (2001). *Global Information Technology Outsourcing: In search of business advantage*, Chichester: John Wiley & Sons.

Laing, R.D (1971). *Self and Others*, Harmondsworth: Penguin.

Levina, N (2005). The Emergence of Boundary Spanning Competence in Practice: Implications for implementation and use of information systems, *MIS Quarterly* **29**: 335–363.

Lorenz, E.H (1988). Neither Friends nor Strangers: Informal networks of subcontracting in French industry, In D. Gambetta (ed.) *Trust: Making and Breaking Cooperative Relations*, Oxford: Basil Blackwell.

Mayer, R.C, Davis, J.H, and Schoorman, F.D (1995). An Integrative Model of Organizational Trust, *Academy of Management Review* **20**: 709–734.

Mcallister, D.J (1995). Affect- and Cognition-Based Trust as Foundations for Interpersonal Cooperation in Organizations, *Academy of Management Journal* **38**: 24–59.

Mcfarlan, F.W, and Nolan, R.L (1995). How to Manage an IT Outsourcing Alliance, *Sloan Management Review* **36**: 9–23.

Mcgrath, K (2006). Affection not Affliction: The role of emotions in information systems and organizational change, *Information and Organization* **16**: 277–303.

Menzies-Lyth, I (1988). *Containing Anxiety in Institutions: Selected essays*, London: Free Association Press.

Miller, P, and O'Leary, T (1987). Accounting and the Construction of the Governable Person, *Accounting, Organizations and Society* **12**: 235–265.

Misztal, B.M (1996). *Trust in Modern Societies*, Cambridge: Polity.

Nicholson, B, and Carmel, E. (2003). Offshore Software Sourcing by Small Firms: An analysis of risk, trust and control, IFIP TC8 & TC9/WG8.2 & WG9.4 Working Conference on Information Systems Perspectives and Challenges in the Context of Globalization, Athens, Greece, International Federation for Information Processing: Laxenburg, Austria.

Nicholson, B, and Sahay, S (2001). Some Political and Cultural Issues in the Globalisation of Software Development: Case experience from Britain and India, *Information and Organization* **11**: 25–43.

Nicholson, B, and Sahay, S (2004). Embedded Knowledge and Offshore Software Development, *Information and Organization* **14**: 329–365.

Pawlowski, S.D, and Robey, D (2004). Bridging User Organizations: Knowledge brokering and the work of information technology professionals, *MIS Quarterly* **28**: 645–672.

Pettigrew, A.M (1990). Longitudinal Field Research on Change: Theory and practice, *Organization Science* 1: 267–292.

Reed, M.I (1992). *The Sociology of Organizations: Themes, perspectives and prospects*, Hemel Hempstead: Harvester Wheatsheaf.

Ring, P.S (1996). Fragile and Resilient Trust and their Roles in Economic Exchange, *Business and Society* 35: 148–175.

Ring, P.S., and Van De Ven, A.H (1994). Developmental Process of Cooperative Interorganizational Relationships, *Academy of Management Review* 19: 90–118.

Rousseau, D.M, Sitkin, S.B, Burt, R.S, and Camerer, C. (1998). Not so Different after All: A cross-discipline view of trust, *Academy of Management Review* 23: 393–404.

Sahay, S (2003). Global Software Alliances: The challenge of 'standardization, *Scandinavian Journal of Information Systems* 15: 3–21.

Sahay, S, Nicholson, B, and Krishna, S (2003). *Global IT Outsourcing: Software development across borders*, Cambridge: Cambridge University Press.

Segal, H (1989). *Klein*, London: Karmac Books.

Strauss, A.L, and Corbin, J (1990). *Basics of Qualitative Research: Grounded theory procedures and techniques*, Newbury Park: Sage.

Strauss, A.L, and Corbin, J (1997). *Grounded Theory in Practice*, London: Sage.

Sturdy, A (1997). The Consultancy Process – An insecure business?, *Journal of Management Studies* 34: 389–413.

Tsoukas, H. (1989). The Validity of Idiographic Research Explanations, *Academy of Management Review* 14: 551–561.

Tushman, M.L (1977). Special Boundary Roles in Innovation Processes, *Administrative Science Quarterly* 22: 587–605.

Van De Ven, A.H, and Poole, M.S (1995). Explaining Development and Change in Organizations, *Academy of Management Review* 20: 510–540.

Van De Ven, A.H, and Poole, M.S (2005). Alternative Approaches for Studying Organizational Change, *Organization Studies* 26: 1377–1400.

Walsham, G (1995). Interpretive Case Studies in IS research: Nature and method, *European Journal of Information Systems* 4: 74–81.

Wastell, D. (1999). Learning Dysfunctions in Information Systems Development: Overcoming the social defences with transitional objects, *MIS Quarterly* 23: 581–600.

Wastell, D (2003). Organizational Discourse as Social Defence: Taming the tiger of electronic government, In E. Wynn, E. Whitley, M.D.

Myers, and J.I. Degross (eds.) *Global and Organizational Discourse about Information Technology*, Boston: Kluwer Academic Publishers.

Wastell, D.G. (1996). The Fetish of Technique: Methodology as a social defence, *Information Systems Journal* **6**: 25–40.

Wenger, E (1998). *Communities of Practice: Learning, meaning and identity*, Cambridge: Cambridge University Press.

Willcocks, L.P, Lacity, M, and Kern, T (1999). Risk Mitigation in IT Outsourcing Strategy Revisited: Longitudinal case research at LISA, *Journal of Strategic Information Systems* **8**: 285–314.

Willcocks, L.P, and Kern, T (1998). IT Outsourcing as Strategic Partnering: The case of the UK inland revenue, *European Journal of Information Systems* **7**: 29–45.

Willcocks, L.P, and Lacity, M (1999). IT Outsourcing in Insurance Services: Risk, creative contracting and business advantage, *Information Systems Journal* **9**: 163–180.

Willcocks, L.P, and Margetts, H (1994). Risk Assessment in Information Systems, *European Journal of* Information *Systems* **4**: 1–12.

Williams, B (1988). Formal Structures and Social Reality, In D. Gambetta (ed.) *Trust: Making and Breaking Cooperative Relations*, Oxford: Basil Blackwell.

Winnicott, D.W. (1987). *Babies and Their Mothers*, New York: Addison-Wesley.

Wittgenstein, L (1953). *Philosophical Investigations*, Oxford: Blackwell.

Zollo, M, Reuer, J.J, and Singh, H (2002). Interorganizational Routines and Performance in Strategic Alliances, *Organization Science* **13**: 701–713.

Zucker, L.G (1986). Production of Trust: Institutional sources of economic structure 1840–1920, *Research in Organizational Behaviour* **8**: 53–111.

Séamas Kelly was a lecturer at the UCD School of Business and Director of the Centre for Innovation, Technology & Organisation (CITO). He holds a Ph.D. in Management Studies/Information Systems from the University of Cambridge. His primary research interests are in the area of ICT-enabled organizational innovation, with a particular emphasis on the social and organizational aspects of information systems implementation and use. Key themes, here, include the management of IS innovation, the role of ICT in facilitating novel modes of organizing, and the relationship between knowledge, technology, and organization.

Camilla Noonan was a lecturer in Strategy and International Business at the UCD School of Business and a member of the Centre for Innovation, Technology & Organisation (CITO). She has also held visiting appointments at Rutgers Business School, USA. She holds a Ph.D. in Economics/ International Business from the University of Reading, UK. Her research focuses on spatial and organizational issues associated with corporate technological activity.

11

Cross-cultural (Mis)Communication in IS Offshoring: Understanding Through Conversation Analysis

David Avison and Peter Banks

Introduction

Information systems (IS) offshoring is the performing of IS-related work by a third party organisation from a location that is geographically and culturally distant from the host organisations prime locations (BCS, 2004). Offshoring IS roles to developing world countries has seen phenomenal growth recently with further rapid growth predicted for the next decade (McManes, 2003) and in the particular context of India (BCS, 2004). As Gorlenko (2006) puts it: 'Whether you like it or not, offshoring is here to stay "if" or "when" to offshore is no longer an issue.'

D. Avison (✉)
Department of Information Systems, ESSEC Business School, Paris, France
e-mail: avison@essec.fr

P. Banks
School of Information Systems and Computing, Brunel University, Uxbridge, UK

© The Author(s) 2017   367
L.P. Willcocks et al. (eds.), *Outsourcing and Offshoring Business Services*, DOI 10.1007/978-3-319-52651-5_11

The heart of the discussion is "how much" – how much we can afford to offshore or more precisely how much we can afford to keep'.

This trend means that IS professionals in the West must deal frequently with their counterparts from lower cost and culturally different peoples such as those of India. 'An appreciation of the culture gap is essential . . . the gap can be huge and exists at all stages of the manager/ team member relationship, causing miscommunication and frustration' (Kobayashi-Hillary, 2003). Other studies looking at offshore suppliers in particular include Oshri *et al.* (2007) and Oza and Hall (2005), and articles based on first-hand experience working in an offshoring environment show unexpected issues when dealing with vendor staff despite having experienced IS project and service managers. Borchers (2003) admits that 'until we studied some of the cultural factors, we had difficulty in understanding software development problems that we were having'.

The following citations explain people's lack of awareness. 'The primary conclusion from our research is that working across cultures when outsourcing software productions is not a trouble-free process . . . . Challenges not only concern the need to adapt to different ways of working but to cultural norms of social behaviour, attitudes toward authority, and language issues' (Krishna *et al.*, 2004). As 'people don't think of themselves as having values or culture; they simply imagine that the qualities they hold dear are those that matter to all mankind' . . . [and that] . . . 'our own culture is invisible to us. We don't see our own ways of doing things as conditioned in the cradle . . . we see them as correct and we conclude that people from other countries have grave failings' (Olson and Olson, 2003).

Given the expansion of offshoring and the apparent importance of cultural issues, we first examine to what extent this has been reflected in the IS literature. Cross-cultural issues exist within many areas. However, Meso *et al.* (2005) argue that 'although research on culture in the context of IS has been conducted, most of it focuses on how culture impacts technology acceptance and diffusion or on the customisation of IS solutions to fit specific culture[s]'.

Relatively little work has been done on the deeper effects of cross-cultural communication within the delivery of offshore projects or services. Available literature appears to focus on either high-level surveys, for example, those that attempt to identify 'Indian culture' to suggest potential challenges to offshoring, such as Rottman and Lacity (2004, 2006), or surveys and anecdotal-based research to investigate the 'culture problem' (Nicholson and Sahay, 2001; Weisinger and Trauth, 2002; Borchers, 2003; Krishna et al., 2004; Narayanaswamy and Henry, 2005). Nevertheless, practitioners need further evidence and understanding of the problems they face in practice.

However, looking at other fields, for example, anthropology, communications and linguistics, there are techniques that have been used successfully to analyse communications across cultures empirically, principally within the arena of ethnographic research. Ethnography is analysis based on observation of subjects within their 'natural environment', taking an anthropological view that in order to understand a group of people, the researchers must engage in an extended period of observation (Silverman, 2000).

An area of focus is the linguistics technique of 'conversation analysis' (CA). Key to CA is detailed transcription of conversations observed in their natural environment. This 'make[s] what was said and how it was said available for analytic consideration, at first for the analyst who does the transcribings, and later for others, colleagues and audiences' (Ten-Have, 1999).

Through this analysis of conversation, a 'window' can be gained on the underlying cultural values because 'in every moment of talk, people are experiencing and producing their cultures, their roles, their personalities .... Conversation Analysis has some promise of precisely locating and describing how that world of talk works [and] how the experienced moments of social life are constructed' (Moerman, 1988). In his recent book, Carbaugh (2005) shows how it is possible to use 'Culturally Contexted' CA to gain an insight into the cultural modes of the participants and on the visible and invisible cultural misunderstandings that occur.

The focus of our research is a case study of one of the leading multinational pharmaceutical organisations (Pharma), currently engaged in offshoring with two Indian vendors, both of which are in the top 10 of Indian outsourcing companies (Vendors 1 and 2).

CA is an underused yet complementary approach to studying social aspects of IS. Yet, the approach is applicable for the study of any social interactions among users, developers, senior managers, job applicants, etc. The aim of our research is therefore to use CA to give a more in-depth understanding of cross-cultural communication issues that can occur with IT offshoring projects and suggest further research in this important domain.

We look next at the literature in more detail and in the subsequent section describe our research approach followed by a discussion of the data collected. We then discuss our research that revealed two major phenomena in terms of asymmetries of participation (in the further section), and then we discuss cohesion and flow in another section. These exposed seven findings, four related to asymmetries of participation and three related to cohesion and flow. Finally, in our conclusion, we summarise our contributions, discuss limitations and suggest further work.

Previous Work

We divide our literature review into three broad areas:

- literature directly focused on culture and communication within IS offshoring;
- general literature related to cross-cultural communications;
- CA and its use to analyse cross-cultural communications.

Culture and IS Offshoring

As discussed in the introduction, a relatively large number of works have described the challenges of cross-culture work within IS offshoring. Lacity and Willcocks (1998) and Rottman and Lacity (2004) have investigated offshoring and highlighted communication and cultural issues as key challenges. However, none of these works have provided tangible evidence of these 'cultural problems'. Instead, they rely on anecdotal evidence from predominantly Western staff working on offshoring engagements.

More journalistic material identifies communications problems or cultural issues as key when managing offshoring engagements but fails to substantiate the claims of 'Culture Surprise' (Olson and Olson, 2003); 'Pitfalls that the outsourcing vendor forgot to mention' (Kobayashi-Hillary, 2005) and 'The Hidden Costs of Offshore Outsourcing' (Overby, 2003) because of the lack of research content.

Borchers (2003), Narayanaswamy and Henry (2005) and Krishna *et al.* (2004) provide valuable contributions to the body of knowledge, showing how differences in culture have created issues in offshoring engagements. However, these papers are somewhat reductionist either by using broad national culture models or wide stereotypes. For example, in India, 'team members prefer to obtain consensus of their subordinates and the project manager before implementing any decisions/ changes' (Narayanaswamy and Henry, 2005). This generalisation is an oversimplification because, as Hill (2001) argues, 'the relationship between culture and country is often ambiguous ... national culture is a mosaic of subcultures'.

These papers and others (Little *et al.*, 2000; Nicholson and Sahay, 2001; Weisinger and Trauth, 2002; Meso *et al.*, 2005), all make valuable contributions but rely on interviews or questionnaires with various sample sizes. The key limitation of this approach, particularly in cultural studies, is highlighted by Ten-Have (1999): 'experience shows that participants may not afterwards "know" what they have been doing or why, and furthermore tend to justify their behaviours in various ways'. This is particularly important in something as difficult to define as culture. How can a respondent know from memory that an issue experienced was caused by cultural differences or provide more than a superficial assessment of an event?

MacGregor *et al.* (2005) describes an ongoing piece of research attempting to explore 'issues surrounding culture and its role in Global Software Development efforts'. It does so by applying discourse analysis, which is related to CA. However, by analysing semi-structured interview transcripts, they are not analysing naturally occurring data. This is contrary to the recommendation of CA (Ten-Have, 1999; Drew and Heritage, 2002), but if complete would have provided a useful comparison to the findings of our research.

Cross-cultural Communications

Culture is 'a nebulous construct that is difficult to define' according to Barkema and Vermeulem and 'scholars have never been able to agree on a simple definition of culture' (Hill, 2001). Hence, there is an intrinsic appeal of models that appear to break down culture into manageable categories. Hofstede's seminal study, conducted in 1980 and updated in 2001, compared the culture of IBM staff across 40 countries, showing variations in their culture over five cultural dimensions (Hofstede, 2001).

The primary criticism of Hofstede's research is the accusation of cultural determinism (Hill, 2001), that is, culture can vary significantly within a nation while Hofstede's research implies a constant national culture (Fernandez *et al.*, 1997; Hill, 2001; Ford *et al.*, 2003). Other models have been proposed, but 'to grasp a concept as vastly complex as national culture without succumbing to reductionist instrumental treatment is potentially overwhelming' (Nicholson and Sahay, 2001). As a result, no one model alone is entirely satisfactory. The key element is to use models such as Hofstede's to 'gain a "handle" on the difficult concept of culture' (Ford *et al.*, 2003), while keeping at the forefront of your mind that they are inherently a generalisation.

One reaction to this criticism is to change how we view culture. As Cowan (1990) argues, 'When culture is defined as that which is shared, questions about this sharedness – Is it actually shared? To what extent? By whom? How does it come to be shared? – disappear by definition'. We may align to the national dimensions proposed by authors such as Hofstede, to a greater or lesser extent, but we will also align to other values and characteristics, such as generation, organisational culture, profession and many other factors. This can be developed further by seeing that 'culture is not perceived as a rigid or static entity, but is in constant flux across individuals within cultural groups, and over time within individuals' (Maznevski and Peterson, 1997).

A broad range of literature shows the intrinsic relationship between communication and culture. They are not separate domains but produced through a dynamic relationship with the other. Communication across cross-cultural boundaries produces the situation where 'markers of communication (words and gestures, for instance) will be read and evaluated differently by different people, depending on the cultural contexts they bring to any communication practice, and on the specific contexts in which that practice takes place' (Schirato and Yells, 2000). This can lead to cultural misunderstandings, as each party to the communication presumes that the other shares a different frame of reference (Carbaugh, 2005). Hinnenkamp (1999) provides a clear summary of how misunderstandings occur within intercultural communication, showing how most misunderstandings are managed and resolved within the communication process, through different forms of 'repair'.

A number of papers explore the culture within India, in particular Nicholson and Sahay (2001) and Fusilier and Durlabhji (2001) that provide a useful comparison for our findings but are at a much more general level, being about Indian culture as a whole, when compared to our study.

CA and Cross-cultural Communications

CA developed as a field of study in the 1960s through collaboration between Harvey Sacks, Emanuel Schegloff and Gail Jefferson (Goodwin and Heritage, 1990). Using highly detailed transcripts of naturally occurring conversation 'CA sees talk as an analysable form of human interaction that reveals the basic fabric of social organization in process' (Tulin, 1997). CA has moved on to 'Applied CA', through use in institutional settings, primarily medical, legal and broadcast news (Drew and Heritage, 2002). More recently, it is being applied to cross-cultural conversations (Carbaugh, 2005).

Detailed transcriptions are used to enable the analyst (and reader) to 'consider talk in its totality as a collaborative production: Seemingly inarticulate or meaningless utterances can be shown to be quite relevant to the exchange' (Tulin, 1997). It is important for analytic finding to be derived from within the talk, as opposed to presenting hypothesis and looking for data that support or refute those hypotheses (*ibid*).3

A relatively small but expanding base of research using CA to analyse culture exists, with articles such as Sidnell (2006) and Carbaugh (2005), explicitly encouraging further utilisation of CA in a cross-cultural context. 'Quite a few well-known and widely-read books on intercultural communication do not provide a single real case analysis, not even a single example of real-life data of people talking to one another' (Blommaert, 1998). There is a 'paucity of research focused on actual communication practices in which cultural differences are apparent and active' (Carbaugh, 2005).

Nevertheless, Gumperz (2002) uses CA to analyse cross-cultural communication in a number of settings, including recorded interviews for a work skills training course in Northern England. This demonstrates clearly how differences in culture put non-native speakers of Northern Indian origin at a distinct disadvantage. Carbaugh (2005) also demonstrates a number of culturally mediated situations. One example suggests what to some Finnish people is seen as a comfortable silence can be profoundly uncomfortable to some Americans. This leads to comments such as 'Superficial Americans' and 'Silent Finns'.

However, no direct comparison has been found to our current study of cross-cultural communication within an organisational workplace setting in an IS context. Drew and Heritage (2002) called for more research in this area, a plea that does not appear to have been clearly answered. 'How people talk together is how they organise … the study of organisational talk [using CA] could thus provide insights into the dynamic features of an organisation as well as organising in general'.

Garcez (1997) looks at other ethnographic research. This summarises articles from CA, discourse analysis and linguistics as they relate to cross-cultural communication. A key concept is the requirement for 'shared understanding' underlying communication and the difficulty of analysis, because 'communication patterns lack the tangible visible quality of house, clothing, and tools, so that it is less easy to recognise their existence as culturally distinct phenomena' (Philips, 1987). We will now turn to our own research approach.

Research Approach

Most previous research on cultural aspects of offshoring has relied on interviews and questionnaires but they inevitably show either what people 'intended to do' or suggest a sanitise-biased version of events, which may hide or distort the true communications issues that are being experienced (Ten-Have, 1999). Our study using CA attempts to 'cut across basic problems associated with the gap between beliefs and action and between what people say and what they do' (Drew and Heritage, 2002).

As Ten-Have (1999) has argued, the CA methodology places less emphasis on sampling than other types of social research because the focus of the analysis is on showing examples of what can occur in certain environments, as opposed to a factual/statistical perspective of what will happen in set environments. The issue of proving a 'representative' sample through complex sampling methodologies is seen as less important than gaining 'specimens' for analysis.

Owing to the size of Pharma, this study has potential access to over 90 different offshoring engagements across 9 different business units and with 2 separate offshore vendors. These engagements are very varied, including the covering of specific projects and ongoing services over a short period to over 5 years. Selecting engagements from different business units, with different roles and ways of working, maximises the variation available and sample richness. Using one organisation limits the generalisability of the research, because we may ask whether the findings are specific to the pharmaceutical industry or to a particular organisational culture. While accepting this criticism, we propose Pharma is representative of many large multinational organisations. However, issues such as the effect of individual organisational cultures cannot be isolated. Therefore, issues highlighted there can only be seen as examples of phenomena that *can* occur, instead of what *will* occur in all offshoring scenarios.

This research focuses on recording a corpus of pre-organised audio telephone conferences, which is the primary communication method between geographically distant staff at Pharma. This limits the research as we exclude other communication channels, such as individual telephone calls, instant messenger conversations, asynchronous group-ware (e.g., e-mail or Lotus Notes databases), videoconferencing or systems/business documentation.

Recording regular team meetings allows this research to capture conversation occurring in its normal setting without interference from the researcher. This is conversation occurring in its normal setting without interference from the researcher. This avoids adding bias caused by prior beliefs of the researcher or participants. We created a bank of recordings and then transcribed sections of the recorded data. The detailed transcriptions 'make what was said and how it was said available for analytic consideration, at first for the analyst who does the transcribings, and later for others, colleagues and audiences' (Ten-Have, 1999).

Given our findings in the literature review on the variability of culture and its state of constant change across individuals within cultural groups, and over time within individuals (Maznevski and Peterson, 1997), this specimen approach appears appropriate. We could never capture every cultural variable, therefore we must focus on what can and has happened, allowing the reader/practitioner to interpret and apply those findings.

It is not possible to transcribe and fully analyse all of the data collected. Transcribing conversations takes a long time (as researchers using interviews will agree), but CA has the additional time-taking task of analysing and transcribing the features within the talk (see Appendix). Sometimes the specimens are unclear and are therefore rejected for analysis. Even where the text is clear, it takes much time looking for each of the features of the talk once transcribed.

There are various possible approaches to focus the work depending on objectives. This study focuses on pulling out the key 'specimens', or what Ten-Have (1999) describes as 'virtuoso moments', providing particular insight into the issues experienced in cross-cultural communication. By focusing on these, we attempt to provide greater insight into the whole body of data.

The transcription process does not focus purely on the words or content, 'the point is to consider talk in its totality as a collaborative production. Seemingly inarticulate or meaningless utterances can be shown to be quite relevant to the exchange' (Tulin, 1997). Therefore,

CA uses a highly detailed transcription conventions system devised by Gail Jefferson to capture the actual vernacular pronunciation, speed changes, emphasis and pauses in the speech production (see Appendix).

Perakyla (2004) explores a number of defined methodological approaches to improve the reliability of findings within CA. Primarily, she recommends relying on 'naturally occurring' data, to reduce the introduction of researcher bias and 'catch "natural interaction" as fully and faithfully as is practically possible ... the ideal is to (mechanically) observe interactions as they would take place without research observation' (Ten-Have, 1999).

During the analysis phase, it is important for the data to lead instead of allowing pre-existing theories to guide us. This avoids introducing researcher bias at the analysis stage. 'Key to the use of CA as a research method in organisational studies is to draw directly from the data, noting phenomena that appear relevant to speakers' (Tulin, 1997). Through these precautions, a later researcher should be able to 'obtain the same findings if he or she tried again in the same way' (Pera"kyla", 2004: 285).

However, despite these precautions, there are criticisms of CA. We cannot prove the validity of the findings themselves. Key to this is the correct interpretation of observations, whether 'the researcher is calling what is measured by the right name' (Kirk and Miller, 1986). Therefore, interpretation of observations should show very clearly that they have 'apparent validity: once you have read them you are convinced that they are transparently true' (Kirk and Miller, 1986). Secondly by making recordings and transcriptions available, 'others could look at what I had studied and make of it what they could, if, for example, they wanted to be able to disagree with me' (Sacks, 1984).

CA is also criticised for lack of generalisability. Perakyla (2004) showed CA's limited ability to generalise observed phenomena, due to inherently limited sample sizes. However, it can be used as a series of examples to demonstrate that the issues observed do occur in communication and evidence how the participants overcome or address them.

Therefore, this research will not provide data on the extent of communications issues within offshoring or validate the best ways to handle them. It will instead provide documented examples of issues that can arise and ways participants have sought to address them. With regard to the issue of generalisability, this paper presents a series of *findings* intended to be the stimulus for further research.

Before looking at the data collected itself, we will briefly consider the ethical issues in the recording of telephone conversations. As Ten-Have (1999) has argued, 'one needs to consider the rights of the participants in the interaction ... rights to refuse: to be recorded or give access to the situation for recording purposes'.

- Consent was gained at an organisational level, from the heads of the offshoring initiatives for both Pharma and the two vendor organisations.
- Consent was gained from all participants at the start of meetings.
- All transcripts were made anonymous.

Data Collection

As stated in the previous section, the objective of the data collection phase was to maximise the variation of engagement types and meetings to record within the case study organisation. This included gaining access to

- offshore projects and offshore application support services;
- engagements representing a range of Pharma's business units;
- different engagements involving both Indian offshore vendors;
- members of staff with a mixture of experience both of managing offshore engagements and 'traditional' IS work.

This process is obviously constrained by access to data, because meetings could only be recorded with the agreement of all participants. Additionally, the process was limited by the time available to the researchers.

Permission was gained to record a series of weekly team meetings for two different teams across the organisation. Additionally, a small pilot study was performed at the start of the research that recorded the meetings of a third engagement within the US sales and marketing business unit. The two engagements used in the research are summarised in Table 11.1. The research was carried out part time over a 6-month

Table 11.1 Summary of offshore engagements studied

Engagement name/business unit	Summary	Type of engagement/ vendor
Development/ Central IT	The Offshore Development Team (ODT) Provide a centralised development service for all Pharma IT This focused on recording a series of weekly team meetings	Central service/ Vendor 2
Sales Force Automation (SFA)/Global IT	Offshore project team, deploying a centralised offshore support model for the Sales Force Automation/tool This focused on recording the weekly program board meetings	Support service- project team/ vendor 1

period from January 2006 although we chose only a few specimens for analysis.

As discussed above, due to the time-consuming nature of the CA technique, it is not possible to analyse all the data collected in detail. To address this limitation we followed the suggestion to make an inventory or summary of recordings made and then from that to select episodes to consider for more detailed consideration or transcription (Ten-Have, 1999).

Table 11.2 summarises each meeting that was recorded and particular observations about the communication within that meeting. By looking across the range of meetings, four phenomena can be seen to occur in different situations and in different meetings:

- *Asymmetry of participation* – The most common observation across all the engagements was that the conversations tended to be dominated by the UK/US parties, who tended to lead discussion, with the Indian vendor staff providing much shorter contributions.
- *Lack of cohesion and flow to conversation* – A general lack of flow and cohesion can be seen within many sections of the conversations and this seems to lead to a high incidence of misunderstandings.
- *Need for mediators to translate communications problems* – Within the discussions, there appeared to be key people who would frequently 'mediate' or 'translate' discussions between the Pharma and vendor

Table 11.2 Summary of meetings recorded

Meeting	Length	Summary	Conversation themes
Development Weekly Update Meeting 1	1 h	Review of outstanding projects. Discussion of each project. Managing each current request and what has been performed on each. Discussion of implication of a new business model	• Asymmetry of conversation • Shared leadership of the meeting • Deflection of question to avoid a direct negative answer • Probing for fuller response by Pharma
Weekly Update Meeting 2	1 h	Review of the open projects. Problems with the promotion of changes to the development environment	• Reluctance to give a direct negative answer • Asymmetry of conversation
Weekly Update Meeting 3	1 h	Review of outstanding projects. Long section reviewing a compliant e-mail	• Asymmetry of conversation • Sharing the leadership of the meeting • Translation of what the problem means
SFA Program Board Meeting 1	1 h	Discussion of support model in the new system. Long discussion about process and disagreement over responsibilities	• Very difficult to follow the flow of the discussion • Conversation dominated by Pharma staff
Program Board Meeting 2	1 h	Support meeting reviewing the open actions. Long discussion over a particular element of the support model and significant misunderstandings between participants	• Conflict within the communication • Lack of flow to individual turns • Translation of issue by Pharma
Program Board Meeting 3	1 h	Review of key problem surrounding the change control process. Further discussion around how the SLAs are measured	• General lack of flow to the discussion • Use of 'non-standard' English • Long discussion of a misunderstanding

Table 11.2 (continued)

Meeting	Length	Summary	Conversation themes
Program Board Meeting 4	15 min	Discussion review of the progress of the project in one market. Discussion of the training completed by new staff member	• Reluctance to give a negative answer • Long very specific answers missing the underlying questions • Asymmetry in conversation

staff. For the Indian staff, this was normally the most senior person present in the exchange.

• *Deflection and when yes does not mean yes* – A tendency by some vendor staff to avoid saying a direct 'no' to requests or use deflective answers to respond to potentially negative questions.

Each of these phenomena needs more detailed analysis to investigate whether it is valid. In order to focus the research, this report will only investigate further the first two phenomena (asymmetries of participation and a lack of cohesion and flow to conversation), as they are seen to be the most frequently occurring in our specimen conversations and because they have embedded within the elements of the latter two themes. We look at both of these phenomena in the next two sections.

Asymmetries of Participation

The study of the structure of how participants orientate between speaking and listening in a conversation or 'turn-taking organisation' is a major area of CA research. Schegloff and Sacks (1973), in their seminal paper, identified key functions showing how we balance our 'turns at talk' and therefore manage the overall conversation.

Within the study of ordinary conversation, for example, conversations between friends outside of an institutional setting or other controlled environment, turn design over the course of the conversation have been shown to be based on a 'standard of equal participation' and is therefore seen to be to an extent 'symmetrical' (Drew and Heritage, 2002).

However, within certain institutional settings, for example, workplaces and professional–lay person interactions, there have been studies that document 'asymmetries of participation' in the interaction, that is, one participant dominating the conversation (Linell and Luckmann, 1991). These have been shown to be highly important to the overall management of the interaction and in understanding the underlying social behaviours that are causing these asymmetries.

We should be clear at this point of two things. Firstly, even within ordinary conversation, some level of asymmetry is always present. Obviously, on a moment-by-moment basis, one participant will be transmitting knowledge to the other. However, in institutional settings, the asymmetries that are observed have a special prevalence and particular significance to the underlying conversation (Linell and Luckmann, 1991; Drew and Heritage, 2002).

Secondly, the presence of asymmetries does not in itself imply problems in the interaction, 'there is no logical relationship between asymmetries and problematic talk' (Drew and Heritage, 2002). However, what is of analytical importance is the reason for these asymmetries and what they tell us about the underlying relationship of the participants in the interaction. There are instances where these asymmetries do lead to problems in the communication (Linell and Luckmann, 1991).

Across the whole corpus of data, there appears to be a clear asymmetry of participation between the Pharma staff and the vendor staff. The participation of the vendor staff in the interaction appears to be significantly less, and most of the interactions appear to be controlled by the Pharma staff.

To illustrate this and investigate potential explanations, the first 'specimen' that we are going to focus on is that of key sections within one of the weekly update meetings of the Offshore Development Team. This is shown as Fig. 11.1 and instances an apparent breakdown in their processes that has resulted in a complaint from an internal customer and a resultant conversation to resolve the issue.

We will start by reviewing the discussion, noting key features of what is said, then we will attempt to pull these together. Present on the call are: Steve who is the Pharma service manager, and the team of six

Present are:
Pharma Service Manager: Steve   *Offshore Analyst:*   Venu
Offshore Analyst: Babu

16	Steve:	I just wanted to share this with the team here. um:: have had an e-mail
17		from John Doe, regarding some um: support issues they been face-
18		facing this is regarding the Profile database, um the full
19		details of this conversation chain are in that brown- um in that mail section
20		((of the Meeting Database)) you needn't read it now. But um:: what
21		I just wanted to do is to get a bit of an understanding of where things are on
22		this particular project. A few things seem to have been a little bit different
23		to standard process and I just want to understand what was happening and
24		whether we can resolve them differently in the ↑future↑. Um the particular
25		issue here is umm- Tammy Callaghan I think it's off, um:: I'll just get the
26		name right bear with me, um:: yes Tammy CALLAGHAN is the um
27		custodian of a database called the Employee Profile database and
28		that sends information through to the Employee Review database and
29		there have been sort of a few issues about who resolves what tickets and
30		how to get them resolved. Umm the first one, (.) um and I apologise I'm
31		going to have to pick on Venu here because I know you've handling a lot of
32		these.
		(0.2)
33		(0.2)
34		in the mail thread it talks about um: a Request-First request sorry a:: Remedy
35		ticket was raised on the 10th of April and then we sent an e-mail to- to
36		Tammy Callaghan and me on the 21st of April asking her to raise a Request-
37		First request to track the work. But I couldn't find any Request-First requests
38		created under her name, so it was just a query first of all.
39		(.)
40		Did you create a Request-First request for this project?
41	Venu:	N::o Steve in fact, I've sent her our standard e-mail uh: with the instructions
42		say we're going create um: have a Request-First request instead of a Remedy
43		ticket for the issues because it took more than two hours to address (.)[
44	Steve:	[Uh::
45	Venu:	[I'm waiting
46		for her reply but I didn't get any reply them even from Tammy or John.
47		I waited even I phone to discuss with the Tammy regard that issues also,
48		but I haven't received any reply so far (.)
49		please can you expand that e-mail section at the end of the team mail ok,
50		um: scroll down, at the end of the mail.
51		(2.2)
52		I mentioned about the two:: hours and yeh twenty first "if you have any
53		question or tension regarding this transfer, or would prefer that the request
54		not be transferred to Request-First for completion please contact me as soon
55		as possible". There is the message I have sent to the client but they didn't
56		come back to-[
57	Steve:	[Yes if we keep it on the screen Babu, and if we read through
58		this message and see what it actually says.
59	Babu:	Yeh um:
60	Steve:	What in effect your saying here is after you've reviewed the request you've
61		determined it's going to take more than two hours to complete (.) [
62	Venu:	[Yeh
63	Steve:	[and "the ODT works on Remedy tickets for up to two hours
64		for no charge, in order to track this request to completion the ODT is
65		transferring your Remedy ticket:- request to Request-First to be completed,
66		please note that same request will be handled on a chargeable basis
67		ODT Analysts will work with you to confirm the full details of your request
68		and an abbreviated project proposal will be sent – project proposal will
69		detail costs and estimated time to complete your project. If you have any
70		questions or concerns regarding this transfer or would prefer that your
71		request not be transferred to Request-First for completion please contact me
72		as soon as possible".
73		(0.2)
74		So what your saying there in that e-mail is "we are transferring your
75		Remedy ticket into Request-First and we will contact you to discuss the
76		project and we will give you all the details and we will come up with the
77		quotations, (.) if you have got a problem with that ↑contact us↑, but if
78		if we don't hear from you we'll assume your ok with that an will continue
79		with the Request-First request.
80		(0.2)
81		But what's actually happened here is you've, you've said- (.) you've said that
82		to the client in the e-mail but what your actually doing is waiting for the
83		client to raise a Request-First request.
84		But the client- you haven't told the client to raise a Request-First request. So
85		the clients sitting there going– "what's going on" where is my Request-First
86		request, where is my project.

Fig. 11.1 Conversation analysis – an apparent breakdown in processes

Vendor 1 developer/analysts, with Venu and Babu, two analysts/developers in the team, the principal speakers (all names are anonymised).

There are two systems mentioned in the discussion: 'Request-First', a small project request tool used to initiate the majority of the work performed by Steve's team, and Remedy, the Pharma incident management tool, from where support requests are raised through the IT help desk. (The meanings of the symbols used are shown in Appendix and are based on the original conventions developed by Gail Jefferson.)

Within the first fairly long turn, we see how Steve seeks to discuss the issues arising from the complaint e-mail. Steve is using very open language – 'share ... with the team' (line 16), 'understand what was happening' (line 23). The message here is non-accusatory, to try and understand the process in order to improve it in the future.

Venu does not respond immediately to Steve's turn, leaving Steve to prompt for a response. While a little confused at first and sticking to specifics of what he has done, it is clear that Venu has tried on a number of occasions to contact the client, but they have not come back to him. The significance that he does not appear to have picked up is that he should have raised the request anyway and has in fact told the customer that he would. At this stage, there is a level of symmetry to the overall conversation; however, the questioning is being led by Steve, and Venu is taking a response-orientated role. Steve now moves into a long explanation of what has occurred, directly translating the significance of what was stated in the e-mail to the customer.

In the next extract (Fig. 11.2), we see that Steve attempts to summarise what he has said, and what the process should be. The long pause at line 93 indicates that he expects some kind of response from Venu, to confirm that he has understood what is said. When that is not forthcoming, Steve follows-up probing for a response. The response provided by Venu, is very short and while polite, appears to miss the wider point, he shows no outward sign that he has understood the underlying original question about why this Request-First request was not raised, and that for future similar incidents he should raise the Request-First ticket himself.

Steve's polite 'Thank you very much' (line 97) response is almost instinctive, flowing straight from Venu's turn with minimal pause. It is

87		(0.1)
88		↓So it's done the wrong way around ↓and the process should be, if you get
89		it in a Remedy ticket and if needs to go into Request-First because it's going
90		to take longer than 2 hours to resolve you need to raise a Request-First
91		request to track it though on behalf of the customer and inform them that
92		that's what you've done.
93		(2.1)
94		does that make sense?
95	**Venu:**	↑Yes↑ Steve, I will take advice and I will do the ticket from there.
96		(0.1)
97	**Steve:**	↑Thank you very much↑ (0.2) I mean have you been doing that for other
98		customers?
99		(1.4)
100	**Venu:**	Yeh (.) most of the customers I ask to create, but it is confused when it's
101		like that, uh: I went by Instant Messenger - I sent a
102		message through IM, I left a message, but they came back if there
103		are issues-(.) like raising the Request-First request. I think I'm having some
104		IM chat windows I think I've saved (.) I can share with you later.
105	**Steve:**	Yeh, cause at the moment I can't see- why you've not raised a
106		Request-First request at this stage, so if you can perhaps come back to me
107		and indicate why that hasn't happened. I just want to understand, the
108		process flow of what happened here so that we can be clear to Tammy and
109		John how we can handle it in the future
110	**Venu:**	Sure
111	**Steve:**	Does that seem ok?
112	**Venu:**	Yes

Fig. 11.2 Conversation analysis – an attempt to summarise

also louder than the surrounding talk, implying surprise. Underlying this and after a short pause, he tries to reframe the question to try to ascertain in a different way if this was an exception or if Venu has misunderstood the whole process. We also see in line 105 his real feelings, stating 'I can't quite see why you've not raised a Request-First request at this stage'.

Venu's response in lines 100–105 is very detailed about the specifics of what he has done. What is left unsaid, however, is any confirmation that he understands that in these circumstances he should always raise the Request-First request unless specifically told not to. In his last two turns of this extract, Venu reverts to single-word answers 'Sure' and 'Yes' (lines 110 and 112) even after Steve probes for a fuller answer (line 112).

Within this final extract shown as Fig. 11.3, the conversation is almost entirely one-sided, with only a small section of talk from Venu. Increasingly, apparent frustration and more direct questioning are appearing in the terminology and tone of Steve's voice.

113	Steve:	If you can just go back to the proposal section Babu and just sort of
114		collapse this, leave this document open, but if you close the actual section,
115		and can highlight the proposal section. The next question I've got is how
116		come it took 10 days to get from the Remedy ticket being raise to a closing
117		the Remedy ticket telling them to open a Request-First request?
118		(0.2)
119		um it ↓seems to have been opened on the 10th ↓ I think it was the 10th of
120		April then it was the 21st of April that we wrote to them to say please enter a
121		Request-First request
122	Venu:	um: I think you, I wrote to them on the 11th April, I replied to Tammy
123		regarding her availability I-(.) can you see that Remedy ticket working diary
124		information. I sent a mail to (her) 11 of April
125		(0.4)
126		Tammy asking about her availability to discuss, several issues.
127	Steve:	Right and what was the answer from that?
128		(.)
129	Venu:	Steve no, after that, after three four days I think the fourth day I got the
130		reply from her.
131	Steve:	Ok um[-
132	Venu:	[You can see that in the working diary section of the Remedy ticket, I
133		left a small (.) mail sent on 11 April.
134	Steve:	Yeh, I mean this comes down to my next question, is what does the diary
135		entry mail sent mean? Um: you need to be more explicit in the diary entry,
136		so you can und- so that people who reading this will understand what's
137		happened with the ticket. Just to say "mail sent" isn't really enough for me
138		to und- anyone to understand what happened. What has happened here.
139		<u>What it should be is</u> you should say: "sent mail to the customer asking if
140		they were available to talk, because I have tried to phone- (.) contact them
141		via phone, then when I tried to IM them they were unavailable so
142		that it clearly shows what you've done. Um:: at the moment say sent
143		them a mail, I've got no idea what the contents of the mail, is what's
144		expected and what the response was.
145	Venu:	Sure Steve
146	Steve:	I think that's the key causes very much um:: when we're- at the moment
147		we're very much working in a mode where it's sort of Venu you take a lead
148		on most of these tickets, um: but when we move across into the OAS
149		((Offshore Application Service – a much larger centralised Offshore
150		development model including all application development and second line
151		support)) model we're going to be dealing with lots of different people
152		working on different tickets and maybe different people on the same tickets.
153		So we need to be very clear (.) exactly what's happened on all of the
154		projects.
155	Venu:	Yes sure Steve I'll do that
156	Steve:	Thanks
157		
158		((Continuation of the meeting about other topics))

Fig. 11.3 Conversation analysis – a one-sided conversation

When asking why it took so long to handle the request (only 2 h work should be done on the request before it is escalated into a Request-First ticket), Steve asks his question (lines 115–117). There follows a pause and he does not receive a response so he clarifies the dates. However, the answer he receives is a statement of fact of what was done, instead of a fuller answer of why it took so long (that he was waiting for the customer to respond).

Steve's response is much more abrupt than we have seen before, showing his dissatisfaction with the response. He has moved from an open approach trying to understand the process, to direct individual statements 'you need to be more explicit' (line 135) and 'you should say' (line 139). Venu's next turn shows his own frustration and from then on he reverts to a fairly formulistic 'Sure Steve' response in lines 145 and 155. These responses miss the implicit request for more information or a clear explanation and instead are used as a device to close down the conversation.

The overall impression of this whole discussion is one where there is not a very satisfactory communication for either party. Steve overtly wished to gain more of an understanding of where the service was having difficulties and prevent further occurrences of the same problems. Venu repeatedly wanted to get across the message that he had tried to contact the client, but that they had not got back to him. Therefore, he felt there was nothing else he could do. Neither appears to have succeeded in their objective.

Neither this one extract nor the corpus of data can provide sufficient evidence to validate that asymmetries are persistent across offshoring engagements. Therefore, before moving into more detail exploring the observed asymmetries, we present our first finding.

Finding 1: That a clearly identifiable asymmetry of participation tends to exist within onshore–offshore vendor meetings.

We can see that as the conversation progressed, it became more and more asymmetrical, with Steve dominating the talk and Venu reverting to very short submissive answers.

Why did the conversation degenerate into such an asymmetric discussion? In this instance, the asymmetric nature of the conversation does appear to have reduced the quality of the interaction. It started as an open discussion but changed into a straight question-and-response scenario that does not appear to have been meeting the needs of either participant. There are two different areas of theory that we will explore in trying to understand this further, and what the observed asymmetries can tell us about the conversation. These are

* lack of shared understanding and listenership;
* the effect of social hierarchies.

Lack of Shared Understanding and Listenership

Is the observed asymmetry in participation, simply due to a lack of understanding by Venu, that fuller explanations were expected in response to questions asked? At key points within this 'specimen' Steve asks direct questions to Venu but receives what can only be regarded as minimal responses. These minimal responses, while answering the explicit question (Steve: Does that seem OK? Venu: Yes [lines 111–112]) appear to miss the underlying request for more information.

This observation has interesting parallels to research by Gumperz (2002) also with Indian-decent participants. He researched intercultural interview situations in England. The first candidate who was of similar decent to the interviewers 'does not just answer the questions but also takes advantage of unfilled pauses and interviewers' hints to make additional elaborative comments that serve to put him in a more favourable light than the [Northern Indian] electrician who provides only minimal replies and does not volunteer any new information. Even direct follow up probes ... produce only brief acknowledgements'.

This is explained by a lack of shared understanding of the wider questions and invitations to talk provided by the interviewer. 'Interviewers and candidates rely on shared interpretations of into national and other contextualisation cues for purposes of conversation management' (Gumperz, 2002). Therefore, by not having the shared understanding that more elaboration on the answer was expected, the speaker does not fulfil the expectations of the listener. Thus, the Northern Indian candidate 'is seen as relatively passive [and] unnecessarily stiff'.

In our example, the expectation of Steve could be seen from his framing of the discussion to be looking at what happened to improve the process for the future. Venu's answers, however, stuck to providing specifics of what happened or short minimal answers. This failed to get across the message that he understood he should have raised the Request-First request and would do so in the future, or that he had previously misunderstood the process but had done everything in his power to ensure the project moved forward. The explicit question is answered, but it does not meet Steve's need of a wider explanation, as a result the quality of the interaction deteriorated.

Paired with the concept of shared understanding is 'listenership', showing that listening is not a passive act. Through subconscious or conscious acts we show understanding, involvement and pass cues to the speaker. However, 'the ways of showing and interpreting listening behaviour can vary cross-culturally' (Garcez, 1997).

Research by Erickson (1998) shows that in cross-cultural situations the speaker can get insufficient cues and listener responses or misinterpret them. This can result in the 'person doing the explaining taking these absences as signs of lack of understanding, and then produce[ing] hyperexplanations, which corrode the quality of these interactions'.

This concept of hyperexplanation may be the reason for Steve's expansions of his explanation in lines 88–93, and also his very long and possibly unnecessarily long explanations in lines 107–110 and 146–154, of why a more detailed entry in the ticket log is required. These explanations all elicited the very short closing statements of 'Sure Steve' (lines 110, 135 and 145) that could have compounded the asymmetry within the conversation. There is insufficient evidence to show conclusively that a lack of shared understanding and missing listener cues contributed to the overall asymmetry of participation observed. However, they are both factors that can vary across cultures and based upon the data presented, there is some evidence to suggest that these factors were present. Therefore, this leads to our next two findings for further research.

Finding 2: That a lack of shared understanding of expected responses results in an increase in asymmetry of participation between Indian vendor staff and UK/US client staff.

Finding 3: That a lack of cues and listener responses results in a disproportionately high occurrence of hyperexplanations within IS offshoring communications.

Social Hierarchy

A key aspect of asymmetry of participation has been shown to be social structure. Asymmetries are not only related to the characteristics of the individuals in the conversation but also of social structures. 'Some aspects of asymmetries are clearly correlated with, even predefined by, positions in social hierarchies' (Linell and Luckmann, 1991: 11).

Given that, we know social hierarchy has been shown to influence asymmetries within conversation to what extent can the asymmetries we have observed be explained by the effect of hierarchy?

Hofstede's 'power distance' dimension that measures perceived inequality between managers and employees shows India has a very high score (77) compared to very low scores in the UK and USA (35 and 40, respectively). As discussed in our literature review, we do not want to succumb to the reductionism of national cultures; however, there is clear evidence that hierarchical relationships are a clear trait throughout Indian society, possibly due to the legacy of the caste system. For example, Sinha and Sinha (1990) state that 'the extent to which Indians are disposed to structure all relationships hierarchically is phenomenal'.

This could explain some of the observed asymmetry in the conversation. Venu can be seen to be deferring to Steve without challenging or expanding on what is said, 'Yes, Steve I will take advice' (line 95), 'Sure Steve' (line 145) 'Yes sure Steve I'll do that' (line 155). When Venu does give a longer response (e.g., in lines 122–125 and 129) he gives very specific answers and does not give supporting arguments. For example, 'I sent a mail to her 11 of April, to Tammy asking about her availability to discuss several issues' (line 129). We can infer that Venu's expectations of appropriate responses to a manager are leading to this.

Of particular interest is how the asymmetry became more pronounced as the conversation progressed. Early on, Venu gave fairly long, specific responses to Steve's questions (e.g., in lines 45–56). However, as the conversation progresses, he moves into more of an acceptance mode.

Owing to the minimal answers Steve receives, he adopts a more direct questioning style for example, 'Right and what was the answer from that?' (line 127). The effect of this is that the asymmetry is reinforced. This is similar to the observation of asymmetries in law courts that are seen to be self-reconstructing. 'If defendants are unwilling or feel incapable of volunteering expanded answers to questions, professionals will then be forced to fall back into habits of posing highly specific and constraining questions permitting the interviewees to respond only minimally' (Linell and Luckmann, 1991: 12). The difference here is that both participants are professionals. However, due to different expectations for leadership (Borchers, 2003), Venu adopts a deferential approach, while Steve continues to try and engage in what could be seen as an open discussion of peers. The effect observed is that the asymmetry becomes self-reconstructing and more pronounced.

As with our discussion of shared understanding previously, there is insufficient evidence to conclusively show a connection between the hierarchical nature of Indian culture (and relatively non-hierarchical UK/US cultures) and the observed asymmetries. However, the observed evidence provides useful supporting evidence for other studies which has suggested the importance of hierarchy within offshoring relationships but provide no substantial evidence from practice (e.g., Borchers, 2003; Kobayashi-Hillary, 2005; MacGregor et al., 2005). This leads to our next finding:

Finding 4: That a major factor of observed asymmetries of participation is perceived hierarchical differences between Indian vendor staff and UK/US client staff.

Summary – Asymmetries of Participation

The asymmetry of participation observed in the 'specimen' shows a pattern that has been identified across the corpus of data, with the Pharma staff tending to dominate the conversation, and the vendor staff taking a deferential approach in the conversations. This asymmetry is not always positive and, as is seen in this case, can at times result in misunderstandings and less than satisfactory interactions. There are, however, insufficient data in our corpus that we have analysed in detail to validate this position. It requires validation by further research. Indeed, it would be particularly interesting for such conversations to be interpreted by Indian researchers to see if their interpretations (of the implications of different Indian social hierarchies, for example) are similar to our Western interpretations.

What we have demonstrated is that beneath the surface of a relatively simple conversation, there are potentially numerous cultural interactions taking place, and that the observed asymmetries can be explained in many different ways, and in reality will be the result of a complex combination of factors.

The importance of this observation is that these differences in cultural preferences can result in misunderstandings, which if not addressed can affect the quality of the whole relationship (Gumperz, 2002; Carbaugh, 2005). The lack of shared understanding about the expected responses in an interaction or behaviours expected in a discussion can result in cultural misunderstanding. The vendor staff can come across as unnecessarily defensive or closed (Gumperz, 2002: 318) and the Pharma staff could come across as aggressive or abrasive (Vallaster, 2005). This has the potential to materially affect the outcome of the offshore engagements. This may explain in part the frequent articles in the trade press containing criticisms of offshore workers due to a perceived reluctance to challenge decisions or ask for clarification (Overby, 2003).

As seen in our example, an open discussion about a breakdown in the process degenerated into a highly asymmetrical, strict question and answer format, which gave Venu little opportunity to shape the discussion or present his perspective. Through greater awareness of this dynamic, it may be possible to adopt strategies to address these observed asymmetries, and maximise the benefits that different team members can bring to the discussion.

Cohesion and Flow

Naturally occurring conversation between people of a similar cultural background can be seen to have a natural flow, rhythm and order (Garcez, 1997). This is demonstrated through discussion of dimensions such as the turn-taking mechanisms and symmetry discussed in the 'Asymmetries of participation' section.

However, the rules as to how conversation should flow and how to construct and manage a conversation can vary across cultures and therefore cause problems when cultural groups cross. Authors, such as Erickson and Shultz (1982), have demonstrated how disturbances in the basic conversational rhythm can cause problems in the underlying conduct of the interaction.

The scope of this discussion can only address a very limited number of these different aspects of cross-cultural elements within conversation, but we hope to show how underlying cultural expectations could be affecting the construction of the discussions and how differences in the way in which the conversation is constructed affects the 'illocutionary force' (Gumperz, 2002) of what is said.

Sales Force Automation Specimens

The next specimen conversation shown as Fig. 11.4 will focus on the weekly project meeting of a team that is implementing a shared offshore support contract for their Sales Force Automation system. The key participants are Neil – the Pharma Programme Office Manager, Hari – the Vendor 1 Lead Project Manager and Joby – his Technical Lead.

The background to this discussion is that over the previous 4 weeks there had been a long-running debate with no agreement over the process for managing change controls within the new support model. This meeting has been specifically set aside to resolve this issue.

PHARMA IT Director:	Bill	PHARMA Programme Manager:	Neil
Vendor 1 Lead PM:	Hari	Vendor 1 Technical Lead:	Joby
PHARMA Local Market Lead:	Hussain	PHARMA Local Market Lead:	Samma

((Before recording starts, the meeting was started and the Vendor 1 Lead was asked to summarise their proposal of how change requests should be managed in their service. N.B. CCR = Change Control Record))		
1	**Hari:**	The purpose of the CCR's is to have the clear control over::: dev
2		and ur test environment
3		(0.5)
4	**Hari:**	er: if: e::r (.) correct me if my understanding is clear.
5		(2.5)
6	**Neil:**	↑Y:es↑ (.) thats true
7		(0.1)
		((Continued on next extract))

Fig. 11.4 Conversation analysis – the weekly project meeting

We start from Hari's first comment. He has been asked to explain their proposed process for managing change controls. Right from the start, this example shows the effect of non-standard 'Indian English' with the slight lack of flow in the sentence and a very old fashioned 'correct me if my understanding is clear' (line 4).

From the pause and the stuttered response, we can see that this surprises Neil who does not at first interpret it as a question. Then he is able to translate the sentence and provide an appropriate answer.

While a trivial example, this demonstrates some of the issues that can arise out of unexpected terminology. This makes even a simple statement difficult to understand. Occurrences like this have been shown to be important within cross-cultural communication. Gumperz's (2002) study of cross-cultural interviews also showed that non-standard responses during the introductions 'significantly affected the quality of the interaction, so that the initial informality has by now been replaced by an air of tenseness'.

The serious note for our study is that through the integration of these non-standard or surprising phrases into more complex or longer sentence structures the coherence of the overall discussion is affected because 'small differences in the use of cohesive devices amount to great systematic communicative problems at the level of coherence' (Garcez, 1997).

However, we should not overplay their impact. As we have seen, Neil quickly overcomes his initial confusion. We could see a parallel perhaps with a strong regional accent. A native speaker might be confused at first but will normally quickly recover. Interestingly, these overt language differences are highlighted in numerous papers (e.g., Krishna *et al.*, 2004; Rottman and Lacity, 2004; Kobayashi-Hillary, 2005).

The next extract shown as Fig. 11.5 is substantially longer and appears to show more substantive issues occurring within the communication. The first observation from the perspective of a reader or anyone listening to the recording is that this whole section is very difficult to follow.

There appears to be very little flow or cohesion to the description, and we can see repeated sections where Hari is building up the speed of his talk (indicated by <bracketed sections>), outlays of breath (indicated by hhh) and prolongation of sounds within words at the end of words (indicated by :: with number of colons indicating length). There are also two instances of latching (shown by an =) which is a mechanism of maintaining or regaining control of talk and serves to break down the natural flow of the conversation. This all indicates that the talk is very rushed and serves to break up the flow and rhythm of the explanation.

The turn-based structure of the conversation and the flow appear to have broken down, with multiple instances when Neil does not recognise immediately that Hari has paused for a continuer or clarification, so that Hari has to probe for a response or there is a long delay (e.g., lines 18, 48 and 55). Equally, there are also frequent overlaps and interruptions as Neil seeks to make clarifications (e.g., lines 10, 20 and 26).

The overall feeling at this point is of a highly asymmetrical conversation in which what Hari is expressing makes abundant sense to him, so he is trying very hard to keep the floor and explain all the way through. In an interesting contrast to the ODT example, the asymmetrical dominance is on the vendor side. However, as is seen in the interruptions in this extract and during the next extract, Neil appears to maintain control of the conversation directing its course, while saying less than Hari.

The extract shown as Fig. 11.6 appears to start in the same vein as the previous conversation, with very fast turns from both Hari and Joby. At

7		(0.1)
8	Hari:	So the whole objective of creating this CCRs (.) to have better control
9		on errm (.) dev an<u>d</u> test environment (0.1)[now if we create
10	Neil:	[Actually technically the
11		test environment-]
12	Hari:	] um::: say urrm (0.2) a change record against (.)
13		see erm there is no ambiguity in taking the change request (.) right
14		from the beginning <let me come from the er::> (process) ↑Change
15		request will be created urrm (.) single change requests .hhh or urm (.)
16		any changes <which will come from the market>
17		(1.2)
18	Hari:	That is clear right?
19		(0.3)
20	Neil:	Y:es:: however ur::m-]
21	Hari:	[where we will in that request mention
22		very clearly that urm ur::m because of this change this, I mean,
23		effectively that change has to be made onto the production
24		environment (.) where in other two environments will be effected
25		because of this cha[nge–
26	Neil:	[°and .. thats fine and I understand°↑ let me just be
27		clear at this point. Are you talking about a change request purely in
28		the form of a word document?
29		(0.3)
30	Hari:	Yeh lets see so far:::r um:: initially when the change request comes
31		that is in the form of err the word document itself, <he'll be initiate
32		then processes onto Change-Trak> ((the Pharma change management
33		tool))
34	Neil:	Yeah
35		(0.3)
36	Hari:	so in that document we are maintaining the activities what we are
37		going to do into (.) um:: regarding the change.
38	Neil:	Ok thats clear thankyou (.)
39	Hari:	Ok we move into Change-Trak, (.) so in order to ( ) that first of all
40		we need to create a change record=
41	Hari:	=now it has to be eit::her either in
42		three different environment or in two single environment. .hhh now if
43		we start from the dev um: Vendor 1 starts working from the Dev. Now
44		we create the change record on to Dev, then it goes for:: the whole
45		cycle of ↑approval↑ and one the approval is done then er:: get into er::
46		the um:: development of the change.
47		(0.2.)
48		Right?
49	Neil:	Yep=
50	Hari:	=so they complete the changes then they move it onto er: test
51		<then again they create a change record> then um: after the approval
52		that task is completed. (.) ag::ain another record has to be now
53		created into er: production. Now the question is who will create that
54		record?
55		(2.3)
56	Neil:	↑OK↑ so this where it comes back to this discussion about release
57		management and that being the responsibility of market leads? Yes?
58		(0.1)

Fig. 11.5   Conversation analysis – more substantive issues

59	Hari:	Cur:::correct <see I mean now I'd say, in fact it's release management
60		now moving onto to production environment> ideally uh: releas:
61		management. Now we need to first of all um: first of all ur:::mm: track
62		the changes also into the production environment.[
63	Neil:	[umhm:
64	Hari:	[cause we are
65		changing the environment of the production, because we are now
66		making the changes into the err:: n::: <production environment> (.)
67		°now Vendor 1 team° will say that they have the urr: responsibility of dev
68		and test. So thats right from beginning, and you know the best
69	Hari:	=<now go away an look at
70		request> (0.3) this what uh Joby
71	Joby:	Yeh actually b: .hh here's one thing Neil, you know, eh for any change
72		we create three records you know[
73	Neil:	[Ye::h
74	Joby:	[↑For three records we have finally. you
75		know what is our aim is <we are creating a (environment) based on
76		production environment. .hh OK we have not taken any SLA for
77		development one thing, test one thing, and uh: finally for production
78		one SLA. So thats right from beginning, and you know the best
79		practices these people have defined, and ah: uh: subsequently <we
80		know the other where they been created, project manager and who
81		created this partic::ular area of Vendor 1 model>. and <he was also
82		telling that we had to do again, to raise only one change request .hhh
83		but two agains:t you know production envir[onment>
84	Neil:	[So::
85	Joby:	[<we had to work only
86		on that> (.)
87	Hari:	it is,
88	Joby:	so you know, but uh:: you know because of the ambiguity and the uh: it
89		is ( ) we are uh speaking on this particular thing: from last
90		four weeks, now you know we have decided it's up to you people how
91		you decide. We don't mind to work it development environment
92		creating one and separately creating in test one ... we don't mind .hh
93		(.) ok we are open for that, because basically we don't want to leave
94		any ambiguity. We just leave this activity to the market leads to
95		decide, whether they want to have three. If they want to have three
96		then we will update only two and the remain third one Market leads
97		have to do in production environment.
98	Neil:	[uh:]
99	Joby:	[but you know for some example I'll tell you, when somebody
100		measured this metric () we:: for each change there will be change
101		requests will be-[
102	Hari:	[three: records]
103	Joby:	[there against each change, three records in
104		Change-Trak-[
105	Neil:	[Yeh I understand (.) .h Hari let me comment here
106		because I think we might be being the victims of terminology here,
107		over the last four weeks. um:: (0.3) Samma, Husain I'll ask you to
108		comment in a second but, (0.2)
109		.hh my worry was always this that uh one change request for a
110		change thats fine that makes sense. Uh::m I always thought umm:
111		through the past that °in one change request only one ↑change↑record
112		(.) would be created in just ↑one of the ↑three environments° and that
113		was deemed as suitable. So .h my concern was that three
114		environments only one change record has been made. Now what
115		you've described is ↓if you take a ↓patch ↓update as an example in
116		one market, the one change request is created for that patch update.
117		and as you go through the work to do that change then three change
118		records are eventually produced. One [for dev
119	Joby:	[°one for dev, one for test°
120	Neil:	[one for test, one for
121		production. Now from my point of view that means the configuration
122		management, for our system is kept up to date, because all three
123		environments are kept up to date with what changes they made. I
124		think and Hussain and Samma I need you to verify this, I think in the
125		past we thought that only one change record would be produced. But
126		it sounds like three, as we want them are being produced and quite
127		sensibly it's only being related to one planned change request, i.e. the
128		word document. So if I:: said Samma, Hussain does it sound like this
129		process is actually ok but we've just been understanding it wrong?
130		
131		((There follows a discussion between Neil and the market leads
132		confirming that this was the cause of the confusion))

133		
134	Neil:	So; uh: Hari, Joby I know you've been listening, um: I personally
135		think that the process your following is ok, I think really the terminology
136		was the problems in the past (.) that we didn't differentiate between
137		changes request and change record
138		(1.0)
139	Hari:	Correct:: uh:::e uh three phasing altogether into the overall changes,
140		um:: there ar:::e uh three phasing the changes, (.) then test the changes (.)
141		like first of all uh:: develop the changes, (.) then test the changes (.)
142		and then release the changes, now every time um what ever activity
143		these guys are doing there is a diary available in the Change-Trak where
144		they:: can:: uh: always keep updating that where they are and what
145		they are doing (.) so there we will have the control like: .hh when the
146		development was done and when the test was completed and when
147		urr: it is ready to raise onto the production
148		(1.2)
149	Neil:	Yes (.) and THAT comes from the change record process[─

Fig. 11.6 Conversation analysis – a highly asymmetrical conversation

line 105, Neil succeeds in interjecting, he uses the same entrance as previously 'Yeh I understand' seemingly trying to assure Hari he has taken his points on board. His approach now is interesting as he prepares the floor for a longer turn-at-talk, so that he will not have to hurry like Hari did to avoid interruption. He informs each participant what he is expecting of them, therefore asking them not to interrupt him. He also sets the scene for what he is about to say 'I think we might be being the victims of terminology here' (line 106). The effect of this is that he is able to speak for significantly longer than any other single turn in the whole conversation.

The luxury of this time allows him to build up and express his thought pattern logically to the whole team. He makes clear what the important aspects of change control were to him and how the proposed process matched it. Having set the scene, he is able to translate the process that Hari was trying to explain 'Now what you've described is...' (line 114–118). At the end of this description, he gets the only interruption of the whole long term, which is taken as a continuer.

The essence of this misunderstanding, which has been going on for over 4 weeks, turns out to be the simple case of misunderstanding terminology between a 'Change Request' and a 'Change Record'. What is most interesting for our present study, however, is not how this misunderstanding came about, but how the parties to the conversation recognised and approached resolving it.

What follows Neil's extended turn-at-talk essentially confirms agreement of this process and that was where the misunderstanding lay.

Discussion

What is interesting from a CA perspective and the effect it had on the coherence of the whole conversation is how Neil managed to set up his turn so that he had sufficient time to explain the process fully, and the contrast in how he was able to explain the same process as Hari in a much clearer manner (to a Western ear/eye).

The first aspect that appears to have affected the coherence of the two explanations is how they manage the conversation. Neil starts his turn-at-talk by framing what he was about to say before explaining it. This has parallels to the analysis by Harvey Sacks of storytelling within conversation where he showed a two-move sequence by which participants gain themselves sufficient time to tell their story without interruption and inform the listeners of their expected response. Thus, by use of this story preface, they are able to maintain control of the conversation.

This is exactly what Neil was able to do during his introductory context setting. By achieving this shared understanding that he needs an extended turn to explain what is happening, he is able to control the conversation and manage his response in a clear logical way.

This approach contrasts to Hari's who moves straight into his attempt to explain the same process. Because the expectations of the rest of the group were not set in advance, he faces continual interruptions, as the other participants continue their natural turn-taking process. This results in him having to use other mechanisms, such as 'latching' and increasing the speed, in order to maintain control. These mechanisms severely impact the coherence of the explanation, making it harder to follow and the message comes across as rushed and confused.

The second aspect, we will discuss is how each speaker organised what they actually said. This is an aspect of rhetorical organisation, and there are interesting contrasts that make Neil's explanation much easier to follow from a Westerner's perspective.

Hari moves directly into the detail of the process, explaining the detail of each step. 'OK so we move into Change-Trak so in order to do that first of all we need to create a change record, now it has to be in either three different environments or in two single environments...' (lines 39–42). The feeling he gives is of building up a story, providing increasing levels of detail, so that everyone can understand what is involved. However, he does not clearly show the importance of each step or their connection to the whole.

This is analogous to what Vallaster (2005) describes as circling the target: 'The style of "logic" of the average Asian person seems to be more intuitive than that of Western people'. The Asian logic is not to head straight towards the goal but to 'circle' it, involving a lot of 'learning by rote'. ... In contrast, Western philosophy with its analytical approach tends to be mainly interested in the 'Why and how?'. In Hari's description, the explicit connections to the wider problem are glossed over and are not clearly dealt with.

By contrast, Neil's focus is on the wider problem. He shows you the connections to the wider problem and his thought process explicitly, 'So my concern was' (line 113) and 'now what you've described is' (line 114), before giving his brief overview of the same process, but at a much higher level.

The way Hari attempts to manage this discussion for this audience causes a problem. Because he does not give these explicit connections to the wider area, they have less 'mental hooks' on which hangs the detail he provides. This is described by Tannen as 'explicit syntactic connections' (Tannen, 1984). This expectation of explicit syntactic connection is not fulfilled by speakers whose overall rhetorical organisation pattern is inductive/collaborative. Therefore, within Hari's explanation, because the listener does not have these connections, they are quickly lost, which leads to interruption for clarifications. These break down the flow of the explanation further, until it looses all of its cohesion. This is demonstrated by the fact that it is left to Neil to deduce the connections. 'OK, so this is where it comes back to this discussion about release management?' (lines 56 and 57).

When comparing Hari's approach of building up the story to Neil's of setting out the problem, we should ask whether this difference is cultural or due to the relative experience of the two speakers.

We should however ask whether this difference is cultural or due to the relative experience of the two speakers. Background information shows that they are of a similar experience level (3–6 years) and a similar age group (both late 20 s/early 30 s), with Neil being the slightly younger and less experienced. Thus, difference in experience is unlikely to be the cause of the contrast.

However, from one specimen conversation, we cannot show that this is a cultural difference. Similar observations of difficulties in explaining complex topics were observed in other areas of the corpus of data and interestingly, there are some potential comparisons with the problems that Venu was having explaining his position in the previous example. In each of his descriptions, he focuses on the process and the actual steps he took. Steve on the other hand uses a similar technique to Neil. 'So what your saying there in that e-mail is'. 'You need to be more explicit in the diary entry so that people who are reading this will understand what's happened with the ticket'.

Overall, we can build a picture that demonstrates how cultural difference could be affecting an individual's approaches to organising their conversation, and therefore their ability to get across their point with the same 'illocutionary force' (Gumperz, 2002). However, before any firm conclusions can be built from this, much more detailed comparative analysis of multiple speaking pairs would be required, hence, our next two findings:

Finding 5: That the rhetorical organisation of turns during conflict/negotiation is culturally contexted and exhibits key contrasts between Indian vendor and UK/US client staff and commonality within these groups.

Finding 6: That cultural differences in the rhetorical organisation by many Indian vendor staff reduce the illocutionary force of their arguments with UK/US client staff.

The fact that there are interactants from different cultural backgrounds does not make a misunderstanding intercultural (Hinnenkamp, 1999), and as the issue had been under discussion for over 4 weeks, we are unlikely to be able to understand what initially caused it. What we can see, however, is that cross-cultural issues are likely to have prolonged the misunderstanding. It is surprising that a problem as simple as the terminology between a change request and a change control has taken 4 weeks to resolve. While we have not shown that actual misunderstanding was due to cultural differences, we have shown that cultural differences may have been impacting the quality of the interaction between the participants, and their ability to resolve the original misunderstanding.

Finding 7: That misunderstandings within cross-cultural communications take longer and more effort to repair than would be expected within 'mono' culture communications.

We have seen from the above discussion that the way in which participants structure their conversation can have cultural relevance. We have not, however, been able to show explicitly that the variance in the rhetorical organisation between Neil and Hari is caused by cultural differences. However, the parallels to the exchange between Steve and Venu might add weight to this potential claim.

This claim is summarised by the two findings for future research. If validated they would mean that in intercultural situations, such as offshoring, a key challenge becomes ensuring that opinions expressed from different cultural backgrounds are included within decisions.

Conclusion

Through this discussion, we have shown the need for more research into the nature of cross-cultural communication within IS offshoring. Emerging issues of cross-cultural conflicts are apparent with the rapid expansion of this field (Borchers, 2003; Rottman and Lacity, 2004; Vallaster, 2005).

We have seen that the current IS literature on cross-cultural organisation is dominated by the use of surveys and a reliance on reductionist national culture models. There have been no concerted efforts to apply ethnographic techniques, such as CA to IS off-shoring. Our research represents a small effort to address that gap.

Our analysis has explored both the use of CA to analyse cultural behaviour in this environment and two key cultural phenomena observed across the corpus of data.

Through the detailed exploration of one example, we have investigated the existence of asymmetries of participation within IS offshoring, demonstrating potential causes of this and the impact that it could have on the quality of communication within IS offshoring. Based on this, we have identified four findings for validation.

Finally, we explored different rhetorical styles of the vendor and client staff showing the impact that they have on the overall cohesion of the conversation and therefore the 'illocutionary force' of their arguments. This identified the final three findings.

As discussed, a key limitation of CA is the ability to generalise findings. Therefore, it has not been possible to assess the scale or impact of cultural differences on IS offshoring engagements. However, we have clearly demonstrated instances where it is believed that cultural differences are impacting communication within offshoring and presenting seven findings for future research.

If we accept that Pharma is not unique in its IS offshoring engagements, and is broadly representative of other similar size multinationals, then we can suppose that other companies may experience similar issues within their offshore engagements.

The key caveat of the above is that given our findings in the literature review on the variability of culture, and its state of 'constant flux across individuals within cultural groups, and over time within individual' (Maznevski and Peterson, 1997), no research on culture could ever claim to do more than capture a picture of the situation within a given context at a given time.

As for contribution, we have demonstrated the existence of asymmetries of participation within the offshoring communication process. While we cannot identify the scale or persistence of these asymmetries (hence Finding 1), we have been able to explore potential explanations for them.

The discussions around a lack of shared understandings and problems within listenership, while not conclusive, provide evidence of phenomena identified in other areas of intercultural research, thus providing evidence of their existence within IS offshoring and further information for practitioners to be aware of within their communications.

Of particular importance are the findings around the effect of social hierarchies on the quality of the interaction. These are again not complete and Finding 3 requires detailed investigation to establish their relative importance. However, the presentation of observed and analysable evidence of deferential behaviour by vendor staff, and the self-reconstructing nature of the asymmetrical relationship, can be seen as a potentially significant contribution.

This research has provided support for prior literature which has suggested that discussions with Indian staff are often dominated by US/UK staff. Nicholson and Sahay (2001) stated 'India is not a very assertive culture, Indians tend to go along with what other people say, especially authority figures'. Prior studies were primarily based on surveys or personal experience, and thus open to the accusation that respondent's biases were incorporated within the data. With the CA research approach, a reader may disagree with the findings presented, but the presence of the transcripts from naturally occurring interactions, makes the data available for all to see and come to their own conclusions.

In the 'Cohesion and flow' section, we have documented a specimen conversation that contains clear communication difficulties. Through our analysis, we have attempted to break these down and gain greater insight into the nature of the problems experienced. Whether the rhetorical differences observed are due to cultural differences of the participants or other unobserved factors, we cannot tell. However, we have presented sufficient evidence, to warrant further investigation of Findings 4 and 5. The value of this insight within IS offshoring is fundamental because, if validated, it will lead to greater understanding of how discussion is formulated across cultures and hence to a greater ability to manage these differences, leading to better decisions.

Finally, addressing the third objective, we have demonstrated the ability of ethnographic research (and specifically CA) to provide a methodology for analysing cross-cultural communication within offshoring and shown its ability to gain greater insight into these cultural challenges. CA allowed us to address some of the weaknesses of interviews and surveys, which could not in any constructive way have demonstrated the asymmetries of communications observed or have provided a vehicle for exploring differences in the rhetorical organisation of discussions.

The findings outlined in this research are designed to stimulate future research efforts. There is no way that one study can cover all of a subject as wide as cross-cultural communication, but through the presentation of these findings, it can hopefully focus future work and highlight the strengths and weaknesses of its chosen methodology.

- *Finding 1*: That on average a clearly identifiable asymmetry of participation exists within onshore–offshore vendor meetings.
- *Finding 2*: That a lack of shared understanding of expected responses results in an increase in asymmetry of participation between Indian vendor staff and UK/US client staff.

• *Finding 3*: That a lack of cues and listener responses results in a disproportionately high occurrence of hyperexplanations within off-shoring communications.

• *Finding 4*: That a major factor of observed asymmetries of participation is perceived hierarchical differences between Indian vendor staff and UK/US client staff.

• *Finding 5*: That the rhetorical organisation of turns during conflict/negotiation is culturally contexted and exhibits key contrasts between Indian vendor and UK/US client staff and commonality within these groups.

• *Finding 6*: That cultural differences in the rhetorical organisation by many Indian vendor staff reduce the illocutionary force of their arguments with UK/US client staff.

• *Finding 7*: That misunderstandings within cross-cultural communications take a longer and more effort to repair than would be expected within 'single' culture communication.

Limitations of this research have been integrated in the discussion as we have progressed through this research. However, we should revisit these now.

The size of the corpus of data collected, while sufficient for the scope of this study, was limited, despite the attempt to maximise variation in the meetings chosen. To address some of the findings successfully, a much larger corpus of data may be required.

The focus on one case study organisation (Pharma) results in the potential for organisational culture aspects affecting the findings. This was managed to some extent by selecting data from different business units across a large multinational organisation.

As discussed in the methodology section, CA has inherent limitations due to the time-intensive nature of transcribing and analysing the data. In this paper we only have space to analyse two key specimens. An important criticism of CA is that through the researchers' selection of specimen conversations, the researchers' own interpretations can be veiled as empirical claims (Tulin, 1997). This has been managed through the efforts to show the data collected and through the provision of full transcripts of the specimen discussions. However, this criticism cannot be entirely ruled out.

This study has focused on telephone conversations within organised meetings. Therefore, interactions outside of these meetings have not been taken into account. Our choice was seen as appropriate due to the availability of the data and scope of this study. However, future research may choose to include other interactions. In particular, investigation of asymmetries and hierarchy (Findings 1 and 4) may benefit from these extra data because offline discussions can be an important way in which a lack of contribution during meetings might be balanced (Vallaster, 2005).

It may also be important to include other communications, for example, e-mail, in the analysis. The lack of visibility of the Lotus Notes database used to manage the ODT meeting prevented us reviewing the e-mails at the centre of the misunderstanding. Some companies may use videoconferencing, and eye contact and body language that this form of communication enables may help to resolve miscommunication (or indeed may not, as cultural differences might impact here as well).

Other implications of the findings were not pursued in this study but are potentially important. To give one example, with IS off-shoring being driven by the perceived labour-cost savings, the hidden costs of cultural differences implied by this study need to be considered in any future study comparing costs and benefits of offshoring initiatives.

Through this report, we have demonstrated the complexity of culture and how differences in culture manifest themselves in our conversations. Moerman (1988) sums this up neatly stating: 'In every moment of talk, people are experiencing and producing their cultures, their roles, their personalities'.

Because talk is critical to organising the successful management of IS offshoring relationships, much will depend on IS professionals over-coming these cultural 'barriers' to communication. Therefore, continued study is critical to improve our understanding of cross-cultural communication and to help meet this challenge.

Acknowledgements We are grateful to Shirley Gregor who provided some insightful comments on an earlier draft.

Appendix

Transcription conventions

The following is a summary of the transcription conventions developed for use within CA. Their purpose is to clearly identify all the features of the talk. The following table is taken from Ten-Have (1999) and based on the original conventions developed by Gail Jefferson.

Sequencing

[A single left bracket indicates the point of overlap onset.

]   A single right bracket indicates the point at which an utterance or utterance-part terminates *vis-à-vis* another.

=   Equals signs, one at the end of one line and one at the beginning of a next, indicate no 'gap' between the two lines. This is often called latching.

Timed intervals

(0.0)   Numbers in parentheses indicate elapsed time in silence by tenth of a second, so (7.1) is a pause of 7 s and one-tenth of a second.

(.)   A dot in parentheses indicates a tiny 'gap' within or between utterances.

Characteristics of speech production

word   Underscoring indicates some form of stress, via pitch and/or amplitude.

::   Colons indicate prolongation of the immediately prior sound. Multiple colons indicate a more prolonged sound.

-          A dash indicates a cut-off.

↓ ↑   Arrows indicate marked shifts into higher or lower pitch in the utterance part immediately following the arrow.

WORD   Upper case indicates especially loud sounds relative to the surrounding talk

°   Utterances or utterance parts bracketed by degree signs are relatively quieter than the surrounding talk.

< >   Right/left carets bracketing an utterance or utterance-part indicate speeding up.

.hhh   A dot-prefixed row of hs indicates an inbreath. Without the dot, the hs indicate an outbreath.

w(h)ord A parenthesised h or a row of hs within a word, indicates breathiness, as in laughter, crying, etc.

Transcriber's doubts and comments

()   Empty parentheses indicate the transcriber's inability to hear what was said. The length of the parenthesised space indicates the length of the untranscribed talk.

(word) Parenthesised words are especially dubious hearings or speaker identifications.

(())   Double parentheses contain transcriber's descriptions rather than, or in addition to, transcriptions.

References

BCS (2004). Offshoring – A challenge or opportunity for British IT professionals? The Report of the BCS Working Group on Offshoring, British Computer Society London.

Blommaert, J (1998). Introduction: Language and politics, language politics and political linguistics, In J. Blommaert and C. Bulcaen (eds.) *Political Linguistics*, Amsterdam: John Benjamins.

Borchers, G. (2003). *The Software Engineering Impacts of Cultural Factors on Multi-Cultural Software Development Teams*, IEEE, NJ: Hoboken.

Carbaugh, D (2005). *Cultures in Conversation*, Mahway, NJ: Lawrence Erlbaum Associates.

Cowan, J (1990). *Dance and the Body Politic in Northern Greece*, Princeton: Princeton University Press.

Drew, P. and Heritage, J (2002). *Talk at Work*, Cambridge: University Press.

Erickson, F. and Shultz, J (1982). *The Counselor as Gatekeeper: Social interaction in interviews*, New York: Academic.

Erickson, K.G (1998). The Impact on Cultural Status Beliefs on Individual Task Performance, In Evaluative Settings, Ph.D. dissertation, Department of Sociology, Stanford University: CA.

Fernandez, D.R., Carlson, D.S., Stepina, L.P. and Nicholson, J.D (1997). Hofstede's Country Classification 25 Years Later, *Journal of Social Psychology* **137**(1): 43–54.

Ford, D., Connelly, C. and Meister, D (2003). Information Systems Research and Hofstede's Cultures Consequences: An uneasy and incomplete partnership, *IEEE Transactions on Engineering Management* **50**(1): 8–25.

Fusilier, M. and Durlabhji, S. (2001). Cultural Values of Indian Managers: An exploration through unstructured interviews, *International Journal of Value Based Management* **14**(3): 223–236.

Garcez, P (1997). Invisible Culture and Cultural Variation in Language Use, Why Language Educators Should Care, *Linguagem and Ensino* **1**(1): 33–86.

Goodwin, C. and Heritage, J (1990). Conversation Analysis, *Annual Review Anthropology* **19**: 283–307.

Gorlenko, L. (2006). The Moment of Truth: How much does culture matter to you?, *Communications of the ACM* **13**: 29–31.

Gumperz, J.J (2002). Interviewing in Intercultural Situations, In P. Drew and J. Heritage (eds.) *Talk at Work*, Cambridge: University Press, pp. 302–330.

Hill, C (2001). *International Business: Competing in the global marketplace*, New York: McGraw-Hill.

Hinnenkamp, V (1999). The Notion of Misunderstanding in Intercultural Communication, *The Journal of* Intercultural *Communication* **1**(1): 7–12.

Hofstede, G (2001). *Cultures Consequences*, 2nd edn London: Sage.

Kirk, J. and Miller, M.L (1986). *Reliability and Validity in Qualitative Research*, In Qualitative Research Methods Series, Vol. 1, Newbury Park, CA: Sage.

Kobayashi-Hillary, M. (2003). There's More to Offshore Outsourcing than Getting Skilled Employees at a Knockdown Price, *Computing*, 27 March.

Kobayashi-Hillary, M (2005). Pitfalls that the Outsourcing Vendor Forgot to Mention, *ACM Queue* **3**(1): 54–60.

Krishna, S., Sahay, S. and Walsham, G (2004). Managing Cross-Cultural Issues in Global Software Outsourcing, *Communications of the ACM* **47**(4): 62–66.

Lacity, M.C. and Willcocks, L.P (1998). An Empirical Investigation of Information Technology Sourcing Practices: Lessons from experience, *MIS Quarterly* **22**(3): 363–608.

Linell, P. and Luckmann, T (1991). Asymmetries in Dialogue: Some conceptual preliminaries, In I. Markova and K. Foppa (eds.) *Asymmetries in Dialogue*, Harvester Wheatsheaf: Hemel Hempstead, pp. 1–20.

Little, J., Granger, M., Adams, E., Holvikivi, J., Lippert, S., Walker, H. and Young, A. (2000). Integrating Cultural Issues into the Computer and Information Technology Curriculum, ITiCSB 2000 Working Group Reports.

MacGregor, E., Hsish, Y. and Kruchten, P (2005). Cultural Patterns in Software Process Mishaps: Incidents in global projects, *Human and Social*, In *Factors of Social Engineering (HSSE)*, May, pp. 1–5.

Maznevski, M.L. and Peterson, M.F (1997). Societal Values, Social Interpretation, and Multinational Teams, In C.S. Granrose and S. Oskamp (eds.) *Cross-Cultural Work Groups*, Thousand Oaks, CA: Sage, pp. 61–89.

McManes, C. (2003). H-1B And L-1 Visas Accelerate Offshore Outsourcing, 7 July, http://www.ieeeusa.org/newspubs/features/070703.htm.

Meso, P., Kim, J. and Kim, D. (2005). Cultural Effects on Offshore-Outsourced System Development, 14th Annual Cross-Cultural Meeting in Information Systems, AIS Special Interest Group on Cross-cultural Research in Information Systems, December.

Moerman, M (1988). *Talking Culture: Ethnography and conversation analysis*, Philadelphia: University of Pennsylvania.

Narayanaswamy, R. and Henry, R (2005). Effects of Culture on Control Mechanisms in Offshore Outsourced IT Projects, SIGMIS-CPR 05, April 14–16, Atlanta, Georgia, USA.

Nicholson, B. and Sahay, S (2001). Some Political and Cultural Issues in the Globalisation of Software Development: Case experience from Britain and India, *Information and Organisation* **11**: 25–43.

Olson, J.S. and Olson, G.M (2003). Culture Surprises in Remote Software Development Teams, *ACM Queue* **1**(9): 52–59.

Oshri, I., Kotlarsky, J. and Willcocks, L (2007). Managing Dispersed Expertise in IT Offshore Outsourcing: Lessons from Tata Consultancy Services, *MIS Quarterly Executive* **6**(2): 53–65.

Overby, S. (2003). The Hidden Costs of Offshore Outsourcing, *CIO Magazine*, September.

Oza, N. and Hall, T (2005). Difficulties in Managing Offshore Software Outsourcing Relationships: An empirical analysis of 18 high maturity Indian software companies, *Journal of Information Technology Case and Application Research* **7**(3): 25–41.

Pera"Kyla", A (2004). Reliability and Validity in Research Based on Naturally Occurring Social Interaction, In D. Silverman (ed.) *Qualitative Research: Theory, Method and Practice*, London: Sage.

Philips, S.U (1987). Warm Springs 'Indian Time', In R. Bauman and J. Sherzer (eds.) *Explorations in the Ethnography of Speaking*, Cambridge: Cambridge University Press, pp. 92–108.

Rottman, J. and Lacity, M (2004). Twenty Practices for Offshore Sourcing, *MIS Quarterly Executive* 3(3): 117–130.

Rottman, J. and Lacity, M (2006). Proven Practices for Effectively Offshoring IT Work, *Sloan Management Review* 47(3): 56–63.

Sacks, H (1984). Notes on Methodology, In J.M. Atkinson and J. Heritage (eds.) *Structures of Social Action. Studies in Conversation Analysis*, Cambridge: Cambridge University Press, pp. 21–27.

Schegloff, E.A. and Sacks, H (1973). Opening Up Closings, *Semiotica* VIII(4): 290–327.

Schirato, T. and Yells, S (2000). *Communication and Culture, An Introduction*, London: Sage.

Sidnell, J. (2006). Conversational Analytic Approaches to Culture, In C. Volegelin (ed.) *Language Situation*, London: Elsevier.

Silverman, D (2000). *Doing Qualitative Research*, London: Sage.

Sinha, J. and Sinha, D. (1990). Role of Social Values in Indian Organisation, *International Journal of Psychology* 25: 705–714.

Tannen, D (1984). *Coherence in Spoken and* Written Discourse. *Advances in Discourse Processes*, Norwood, NJ: Ablex.

Ten-Have, P (1999). *Doing Conversation Analysis – A practical guide*, London: Sage.

Tulin, M (1997). Talking Organisation – Possibilities for Conversation Analysis in Organisational Behaviour Research, *Journal of Management Inquiry* 6(2): 101–119.

Vallaster, C (2005). Cultural Diversity and Its Impact on Social Interactive Processes – Implications from an empirical study, *International Journal of Cross-cultural Management* 5(2): 123–138.

Weisinger, J. and Trauth, E (2002). Situating Culture in the Global Information Sector, *Information Technology and People* 15(4): 306–320.

David Avison was distinguished professor of Information Systems at ESSEC Business School, near Paris, France. He is president of the *Association of Information Systems (AIS)*. He is joint editor of Blackwell Science's

Information Systems Journal. His book publications include the fourth edition of the well-used text *Information Systems Development: Methodologies, Techniques and Tools* (jointly authored with Guy Fitzgerald) and a new book *Project Management in Information Systems* (jointly authored with Reza Torkzadeh). He was Chair of the *International Federation of Information Processing* (*IFIP*) *8.2* group on the impact of IS/IT on organisations and society. He was joint program chair of the *International Conference in Information Systems* (*ICIS*) in Las Vegas and most recently, joint program chair of the *IFIP TC8* conference in Milan, Italy. He researches in the area of information systems development and more generally on information systems in their natural organisational setting.

Peter Banks has a B.Sc. (Hons.) in Business Administration from the University of Bath. For the past 6 years, he has been working in industry in FTSE 100 organisations. Much of this time has been with a large pharmaceutical company where the research described in this paper was carried out. Most recently, he studied part-time to gain an M.Sc. in Information Management from Brunel University.

12

Applying Multiple Perspectives to the BPO Decision: A Case Study of Call Centres in Australia

Mark Borman

Introduction

Business process outsourcing (BPO) occurs where a supplier takes over responsibility for one or more of an organisation's business processes. BPO is seen as particularly suited for well defined, self-contained and measurable process-based activities (Tas and Sunder 2004). Such activities can be generic, such as customer management, human resources and finance, or industry specific, such as loan application processing.

While academic research specifically focused on BPO is emerging (see e.g. Feeny et al. 2003; Ramachandran and Voleti 2004), the field appears somewhat neglected compared to information technology (IT) outsourcing. The literature review of Dibbern et al. (2004) highlighted that 'current outsourcing research appears to be heavily tied to IS' (p. 90). Rouse and Corbitt (2004) similarly comment on the absence of academic publications on BPO. Yet, Codling and

M. Borman (✉)
School of Business, University of Sydney, Sydney, Australia
e-mail: m.borman@econ.usyd.edu.au

© The Author(s) 2017   **413**
L.P. Willcocks et al. (eds.), *Outsourcing and Offshoring Business Services*, DOI 10.1007/978-3-319-52651-5_12

Miller (2004) suggest that, for the UK at least, BPO will represent a market 75% as large as IT outsourcing by 2007. Technology Partners (2004) suggest that increasingly BPO and IT outsourcing will be bundled with 'the business process ruling the decision making' (p. 1). The importance of aligning an organisation's IT with its business operations has long been recognised (Sabherwal et al. 2001). BPO, by subsuming IT considerations into a broader business decision, rather than being a focus in their own right *à la* IT outsourcing, reinforces that importance.

Dibbern et al. (2004) suggest there is a relatively even split between IT outsourcing research that has focused on questions of *why* outsource, *what* to outsource and *how* to manage the relationship with the outsourcing service provider.[1] When considering the timeline of the various publications though it appears that researchers have moved on from the why and what questions to focus on how to make relationships successful. Increasingly, research papers focus on the critical factors for a successful relationship (Kern and Willcocks 2000) or the construction of effective outsourcing contracts (Saunders et al. 1997).

In focusing on BPO, this paper reflects the starting point of much of the research in IT outsourcing by seeking to address the questions of why outsource and what activities should be outsourced. Much of the early research into IT outsourcing applied a single theoretical lens to frame the outsourcing decision (e.g. Lacity and Hirschheim 1993 and transaction cost theory). Dibbern et al. (2004), however, suggest that as researchers sought to better understand the complexity of outsourcing, they increasingly embraced the application of multiple theoretical lenses. Such a multi-perspective approach will be applied here. With regard to the capabilities suppliers need to deliver the outsourced activities, there is little existing research to build upon. Furthermore, where research has considered capabilities, it has primarily done so from the client perspective – the capabilities a client requires to manage its outsourcing relationship effectively.

---

[1] Dibbern et al. (2004) identified 28 papers in the *what* category, 46 in the *why* and 36 in the *how* for the period 1988–2000.

Saunders et al. (1997), for example, highlight the role of an effective contract, while Alborz et al. (2004) emphasise the process of constructing an effective relationship and Lacity et al. (1996) highlight the ability to assess changing needs.

The remainder of the paper comprises three sections. The first proposes and outlines a multi-perspective approach to the BPO decision. The second reports an empirical study of outsourced call centres in Australia. The rationale for focusing on call centres was twofold. Firstly, customer management has been recognised by Codling and Miller (2004) as the fastest growing BPO segment with an annual growth rate of 15.1%, and call centres are the core of customer management. Secondly, IT plays a significant and increasing role in supporting call centres (Bousfield 2003). The final section of the paper outlines the implications and limitations of the current work and suggests opportunities for future research.

The paper contributes to the literature in three principal ways. Firstly, it extends outsourcing research to the BPO context. Secondly, it proposes a multi-perspective approach to analysing BPO that combines transactional, organisational and environmental level considerations. Thirdly, it identifies specific capabilities required of suppliers for BPO.

A Multi-perspective Approach to BPO Decision-Making

IT is seen by many as a key enabler of BPO (Edwards 2004; Tornbohm and Andrault 2005). Indeed, Tornbohm and Andrault (2005) have defined BPO as 'the delegation of one, or more, information and communication technology intensive business processes to an external service provider' (p. 3). Here IT-enabled reductions in transaction costs are proposed as the primary motivator behind BPO. However, it is suggested that the specific choice for a particular organisation will also be shaped by a combination of firm specific and environmental factors. With regard to the supplier capabilities required for the resultant BPO initiative, it is proposed that the work of Feeny et al. (2003) serve as a starting point. The complete set of influences on the BPO decision is illustrated in Fig. 12.1.

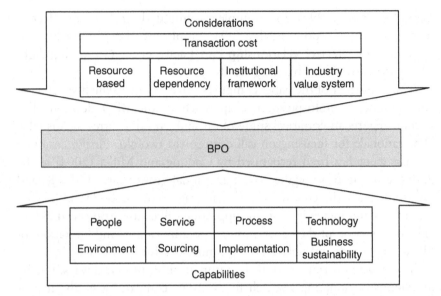

Fig. 12.1 Decision-making approach for BPO

BPO Decision Considerations

While research examining the motivation for, and objective of, IT outsourcing draws from many theoretical perspectives, four dominate: transaction cost theory, agency theory, and resource-based and resource-dependency theories (Cheon et al. 1995; Klein 2002; Dibbern et al. 2004). Given there are many similarities between agency and transaction cost theory (Dibbern et al. 2004), yet only the latter explicitly focuses on whether to outsource or not (Hancox and Hackney 1999), agency theory will not be considered further.

The resource-based and resource-dependency theories do not inherently conflict with each other, nor with transaction cost theory (Duncan 2002). Rather, the three theories can be seen as complementary.[2]

---

[2] Melville et al. (2004) suggest that adopting such a synthesising approach is beneficial. While the existence of multiple competing theoretical approaches can provide varied insights, the resulting fragmentation and isolation can also limit the overall development of understanding in an area.

Previously, for example, Grover et al. (1994) combined resource-based and resource-dependency theories, while Poppo and Zenger (1998) integrated transaction cost and resource-based theories. Here, it is proposed that the addition of resource dimensions moves any decision beyond pure transactional analysis to take into account the strategic contribution of an activity to an organisation and how the relationship with the supplier will be managed.

The transaction cost, resource-based and resource-dependency theories are briefly outlined below. It is then suggested that understanding of BPO decision-making will be improved if two further perspectives are added. Propositions are suggested based on the individual perspectives together with a meta-proposition that seeks to combine them.

Transaction Cost Theory

Transaction cost theory seeks to explain when organisations will externalise activities. From a production cost point of view, the market (external supply) is always seen as the preferred mode for organising production, as specialist producers have lower cost structures. Authors such as Levina and Ross (2003), Rouse and Corbitt (2004) and Kakabadse and Kakabadse (2005) suggest that the primary motivation for outsourcing is to cut costs. However, whether activities are actually externalised depends upon the transaction costs involved. Transaction costs are those costs incurred through putting in place, and operating, the necessary governance structure. Williamson (1986) argues that it is the interaction of human constraints and failings, bounded rationality and opportunism, with the specific qualities of a transaction, asset specificity, uncertainty and frequency of the transaction, that determine actual transaction costs. It has been extensively argued that IT reduces the transaction costs associated with using external suppliers (Ciborra 1987; Clemons et al. 1993), and it is suggested here that such a reduction will encourage outsourcing.

Proposition 1: IT facilitates BPO by reducing the associated transaction costs allowing organisations to engage with lower cost suppliers.

Resource-based Theory

Resource-based theory suggests that firms secure success by utilising their *unique* resources comprised of intangible and tangible assets that are tied semi-permanently to the firm (Wernerfelt 1984). However, such resources provide a sustained competitive advantage only when competitors are unable to acquire and deploy similar resources (Mata et al. 1995). Furthermore, according to Coyne (1986), to provide an advantage, the resources must contribute to 'a consistent difference in important attributes between the producer's product and those of his competitors' (p. 51). From the resource-based perspective, success is maximised where organisations focus their attention on those areas where their distinctive capabilities lie (Hagel and Seely Brown 2001) and rely on others for the provision of ancillary activities. Within the IS outsourcing domain, Halvey et al. (1996) and Dibbern et al. (2004) suggest that organisations are outsourcing to focus on key value-adding activities, hence Proposition 2.

Proposition 2: Organisations will use BPO for non-core activities.

Resource-dependency Theory

Resource-dependency theory states that organisations are dependent upon their environment and are faced with choices regarding how they manage that dependency (Thompson 1967). Kotter (1979) suggests that organisations need to adopt strategies to manage their dependency on external parties and ensure access to the resources they supply is stable and secure. There appears to be limited research in an outsourcing context though regarding the active management of dependency. Where a resource-dependency perspective has been adopted, it has typically been from a static point of view. For example, Ang and Cummings (1997) considered the influence of the number of potential suppliers but did not consider whether and how that number, and hence the associated dependency, could be modified.

Proposition 3: Organisations will seek to minimise supplier dependency when using BPO.

Combining the transaction cost, resource-based and resource-dependency approaches provide a rationale for identifying candidate activities for BPO *from the perspective of the focal firm* – the outsourcer. Drawing from the work of Melville et al. (2004), it is suggested that the operating environment in which that firm sits – specifically its institutional and industry context – should also be considered. The influence of such factors, however, appears to have largely been neglected by the outsourcing literature to date. Notable exceptions include Ang and Cummings (1997) who examined the influence of regulators on IT outsourcing and Ang and Straub (2002) who examined the competitiveness of the supplier market.

Institutional Context

According to Perez (1983), the political, economic and judicial institutions of a society function as a web of interconnected formal rules and informal constraints that establish a structure for organisational interactions – the so-called rules of the game. By regulating relationships, the institutional context serves to promote particular modes of organising activities (North 1990). Of particular interest, here is how the prevailing institutional context may influence BPO.

Proposition 4: The nature and extent of BPO will be shaped by an organisation's institutional context.

Industry Value System

Porter (1985) suggested that the competitive success of an organisation is determined by a combination of the value chain of that organisation and the broader value system within which it is positioned.[3] When considering BPO, therefore, an organisation should consider the potential impact on its standing within the value system, and in particular whether it will weaken it, for example, by reducing barriers to entry. Dibbern *et al.*'s (2004) review of the literature suggests that there has been limited research considering the influence of an organisation's competitive milieu on outsourcing decisions. One exception is the work of Sharma and Yetton (1996) regarding the striking of an alliance-based deal with a vendor, but this has a very narrow focus.

> **Proposition 5:** Organisations will not use BPO if it is detrimental to their standing in the industry value system.

From the perspective of this paper, perhaps more important than any of the preceding hypotheses is a final meta-proposition related to combining the perspectives.

> **Proposition 6:** Applying multiple theoretical perspectives increases understanding of the BPO decision.

BPO Capabilities Sought

In order to deliver BPO certain capabilities will be sought from a prospective supplier. Such capabilities represent the set of skills that will enable the outsourced activity to be delivered effectively over time. Some research in the IT and BPO outsourcing domains has been conducted with regard to capabilities (Lacity et al. 1996; Feeny and Willcocks 1998). However, it has focused primarily on the client perspective – the capabilities a client requires to manage its

---

[3] Porter argued that five forces determine the attractiveness of an industry to a firm: bargaining power of buyers; bargaining power of suppliers; threat of new entrants; threat of substitute products or services and rivalry among existing firms.

outsourcing relationship. Dibbern et al. (2004) review of the literature suggests that the supplier perspective has largely been neglected, and that where it has been considered, the primary focus has been on structuring the client–supplier relationship with only limited research conducted in the area of vendor selection. There are of course exceptions. Ramachandran and Voleti (2004) identify the need for a combination of business development and operational capabilities. Goles (2001) considers the business understanding, technological and relationship management capabilities of suppliers. McFarlan and Nolan (1995) emphasise the importance of the financial stability of vendors and their ability to keep pace with technological advances. Michell and Fitzgerald (1997) examine the varied characteristics of outsourcing suppliers based upon their backgrounds and start to consider how the client's and the supplier's views of the capabilities sought may differ. The research, however, is typically restricted to IT outsourcing.

Perhaps, the most comprehensive research that specifically addresses BPO is the work of Feeny et al. (2003) which identified seven critical business capabilities for BPO providers:

- People – the ability to draw upon the commitment, energy and talents of staff.
- Service – the ability to regard end users as customers, understand what good service represents and deliver it.
- Process – the ability to improve existing business processes within client companies.
- Technology – the provision of a technology platform that is core to the service delivered.
- Environment – the ability to develop an effective working environment that reinforces the distinctiveness of the provider.
- Sourcing – expertise in procurement and an ability to leverage aggregate purchasing power.
- Implementation – the ability to implement a BPO initiative and deliver it over time.

Table 12.1 Capabilities required of BPO suppliers

Feeny et al. (2003)	Feeny et al. (2005)
Supplier capabilities	
People	Behaviour management
Service	Customer development
Process	Domain expertise process re-engineering
Technology	Technology
Environment	–
Sourcing	Sourcing
Implementation	Programme management
	Leadership
	Organisation design
	Governance
Business sustainability	Business management
	Planning and contracting

A subsequent article, Feeny et al. (2005), increases the number of capabilities to 12. As expected, and as illustrated in Table 12.1, many of those capabilities map directly to those of Feeny et al. (2003).

It is suggested here that the original set of seven capabilities represents the better starting point to build upon. Feeny et al. (2003) more clearly draw the line connecting the empirical work conducted and the capabilities identified. Furthermore many of the additional capabilities appear too narrow in definition, or applicability, to serve as core supplier capabilities. For example, governance as defined by Feeny et al. (2005) refers primarily to the use of jointly staffed governance mechanisms for large relationship-oriented deals. Larsson et al. (2003) and Kakabadse and Kakabadse (2005), however, suggest that such relationship-based deals are both rare and require a different set of skills to more traditional ones. Only together do programme management (the ability to manage a series of interrelated change projects), leadership (the person in charge of the supplier account team) and organisation design (the organisational structures and processes to deliver the BPO business plan) start to approximate the requirements to successfully initiate and manage a BPO initiative that were earlier addressed by the implementation capability. As such, Feeny et al. (2003) will form the basis for the study of capabilities here. Business sustainability will be appended to the list as it is a capability identified by other researchers (McFarlan and Nolan 1995) as well as Feeny et al. (2005) that does map easily to any of the existing capabilities. The resultant propositions are as follows:

Proposition 7: Suppliers must have the ability to draw upon the commitment, energy and talents of staff.

Proposition 8: Suppliers must have the ability to regard end users as customers, understand what good service represents and deliver it.

Proposition 9: Suppliers must have the ability to improve existing business processes within client companies.

Proposition 10: Suppliers must have the ability to provide a technology platform that is core to the service delivered.

Proposition 11: Suppliers must have the ability to develop an effective working environment that reinforces the distinctiveness of the provider.

Proposition 12: Suppliers must have expertise in procurement and an ability to leverage aggregate purchasing power.

Proposition 13: Suppliers must have the ability to implement a BPO initiative and deliver it over time.

Proposition 14: Suppliers must have the ability to maintain a viable business over time.

Methodology

The case study method is well established in information systems research, especially where the aim is to enhance understanding in circumstances where research and theory are at a formative stage and a phenomenon is not well understood (Benbasat et al. 1987). The case work presented here is primarily explanatory (Yin 1984) and draws upon the work of Yin (1984) and Dubé and Paré (2003) with regard to the approach followed. Essentially, propositions were developed based upon the theory presented, and data were then collected and analysed in order to evaluate them. By adopting multiple theoretical lenses, the research is also aligned with Yin's (1984) recommendation to test alternative explanations. Rather than seeing if one perspective is better than another, the objective was to determine whether a combination of perspectives yielded a better understanding than a single one.[4,5]

A multi-case research design, based upon a literal replication logic (Yin 1984), was adopted with the aim of determining whether findings were industry-specific or more generalisable. The selection of cases was purposeful (Miles and Huberman 1994) to cover industries active in BPO. The unit of analysis was the set of related outsourced activities provided by a supplier to a client.

Suppliers were first selected on the basis of being the largest providers of outsourced call centre services in Australia.[6] Tas and Sunder (2004) suggest that BPO is particularly common in the financial services, utilities and telecommunications industries. Working with each supplier, a client was approached and engaged in the study to ensure coverage of these industries. Three supplier–client dyads were examined. In each case, the relationship was regarded as successful by both the supplier and the client. The use of supplier–client dyads permitted triangulation, increasing confidence in the findings (Dubé and Paré 2003). Further triangulation was achieved through seeking two interviewees in each organisation, one at a strategic level and the other at an operational one, by reviewing documentation and reports and walking through and observing call centres operated by each supplier. Table 12.2 provides an overview of each supplier–client dyad. The specific activities outsourced varied between clients. Acquisition refers to the acquiring of new customers. It can be an outbound activity (whereby the call centre contacts potential customers) or an inbound one (whereby potential customers contact the centre, e.g. in response to a direct mail offer). The remaining activities are inbound. Customer service refers to non-technology-related customer communications, for example, to activate a new credit card or phone service, to upgrade a service or to query a bill. Help desk refers

---

[4] A commingled rival approach according to Yin (1984).

[5] With regard to the capabilities sought of suppliers, the underlying proposition in each case was that the capability was sought.

[6] Together they represent over 50% of the market.

Table 12.2 Supplier and client case details

Dyad	Supplier	Interviewees	Client	Interviewees	Activities outsourced	Length of relationship (years)
A	SUPPLIER1 – Founded in 1996 and operating at multiple sites in Australia and New Zealand with a total seat capacity in excess of 1,500	General manager sales (GMS) Client services manager (CSM)	CLIENT1 – A major Australian financial services provider	Head of channel management (HCM)	Acquisition customer service	5
B	SUPPLIER2 – Founded in 1998 and currently operating nine call centres in Australia with a total number of seats in excess of 1,500	Director business development (DBD)	CLIENT2 – An established utility supplier that has recently expanded the range of services it provides	Commercial director (CD) General manager marketing (GMM)	Acquisition customer service	3
C	SUPPLIER3 – Local subsidiary of a multinational provider launched in 1996 with six sites in Australia providing a total number of seats in excess of 1,500	Senior VP business development and marketing (BDM) Regional account manager (RAM)	CLIENT3 – A major provider of telecommunications with operations in Australia and overseas	National manager customer services (MCS) Outsourced services relationship manager (SRM)	Acquisition customer service Help desk	8

to technology-related communications, for example, to seek assistance in configuring a Blackberry.

A total of 10 interviews were conducted. Interviews were between 1 and 2 h in duration, and a semi-structured interview protocol was followed with questions across three principal themes: Why outsource, what to outsource and what capabilities are sought in suppliers. While the underlying rationale was purposeful, to collect data pertinent to the theoretical lenses and related propositions, it was deliberately non-directive so as not to preclude the emergence of concepts not previously considered (Patton 2002). As such, it is in line with the methodology presented by Eisenhardt (1989). With regard to analysis, data were first reviewed and coded in line with the principal dimensions of each theoretical lens.[7] Descriptive codes were used and interview transcripts coded in sentence or multi-sentence chunks. It was possible for the same piece of text to be multi-coded if it was related to more than one perspective and proposition. Such an approach is in accord with the recommendations of Miles and Huberman (1994) who suggest that the level of coding detail should be aligned with the objectives of the research. As also suggested by Miles and Huberman (1994), the data were then collated into conceptually clustered data displays in order to make it readily accessible. Where interview data did not code to the concepts identified *a priori* as of interest, it was further assessed to determine if additional concepts could be formed.

Case Study Results

As outlined in the methodology, the results of the case study interviews were codified and collated into data display tables – see Tables 12.3 and 12.4. Here the key aspects of the content of those tables will be described and the propositions outlined earlier assessed.

---

[7] For example, codes related to Transaction cost theory included: TC-C (cost), TC-IT (information technology), TC-AS (asset specificity) and TC-U (uncertainty).

Table 12.3 Why outsource and what activities?

Why outsource and what activities	Client			Supplier		
	CLIENT1	CLIENT2	CLIENT3	SUPPLIER1	SUPPLIER2	SUPPLIER3
Transaction cost	• IT enables separation of activities and external provision at reduced cost • Lack of space key excuse/driver • Expect supplier to regularly update technology	• IT enables separation of activities and external provision at reduced cost • Minimise cost and risk of expansion into new markets by outsourcing	• IT enables separation of activities and external provision at reduced cost • Virtual call centre permits load distribution and benchmarking • Cost saving primarily derived from labour • Activities with fluctuating demand • IT facilitates reporting	• IT enables separation of activities and external provision at reduced cost • Lack of space key driver • IT facilitates reporting	• IT enables separation of activities and external provision at reduced cost • Provide call centre function • Can deliver and source regardless of location • Migrate to more cost-effective technology as appropriate • IT facilitates reporting	• IT enables separation of activities and external provision at reduced cost • Call centre technology and process focus • IT facilitates reporting • Limited knowledge of existing costs at outset • Outbound first • Global diktats
Resource based	• Non-core activities that are routine and high volume • Core/Non-core divide shifts over time	• Non-core activities	• Non-core activities (and non-core business segment) • Help desk activities • Core/Non-core divide shifts over time	• Overspill of activities as a result of growth Maintain internal call centre operational and management skills • Core/Non-core divide shifts over time	• All customer service seen as non-core and nonstrategic	• Accommodate growth of non-core activities (permanent) and improve internal operations through benchmarking • Core/Non-core divide shifts over time

(continued)

Table 12.3 (continued)

Why outsource and what activities	Client			Supplier		
	CLIENT1	CLIENT2	CLIENT3	SUPPLIER1	SUPPLIER2	SUPPLIER3
Resource dependency	• Single supplier • Call centres considered a non-growth area relative to online (primary contact channel) • Stable long-term relationship founded upon a well-established procurement process	• Use of multiple suppliers (for a variety of tasks) • Regular renegotiation and extension of contracts	• Use of multiple suppliers (for the same tasks) • Recognise switching difficult (especially as outsourcing expands) • Long-term contracts	• Open book accounting • Upgrade of platforms • Sophistication with regard to expectations, approach and contract • Contracts contain KPIs and performance-related penalties and incentives • Competitive (supply side) • CLIENT3 dominates (client side) • Client-provided business processes and IT systems	• Use of multiple suppliers	• Use of multiple suppliers • Client-provided business-specific processes and IT systems

Institutional framework	• Regulatory changes allow expansion and increased competition	• Regulatory changes allow expansion into new markets	• Labour relations framework allows outsourcing service providers access to labour on better terms	• Deregulation increasing competition • Flexible employment and contractors • Treatment of GST	• Flexible employment agreements and use of contractors	• Flexible employment agreements and use of contractors
Industry value system	• Separation from competition	• Concern if supplier sought to service principal competitors	• Increased pressure to maximise efficiency and increase competitiveness • Separation from competition	• Industry wide shift • Levels the playing field	• Industry wide shift	• Industry wide shift • Cycle through industries

Table 12.4 Supplier capabilities sought

Supplier capabilities sought	Client			Supplier		
	CLIENT1	CLIENT2	CLIENT3	SUPPLIER1	SUPPLIER2	SUPPLIER3
People	• Client provides task variety	• CSRs seen as an important part of the business • Shared client/supplier events	• Change culture	• Awards focus • Recruits with traits that map to the client (flair) • Client interactions with CSRs (ownership)	• Recruitment difficult • Performance-related pay • Recruits with traits that map to the client (flair) • Client interactions with CSRs (ownership)	• Performance-related pay • Generic client culture • Growth allows progression
Service	• Test performance through mystery shopping	• 'Delight' the customer • Work with supplier to communicate culture	• Commitment to service, technology and reporting • Efficiency over service	• Importance of reporting • Transfer of client staff • Replicate client culture • Promote staff within client portfolios	• Importance of reporting • Capture 'essence' of client culture	• Importance of reporting • Transfer of client staff • Promote staff within client portfolios
Process	• Simple tasks – little understanding of business required	• Simple business model • Customer management capability • Design processes and audit supplier use (except where simple and standalone)	• Processes need to be tidy before handing over • Rely on supplier where help desk skills required	• Poorly documented processes – can be improved	• Core skill seen as call centre process management and redesign • Micro-management makes improvement difficult	• General process understanding and expertise • Separation between task and call centre processes • Provide technical help desk expertise

Technology	• Expect supplier to regularly update technology	• Match technology to customer and transaction	• Precise mix of client/supplier technology varies	• Use clients core technology (customers use same via Internet)	• Migrate to more cost-effective technology as appropriate • Location mixture of planning and history	• Challenge process • Fill in call centre and management related technology • Specialised call centre design • Location driven by costs/incentives
Environment	• Lack of space key excuse/driver	• Close location to promote information exchange	• Design less important than management • Location largely unimportant	• Reflect and reinforce who the client is • Specialised call centre design		
Sourcing	• Unimportant as clients have scale themselves	• Provide knowledge of what is required	• Unimportant as clients have scale themselves	• Unimportant as clients have scale themselves	• Provide knowledge of what is required	• Unimportant as clients have scale themselves
Implementation	• Retain management role • Flexibility key • Cost not outcome driven	• Clear outcomes established • Senior level oversight • Dedicated manager • Dedicated client service manager required • Separation from competition • Open communication key • Limited communication required for simple activities	• Dedicated client team to manage outsourced operations • Separation of operational and relationship roles • Mid-level oversight • Maintain management capabilities	• Contacts and relationships key • Criticality of maintaining high-level relationships (lack of commitment) • Multiple levels of open communication • Separate business streams • Dedicated team for implementation and operation	• Thin structure reflecting price orientation • Central point of contact/management aids coordination (but bureaucratic) • Need to maintain high-level relationships (change) • Open communication	• Client silos – inhibit communication (shadow organisation) • Trust paramount – have access to business plans of multiple clients • Separate business streams • Dedicated implementation team • Top management pairings

(continued)

Table 12.4 (continued)

Supplier capabilities sought	Client			Supplier		
	CLIENT1	CLIENT2	CLIENT3	SUPPLIER1	SUPPLIER2	SUPPLIER3
			• Trust/confidentiality key • Separation from competition • Robust internal systems • Experience • Non-standard contracts	• Importance of team leaders within call centres • Open book accounting • Long-term contracts • Balance long/short term	• Dedicated team (initiation operation) • TQM • Open book accounting • Stability of long-term relationships	• Difficulty of managing only part of a function • Increasingly marginal • Balance long/short term
Business sustainability	• Stable business	• Successful business track record • Centralised contracts				

Considerations Shaping the Outsourcing Decision

Proposition 1: IT facilitates BPO by reducing the associated transaction costs allowing organisations to engage with lower cost suppliers

While various reasons for why outsourcing was on an organisation's agenda were given, lack of space for CLIENT1, for example, cost reduction was the universal reason for it being chosen.

customers typically looking for savings of 20% to be worth the risk. SUPPLIER1-GMS

All of the suppliers saw access to cheaper labour[8] as a principal source of that reduction while SUPPLIER1 and SUPPLIER2 also looked to their abilities to improve processes and make greater use of technology.

All the interviewees acknowledged that outsourcing had been facilitated by IT-enabling access to systems and data regardless of location. At the extreme, CLIENT3 had established a virtual call centre, combining separate call centres provided by different providers and accessed by a single telephone number. There was also evidence of IT being used to manage the determinants of transaction costs. CLIENT3 and SUPPLIER3, for example, cited the ability to collect and supply performance-related data (reducing uncertainty). The expectation of CLIENT1 and SUPPLIER2 for IT to be regularly refreshed and updated can be seen as a means of managing asset specificity by treating IT as 'disposable' reducing the possibility of 'lock-in'. The initial choice for outsourcing of campaign-based outbound call activities by CLIENT3 also aligns with expectations that infrequent, that is, non-continuous activities are best sourced via the market.

The case studies provide support for Proposition 1 while also suggesting that clients follow different approaches to manage transaction costs.

---

[8] See the section related to Proposition 4 for details on how these cost savings arise.

Proposition 2: Organisations will use BPO for non-core activities

All of the client organisations stated that only non-core activities were outsourced. However, what is seen as non-core varies between organisations and may shift over time. The examples of CLIENT1 and CLIENT3 suggest that there are two types of non-core activities seen as suitable for outsourcing. Those that are simple and high volume and those that require specific skills sets – for example, second-level technical help for the support of Blackberry devices.

> outsourced services are those that are short, routine and high volume. CLIENT1-HCM

The core/non-core decision appears more complex than a one-time assessment. In both the CLIENT1 and CLIENT3 cases, there was a progression regarding what was outsourced with a common starting point of telemarketing.

> outbound services typically go first ... they are campaign based and requirements fluctuate making them hard [for clients] to manage. SUPPLIER3-BDM

With CLIENT1 initially, it was only those activities related to its recently established home insurance operations that were outsourced. Those related to its established primary lines of business were off limits. Over time, however, CLIENT1 became amenable to outsource an increasing range of call centre-based activities across all business lines.

> we have moved away from seeing much of customer service as core as other areas have taken precedence with regard to money and management focus. CLIENT1-HCM

CLIENT2 and CLIENT3 also initially introduced outsourcing outside of their mainstream business. For CLIENT2, the focus was on call centre-oriented customer service activity related to its expansion into new geographical territories while CLIENT3 first outsourced activities related to new product lines.

While providing support for Proposition 2, the case studies suggest that what is regarded as core may change over time and the decision may consider the line of business as well as the activity.

Proposition 3: Organisations will seek to minimise supplier dependency when using BPO

Clients seek various ways to manage their relationships with suppliers. CLIENT1 is focused on careful initial selection with SUPPLIER1 suggesting that this included an emphasis on open book accounting and the establishment of key performance indicators (KPIs). CLIENT2 and CLIENT3 by contrast maintain a portfolio of suppliers. Such arrangements can provide backup – in the case of CLIENT3 where two suppliers perform the same activity – and permit comparison in terms of service and price. Not having all or nothing contracts is seen as providing leverage to clients. It becomes practical for them to threaten to, or actually, move business between suppliers as a means of signalling that an improvement in service is required.

> ... it can be difficult for a supplier if they loose a chunk of business but generally suppliers look to the long term and have multiple streams of business with [CLIENT3]. CLIENT3-MCS

Moving between suppliers though is seen as difficult by CLIENT3 and becoming more so as the extent of the services outsourced increases. CLIENT3 related the example where the initial implementation of a BPO initiative failed and they had to take the service back in-house for 3 weeks. They doubted that they could do this now as they no longer have the necessary skills internally. Actual change also appears to be infrequent. SUPPLIER2 claimed to have never lost a major client. Furthermore, in all cases clients have focused on long-term contracts and relationships with suppliers. CLIENT3, for example, has had a relationship with SUPPLIER3 for 8 years.

From the supplier perspective, SUPPLIER1 saw the market as competitive while SUPPLIER3 suggested that the size of CLIENT3 made them the dominant partner. SUPPLIER3 also saw the use of multiple suppliers as problematic from a coordination and quality perspective.

> Having multiple suppliers is messy because problems and solutions are often interconnected across activities. SUPPLIER3-RAM

From the perspective of Proposition 3, clients appear to have actively taken steps to manage their dependency on suppliers. The experience of CLIENT3, however, suggests it may become harder to do this in future.

Proposition 4: The nature and extent of BPO will be shaped by an organisation's institutional context

The institutional framework appears to influence BPO in a variety of ways. It can provide the jolt that leads to a client considering BPO. For CLIENT2 it was changes in legislation that allowed it to expand into new products and geographical areas. BPO was seen as a means both to reduce the time to establish new operations and to minimise the upfront expense. For CLIENT1 it was similar changes exposing it to new competition that provided the motivation to examine BPO as means of reducing costs.

The institutional framework can also impact on the attractiveness of BPO. CLIENT1 and SUPPLIER1 cited the case of the introduction of the Goods and Service Tax (GST) – a fixed rate consumption tax – which exempted many financial services from the tax and denied financial service providers input tax credits related to the supply of those services. As such there was a bias towards self-supply. The tax legislation was subsequently amended to allow a reduced input tax credit, 75%, which encouraged outsourcing.

All of the suppliers, and CLIENT3, also saw legislation as one of the primary reasons for the success of outsourcing through the opportunity it provided suppliers to lower labour costs. Since the late 1980s, in Australia, there has been a move away from a collective award system, whereby all the workers within an industry are granted the same conditions of employment and wages, to allow for more local flexibility. That shift is perhaps best symbolised by the 1996 Workplace Relations Act which provided employers with the opportunity to negotiate Enterprise Bargaining Agreements (EBA) with their staff collectively or hire staff on individual contracts, Australian Workplace Agreements (AWA). Suppliers have taken full advantage of the new regime. SUPPLIER1, for example, cited its ability to establish a labour vehicle that gave it flexibility with regard to the contracting of staff as a significant source of competitive advantage. SUPPLIER2 believed the same was true with regard to its ability to negotiate an EBA. SUPPLIER3 suggested that the impact of legislation was twofold. It allowed suppliers to construct their businesses to minimise costs, and it allowed clients to use it as leverage with their internal operations.

> outsourcing allows clients to do something different break up their existing labour environment and drive different relationships. SUPPLIER2-DBD.

The cases provide evidence to support the proposition that the institutional framework influences outsourcing by allowing, or requiring, organisations to do something differently and by shaping the attractiveness of outsourcing.

Proposition 5: Organisations will not use BPO if it is detrimental to their standing in the industry value system

Suppliers saw the penetration of outsourcing occurring at an industry level with SUPPLIER1 and SUPPLIER3 suggesting that deregulation was the impetus.

> telecommunications leads the way followed by financial services and utilities. SUPPLIER3-BDM
>
> outsourcing levels the playing field. nothing different except brand and perceptions and strategy. SUPPLIER1-GMS

CLIENT1 and CLIENT3 recognised that the 'sharing of suppliers' – and hence, the commodification of activities – was inevitable and that such arrangements were manageable.

> Australia is a small business environment with a limited pool of expertise.... CLIENT3-MCS

CLIENT2, however, stated it would be concerned if a supplier also worked for a major competitor.

The cases suggest that BPO is an industry-wide phenomenon and organisations are outsourcing aware, and largely unconcerned, that their competitors are following the same path with the same suppliers. The result, however, may be that organisations are making it more difficult to differentiate themselves.

Proposition 6: Applying multiple theoretical perspectives increases understanding of the BPO decision

Based upon the preceding analysis, it is suggested that the evidence supports Proposition 6 and that a better understanding of the BPO decision will be gained by applying multiple perspectives rather than a single one; each perspective on its own revealing only part of the story. However, the cases suggest that the situation may be more complex than anticipated. For example, an IT-enabled ability to minimise transaction costs appears *prima facie* to be in accord with transaction cost theory. However, the cases of CLIENT1 and CLIENT2 also suggest that there may need to be some impetus for organisations to take advantage of the opportunity – provided by deregulation and increased competition. As another example, while organisations are outsourcing non-core activities, as resource-based theory would predict, the perception as to what is core and non-core appears to be fluid with CLIENT1 and CLIENT3 deciding over time that an increasing proportion of activities do not need to be performed in-house.

Capabilities Sought in Outsourcing Suppliers

Interviewees were asked to identify the capabilities that were sought from suppliers. As Table 12.4 illustrates many map to those proposed by Feeny et al. (2003) and help to refine and elaborate on them.

Proposition 7: Suppliers must have the ability to draw upon the commitment, energy and talents of staff

Suppliers valuing, motivating and retaining transferred and recruited staff was seen as important by CLIENT1 and CLIENT2. For CLIENT3, however, outsourcing was seen much more as an opportunity to change the existing culture both directly with the outsourced activities and indirectly with the retained call centres.

CLIENT2 recognised that they are managing a conundrum. While stressing the importance of suppliers 'treating employees well since these are ultimately the people who deliver the service' CLIENT2 also acknowledged:

> we spend time training staff, ensuring they are well paid with good superannuation and holidays within a value driven, community and family oriented working environment ... [providers] don't do that. CLIENT2-GMM

Sources of staff motivation varied. SUPPLIER1 was heavily focused on awards. SUPPLIER2 'carved up contracts' making a proportion of each month's gross margin available to call centre staff subject to them hitting predefined targets. CLIENT1 played a more active role than CLIENT3 or CLIENT2 seeking to motivate its supplier's staff by providing opportunities for them to perform alternative tasks.

> we use them beyond the telephone as promotional staff – they know the product.... Gives them variety and a break from the phone while still getting paid. CLIENT1-HCM

SUPPLIER2 suggested that recruitment is difficult and all suppliers invest considerable time and resources in the selection process.

> six interviews ... and select based on skills, charisma and likelihood of staying. SUPPLIER2-DBD

Overall, the cases provide support for Proposition 7. While illustrating alternative approaches they also highlight the difficulties suppliers face. An additional focus on recruitment to ensure a ready supply of staff appears to be required.

Proposition 8: Suppliers must have the ability to regard end users as customers, understand what good service represents and deliver it

While CLIENT1 and CLIENT2 have a focus on high levels of customer service CLIENT3 was more focused on efficiency, subject to delivering a *minimum* level of service. CLIENT1 and CLIENT2 thought it important that suppliers replicated their organisational culture. Various steps are taken by suppliers to ensure this. SUPPLIER2, for example, has a process to instil a client's culture in its staff while SUPPLIER1 focuses on promoting staff within, rather than across, client silos, for example, from being a customer representative for CLIENT1 to being a team leader for them.

Table 12.5 Core capabilities sought from BPO suppliers of call centre service

People	Recruit and motivate staff
Service	Demonstrably deliver the client's desired level of service to customers
Process	Improve call centre-related processes
Technology	Evolve call centre-related technology
Implementation	Establish and maintain multilevel client relationships
Business sustainability	Maintain a viable business over time

work with the client to spell out their culture. often difficult to know what it is especially where it is represented by a person. We sit down with them and determine what it means and then instil it into activities, behaviours and quality. SUPPLIER2-DBD

we have workshops over two days with our trainers where we tell them about who we are, our values and the importance of the customer experience, what we want and how we measure it. It is very experiential with mystery shopping where we call up inhouse and competitors and see how what we want differs from what they are doing. CLIENT2-GMM

SUPPLIER1 and SUPPLIER2 also stated that they tried to recruit staff with characteristics that reflected the culture of their clients.[9]

All of the suppliers suggested that the collection and communication of performance data were key to ensuring a customer focus to their operations.

we have continuous process improvement for each contract and manage via statistical control across multiple KPIs. SUPPLIER2-DBD

Support is provided for Proposition 8 with an emphasis on customer service that reflects the client. Suppliers also focus on measuring satisfaction and performance to demonstrate this. It should be noted that the level of customer service sought may vary across clients.

Proposition 9: Suppliers must have the ability to improve existing business processes within client companies

With the exception of technical help desk services, the ability to improve existing *business-specific* processes appeared a minor consideration for all clients.

we have an internal team that writes all processes and procedures and regularly audit suppliers to make sure that they are up to date in the ones they are using. CLIENT2-CD

---

[9] By contrast, SUPPLIER3 and CLIENT3 were focused on changing the organisational culture.

CLIENT3 also suggested that it is unrealistic to expect a BPO provider to be able to improve a problematic process.

> we expected outsourcing to solve problems in the past … but you have to know what you want and how to do it … [in one case] problems were exacerbated by having a third party and we ended up bringing it back in house. CLIENT3-MCS

Of more importance to clients was the ability of suppliers to operate and continually improve a call centre, that is, how calls are handled. This was recognised by suppliers.

> [CLIENT1] understand their own business and have their own highly defined call management processes as specified in their tender documents … we look at what they do and see if we believe there are opportunities for realising gains based on our experience and best practice by tweaking processes or technology … and we make sure that we build the ability to change those things into the contract. SUPPLIER1-GMS

SUPPLIER2 also suggested that for the best results clients needed to recognise that they were the experts in running call centres and avoid micromanagement.

> makes it difficult … client knows best … give us the freedom to do out job … increased sales when changed and allowed to do it our way. SUPPLIER2-DBD

The cases suggest an amendment to Proposition 9 restricting it to call centre-related processes. Clients are seen as the source of industry or business-specific process expertise.

Proposition 10: Suppliers must have the ability to provide a technology platform that is core to the service delivered

SUPPLIER1 and SUPPLIER3 make use of their client's core business technology while providing the delivery technology to operate a call centre, including telecommunications switches, call routers, reporting software.

> we provide the core technology ... billing, activation.... CLIENT3-SRM

> we use the same [client provided, credit card application] software that customers do when applying in via the web. SUPPLIER1-GSM

> There are often gaps in the client's technology ... they often have good activity systems but poor management systems, lacking knowledge management or workflow so we apply our own tools. SUPPLIER3-BDM

CLIENT1 and CLIENT2 expect their suppliers to continually upgrade their technology migrating to lower cost platforms – automated and database-driven response systems, for example. CLIENT1 cited their transition of business from one supplier to another because the incumbent, while effective at providing the service based on the existing technology platform, had not sought to develop or update it at all. SUPPLIER2 suggested through that the ability to move to more cost-effective technology was influenced by a combination of the nature of the activity and customer sophistication.

> Multiple channels available – speech recognition, IVR, agents, website, fax, email – are customers ready to handle? SUPPLIER2-DBD

Similarly to Proposition 9, clients are seen as the primary source of business or industry-specific technology. As such, Proposition 10 should be restricted to the operation and evolution of call centre-related technology.

Proposition 11: Suppliers must have the ability to develop an effective working environment that reinforces the distinctiveness of the provider

SUPPLIER1 and SUPPLIER3 suggested that it was important for the environment to reflect and reinforce who the client was. Clients however did not support this perspective. Location was seen as important by all suppliers – from the perspective of availability of, and accessibility for, labour. SUPPLIER1 though accepted that some of their locations were less than ideal.

> we are gradually moving to new locations … this building was not designed to be a call centre, there are not enough lifts and we are on the wrong train line for staff to come in from the West. SUPPLIER1-GMS

City locations were seen as providing a large labour pool but with high costs and retention difficulties while in country locations staff were viewed as easier to retain but less career oriented and motivated.

> Sydney is competitive and staff churn … partly because inhouse centres pay more than outsourced ones. SUPPLIER2-DBD

> in the country staff stay but they are not motivated to move [i.e. be promoted]. SUPPLIER1-CSM

Only CLIENT2 viewed proximity to their supplier as important.

> [being located in the same building] gives us a heads up of issues in the marketplace because of proximity. CLIENT2-GMM

> being there doesn't tell you that much … we get feedback through customer mystery shopping. CLIENT3-SRM

The cases suggest that environment is not important from a client's perspective. Ensuring access to labour emerged as the most important environment-related issue, though this may perhaps best be subsumed within the recruitment aspect of the people capability.

Proposition 12: Suppliers must have expertise in procurement and an ability to leverage aggregate purchasing power

With regard to cost savings, sourcing expertise was not generally seen as important by clients or suppliers.

small end – 60–100 seats – get the benefits of scale. Client Z have scale themselves. SUPPLIER3-BDM

According to CLIENT2 and SUPPLIER2, however, clients could benefit from suppliers' knowledge regarding what technology was available and appropriate.

No support was provided for Proposition 12.

Proposition 13: Suppliers must have the ability to implement a BPO initiative and deliver it over time

The ability to successfully implement and manage a BPO initiative was seen as critical by clients and suppliers. For SUPPLIER1 and SUPPLIER3, the approach was largely consistent with the establishment of multiple levels of communication with their clients encompassing contacts at director, operational (day-to-day) and relationship level. CLIENT1 and CLIENT3 had also established their own dedicated internal role with responsibility for managing outsourced services, though this was at an overarching, rather than individual supplier, level.

> miscommunication can impact the relationship so we have multiple levels of interaction to try and mitigate the impact and seek to manage through the client. SUPPLIER1-GMS
> need close relationships as open and upfront as possible. We prefer warts and all, to know problems rather than not – can then address. CLIENT3-MCS

There was more limited communication between CLIENT2 and SUPPLIER2 – and there was some disagreement as to why this was the case:

> horses for courses ... a thinner structure reflecting their price orientation. SUPPLIER2-DBD
> its not rocket science we do not need to speak everyday. CLIENT2-GMM

Where management oversight of BPO sat in the client organisational hierarchy varied – for example, mid-tier in CLIENT3, more senior in CLIENT2. All suppliers use dedicated implementation teams – though only in the case of SUPPLIER1 and SUPPLIER2 did some members of that team also acquire responsibility for the operation of the call centre once it was up and running.

SUPPLIER1 suggested that effective relationship management requires competency on both the supplier and client side. CLIENT2 mirrored such comments recognising that each contract with SUPPLIER2 was drawn up afresh with content heavily dependent upon who in their legal team worked on it.

> we have no concept of consistency regarding service levels for example. CLIENT2-CD

Proposition 13 was supported with effective communication and the development of close working relationships seen as key to successful service delivery.

Proposition 14: Suppliers must have the ability to maintain a viable business over time

All clients suggested that they wanted an experienced supplier with a successful track record.

> it is expensive to change ... we don't want a failure. CLIENT2-CD

Open-book accounting was the standard approach suppliers took to achieve and demonstrate a fair and sustainable price. It was required by CLIENT1. SUPPLIER3 went further posting profit and loss accounts for individual clients within call centres so staff, and clients, could see how they were performing. Suppliers though suggested that clients often focused on getting the absolute lowest price. SUPPLIER1, for example, suggested that CLIENT1 had moved to shorter term contracts and to price them so that it was questionable to whether they were commercially viable. SUPPLIER3 also suggested that CLIENT3 'wields a big stick'.

To try and ensure the long-term viability of their businesses all of the suppliers looked to establish long-term contracts with clients.

It would appear that the validity of Proposition 14 is recognised. However, suppliers *claim* that the actions of clients may undermine it.

From a capability perspective, the research suggests that while there is some variation between individual clients, there is considerable consensus regarding the capabilities sought from suppliers. Fortunately, this is also largely in line with what suppliers think clients expect from them. A clear area of difference between suppliers and clients though relates to the working environment. Clients appear much less interested in it than suppliers expect them to be.[10]

The capabilities identified map reasonably well to the list proposed as a synthesis of the work of Feeny et al. (2003, 2005). They do however suggest some refinements. For example, there is a clear need for suppliers to be able to measure and report on the levels of service they provide. With regard to process and technology, there also appears to be a distinction between business activity-specific capabilities and those associated with operating call centres. The former relate to what should be done and the latter to how it should be delivered. It is in the call centre space that clients seek proficiency from providers.

The cases also suggest that capabilities related to sourcing may not be a widespread requirement. Furthermore, there is some evidence that the ability of suppliers to fully apply their capabilities is affected by the clients themselves – for example, if they seek to micromanage. Table 12.5 summarises the core capabilities identified with refined descriptors.

---

[10] It might be interesting to determine whether this is because the working environment is largely irrelevant or whether clients take it for granted.

Implications, Limitations and Future Research

Synthesising and extending existing work in the IT and BPO domains, an approach was proposed to apply multiple theoretical perspectives to better understand the BPO decision. Subsequent empirical work suggested that greater insight into the *why* and *what* of outsourcing is indeed achieved than could be realised through the use of a single perspective. Organisations also appear to have broadly similar objectives and considerations when outsourcing, suggesting that it is a useful objective to seek to develop a decision-making guide rather than having to treat each BPO decision as unique. There appears, however, to be a more complex interaction between the perspectives than anticipated. At the outset, for example, it was thought that transaction cost theory would supply the underlying rationale, that IT reduces the transaction costs associated with using external suppliers promoting BPO. The role of the other perspectives was thought to be to explain the nature and limits of that BPO; specifically that

- BPO will be restricted to non-core activities;
- organisations will seek to minimise supplier dependency;
- BPO is shaped by the institutional context;
- organisations will ensure BPO does not negatively impact their value system position.

While the first two influences were as expected, the research suggests that an organisation's institutional system, and in particular changes to it such as deregulation, may also play a role in providing the initial motivation to outsource. As such, the possibility emerges that IT-enabled reductions in transaction costs are a necessary, but not necessarily sufficient, condition for BPO.[11] There needs to be some stimulus to cause organisations to act. Organisations also appear to pay less attention

---

[11] The cases thus appear to lend support to the aside of Dibbern et al. (2004) that the *why* and *what* of outsourcing are interdependent.

to the impact of BPO on their position in the industry value system than was expected.

The research also suggests that it may be valuable for organisations to consider the consequences of outsourcing over the long term. There is some evidence to suggest that BPO may, over time, reduce the ability of organisations to differentiate themselves and that the ability to manage supplier dependency may be reduced as more activities are outsourced.

Turning to the capabilities sought of suppliers, the research suggests that there are some common requirements across clients (and that suppliers, as well as clients, recognise those requirements in most cases). A number of the capabilities identified by Feeny et al. (2003, 2005), however, are questioned and a narrower set proposed. Reassuringly, a capability regarding technology remains providing additional support for positioning of IT as a key force driving BPO. Similarly, the close communication associated with implementation can be seen as contributing to the management of supplier dependency by ensuring clients are cognisant of the plans and actions of their suppliers (Sheffi 2005). Additional research is required to test the set of capabilities identified to determine if it is robust and further elaborate on the details of the capabilities. It would also be of value to investigate whether the lack of any industry-specific process or technology expertise, exemplified here by the split between business-specific and call centre processes, holds for other types of generic BPO.

A weakness of the research is that it is focused on one BPO activity, call centres, in one location, Australia. In addition, it has considered only large suppliers and clients in the private sector. More extensive empirical work across a broader range of organisations is needed to determine whether the findings can be generalised. It is possible, for example, that the factors influencing BPO may differ significantly between the private and public sectors. It may also be the case that the perspectives adopted may not be sufficiently comprehensive. It might be valuable, for example, to also consider the influence of an organisation's internal context. The research as it stands has also accepted one dimensional, unquantified, assessments of the capabilities and the success of the outsourcing initiatives. It would be useful to combine a comprehensive satisfaction instrument (such as that used by Sengupta and Zviran 1997 or Jiang et al. 2002) with quantified measures of each capability to investigate in greater detail the principal relationships that exist. Finally, and returning to the research of Dibbern et al. (2004), work also remains to be done in understanding the process through which BPO is implemented successfully – the *how*. How, for example, are relationships best developed? It is likely that multiple approaches are possible and research that provides a greater understanding of the options would be of great value to practitioners.

References

Alborz, S, Seddon, P.B, and Scheepers, R (2004). Impact of Configuration on IT Outsourcing Relationships, Proceedings of the Tenth Americas Conference on Information Systems, (New York, August 2004). 3551–3560.

Ang, S, and Cummings, L.L (1997). Strategic Responses to Institutional Influences on Information Systems Outsourcing, *Organization Science* **8** (3): 235–256.

Ang, S, and Straub, D (2002). Costs, Transaction Specific Investments and Vendor Dominance of the Marketplace: The economics of IS outsourcing, In R. Hirschheim, A. Heinzl, and J. Dibbern (eds.) *Information Systems Outsourcing*, Berlin: Springer, pp. 47–76.

Benbasat, I, Goldstein, D.K, and Mead, M (1987). The Case Study Research Strategy in Studies of Information Systems, *MIS Quarterly* **11**(3): 369–386.

Bousfield, P. (2003). The Business Case for Call Centre Outsourcing, *Interactive Marketing* **5**(2): 111–116.

Cheon, M.J, Grover, V, and Teng, J.T.C (1995). Theoretical Perspectives on the Outsourcing of Information Systems, *Journal of Information Technology* **10**(4): 209–220.

Ciborra, C.U (1987). Research Agenda for a Transaction Costs Approach to Information Systems, In R.J. Boland and R.A. Hirschheim (eds.) *Critical Issues in Information Systems Research*, London: John Wiley & Sons, pp. 253–274.

Clemons, E.K, Reddi, S.P, and Row, M.C (1993). The Impact of Information Technology on the Organization of Economic Activity: The move to the middle hypothesis, *Journal of Management Information Systems* **10**(2): 9–35.

Codling, P, and Miller, A (2004). *Trends and Opportunities in the* UK *Market,* London: Ovum.

Coyne, K.P (1986). The Anatomy of Sustainable Competitive Advantage, *The McKinsey Quarterly* **22**(2): 50–65.

Dibbern, J., Goles, T., Hirschheim, R., and Jayatilaka, B. (2004). Information Systems Outsourcing: A survey and analysis of the literature, *The Data Base for Advances in Information Systems* **35**(4): 6–102.

Dubé, L., and Paré, G (2003). Rigor in Information Systems Positivist Case Research: Current practices, trends, and recommendations, *MIS Quarterly* **27**(4): 597–635.

Duncan, N.B (2002). IS Integration in the Internet Age, In R. Hirschheim, A. Heinzl, and J. Dibbern (eds.) *Information Systems Outsourcing,* Berlin: Springer, pp. 395–414.

Edwards, B. (2004). A World of Work, *Economist* 3–16 13th November.

Eisenhardt, K.M (1989). Building Theories form Case Study Research, *Academy of Management Review* **14**(4): 532–550.

Feeny, D, Willcocks, L, and Lacity, M (2003). *Business Process Outsourcing: The promise of the 'enterprise partnership' model,* (http://www.templeton.ox.ac.uk/oxiim/bpo.htm) Templeton College, University of Oxford.

Feeny, D, Lacity, M, and Willcocks, L. (2005). Taking the Measure of Outsourcing Providers: Successful outsourcing of back office business functions requires knowing not only your company's needs but also the 12 core capabilities that are key criteria for screening suppliers, *Sloan Management Review* **46**(3): 41–49.

Feeny, D, and Willcocks, L. (1998). Core IS Capabilities for Exploiting Information Technology, *Sloan Management Review* **39**(3): 9–20.

Goles, T. (2001). The Impact of the Client/Vendor Relationship on Outsourcing Success, unpublished dissertation, University of Houston.

Grover, V., Cheon, M.J, and Teng, J.T.C (1994). An Evaluation of the Impact of Corporate Strategy and the Role of Information Technology on IS Functional Outsourcing, *European Journal of Information Systems* **3**(3): 179–190.

Hagel, J, and Seely Brown, J. (2001). Your Next IT Strategy, *Harvard Business Review* **79**(9): 105–113.

Halvey, J.K, Halvey, J.H, and Melby, B.M (1996). *Information Technology Outsourcing Transactions: Process, strategies and contracts,* New York: John Wiley.

Hancox, M., and Hackney, R. (1999). Information Technology Outsourcing: Conceptualizing practice in the public and private sector, Proceedings of the

32nd Annual Hawaii International Conference on System Science (Maui, Hawaii, January 1999) 5–8.

Jiang, J, Klein, G, and Carr, C (2002). Measuring Information System Service Quality: SERVQUAL from the other side, *MIS Quarterly* **26**(2): 145–166.

Kakabadse, A., and Kakabadse, N (2005). Outsourcing: Current and future trends, *Thunderbird International Business Review* **47**(2): 183–204.

Kern, T., and Willcocks, L. (2000). Exploring Information Technology Outsourcing Relationships: Theory and practice, *Journal of Strategic Information Systems* **9**(4): 321–350.

Klein, H (2002). On the Theoretical Foundations of Current Outsourcing Research, In R. Hirschheim, A. Heinzl, and J. Dibbern (eds.) *Information systems outsourcing*, Berlin: Springer, pp. 24–44.

Kotter, J.P (1979). Managing External Dependence, *Academy of Management Review* **4**(1): 87–92.

Lacity, M, and Hirschheim, R (1993). *Information Systems Outsourcing: Myths, metaphors and realities*, Wiley: Chichester.

Lacity, M.C, Willcocks, L.P, and Feeny, D.F (1996). The Value of Selective IT Sourcing, *Sloan Management Review* **37**(3): 13–25.

Larsson, R, Brousseau, K.R, Driver, M.J, Holmquist, M, and Tarnovskaya, V (2003). International Growth through Co-operation: Brand driven strategies, leadership and career development in Sweden, *Academy Management Executive* **17**(1): 45–51.

Levina, N, and Ross, J.W (2003). From the Vendor's Perspective: Exploring the value proposition in information technology outsourcing, *MIS Quarterly* **27**(3): 331–364.

Mata, F.J, Fuerst, W.L, and Barney, J.B (1995). Information Technology and Sustained Competitive Advantage, *MIS Quarterly* **19**(4): 487–505.

McFarlan, F.W, and Nolan, R.L (1995). How to Manage an IT Outsourcing Alliance, *Sloan Management Review* **36**(2): 9–23.

Melville, N, Kraemer, K, and Gurbaxani, V (2004). Information Technology and Organizational Performance: An integrative model of IT business value, *MIS Quarterly* **28**(2): 283–322.

Michell, V., and Fitzgerald, G. (1997). The IT Outsourcing Market-Place: Vendors and their selection, *Journal of Information Technology* **12**(3): 223–237.

Miles, M.B, and Huberman, A.M (1994). *Qualitative Data Analysis: An expanded sourcebook*, 2nd edn., Thousand Oaks: Sage.

North, D.C (1990). *Institutions, Institutional Change and Economic Performance*, Cambridge: Cambridge University Press.

Patton, M.Q (2002). *Qualitative Research and Evaluation Methods*, 3rd edn., Thousand Oaks: Sage.

Perez, C (1983). Structural Change and Assimilation of New Technologies in the Economic and Social Systems, *Futures* **15**(5): 357–375.

Poppo, L., and Zenger, T. (1998). Testing Alternative Theories of the Firm: Transaction cost, knowledge based and measurement explanations for make-or-buy decisions in information services, *Strategic Management Journal* **19**: 853–877.

Porter, M.E (1985). *Competitive Advantage*, New York: The Free Press.

Ramachandran, K., and Voleti, S. (2004). Business Process Outsourcing (BPO): Emerging scenario and strategic options for IT-enabled services, *Interfaces* **29**(1): 49–62.

Rouse, A.C, and Corbitt, B. (2004). IT Supported Business Process Outsourcing (BPO): The good, the bad and the ugly, Proceedings of Eighth Pacific Asia Conference on Information Systems (Shanghai, China, July 2004) 8–11.

Sabherwal, R., Hirschheim, R., and Goles, T. (2001). The Dynamics of Alignment: Insights from a punctuated equilibrium model, *Organization Science* **12**(2): 179–197.

Saunders, C, Gebelt, M, and Hu, Q (1997). Achieving Success in Information Systems Outsourcing, *California Management Review* **39**(2): 63–79.

Sengupta, K., and Zviran, M. (1997). Measuring User Satisfaction in an Outsourcing Environment, *IEEE Transactions on Engineering Management* **44**(4): 414–421.

Sharma, R., and Yetton, P. (1996). Interorganizational Cooperation to Develop Information Systems, Proceedings of the 17th International Conference on Information Systems (Cleveland, OH, 16–18 December 1996) 122–132.

Sheffi, Y (2005). *The Resilient Enterprise: Overcoming vulnerability for competitive advantage*, Boston: MIT Press.

Tas, J, and Sunder, S. (2004). Financial Services Business Process Outsourcing, *Communications of the ACM* **47**(5): 50–52.

Technology Partners (2004). *BPO/IT Bundling:, Position paper*, Dallas Texas: Technology Partners.

Thompson, R.L. (1967). *Organizations in Action*, New York: McGraw-Hill.

Tornbohm, C, and Andrault, M. (2005). *User Survey: Business process outsourcing, Western Europe, 2004 (executive summary)*, Report ID: G00126191, Gartner Group.

Wernerfelt, B (1984). A Resource-Based View of the Firm, *Strategic Management Journal* 5(2): 171–180.

Williamson, O.E (1986). *Economic Organization: Firms, markets and policy*, Brighton: Wheatsheaf.

Yin, R (1984). *Case Study Research: Design and methods*, Beverly Hills: Sage.

Dr Mark Borman was a senior lecturer in business information systems in the School of Business at the University of Sydney. Prior to joining the University of Sydney, he worked for a number of years in senior consulting and executive roles in the UK, USA and Australia. Mark has published and presented in journals and conferences including JIT, JORS, IJIM, ECIS, AMCIS, PACIS and ACIS. His primary research interest is in understanding the why, the what and the how of outsourcing in all its forms.

13

A Historical Review of the Information Technology and Business Process Captive Centre Sector

Ilan Oshri and Bob van Uhm

Introduction

Offshoring has emerged as a major trend in management in recent years (Farrell 2005; Lampel and Bhalla 2008) though its roots lie in the mercantilism and imperialism of the seventeenth century. The East India Company first established its own factories in India, recognizing the cost-effectiveness, flexibility and viability of having a company foothold in the targeted trade country.[1] The idea of establishing company-owned factories in host countries quickly swept commercial trade endeavours and expanded to such industries as sugar and rum processing and

---

[1] http://www.portcities.org.uk/london/server/show/ConNarrative.136/chapterId/2766/The-East-India-Company.html.

I. Oshri (✉)
Loughborough University, Leicestershire, UK
e-mail: I.Oshri@lboro.ac.uk

B. van Uhm
CEMS Programme, Rotterdam School of Management, Rotterdam, The Netherlands

© The Author(s) 2017   **455**
L.P. Willcocks et al. (eds.), *Outsourcing and Offshoring Business Services*, DOI 10.1007/978-3-319-52651-5_13

trade. In the modern day, this has become more visible since US multinationals began to offshore labour-intensive manufacturing processes to low-cost developing countries, such as Mexico and Panama (Carmel and Tija 2005).

One significant new development within the concept of offshoring began in the mid-1990s. Companies such as Xerox, General Electric and AmericanExpress set up offshore facilities, also known as captive centres (Levina 2006), to carry out enterprise-wide services, such as converting data from one medium to another (e.g. converting paper documents to digital data in corporate databases) (Aron 2002). Since then, significant technological developments, such as telecom bandwidth, satellite technology and the Internet, have eliminated distance issues, enabling information to be sent around the world in seconds at marginal costs. Indeed, in *The World Is Flat*, Thomas Friedman describes how a Web-enabled global playing field has been created as a result of the convergence of 10 flattening factors, among them the introduction of search engines and work-flow applications and the growing tendency to outsource and offshore work (Friedman 2005). Following these developments, information technology requirements, such as software maintenance and development, back-office operations and Research and Development (R&D), could be carried out at lower costs in countries such as Israel, Singapore, India, the Philippines and China (Bierce et al. 2004; Carmel and Tija 2005). Indeed, in late 2010, nearly 500 captive centres had been established by large multinationals in 34 countries representing an economic value of $12.3 billion and employing over 440,000 professionals.[2] Setting up a captive unit in an offshore location is not free from challenges and involves more than simply hiring employees, renting a building and installing hardware. In fact, past research has suggested that over 60% of offshore captive centres do not meet their financial objectives (Apte et al. 2007). Indeed, considering the competitive nature of the offshoring market, many parent firms struggle with ever increasing costs, employee attrition, the lack of integration

---

[2] http://www.nasscom.in/Nasscom/templates/NormalPage.aspx?id=60669.

with the firm's operations and strategies and lack of management support (Oshri et al. 2009a).

Some experts suggest that the nature and purpose of captive centres must transform for them to be successful; for example WNS, a captive centre located in India previously owned by British Airways, has transformed itself from a captive centre that provides services to its parent firm to a larger centre that now provides services to international customers as well.[3] At the same time, small-sized captive centres are hard to maintain because they offer little long-term career growth to employees, resulting in high attrition levels (Oshri 2011). Such effects on both the growth and survival of captive centres have led firms in recent years to explore a wider range of strategic options that offer either a lifeline or an exit strategy (Oshri et al. 2008).

In parallel to these important developments in the offshoring sector, research has taken interest in understanding the offshoring phenomenon and its drivers (e.g. Rottman and Lacity 2006; Contractor et al. 2010; Lacity et al. 2010). One of the areas that gained much attention relates to the factors affecting country attractiveness for offshoring. In this stream of studies, several factors were discovered to affect country attractiveness for offshoring such as the supply of talent, low-cost workforce, quality of the infrastructure and government policies promoting foreign direct investment (FDI) (Joshi and Mudigonda 2008; Kotlarsky and Oshri 2008). In shaping research around the resources a country can offer as the source of attractiveness for offshoring investments, the extant literature has mainly been interested in understanding the supply side of offshoring while shedding little light on how the offshoring sector has responded to such propositions (Gospel and Sako 2010). In this regard, while the body of knowledge about offshoring has significantly grown in recent years, we still know very little about the changes that the offshore captive centre sector has gone through in modern times. Such a quest is in particular relevant in light of recent studies that suggest that captive centre models have changed from solely providing services to the parent

---

[3] http://articles.economictimes.indiatimes.com/2006-07-27/news/27439112_1_wns-global-services-wns-holdings-trinity-partners.

firm to multiple forms in which (i) the captive has been providing services to external clients, (ii) outsources tasks to local vendors or even (iii) being divested to a local firm (Oshri 2011). Considering these strategic changes, one could argue that from a historical viewpoint, it is imperative to understand how the captive sector has changed over time in terms of functions offshored, to which country and through which captive centre model. However, there can also be an argument to understand whether such changes in captive investments can be explained vis-à-vis existing country selection frameworks (Carmel and Tija 2005; Farrell 2006; Joshi and Mudigonda 2008) that have traditionally focused on assessing country attractiveness separate from strategic changes in the destiny of the captive centre and the actual investments made by the multinational.

To address this gap, this paper examines investments made by Fortune 250 global firms regarding their captive centres between 1985 and 2010 within the context that shaped their offshoring decision. We review the development of the captive sector by considering the environmental factors that shaped changes in the way multinationals made decisions about their captive investments. By examining 25 years of captive centre investments, this study seeks to extend our understanding about the interactions between the supply and demand sides in offshore captive decisions as well as to assess whether extant country selection frameworks provide an explanation for changes in multinational captive investments over the years.

The remainder of the paper is structured as follows. Following this introduction, we review the literature on captive centre models and country selection frameworks. The subsequent sections provide a historical review and analysis of the offshore captive centre sector between 1985 and 2010. We divide the analysis into four phases, each representing a significant change in the offshore captive centre's historical trajectory. Further, the historical review and analysis provides a detailed account of the captive centre models, function offshored and location chosen by the Fortune 250 global firms. We conclude the paper by examining the forces that shaped changes in the historical trajectory of the offshore captive centre sector.

A Review of Strategic Captive Centre Models

While offshoring has attracted the attention of academics since the middle of the 1980s, the concept of captive centres has not been studied until recently (Aron and Singh 2005). Indeed, recent years have witnessed growth in the number of academic publications that refer to the captive centre as one of the sourcing models (Aron and Singh 2005; Carmel and Tija 2005). Yet, such studies on captive centres tended to treat this sourcing model as a single dimension option in which the focus of research is whether to offshore using a third-party service provider or set up a wholly owned captive centre (Aron and Singh 2005; Levina 2006). It is only recently that evidence has emerged that while most captive centres are set up to provide services for the parent firms, many of them change their destiny over time and pursue various growth and development strategies (Oshri et al. 2008). Indeed, a recent study has considered four fundamental offshore captive centre models (Oshri et al. 2008; Oshri 2011). The first is *basic captive centre*, which provides services to the parent firm only; the second is *shared captive centre,* which provides services to both parent firm and external clients; the third is *hybrid captive*, which provides core business process services to the parent firm but outsources non-core processes to a third-party service provider and the fourth is *divested captive*, which represents a divesture of part or the entire offshore captive centre (Oshri et al. 2008). Each offshore captive centre model represents a strategic choice for the parent firm regarding the value created by the offshore captive centre as well as the value created for the parent firm, the offshore captive centre and its extended network.

Table 13.1 describes the four types of captive centres and the value each type may bring to the parent firm.

Captive centre models are by no means constant and long lasting. They change as firms attempt to align their offshoring strategy with changes in the environment, in particular with regard to the benefits that the offshore location is offering as compared with alternative locations. Thus, the development of the captive centre sector depends on the parent firm's ability to first properly select the offshore location, and if

Table 13.1 Captive centres models and their value proposition

Captive centre model	Definition	Value for the parent firm
Basic captive	Provides service to the parent firm	Maintains control over operations, ensures service quality and benefits from low-cost economies
Hybrid captive	Provides service of core processes to the parent firm while outsourcing non-core processes to a third-party provider	In addition to the basic captive value propositions, hybrid captive improves operational efficiencies through the outsourcing of non-core activities to a third-party vendor
Shared captive	Provides services to both parent firm and external clients	Improves parent firm's market share through the acquisition of external clients. Speeds up learning regarding market and product demand and better positioned to address local needs
Divested captive	The divestment of either part or entire offshore captive centre	Improves the parent firm's ability to manage risk of offshore and near-shore assets. Alternatively, if the captive centre is successful, improves the firm's return on offshore and near-shore investments

needed, re-adjust its initial decision subject to changes in the offshore location or the alternatives (Doh et al. 2009).

A Review of Country Selection Frameworks

Many countries are now competing for a share of the growing offshore services market. Alongside such jostling, several frameworks have been proposed by academics and practitioners attempting to explain the factors that shape country attractiveness for offshoring services. Indeed, past research has identified a number of factors affecting offshoring decisions such as cost (Carmel and Tija 2005), the pool of skills available in the offshore location (Farrell 2006), government support and living environment (Carmel and Tija 2005), the attractiveness of the local market (Farrell 2006) and the risk profile of the offshore location (Doh et al. 2009). Factors affecting the attractiveness of a location for offshoring services have been incorporated into various selection frameworks in order to guide managers in their offshoring decisions (e.g. A.T. Kearney 2004; Carmel and Tija 2005). While such country selection frameworks have been helpful in guiding firms regarding their offshoring decisions, they have suffered from two limitations. First, selection frameworks consider the supply side in the offshoring decision, for example the offering of offshoring locations (Gospel and Sako 2010) failing to incorporate in their analysis aspects relating to the strategic investment and later change in the initial investment made by multinationals over the years. As a result, extant country selection frameworks have evolved as a supply-driven list of factors that endow little attention to the changes in the strategic offshoring decision that multinationals pursue over time or to their selectivity regarding which functions should be offshored to which location (Contractor et al. 2010; Gospel and Sako 2010). Second, most country selection frameworks do not consider the possibility of multinationals changing their offshoring decisions over time. Further, such frameworks shy away from examining changes in offshore captive investments as part of understanding offshoring decisions. In this regard, existing country selection frameworks are rather static in nature, providing a snap-shot image of the attractiveness of a location for the initial offshoring decision. Yet, with mounting evidence that multinationals tend to change their initial offshoring decision by either terminating their captive investment, bringing back offshored function to an onshore location, migrating a captive to a different offshore location, divesting part of the captive or even changing the strategic destiny of the captive, a rather dynamic framework is needed, in which a multinational can reconsider its offshore captive investment over time based on the strategic importance of its offshore unit and the alternatives. A study by Joshi and Mudigonda (2008), an exception within the rather broad offering of country selection frameworks, has incorporated into the primary country attractiveness factors both inhibiting and facilitating factors. The authors describe facilitating factors as those that 'support convenient initial entry, smooth transition, and efficient, trouble-free delivery of services from the offshore location' (p. 217) while inhibiting factors are 'responsible for the slow take-off of offshoring, despite some of the advantages that it may offer' (p. 216). While the inhibiting and facilitating factors improve our understanding regarding the dynamics of offshoring attractiveness, in particular with regard to why a specific location may become either more or less attractive for offshoring over time, we still lack the analysis and tools under which change in offshore captive investment can be explored by multinationals. To contribute to this gap, this paper examines the history of captive centre investments of Fortune 250 global firms by considering the nature of the strategic investment in the captive centre, the location and function offshored. We explore offshore captive investments vis-à-vis the supply factors that shaped the development of this sector. Data were collected from secondary sources available in the professional media about offshoring investments.[4] The researchers sought for relevant information about the 2010 Fortune 250 global firms.[5] In order to identify the initial investment in an offshore captive centre, the researchers searched for information about investments made by Fortune 250 global firms between 1985 and 2010 using specific keywords such as captive centre/center, offshore/offshoring, shared service centre/center, information technology outsourcing (ITO), and business process outsourcing (BPO). Information about new captive centre set ups and changes made in captive centres in the following years were sought in particular with regard to location, function offshored and the captive model. The information collected on each captive centre was then populated into an Excel spreadsheet that served as the database for both the narrative and computed results presented below.

---

[4] For example: Forrester Market research, *CIO Magazine*, Outsourcing Institute, National Outsourcing Association, NASSCOM, Everest Research Institute, *The Hindu Business Line, Offshore Magazine, Computer Weekly* and others.

[5] List of Global 250 global firms in 2010 can be found on the following link: http://money.cnn.com/magazines/fortune/global500/2010/.

Phase 1: 1985–1997

If a foreign country can supply us with a commodity cheaper than we ourselves can make it, better buy it off them with some part of the produce of our own industry employed in a way in which we have some advantage.[6]

It is believed that Texas Instruments' R&D centre, set up in 1985, was the first multinational with a captive centre in India.[7] After Texas Instruments' move into India, it took several years for additional large multinationals to consider their offshoring strategy. Only in 1992, Deutsche Bank and Citigroup set up captive centres in India. Deutsche Bank's captive focused on providing IT and business process services to the parent firm with the intention of reducing its onshore costs.[8] Citigroup on the other hand set up six captive centres that provided IT, finance and accounting, and customer support services to both the parent firm and external clients from facilities in Chennai, Mumbai, Delhi, Bangalore, Hyderabad and Kolkata.[9]

Samsung, the South Korean multinational, was the fourth large multinational to set up a captive centre in 1993. Samsung's captive centre, located in Moscow (Russia), provided R&D services to the parent firm.[10] The captive was set up as a hybrid captive collaborating with local governmental and academic research organizations.

In 1995, IBM, the well-known US-based multinational, set up a captive centre in China.[11] The captive centre provided R&D services to the parent firm. The French bank Societé Generale set up a shared captive in Dublin (Ireland) to carry out financial activities for both the

---

[6] Adam Smith's 'The Wealth of Nations' in 1776.

[7] http://www.ti.com/ww/in/company_info.html.

[8] http://www.computerweekly.com/Articles/2007/11/08/227955/Deutsche-Bank-outsources-to-HCL-Technologies.htm.

[9] http://www.copc.com/media/pdf-case-studies/COPC001_Citigroup_CaseStudy_03.pdf.

[10] http://www.research.samsung.ru/srcinfo/srcprofil-history.html.

[11] http://www-31.ibm.com/cn/crl/en/.

parent firm and external clients.[12] LG opened a shared captive centre in Russia providing IT services,[13] while United Technologies set up a basic captive in India for a similar line of services.[14]

In 1996, Exxon Mobile set up a basic captive in India to provide IT support and customer services.[15] Daimler, the German conglomerate, also set up a basic captive centre in India to provide IT support and R&D services to the parent firm.[16] Samsung added another hybrid captive to provide R&D services, this time from India,[17] while HSBC opened its first captive centre, a basic type, in India to provide the firm with IT, finance and accounts, and customer support services.[18] Panasonic, the Japanese multinational, set up in Singapore an R&D centre, which worked with local providers.[19]

In 1997, General Electric set up its first captive centre in India, now known as the largest BPO company, Genpact.[20] The captive was set up as a basic type providing IT and finance services to General Electric. Hewlett-Packard set up an R&D centre in Israel[21] and Honda Motors set up an R&D centre in Brazil.[22] LG established a hybrid captive centre in Russia to provide IT support and R&D services, closely working with local providers.[23] Unilever set up its first R&D centre in India, forming

---

[12] http://www.captive.com/showcase/dublin.html.

[13] http://www.intsoft.spb.ru/article-An-interview-with-Yuri-Leethe-head-of-LG-Soft-Lab-a-St-Petersburg-based-branch-of-LGElectronics.html.

[14] http://www.netpicker.net/ButdespiteitspopularitysuIndi.html; http://www.cio.com/article/31928/Inside_Outsourcing_In_India.

[15] http://www.exxonmobil.com/AP-English/about_where_india.aspx.

[16] http://www.mercedes-benz.co.in/content/india/mpc/mpc_india_website/enng/home_mpc/passengercars/home/passengercars_world/Our_Presence_in_India/1.html.

[17] http://www.samsungindiasoft.com/default.asp?page=india.

[18] http://www.businessweek.com/magazine/content/06_05/b3969426.htm.

[19] http://www.psl.panasonic.com.sg/.

[20] http://www.genpact.com/home/aboutgenpact.aspx; http://www.atimes.com/atimes/South_Asia/FK12Df03.html.

[21] http://www.hpl.hp.com/israel/.

[22] http://hondanews.com/channels/corporate-worldwide-operations/releases/south-america-operations-overview.

[23] http://www.intsoft.spb.ru/article-An-interview-with-Yuri-Leethe-head-of-LG-Soft-Lab-a-St-Petersburg-based-branch-of-LGElectronics.html.

collaborations and acquiring services from local firms.[24] United Technologies opened its second R&D centre, this time in China, which provided services only to the parent firm.[25] Shell opened its first captive centre to provide IT and customer support services from Malaysia.[26]

Key Trends in Phase 1: The Rise of India

Fortune global 250 firms set up 21 captive centres between 1985 and 1997 (see Fig. 13.1). The vast majority of these multinationals applied a basic captive model (see Fig. 13.2). Also, most of the captive centres in Phase 1 provided either BPO or R&D services to the parent firm. In terms of location, captive centres were established during Phase 1 in eight countries and three continents, but the vast majority of them were set up in India (see Fig. 13.3). Indeed, in the 1980s and 1990s, India had just started becoming attractive for offshoring (Metters and Verma 2007).

The rise of the IT service sector in India is also linked to the country's British colonial past, which resulted in the British Empire founding the first universities and scientific institutes in India. These universities later became the Indian Institutes of Technologies and the Indian Institute of Management, now known for their quality graduates in the field of engineering and general management. The leading position of India in the captive sector is also attributed to the Indian government's investment in education in the 1980s and the long-term development of science and engineering (S&E) talent (Manning et al. 2008). At the political and economic level, India experienced significant changes in the 1990s. Until 1991, a socialist economic philosophy prevailed in India, which discouraged FDI in many sectors including the captive centre sector. However, in July 1991, the Indian government introduced a

---

[24] http://www.hul.co.in/careers-redesign/carreerschoices/researchanddevelopment/OverviewofResearchCentres/?WT.LHNAV=Overview_of_Research_Centres.
[25] http://www.thefreelibrary.com/UNITED+TECHNOLOGIES+-RESEARCH+CENTRE+TO+BEGIN+COLLABORATIVE+R%26D+IN . . .-a016927550.
[26] http://mrem.bernama.com/viewsm.php?idm=2421.

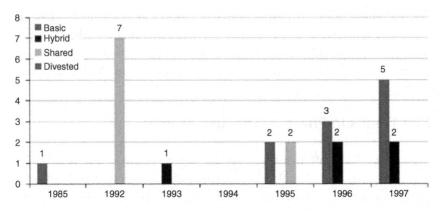

Fig. 13.1   Number of captive set-ups per type, 1985–1997

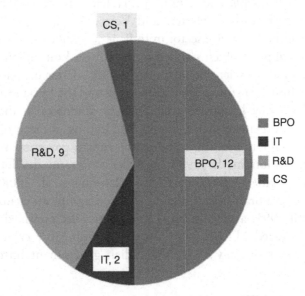

Fig. 13.2   Number of captive set-ups per function, 1985–1997

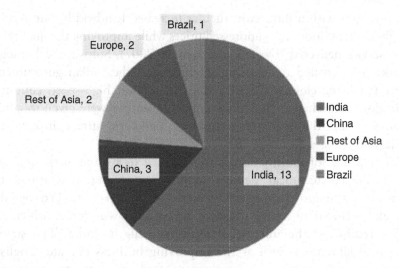

Fig. 13.3 Number of captive set-ups per geographic location, 1985–1997

series of reforms that liberalized trade and foreign investments across the economy (Metters and Verma 2007).

These changes in the Indian economy coincided with two events in the global economy and IT industry. First, there was a growing concern from multinationals that the so-called millennium bug would result in a major disturbance to their operations and therefore solutions to this matter and resources to deliver adequate solutions were sought beyond firms' boundaries, including in offshore locations such as India. Second, following the 'dot-com bubble', the global economy entered a recession period that pressed multinationals to seek new sources of efficiencies (Nassimbeni and Sartor 2008). India, with its growing pool of talent at low costs, had become very attractive to certain offshore activities, such as IT services and customer support.

With the march of some of the largest multinationals to India, the Indian government realized the importance of its telecommunications sector. In 1994, the government privatized the telecommunications sector in order to enable investment by private firms and thus support the development of the IT sector. This deregulation resulted not only in innovations within the sector, such as increased bandwidth, but also in higher competition that suppressed prices while improving the quality of the service delivered (Dossani and Kenney 2007). Software technology parks were created to host foreign firms and the Indian government invested in developing infrastructures to support high-speed communication technologies. In addition, fiscal incentives were given to companies using the software technology parks to attract investment (Nassimbeni and Sartor 2008).

The arrival of multinationals to India led to a surge in the pursuit of advanced technical degrees among the young generations to improve their growth potential relative to their parents' (Youngdahl et al. 2010). This trend resulted in a skilled workforce, which in turn reinforced the interest of multinationals in India. The stable political climate, as well as the improving business climate, English language proficiency, the pressure to find resources to solve the Millennium Bug threat and the success of captive pioneers, such as Texas Instruments, resulted in increased attention of executives to the potential of India by 1997 (Oshri et al. 2009b).

Phase 2: 1998–2002

Came to India for costs, stayed for quality.[27]

The year 1998 marked the beginning of a new wave of setting up offshore captives in India and in other locations. Further, during Phase 2, the range of services offshored to captive centres significantly expanded. One of the reasons for this growth is attributed to the 'General Electric Effect', as its captive centre set up in 1997, attracted the attention of both competitors and potential clients. Indeed, while General Electric was not the first to open a captive centre in India, its presence resulted in rising confidence in the offshore captive option (Metters and Verma 2007).

---

[27] The citation is found in an interview from McKinsey with the head of operations for Dell India. Retrieved from http://www.mckinsey.com/clientservice/bto/pointofview/pdf/MoIT8_Dell_F.pdf.

Eleven captives were set up in 1998[28] by large multinationals including Chevron's basic captive centre in the Philippines, which provided a range of business processes and IT services, Hewlett-Packard's basic captive centre in the Czech Republic,[29] IBM's hybrid captive in India[30] and Procter and Gamble's hybrid captive in China.[31] In 1999, six captive centres were established including Verizon's basic captive in the Philippines,[32] another Procter and Gamble hybrid captive in the Philippines[33] and LG's basic captive centre in Israel.[34] In 2000, 13 captive centres were established by various multinationals, such as Shell's basic captive in Malaysia,[35] AXA's basic captive in India[36] and GE's R&D centre in India.[37] In this year, IBM set up a shared captive centre in Slovakia that provided IT and finance and accounting services.[38] In 2001, 15 captive[39] centres were set up consisting of 12 basic captives and three hybrid captives. Among the multinationals that set up basic captives in this year were Ford Motors and HSBC in India[40] and Toshiba in China.[41] Hybrid captive centres were set up by Verizon[42]

---

[28] The complete list of Fortune firms that set up captive centres during Phases 1–4 can be obtained from the corresponding author upon request.

[29] http://h10134.www1.hp.com/contacts/locations/czech/.

[30] http://www-07.ibm.com/in/research/laboverview.html.

[31] http://www.allbusiness.com/company-activities-management/company-structures-ownership/10625962-1.html.

[32] http://www.verizonbusiness.com/resources/newsletters/an-offshoring-checklist-improve-your-chances-for-success_en_xg.pdf.

[33] http://www.mb.com.ph/articles/265215/pg-s-manila-servicecentre-leads-way-business-technology-innovations.

[34] http://www.lgtci.net/.

[35] http://www.shell.com.my/home/content/mys/aboutshell/careers/other_opportunities/.

[36] http://www.cbronline.com/companies/axa_business_services.

[37] http://www.ge.com/in/company/jfwtc/index.html.

[38] http://www-05.ibm.com/employment/sk/about/about_us.html.

[39] http://techon.nikkeibp.co.jp/NEA/archive/200206/188420/.

[40] http://www.hsbcglobalresourcing.com/country.aspx?gsc=GSC_HYD1.

[41] http://techon.nikkeibp.co.jp/NEA/archive/200206/188420/.

[42] http://www.computerworlduk.com/advice/outsourcing/827/using-service-providers-to-improve-off-shoring/.

and Nokia in India,[43] and Panasonic in China.[44] For the first time, a multinational divested its captive centre. Deutsche Bank's shared captive centre, which was set up in 1992 in India to provide IT and BPO services, was divested to HCL Technologies, which bought out a majority stake.[45] The growth trend of setting up captive centres continued in 2002 with 20 captives set-up around the globe. The dominating model in 2002 was the basic captive centre with 15 new start-ups by various multinationals such as HP in Poland,[46] Samsung in India[47] and Citigroup in Chile.[48] There were also four hybrid captives set-up in this year, among them, HSBC's hybrid captive in India[49] and Dell's in Brazil.[50] One shared captive was set up in 2002 by Vodafone in Egypt to provide customer support services.[51] Figure 13.4 presents the distribution of captive types during Phase 2.

During Phase 2 (1998–2002), a total of 66 captive centres were established and one divested (see Fig. 13.4). They varied in terms of the services that were offshored, with 28 captives established as R&D centres, 17 providing various BPO services, 11 captives providing IT services and 10 captives providing customer support (see Fig. 13.5). Locations also expanded in Phase 2 in comparison to Phase 1. While India was still the most attractive location for captive centres, with 21 new start-ups in Phase 2, China and Central-Eastern Europe (CEE) emerged as contenders with 12 new captives in each location and 10 new captives in South America (see Fig. 13.6).

[43] http://techon.nikkeibp.co.jp/NEA/archive/200206/188420/.

[44] http://panasonic.cn/prdcc/english/intro/index.html.

[45] http://sip-trunking.tmcnet.com/news/2007/11/09/3084544.htm.

[46] http://h10134.www1.hp.com/contacts/locations/poland/.

[47] http://www.businesstrendsasia.com/index.php?cat=2:24:86 &art=624.

[48] http://www.investchile.cl/rps_corfo_v57/OpenSite/Investchile/Publications/Publications/carga/Chile,%20International%20Services%20Centres,%20Success%20Stories.pdf.

[49] http://www.businessweek.com/magazine/content/06_05/b3969426.htm.

[50] http://www.revistapesquisa.fapesp.br/%3Fart=1981&bd=1&pg=1&lg=en.

[51] http://vis.vodafone.com.eg/CorporateProfile.aspx.

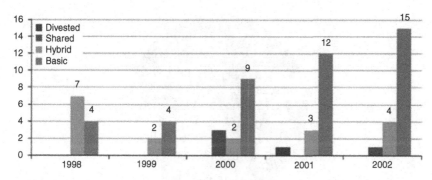

Fig. 13.4 The number of captive set-ups per type, 1998–2002

Key Trends in Phase 2: The Hybrid Model and the Rise of R&D Centres in China

We observe two key trends during Phase 2 (1998–2002). First, while the basic captive model was still the dominating offshore captive sector in Phase 2, we notice that compared with Phase 1, a larger number of multinationals adopted the hybrid model when setting up an offshore captive centre. The growth in the number of hybrid captives in Phase 2 suggests that multinationals sought to benefit from access to resources available in the local market as well as to enable the captive centre to specialize in its line of services while outsourcing non-core activities to local vendors. This trend was supported by the growing maturity of the captive sector. Indeed, during Phase 2, several captive centres gained the highest capability maturity model level, a certificate that signals a high-quality assurance process within the captive. This advancement in process methodologies within some captive centres legitimized the captive option against the third-party outsourcing alternative. For example, LG Soft India (LGSI), a subsidiary of LG Electronics (LGE) based in Bangalore, India, received its CMM Level 5 and ISO 9001 certified global software service provider in November 2001.[52] With India's

---

[52] www.lgsoftindia.com.

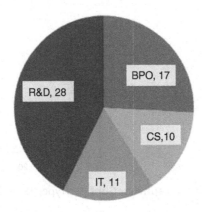

Fig. 13.5 The number of captive set-ups per function, 1998–2002

deregulation and liberalization of its economy, multinationals also found the conditions to invest more appealing than in the past. Similarly, following China's joining the World Trade Organization in 2001, many of the regulations restricting FDI had been removed or relaxed regarding certain sectors. Therefore, multinationals had the freedom, in some sectors, to set up a wholly owned subsidiary without having to enter a joint venture with a Chinese firm. Alongside the deregulation regarding FDI, China invested in developing technological competencies through the investment in higher education programmes, making China attractive for R&D captive centres. Further, major investments in improving and expanding the talent pool led to the increasing attractiveness of China. Between 1995 and 2003, for example the number of first-year doctoral students in S&E in Chinese universities increased six fold (Ernst 2006). Moreover, the quality of education was improved by establishing partnerships with Western universities. Last but not least, the 'brain drain', which countries such as India and China suffered from for many decades, was replaced by a 'reverse brain drain'; individuals who left these countries to pursue education and business opportunities abroad noticed the increasing attractiveness of the home country and came back (Youngdahl et al. 2010).

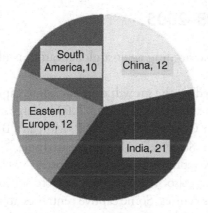

Fig. 13.6   The number of captive set-ups per geographic location, 1998–2002

The second trend observed in Phase 2 concerns the rise of R&D centres and in particular in China. While India attracted more captive centres than any other location, China, as a single country, became more attractive for R&D activities. China attracted eight R&D captives out of the total 23 R&D centres set up during Phase 2, more than India and any other region. Further, we observe that in Phase 2, more captive centres were set up for R&D activities than any other function.

While India and China were the most attractive countries for offshoring, CEE also attracted a large number of captive centres, 12 in total, during Phase 2. In particular, Poland attracted five captive centres in 1999 and 2000. One reason for this is that the Polish government took initiatives to make the country attractive for FDI. The Krakow Technology Park (KTP), for example an economic investment zone established in 1998, was set up to provide incentives in the form of significant depreciation write-offs and tax exemptions. In addition, the KTP hosted 15 higher education institutes and over 140 research centres to ensure an ongoing flow of talent to those centres. HSBC is one of the companies that established a captive centre in Krakow while HP and Siemens set up their captives in Warsaw, Wroclaw and Lodz.

Phase 3: 2003–2005

It has been said that arguing against globalization is like arguing against the laws of gravity.[53]

Phase 3 is marked by the growth of the offshore captive sector. Thirty-seven captive centres were established in 2003 by large multinationals such as Shell's Customer Centre in Chile,[54] J.P. Morgan's BPO in India[55] and the Royal Bank of Scotland's IT captive in India.[56] Of the 37 newly established, 30 were set up as basic captive centres, 5 as hybrid captives and 2 as shared captives. Also, BPO and R&D were still the main functions offshored to captive centres. Some captive centres established in 2003 were divested or terminated later on, for example AXA's basic captive, which provided customer support services from India was divested in 2005[57]; Banco Santander's basic captive centre that provided customer support from India was terminated in 2006[58] and Unilever's basic captive centre providing BPO services from India was divested in 2006.[59] In 2004, 43 captive centres were set up around the globe by multinationals. Among these were Deutsche Telekom's IT support centre in Russia; Arcelor Mittal's shared captive providing BPO services from South Africa[60] and Credit Suisse's basic captive that provided BPO services from Singapore.[61] Thirty of the newly established captives in 2004 were basic captives and the remaining were hybrid and shared (nine and four, respectively). The

---

[53] Kofi Annan, Statement of the former Secretary General of the United Nations, during an international conference of nongovernmental organizations in 2000. Retrieved from www.corpwatch.org/article.php?id=589.

[54] http://www.investchile.cl/rps_corfo_v57/OpenSite/Investchile/Publications/Publications/carga/Chile,%20International%20-Services%20Centres,%20Success%20Stories.pdf.

[55] http://dqindia.ciol.com/content/DQTop20_2006/SASnBPO06/2006/206082843.asp.

[56] http://www.naukri.com/gpw/rbs/home.htm.

[57] http://www.atimes.com/atimes/South_Asia/HG14Df02.html.

[58] http://www.thisismoney.co.uk/money/news/article-1594301/Abbey-closes-Indian-call-centres.html.

[59] http://www.computerworlduk.com/news/outsourcing/8424/unilever-sells-financial-shared-services-to-capgemini/.

[60] http://www.arcelormittal.com/index.php?lang=en&page=730.

[61] http://www.thefreelibrary.com/CSFB+Opens+Singapore+Services+Centre.-a0113162917.

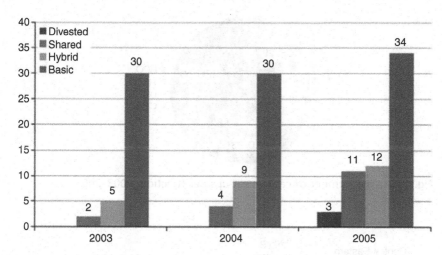

Fig. 13.7   The number of captive set-ups per type, 2003–2005

majority of the captives set-up in 2004 were providing BPO services (16). The growth trend of setting up captives continued in 2005 with the announcement of 58 new captives established around the world. Volkswagen set up an R&D centre in China;[62] Citigroup established a basic captive providing BPO services from the Philippines[63] and Tesco opened a captive centre in India to provide IT services.[64] Thirty-four of the newly established units were basic captive centres and the remaining were hybrid and shared. The functions offshored through captive centres were still dominated by BPO services (22) and R&D centres (17). Two GE captive centres were divested in 2005: a basic captive centre providing BPO services, which was established in 1997 in India and a basic captive centre providing BPO services, which was set up in China in 2000.

In total, 137 captive centres were set up and three were divested during Phase 3 (see Fig. 13.7). The dominating functions offshored through captive centres were still BPO and R&D with 53 and 36 new

---

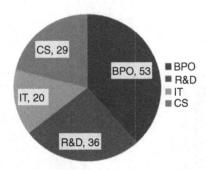

Fig. 13.8 The number of captive set-ups per function, 2003–2005

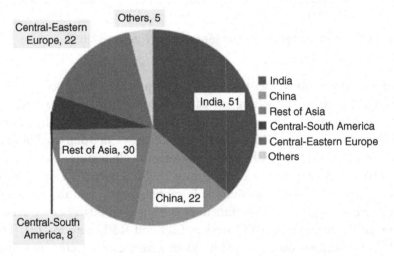

Fig. 13.9 The number of captive set-ups per geography geographic location, 2003–2005

start-ups during this phase (see Fig. 13.8). There was also an additional expansion of the number of locations to which work was offshored, in which Asian countries (excluding China and India) accounted for 30 new captives in this period, while China and CEE maintained their relative attractiveness in the market though India, indeed, was still the most attractive location for offshoring in Phase 3 (see Fig. 13.9).

Key Trends in Phase 3: The Expansion of Offshoring Locations

Basic captive business models dominated the firms' logic in Phase 3 (2003–2005). However, at the same time, multinationals expanded their search for attractive offshore locations to set up captive centres in 26 countries (compared with 19 countries in Phase 2 and 11 in Phase 1). Indeed, with the increase in the offshoring of BPO and R&D activities, multinationals needed to seek new sources of talent (Rutherford and Mobley 2005). In particular, US-based multinationals were pressed to seek talent outside the USA as the government significantly reduced the quota of H1B visas in 2003 (Lewin et al. 2009). The H1B visa is a non-immigrant visa for temporary work that requires specialized knowledge not readily available in the USA. This cutback in H1B visas combined with the 'reversed brain drain' from the Western world to India, high costs of domestic talent, the ageing of the population and the retirement of baby boomers and the decline in number of S&E talent in the Western world (Lewin and Couto 2007) drove multinationals to fill critical positions outside the USA.

For example, Taiwan, which was not a destination for offshoring through captive centres in Phase 1 and 2, attracted five R&D captive centres in Phase 3 set up by Sony, Ford Motors, Dell, IBM and Fujitsu. Taiwan had become an attractive location for offshored R&D activities mainly because of government incentives to improve the business climate with the flow of engineering talent from Taiwanese universities. Similarly, Panama set up the 'Panama-Pacific Special Economic Area' in 2001, which offered multinationals taxation benefits and discounted international calls, having set up their call centres in this economic area. However, government incentives to attract R&D investment did not always work. For example, the Malaysia R&D Grant Scheme, introduced in 1996,[65] attracted only one multinational, Panasonic, to open a hybrid R&D captive in the multimedia super corridor, despite a massive media campaign and very generous benefits.

---

[65] www/nitc.my/index.cfm?&menuid=28.

While India maintained its leading position, rising costs deterred some multinationals from setting up their captives in the country. In addition, several countries became more attractive for offshoring as their governments introduced incentives for FDI and their universities provided a healthy supply of talent. For example, South Africa attracted three captive centres while Romania and Sri Lanka attracted two captives each. Guatemala, El Salvador and Thailand attracted one captive centre each. However, rising costs in India did not always result in multinationals seeking alternative countries for their captives. For example, Allianz, the German insurance company, looked for alternatives within India to deal with cost pressures in some 'tier 1' cities (e.g. Mumbai and Bangalore). Their alternative was a 'tier 3' city, called Trivandrum, in which they set up their captive centre in 2003.

China continued to maintain its position as an attractive offshoring location in Phase 3, mainly attracting R&D centres. Improvements in the number of Chinese firms qualifying for quality standards such as CMM and ISO certifications increased in Phase 3. Further, ongoing improvements in the education system, the introduction of English lessons as part of the education system and the increase in the number of graduates from Chinese universities caught the attention of multi-nationals (A.T. Kearney 2007). As an ongoing trend from Phase 2, multinationals mainly set up R&D captive centres in China, seeking to benefit from low-cost talent as well as position their products for the Chinese market (Crosman 2008). Hitachi, the Japanese electronics giant, for example set up two R&D centres in China in order to access the Chinese market and General Electric set up a basic R&D captive in Shanghai to ensure its leading position in the region.

The ongoing growth in captive centres in CEE was attributed to the rapid economic development in this region and to their accession to the European Union. Countries such as Poland, the Czech Republic, Hungary and Slovakia joined the European Union in 2004 while Romania and Bulgaria followed in 2007.[66] The data set indeed confirms increased captive activity in these countries since 2004.

---

[66] The information is obtained from the official website of the European Union. The data are retrieved from http://europa.eu/abc/european_countries/eu_members/index_en.htm.

Although the period between 2003 and 2005 can be characterized by rapid growth in setting up captive centres, it also brought to light the first signs of reservation to offshoring activities (Mordecai 2006). While the public debate and demonstrations in the USA attracted the attention of the media during the 2004 elections, some legislators took a clear stand against offshoring. One of them, Senator John Kerry, promoted legislation that required a mandatory notification by companies who were moving jobs offshore. His activities also included the setting up of the Call Center Consumer's Right to Know Act in which representatives initiating a call from a call centre outside the USA to individuals located in the United States needed to disclose their physical location at the beginning of each call. Another prevention measure was the United States Workers Protection Act, introduced in 2004 and adopted in several states, which required US firms to show a positive net gain in jobs inside the state in order to qualify for tax preferences. At the same time, penalties were imposed on firms that laid off employees in the USA in order to create these jobs overseas. The government also restricted trade with contractors and subcontractors, who were providing the service from a site outside the USA (Mordecai 2006). Clearly, legislators and part of the public in the USA were concerned with offshoring, and some measures were introduced to reduce its impact on the job market.

Phase 4: 2006–2010

The concept of owning an offshore services unit may have outlived its value for most companies.[67]

While 2005, the last year in Phase 3, witnessed the setting up of 57 new captive centres around the globe, Phase 4 started with only 30 new captive set-ups. Indeed, Phase 4 is characterized by a major drop in new start-ups of captives around the globe as well as with a dramatic rise in

---

[67] Stephanie Overby, a business journalist commenting on the state of captive centres in CIO Magazine, 30th June 2009: http://www.cio.com/article/496322/Outsourcing_The_Demise_of_the_Offshore_Captive_Centre.

the number of captive divestments in 2008. There was also an increase in the number of shared captive set-ups in 2006 and 2007 in comparison to previous years.

In 2006, multinationals set up 19 basic captives in 10 different countries. This included Deutsche Telekom setting up a customer service centre in Slovakia,[68] Johnson & Johnson's BPO in the Czech Republic[69] and United Health Group's BPO in India.[70] Nine hybrid captives were set up in 2006, which were predominantly focusing on R&D activities while 11 shared captives were mainly providing BPO services to multiple clients. In this year, Unilever divested its 2003 BPO captive centre in India.[71] In 2007, multinationals set up a total of 39 captive centres, nine captive centres more than the previous year. Twenty-two new start-ups were basic captives by firms such as Samsung's R&D centre in Israel,[72] the Royal Bank of Scotland's BPO in India[73] and Nokia's R&D centre in China.[74] Six hybrid captives were set up in 2007 by firms such as Panasonic's R&D centre in Vietnam[75] and Credit Suisse's BPO in India.[76] Eleven shared captive centres were established in 2007 with Robert Bosch setting up four BPOs in India,[77] Romania[78] and Argentina.[79] Only one captive was divested in 2007: Barclays' BPO in India, which was established in 2004.[80] In 2008, a total of 34 captives were established by large multinationals. This is the second drop in the number of new established

---

[68] http://www.t-systems.com/tsip/en/225332/locations/international/slovakia.

[69] http://www.czechinvest.org/data/files/bss-764-de.pdf.

[70] http://www.uhgi.com/products/businesses/india.html.

[71] http://economictimes.indiatimes.com/articleshow/1967649.cms.

[72] http://www.manufacturing.net/Samsung-Buys-TransChip.aspx.

[73] http://articles.economictimes.indiatimes.com/2007-12-12/news/27669175_1_rbs-paul-abraham-dutch-bank.

[74] http://www.v3.co.uk/v3-uk/news/1991305/nokia-siemens-expands-r-d-china.

[75] http://panasonic.co.jp/corp/news/official.data/data.dir/en070405-8/en070405-8.html.

[76] http://www.thehindubusinessline.com/todays-paper/article1652045.ece?ref=archive.

[77] http://news.oneindia.in/2007/08/15/robert-bosch-india-to-investrs-250-cr.html.

[78] http://www.romania-insider.com/bosch-to-expand-production-centre-in-blaj-romania-with-eur-100-mln-investment/26458/#.

[79] http://www.boschcommunicationcentre.com/content/language1/html/argentina.aspx.

[80] http://bpotiger.com/2007/06/hdfcbarclays_selling_intelenet.html.

captives since 2005. Further, in 2008, 19 captives were divested by large multinationals. These included Citigroup's BPO in India,[81] Unilever's BPO in Brazil and Chile,[82] Aviva's BPO in India[83] and Dell's customer service centre in El Salvador.[84] Only four shared captives were established in this year, by HP in Panama[85] and IBM in India[86] and Mexico.[87] There were 12 hybrid captives set-up in 2008 including Nestlé's R&D centre in China,[88] Microsoft's R&D centre in Israel[89] and Siemens' R&D centre in Singapore.[90] In 2009, 21 captives were established by large multinationals around the globe. Thirteen of them were basic captives and the remaining hybrid captives. No shared captives were established in this year. Also, only four captives were divested in 2009: two AIG IT captives in India that were set up in 2003,[91] Siemens' IT captive in India from 2004[92] and Sony's R&D centre in India from 2007.[93] The year 2010 witnessed an increase in the number of captive centre set-ups. In total, 33 captives were established by large multinationals with 21 basic captives, six hybrids and six shared captives. There was only one divestment of a captive by Target of its 2005 BPO in India.[94]

---

[81] http://www.thaindian.com/newsportal/uncategorized/citi-sellsindian-it-arm-to-wipro-for-127-mn_100134435.html.

[82] http://www.computerworlduk.com/news/outsourcing/8424/unilever-sells-financial-shared-services-to-capgemini/.

[83] http://www.dnaindia.com/money/report_you-ll-see-more-captive-bpo-units-being-sold_1178761.

[84] http://www.bloggingstocks.com/2008/10/21/dell-sells-900-personcall-centre-in-el-salvador/.

[85] http://www.hp.com/hpinfo/newsroom/press/2007/071010b.html.

[86] http://www.efytimes.com/e1/fullnews.asp?edid=21277.

[87] http://www.redorbit.com/news/technology/1399494/ibm_opens_mexico_archiving_centre/.

[88] http://www.redorbit.com/news/business/1595859/nestle_opens_new_rd_centre_in_beijing.

[89] http://www.globes.co.il/serveen/globes/docview.asp?did=1000343640.

[90] http://sg.siemens.com/press/corporate/Pages/SiemensOpens-FirstCorporateRDCentreinSouthEastAsia.aspx.

[91] http://www.cio.com/article/499483/HP_Subsidiary_Acquiring_AIG_s_Software_Operation_in_India.

[92] http://www.indiabusinessview.com/news/51/siemens-it-unit-sislsold-low-valuation.

[93] http://articles.timesofindia.indiatimes.com/2009-11-20/chennai/28068006_1_sony-ericsson-mobile-communications-r-d-facilityr-d-centres.

[94] http://www.deccanherald.com/content/47333/wipro-buy-targetindia-centre.html.

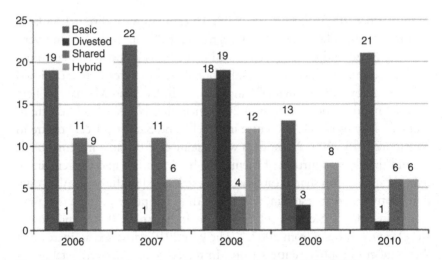

Fig. 13.10   The number of captive set-ups per type, 2006–2010

Phase 4 witnessed a major drop in the number of captive centre start-ups, which made some commentators such as the business journalist Stephanie Overby predict the demise of the offshore captive centre[95] (see Fig. 13.10). Indeed, the financial crisis in 2008 is strongly associated with multinationals' decisions to divest captive centres and on some occasions delay additional FDIs. However, 2010 witnessed a slight increase in the number of captive start-ups, which may indicate a recovery in the captive sector. Further, Phase 4 also experienced an ongoing expansion of offshoring locations in which, for the first time, India and China together attracted less than 50% of the new established captives (see Fig. 13.11). Central and Eastern Europe, in this regard, emerged as a viable contender to China and as an alternative to India (Fig. 13.12).

---

[95] http://www.cio.com/article/496322/Outsourcing_The_Demise_of_the_Offshore_Captive_Centre.

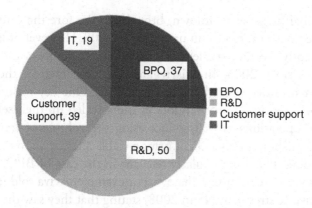

Fig. 13.11   The number of captive set-ups per geographic location, 2006–2010

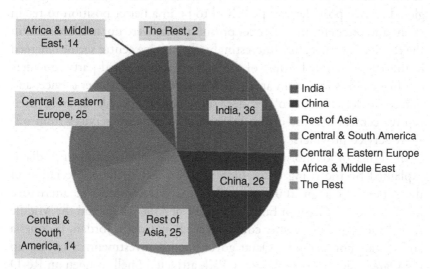

Fig. 13.12   The number of captive set-ups per function, 2006–2010

Key Trends in Phase 4: Slowdown in New Start-ups, Captive Centre Sell-offs and the Rise of CEE

While the basic business model still dominated the captive sector, the challenges multinationals faced during Phase 4 (2006–2010), induced by the global financial meltdown, brought to the fore the centrality of the divested business model, in particular in 2008. However, it is evident that the captive sector experienced a slowdown in terms of the number of start-ups since 2006. In this regard, the slowdown in the captive sector started prior to the global financial crisis. One key reason for this trend is because third-party vendors in India scaled up their services by improving operations as well as increasing the volume of transactions performed offshore to offer client firms a viable alternative to the captive centre option. This is particularly relevant in the case of BPO, as fewer BPO captives were set up in Phase 4. For example, Aviva sold its Indian BPO captive centres to WNS in 2008, stating that they saw the buyer as a partner who 'truly understands the insurance industry and has a tireless commitment to process excellence and customer care'.[96] In this regard, a global service provider was perceived to be in a better position to retain talent and offer employees career prospects that were not available within the captive centre sector. Interestingly, the captive centre sector emerged in the 1990s mainly because of the lack of credible third-party providers to offer services in certain areas, such as BPO and customer service, and indeed in less than two decades, some multinationals divested their captive centres because of the availability of superior services from offshore service providers.

In terms of offshoring locations, the ongoing decline of India is explained by the rising costs, high attrition levels, the appreciation of the rupee (Crosman 2008) as well as the attractiveness of alternative locations such as Eastern Europe, the rest of Asia, Africa and the Middle East. Among the newcomer countries are Bangladesh, Jordan, Indonesia and Qatar. For example, Qatar government's investment in setting up the Qatar Science & Technology Park attracted Shell to open an R&D centre in the country. In this regard, government regulation and incentive programmes play a major role in improving the attractiveness of the country for offshoring.

---

[96] Cathryn Riley, Chief Operating Officer of Norwich Union Life, and Chairman, Aviva Global Services, both business divisions of Aviva.http://ir.wns.com/phoenix.zhtml?c=200768&p=irolnewsArticle&ID=1173750&highlight=.

While evidence suggests that improvements in third-party offerings have led to the decline in new captive start-ups and the ongoing competition between countries for offshore work intensifies, the impact of the financial crisis on the captive sector is also evident with the sell-off of 19 captives in 2008 alone. We review the impact of the financial crisis on the captive sector in the following section.

The Impact of the Global Recession on the Captive Centre Sector

The year 2008 marked the beginning of the global financial crisis during which significant changes were evident in terms of the offshoring business models. First, in 2008, a record number of 19 captive centres were divested, followed by four divestments in 2009. At the same time, in 2008, a drop in the number of captives set-up, from 39 in 2007 to 34 in 2008, is evident, followed by a major fall in 2009 to only 21 captive start-ups. Our analysis suggests that the vast majority of divestures that took place in 2008 can be attributed to the financial crisis (see Table 13.2). Table 13.2 provides several examples of captive centres which were divested during Phase 4.

For example, Citigroup, a struggling financial institution during the early years of the crisis, decided to opt for a third-party arrangement and as a result sold six global service centres to TCS for $505 million. In the acquisition contract, both parties agreed that TCS would provide services for the bank for at least another 9 years in a contract that was worth about $2.4 billion.[97] In 2008, Citigroup also sold its four IT centres (CTS) to Wipro for $127 million.[98] Wipro agreed to provide technology infrastructure services to Citigroup for 6 years worth over $500 million. In 2009, Siemens and AIG divested three captive centres mainly for cost and restructuring reasons induced by unfavourable economic conditions.

While the captive sector suffered from a decline and an unprecedented sell-off in 2008 and 2009, 2010 in fact witnessed a growth spurt with 33

---

[97] http://www.tcs.com/news_events/press_releases/Pages/TCS-To-Acquire-Citigroup-Global-Services.aspx.

[98] http://www.rediff.com/money/2008/dec/23citigroup-sells-cts-towipro.htm.

Table 13.2 Divested captive centres in 2008

Company	Amount of divested captives	Location(s)	Sold to	Reasons as indicated in press releases
Aviva	5	India/Sri Lanka	WNS	Global economic recession, raise capital, capitalize on experience of third-party providers
Citigroup	10	India	Wipro & TCS	Global economic recession, focus on core operations, rising costs, to free up capital, unrealistic expectations, attempt to recover from economic downturn
Dell	1	El Salvador	Stream Global Services Inc.	Cut costs, increase efficiency, improve quality
Prudential	1	India	Capita	Financial difficulties
Unilever	2	Chile/Brazil	Capgemini	Reduce complexity, cut costs, increase efficiency, extend expertise outside own group, capitalize on third-party providers

start-ups. Our observation is supported by research published by Evert Research claiming that, as of the fourth quarter of 2009, captive start-ups were in fact beginning to rebound (Goolsby 2010).

Trends in Phases 1–4: Captive Models, Attractiveness of Locations and Functions Offshored

The aim of this paper was to study changes in the captive centre sector in order to understand the forces that shaped its growth between 1985 and 2010. Several trends have been identified based on the historical review

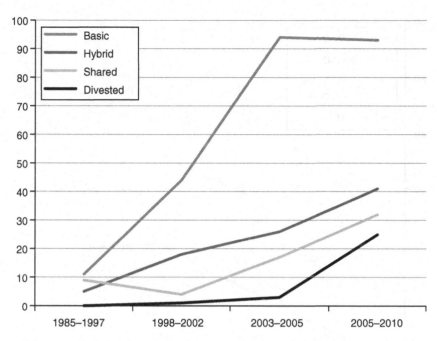

Fig. 13.13   Number of captive set-ups per type, 1985–2010

and analysis of the four phases. First, while the basic captive model dominated the captive centre sector, it is evident that the application of this model has declined in Phase 4 (see Fig. 13.13) and the use of hybrid and shared captive models has intensified in Phases 3 and 4. One reason for this trend is that multinationals have gained imperative experience in managing captives offshore to allow them to experiment with other captive models such as the hybrid and the shared. In particular, multinationals have realized the potential in emerging markets such as India and China where opportunities to attract external clients were present through the shared captive model as well as opportunities to improve operational costs through the outsourcing of non-core activities to local vendors in the hybrid captive model. While multinationals have experimented with the hybrid and shared captive models, they also divested quite a few captive centres during Phase 4, mainly because of the worsening economic conditions in 2008. However, not all captive

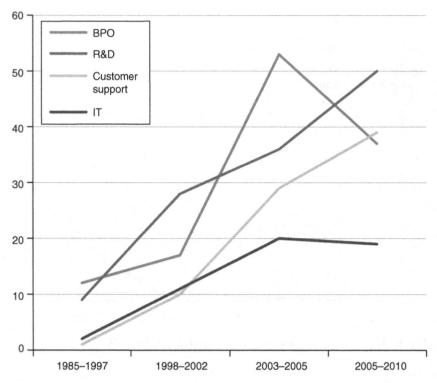

Fig. 13.14 Number of captive set-ups per function, 1985–2010

divestures in Phase 4 were because of worsening economic conditions. Some divestures were pursued simply because the maturity of the captive centre, which signalled to the parent firm an opportunity to offload the asset without having to risk service quality.

The second trend concerns the type of activities that have been offshored through the captive model (see Fig. 13.14). In this regard, more captive centres were set up to carry out R&D activities than for any other function. Also, until Phase 3, BPO captives grew steadily; however, the number of new BPO start-ups declined in Phase 4, suggesting that multinationals may have preferred using third-party service providers instead of owning BPO captive centres. This can be explained by the maturity level of the BPO service offered by offshore

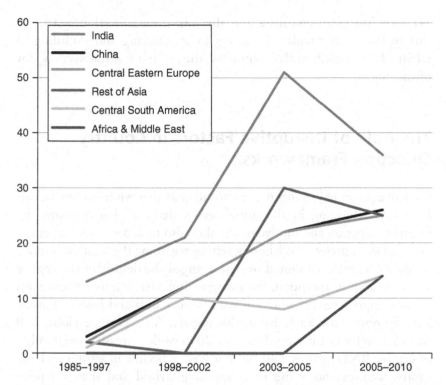

Fig. 13.15   Number of captive set-ups per geographic location, 1985–2010

third-party vendors, which only became attractive for client firms in Phase 4. Customer support has demonstrated ongoing growth throughout the four phases mainly driven by cost-saving considerations and access to multilingual talent in regions such as CEE (for entire Europe), North Africa (for French- and Arabic-speaking countries) and South America (for Spanish-speaking countries and the Spanish population in the USA).

The third trend is the decline of India as the most attractive offshoring location while Central and Eastern Europe improved its attractiveness throughout the four phases (see Fig. 13.15). Rising costs in India have affected the attractiveness of the country while governments in CEE countries offered tax benefits to multinationals willing to invest in their countries. Further, the physical proximity of CEE to

Western European countries and the improved education system in this region, in particular the access to engineering and multilingual talent, have significantly improved the region's attractiveness for offshoring.

The Role of Disruptive Factors in Country Selection Frameworks

Evidence presented in this paper also suggests that while multinationals have been engaging in the initial set-up decision that concerns the location, function and captive mode, they also took decisions that either changed their preferred offshoring setting regarding the location, captive model or function offshored or that changed the destiny of the captive few years after its inception. For example, India has lost its attractiveness for new captive set-ups in recent years while China and Eastern Europe have become more attractive in this respect. Also, Fortune global 250 firms set up fewer BPO captives since 2006 while increasing the number of captive R&D centres. Last but not least, a decline in setting up basic captive centres and a rise in establishing hybrid and shared captive centres indicate that multinationals have been experimenting with more complex captive models following the acquisition of experience over the years. Evidence reported here also shows that several firms changed the destiny of their captive units. Deutsche Bank set up a captive centre in India 1992, but then decided to divest it in 2001. Citigroup set up a shared captive in 1992 in India and divested it to TCS in 2008. In total, out of 418 captives set-up between 1985 and 2010, 31 captives have been divested, 4 have been migrated and 4 more have been terminated. Our findings confirm Joshi and Mudigonda's observation that some factors act as facilitating offshoring. In the case of captive centres facilitating factors may include low-cost labour, the supply of talent and the availability of incentives provided by the government. However, as multinationals may change initial offshoring decision, we propose considering *disruptive factors* as complementary to inhibiting factors (Joshi and Mudigonda 2008) in the context of captive centres. Disruptive factors motivate multinationals to change their off-shoring strategy by either switching between captive models or by relocating offshored functions to another location. These factors can be related, on the one hand, to worsening economic conditions at the offshore location or alternatively improving economic conditions in an alternative offshore location.

In terms of facilitating factors in the captive centre sector, many countries benefited from their effect, making their offshoring services more attractive to multinationals. For example, for many years, India has benefited from a wide range of inducing factors, which turned the country into the most attractive offshore destination for captive centres from the mid-1980s. India's low-cost, highly skilled talent and generous government incentives promoting FDIs are among the more prominent inducing factors that transformed its offshoring industry. In recent years, China has emerged as a serious contender to India, mainly because of the advantage gained through several inducing factors such as the supply of low-cost talent and government deregulation programmes promoting FDI. However, while India has kept its leadership in the captive centre sector, China has emerged as an attractive offshore destination for R&D facilities for multinationals that perceived China to be a growth market for their products and therefore sought to physically locate their R&D activities to the local market. In this regard, the specialization of the Chinese captive centre sector in R&D was driven by a demand factor (e. g. growth market) while the specialization of the Indian captive centre sector in BPO was mainly driven by a set of supply factors (e.g. supply of low-cost talent). In a similar manner, Central and Eastern European countries, in particular Poland and Hungary, have benefited from access to multilingual personnel, which was needed for captive centres providing customer support to European clients.

Disruptive factors in the captive centre sector were also evident, in particular where changes in trends have been observed. For example, during Phases 3 and 4, the number of start-ups of certain captive models such as hybrid, shared and divested has increased while the number of new basic captives has levelled. As the captive sector has gained experience in setting up and operating an offshore captive centre, multinationals gradually diverted from the basic captive model to experiment with other business models through which additional value can be delivered to the parent firm including a growth approach through the shared captive model or a cost-driven approach through the hybrid model. In this regard, the maturity of the captive sector disrupted the dominant position of the basic captive model and enabled multinationals to consider alternative paths as to how the captive centre can deliver value including the divestment option. WNS, previously fully owned by British Airways, is a good example of a captive that its growth potential has been exploited by its parent firm. A business plan presented by the captive former general manager, which requested a significant investment from British Airways in order to finance its next growth spur, has been rejected by top management followed by the divestment of 70% stake in the captive in 2002. In taking this strategic decision, British Airways sought to extend the value its captive delivered by switching from ownership to an outsourcing contract with the acquiring party. General Electric (2005), AXA (2005), Citigroup (2008), Barclays (2007) and Nokia (2001) are additional examples in our sample where the parent firm had sought to benefit from the captive by replacing ownership with a long-term outsourcing contract.

We have also observed significant changes in terms of the functions offshored through the captive model since 1985. In particular, in Phases 3 and 4 there has been a significant decline in the number of BPO captive set-ups and a mild decline in the number of IT captive set-ups. Yet, we have observed an ongoing increase in the number of R&D captives over the entire period of this study. We explain the decline in IT and BPO start-ups by considering the maturity level of local IT and BPO vendors, in particular in India. In this regard, the IT vendor sector in India has achieved maturity much earlier than the BPO sector, explaining the fewer IT captive set-ups and the modest growth over years (and a decline in Phase 4). On the other hand, the maturity of the third-party BPO sector has only recently reached the level in which multinationals would consider relying on a vendor for BPO services as an alternative to the BPO captive option. In this respect, the maturity of the third-party BPO sector acted as a disruptive factor to divert multinationals from setting up and owning a captive centre to the contractual approach for services for fees.

Last but not least, we have also observed a decline in the number of captive start-ups in India during Phase 4 while other geographic locations such as Eastern Europe have become more attractive. We attribute the decline in India to both the attractiveness of other locations for certain functions, such as access to multilingual staff for customer support functions in Europe, as well as to the rising costs and other factors such as distance and time zone differences, which are challenging for multinationals. In this regard, some multinationals realized the relatively high management costs involved in coordinating work over distance and time zones to eventually decide to relocate their captive centres to near-shore locations such as Eastern Europe. Two prominent examples are Dell and Maersk that migrated their customer support operations from India and China, respectively, to their domestic markets.

Conclusion

The case of offshore captive centres presents a challenging setting for extant country selection frameworks. While existing country selection frameworks inform multinationals about the considerations for setting up their captive centres, the existing literature is rather silent about the consequent changes, perceiving the captive centre set-up to be a single-dimension decision. In this paper we sought to shed light on the development of the captive centre sector by first documenting the changes that took place in this sector and second examining whether changes in captive centre settings could be explained by extant country selection frameworks. Our contribution to the IS outsourcing literature is twofold: First, we provide a detailed account of captive centre investments pursued by Fortune 250 global firms. This historical review provides an insight into the key considerations that led multinationals change their offshoring decisions. Indeed, while the outsourcing literature has predominantly focused on understanding offshoring investments from the supply side (Gospel and Sako 2010), this study included also the demand side by considering the actual investments made by multinationals as a response to certain attractive country resources. Our second contribution is in the extension of existing country selection frameworks that have tended to be rather static, mainly focusing on the current offshoring conditions in a specific country, while providing little guidance regarding the possibility to make changes in the initial offshoring investment. In this regard, we propose to extend existing country selection frameworks (Carmel and Tija 2005; Farrell 2006) by considering *disruptive* factors along with facilitating factors for those occasions when managers revisit their initial offshoring decisions.

From a practical viewpoint, while the professional and academic literature is by and large implying that a captive investment is a single-dimension decision that does not require an update over time (Aron and Singh 2005; Levina 2006), evidence presented above suggests that the captive centre sector has undergone significant changes in terms of the preferred location for captive investments, the functions offshored through captives and even the mode of setting up captives. We therefore argue that managers need to assess their initial offshore captive investment in terms of functions offshored, preferred location and the optimal captive model, every 3–5 years. In such an assessment, managers should be looking for disruptive events in the current settings of the captive such as the maturity of the service offered by a third-party vendor as an alternative for the current setting by a wholly owned captive as well as disruptive factors that may improve the attractiveness of an alternative location or captive model. The outcome of such assessment exercises should inform managers whether a migration of the captive to a new location will potentially result in better returns on the offshoring investment or changing the captive model from a basic to a shared may allow the captive to grow and become a source of expansion in this region.

As the study of captive centre is in its infancy, there are numerous opportunities for researchers to advance our understanding of the phenomenon at the sector and firm level. At sector level, the captive models (Oshri 2011) used in this paper have been developed based on several case studies dated 2010. Additional contemporary studies are needed to examine current captive models and the value they bring to the parent firm. Further, as multinationals embark on designing their global business service organization by considering disruptive factors that will drive them to relocate certain activities, research needs to model and test the effect of factors mentioned in this paper on captive migration decisions. At the firm level, changes in the destiny of a captive from basic to shared or from basic to hybrid may result in tension between the captive and the parent firm. Research has so far fallen short from understanding the governance structure between the captive and its parent firm and how such governing structure may best facilitate the success of the captive centre.

References

Apte, S., Mccarthy, J., Ross, C., Bartolomey, F., and Thresher, A. (2007). Shattering the Offshore Captive Center Myth, [WWW document] http://www.forrester.com/Research/Document/Excerpt/0,7211,42059,00.html.

Aron, R. (2002). *Business Processes Are Moving from the West to other Parts of the World, Knowledge@Wharton*, Pennsylvania: University of Pennsylvania.

Aron, R., and Singh, J.V. (2005). Getting Offshoring Right, *Harvard Business Review* **83**(12): 135–140.

Bierce, A., Spohr, S, and Shah, R (2004). Captive No More, *Executive Agenda* 7 (2): 5–10.

Carmel, E., and Tija, P. (2005). *Offshoring Information Technology*, Cambridge, UK: Cambridge University Press.

Contractor, J.F., Kumar, V., Kundu, S.K., and Pedersen, T. (2010). Reconceptualizing the Firm in a World of Outsourcing and Offshoring: The organizational and geographical relocation of high-value company functions, *Journal of Management Studies* **47**(2): 1417–1433.

Crosman, P (2008). Worldsourcers; While India still Rules the World of IT Offshoring, *Wall Street and Technology* **26**: 26–30.

Doh, J.P., Bunyaratavej, K., and Hahn, E.D. (2009). Separable but Not Equal: The location determinants of discrete services off shoring activities, *Journal of International Business Studies* **40**(6): 926–943.

Dossani, R., and Kenney, M. (2007). The Next Wave of Globalization: Relocating Service Provision to India, *Ideas* **35**(5): 772–791.

Ernst, D. (2006). Innovation Offshoring; Asia's Emerging Role in Global Innovation Networks, in http://Scholarspace.Manoa.Hawaii.Edu/Bitstream/10125/12531/3/Sr010.Pdf.Txt (ed.)East-West center Special report.

Farrell, D. (2005). Offshoring: Value creation through economic change, *Journal of Management Studies* **42**(3): 675–682.

Farrell, D. (2006). Smarter Offshoring, *Harvard Business Review* **84**(6): 84–92.

Friedman, T.L. (2005). *The World Is Flat: A brief history of the twenty-first century*, New York: Farrar: Straus and Giroux.

Goolsby, K. (2010). Part I–trends in offshore captive services centres: interview of Everest Research Institute's Salil Dani, Outsourcing Buzz Blog, 10th February 2010, [WWW document] http://www.outsourcing-buzz-blog. com/2010/02/interview_of_ev.html.

Gospel, H., and Sako, M. (2010). The Unbundling of Corporate Functions: The evolution of shared services and outsourcing in human resource management, *Industrial and Corporate Change* 19(5): 1–30.

Joshi, K., and Mudigonda, S. (2008). An analysis of India's future attractiveness as an offshore destination for IT and IT-enabled services, *Journal of Information Technology* 23(4): 215–227.

Kearney, A.T. (2004). *Making Offshore Decisions: A.T. Kearney's 2004 offshore location Attractiveness index*. [WWW document] http://kdi.mscmalaysia.my/ static/reports/AT%20Kearney%202004%20Report.pdf (accessed 20 October 2012).

Kearney, A.T. (2007). Offshoring for Long-term Advantage: The 2007 A.T. Kearney global services location index, Chicago. [WWW document] http:// www.atkearney.com/documents/10192/e604b639-2925-4a44-9a15- a872b9729407 (accessed 20 October 2012).

Kotlarsky, J., and Oshri, I. (2008). Country attractiveness for offshoring and offshore-outsourcing, *Journal of Information Technology* 23(4): 228–231.

Lacity, M.C., Khan, S., Yan, A., and Willcocks, L.P. (2010). A Review of the IT Outsourcing Empirical Literature and Future Research Directions, *Journal of Information Technology* 25(4): 395–433.

Lampel, J., and Bhalla, A. (2008). Embracing Realism and Recognizing Choice in IT Offshoring Initiatives, *Business Horizons* 51(5): 429–440.

Levina, N. (2006). In or Out in an Offshore Context: The choice between captive centers and third-party vendors, *Cutter IT Journal* 19(12): 24–28.

Lewin, A., and Couto, V. (2007). Next Generation Offshoring: The globalization of innovation, CIBER/Booz Allen Hamilton Report. Durham: Duke University.

Lewin, A.Y., Massini, S., and Peeters, C. (2009). Why Are Companies Offshoring Innovation? The Emerging Global Race for Talent, *Journal of International Business Studies* 40(6): 901–925.

Manning, S., Massini, S., and Lewin, A. (2008). A Dynamic Perspective of Next-Generation Offshoring; The Global Sourcing of Science and Engineering Talent, *Academy of Management Perspectives* 22(3): 35–54.

Metters, R., and Verma, R. (2007). History of Offshoring Knowledge Services, *Journal of Operations Management* **26**(2): 141–147.

Mordecai, A. (2006). Anti-offshoring Legislation: The new wave of protectionism. The backlash against foreign outsourcing of American service jobs, *Richmond Journal of Global Law and Business* **4**(10): 85–105.

Nassimbeni, G., and Sartor, M. (2008). *Sourcing in India; Strategies and Experiences in the Land of Service Offshoring*, New York, NY: Palgrave Macmillan.

Oshri, I., Kotlarsky, J., and Liew, C.M. 2008. Four Strategies for 'Offshore' Captive Centers. *Wall Street Journal* Business Insight section, R4

Oshri, I., Kotlarsky, J., Rottman, J.W., and Willcocks, L. (2009a). Global Outsourcing: Recent trends and issues, *Information Technology & People* **22** (3): 192–200.

Oshri, I., Kotlarsky, J., and Willcocks, L. (2009b). *The Handbook of Global Outsourcing and Offshoring*, London: Palgrave Macmillan.

Oshri, I. (2011). *Offshoring Strategies: Evolving captive center models*, Boston, MA: The MIT Press.

Rottman, J., and Lacity, M.C (2006). Proven Practices for Effectively Offshoring IT Work, *Sloan Management Review* **47**(3): 56–63.

Rutherford, B., and Mobley, S. (2005). The Next Wave: Refining the future of offshoring, *Journal of Corporate Real Estate* **7**(1): 87–95.

Youngdahl, W., Ramaswamy, K., and Dash, K. (2010). Service Offshoring: The evolution of offshore operations, *International Journal of Operations and Production Management* **30**(8): 798–799.

Ilan Oshri is a professor of Globalisation and Technology at Loughborough School of Business and Economics, UK. Oshri is the author and co-author of nine books and over 30 journal articles on global sourcing. He is also the cofounder of the Global Sourcing Workshop, Director of Research Centre for Global Sourcing and Services, and a regular contributor to professional magazines.

Bob van Uhm graduated from the CEMS programme at Rotterdam School of Management in 2011. He is currently junior client executive at Nielsen, The Netherlands.

14

Review of the Empirical Business Services Sourcing Literature: An Update and Future Directions

Mary C. Lacity, Shaji A. Khan and Aihua Yan

Introduction

During the last few decades, researchers from information systems, business strategy, international business, and economics have examined the sourcing of business process (BP) and information technology (IT) services. Sourcing remains an important issue to study because the market continues to grow in size. Gartner, for example, estimated that the combined global information technology outsourcing (ITO) and business process outsourcing (BPO) markets were worth US$373 billion

M.C. Lacity (✉)
University of Missouri, College of Business Administration, Saint Louis, Missouri, USA
e-mail: Mary.Lacity@umsl.edu

S.A. Khan · A. Yan
College of Business, City University of Hong Kong, Tat Chee Ave, Hong Kong
e-mail: shajikhan@umsl.edu; aihuayan@cityu.edu.hk

© The Author(s) 2017   499
L.P. Willcocks et al. (eds.), *Outsourcing and Offshoring Business Services*, DOI 10.1007/978-3-319-52651-5_14

in 2011 and $424 billion in 2014, with a compound annual growth rate of 4.4% (auriga.com/blog/outsourcing-industry-experts-gathered-in-the-city-of-the-eternal-spring/). Another consulting firm, Horses for Sources, sized the 2013 combined ITO and BPO market at $952 billion (www.horsesforsources.com/hfs-index-q12013_02221), over twice as large as Gartner's size estimate.

As academic research kept pace with the market growth through an increasing number of studies, reviews of the literature were conducted to summarize the results, mostly on IT sourcing decisions (e.g., Dibbern et al., 2004; Fjermestad and Saitta, 2005; Mahnke et al., 2005). Two reviews stand out for using the same method so that ITO and BPO research results could be compared (Lacity, Khan, Yan, & Willcocks, 2010; Lacity, Solomon, Yan, & Willcocks, 2011). The 2010 *Journal of Information Technology* (*JIT*) article, 'A Review of the IT Outsourcing Empirical Literature and Future Research Directions', analyzed 741 findings on the determinants of ITO decisions and outcomes from 164 empirical articles published between 1992 and 2010. Using the same coding method, the 2011 *JIT* article, 'Business Process Outsourcing Studies: A Critical Review and Research Directions', analyzed 615 findings on the determinants of BPO decisions and outcomes from 67 empirical articles published between 1996 and 2011. Both ITO and BPO research reviews found that the major categories of the determinants of sourcing decisions and outcomes for IT and BP services were similar (Lacity, Khan, Yan, & Willcocks, 2010; Lacity, Solomon, Yan, & Willcocks, 2011). The main differences between the research streams occurred at the level of specific independent variables within each broad category. Researchers have recently included both IT and BP services within single studies (e.g., Mann et al., 2011; Freytag et al., 2012; Narayanan and Narasimhan, 2014). For this paper, we therefore pooled the sourcing of IT and BP into the broader category we called 'business services'. Business services include, but are not limited to, financial and accounting, human resources, procurement, research and development (R&D), call centers/customer service, software development, software support, infrastructure management services, systems integration services, and legal services.

Elaborating on the results from the two prior *JIT* reviews, Lacity, Khan, Yan, and Willcocks (2010) and Lacity, Solomon, Yan, and Willcocks

(2011) found that ITO and BPO *decisions* were both determined by the broad categories of sourcing motivations (e.g., cost reduction and access to skills), transaction attributes (e.g., criticality of the service), and client firm attributes (e.g., prior performance). As noted above, the main differences occurred at the level of specific independent variables within each broad category. The *JIT* reviews examined research results on simple 'make or buy' decisions (Williamson, 1975), also called 'insourcing or outsourcing' decisions. Lacity, Khan, Yan, and Willcocks (2010) and Lacity, Solomon, Yan, and Willcocks (2011) also reviewed studies that examined hybrid modes (Williamson, 1991), degrees of outsourcing (e.g., Koh *et al.*, 2004), and offshoring (e.g., Dutta and Roy, 2005). The authors also reviewed research on how organizations made renewal decisions when initial outsourcing contracts were about to expire, including sourcing decisions that led to resigning with the incumbent provider, switching providers, and backsourcing (e.g., Whitten and Leidner, 2006). As the JIT reviews, has research continued to study the same sourcing decisions and continued to find the same determinants, or have new insights emerged? More formally, we ask the first two research questions:

RQ1: What has the recent empirical academic literature found about the determinants of sourcing *decisions* for business services?

RQ2: How do recent findings compare with previous findings?

The two *JIT* reviews also reviewed studies on sourcing *outcomes*, such as identifying the determinants of client satisfaction (e.g., Levina and Ross, 2003), service quality (e.g., Park and Kim, 2005), and business impact (e.g., Agarwal *et al.*, 2006). Lacity, Khan, Yan, and Willcocks (2010) and Lacity, Solomon, Yan, and Willcocks (2011) found that outcomes were determined by similar categories of independent variables. Transaction attributes (e.g., uncertainty), contractual governance (e.g., contract detail), relational governance (e.g., knowledge sharing), client firm capabilities (e.g., the ability to manage providers), and provider firm capabilities (e.g., human resource management) determined sourcing outcomes in both reviews (Lacity, Khan, Yan, & Willcocks, 2010; Lacity, Solomon, Yan, & Willcocks, 2011). Again, the main differences occurred at the level of specific independent variables within each broad category. Since the *JIT* reviews, has research continued to study the same sourcing outcomes and continued to find the same determinants, or have new insights emerged? More formally, we ask

RQ3: What has the recent empirical academic literature found about the determinants of sourcing *outcomes* for business services?
RQ4: How do recent findings compare with previous findings?

One purpose of a traditional literature review is to develop an argument that certain areas or topics warrant further research (Boell and Cecez-Kecmanovic, 2015). The two previous *JIT* reviews addressed a number of gaps in knowledge, leading to the research question:

RQ5: What progress has been made on previously recognized gaps in knowledge?

To answer the first five research questions, we investigated the most current research on sourcing decisions and outcomes for business services. This updated review of the published research began where the previous *JIT* reviews had stopped, which was the 1st quarter of 2010 for the ITO review (Lacity, Rottman, & Khan, 2010) and the 2nd quarter of 2011 for the BPO review (Lacity *et al.*, 2011). In this update, we examined 174 new empirical Business Services Sourcing (BSS) articles across 78 academic journals spanning a multitude of disciplines and published between the 2nd quarter of 2010 and 2014.

The remainder of this paper is structured as follows. First, we explain the research method, which is identical to the previous *JIT* reviews so we could compare the results to answer research questions 2, 4, and 5 (Lacity, Khan, Yan, & Willcocks, 2010; Lacity, Solomon, Yan, & Willcocks, 2011). Then, we answer the first five research questions by using the coded findings. Overall, this review found a proliferation in the types of sourcing decisions covered and a richer picture of the independent variables that affected sourcing decisions and outcomes. While researchers continued to study traditional sourcing decisions like make-or-buy, offshoring, and renewal decisions, they also explored new sourcing decisions including captive centers (e.g., Oshri and Van Uhm, 2012), shared services (e.g., McKeen and Smith, 2011), impact sourcing (Lacity *et al.*, 2014), and rural sourcing (Lacity, Rottman, & Khan, 2010). Besides answering the first five questions, we also present additional findings that were exceptionally interesting in a discussion section. We discuss, for example, the overall 'batting averages' of outsourcing relationships and the global expansion of research to include clients from 23 countries and providers from 34 countries. We also highlight fascinating research that showed the complex and oscillating interplay between contractual and relational governance that contradicts previous research. Much work has been done, but as the sourcing of business services changes so much in practice, there is much more research to do. Therefore, our final question is

RQ6: What are promising areas for future research?

To answer this, we examine pressing practitioner challenges, like the roles of sourcing clients, providers, and advisors who have to protect our world and to uplift its inhabitants. Finally, we conclude with an overall summary of findings and identify the limitations and contributions of this review.

Research Method

We followed the method used in Lacity, Khan, Yan, and Willcocks (2010) and Lacity, Solomon, Yan, and Willcocks (2011) to find publications, code, analyze, and present findings. We conducted keyword searches in the ABI Inform, EBSCOHost, JSTOR, and Science Direct databases restricting the publication dates to be within the year 2010 and after. Through cursory examination of many hundreds of search results, we identified an initial pool of 386 journal articles. As the coding process progressed, we conducted manual searches to include articles published after our initial searches until the end of year 2014. These manual searches resulted in an additional 42 articles making the pool of articles examined at 428 articles. Through more careful examination of these articles, we eliminated 254 articles which did not directly pertain to sourcing, were not empirical, or were considered in the previous *JIT* reviews. Thus, this review is based on a final set of 174 articles (see Table 14.1).

Coded Articles

The final set of papers includes 92 IT sourcing studies, 54 BP sourcing studies, and 28 studies that examined sourcing for both types of services (see Table 14.1). These studies crossed disciplines and were published in 78 refereed journals from the disciplines of management, information systems, marketing, economics, and supply chain management. As in the prior *JIT* reviews, we examined and coded qualitative (73 studies), quantitative (96 studies), and mixed-methods (5 studies) research. Further, we coded articles based on whether an article was from the 'client' perspective (111 studies), 'provider' perspective (31 studies), or both perspectives (32 studies).

Coding Variables

We first created a relational database of all the 174 articles. In order to aggregate findings across studies and to abstract the particular variables used within studies at a higher level, we drew upon master codes of variables used in Lacity, Khan, Yan, and Willcocks (2010) and Lacity, Solomon, Yan, and Willcocks (2011) as a starting point. Using variables and descriptions from these prior reviews helped to keep findings from this review comparable to the prior reviews and to extent codes as applicable. Whenever we observed new concepts and variables (that were not part of existing master code lists), we iteratively added variables to our list.

In total, we coded 219 variables, of which 150 (68%) were used in the prior *JIT* reviews. However, we renamed some variables used in Lacity, Khan, Yan, and Willcocks (2010) and Lacity, Solomon, Yan, and Willcocks (2011) to reflect the progression of outsourcing practice. For example, we now use the term 'provider' instead of 'supplier' or 'vendor'. Thus, we renamed variables like 'supplier size' and 'supplier reputation' to 'provider size' and 'provider reputation' in this update. Because we combined IT and BP services under the generic term 'business services', we also renamed some

Table 14.1 Empirical research base

Publication name	Year of publication						Study methods Qualitative: L Quantitative: T Mixed: M			
	2010	2011	2012	2013	2014	Total	L	T	M	Total
1 Administrative Science Quarterly				1		1		1		1
2 Business Horizons					1	1			1	1
3 California Management Review	1					1	1			1
4 Clinical Governance				1		1	1			1
5 Communications of the ACM	2	1				3	2	1		3
6 Communications of the AIS	1	3			1	5	4	1		5
7 Computers & Security					1	1			1	1
8 Creativity and Innovation Management					1	1		1		1
9 Decision Sciences	2				1	3		3		3
10 Decision Support Systems		1	1			2	1	1		2
11 Economics of Innovation & New Technology				1		1		1		1
12 European Journal of Information Systems	2					2		2		2
13 European Management Journal		1	1			2	2			2
14 Expert Systems					1	1	1			1
15 Human Resource Development International					1	1		1		1
16 Human Resource Management Journal					1	1	1			1
17 Human System Management	1					1	1	1		1
18 IEEE Transaction on Engineering Management		6		1		7	4	3		7
19 Industrial & Corporate Change		1				1	1			1
20 Industrial Management & Data Systems			1			1	1			1

(continued)

(continued)

	Publication name	Year of publication						Study methods Qualitative: L Quantitative: T Mixed: M			
		2010	2011	2012	2013	2014	Total	L	T	M	Total
21	Industrial Marketing Management	1	2	1		1	5	4	1		5
22	Industrial Relations Journal	1					1	1			1
23	Industry & Innovation	3			1		4	1	3		4
24	Information & Management				1	2	3		3		3
25	Information and Software Technology		1	1			2	1	1		2
26	Information Resources Management Journal			1			1		1		1
27	Information Systems Frontier	1		2			3	2	1		3
28	Information Systems Journal				1	2	3	3			3
29	Information Systems Management	1	1	1			3	2	1		3
30	Information Systems Research	3	1			1	5		5		5
31	Information Technology & People				1		1		1		1
32	Information Technology Management			1			1	1			1
33	Intelligent Systems in Accounting, Finance and Management					1	1	1			1
34	International Journal of Accounting Information Systems	1		1			2		2		2
35	International Journal of Business and Management			1			1		1		1
36	International Journal of Human Resource Management		1				1		1		1
37	International Journal of Information Management				1		1		1		1

No.	Journal						Total
38	International Journal of Innovation Management				1		1
39	International Journal of Management					2	2
40	International Journal of Management & Information Systems	1			1		1
41	International Journal of Public Administration	1		1	1		1
42	Journal of Applied Business Research					1	1
43	Journal of Computer Information Systems					1	1
44	Journal of Global Information Technology Management	2				2	2
45	Journal of Information Systems and Technology Management		1	1	1	1	1
46	Journal of Information Technology	2			1	1	2
47	Journal of Information Technology Case and Application Research	2			2		2
48	Journal of Information Technology Theory and Application			1	1		1
49	Journal of International Business Studies	1	1			2	2
50	Journal of International Management	2	2		1	2	3
51	Journal of Management Information Systems	4	2	2	2	8	10
52	Journal of Management Research		1		1		1
53	Journal of Management Studies	1			1	1	1
54	Journal of Operations Management	2		2		4	4
55	Journal of Purchasing and Supply Management		2		2	2	2
56	Journal of Strategic Information Systems	2	1	2		3	5
57	Journal of Supply Chain Management	1		1		1	2
58	Journal of the Association for Information Systems	1	1			1	1

(continued)

(continued)

Publication name	Year of publication						Study methods *Qualitative: L Quantitative: T Mixed: M*			
	2010	2011	2012	2013	2014	Total	L	T	M	Total
59 Journal of World Business					1	1	1			1
60 Management International Review		2	1			3		3		3
61 Management Science	1					1		1		1
62 MIS Quarterly			1	3	1	5	1	4		5
63 MIS Quarterly Executive	2	1				3	3			3
64 Organizacija				1		1		1		1
65 Organization Science	2		3			5	3	2		5
66 Organizational Dynamics		1				1	1			1
67 Personnel Review		1				1		1		1
68 Production and Operations Management		1		1		2		2		2
69 Project Management Journal		1	1			2		2		2
70 Qualitative Research in Accounting and Management				1		1	1			1
71 R&D Management		1				1		1		1
72 Research Policy					1	1		1		1
73 Review of Development Economics		1				1		1		1
74 Service Business	2			1		3	2		1	3
75 Skyline Business Journal				1		1	1			1
76 Strategic Management Journal	1	1	2	1		5		5		5
77 Strategic Outsourcing: An International Journal	5	4	3	1	1	14	8	4	2	14
78 Technology Analysis & Strategic Management	1					1	1			1
Grand total	48	43	35	22	26	174	73	96	5	174

	Study perspectives Clients: C Providers: P Both: C/P				Type of business service Business processes: BP Information technology: IT Both: IT and BP combined			
	C	P	C/P	Total	BP	IT	Both	Total
1 Administrative Science Quarterly		1		1	1			1
2 Business Horizons	1			1	1			1
3 California Management Review	1			1	1			1
4 Clinical Governance	1			1	1			1
5 Communications of the ACM	2		1	3	1	1	1	3
6 Communications of the AIS	3	2		5	1	3	1	5
7 Computers & Security			1	1		1		1
8 Creativity and Innovation Management	1			1	1			1
9 Decision Sciences	2		1	3		1	2	3
10 Decision Support Systems	2			2		1	1	2
11 Economics of Innovation & New Technology	1			1	1			1
12 European Journal of Information Systems	1	1		2		2		2
13 European Management Journal	2			2	1		1	2
14 Expert Systems	1			1		1		1
15 Human Resource Development International	1			1	1			1
16 Human Resource Management Journal	1			1	1			1
17 Human System Management	1			1		1		1
18 IEEE Transaction on Engineering Management	4	2	1	7		6	1	7
19 Industrial & Corporate Change		1		1			1	1
20 Industrial Management & Data Systems	1			1		1		1
21 Industrial Marketing Management	1	2	2	5	3		2	5
22 Industrial Relations Journal		1		1	1			1
23 Industry & Innovation	4			4	2		2	4
24 Information & Management	3			3		3		3
25 Information and Software Technology	1	1		2		2		2

(continued)

Publication name	Study perspectives Clients: C Providers: P Both: C/P				Type of business service Business processes: BP Information technology: IT Both: IT and BP combined			
	C	P	C/P	Total	BP	IT	Both	Total
26 Information Resources Management Journal	2			2	1	1		2
27 Information Systems Frontier	2		1	3		3		3
28 Information Systems Journal	1		2	3		3		3
29 Information Systems Management	3			3		3		3
30 Information Systems Research	3		2	5		5		5
31 Information Technology & People			1	1		1		1
32 Information Technology Management	1			1		1		1
33 Intelligent Systems in Accounting, Finance and Management	1			1			1	1
34 International Journal of Accounting Information Systems	2			2		1	1	2
35 International Journal of Business and Management	1			1		1		1
36 International Journal of Human Resource Management		1		1	1			1
37 International Journal of Information Management		1		1		1		1
38 International Journal of Innovation Management			1	1		1		1
39 International Journal of Management	2			2		2		2
40 International Journal of Management & Information Systems	1			1	1			1
41 International Journal of Public Administration	1			1	1			1
42 Journal of Applied Business Research	1			1		1		1
43 Journal of Computer Information Systems	1			1		1		1
44 Journal of Global Information Technology Management	1	1		2		2		2

#	Journal					
45	Journal of Information Systems and Technology Management	1		1		1
46	Journal of Information Technology	2		1		2
47	Journal of Information Technology Case and Application Research	1	1	2		2
48	Journal of Information Technology Theory and Application	1		1		1
49	Journal of International Business Studies	2	1	1		2
50	Journal of International Management	2	2		1	3
51	Journal of Management Information Systems	5	3	7		10
52	Journal of Management Research	1		1		1
53	Journal of Management Studies	1	1			1
54	Journal of Operations Management	3	1		3	4
55	Journal of Purchasing and Supply Management	2	2			2
56	Journal of Strategic Information Systems	4		5		5
57	Journal of Supply Chain Management	2			1	2
58	Journal of the Association for Information Systems	1	1		1	1
59	Journal of World Business	2		1	1	1
60	Management International Review	2		1	2	3
61	Management Science	1		5		1
62	MIS Quarterly	2		1		5
63	MIS Quarterly Executive	1	1	1	1	3
64	Organizacija	1				1
65	Organization Science	5	2	3		5
66	Organizational Dynamics		1			1
67	Personnel Review	1	1			1
68	Production and Operations Management	1	1			2
69	Project Management Journal	1	1		1	2
70	Qualitative Research in Accounting and Management	1	1			1
71	R&D Management	1	1			1

(continued)

(continued)

Publication name	Study perspectives Clients: C Providers: P Both: C/P				Type of business service Business processes: BP Information technology: IT Both: IT and BP combined			
	C	P	C/P	Total	BP	IT	Both	Total
72 Research Policy	1			1	1			1
73 Review of Development Economics	1			1	1			1
74 Service Business	3			3	3			3
75 Skyline Business Journal		1		1		1		1
76 Strategic Management Journal	4		1	5	2	1	2	5
77 Strategic Outsourcing: An International Journal	5	3	6	14	6	5	3	14
78 Technology Analysis & Strategic Management	1			1	1			1
Grand total	111	31	32	174	54	92	28	174

Note: This table indicates the number of empirical research papers included in this review by publication name, year of publication, study methods, study perspectives, and type of business service studied variables as appropriate. For example, we renamed variables in Lacity *et al.* (2011) like 'process complexity' and 'process integration' to 'service complexity' and 'service integration'.

Appendix A lists the names and descriptions of the 219 variables used in this review to code individual studies, identifies the 69 new variables with an asterisk, and indicates any minor name changes as Lacity, Khan, Yan, and Willcocks (2010) and Lacity, Solomon, Yan, and Willcocks (2011).

Dependent Variables

We coded 105 unique variables that were used as dependent variables in the studies. Appendix B indicates the frequency with which each dependent variable was studied categorized by the type of business service studied (IT or BP or both). In total, we coded 1,304 relationships involving these 105 dependent variables. Among the 1,304 relationships, 731 (56%) examined IT services, 365 (28%) examined BP services, and 208 (16%) examined both. Rows in Appendix B indicate dependent variables grouped together by three of the broad categories used by Lacity, Khan, Yan, and Willcocks (2010) and Lacity, Solomon, Yan, and Willcocks (2011): dependent variables that examined sourcing outcomes (566 out of 1,304 relationships; 43%), dependent variables that examined sourcing decisions (383 out of 1,304 relationships; 29%), and a miscellaneous set of dependent variables that examined various outcomes such as effects of sourcing decisions on adaptability, provider employee turnover, and client power (191 out of 1,304 relationships; 15%).

In addition, we included two additional broad categories of dependent variables that examined relational governance (99 out of 1,304 relationships; 7.5%) and dependent variables that examined contractual governance (65 out of 1,304 relationships; 4.5%). In the previous *JIT* reviews, relational and contractual governance were independent variable categories but not dependent variable categories. Since the previous *JIT* reviews, research on how clients and providers govern relationships has become more prevalent and these two new categories were created to accommodate these developments.

Independent Variables

Appendix C lists the 203 variables that appeared as independent variables in the studies coded and the frequency with which they were broken down by the type of business service studied. The independent variables were grouped together into 16 broad categories, 14 of which were found in the previous *JIT* reviews (Lacity, Khan, Yan, & Willcocks, 2010; Lacity, Solomon, Yan, & Willcocks, 2011). The 16 broad categories are transaction attributes, relational governance, client firm characteristics, sourcing motivations, sourcing decisions, provider firm capabilities, client firm capabilities, contractual governance, country characteristics, provider firm characteristics, relationship characteristics, sourcing outcomes, environment, influences, decision characteristics, and employee level. The new categories are relationship characteristics and employee level. Relationship characteristics capture the attributes of the relationship between a client and provider that are broader than just a single transaction between them, such as the length of the relationship (e.g., Handley and Benton, 2012), client power (e.g., Rai *et al.*, 2012), and provider power (e.g., Barthélemy, 2011). The employee-level category includes practical intelligence (e.g., Langer *et al.*, 2014) and task variety (e.g., Sengupta and Gupta, 2011). In contrast to Lacity, Khan, Yan, and Willcocks (2010) and Lacity, Solomon, Yan, and Willcocks (2011), the various motivations to source are no longer the most frequently appearing independent variables in the relationships we coded. Instead, various variables in the transaction attributes were most prevalent.

Coding Direct Relationships

Following Lacity, Khan, Yan, and Willcocks (2010) and Lacity, Solomon, Yan, and Willcocks (2011), we coded the *nature* of the relationships between study variables as follows. A positive 'significant' relationship was coded as '+1', a negative relationship was coded as '−1', a 'not significant' relationship was coded as '0'. The code 'M' was used to indicate a relationship that 'mattered'. The 'M' code was needed because some significant relationships were categorical (i.e., not ordinal, interval, or continuous), but a relationship clearly mattered between the independent and dependent variable. For example, Langer *et al.* (2014) found that project type (maintenance *vs* new development) had significantly different effects on offshoring project success in terms of client satisfaction. The relationship between transaction type and offshore outsourcing success was, therefore, coded as 'M' for 'mattered'. Table 14.2 summarizes the coding schema.

The three authors coded articles individually and met weekly to discuss their codes. Once consensus was achieved for each relationship in terms of the variables, as well as the nature of the relationship, we recorded that relationship into our master database. After the first round of coding was completed, the second author then manually examined the codes to identify inconsistent codes and/or data entry errors. Any issues raised were resolved with input from all authors. This iterative process of assigning codes to the nature of the relationships and placing each study's particular variables into our broader coded variables resulted in a total of 1,304 relationships between 219 coded variables from 174 studies. At this level of detail, it is difficult to discern meaningful patterns because the number of dyadic relationships becomes unwieldy. Following Lacity, Khan, Yan, and Willcocks (2010) and Lacity, Solomon, Yan, and Willcocks (2011), we collapsed the dependent variables into five broader-dependent variable categories. Appendix D presents all the specific independent variables, as rows, sorted by frequency within each of the 16 independent variable categories. The five categories of dependent variables (1) sourcing outcomes, (2) sourcing decisions, (3) miscellaneous variables, (4) relational governance, and (5) contractual governance appear as column groupings sorted by total

Table 14.2 Coding schema for relationships

Relationship	Code	Meaning
Significant (Only P<0.05 for quantitative studies or strong argument by authors for qualitative studies coded as significant)	+1	Positive relationship between independent and dependent variable
	−1	Negative relationship
	M	A relationship between a categorical independent variable and a dependent variable mattered
Not significant	0	Relationship was studied and no significant relationship was found

frequency. For each relationship between the independent variables and dependent variable category as described above, cells indicate the frequency with which a relationship was found to be positive, negative, 'not significant', or whether it 'mattered' as described in Table 14.2.

Appendix D answers in detail the question: Which variables have BSS researchers studied most frequently and what have they found pertaining to the determinants of BSS decisions, outcomes, and governance? To facilitate a discussion of these findings, we created Fig. 14.1 by extracting the evidence from Appendix D in terms of *multiple examinations* of a relationship that produced *consistent results* by replicating the criteria used in the prior *JIT* reviews. In terms of multiple examinations, we replicated the decision rule to extract the relationships that have been examined by BSS researchers at least 5 times (Jeyaraj *et al.*, 2006; Lacity, Khan, Yan, & Willcocks, 2010; Lacity, Solomon, Yan, & Willcocks, 2011). In terms of consistent results, we also extracted variables in which at least 60% of the evidence was consistent. This minimum threshold ensures that more than half the evidence produced the same finding; it also follows the decision rule from prior *JIT* reviews for comparative purposes. We also wanted to identify the most robust findings and thus created a tiered legend. Consistent with Lacity, Khan, Yan, and Willcocks (2010) and Lacity, Solomon, Yan, and Willcocks (2011), we used double symbols (++, --, MM, 00) to indicate when more than 80% of the findings were consistent. We used single symbols (+, -, M, 0) when more than 60% and up to 80% of the findings were consistent. To be clear, double symbols indicate greater consistency among repeated findings across studies; they do not indicate the magnitude or strength of a particular relationship.

Specifically, for each of these independent variables, a '++' in parentheses next to the total frequency denotes that more than 80% of the relationships found a positive relationship with a particular dependent variable category (Lacity, Khan, Yan, & Willcocks, 2010; Lacity, Solomon, Yan, & Willcocks, 2011). Similarly, a '--' denotes that more than 80% of the relationships found a negative relationship. 'MM' accordingly suggests that more than 80% of the relationships found a categorical independent variable 'mattered' in terms of the dependent category. Finally, a '00' indicates that more than 80% of the relationships coded did not find any 'significant' relationship between the independent variable and dependent category. When only between 60% and 80% of the evidence (> = 60 and < = 80%) was consistent, we used single, '+', '–', 'M', and '0' to denote the respective relationships. All other total frequencies remain not highlighted, suggesting a lack of clear discernable pattern in terms of the nature of these relationships.

Findings on the Determinants of Sourcing Decisions

This section answers the first research question: What has the recent empirical academic literature found about the determinants of sourcing decisions for business services? We answered Question 1 using the criteria of at least 60% consistent findings from at least five examinations of a relationship between an independent variable and a sourcing decision (Lacity, Khan, Yan, & Willcocks, 2010; Lacity, Solomon, Yan, & Willcocks, 2011). Fig. 14.1 depicts the empirical evidence that meets these criteria. The figure captures 19 independent variables that affected sourcing decisions, organized by the 6 broad categories of transaction attributes, client firm characteristics, sourcing motivations, provider firm capabilities, client firm capabilities, and country characteristics. Each broad category and the independent variables within them are discussed below.

Transaction Attributes

Under the broad category 'transaction attributes', researchers sought to answer the question: Are there general attributes of business services that are more likely to influence sourcing decisions than others? In Fig. 14.1, five transaction attributes were examined at least 5 times and produced consistent results in the current review: transaction costs, knowledge formalization, service standardization, service complexity, and external production cost advantage.

Transaction costs are defined as the effort, time, and costs incurred to search, create, negotiate, monitor, and administer a business services contract between a client and provider (Williamson, 1991; Levina and Su,

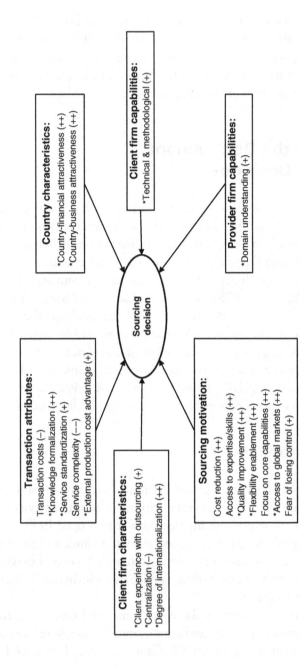

Fig. 14.1 The determinants of sourcing decisions. *Note:* *New variable since previous ITO and BPO review. More than 80% of the evidence was positively significant (++), negatively significant (−−), not significance (00), or mattered (MM); 60%–80% of the evidence was positively significant (+), negatively significant (−), not significance (0), or mattered (M).

2008). Transaction costs were examined 5 times in the current review. Three tests of the effects of transaction costs on sourcing decisions found that they were negatively associated with outsourcing and offshoring decisions, which is consistent with transaction cost economics (TCE) (e.g., Gonzalez *et al.*, 2010a; Gefen *et al.*, 2011; Dibbern *et al.*, 2012). Transaction costs were also found to be positively associated with the decision to create shared services in one relationship (Gefen *et al.*, 2011). One relationship found no association between transaction costs and sourcing decision (Dibbern *et al.*, 2012).

Knowledge formalization is the degree to which clients and providers can formalize/codify requirements (e.g., Aubert *et al.*, 2011). All six empirical examinations of knowledge formalization found that it was positively associated with decisions to outsource, both domestically (e.g., Whitaker *et al.*, 2010) and offshore (e.g., Dedrick *et al.*, 2011). For example, Whitaker *et al.* (2010) found that process formalization (which the authors call 'process codification') was significantly related to decisions to outsource business services, both on and offshore.

Service standardization is the degree to which a service is standard across users (e.g., Tate and Ellram, 2009). Examined 6 times, four empirical assessments found a positive relationship between service standardization and shared services (e.g., McIvor *et al.*, 2011), out-sourcing (e.g., Sako, 2010), and offshoring (e.g., Mudambi and Venzin, 2010). One case study found a negative association between service standardization and shared services (Sako, 2010). One study found no discernable relationship (Aubert *et al.*, 2012). *Service complexity* is the degree to which a service or project requires compound steps, the control of many variables, and/or where cause and effect are subtle and dynamic (e.g., Ventovuori and Lehtonen, 2006; Penfold, 2009). Among six empirical examinations, we coded five negative relationships between service complexity and outsourcing (e.g., Jain and Thietart, 2014), offshoring (e.g., Poston *et al.*, 2010), and degree of outsourcing (e.g., Aubert *et al.*, 2012). One study found no discernible relationship (Susarla *et al.*, 2010b).

External production cost advantage is the degree to which a provider is perceived to have an advantage over a client organization in production cost economies (e.g., Williamson, 1991; Rajeev and Vani, 2009). TCE suggests that the market's external production cost advantage should be positively associated with outsourcing decisions, and indeed four out of five empirical tests found that relationship (e.g., Dibbern *et al.*, 2012; Freytag *et al.*, 2012; Jain and Thietart, 2014). One study found that external production cost advantage was negatively associated with IT-shared services (Gefen *et al.*, 2011), which was also a consistent finding with TCE. Thus, clients tended to outsource services when providers had a production cost advantage and insourced (including shared services) when the client had the production cost advantage.

Client Firm Characteristics

Under this broad category, researchers sought to answer the question: Are certain types of clients more likely to make particular sourcing decisions for business services than others? In the current study, three client firm characteristics produced consistent results after repeated examinations: client experience with outsourcing, centralization, and the client's degree of internationalization.

Five empirical examinations out of seven found that a *client's prior experience with outsourcing* was positively associated with more outsourcing and more offshoring (e.g., Mayer *et al.*, 2012; Whitaker *et al.*, 2010; Mithas *et al.*, 2013). Two studies found no relationship (Alvarez-Suescun, 2010; Martins and Martins, 2012).

Centralization is the degree to which an organization's resources, services, or decision-making are concentrated within a particular group or location (e.g., Delmotte and Sels, 2008). Examined 5 times, centralization was negatively associated 4 times with outsourcing (e.g., Sako, 2010), multisourcing (e.g., Su and Levina, 2011), and shared services (e.g., Iveroth, 2010). One case study found that centralization was positively associated with shared services (Sako, 2010). These findings suggest that decentralized services were more likely to be outsourced or multisourced. Degree of centralization had mixed effects on shared services decisions depending on the case study (Sako, 2010).

A *client firm's degree of internationalization* is defined as the geographic reach of a client – local, regional, country, international, or global (e.g., Whitaker *et al.*, 2010). Researchers found 6 out of 7 times that higher levels of internationalization were positively associated with the creation of offshore captive centers (e.g., Martinez-Noya *et al.*, 2012) and with greater degrees of outsourcing (e.g., Whitaker *et al.*, 2010) and offshoring (e.g., Martinez-Noya *et al.*, 2012).

Sourcing Motivations

Under this broad category, researchers sought to answer the question: What are the main motives that drive sourcing decisions? In Fig. 14.1, seven sourcing motivations were examined at least 5 times and produced consistent results in the current review: cost reduction, access to expertise/skills, quality improvement, flexibility enablement, focus on core capabilities, access to global markets, and fear of losing control.

Cost reduction, a client organization's need or desire to reduce the costs of providing a service, was examined 22 times and 19 times it was found to be an important and positive motivation for all types of sourcing decisions including outsourcing (e.g., Gefen *et al.*, 2011), offshoring (e.g., Mudambi and Venzin, 2010), shared services (e.g., Amiruddin *et al.*, 2013), multisourcing (e.g., Su and Levina, 2011), captive centers (e.g., Angeli and Grimaldi, 2010), and rural sourcing (Lacity, Rottman, & Khan, 2010). One study found that cost reduction 'mattered' when selecting among different countries for offshoring (Martinez-Noya *et al.*, 2012). One study found that some clients outsourced even if it costs them more money when knowledge integration was the main objective (Jorgensen, 2010). One study of Spanish firms found that reducing costs did not matter (i.e., was insignificant) when sourcing R&D capabilities; lack of necessary resources and capabilities to enable the firm to carry out the activity effectively was the primary motive (Redondo-Cano and Canet-Giner, 2010). Overall, costs are a main driver of sourcing decisions, but clearly not the only motive as six other motives were also repeatedly found to be significant.

A client organization's desire or need to *access provider skills/expertise* was examined 19 times, and 17 times it positively drove all sorts of outsourcing decisions, including offshoring (Tambe and Hitt,

2010), multisourcing (e.g., Su and Levina, 2011), and impact sourcing (e.g., Sakolnakorn, 2011). Clients were also motivated by *quality improvement*, a client organization's desire or need to improve the quality of the client's business, processes, or capabilities. Examined 9 times, quality improvement positively motivated sourcing decisions 8 times (e.g., Premuroso *et al.*, 2012; Kuula *et al.*, 2013). *Flexibility enablement*, a client organization's desire or need to increase the flexibility of the use and allocation of resources for business services, was the fourth most frequently studied sourcing motivation and it was always found to be an important driver of sourcing decisions (e.g., Ceci and Masciarelli, 2010). There is also strong evidence that clients wished to *focus on core capabilities*, which led to offshoring or outsourcing noncore capabilities (e.g., Premuroso *et al.*, 2012). A client organization's desire or need to gain *access to global markets* by outsourcing to providers in those markets was another robust finding (e.g., Premuroso *et al.*, 2012). Finally, *fear of losing control* over the service was positively associated with backsourcing (e.g., Bhagwatwar *et al.*, 2011) and shared services (e.g., McKeen and Smith, 2011). Another way to interpret this finding is that fear of losing control led to insourcing decisions.

Provider Firm Capabilities

Under the broad category 'provider firm capabilities', researchers sought to answer the question: How do a provider's capabilities influence a client's sourcing decision? This particular question was not investigated often – researchers only investigated the question 11 times using five variables in the current review. Only a provider's domain understanding was examined at least 5 times and produced consistent results (see Fig. 14.1).

Domain understanding is the extent to which a provider has prior experience and/or understanding of the client organization's business and technical contexts, processes, practices, and requirements (e.g., Luo *et al.*, 2012). Three of the 5 times it was examined; domain understanding was positively associated with outsourcing (Bidwell,

2012; Mayer *et al.*, 2012) and offshoring decisions (Dedrick *et al.*, 2011). One study found a negative relationship between a provider's domain understanding and backsourcing decisions. Thus, four of the positively or negatively significant results are consistent; clients outsourced and offshored more when providers had strong domain understanding and one client backsourced accounting services when the provider was deemed to have had weak domain understanding (Maelah *et al.*, 2010).

Client Firm Capabilities

Under the broad category 'client firm capabilities', researchers sought to answer the question: How do a client's capabilities influence a client's sourcing decision? This question was examined 23 times using 8 independent variables. Only one independent variable – a client's technical and methodological capability – was examined enough times and produced consistent results to be included in Fig. 14.1.

A *client's technical and methodological capability* is defined as a client organization's level of maturity in terms of technical or process-related standards and best practices (e.g., Bardhan *et al.*, 2007). Examined 11 times, 7 times it was found that higher levels of a client's technical and methodological capability were associated with more offshoring (e.g., Dedrick *et al.*, 2011), outsourcing (e.g., McIvor *et al.*, 2011), and captive centers (e.g., Martinez-Noya *et al.*, 2012). Four studies found no relationship between a client's technical and methodological capability and decisions pertaining to domestic sourcing (e.g., Martinez-Noya *et al.*, 2012) and offshoring (e.g., Whitaker *et al.*, 2010).

Country Characteristics

Under the broad category 'country characteristics', researchers sought to answer the question: How does a country's characteristics influence sourcing decisions? In Fig. 14.1, two country characteristics were examined at least 5 times and produced consistent results in the current review: financial attractiveness and business attractiveness.

A *country's financial attractiveness* is the degree to which a country is attractive to outsourcing clients or providers because of favorable financial factors such as labor costs, taxes, regulatory, and other costs (e.g., Doh *et al.*, 2009; Malos, 2010). Examined 7 times, a country's financial attractiveness was always positively associated with decisions related to offshoring and country selection (e.g., Hahn and Bunyaratavej, 2010; Massini *et al.*, 2010).

A *country's business attractiveness* is the degree to which a country is attractive to outsourcing clients or providers because of favorable business environmental factors such as economic stability, political stability, cultural compatibility, infrastructure quality, security of intellectual property (IP) (e.g., Doh *et al.*, 2009; Malos, 2010). Examined 7 times, a country's business attractiveness was positively associated with decisions related to offshoring and country selection 6 times (e.g., Gonzalez *et al.*, 2010b; Hahn and Bunyaratavej, 2010).

In summary, 19 independent variables pertaining to transaction attributes, client firm characteristics, sourcing motivations, provider and client firm capabilities, and country characteristics were repeatedly examined and produced consistent effects on sourcing decisions in the current review. Next, we compare these results with the results from the prior *JIT* reviews (Lacity, Khan, Yan, & Willcocks, 2010; Lacity, Solomon, Yan, & Willcocks, 2011).

Comparison of Sourcing Decision Determinants with Prior Research

This section answers the second research question: How do recent findings on determinants of sourcing decisions compare with previous findings? To help communicate the answer to Question 2, we included an asterisk in Fig. 14.1, next to the new independent variables that had not previously met the inclusion criteria in the prior *JIT* reviews (Lacity, Khan, Yan, & Willcocks, 2010; Lacity, Solomon, Yan, & Willcocks, 2011). Among the 19 independent variables in Fig. 14.1, 13 are new. We also compare more detailed results from the current review with the ITO review and BPO review in Table 14.3.

Table 14.3 Comparison of findings on determinants of sourcing decisions

Broad IV category	Independent variable (IV)	ITO review (Lacity, Rottman, & Khan, 2010)	BPO review (Lacity et al., 2011)	This review
Transaction attributes	Transaction costs	−		−
	Knowledge formalization			++
	Service standardization		−	+
	Service complexity			−
	External production cost advantage			+
	Critical role of business service	−	−	
	Uncertainty	−		
	Risk	−		
Client firm characteristics	Client experience with outsourcing			+
	Centralization			−
	Degree of internationalization-client			++
	Prior firm performance-client		+	
	Department performance	−		
	Industry		0	
	Client firm age		0	
Sourcing motivations	Cost reduction	++	++	++
	Access to expertise/skills	++	++	++
	Quality improvement	++	++	++
	Flexibility enablement	++		++

(continued)

Table 14.3 (continued)

Broad IV category	Independent variable (IV)	ITO review (Lacity, Rottman, & Khan, 2010)	BPO review (Lacity et al., 2011)	This review
	Focus on core capabilities	++	++	++
	Access to global markets			++
	Fear of losing control	– –	+	
	Scalability		++	
	Rapid delivery		++	
	Concern for security/IP	–	– –	
	Political reasons	+		
	Technology upgrade	++		
Provider firm capabilities, client firm capabilities, country characteristics	Domain understanding			+
	Technical and methodological	++		+
	Country-financial attractiveness			++
	Country-business attractiveness			++
Influences	Mimetic	++		
Total significant IVs		14	12	19

Note: More than 80% of the evidence was positively significant (++), negatively significant (––), found no significance (00), or mattered (MM); 60–80% of the evidence was positively significant (+), negatively significant (–), found no significance (0), or mattered (M)

Each broad category and the significant independent variables from all three reviews are compared below.

Comparison of Transaction Attributes

How do the five important transaction attributes found in the current review compare with the prior *JIT* reviews? Table 14.3 helps to answer this question by listing all the transaction attributes that were examined at least 5 times and produced consistent results for all three reviews. Both this current review and the ITO review in Lacity, Rottman, and Khan, (2010) repeatedly found a negative relationship between *transaction costs* and outsourcing decisions. *Service complexity* was also negatively associated with outsourcing decisions in this current review and in the BPO review in Lacity *et al.* (2011).

Unlike the current review, the previous ITO and BPO reviews repeatedly found a negative relationship between the criticality of the service and outsourcing. *Criticality of service* is the degree to which a client organization views the business service as a critical enabler of business success (e.g., Klaas *et al.*, 2001; Wahrenburg *et al.*, 2006). In the current review, criticality of the service was studied 12 times, and results were mixed yet consistent. Results were mixed in that four findings reported a positive relationship, six findings reported a negative relationship, and two findings reported no significant relationship between criticality of service and sourcing decisions. However, when one examines the richness of the sourcing decisions studied in this current review, the mixed findings are consistent and make sense. The studies that found a positive relationship between criticality of the service and sourcing decisions were examining decisions to commercialize (e.g., Freytag *et al.*, 2012), create shared services (McKeen and Smith, 2011), or backsource (Freytag *et al.*, 2012). Thus, critical services were kept internally or exploited through commercialization. The studies that found a negative relationship examined outsourcing (e.g., Bidwell, 2012), multisourcing (e.g., Su and Levina, 2011), and offshoring decisions (e.g., Mudambi and Venzin, 2010). Thus, non-critical services were more likely to be outsourced.

Uncertainty, defined as the degree of unpredictability or volatility of future states as it relates to the definition of requirements, emerging technologies, and/or environmental factors (Williamson, 1991; Mani *et al.*, 2010), was studied 12 times in the current review and results were mixed and inconsistent. Unlike the ITO review that consistently found a negative relationship between uncertainty and sourcing decisions, the current review found the following: Half of the studies found no relationship (e.g., Mithas *et al.*, 2013). Three studies found a negative relationship between uncertainty and outsourcing (e.g., Weigelt and Sarkar, 2012), and offshoring (e.g., Poston *et al.*, 2010). Two studies found a positive relationship between uncertainty and outsourcing (Barthélemy, 2011; Aubert *et al.*, 2012).

Comparison of Client Firm Characteristics

Table 14.3 compares the client firm characteristics found in this current review with the prior *JIT* reviews (Lacity, Khan, Yan, & Willcocks, 2010; Lacity, Solomon, Yan, & Willcocks, 2011). While the broad category of client firm characteristics was evidenced across all three reviews, there was no overlap at the level of independent variables. Interestingly, the ITO review found that 'unhealthy' client firms were more likely to outsource IT than 'healthy' firms but the BPO review found that 'healthy' client firms were more likely to outsource BPs than 'unhealthy' firms. Specifically, the ITO view found that *poor IS department performance* was positively related to outsourcing decisions – a situation practitioner's sometimes called 'outsource your mess for less' (e.g., Strassmann, 1995). Department performance is defined and measured as a CXO's, CEO's, or organizational members' perceptions of the function's performance or competence (e.g., Klaas *et al.*, 2001). In contrast, the BPO review found that good *financial performance* was positively associated with the outsourcing of BPs (e.g., Dunbar and Phillips, 2001). Client firm performance was usually measured as net profits, return on assets, expenses, earnings per share, number of patents, and/or stock price prior to an outsourcing decision (e.g., Dunbar and Phillips, 2001; Gilley *et al.*, 2004). In the current review, prior firm performance was assessed 2 times and all

3 times it was not found to be a significant determinant of sourcing decisions (e.g., Spithoven and Teirlinck, 2015). Also in the current review, department performance was examined 4 times as a determinant of sourcing decisions. Twice it was found to be not significant (e.g., Ali and Green, 2012) and twice it was negatively associated with outsourcing (e.g., Blaskovich and Mintchik, 2011).

Comparison of Sourcing Motivations

Table 14.3 compares the sourcing motivations found in this current review with the prior *JIT* reviews (Lacity, Khan, Yan, & Willcocks, 2010; Lacity, Solomon, Yan, & Willcocks, 2011). *All three reviews found robust and consistent evidence that sourcing decisions were motivated by a client's desire to reduce costs, assess expertise and skills, improve service quality, and focus on core capabilities.* The ITO review found a negative relationship between *fear of losing control* and sourcing decisions (e.g., Patane and Jurison, 1994) while the current review found a positive relationship. However, the different findings in the current review and the ITO review are consistent and make sense: Clients who feared losing control outsourced less (as found in the ITO review) and backsourced and created internal shared services more (as found in the current review).

We also note that the current review found some evidence that the other motivations found in prior *JIT* reviews such as *scalability, rapid delivery, concern for security and IP*, and *technical upgrades* were found to motivate sourcing decisions, but these motivations were not examined at least 5 times in the current review. (See Appendix A for definitions.) Perhaps after repeated tests, the current list of sourcing motivations will become quite extensive.

Comparison of Provider Firm Capabilities

Neither the ITO review nor the BPO review tested any independent variable associated with provider firm capabilities at least 5 times with consistent results, so the broad category 'provider firm capabilities' was not included as a determent of sourcing decisions in Lacity, Khan, Yan, and Willcocks (2010) and Lacity, Solomon, Yan, and Willcocks (2011). Pertaining to the specific prior examinations of *domain understanding*, two studies in the ITO review and one study in the BPO review examined the relationship between domain understanding and a sourcing decision and all three were positive (Lacity, Khan, Yan, & Willcocks, 2010; Lacity, Solomon, Yan, & Willcocks, 2011).

Comparison of Client Firm Capabilities

Neither the ITO review nor the BPO review tested any independent variable associated with client firm capabilities at least 5 times with consistent results, so the broad category 'client firm capabilities' was not included as a determent of sourcing decisions in Lacity, Khan, Yan, and Willcocks (2010) and Lacity, Solomon, Yan, and Willcocks (2011). Pertaining to the specific prior examinations of a *client's technical and methodological capability*, three studies in the ITO review and one study in the BPO review examined the variable's effects on sourcing decisions. Results in the prior reviews were mixed: Two studies found a positive relationship, one study found a negative relationship, and one found that the client's capability 'mattered' (Lacity, Khan, Yan, & Willcocks, 2010; Lacity, Solomon, Yan, & Willcocks, 2011).

Comparison of Country Characteristics

Neither the ITO review nor the BPO review included tests of any independent variable associated with country characteristics at least 5 times with consistent results; so 'country characteristics' was not included as a broad category that determined sourcing decisions in Lacity, Khan, Yan, and Willcocks (2010) and Lacity, Solomon, Yan, and Willcocks (2011). In the ITO review, no studies examined the relationship between any country characteristics and sourcing decisions (Lacity, Rottman, & Khan, 2010). The BPO review included four studies of a *country's financial attractiveness* and all were positively associated with sourcing decisions. Three BPO studies examined a *country's business attractiveness*, with one finding reporting no significant relationship, one finding a positive relationship, and one relationship that 'mattered' (Lacity *et al.*, 2011).

Comparison of Influence Sources

As a broad category, the ITO review included, 'influence sources' as a determinant of sourcing decisions. Influence sources as a broad category ask the question: What sources influence a client's sourcing decision? The theory of Institutional Isomorphism posits that firms may experience three types of influences: mimetic, normative, and coercive (DiMaggio and Powell, 1991). *Mimetic influence* was the only independent variable in the ITO review studied at least 5 times and produced consistent results (Lacity, Rottman, & Khan, 2010). Influences that arose from the perception that peer organizations were more successful were found to positively and significantly affect IT outsourcing decisions every time it was examined (e.g., Loh and Venkatraman, 1992; Pinnington and Woolcock, 1995; Ang and Cummings, 1997; Benamati and Rajkumar, 2002). In the current review, mimetic influences were examined 4 times with mixed results. Mimetic influences were positively significant twice (Mudambi and Venzin, 2010; Khan and Lacity, 2012), insignificant once (Blaskovich and Mintchik, 2011), and mattered once (Manning *et al.*, 2010).

In summary, the current review and the previous *JIT* reviews repeatedly and consistently found that sourcing decisions were determined by transaction attributes, client firm characteristics, and sourcing motivations. The current review also found that provider capabilities and client capabilities affected sourcing decisions. For a more detailed analysis of the comparisons across studies, please see the section 'Comparison to previously studied determinants of sourcing decisions' in the Conclusion.

Findings on Sourcing Outcomes

In this section, we answer the third research question: What has the recent empirical academic literature found about the determinants of sourcing outcomes for business services? Again, we answered Question 3 using the criteria of at least 60% consistent findings from at least five examinations of a relationship between an independent variable and a sourcing outcome. Fig. 14.2 depicts the empirical evidence that meets

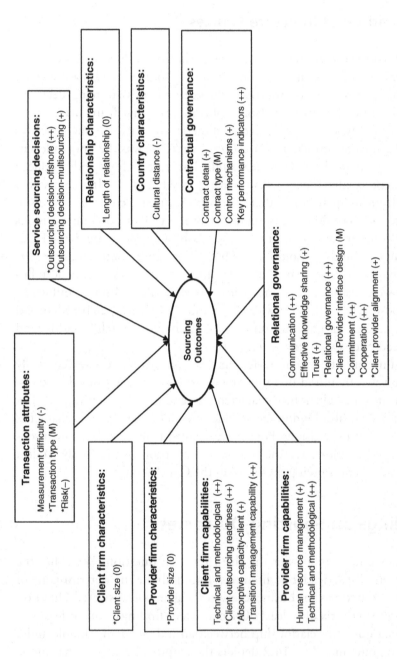

Fig. 14.2 The determinants of sourcing outcomes *Note:* *New variable since previous ITO and BPO review. More than 80% of the evidence was positively significant (++), negatively significant (--), not significance (00), or mattered (MM); 60–80% of the evidence was positively significant (+), negatively significant (-), not significance (0), or mattered (M).

these criteria. The figure captures 27 independent variables that have affected sourcing outcomes, organized by the broad categories of transaction attributes, relational governance, client firm characteristics, sourcing decisions, provider firm capabilities, client firm capabilities, contractual governance, country characteristics, provider firm characteristics, and relationship characteristics. Each broad category and the independent variables within them are discussed below.

Transaction Attributes

Under the broad category 'transaction attributes', researchers sought to answer the question: Are there general attributes of business services that are more likely to influence sourcing outcomes than others? In Fig. 14.2, three transaction attributes were examined at least 5 times and produced consistent results in the current review: measurement difficulty, transaction type, and risk.

Measurement difficulty is the degree of difficulty in measuring the performance of exchange partners in circumstances of joint effort, soft outcomes, and/or ambiguous links between effort and performance (e.g., Tate and Ellram, 2009). Examined 8 times, 5 times measurement difficulty was negatively associated with outsourcing outcomes for both clients (e.g., Rai et al., 2012) and providers (e.g., Vitasek and Manrodt, 2012). Two times, measurement difficulty was positively associated with outcomes associated with a client's loss of control (Mathew, 2011) and with increased business risk (Mathew, 2011). Together, seven of the eight negatively or positively significant findings consistently showed that measurement difficulty was a bane for sourcing outcomes. Only one study found that measurement difficulty had no effect on the project performance of outsourced IT projects (Tiwana, 2010).

Transaction type is the type of work, usually operationalized as a categorical variable, such as delineating among transactions involving development, maintenance, and reengineering work (e.g., Gopal and Koka, 2010) or between ITO and BPO (e.g., Lee and Kim, 2010). In the current study, 19 different types of services were examined across all the studies (see Table 14.4).

Table 14.4 Business services studied[a]

Business service	Total
1. Information technology – generic	92
2. Business processes – generic	39
3. Software development	33
4. Research and development	20
5. Manufacturing support services	11
6. Call left/customer service	10
7. Systems maintenance	9
8. Human resources	9
9. Finance and accounting	8
10. Logistics and supply chain management	6
11. IT infrastructure management services	4
12. Systems integration	3
13. Legal processes	3
14. Marketing	3
15. Generic consulting	3
16. Business intelligence	3
17. Sales	2
18. Staff augmentation	1
19. Procurement	1
Total	260

[a]Cells indicate frequency with which a business service is studied. Total is greater than number of articles as some articles mentioned more than one business service

The most common types of services were general IT and BP services, software development, and R&D. Within a study, some researchers compared the sourcing outcomes of just two types of services (e.g., Handley, 2012), while others considered five or more (e.g., Doloreux and Shearmur, 2013).

Examined 17 times, 11 times transaction type 'mattered' in that the transaction type affected sourcing outcomes such as innovation effects (like number of patents files) (e.g., Doloreux and Shearmur, 2013), outsourcing success (e.g., Handley, 2012), and offshoring success (e.g., Narayanan et al., 2011). For example, Doloreux and Shearmur (2013) found that outsourcing external R&D services, knowledge validation services, general business support services, patent services, and accounting services had different effects on product, process, managerial, and marketing innovations. Handley (2012) found that outsourcing IT had different effects on provider satisfaction than outsourcing logistics.

Six times, transaction type did not matter. For example, Gopal and Koka (2012) found that project type (new software development or reengineering of existing systems) did not affect the outcome of project profitability. Rai *et al.* (2012) found that process type (securities, consumer credit, credit card, or domestic payments) did not significantly affect BPO satisfaction when the main effect variables were considered in the regression models.

Risk is the extent to which a transaction exposes a party (client or provider) to a chance of loss or damage (e.g., Wullenweber *et al.*, 2008; Mathew and Das Aundhe, 2011). Examined 5 times, 4 times risk was found to negatively affect outsourcing outcomes. For example, Qin *et al.* (2012) found that eight types of risks negatively affected IT outsourcing outcomes in China. Gholami (2012) studied the effects of five types of risks on IT outsourcing projects in a case study and found that risks negatively affected outcomes. One study, however, found that financial risk did not significantly affect a provider manager's subjective evaluation of project performance (Ramchandran and Gopal, 2010).

Client Firm Characteristics

Under this broad category, researchers sought to answer the question: Are certain types of clients more likely to experience successful sourcing outcomes than others? In the quest to identify and/or control for between firm differences that may account for sourcing outcomes, researchers have incorporated a variety of client firm characteristics in their studies (see Appendix D). However, this review found an overall paucity of evidence linking client firm characteristics with sourcing outcomes. In Fig. 14.2, only one client firm characteristic was consistently coded at least 5 times: client size. Client size was repeatedly found to be not significant.

Client size was typically operationalized as total firm assets, sales, and/or number of employees (e.g., Handley and Benton, 2012).

A majority of studies incorporated firm size as a statistical control variable. Client size was coded in relationships with sourcing outcomes for a total of 10 times. Six of those relationships showed no significant effects, three showed a positive link, and none of them reported a negative effect. For example, Teo and Bhattacherjee (2014) reported a significant and positive effect of client firm size on operational IT performance, while Narayanan and Narasimhan (2014) reported no relationship between client firm size and client outsourcing cost performance.

Provider Firm Characteristics

Under this broad category, researchers sought to answer the question: Are certain types of providers more likely to deliver successful sourcing outcomes to clients than others? In Fig. 14.2, only one provider firm characteristic, provider size, was consistently coded as least 5 times. Like client size, provider size was repeatedly found to be not significant.

Similar to client size, a *provider's size* was typically operationalized as total firm assets, sales, and/or number of employees (e.g., Handley and Benton, 2012). A majority of studies incorporated provider size as a statistical control variable. Provider size was coded in relation to sourcing outcomes for a total of 6 times, out of which four relationships found no significant relationship between provider size and outsourcing outcomes. For example, Gao *et al.* (2010) found no effect of provider firm size on the export performance of the provider firm.

Client Firm Capabilities

Under the broad category 'client firm capabilities', researchers sought to answer the question: How do a client's internal capabilities influence sourcing outcomes? In Fig. 14.2, we found four variables associated with client firm capabilities that were examined at least 5 times with consistent results: a client firm's technical and methodological capability, their outsourcing readiness, absorptive capacity, and transition management capability. Overall, the four client firm capabilities positively related to sourcing outcomes.

A *client's technical and methodological capability* is a client organization's level of maturity in terms of technical or process-related standards and best practices (e.g., Bardhan *et al.*, 2007). Examined 12 times, 10 findings reported a positive link between a client firm's technical and methodological capabilities and sourcing outcomes such as performance improvements in client firms (e.g., Teo and Bhattacherjee, 2014), project performance (e.g., Devos *et al.*, 2012), and outsourcing success in general (e.g., Vitasek and Manrodt, 2012). These findings suggest that a client is more likely to experience better sourcing outcomes when they themselves have mastered the technologies and processes associated with providing the service.

A *client firm's outsourcing readiness* is the extent to which a client organization is prepared to engage an outsourcing provider by having realistic expectations and a clear understanding of internal costs and services compared with outsourced costs and services (e.g., McIvor *et al.*, 2009). Examined 10 times, a client's firm readiness was always found to positively impact sourcing outcomes pertaining to project performance (e.g., Verner and Abdullah, 2012), client success with outsourcing (e.g., Hodosi and Rusu, 2013), offshoring (e.g., Poston *et al.*, 2010), and provider success (e.g., Palvia *et al.*, 2011). Again, these findings suggest that a client is more likely to experience better sourcing outcomes when they themselves have considerable understanding about providing the service themselves.

A *client's absorptive capacity* is a client organization's ability to scan, acquire, assimilate, and exploit valuable knowledge (e.g., Grimpe and Kaiser, 2010; Reitzig and Wagner, 2010). This relationship was examined 5 times out of which four relationships found a positive impact on outsourcing outcomes such as a client firm's business performance (e.g., Bustinza *et al.*, 2010) and business service improvements (e.g., Ippolito and Zoccoli, 2010). For example, Bustinza *et al.* (2010) found that a client's absorptive capacity (operationalized as 'learning capability') positively affected outsourcing business outcomes such as cost savings, flexibility, and compliance among 112 Spanish firms represented in the survey. These findings suggest that client's cannot be passive recipients of services when outsourcing. Rather, clients must be able to absorb the knowledge providers generate in outsourcing relationships in order to achieve maximum results.

A *client's transition management capability* is the extent to which a client organization effectively transitions services to or from outsourcing providers or integrates client services with provider services (e.g., Luo *et al.*, 2010). Examined 5 times, all relationships found a positive impact of a client firm's ability to transition services on sourcing outcomes associated with backsourcing (Bhagwatwar *et al.*, 2011), switching providers (Weiner and Saunders, 2014), outsourcing (e.g., Svejvig, 2011), and offshoring (Beulen *et al.*, 2011). Beulen *et al.* (2011) provided the deepest exploration of transition management capabilities among the coded studies. Using a case study, the authors described multiple activities the client performed well during a transition to outsourcing, including transition planning, knowledge transfer, interim governance, and preparing the retained organization for life after outsourcing.

Provider Firm Capabilities

Under the broad category 'provider firm capabilities', researchers sought to answer the question: How do a provider's internal capabilities influence sourcing outcomes? In Fig. 14.2, two provider firm capabilities were examined at least 5 times and produced consistent results: human resource management capabilities and technical and methodological capabilities. Both provider firm capabilities were positively related to sourcing outcomes.

A provider's *human resource management capability* is the provider's ability to identify, acquire, develop, retain, and deploy human resources to achieve both provider's and client's organizational objectives (e.g., Kuruvilla and Ranganathan, 2010). Examined 10 times, this capability was found to positively affect sourcing outcomes 8 times. Researchers found a positive association between a provider's human resource management capability and sourcing outcomes associated with project performance (e.g., Verner and Abdullah, 2012), client firm performance (e.g., Narayanan and Narasimhan, 2014), and business performance of provider firms (Agrawal *et al.*, 2012), among others. One negative relationship found that the provider's HR management capability was negatively related to a client's loss of control (Gorla and Lau, 2010). One negative relationship found that the provider's presence of trained personnel was negatively associated with time and material contracts (Gopal and Koka, 2010).

A *provider's technical and methodological capability*, a provider organization's level of maturity in terms of technical or process-related standards, and best practices (e.g., Bardhan *et al.*, 2007) were examined 11 times and 9 times, and a positive link was found between a provider firm's technical and methodological capabilities, and outsourcing outcomes from both client and provider perspectives. This capability positively affected outsourced project performance (e.g., Verner and Abdullah, 2012), provider firm performance (e.g., Gao *et al.*, 2010), client firm performance (e.g., Bachlechner *et al.*, 2014), overall success with outsourcing (e.g., Vitasek and Manrodt, 2012), and service quality (Palvia *et al.*, 2010). The one negative relationship found that the provider's technical and methodological capability was negatively related to a client's loss of control (Gorla and Lau, 2010). Thus, all positively or negatively significant findings suggested that the provider's technical and methodological capability produces beneficial effects.

Relational Governance

Under the broad category of 'relational governance', researchers sought to answer the question: How does relational governance influence sourcing outcomes? Relational governance is the unwritten, noncontractual, worker-based controls, designed to influence interorganizational behavior (Macneil, 1980; Kim, 2008). In Fig. 14.2, eight relational governance variables were examined at least 5 times and produced consistent results in the current review: communication, knowledge sharing, trust, relational governance, client provider interface design, commitment, cooperation, and client provider alignment. All of these independent variables positively affected sourcing outcomes.

Communication is the degree to which parties are willing to openly discuss their expectations, directions for the future, their capabilities, and/or their strengths and weaknesses (e.g., Gainey and Klaas, 2003). Examined 15 times, communication positively affected outsourcing outcomes 14 times. For example, Jain *et al.* (2011a, b) found that communication positively affected offshoring success from the client's perspective. Palvia *et al.* (2011) found that communication positively affected outsourcing success from the provider's perspective.

Knowledge sharing is the degree to which clients and providers share and transfer knowledge (e.g., Mahmoodzadeh *et al.*, 2009). Examined 18 times, 11 times it was positively associated with outsourcing outcomes associated with offshoring (e.g., Dedrick *et al.*, 2011) and outsourcing success (Qi and Chau, 2012). Five studies did not find a significant relationship between knowledge sharing and outsourcing outcomes associated with offshore project performance. For example, Srikanth and Puranam (2011) found that knowledge transfer effort did not significantly affect post-offshoring process performance.

In general, *trust* is the confidence in the other party's benevolence (e.g., Gainey and Klaas, 2003). Examined 10 times, trust positively affected all types of sourcing outcomes 8 times, including service quality (e.g., Deng *et al.*, 2013), outsourcing success (e.g., Swar *et al.*, 2012), captive center success (e.g., Prikladnicki and Audy, 2012), and innovation effects (Whitley and Willcocks, 2011). The one study that found a negative relationship between trust and sourcing outcomes found that trustworthiness of providers in prior engagements mitigated the risk of loss of control over information assets (Mathew, 2011). Thus, all the positively and negatively significant findings suggested that trust helped to ensure better sourcing outcomes.

Within the broad category of 'relational governance', there is a general independent variable that is also called *relational governance*. This is because some studies measured an independent variable that was simply called *relational governance* (e.g., Srivastava and Teo, 2012). Examined 16 times, relational governance positively affected sourcing outcomes 13 times. In particular, relational governance positively affected outsourcing outcomes (e.g., Ji-Fan Ren *et al.*, 2011), offshoring outcomes (e.g., Srivastava and Teo, 2012), and innovation effects (e.g., Weeks and Thomason, 2011). One study found a negative relationship between relational governance and risk (Mathew, 2011). Thus, all the positively and negatively significant findings suggested that relational governance improved sourcing outcomes.

Client/provider interface design is the planned structure on where, when, and how client and provider employees work, interact, and communicate (e.g., Sen and Shiel, 2006). Studied 5 times, 3 times client/provider interface design mattered and 2 times it was positively associated with sourcing outcomes. For example, Kotlarsky *et al.* (2014) found that structured coordination modes significantly affected offshore outsourcing project outcomes.

Commitment is the degree to which partners pledge to continue the sourcing relationship (e.g., Levina and Su, 2008). Examined 5 times, it was always found to positively affect sourcing outcomes. For example, Qi and Chau (2012) found a positive relationship between commitment and IT outsourcing success in two case studies. Uriona-Maldonado *et al.* (2010) also found a positive relationship between commitment and a client's outsourcing success in a Brazilian case study; lack of commitment also contributed to failure in an initial outsourcing relationship in this study.

Cooperation is the degree to which client and provider employees are willing to work together in common pursuit (e.g., Wullenweber *et al.*, 2008). Examined 5 times, cooperation was always found to positively affect sourcing outcomes. For example, Jean *et al.* (2010) found that cooperativeness was positively associated with a provider's innovativeness and market performance in IT outsourcing relationships. Palvia *et al.* (2011) found that Indian providers perform optimally when they developed effective relationships with their clients based on cooperation (as well as on trust and communication).

Client/provider alignment is the degree to which client and provider incentives, motives, interests, and/or goals are aligned (e.g., Sen and Shiel, 2006). Examined 5 times, client/provider alignment was positively associated with sourcing outcomes 4 times. For example, Lacity and Willcocks (2014) found that mechanisms that align client and provider incentives, like gainsharing, were positively associated with innovation outcomes. Vitasek and Manrodt (2012) found that alignment was a key feature of vested outsourcing relationships.

Contractual Governance

Under the broad category 'contractual governance', researchers sought to answer the question: How does contractual governance, that is, the formal, written, and agreed upon forms of control, influence sourcing outcomes? In Fig. 14.2, four contractual governance independent variables were examined at least 5 times and produced consistent results in the current review: contract detail, contract type, control mechanisms, and key performance indicators. All of these independent variables positively affected sourcing outcomes.

Contract detail is the number or degree of detailed clauses in the written outsourcing contract, such as clauses that specify prices, service levels, key process indicators, benchmarking, warranties, and penalties for nonperformance (e.g., Handley and Benton, 2009; Luo *et al.*, 2010). Examined 11 times, 7 times contract detail was positively associated with outcomes pertaining to outsourcing (e.g., Qi and Chau, 2012) and offshoring success (e.g., Srivastava and Teo, 2012). For example, Srivastava and Teo (2012) found that contract detail positively related to both quality and cost performance in projects performed by Indian-based providers. Two examinations found that contract detail was negatively related to outcomes associated with loss of control and risk (Mathew, 2011). Thus, all positively and negatively significant findings found beneficial outcomes from detailed contracts.

Contract type is a term denoting different forms of contracts used in outsourcing. Examples include customized, fixed-priced, time and materials, fee-for-service, gainsharing, and partnership-based contracts (e.g., McFarlan and Nolan, 1995; Poppo and Zenger, 2002; Ross and Beath, 2006; Gopal and Koka, 2010). Examined 15 times, contract type 'mattered' 9 times in that different types of contracts affected outcomes differently. Contract type significantly affected outcomes associated with client outsourcing success (e.g., Vitasek and Manrodt, 2012), offshoring project performance (e.g., Srivastava and Teo, 2012), and provider business performance (e.g., Gopal and Koka, 2012). For example, Srivastava and Teo (2012) found that contract type (fixed-price or time and materials) affected *cost* performance in projects performed by Indian-based providers. Six times, contract type was not significant. Srivastava and Teo (2012) found that contract type (fixed-price or time and materials) did not significantly affect *quality* performance in projects performed by India-based providers.

Control mechanisms are certain means or devices a controller uses to promote desired behavior by the controlee (e.g., Daityari *et al.*, 2008). Examined 10 times, 6 times control mechanisms positively affected client and provider outcomes. For example, Jayaraman *et al.* (2013) examined data collected from 205 BPO service providers in India and found that more control mechanisms (contractual, administrative, and relational) had complementary effects on a provider's business performance. Two examinations found that control mechanisms mattered (Gopal and Gosain, 2010; Jain *et al.*, 2011b). For example, Gopal and Gosain (2010) found that different control modes (software process control, quality outcome control, efficiency outcome control, and clan control) affected outsourcing project performance differently.

Key performance indicators are a set of measures to assess performance (e.g., De Toni *et al.*, 2007; Mahmoodzadeh *et al.*, 2009). Examined 6 times, key performance indicators were always found to positively affect sourcing outcomes associated with outsourcing (McIvor *et al.*, 2011), offshoring (e.g., Kuula *et al.*, 2013), and shared services (e.g., Amiruddin *et al.*, 2013). For example, Iveroth (2010) found that key performance indicators were a significant factor in leading IT-enabled changes in Ericsson's financial and accounting shared services organization.

Country Characteristics

Under the broad category 'country characteristics', researchers sought to answer the question: How does a country's characteristics influence sourcing outcomes? In Fig. 14.2, one country characteristic was examined at least 5 times and produced consistent results in the current review: cultural distance.

Cultural distance is the extent to which the members of two distinct groups (such as client and provider organizations) differ on one or more cultural dimensions (e.g., Mehta *et al.*, 2006). Examined 5 times, cultural distance was negatively related to outsourcing outcomes 3 times. Specifically, cultural distance hurt the performance of offshoring (Jain *et al.*, 2011b), captive centers (Prikladnicki and Audy, 2012), and the provider's business performance (Sakolnakorn, 2011). For example, Prikladnicki and Audy (2012) found that cultural differences were a major challenge experienced by case companies with captive centers (which the authors called 'internal offshoring'). In particular, national cultural differences were identified as the main cultural challenge for captive centers. In offshore outsourcing, both organizational and national cultural differences were challenges in that study.

Relationship Characteristics

Under the broad category of 'relationship characteristics', researchers sought to answer the question: How does a relationship's characteristics influence sourcing outcomes? In Fig. 14.2, one relationship characteristic was examined at least 5 times and produced consistent results in the current review: length of relationship.

Length of relationship is the number of years a client and a provider organization has worked together (e.g., Gainey and Klaas, 2003). Examined 5 times, 4 times it was found to be not significant. In particular, length of relationship had no significant effect on either a client's or provider's assessment of outsourcing success (e.g., Ee *et al.*, 2013; Hodosi and Rusu, 2013). For example, Handley and Benton (2012) did not find a significant relationship between longevity of the outsourcing relationship and the client's reliance on mediated power.

Sourcing Decisions

Under this broad category, researchers sought to answer perhaps the most interesting among all the research questions: Do outsourcing, offshoring, multisourcing, shared services, and other sourcing decisions improve performance? In the current study, two sourcing decisions produced consistent results after repeated examinations: offshore outsourcing decisions and multisourcing decisions.

An *offshore outsourcing decision* is a client organization's decision to engage an offshore provider (e.g., Fifarek *et al.*, 2008; Lee and Kim, 2010). Examined 8 times, offshore outsourcing produced positive outcomes 7 times pertaining to client perceptions (e.g., Khan and Lacity, 2012), innovation effects (e.g., Tate and Ellram, 2012), and a client's business performance (e.g., Lee, and Kim, 2010). For example, Khan and Lacity (2012) surveyed 84 BPO and ITO buyers and found that the majority was satisfied with the overall benefits from offshoring. The majority of buyers also reported that offshoring helped to reduce costs.

A *multisourcing decision* is a client organization's decision to engage multiple service providers (e.g., Sia *et al.*, 2008), primarily aiming for breath of providers (e.g., Su and Levina, 2011). Examined 5 times, 3 times multisourcing as an independent variable was positively related to an outsourcing outcome, but only one finding can be considered truly beneficial. Svejvig (2011) found that multisourcing was positively related to the client's ability to shift work to another provider when one provider was not performing well. Two other studies found that multisourcing was positively related to risks, which meant that multisourcing increased certain types of risks studied (Mathew and Das Aundhe, 2011; Su and Levina, 2011). Mathew and Das Aundhe (2011), for example, found that multisourcing increased the risk of vendor conflict. Su and Levina (2011) found in one case study that multisourcing reduced a provider's commitment to the client and the provider started to underinvest in the relationship. One study by Bachlechner *et al.* (2014) found that making sure that all providers were secure became increasingly difficult with higher numbers of providers. Thus, because of the nature of the outsourcing outcomes studied, we think it more accurately conveys to readers that 60% of multisourcing findings were not beneficial to sourcing outcomes.

In summary, 27 independent variables pertaining to transaction attributes, client and provider firm characteristics, client and provider firm capabilities, contractual and relational governance, country characteristics, relationship characteristics, and service sourcing outcomes were repeatedly examined and produced consistent effects on sourcing outcomes in the current review. Next, we compare these results with the results from the prior *JIT* reviews (Lacity, Khan, Yan, & Willcocks, 2010; Lacity, Solomon, Yan, & Willcocks, 2011).

Comparison of Sourcing Outcome Determinants with Prior Research

This section answers the fourth research question: How do recent findings on determinants of sourcing outcomes compare with previous findings? To communicate the answer to Question 4, we included an asterisk in Fig. 14.2, next to any new independent variable that had not previously met the inclusion criteria in the prior *JIT* reviews (Lacity, Khan, Yan, & Willcocks, 2010; Lacity, Solomon, Yan, & Willcocks, 2011). Among the 27 independent variables in Fig. 14.2, 16 are new. We also compared more detailed results from the current review with the ITO review and BPO review in Table 14.5. Each broad category and the significant independent variables from all three reviews are compared below.

Comparison of Transaction Attributes

Only the ITO review tested any independent variable associated with transaction attributes at least 5 times and found consistent results (see Table 14.5). In the ITO review, *measurement difficulty* and *uncertainty* were negatively associated with outsourcing outcomes (Lacity,

Table 14.5 Comparison of findings on determinants of sourcing outcomes

Broad IV category	Independent variable	ITO review (Lacity, Rottman, & Khan, 2010)	BPO review (Lacity et al., 2011)	This review
Transaction attributes	Measurement difficulty	—		—
	Transaction type			M
	Risk			—
	Uncertainty	—		
Client firm characteristics	Client size			0
	Client experience with outsourcing	++		
Provider firm characteristics Client firm capabilities	Provider size		0	0
	Technical and methodological	++		++
	Client outsourcing readiness			++
	Absorptive capacity – client			+
	Transition management			++
	Provider management	++	++	
	Contract negotiation	++		
	Cultural distance management	+		
	Risk management	+		
Provider firm capabilities	Business service management	++	+	+
	Human resource management	++	++	++
	Technical and methodological	++		++
	Domain understanding	++		+
Relational governance	Communication	++	++	++
	Knowledge sharing	++	++	+
	Trust	++		+
	Relational governance			++
	Client Provider interface design			M
	Commitment			++
	Cooperation			++
	Client provider alignment			+

(continued)

Table 14.5 (continued)

Broad IV category	Independent variable	ITO review (Lacity, Rottman, & Khan, 2010)	BPO review (Lacity et al., 2011)	This review
	Partnership view	++	++	
	Relationship-specific investment		+	+
Contractual governance	Contract detail	++	+	
	Contract type	MM		M
	Control mechanisms	MM		+
	Key performance indicators			++
	Contract size	++		
Country characteristics Relationship characteristics	Cultural distance	--	--	-
	Length of relationship			0
	Relationship quality	++		
	Prior client/provider working relationship	++		
Decision characteristics	Top management commitment/support	++		
	Evaluation process	MM		
Sourcing decisions	Outsourcing decision-offshore		+	++
	Outsourcing decision-multisourcing			+
	Outsourcing decision-make or buy	+		
	Configurational approach		MM	
	Total Significant IVs	25	12	27

Note: More than 80% of the evidence was positively significant (++), negatively significant (--), found no significance (00), or mattered (MM); 60–80% of the evidence was positively significant (+), negatively significant (-), found no significance (0), or mattered (M).

Khan, Yan, & Willcocks, 2010; Lacity, Solomon, Yan, & Willcocks, 2011). Measurement difficulty was the only common transaction attribute in the current review and in the ITO review.

Comparison of Client Firm Characteristics

Only the ITO review tested any independent variable associated with client firm characteristics and sourcing outcomes at least 5 times with consistent results (Lacity, Rottman, & Khan, 2010). In the ITO review, *client experience with outsourcing* positively affected outsourcing outcomes (see Table 14.5). While the previous ITO and BPO reviews included *client size* effects on sourcing outcomes, both reviews indicated a lack of consistent patterns. Lacity *et al.* (2011) coded nine client size relationships without any consistent patterns and Lacity, Rottman, and Khan (2010) found only three relationships.

Comparison of Provider Firm Characteristics

Besides the current review, only the BPO review tested any independent variable associated with provider firm characteristics and sourcing outcomes at least 5 times with consistent results (Lacity, Rottman, & Khan, 2010). *Provider size* was examined 5 times in the BPO review (Lacity *et al.*, 2011) where a majority of evidence suggested no significant relationships between firm size and sourcing outcomes. Provider firm size was examined only 2 times in the ITO review (Lacity, Rottman, & Khan, 2010). In summary, these codes suggest that firm differences in terms of provider size are not a meaningful predictor of sourcing outcomes.

Comparison of Client Firm Capabilities

The previous ITO and BPO reviews tested several independent variables associated with client firm capabilities at least 5 times and found consistent results (see Table 14.5). Both the ITO review and BPO review found that the client's *provider management capability*, the extent to which a client organization is able to effectively manage outsourcing providers, positively affected outsourcing outcomes (Lacity, Khan, Yan, & Willcocks, 2010; Lacity, Solomon, Yan, & Willcocks, 2011). In the current review, provider management capability was only studied 4 times, but all 4 times it was positively associated with outsourcing outcomes (e.g., Bachlechner *et al.*, 2014).

In the ITO review, the client's *contract management capability*, the extent to which a client organization is able to effectively prepare, negotiate, and manage contracts with providers, was repeatedly tested and found to positively affect outsourcing outcomes (Lacity, Rottman, & Khan, 2010). The current review also found a positive relationship in the 4 times it was examined.

The ITO review also found that a client's *cultural distance management capability*, the extent to which a client understands, accepts, and adapts to cultural differences, positively affected outsourcing outcomes (Lacity, Rottman, & Khan, 2010). In the current review, this variable was moved from the client firm capability category to the relational governance category because new studies suggest that cultural distance management is a shared capability – clients and providers have to adapt to each other's culture. For example, Lacity and Willcocks (2014) described how acculturation, the process by which two or more cultures merge to form a cohesive culture, led to positive outsourcing outcomes.

The ITO review found that a client's *risk management capability*, a client organization's practice of identifying, rating, and mitigating potential risks associated with outsourcing, positively affected outsourcing outcomes (Lacity, Rottman, & Khan, 2010). In the current review, it was only examined once and found to positively affect outsourcing success (Gholami, 2012).

The BPO review found that a client's *business service management capability*, the ability of a client organization to efficiently and effectively manage a BP/service using in-house resources, was positively related to outsourcing outcomes. In the current review, all three examinations of a client's business service management capability were also positively related to outsourcing success (e.g., Amiruddin *et al.*, 2013).

Comparison of Provider Firm Capabilities

In terms of provider firm capabilities, current findings on *HR management capabilities* were consistent with the previous reviews. While the ITO review found a positive influence of a provider firm's *technical and methodological capability* (consistent with this review), the BPO review did not. The ITO review also found that a provider's *domain understanding* positively affected outsourcing outcomes (Lacity, Rottman, & Khan, 2010). In the current review, domain understanding was only examined 3 times as a determinant of outcomes. Twice it was not significant. For example, Tiwana (2010) did not find a significant relationship between a vendor's domain understanding and outsourced project performance among a sample of 120 outsourced projects. Deng *et al.* (2013) did not find a significant relationship between learning about a particular client and service quality among a sample of 119 people representing 8 Chinese IT outsourcing providers.

Comparison of Relational Governance

The previous ITO and BPO reviews tested several independent variables associated with relational governance at least 5 times and found consistent results (see Table 14.5). All three reviews found that *communication, knowledge sharing,* and *trust* positively affected sourcing outcomes. Both the ITO review and BPO review found that the *partnership view* was an important determinant of sourcing outcomes (Lacity, Khan, Yan, & Willcocks, 2010; Lacity, Solomon, Yan, & Willcocks, 2011). A partnership view is a client organization's consideration of providers as trusted partners rather than as opportunistic vendors (e.g., Willcocks *et al.*, 2004; Sen and Shiel, 2006). In the current review, partnership view was only studied twice; both times, it was positively associated with outsourcing success (Uriona-Maldonado *et al.*, 2010; Quayle *et al.*, 2013). The BPO review also repeatedly and consistently found that *relationship-specific investment* – specific investments made over time which discourage opportunism, reinforce signals of the client firms, and create extendedness of the relationships (e.g., Tate and Ellram, 2009) – positively affected sourcing outcomes.

Comparison of Contractual Governance

The previous ITO and BPO reviews tested several independent variables associated with contractual governance at least 5 times and found consistent results (see Table 14.5). All three reviews found that *contract detail* was positively related to sourcing outcomes (Lacity, Khan, Yan, & Willcocks, 2010; Lacity, Solomon, Yan, & Willcocks, 2011). In the ITO review and in the current review, *contract type* and *control mechanisms* were important determinants of sourcing outcomes. In addition, the ITO review found that larger sized contracts were positively related to sourcing outcomes. Examined 3 times in the current review, *contract size* was always found to be not significant (e.g., Handley and Benton, 2012; Nagpal *et al.*, 2014). Contract size is defined as the size of the outsourcing contract usually measured as the total value of the contract in monetary terms (e.g., Gewald and Gellrich, 2007). For example, Nagpal *et al.* (2014) report no significant effects of contract size on a client's business performance in terms of abnormal stocks returns.

Comparison of Country Characteristics

The previous ITO and BPO reviews tested only one independent variable associated with country characteristics at least 5 times and found consistent results (see Table 14.5). All three reviews found that *cultural distance* was negatively related to sourcing outcomes (Lacity, Khan, Yan, & Willcocks, 2010; Lacity, Solomon, Yan, & Willcocks, 2011).

Comparison of Relationship Characteristics

In the current review, the *length of relationship*, where researchers considered age of a client/provider relationship in a temporal sense, was repeatedly and consistently found to have no significant effects on sourcing outcomes. The BPO review did not examine any relationship characteristics frequently enough to be included as a broad determinant of sourcing outcomes. The ITO review, however, found two relationship characteristics to be positively associated with sourcing outcomes after repeated examinations: prior client/

provider working relationship and relationship quality. In the ITO review, a *prior client/provider working relationship*, where researchers considered variables that connote a client and provider had worked together in the past without invoking temporal length (see Appendix A for definition), had positive effects on sourcing outcomes in five of the 6 times it was studied (e.g., Mayer and Salomon, 2006). In the current review, this variable was studied 9 times but no consistent patterns were discernible. Thus, it is not included among variables in Fig. 14.2 and Table 14.5. Similarly, the ITO review suggested that *relationship quality* was also positively and significantly related to sourcing outcomes five out of 5 times it was empirically studied (Lacity, Rottman, & Khan, 2010). In the current review, this variable was coded only one time with respect to sourcing outcomes and hence not included in Fig. 14.2 and Table 14.5.

Comparison of Decision Characteristics

Decision characteristics examine who participates in sourcing decisions and what processes are used to make sourcing decisions. The current review and the BPO review did not examine any decision characteristics frequently enough to be included as a broad determinant of sourcing outcomes. The ITO review, however, found two decision characteristics to be significantly associated with sourcing outcomes after repeated examinations: top management support commitment/support and the evaluation process. *Top management commitment/support* is the extent to which senior executives from the client organization provide leadership, support, and commitment to sourcing. Of the 7 times this variable was examined, it was always found that higher levels were associated with better ITO outcomes. The *evaluation process* is the client organization's process for evaluating and selecting suppliers. Of the six relationships studied in the ITO review, all six were significant or mattered (e.g., Baldwin *et al.*, 2001; Kern *et al.*, 2002; Cullen *et al.*, 2005). For example, Cullen *et al.* (2005) identified 54 key outputs from processes that ITO practitioners use to manage ITO. Their major contribution was to link evaluation processes to ITO outcomes. They concluded that 'our major finding is that the more of these processes an outsourcing organization conducts, and conducts well, the greater its success, regardless of its outsourcing objectives' (Cullen *et al.*, 2005, p. 229).

Comparison of Sourcing Decisions

Sourcing decisions examine what sourcing options were chosen. The previous ITO and BPO reviews tested several independent variables associated with outsourcing decisions at least 5 times and found consistent results (see Table 14.5). Like the current review, the BPO review found that *offshoring* resulted in positive outcomes in the majority of findings (Lacity *et al.*, 2011). The BPO review also found that a *configurational approach* mattered. With a configurational approach, the client firm matches multiple factors in configurations that maximize their chances of outsourcing success. For example, matching strategic intent with contractual governance, matching transaction attributes with contractual governance (e.g., Sen and Shiel, 2006; Saxena and Bharadwaj, 2009). In the current review, only two studies examined a configurational approach, once it was positively associated with a client's business performance (Kroes and Ghosh, 2010) and once it mattered (Uriona-Maldonado *et al.*, 2010). The ITO review found that *make-or-buy decisions* were positively associated with outsourcing outcomes (Lacity, Rottman, & Khan, 2010).

In summary, the current review and the previous *JIT* reviews repeatedly and consistently found that transaction attributes, client firm characteristics, client and provider capabilities, relational and contractual governance, and country characteristics determined sourcing outcomes. For a more detailed analysis of the comparisons across studies, please see the section 'Comparison to previously studied determinants of sourcing outcomes' in the Conclusion.

Gaps in Knowledge Assessment

This section seeks to answer the fifth research question: What progress has been made on previously recognized gaps in knowledge since the ITO and BPO reviews? Lacity, Khan, Yan, and Willcocks (2010) and Lacity,

Solomon, Yan, and Willcocks (2011) identified research gaps pertaining to empirical gaps on the direct determinants of sourcing decisions and outcomes, empirical gaps on interactive/dynamics effects, and theoretical gaps. In this review, we only can assess progress pertaining to direct determinants of sourcing decisions and outcomes as we did not review interaction effects or theories. Table 14.6 captures 10 empirical gaps in Lacity, Khan, Yan, and

Table 14.6 Assessment of progress made on previously identified gaps in knowledge

Empirical gaps on the direct determinants of sourcing decisions and outcomes	Empirical gap identified in ITO review (Lacity, Rottman, & Khan, 2010)	Empirical gap identified in BPO review (Lacity et al., 2011)	Is progress evident in this review?
1. Strategic motivations of sourcing decisions	X		Yes, some progress
2. Strategic outsourcing outcomes/ innovation effects	X	X	Yes, good progress
3. Environmental influences on outcomes	X	X	Yes, some progress
4. Configurational approaches on outcomes	X		No, little progress
5. Client firm capabilities on outcomes		X	Yes, good progress
6. Provider firm capabilities on outcomes		X	Yes, good progress
7. Pricing models on outcomes		X	Yes, good progress
8. Business analytics/ knowledge process outsourcing		X	No, little progress
9. Destinations besides India	X	X	Yes, considerable progress
10. Emerging models and trends	X		Yes, considerable progress

Willcocks (2010) and Lacity, Solomon, Yan, and Willcocks (2011). Each gap and progress evidenced in this review is discussed next.

Strategic Motivations of Outsourcing Decisions

In the ITO review, the authors called for more studies of strategic motivations of sourcing decisions (Lacity, Rottman, & Khan, 2010). The authors noted that researchers frequently studied and frequently found strong empirical support that what drove most outsourcing decisions was the desire to reduce costs on what was viewed as a noncore IT activity or a poor performing IS service which could be better provided by providers with superior skills, expertise, and technology. The authors found that researchers had under-examined the more strategic drivers of sourcing decisions including access to global markets, innovation, and commercial exploitation. In the current review, some progress was evident. Researchers have made the most progress on examining *access to global markets* as a strategic motivation of sourcing decisions, and indeed, it was examined frequently enough to be included in Fig. 14.1 as a major determinant of sourcing decisions (e.g., Angeli and Grimaldi, 2010; Ceci and Masciarelli, 2010; Gonzalez *et al.*, 2010b; Tambe and Hitt, 2010; Tajdini and Nazari, 2012). Other strategic motivations in the current review include *innovation* (examined 3 times) and *strategic intent* (examined 3 times). If one considers nimbleness as a strategic motivation, then the current review made good progress on examining *flexibility enablement* (examined 8 times) and *scalability* (examined 3 times). (See Appendix A for definitions.)

Strategic Outsourcing Outcomes/Innovation Effects

Both the ITO and BPO reviews called for more empirical research on strategic outsourcing outcomes/innovation effects (Lacity, Khan, Yan, & Willcocks, 2010; Lacity, Solomon, Yan, & Willcocks, 2011). The authors argued that practitioner surveys (e.g., surveys conducted by the International Association of Outsourcing Professionals [IAOP] and

Horses for Sources) found that clients increasingly expected service providers to deliver innovations, but that academics had only closely examined the innovation effects of outsourcing R&D (e.g., Ciravegna and Maielli, 2011; Lucena, 2011; Nieto and Rodriguez, 2011). They called for more studies on innovation effects from outsourcing other services besides R&D. In the current review, *innovation effects* were examined 33 times as a dependent variable (see Appendix B), and 19 findings examined business services other than R&D (e.g., Weeks and Thomason, 2011; Whitley and Willcocks, 2011; Tate and Ellram, 2012; Lacity and Willcocks, 2014). Overall, the non-R&D and R&D studies found that clients experienced increased levels of innovation effects when certain independent variables were present, such as strong relational governance (e.g., Weeks and Thomason, 2011; Doloreux and Shearmur, 2013), strong contractual governance (e.g., Whitley and Willcocks, 2011), and strong client firm capabilities (e.g., Mihalache *et al.*, 2012; Lacity and Willcocks, 2014).

We also know that there are more studies on innovation in sourcing relationships on the horizon. Specifically, the *Journal of Strategic Information Systems* issued a call for papers in 2014 for a special issue on understanding strategic innovation in IT and BPO. The special issue is edited by Julia Kotlarsky, Ilan Oshri, Sirkka Jarvenpaa, and Jae-Nam Lee.

Environmental Influences on Outcomes

Both the ITO and BPO reviews called for more empirical research on effects of environmental factors on sourcing outcomes (Lacity, Khan, Yan, & Willcocks, 2010; Lacity, Solomon, Yan, & Willcocks, 2011). Environmental influences are factors that exist in the external environment for which parties have little control, such as the level of competition and public opinion about outsourcing/offshoring, that can affect sourcing outcomes for clients or providers. In the ITO review, only three environmental variables were examined – *provider competition, legal and political uncertainties*, and *ethnocentrism*. In total, these variables were examined 11 times. In the BPO review, only three environmental variables were examined – provider competition, *public awareness*, and *public perceptions of outsourcing*. In total, these variables were examined only 8 times. In the current review, five environmental variables were examined – provider competition, *environmental uncertainty*, public perceptions of outsourcing, competition in client firm environment (i.e., *client competition*), and *industry growth*. (See Appendix A for definitions.) These variables were examined 24 times in the current review (see Appendix D). Researchers had made the most progress on examining provider competition (examined 15 times) (e.g., Cordella and Willcocks, 2012; Wiener and Saunders, 2014) and environmental uncertainty (examined 3 times) (e.g., García-Vega and Huergo, 2011; Mithas *et al.*, 2013). Overall, some progress has been made.

Configurational Approaches on Outcomes

The ITO review called for more configurational and portfolio approaches to outsourcing (Lacity, Rottman, & Khan, 2010). The authors argued that some of the most interesting work in ITO considered how organizations matched multiple factors in configurations that maximized their chances of success. For example, matching strategic intent with contractual governance, matching transaction attributes with contractual governance, or matching IT's value proposition, IT's asset position, relational asset position, and relational capabilities with ITO decisions (e.g., DiRomualdo and Gurbaxani, 1998; Lee *et al.*, 2004; Fink, 2010). Some progress had already been made by the time the BPO review was conducted. The BPO review reported on 14 examinations of *configurational approaches* on outsourcing outcomes and found that it 'mattered' 11 times (Lacity *et al.*, 2011). In the current review, a configurational approach was only examined twice (Kroes and Ghosh, 2010; Uriona-Maldonado *et al.*, 2010). Both studies found significant effects on sourcing outcomes. Overall, the current review indicates a backslide.

Client Firm Capabilities on Outcomes

The BPO review called for more empirical research on retained client capabilities (Lacity *et al.*, 2011). In the BPO review, only a *client firm's business service management* and *provider management capabilities* were examined at least 5 times. Also in the BPO review, a *client's absorptive capacity, client outsourcing readiness, proactive sense-making, change management, contract management, HR management,* and *risk management capabilities* were all found to positively affect BPO decisions, but none of these were replicated at least 5 times. (See Appendix A for definitions.) Has progress been made? In the current review, four client firm capabilities were examined at least 5 times and produced consistent results: technical and methodological, a client's absorptive capacity, client outsourcing readiness, and transition management capabilities. Also, as evidenced in Appendix D, three more client firm capabilities were examined 4 times and were all found to positively affect sourcing outcomes: HR management, contract management, and provider management capabilities. Overall, good progress has been made.

Provider Firm Capabilities on Outcomes

The BPO review argued that there was a severe gap in the study of provider firm capabilities because only one capability, a *provider's HR management capability*, had been studied at least 5 times with consistent results. Lacity *et al.* (2011) wrote that outsourcing must, by definition, be highly dependent on a provider's ability to perform and clearly more capabilities contribute to performance than just HR management. In the current review, a provider's HR management capability was once again examined repeatedly and found to positively affect sourcing outcomes. In addition, a provider's technical and methodological capability was examined 11 times and found to significantly affect outcomes. An additional 16 provider capabilities as determinants of sourcing outcomes were examined in this review: *client management capability* (examined 4 times); *contract management capability, project management capability,* and *project scoping accuracy* (each examined 3 times); *provider breadth of service, delivery capability,* and *change management* (each examined twice); and *security/privacy/ confidential capability, business service management capability, technology infrastructure quality, transition management capability, quality management capability, generic provider capabilities, boundary spanning capabilities, employee performance capabilities,* and *organizational learning* (each examined once). (See Appendix A for definitions.) In total, this review includes 50 examinations of 21 types of provider capabilities on sourcing outcomes. Good progress has been made.

Pricing Models on Outcomes

The BPO review called for more studies on pricing models, which at the time focused on comparing fixed-price and time and materials pricing (Lacity *et al.*, 2011). In the current review, different types of contract pricing (i.e., *contract type*) were examined 15 times as determinants of outsourcing outcomes. These predominantly included additional studies on fixed-price *vs* time and materials contracts (see Table 14.7). In general, fixed-price contracts were more risky for providers and time and materials contracts were more risky for clients (e.g., Dey *et al.*, 2010).

In the current review, there were also repeated examinations (14 in total) of what makes a client or provider choose among contract types. In these studies, contract type becomes the dependent variable. For example, Narayanan and Narasimhan (2014) report on seven examinations of the determinants of contract type. They found that supplier asset specificity, firm size, and agility motivation were associated with partnership contracts (revenue sharing). They also found that outsourcing experience, requirements uncertainty, core/noncore, and cost motivation did not affect contract choice at $P<0.05$ level. Susarla *et al.* (2010a, b) reported, based on data from 154 providers, that business analytics services were more likely to be governed with a time and materials contract and that automation tasks were more likely to be governed with a fixed-price contract. Sharma and Iyer (2011) examine pricing policies such as price bundling, solution pricing, component pricing, cost plus pricing, fixed fee pricing, and other pricing models using case studies.

Overall, good progress has been made on the determinants of contract type choice, but the types of contracts still focused mostly on fixed-price and time and materials. (By comparison, the ITO review included only one examination of the determinants of contract type

Table 14.7 Contract type as determinant of outsourcing outcomes: The current review

Contract type	Authors	Number of relationships within the study
Outcome (software licenses) *vs* behavior-based (consulting)	Devos *et al.* (2012)	1
Fixed-price, time and materials, profit sharing, performance-based, hybrid	Dey *et al.* (2010)	1
Fixed-price, time and materials	Gopal and Koka (2010)	1
Fixed-price, time and materials	Gopal and Koka (2012)	1
Fixed-price, time and materials	Langer *et al.* (2014)	2
Standard, incomplete, partnership (revenue sharing)	Narayanan and Narasimhan (2014)	1
Fixed-price, time and materials	Ramchandran and Gopal (2010)	1
Fixed-price, time and materials	Srivastava and Teo (2012)	2
Fixed-price, time and materials	Tiwana (2010)	1
Fixed-price, time and materials, subcontracting	Verner and Abdullah (2012)	1
Outcome-based contracting, subcontracting	Vitasek and Manrodt (2012)	3
	Total	15

and the BPO review did not include any studies that examined the determinants of contract type.)

Business Analytics/knowledge Process Outsourcing

The BPO review called for more studies on the outsourcing of business analytics and knowledge processes (Lacity *et al.*, 2011). Among the 87 papers included in the BPO review, only 3 dealt with knowledge process outsourcing – the outsourcing of knowledge-intensive activities like business analytics (e.g., Sen and Shiel, 2006; Raman *et al.*, 2007; Currie *et al.*, 2008). In a survey of practitioners, the consulting firm Horses for Sources had found that that business analytics and knowledge processes were the top growth areas of client interest in outsourcing during 2010–2011 (Fersht *et al.*, 2011). In the current review, we were able to find only three studies that mentioned business intelligence/business analytics among the types of services studied (see Table 14.4). Susarla *et al.* (2010a) explicitly examined the sourcing of business analytics for customer relationship management services. Two other studies mentioned business intelligence/business analytics as one of the services included in those studies (Aubert *et al.*, 2011; Narayan and Narasimhan, 2014). Overall, little progress has been made beyond these three studies.

Destinations Besides India

Both the ITO and BPO reviews called for more studies of sourcing destinations besides India (Lacity, Khan, Yan, & Willcocks, 2010; Lacity, Solomon, Yan, & Willcocks, 2011). When provider location was specifically mentioned in the ITO review articles, 77% studied providers based in India. When provider location was specifically mentioned in the BPO review articles, 51% of papers studied providers based in India. The next most frequently studied country in the BPO review was Chinese-based BPO providers, with three papers.

Why study other destinations? Practices that were effective in managing Western client–Indian provider relationships did not always work well in other countries (e.g., Lacity *et al.*, 2011). For example, the ITO literature identified onshore liaisons as a best practice for US clients engaging Indian ITO providers (e.g., Gopal *et al.*, 2002; Rottman and Lacity, 2006). Onsite liaisons (i.e., bringing Indian provider employees to US client sites) were not used in other countries. For example, Jarvenpaa and Mao (2008) found that large Japanese clients did not interact directly with Chinese providers but instead preferred to interface through a Japanese-based IT provider.

Table 14.8 Articles that identified provider location

Provider based in	Number of mentions	Percentage of mentions
1. India	41	31
2. The United States	15	11
3. Global	13	10
4. China	9	7
5. The United Kingdom	4	3
6. Russia	4	3
7. Brazil	4	3
8. Canada	4	3
9. Poland	3	2
10. Philippines	3	2
11. Argentina	3	2
12. France	2	2
13. Malaysia	2	2
14. Egypt	2	2
15. Japan	2	2
16. Mexico	2	2
17. Estonia	1	1
18. Singapore	1	1
19. Romania	1	1
20. Italy	1	1
21. Tunisia	1	1
22. Germany	1	1
23. Vietnam	1	1
24. Lithuania	1	1
25. Dominican Republic	1	1
26. Bulgaria	1	1
27. Taiwan	1	1
28. Belgium	1	1
29. Ireland	1	1
30. Pakistan	1	1
31. The United States Territories	1	1
32. Australia	1	1
33. Costa Rica	1	1
34. Israel	1	1
Total mentions of provider location	131	100

Note: Some studies examined several provider locations, so a specific article may be counted more than once in the total and some studies did not mention locations

The current review included articles that examined providers based in 34 countries (see Table 14.8). For each paper, we recorded whether a provider's location was specifically mentioned. Some researchers studied providers based in just one location (e.g., Gopal *et al.*, 2011) while other researchers studied providers from multiple countries within one study (e.g., Arnold *et al.*, 2010). Among the 131 times papers mentioned the provider location(s) in the article, 31% studied providers based in India (e.g., Agrawal *et al.*, 2012), 11% studied US-based providers (e.g., Miozzo and Grimshaw, 2011), 10% studied global suppliers (e.g., Babin and Nicholson, 2011), and 7% studied providers based in China (e.g., Kang *et al.*, 2014). There was also representation of providers based in Russia, the United Kingdom, Canada, and Brazil, studied 4 times each. Overall, the richness of provider locations appears to be enhanced as the prior ITO and BPO reviews.

Emerging Models and Trends

Both the ITO review and BPO review called for more research on emerging models and trends. The prior reviews, particularly, noted the need for academic research on cloud sourcing, shared services, captive centers, bundled services, rural outsourcing, crowdsourcing, and freelance sourcing (Lacity, Khan, Yan, & Willcocks, 2010; Lacity, Solomon, Yan, & Willcocks, 2011). Progress on each is discussed.

Cloud services, including Infrastructure as a Service (IaaS), Platform as a Service (PaaS), and Software as a Service (SaaS), has exploded in the last 4 years in both practice and in academic research. In practice, the size of the cloud services market was estimated by Forrester Research to be over US$100 million worldwide in 2015.[1] As far as academic research on cloud services, an ABI-Inform search revealed 1,203 articles on the subject published since January 2011. Before this date, there were only 269 articles. Academics have clearly excelled at filling the research gap on cloud sourcing. We believe that cloud sourcing represents such a

---

[1] From 'Roundup of Cloud Computing' on http://www.forbes.com/sites/louiscolumbus/2015/01/24/roundup-of-cloud-computingforecasts-and-market-estimates-2015/.

paradigm shift in the provision of services that it warrants its own special review; so cloud services were excluded from this review.

Shared services and *captive centers* are important insourcing options. Shared services appear as a dependent variable in 25 relationships coded in this review (e.g., Sako, 2010) and as an independent variable in six relationships (e.g., Whitaker *et al.*, 2010). Fielt *et al.* (2014) provided one of the most comprehensive reviews conducted on shared services research. The authors examined the definitions, drivers, stakeholder roles, methods, and theories of 18 articles on information systems shared services. As a dependent variable, researchers have examined the determinants of captive centers 7 times in the current review (e.g., Martinez-Noya *et al.*, 2012). As an independent variable, researchers have examined captive centers twice (e.g., Massini *et al.*, 2010). Oshri and van Uhm (2012) wrote the most comprehensive study on captive centers. They examined offshore captive investments made by Fortune 250 Global firms between 1985 and 2010. They studied four different types of captive centers – basic, hybrid, shared, and divested and how these models changed over time. They identified four phases: the rise of India because of cost savings, the shift of India from costs to quality, global proliferation, and disruption.

Bundled services is a client organization's decision to procure multiple services from the same provider, especially as it relates to the decision to deepen an existing provider relationship. In the current review, bundled services were examined 6 times as an independent variable and 4 times as a dependent variable (e.g., Su and Levina, 2011). Bundled services were also examined as juxtapositions to multisourcing decisions. *Multisourcing* is a client organization's decision to engage multiple service providers. For example, Su and Levina (2011) examined how clients made decisions about the breadth (multisourcing) and depth (bundled services) of provider relationships.

Rural sourcing is a client organization's decision to engage a rural-based provider. Rural sourcing was identified in the BPO review as a niche market worth considering. In the current review, rural sourcing was only examined once as an independent variable and 3 times as dependent variable (Lacity, Rottman, & Khan, 2010). Rural sourcing seems to be confined to large countries with considerable cost variations between urban and rural locations in the United States, China, and India (Lacity *et al.*, 2011).

The BPO review also mentioned *crowdsourcing* and *freelance sourcing* as niche markets worth studying, but these topics were not included in the current review. We do note that before January 2011, 23 peer-reviewed articles mentioned 'crowdsourcing' in the abstract and 226 peer-reviewed articles mentioned it in the abstract after this date according to ABI-INFORM. Thus, crowdsourcing has clearly become a mainstream topic. We also note that before January 2011, 10 peer-reviewed articles mentioned 'freelancing' or 'freelance sourcing' and 11 peer-reviewed articles mentioned these terms in the abstracts after this date. Freelance sourcing research is still nascent.

Discussion

Thus far, we have answered the first five research questions. In this section, we focus on four additional findings that were interesting or surprising from the current review.

Overall Batting Averages

In the ITO and BPO reviews, the authors presented overall 'batting averages' based on make-or-buy decision findings. The ITO review found that 63% of the findings reported positive outcomes from outsourcing IT, 22% of the findings reported negative outcomes, and 15% of the findings reported no significant changes in performance (Lacity, Rottman, & Khan, 2010). The BPO review found that 56% of the findings reported positive outcomes from outsourcing BPs, 11% of the findings reported negative outcomes, and 33% of the findings reported no significant changes in performance (Lacity, Rottman, & Khan, 2010). This review needed a more careful calculation as one significantly positive relationship of make-or-buy a decision was actually detrimental (increasing loss of knowledge) and one negative relationship was actually beneficial (reducing spend). Therefore, we closely examined the 33 make-or-buy findings and determined that *48% of the current findings reported beneficial outcomes from outsourcing business services, 30% of the findings reported unbeneficial outcomes, and 21% of the findings reported no significant changes in performance after outsourcing.*

The *degree of outsourcing* can also be used to calculate an overall 'batting average'. In the current review, repeated examinations of the degree of outsourcing on outsourcing outcomes produced mixed results. Examined 14 times, four findings reported that greater degrees of out-sourcing increased outcomes in terms of a client's business performance (e.g., Han and Mithas, 2013) and innovation effects (e.g., Mihalache *et al.*, 2012). Five times, greater degrees of outsourcing had negative effects on sourcing outcomes such as service quality (e.g., Gorla and Somers, 2014), a client's business performance (e.g., Qu *et al.*, 2010), and a provider's business performance (e.g., Reitzig and Wagner, 2010). Five examinations found no significant differences after sourcing deci-sions pertaining to service performance (e.g., Teo and Bhattacherjee, 2014) or business performance (e.g., Sheehan and Cooper, 2011). Through careful examination of all the findings, *29% of the current findings reported beneficial results from greater degrees of outsourcing, 36% of the findings reported unbeneficial outcomes, and 36% of the findings reported no significant changes in performance.*

The Relationship between Contractual and Relational Governance is More Complex than Previously Thought

Although all three reviews focused on studies that treated contractual and relational governance as independent variables, the ITO review made specific mention that research had indicated that contractual and rela-tional governance were *complements*. In the ITO review, Lacity, Rottman, and Khan, (2010) wrote, 'Researchers have also found significant interac-tions between contractual governance and relational governance. Several important papers found that the interaction between contractual and relational governance is positive, and thus contractual and relational governance serve as complements rather than as substitutes (Saunders

Table 14.9 New studies on the relationship between contractual and relational governance

Authors	Findings
Rai *et al.* (2012)	Substitutes
Cao *et al.* (2013)	Substitutes that oscillate over time
Tiwana (2010)	Simultaneously serve as complements and substitutes
Lioliou *et al.* (2014)	Simultaneously serve as complements and substitutes
Huber *et al.*, 2013	Complements and substitutes that oscillate over time

et al., 1997; Sabherwal, 1999; Poppo and Zenger, 2002; Wullenweber *et al.*, 2008; Goo *et al.*, 2009)' (412–413).

In the current review, we found that the relationship between contractual governance and relational governance was examined 5 times, but the findings were more complex than previously found since Lacity, Rottman, and Khan, (2010) (see Table 14.9). In contrast to the findings from the ITO review, Rai *et al.* (2012) found that contractual and relational governance served as *substitutes*. Specifically, the authors found that the relational mechanism, trust, substituted for contractually specified activity expectations, goal expectations, and contractual flexibility. The relational mechanism, information exchange, was also found to substitute for contractually specified activity expectations and goal expectations. The authors also found that the relational mechanism, conflict resolution, substituted for contractually specified goal expectations.

Cao *et al.* (2013) examined the evolution of governance over time and the authors found that contractual and relational governance were *substitutes that oscillated over time* in that sometimes the partners relied more on contractual governance and sometimes they relied more on relational governance. Tiwana (2010) studied 120 outsourced projects and found that formal controls (i.e., contractual governance) and informal controls (i.e., relational governance) were *simultaneously complements and substitutes*. Specifically, the author found 'that informal control mechanisms strengthen the influence of formal behavior control mechanisms on systems development ambidexterity (complementary effects) but weaken the influence of formal outcome control mechanisms (substitutive effects)' Tiwana (2010, p. 87). Lioliou *et al.* (2014) also found that contractual and relational governance were simultaneously complements and substitutes, depending on certain conditions. Using a case study, the authors found that contractual governance can dampen or replace (substitution effects) or compensate (complementary effects) for relational governance in cases of workforce changes and during times of relational conflict. Huber *et al.* (2013) found that the relationship between contractual and relational governance *oscillated between complements and substitutes* based on goal fuzziness, goal conflict, and goal misalignment. These recent studies question the prevailing view of an either/or dichotomy of complementarity or substitution by showing that contractual and relational governance were causally connected over time.

Industry Effects Remain a Mystery

Industry differences among client firms have been examined repeatedly with mixed and inconsistent results in all three reviews. In the current review, industry was examined 19 times. A total of 10 times, a client's industry was not significant, meaning that clients from some industries were equally likely to outsource, offshore, or erect a captive center than clients from other industries (e.g., Alvarez-Suescun, 2010; Spithoven and Teirlinck, 2015). Nine times, industry did matter for outsourcing or for the degree of outsourcing (e.g., Qu *et al.*, 2011; Aubert *et al.*, 2012). Similarly, the ITO review reported that 13 empirical tests of industry on outsourcing found no relationships 7 times, and 6 times industry did matter (Lacity, Rottman, & Khan, 2010). The BPO review found that 6 out of 10 examinations of industry found no effects and 4 times it mattered (Lacity *et al.*, 2011). The BPO review declared 'industry' as a research 'culs de sac'.

Researchers Studied Clients from All Over the World

In this review, we also analyzed client location in addition to provider location. For each paper, we recorded whether a client's location was specifically mentioned. Some researchers studied clients based in just one location (e.g., Amiruddin *et al.*, 2013), while other researchers studied clients from multiple countries within one study (e.g., Khan and Lacity,

Table 14.10 Client locations studied

Client based in	Number of mentions	Percentage of mentions
1. The United States	78	52
2. Global	19	13
3. Germany	10	7
4. The United Kingdom	7	5
5. Canada	7	5
6. Spain	3	2
7. Sweden	3	2
8. China	3	2
9. Australia	3	2
10. Finland	2	1
11. Italy	2	1
12. India	1	1
13. Denmark	1	1
14. Taiwan	1	1
15. Malaysia	1	1
16. Hong Kong	1	1
17. France	1	1
18. Switzerland	1	1
19. Portugal	1	1
20. Iran	1	1
21. Singapore	1	1
22. Japan	1	1
23. Slovenia	1	1
Total mentioning client location	149	100

Note: Some studies examined several client locations, so a specific article may be counted more than once in the total

2014). In all, we were able to code clients based in at least 23 countries (see Table 14.10).

Among the 149 times a client's location was mentioned, 52% were clients based in the United States (e.g., Lacity *et al.*, 2014), 13% were global clients (e.g., Sengupta and Gupta, 2011), 7% were clients based in Germany (e.g., Huber *et al.*, 2013), and 5% were clients based in the United Kingdom (e.g., Weeks and Thomason, 2011) and Canada (e.g., Doloreux and Shearmur, 2013). In addition, clients based in 18 other countries were mentioned. Overall, researchers have clearly covered the globe for both provider and client locations.

Future Research Directions

Finally, we answer Question 6: What are promising areas for future research? So much exciting research has been published since the ITO and BPO reviews (Lacity, Khan, Yan, & Willcocks, 2010; Lacity, Solomon, Yan, & Willcocks, 2011). We have seen a proliferation in the types of sourcing decisions covered, a richer picture of the independent variables that affect sourcing decisions and outcomes, a deeper understanding of the relationship between contractual and relational governance, and an expansion of global research. Much work has been done, but as the sourcing of business services changes so much in practice, there is much more research to do.

As further contributions to 'normal science' (Kuhn, 1970), researchers may continue to make progress on the areas mentioned in the gaps-assessment discussion. More studies on innovation, environmental factors, configurational approaches, client and provider capabilities, pricing models besides fixed-price and time and materials, business analytics sourcing, and emerging models seem worthwhile. Researchers can also replicate the promising, yet understudied, relationships found in Appendix D.

Specifically, we call readers to the determinants of governance in Appendix D. In this review, we included two additional broad categories of dependent variables that examined relational governance (99 relationships) and dependent variables that examined contractual governance (65 relationships). (In the previous *JIT* reviews, relational and contractual governance were independent variable categories but not dependent variable categories.) As the coding process progressed, we were excited to read that researchers were asking, 'What determines how clients and providers govern relationships?' We were hoping to use these two new categories to help answer the question. Unfortunately, there were only two independent variables that were replicated at least 5 times with consistent results to identify as robust determinants of contractual governance: *uncertainty* (+) and *client size* (0). The more the uncertainty is, the more contractual mechanisms were used. Client size, again, was repeatedly found to be not significant. Also, there were only two independent variables that were replicated at least 5 times with consistent results to identify as robust determinants of relational governance: *communication* (+) and *contractual governance* (MM). In the 'Discussion' section, we expanded on the complex connection between contractual and relational. Overall, more research is needed to answer the question on what determines governance.

What research might be truly impactful? We believe researchers can help the world understand how sourcing decisions will increasingly affect jobs, prosperity, safety, and the sustainability of our planet. We propose five rather audacious future research directions, but these questions have gained some validity based on 2014/2015 discussions and presentations at practitioner sourcing group meetings, including meetings of the IAOP, National Association of Outsourcing, Global Sourcing Council, World ITO/BPO Forum, REVAmerica, and the Institute of Robotic Process Automation (IRPA). The questions are

1. What roles do sourcing clients and providers have in uplifting marginalized populations around the world?

According to the US Census Bureau, world population exceeded 7 billion people in 2012. The World Bank estimated that 80% of the world's population – 5.6 billion people – were below the poverty line, living on less than $10 per day. In 2011, 2.2 billion people lived in extreme poverty, living on less than $2 per day (www.globalissues.org/article/26/povertyfacts-and-stats). Caring leaders from the sourcing community realize that all the spending that occurs in sourcing can help alleviate poverty by employing marginalized populations to provide business services. The Global Sourcing Council (www.gsc.clubexpress.com/), for example, was created as a nonprofit organization to help an organization's source goods and services by uplifting humanity through jobs while protecting the environment. In the academic community, there are several researchers beginning to study how sourcing clients and providers alleviate poverty through meaningful work. This research stream is called 'impact sourcing' and it is defined as, 'the practice of hiring and training marginalized individuals to provide IT, BP, or other digitally enabled services who normally would have few opportunities for good employment' (Carmel *et al.*, 2014). Globally, impact sourcing may employ as many as 561,000 people and may generate as much as $20 billion worldwide (Monitor Group/Rockefeller Foundation, 2011; Accenture, 2012; Avasant/Rockefeller Foundation, 2012; Everest Group, 2014).

There are several nonprofits already established to help alleviate poverty through meaningful work in the business services sector. Digital Data Divide trains and employs high school graduates in Cambodia, Laos, Kenya, and the United States. Head Held High and RuralShores focus on disadvantaged populations in India (Monitor Group/Rockefeller Foundation, 2011). Samasource uses work distributed to mobile phones to employ people at the bottom of the pyramid through 16 delivery partners in Haiti, Kenya, India, Cameroon, Zambia, and Uganda (Gino and Staats, 2012). Established service providers, like Accenture, also aim to subcontract some of its services (with full knowledge and approval of clients) to help populations like Native American Indians (Accenture, 2012).

Despite the growing size of the impact sourcing market, there is relatively little research on this developing phenomenon. The research that does exist provides case studies on companies aiming to help such varied marginalized populations as the poor, Native American tribe members, ultraorthodox Jewish women who are not allowed to work with men, and prisoners, of which there are 6 million worldwide (e.g., Heeks and Arun, 2010; Gino and Staats, 2012; Heeks, 2012; Lacity et al., 2012, 2014). More research on impact sourcing is needed to convince customers of the value of such services and to inspire other entrepreneurs and established service providers to pursue social missions.

2. What roles do sourcing clients and providers have in sustaining the planet?

Environmental sustainability is the idea that human survival and well-being depends on the natural environment. Overpopulation, depletion of natural resources, pollution, and nuclear proliferation are all serious threats to environmental sustainability (Rosa et al., 2010). Companies that source business services certainly affect the environment through power consumption in data centers, employees' global travel, consumption of water, and disposal of e-waste, to name a few (Babin and Nicholson, 2011). One way that business services companies can protect the environment is to meet standards set by such organizations as Global Reporting Initiative, the Carbon Disclosure Project, the UN GlobalCompact and the ISO environmental, and social responsibility standards. Babin and Nicholson (2011) assessed the environmental maturity of 19 major ITO and BPO providers and found that Accenture, Infosys, TCS, Wipro, and HP had the most mature sustainability profiles. Beyond this isolated study, we did not find any empirical research that assessed how sourcing clients and providers specifically help or hurt the physical environment. This is perhaps because environmental sustainability is usually not an isolated goal, but rather part of a three-pronged approach known as corporate social responsibility (CSR). CSR aims to simultaneously balance economic, social, and environmental objectives (Porter and Kramer, 2006, 2011).

In business services sourcing, practitioners are very concerned about CSR. For example, the IAOP has made CSR a key theme in its conferences (IAOP, 2009). The Global Sourcing Council (www.gscoun cil.org/we-support-theunited-nations-global-compact/) is working with the United Nations on a policy of 10 universally accepted principles in the areas of human rights, labor, the environment, and anticorruption. A few academic researchers have begun to study CSR capabilities of both sourcing clients and providers (Babin, 2008; Babin and Nicholson, 2009, 2012; Babin *et al.*, 2011; Madon and Sharanappa, 2013; Li *et al.*, 2014). Clearly, more work is needed.

3. What role do advisors play in all of this?

All of the academic reviews (this review and Lacity, Khan, Yan, & Willcocks, 2010; Lacity, Solomon, Yan, & Willcocks, 2011) focused on the roles of clients and providers in making sourcing decisions and in affecting sourcing outcomes. In practice, however, there is another power stakeholder that highly influences sourcing practice: the advisor community. Advisors help clients develop a sourcing strategy, select sourcing locations, develop requests for proposals, evaluate provider bids, negotiate contracts, assist in transitions, build retained capabilities, and review outsourcing relationship health, among other services. Advisors help providers with strategy, finding new locations, crafting pricing models, to name a few of their services. According to the IAOP, some of the top advisors include Quint Wellington Redwood, Avasant, Ernst and Young, PriceWaterhouseCoopers, Deloitte, Alsbridge, Kirkland & Ellis, to name a few (www.iaop.org/content/19/165/3880). According to Influencer Relations Research, the top advisors for 2016 were Gartner,

Forrester Research, Horses for Sources (HfS), International Data Corporation (IDC), Digital Clarity Group, NelsonHall, Information Services Group (ISG), Everest Group, KPMG, and TowerGroup (www. influencerrelations.com/4067/rising-starsin-the-analyst-value-survey). These advisors have never been studied academically; yet, clearly, they are likely to be highly influential because of normative influences (DiMaggio and Powell, 1991). Back in 2006, Poppo and Lacity surmised that one reason outsourcing outcomes had improved over time was because advisors facilitated a client's organizational learning. They wrote 'Another very important factor in customer learning is the wide spread-use of key IT outsourcing consultants and IT outsourcing legal firms. We are witnessing an institutional isomorphic effect where outside experts, such as Technology Partners International (TPI) (now ISG) and Gartner Group, seed client organizations with similar standards and methods ... TPI consultants have assisted in over 300 client sourcing transactions valued at more than $175 billion. Considering that the entire US outsourcing market is $250 billion a year, we certainly understand the impact TPI has had on customer learning' (Poppo and Lacity, 2006, 270). Research into the roles of advisors would be certainly enlightening.

4. *What are the implications of threats to cybersecurity on sourcing and vice versa?*

Arguably, cybersecurity is currently one of the most critical issues facing individuals, organizations, governments, and society (Hoffman et al., 2015), as evidenced by yet another year filled with a spate of spectacular data breaches.[2] An interesting stream of work has recently emerged that examines the outsourcing of information security management (i.e., Managed Security Services) (e.g., Cezar et al., 2014). While studying managed security services as another type of business service being outsourced is certainly important, we believe there are at least two other aspects that deserve urgent attention. First, given most, if not all, business services are IT enabled and IT services are a major portion of outsourced

---

[2] 2015 Verizon Data Breach Investigations Report, http://www.verizonenterprise.com/DBIR/2015/.

business services (Lacity, Khan, Yan, & Willcocks, 2010; Lacity, Solomon, Yan, & Willcocks, 2011), it appears critical to better understand the impacts of outsourcing of business services on organizational security postures, exposure to cyber threats, and their abilities to effectively manage information security. For example, Reitzig and Wagner (2010) argue that as organizations outsource upstream activities, they face the possibility of losing knowledge on conducting downstream activities through the mechanism of 'forgetting by outsourcing vertically related activities' (1196). As organizations continue to disintegrate value chains via globally dispersed service provides, do they risk 'forgetting' how to effectively manage information security in the process? On the other hand, how does increased management focus on cybersecurity shape outsourcing decisions and management of outsourced services?

Second, as both the breadth and depth of outsourcing of business services increase, how can organizations effectively build security into the outsourcing process? How can they effectively stipulate security-related expectations in outsourcing contracts, and more importantly govern and monitor outsourcing relationships to ensure security and compliance? While the first set of issues may be more difficult to address empirically, we believe that outsourcing practice can benefit immensely from research-based guidance on these complex and murky issues.

5. How will service automation affect workers around the globe?

In 2014, Brynjolfsson and McAfee published a best-selling book called *The Second Machine Age*. They argued that the 'first' machine age occurred during the Industrial Revolution when machines replaced humans doing physical labor. During the 'second' machine age – the age happening now – machines are increasingly replacing humans doing highly perceptional tasks (like driving cars) and highly cognitive tasks (like designing financial portfolios to balance risk). According to the authors, some of the positive consequences will be an explosion in the variety and volume of consumption. One huge unanswered question relates to the nature of work: As computers increasingly take over jobs, what work will humans do? This question has been splattered on the covers of such publications as *The Harvard Business Review* (Davenport and Kirby, 2015; Frick, 2015; Reeves *et al.*, 2015), *The Atlantic Monthly* (Thompson, 2015), and *The Wall Street Journal* (Davenport and Iyer, 2015).

In the sourcing industry, we are certainly witnessing the shift from labor to automation for the provisioning of business services. Consider these bellwether events:

- In September 2014, Wipro announced it will reduce headcount by one-third over the next 3 years because of disruptive technologies like automation and AI.[1]
- In December of 2014, Frank Casale launched the IRPA in New York City (www.irpanetwork.com/). In his keynote speech at the event, Casale, also the founder of The Outsourcing Institute (www.outsourcing.com) in 1993, said he launched the IRPA because he saw that automation technology was going to be the next game changer in outsourcing.
- In May of 2015, The REVAmerica conference (www.revamerica.com), designed to build a vibrant business services industry in the United States, presented a panel on why RPA is great for American jobs.
- In June of 2015, The World BPO Forum (www.worldbpoforum.com/ conference_agenda_2015.aspx) and the National Outsourcing Association (http://www.noa.co.uk/events/noa-symposium/) added key-notes and panel discussions on robotic process automation to their agendas.
- In July of 2015, the IAOP launched a chapter dedicated to Robotic Process Automation (www.iaop.org/content/23/162/4295). One provider from a major Indian provider estimated that going forward, 70% of its IT services would be automated and 30% would be labor based.
- During 2014–2015, the major sourcing advisors started developing RPA practices, including the Everest Group, Alsbridge, HfS, KPMG, and ISG.

The research questions are daunting. If ITO and BPO services will be increasingly provided by technology, what happens to countries with labor arbitrage advantages? For example, what will happen to India's middle class, which was largely built on this sector? Will automation lead to more reshoring back to high-cost destinations? Will opportunities to uplift marginalized populations by employing them in the services sector diminish? Bringing all these research issues together, we ask How can sourcing clients, providers, and advisors protect jobs, protect the environment, and ensure security in an increasingly automated world?

Conclusion

This review of the empirical business services sourcing literature aimed to answer six major questions: What has the recent empirical academic literature found about the determinants of sourcing decisions for business services? How do recent findings compare with previous findings? What has the recent empirical academic literature found about the determinants of sourcing outcomes for business services? How do recent findings compare with previous findings? What progress has been made on previously recognized gaps in knowledge? What are the promising areas for future research? The answers to each are summarized in the following sections.

Summary of Sourcing Decisions Determinants in this Review

On the determinants of sourcing decisions in the current review, the empirical evidence found that sourcing decisions were complex as demonstrated by the 19 significant independent variables that were empirically found to repeatedly influence sourcing decisions across the six broad categories of motivations to outsource, transaction attributes, client firm characteristics, client firm capabilities, provider firm capabilities, and country characteristics. Across all the current studies, client organizations clearly had a rich set of motives driving sourcing decisions in addition to *cost savings*, including the desire to improve the *quality* and *flexibility* of existing services, the desire to *access a provider's expertise* and *global markets*, and a strategy to *focus in-house staff on critical services*. When clients *feared losing control*, they tended to select insourcing options. When making sourcing decisions, client organizations also considered a number of transaction attributes that hindered outsourcing and favored insourcing, like high *transaction costs*, difficulty *formalizing knowledge*, high *service complexity*, and lack of *service standards*. Clients selected outsourcing over insourcing when the providers were deemed to possess superior *external production cost advantages*. Client and provider firm capabilities also influenced sourcing decisions. Clients felt more confident outsourcing services when they themselves had mature *technical and methodological capabilities*. Clients tended to only outsource when they thought the provider had a deep *domain understanding* of their business and technical contexts, processes, practices, and requirements. When considering which country to source a service from, clients considered a *country's financial and business attractiveness*. Sourcing experience clearly mattered in that clients with *prior outsourcing experience* relied on that knowledge when making future sourcing decisions. When clients were citizens of the world as indicated by high *degrees of internationalization*, they outsourced and offshored more.

Comparison to Previously Studied Determinants of Sourcing Decisions

Like the current review, the prior ITO and BPO reviews reported that repeated examinations consistently found that sourcing decisions were determined by sourcing motivations, transaction attributes, and client firm characteristics (Lacity, Khan, Yan, & Willcocks, 2010; Lacity, Solomon, Yan, & Willcocks, 2011). Within these three broad categories, there were similarities and differences at the level of independent variables.

For sourcing motivations, all three reviews found robust and consistent evidence that sourcing decisions were motivated by a client's desire to *reduce costs, assess expertise and skills, improve service quality*, and *focus on core capabilities*. In addition, the current review and the ITO review found that *fear of losing control* was a significant motivator. Both the ITO and BPO reviews found that *concern for security/IP* motivated insourcing decisions. The ITO review was the only review that repeatedly examined and consistently found that *political reasons* and the desire to *upgrade technology* motivated sourcing decisions. The BPO review was the only review that repeatedly examined and consistently found that *scalability* and *rapid delivery* motivated sourcing decisions.

For transaction attributes, two of the three reviews repeatedly and consistently found that *transaction costs* (this review and the ITO review), *service complexity* (this review and the BPO review), and *critical role of business service* (the ITO and BPO reviews) were determinants of sourcing decisions. In addition, the ITO review found that *uncertainty* and *risk* were repeatedly found to negatively affect outsourcing decisions, leading to more insourcing.

For client firm characteristics, there was no overlap at the level of individual independent variables across the three reviews. The current review repeatedly examined and consistently found that *client experience with outsourcing, centralization,* and *degree of internationalization* affected sourcing decisions. The ITO review repeatedly examined and consistently found that *department performance* was negatively associated with outsourcing decisions. The BPO review repeatedly examined and consistently found that *client firm performance* was positively associated with outsourcing decisions.

Summary of Sourcing Outcome Determinants in this Review

On the determinants of sourcing outcomes in the current review, the empirical evidence suggested that sourcing decisions were also complex as demonstrated by the 27 significant independent variables that were found repeatedly to influence sourcing outcomes across the 10 broad categories of transaction attributes, client firm characteristics, provider firm characteristics, client firm capabilities, provider firm capabilities, contractual governance, relational governance, country characteristics, relationship characteristics, and service sourcing decisions. Across the current studies, clients struggled to get good sourcing outcomes under conditions of high *uncertainty* and high levels of *risk*. Different *types of transactions* also resulted in different sourcing outcomes, but no discernable pattern can be reported because different authors examined different transaction types. Capabilities were also important determinants of sourcing outcomes. Clients with strong *technical and methodological capabilities, absorptive capacity,* and *transaction management capabilities* had better sourcing outcomes compared with clients with weak or immature capabilities. Also, clients needed to be *ready to outsource* by having realistic expectations and a clear understanding of internal costs and services compared with outsourced costs and services. Provider capabilities were also important, providers with strong *HR management capabilities* and *technical and methodological capabilities* produced better outcomes for clients and themselves compared with providers with weak capabilities. Contractual and relational governance were powerful influencers on sourcing outcomes. When clients signed *detailed contracts* and used more *control mechanisms* and *key performance indicators*, they experienced better sourcing outcomes compared with clients with loose contracts and fewer controls. *Contract type* also influenced outcomes in that fixed-price contracts had different effects on risks, success, and financial performance than time and materials contracts. Higher levels of seven relational governance variables were associated with better sourcing outcomes: *communication, knowledge sharing, trust, relational governance* (generic), *commitment, cooperation,* and *alignment*. The *interface design* also mattered – clients and providers need to actively design how the parties will work together. *Cultural distance* hurt sourcing outcomes, but this, in theory, could be offset with higher levels of a cultural distance management capability.

Comparison to Previously Studied Determinants of Sourcing Outcomes

Like the current review, the prior ITO and BPO reviews reported that repeated examinations consistently found that sourcing outcomes were determined by transaction attributes, client firm characteristics, client firm capabilities, provider firm capabilities, contractual governance, relational governance, country characteristics, relationship characteristics, and service sourcing decisions (Lacity, Khan, Yan, & Willcocks, 2010; Lacity, Solomon, Yan, & Willcocks, 2011). Within these nine broad categories, there were similarities and differences at the level of independent variables. Focusing on the similarities across all three reviews, all reviews found that a provider's strong *HR management capability* was associated with better sourcing outcomes. All three reviews found that *detailed contracts* (part of contractual governance) produced better sourcing outcomes than loose contracts. All three reviews found that high levels of *communication* and *knowledge sharing* between clients and providers (part of relational governance) were associated with good sourcing outcomes.

The Next Moves

Despite the rich body of current research reviewed, the field continues to rapidly evolve and therefore remains a rich field of inquiry. We have suggested areas of future research based on understudied, yet promising variables, and called for continued progress on previously identified gaps in knowledge. We also proposed what we believe to be some bold research questions that might direct future research. As Lacity *et al.* (2011) concluded, 'Much has been accomplished, yet so much remains to be done'.

Limitations

All three literature reviews – this current review and Lacity, Khan, Yan, and Willcocks (2010) and Lacity, Solomon, Yan, and Willcocks (2011) – share the same limitations as they followed the same method. First, we cannot guarantee that we found every empirical business services sourcing article published in a refereed journal. We apologize in advance if we have missed any important work by colleagues. Second, we recognize that we could have made errors in coding the 1,304 findings. We used three independent coders (i.e., the authors) and the second author went through each finding at the end of the coding process to check for errors to ensure reliability. Third, the relationships in all three reviews only capture direct effects, not inter-active effects or dynamic effects. There were simply not enough repli-cations to include these additions in this review. Fourth, the review method is not as statistically rigorous as a meta-analysis. Because we were keen to include the rich base of qualitative research, we coded 73 qualitative studies (out of the 174 total number of articles). Fifth, the selected threshold value for analyzing repeated relationships of 5 times or more and the selected threshold value of extracting consistent findings of greater than 60% are arbitrary. We used these thresholds to compare findings with prior reviews. The detailed data is available in Appendix D, if other researchers want to reexamine the data using different thresholds.

Contributions

By answering the six research questions, this review contributes to the literature in a number of important ways. For researchers new to the study of business services sourcing, we have documented and described 219 variables used in current research. We have captured the results of 1,304 empirical examinations of the relationships between independent and dependent variables. We have highlighted robust findings that were replicated at least 5 times and produced consistent results. The appendices also point to promising findings that need more replications to become robust. We have assessed also where progress still needs to be made on previously identified gaps in knowledge, thus signaling where new researchers can readily contribute. For advanced researchers, we have outlined more ambitious research goals pertaining to the well-being of our planet and its inhabitants.

Appendix A

Master codes

*Indicates a new variable that was not coded before in Lacity, Rottman, and Khan, (2010) or Lacity *et al.* (2011).

1. *Absorptive capacity – client:* A client organization's ability to scan, acquire, assimilate, and exploit valuable knowledge (e.g., Grimpe and Kaiser, 2010; Reitzig and Wagner, 2010).
2. *Absorptive capacity – provider:* A provider organization's ability to scan, acquire, assimilate, and exploit valuable knowledge (e.g., Luo *et al.*, 2010). (Previously called 'Absorptive Capacity – Supplier' in Lacity *et al.*, 2011.)
3. *Access to expertise/skills:* A client organization's desire or need to access provider skills/expertise (e.g., Currie *et al.*, 2008; Lam and Chua, 2009).

4. *Access to global markets:* A client organization's desire or need to gain access to global markets by outsourcing to providers in those markets (e.g., Gorp *et al.*, 2007).
5. *Adaptability:* The extent to which a party is able to adapt a business service to meet changes in the environment (e.g., Sia *et al.*, 2008).
6. *Adherence to environmental standards:* The degree to which an organization has embraced or been certified as following ecological standards such as ISO 26000, Carbon Disclosure Project, UN Global Compact (e.g., Babin and Nicholoson, 2011).
7. *Asset complementarity:* The degree to which a set of assets is uniquely complementary (e.g., Argyres and Zenger, 2012).
8. *Asset Specificity:* The degree to which an asset can be redeployed to alternative uses and by alternative users without sacrifice of productive value (Williamson, 1976; Sia *et al.*, 2008).
9. *Asset specificity – human:* The degree to which a human asset can be redeployed to alternative uses and by alternative users without sacrifice of productive value (e.g., Alvarez-Suescun, 2010).
10. *Asset specificity – physical:* The degree to which a physical asset can be redeployed to alternative uses and by alternative users without sacrifice of productive value (e.g., Alvarez-Suescun, 2010).
11. *Boundary spanning capability – client:* A client firm's external BPs that bridge the internal and external boundaries. That is client firm processes that ease the organizational and national boundaries between clients and service providers (e.g., Du and Pan, 2013).
12. *Boundary spanning capability – provider:* A service provider firm's external BPs that bridge the internal and external boundaries. That is provider firm processes that ease the organizational and national boundaries between clients and service providers (e.g., Du and Pan, 2013).
13. *Business service management capability – client:* The ability of a client organization to efficiently and effectively manage a BP/service using in-house resources (e.g., McIvor *et al.*, 2009). (Previously called 'Business Process Management Capability – Client' in Lacity *et al.*, 2011.)

14. *Business service management capability – provider:* The ability of a provider organization to efficiently and effectively manage a BP/ service (e.g., Saxena and Bharadwaj, 2009). (Previously called 'Business Process Management Capability – Supplier' in Lacity *et al.*, 2011.)

15. *Business strategic type:* An organization's strategy to address three fundamental business problems – entrepreneurial, engineering, and administrative. Categorized under the Miles and Snow typology as defenders, prospectors, analyzers, and reactors (Miles and Snow, 1978; Shih *et al.*, 2005; Kenyon and Meixell, 2011).

16. *Career development of employees:* A client organization's desire or need to provide better career opportunities for employees (e.g., Lacity *et al.*, 2004).

17. *Centralization:* The degree to which an organization's resources, services, or decision-making are concentrated within a particular group or location (e.g., Delmotte and Sels, 2008). (Previously called 'Centralization of Department' in Lacity *et al.*, 2011.)

18. *Change catalyst:* A client organization's desire or need to bring about large scale changes in the organization (e.g., Gospel and Sako, 2010).

19. *Change management capability – client:* The extent to which a client organization effectively manages change (e.g., Lacity *et al.*, 2004). (Previously called 'Change Management Capability' in Lacity *et al.*, 2011.)

20. *Change management capability – provider:* The extent to which a provider organization effectively manages change (e.g., Lacity *et al.*, 2011).

21. *CIO power:* The level of influence of the head of the IT function (e.g., Chakrabarty and Whitten, 2011; Gefen *et al.*, 2011).

22. *Client–Provider alignment:* The degree to which client and provider incentives, motives, interests, and/or goals are aligned (e.g., Sen and Shiel, 2006). (Previously called 'Client–Supplier Alignment' in Lacity *et al.*, 2011.)

23. *Client–Provider interface design:* The planned structure on where, when, and how client and provider employees work, interact, and

communicate (e.g., Sen and Shiel, 2006). (Previously called 'Client–Supplier Interface Design' in Lacity, Rottman, & Khan, 2010).

24. *Client age:* The age of a client organization in years (e.g., Delmotte and Sels, 2008).

25. *Client business change:* The degree to which the client's business structure or leadership change through mergers, acquisitions, divestitures, and/or C-suite turnover (e.g., Mathew and Das Aundhe, 2011).

26. *Client experience with outsourcing:* The situation in which the client has prior outsourcing experience (e.g., Alvarez-Suescun, 2010).

27. *Client management capability:* The extent to which a provider organization is able to effectively manage client relationships (e.g., Howells *et al.*, 2008).

28. *Client outsourcing readiness:* The extent to which a client organization is prepared to engage an outsourcing provider by having realistic expectations and a clear understanding of internal costs and services compared with outsourced costs and services (e.g., McIvor *et al.*, 2009).

29. *Client power:* The degree of power the client has over the provider, measured as a percentage of the provider's revenues (e.g., Susarla *et al.*, 2010b).

30. *Client prestige:* The degree to which a client is widely regarded and respected (e.g., Handley and Benton, 2012).

31. *Client size:* The size of a client organization usually measured as total assets, sales, and/or number of employees (e.g., Handley and Benton, 2012).

32. *Client size – Department:* The size of a client's department or function considering outsourcing, usually measured as total assets, sales, and/or number of employees in that department (e.g., Chakrabarty and Whitten, 2011).

33. *Client-specific knowledge required:* The degree to which a unit of work requires a significant amount of understanding/knowledge about unique client systems, processes, or procedures (e.g., McKenna and Walker, 2008).

34. *Client–Provider coordination processes:* The extent to which coordination and communication processes are present between a provider and its client during project execution. These include aspects such as presence of provider liaisons, accurate and complete project documentation, project status reports, and issue remediation processes (e.g., Gopal *et al.*, 2011).

35. *Commitment:* The degree to which partners pledge to continue the relationship (e.g., Levina and Su, 2008).

36. *Communication:* The degree to which parties are willing to openly discuss their expectations, directions for the future, their capabilities, and/or their strengths and weaknesses (e.g., Gainey and Klaas, 2003).

37. *Competition in client firm environment:* The presence of multiple, reputable, and trustworthy firms within a client's industry (e.g., Mithas *et al.*, 2013).

38. *Compliance:* A client organization's need to desire to improve compliance (e.g., Iveroth, 2010).

39. *Concern for security/intellectual property:* A client organization's concerns about security of information, transborder data flow issues, and protection of IP (e.g., Wullenweber *et al.*, 2008).

40. *Configurational approach:* The client firm matches multiple factors in configurations that maximize their chances of outsourcing success. For example, matching strategic intent with contractual governance, matching transaction attributes with contractual governance (e.g., Sen and Shiel, 2006; Saxena and Bharadwaj, 2009).

41. *Conflict resolution:* The degree to which clients and providers quickly, fairly, and meaningfully resolve disputes (e.g., Wullenweber *et al.*, 2008).

42. *Conflict resolution approach:* The type of approach used to handle a conflict between clients and providers. Types of approaches include integrating, accommodating, compromising, collaborative, and avoiding (e.g., Lacity and Willcocks, 2014).

43. *Contract detail:* The number or degree of detailed clauses in the outsourcing contract, such as clauses that specify prices, service levels, key process indicators, benchmarking, warranties, and

penalties for nonperformance (e.g., Handley and Benton, 2009; Luo *et al.*, 2010).

44. *Contract duration:* The duration of the contract in terms of time (e.g., Willcocks *et al.*, 2004).

45. *Contract flexibility:* The degree to which a contract specifies contingencies and enables parties to change contractual terms (e.g., Sia *et al.*, 2008).

46. *Contract management capability – client:* The extent to which a client organization is able to effectively prepare, negotiate, and manage contracts with providers, including the ability to track service levels and verify invoices (e.g., Sanders *et al.*, 2007). (Previously called 'Contract Management Capability' in Lacity *et al.*, 2011.)

47. *Contract management capability – provider:* The extent to which a provider organization is able to effectively prepare, negotiate, and manage contracts with clients (e.g., Agrawal *et al.*, 2012).

48. *Contract size:* The size of the outsourcing contract usually measured as the total value of the contract in monetary terms (e.g., Gewald and Gellrich, 2007).

49. *Contract type:* A term denoting different forms of contracts used in outsourcing. Examples include customized, fixed-priced, time and materials, fee-for-service, gainsharing, and partnership-based contracts (e.g., McFarlan and Nolan, 1995; Poppo and Zenger, 2002; Ross and Beath, 2006; Gopal and Koka, 2010).

50. *Contractual governance:* A general term that captures the overall formal and legally binding written rules designed to influence interorganizational behavior (e.g., Bachlechner *et al.*, 2014).

51. *Control mechanisms:* Certain means or devices a controller uses to promote desired behavior by the controlee (e.g., Daityari *et al.*, 2008).

52. *Convenience:* A client organization's desire to select a sourcing option based on ease of use, convenience, and less frustration (e.g., McKenna and Walker, 2008).

53. *Cooperation:* The degree to which client and provider employees are willing to work together in common pursuit (e.g., Wullenweber *et al.*, 2008).

54. *Coopetition:* The degree to which competitors cooperate (e.g., Wiener and Saunders, 2014a).

55. *Corporate social responsibility capability – client:* A client organization's ability to behave in a socially responsible way, such as promoting environmental responsibility, promoting fair labor practices, and engaging in philanthropy (e.g., Babin and Nicholson, 2011).

56. *Corporate social responsibility capability – provider:* A provider organization's ability to behave in a socially responsible way, such as promoting environmental responsibility, promoting fair labor practices, and engaging in philanthropy (e.g., Brown, 2008). (Previously called 'Corporate Social Responsibility-Supplier' in Lacity *et al.*, 2011.)

57. *Cost reduction:* A client organization's need or desire to reduce costs of providing a service (e.g., Borman, 2006).

58. *Country:* The nationality of the client or provider organization (e.g., Reitzig and Wagner, 2010).

59. *Country – business attractiveness:* The degree to which a country is attractive to outsourcing clients or providers because of favorable business environmental factors such as economic stability, political stability, cultural compatibility, infrastructure quality, security of IP (e.g., Doh *et al.*, 2009; Malos, 2010).

60. *Country – financial attractiveness:* The degree to which a country is attractive to outsourcing clients or providers because of favorable financial factors such as labor costs, taxes, regulatory, and other costs (e.g., Doh *et al.*, 2009; Malos, 2010).

61. *Country – human resource attractiveness:* The degree to which a country is attractive to outsourcing clients or providers because of favorable people skills and availability factors such as size of labor pool, education, language skills, experience, and attrition rates (e.g., Mehta *et al.*, 2006; Malos, 2010).

62. *Country selection:* A client or provider's decision to locate in a particular country (e.g., Massini *et al.*, 2010).

63. *Country size:* The size of the country, typically measured by GDP, population, or services exports, and so on (e.g., Hahn *et al.*, 2011).

64. *Criticality of service:* The degree to which a client organization views the business service as a critical enabler of business success (e.g., Klaas *et al.*, 2001; Wahrenburg *et al.*, 2006). (Previously called 'Critical Role of Business Process – Organization' in Lacity *et al.*, 2011).

65. *Cultural distance:* The extent to which the members of two distinct groups (such as client and provider organizations) differ on one or more cultural dimensions (e.g., Mehta *et al.*, 2006).

66. *Cultural distance management:* The extent to which client and provider organizations understand, accept, and adapt to cultural differences (e.g., Tate *et al.*, 2009).

67. *Culture:* Shared values, beliefs, practices, and assumptions that characterize a group (e.g., Rajeev and Vani, 2009).

68. *Degree of internationalization – client:* The geographic reach of a client – local, regional, country, international, or global (e.g., Whitaker *et al.*, 2010).

69. *Degree of internationalization – provider:* The geographic reach of a provider – local, regional, country, international, or global (e.g., Cha and Quan, 2011).

70. *Delivery capability:* A provider's ability to deliver a contracted service on time, on budget, and with agreed upon service quality (e.g., Howells *et al.*, 2008).

71. *Department performance:* CXO's, CEO's, or organizational members' perceptions of the function's performance or competence (e.g., Klaas *et al.*, 2001).

72. *Department power:* The level of influence of the department on the organization (e.g., Dunbar and Phillips, 2001).

73. *Department size:* The size of a department or business function usually measured as number of employees (e.g., Calantone and Stanko, 2007).

74. *Domain understanding:* The extent to which a provider has prior experience and/or understanding of the client organization's business and technical contexts, processes, practices, and requirements (e.g., Luo *et al.*, 2010).

75. *Evaluation process – client assessment:* The client organization's process for evaluating its own services to determine which are

critical or outsourcing ready (e.g., Handley, 2012). (Previously called 'Evaluation Process' in Lacity *et al.*, 2011.)

76. *Evaluation process – provider selection:* The client organization's process for evaluating and selecting providers (e.g., Handley and Benton, 2009). (Previously called 'Evaluation Process' in Lacity *et al.*, 2011.)

77. *External production cost advantage:* The degree to which a provider is perceived to have an advantage over a client organization in production cost economies (e.g., Williamson, 1991; Rajeev and Vani, 2009).

78. *Fear of losing control:* A client organization's concerns that outsourcing may result in loss of control over the service (e.g., Lewin and Peeters, 2006; Sanders *et al.*, 2007).

79. **Firm ownership structure – client:* The client's ownership structure: private, public, jointly owned with primary provider (e.g., Rai *et al.*, 2012).

80. *Firm ownership structure – provider:* The provider's ownership structure: private, public, jointly owned with primary client (e.g., Jayaraman *et al.*, 2013). (Previously called 'Supplier Ownership' in Lacity *et al.*, 2011).

81. *Flexibility enablement:* A client organization's desire or need to increase the flexibility of the use and allocation of resources (e.g., Tate and Ellram, 2009).

82. *Focus on core capabilities:* A client organization's desire or need to outsource in order to focus on its core capabilities (e.g., Carey *et al.*, 2006; Gewald and Dibbern, 2009).

83. **Functional spend:* The annual operating budget for a function or department (e.g., Kobelsky and Robinson, 2010).

84. *Geographic distance:* The physical distance between two locations (e.g., Doh *et al.*, 2009).

85. *Human resource management capability – client:* A client organization's ability to identify, acquire, develop, retain, and deploy human resources to achieve its organizational objectives (e.g., Klaas *et al.*, 2001).

86. *Human resource management capability – provider:* A provider organization's ability to identify, acquire, develop, retain, and

deploy human resources to achieve both provider's and client's organizational objectives (e.g., Kuruvilla and Ranganathan, 2010).

87. *Industry:* The primary industry classification of a client organization. Common classifications include service *vs* manufacturing, SIC codes, and so on (e.g., Bardhan *et al.*, 2007; Mani *et al.*, 2010).

88. *Industry growth:* The increase or decrease in the size of a market (e.g., Budhwar *et al.*, 2006).

89. *Influences – coercive:* Influences that result from both formal and informal pressures exerted on an organization by other organizations upon which they are dependent (e.g., DiMaggio and Powell, 1991; Bignoux, 2011).

90. *Influences – external and internal:* The combination of external media, provider pressure, and internal communications at the personal level among managers of companies (e.g., Borman, 2006).

91. *Influences – mimetic:* Influences that arise from the perception that peer organizations are more successful, by modeling themselves based on peer organizations, the mimicking organization aims to achieve similar results (e.g., Klaas *et al.*, 2001).

92. **Information asymmetry:* The degree to which one party has information that is unknown to another party in a transaction (e.g., Devos *et al.*, 2012).

93. **Information quality:* The degree to which information fits its intended use and is accurate, relevant, timely, and complete (e.g., Bustinza *et al.*, 2010).

94. *Innovation:* A client organization's desire or need to use sourcing as an engine for innovation (e.g., Ciravegna and Maielli, 2011).

95. *Innovation effects:* The extent to which outsourcing positively effects a client's innovation, such as the effects on the number of patents filed or granted (e.g., Grimpe and Kaiser, 2010).

96. **Innovativeness – client:* The degree to which a client introduces new technologies, processes, services, and methods in their own organization (e.g., Weigelt and Sarkar, 2012).

97. **Innovativeness – provider:* The degree to which a provider introduces new technologies, processes, services, and methods

in their own organization and/or the client's organization (e.g., Jean *et al.*, 2010).

98. *Key performance indicators:* A set of measures to assess performance (e.g., De Toni *et al.*, 2007; Mahmoodzadeh *et al.*, 2009).

99. *Knowledge formalization:* The degree to which clients and providers can formalize/codify requirements (e.g., Aubert *et al.*, 2011).

100. *Knowledge required:* The degree to which a unit of work requires a significant amount of understanding/knowledge about unique, specialized, or advanced content (e.g., Lam and Chua, 2009).

101. *Knowledge sharing:* The degree to which clients and providers share and transfer knowledge (e.g., Mahmoodzadeh *et al.*, 2009) (Previously called 'Effective Knowledge sharing in Lacity *et al.*, 2011).

102. *Legal and political uncertainties:* The extent to which a location's legal and political environments are uncertain, unstable, or unfamiliar (e.g., Currie *et al.*, 2008; Penfold, 2009).

103. *Length of relationship:* The number of years a client and a provider organization has worked together (e.g., Gainey and Klaas, 2003).

104. *Loss of control:* The degree to which a client loses control over a business service after outsourcing (e.g., Sanders *et al.*, 2007).

105. *Loss of knowledge:* The degree to which a client loses knowledge about a business service after outsourcing (e.g., Kien *et al.*, 2010).

106. *Measurement difficulty:* The degree of difficulty in measuring performance of exchange partners in circumstances of joint effort, soft outcomes, and/or ambiguous links between effort and performance (e.g., Tate and Ellram, 2009).

107. *Middle-management commitment/support:* The extent to which middle managers provide leadership, support, and commitment to outsourcing (e.g., Levina and Su, 2008).

108. *Mutual agreement:* The degree of agreement about behaviors, goals, obligations, and policies among partners (e.g., Lioliou *et al.*, 2014).

109. *Mutual dependency:* The degree to which a client and a provider depend upon one another (e.g., Baraldi *et al.*, 2014).

110. *Mutual understanding:* The degree of understanding of behaviors, goals, and policies among partners (e.g., Sen and Shiel, 2006).

111. *Opportunism:* 'Self-interest seeking with guile' or 'Making of false or empty, that is self-disbelieved, threats and promises' (Williamson, 1976, 1991; Tate and Ellram, 2009).

112. *Organizational boundaries:* The demarcation between the organization and its environment; in outsourcing, the demarcation between the client and provider organizations (e.g., Baraldi *et al.*, 2014).

113. *Organizational learning:* The degree to which organizations learn, often associated with the organization's commitment to learn, open-mindedness and shared vision (e.g., Malik *et al.*, 2012).

114. *Outsourcing decision – backsourcing:* A client organization's decision to bring a previously outsourced service back in-house (e.g., Veltri *et al.*, 2008).

115. *Outsourcing decision – bundled services:* A client organization's decision to procure multiple services from the same provider, especially as it relates to the decision to deepen an existing provider relationship (e.g., Su and Levina, 2011).

116. *Outsourcing decision – captive:* A client organization's decision to operate a captive center in a nondomestic location (e.g., Massini *et al*, 2010).

117. *Outsourcing decision – commercial enterprise:* A client organization's decision to create a new commercial entity to provide outsourcing services to both internal and external customers (e.g., Freytag *et al.*, 2012).

118. *Outsourcing decision – degree of outsourcing:* The amount of outsourcing as indicated by percentage of budget outsourced and/or type and number of business services outsourced (e.g., Gilley *et al.*, 2004; Salimath *et al.*, 2008).

119. *Outsourcing decision – degree of outsourcing – offshore:* The amount of offshore outsourcing as indicated by percentage of budget outsourced and/or type and number of business services outsourced (e.g., Khan and Lacity, 2012).

120. *Outsourcing decision – domestic:* A client organization's decision to engage a domestic provider (e.g., Pearce, 2014).

121. *Outsourcing decision – impact sourcing:* Hiring marginalized individuals (i.e., people who normally would have few opportunities for good employment) to provide IT, BP, or other digitally enabled services (e.g., Lacity *et al.*, 2014).

122. *Outsourcing decision – make or buy:* The fundamental make or buy decision (e.g., Williamson, 1991) in which a client organization decides to keep a business service in-house or decides to engage an outsourcing provider, measured as a binary variable (e.g., Lee and Kim, 2010).

123. *Outsourcing decision – multisourcing:* A client organization's decision to engage multiple service providers (e.g., Sia *et al.*, 2008), primarily aiming for breath of providers (e.g., Su and Levina, 2011).

124. *Outsourcing decision – offshore:* A client organization's decision to engage an offshore provider (e.g., Fifarek *et al.*, 2008; Lee and Kim, 2010).

125. *Outsourcing decision – offshore – county:* A client's decision to select this country as an offshore outsourcing destination; a country's location attractiveness to outsourcing clients in other countries (e.g., Datta and Bhattacharya, 2012).

126. *Outsourcing decision – provider selection:* A client organization's reason(s) for selecting a particular provider (e.g., Howells *et al.*, 2008). (Previously called 'Outsourcing Decision – Supplier Selection' in Lacity *et al.*, 2011.)

127. *Outsourcing decision – renewal:* The client's decision to extend or renew an existing outsourcing contract (e.g., Bharadwaj *et al.*, 2010).

128. *Outsourcing decision – rural:* A client organization's decision to engage a rural-based provider (e.g., Lacity, Rottman, & Khan, 2010).

129. *Outsourcing decision – shared services:* The client's decision to share services across business divisions (e.g., Sako, 2010).

130. *Outsourcing decision – switch providers:* A client organization's decision to switch outsourcing providers (e.g., Freytag *et al.*, 2012).

131. *Outsourcing outcomes – backsourcing:* The degree to which a client organization reports successful backsourcing of a business or IT service (e.g., Bhagwatwar *et al.*, 2011).

132. *Outsourcing outcomes – captive:* The degree to which a client organization reports that the captive center is successful (e.g., Prikladnicki and Audy, 2012).

133. *Outsourcing outcomes – organizational business performance – client:* The degree to which a client organization achieved organizational-level business performance improvements, as a result of an outsourcing decision, such as stock price performance, revenue growth, return on assets, expenses, or profits (e.g., Reitzig and Wagner, 2010).

134. *Outsourcing outcomes – organizational business performance – provider:* The degree to which a provider organization achieved organizational-level business performance improvements, as a result of an outsourcing decision, such as stock price performance, return on assets, expenses, or profits (e.g., Rajeev and Vani, 2009).

135. *Outsourcing outcomes – performance improvements:* The degree to which a client organization reports business service improvements, as a consequence of outsourcing, such as reports of costs savings realized, better quality of services, better compliance, or tighter security (e.g., Mani *et al.*, 2010). (Previously called 'Outsourcing Outcomes – Process Performance Improvements' in Lacity *et al.*, 2011.)

136. *Outsourcing outcomes – performance improvements – offshore:* The degree to which a client organization reports business service improvements as a consequence of offshore outsourcing, such as reports of costs savings realized or better quality of services (e.g., Levina and Su, 2008). (Previously called 'Outsourcing Outcomes – Process Performance Improvements – Offshore' in Lacity *et al.*, 2011.)

137. *Outsourcing outcomes – project performance:* The degree to which a project is delivered on time, within budget, and meets requirements (e.g., Palvia *et al.*, 2010).

138. *Outsourcing outcomes – project performance – offshore:* The degree to which an offshored project is delivered on time, within budget, and meets requirements (e.g., Tate and Ellram, 2012).

139. *Outsourcing outcomes – success – client:* A client organization's general perceptions of success and satisfaction with outsourcing (e.g., Sia *et al.*, 2008). (Previously called 'Outsourcing Outcomes – Success' in Lacity *et al.*, 2011.)

140. *Outsourcing outcomes – success – offshore:* A client organization's general perceptions of success and satisfaction with offshore outsourcing (e.g., Vivek *et al.*, 2008).

141. **Outsourcing outcomes – success – provider:* A provider organization's general perceptions of success and satisfaction with outsourcing/offshoring (e.g., Palvia *et al.*, 2011).

142. **Outsourcing outcomes – success – shared services:* A client organization's general perceptions of success and satisfaction with shared services (e.g., Iveroth, 2010).

143. **Outsourcing outcomes – switch providers:* A client organization's report on the extent of success after switching service providers (e.g., Wiener and Saunders, 2014a).

144. *Partnership view:* A client organization's consideration of providers as trusted partners rather than as opportunistic vendors (e.g., Willcocks *et al.*, 2004; Sen and Shiel, 2006).

145. *Political reasons/influences:* A client stakeholder's desire or need to use a sourcing decision to promote personal agendas (e.g., Maelah *et al.*, 2010).

146. **Practical intelligence:* An individual's ability to resolve project-related work problems that are unexpected, difficult, and cannot be resolved using established processes and frameworks (e.g., Langer *et al.*, 2014).

147. *Prior client/provider working relationship:* The situation in which the client and provider organizations have worked together in the past (e.g., Mani *et al.*, 2010). (Previously called 'Prior Client/ Supplier Working Relationship' in Lacity *et al.*, 2011.)

148. *Prior firm performance – client:* Client firm performance usually measured as net profits, return on assets, expenses, earnings per

share, number of patents, and/or stock price prior to an outsourcing decision. (e.g., Dunbar and Phillips, 2001; Gilley *et al.*, 2004).

149. *Prior firm performance – provider:* Provider firm performance usually measured as net profits, return on assets, expenses, earnings per share, and/or stock price prior to an outsourcing contract. (e.g., Gewald and Gellrich, 2007; Nadkarni and Herrmann, 2010). (Previously called 'Prior Firm Performance – Supplier' in Lacity *et al.*, 2011.)

150. *Product quality:* The quality of the end product delivered as part of an outsourcing/offshoring arrangement (e.g., Whitten and Leidner, 2006).

151. *Project duration:* The duration of the project in terms of time (e.g., Ramchandran and Gopal, 2010).

152. *Project management capability – client:* The ability of retained teams within client organizations to internally manage and coordinate project activities related to planning, execution, and feedback for an outsourced project (e.g., Gopal *et al.*, 2011).

153. *Project management capability – provider:* The ability of delivery teams within provider organizations to internally manage and coordinate project activities related to planning, execution, and feedback for an outsourced project (e.g., Gopal *et al.*, 2011).

154. *Project scoping accuracy – provider:* A provider firm capability to estimate the contract scope accurately (not underbid or overbid) (e.g., Koh *et al.*, 2004). (Previously called 'Project Scoping Accuracy' in Lacity, Rottman, & Khan, 2010).

155. *Project size:* The size of a project, usually measured as number of people or effort (e.g., Langer *et al.*, 2014).

156. *Provider breadth of service:* The degree to which providers offer a wide variety of services (e.g., Gao *et al.*, 2010).

157. *Provider capabilities:* A broad term that captures the overall level of a provider's abilities (e.g., Su and Levina, 2011). (Previously called 'Supplier's Core Competences' in Lacity, Rottman, & Khan, 2010).

158. *Provider competition:* The presence of multiple, reputable, and trustworthy service providers which can provide a range of

choices for the clients (e.g., Levina and Su, 2008). (Previously called 'Supplier Competition' in Lacity *et al.*, 2011.)

159. *Provider dependency:* The degree to which a client depends on a provider (e.g., Borman, 2006). (Previously called 'Supplier Dependency' in Lacity *et al.*, 2011.)

160. *Provider employee – attitude:* Attitude of employees toward their jobs or employers (e.g., Sarker *et al.*, 2010).

161. *Provider employee performance:* The client's perception of the performance of individual provider employees (e.g., Daityari *et al.*, 2008; Lam and Chua, 2009). (Previously called 'Supplier Employee Performance' in Lacity *et al.*, 2011.)

162. *Provider employee satisfaction:* The degree to which provider employees are satisfied with their jobs and employers (e.g., Lacity *et al.*, 2014).

163. *Provider employee turnover:* The percentage of the workers that are replaced in a given time period, frequently measured as turnover intention (e.g., Budhwar *et al.*, 2006) (Previously called 'Supplier Employee Turnover' in Lacity *et al.*, 2011.)

164. *Provider employee work life conflict:* 'The inter-(between) role conflict where the demands created by the job interfere with performing family-related responsibilities'(Netemeyer *et al.*, 2004, p. 50, as cited in Sarker *et al.*, 2010).

165. *Provider firm age:* The age of a provider firm in years (e.g., Lahiri and Kedia, 2009). (Previously called 'Supplier Age' in Lacity *et al.*, 2011.)

166. *Provider management capability:* The extent to which a client organization is able to effectively manage outsourcing providers (e.g., Sanders *et al.*, 2007). (Previously called 'Supplier Management Capability' in Lacity *et al.*, 2011.)

167. *Provider power:* The degree of power the provider has over the client (e.g., Barthélemy, 2011).

168. *Provider reputation:* The public's perception of a provider's capabilities based on past performance and financial status (e.g., Gewald and Gellrich, 2007). (Previously called 'Supplier Reputation' in Lacity *et al.*, 2011.)

169. *Provider size:* The size of a provider organization usually measured as total assets, sales, and/or number of employees (e.g., Nadkarni and Herrmann, 2010). (Previously called 'Supplier Size' in Lacity *et al.*, 2011.)

170. *Public perceptions of outsourcing:* The degree to which the public has a negative perception of outsourcing or offshoring (e.g., Sen and Shiel, 2006).

171. *Quality improvement:* A client organization's desire or need to improve the quality of the client's business, processes, or capabilities (e.g., Gewald and Dibbern, 2009).

172. *Quality management capability – provider:* The degree to which a provider has a total quality management philosophy and a focus on continuous improvement (e.g., Malik *et al.*, 2012).

173. *R&D spend:* The amount of money an organization spends on R&D (e.g., Calantone and Stanko, 2007; Grimpe and Kaiser, 2010).

174. *Rapid delivery:* A client organization's desire or need to speed up service delivery (e.g., Bandyopadhyay and Hall, 2009; Lam and Chua, 2009).

175. *Relational governance:* The unwritten, worker-based mechanisms designed to influence interorganizational behavior (Macneil, 1980; Kim, 2008).

176. *Relationship quality:* The quality of the relationship between a client and provider (e.g., Sia *et al*, 2008; Saxena and Bharadwaj, 2009).

177. *Relationship-specific investment:* Specific investments made over time which discourage opportunism, reinforce signals of the client firms, and create extendedness of the relationships (e.g., Tate and Ellram, 2009).

178. *Risk:* The extent to which a transaction exposes a party (client or provider) to a chance of loss or damage (e.g., Wullenweber *et al.*, 2008; Mathew and Das Aundhe, 2011).

179. *Risk management capability – client:* A client organization's practice of identifying, rating, and mitigating potential risks associated with outsourcing (e.g., Borman, 2006).

180. *Risk spread:* The distribution of risk, typically by assigning work to multiple providers and/or locations (e.g., Su and Levina, 2011).

181. *Scalability:* The ability to scale volume of service up or down based on demand (e.g., Currie *et al.*, 2008; Redondo-Cano and Canet-Giner, 2010).

182. *Security breach:* A significant incident that results in unauthorized access of data, applications, services, networks and/or devices, or loss or theft of IP (e.g., Gorla and Lau, 2010).

183. *Security, privacy, and confidentiality capability – provider:* The proven ability of a provider to protect client data through investments in technology, training, process controls, audits, and other management practices (e.g., Sen and Shiel, 2006). (Previously called 'Security, Privacy, and Confidentiality Capability – Supplier' in Lacity *et al.*, 2011.)

184. *Senior leadership:* The extent to which the senior executives of an organization are effective leaders (e.g., Lacity *et al.*, 2004).

185. *Service complexity:* The degree to which a service or project requires compound steps, the control of many variables, and/or where cause and effect are subtle and dynamic (e.g., Ventovuori and Lehtonen, 2006; Penfold, 2009). (Previously called 'Process Complexity' in Lacity *et al.*, 2011.)

186. *Service integration:* The degree to which clients and providers are able to integrate services (e.g., Sen and Shiel, 2006). (Previously called 'Process Integration' in Lacity *et al.*, 2011.)

187. *Service interdependence:* The level of integration and coupling among tasks; services that are highly integrated are tightly coupled and difficult to detach (e.g., Sanders *et al.*, 2007). (Previously called 'Process Interdependence' in Lacity *et al.*, 2011.)

188. *Service quality:* The quality of a service, frequently measured as a client's perception of a satisfactory service performance by the provider (e.g., Lewin and Peeters, 2006).

189. *Service standardization:* The degree to which a service is standard (e.g., Tate and Ellram, 2009). (Previously called 'Process Standardization' in Lacity *et al.*, 2011.)

190. *Slack resources:* Resources and organization possesses in excess of what is required to maintain the organization (e.g., Koh *et al*, 2004; Hall and Liedtka, 2005). (Previously called 'Financial Slack' in Lacity, Rottman, & Khan, 2010).

191. *Social capital – cognitive dimension:* Social capital arising from the sharing representations, interpretations, and systems of meaning among parties (Nahapiet and Ghoshal, 1998; Willcocks *et al.*, 2004).

192. *Social capital – relational dimension:* Social capital arising from personal relationships people have developed with each other through a history of interactions (Nahapiet and Ghoshal, 1998; Willcocks *et al.*, 2004).

193. *Social capital – structural dimension:* Social capital arising from the patterns of linkages between people or units including network ties, network configuration, and network appropriability (Nahapiet and Ghoshal, 1998; Willcocks *et al.*, 2004).

194. *Social norms:* An individual's perceptions of the social pressures put on him or her to perform or not to perform the behavior in question. (Ajzen and Fishbein, 1980; Raman *et al.*, 2007).

195. *Staff transfer:* The practice of transferring staff from the client to provider organization (e.g., Miozzo and Grimshaw, 2011).

196. *Stakeholder buy-in:* Gaining commitment and support from all parties involved in sourcing-related decisions (e.g., Tate and Ellram, 2009).

197. *Strategic intent:* A client organization's desire or need to source for strategic reasons such as developing new capabilities that can be leveraged in the marketplace (e.g., Sanders *et al.*, 2007).

198. *Switching costs:* The costs incurred when a client organization changes from one provider or marketplace to another (e.g., Wahrenburg *et al.*, 2006).

199. *Task programmability:* The degree to which appropriate behavior by the agent (provider) can be precisely defined in advance (Eisenhardt, 1989) (e.g., Susarla *et al.*, 2010a, b).

200. *Task variety:* The degree to which a task requires various activities, skills, and talents (e.g., Sengupta and Gupta, 2011).

201. *Team dispersion:* The degree to which a team is geographically dispersed, often measured as a percentage of teammates onshore/offshore (e.g., Langer *et al.*, 2014).
202. *Team size:* The number of individuals assigned to a team (e.g., Gopal and Koka, 2012).
203. *Team turnover:* The extent to which team members leave a team (e.g., Narayanan *et al.*, 2011).
204. *Technical and methodological capability – client:* A client organization's level of maturity in terms of technical or process-related standards, and best practices (e.g., Bardhan *et al.*, 2007).
205. *Technical and methodological capability – provider:* A provider organization's level of maturity in terms of technical or process-related and best practices (e.g., Sia *et al.*, 2008; Shah Bharadwaj and Saxena, 2009). (Previously called 'Technical and Methodological Capability – Supplier' in Lacity *et al.*, 2011.)
206. *Technology infrastructure quality – provider:* The degree to which the technology infrastructure the provider uses to support service delivery is nimble, scalable, and state-of-the-art (e.g., Kannabiran and Sankaran, 2011).
207. *Technology integration imperative:* A client organization's need or desire to integrate technologies (e.g., Gefen *et al.*, 2011).
208. *Technology upgrade:* A client organization's need or desire to improve or upgrade technology (e.g., Bhagwatwar *et al.*, 2011). (Previously called 'Technical Reasons' in Lacity, Rottman, & Khan, 2010).
209. *Time zone differences:* The difference in local times between two locations as measured in hours (e.g., Mehta *et al.*, 2006).
210. *Top management commitment/support:* The extent to which senior executives provide leadership, support, and commitment to outsourcing (e.g., Tate and Ellram, 2009).
211. *Training:* The nature or extent of provider employee training by either the client or provider organization (e.g., Raman *et al.*, 2007; Malik, 2009).
212. *Transaction costs:* The effort, time, and costs incurred in searching, creating, negotiating, monitoring, and administrating a

service contract between buyers and providers (Williamson, 1991; Levina and Su, 2008).

213. *Transaction frequency:* The number of times a client organization initiates a transaction typically categorized as either occasional or frequent (e.g., Wahrenburg *et al.*, 2006).

214. *Transaction size:* The size of a transaction often measured in terms of dollar value or effort (e.g., Luo *et al.*, 2010).

215. *Transaction type:* The type of work, usually operationalized as a categorical variable, such as delineating among transactions involving development, maintenance, and reengineering work (e.g., Gopal and Koka, 2010) or between ITO and BPO (e.g., Lee and Kim, 2010).

216. *Transition management capability – client:* The extent to which a client organization effectively transitions services to or from outsourcing providers or integrates client services with provider services (e.g., Luo *et al.*, 2010).

217. *Transition management capability – provider:* The extent to which a provider organization effectively transitions services from a client organization to the provider or integrates client services with provider services (e.g., Saxena and Bharadwaj, 2009). (Previously called 'Transition Management Capability – Supplier' in Lacity *et al.*, 2011.)

218. *Trust:* The confidence in the other party's benevolence (e.g., Gainey and Klaas, 2003).

219. *Uncertainty:* The degree of unpredictability or volatility of future states as it relates to the definition of requirements, emerging technologies, and/or environmental factors (Williamson, 1991; Mani *et al.*, 2010).

Appendix B

Table B.1 Frequency with which dependent variables appear in this review by type of service

Meta category/dependent variable	Frequency by type of service			
	Both	BP	IT	Total
Sourcing outcomes				
Outsourcing outcomes – success – client	27	38	47	112
Outsourcing outcomes – organizational business performance – client	18	11	27	56
Outsourcing outcomes – success – offshore	4	19	32	55
Outsourcing outcomes – organizational business performance – provider	1	29	23	53
Outsourcing outcomes – project performance	3		50	53
Outsourcing outcomes – performance improvements	8	8	27	43
Outsourcing outcomes – project performance – offshore	8	1	30	39
Service quality	3		30	33
Innovation effects	7	21	3	31
Outsourcing outcomes – success – provider	25	1		26
Risk			19	19
Outsourcing outcomes – success – shared services		15		15
Outsourcing outcomes – performance improvements – offshore	9	1		10
Outsourcing outcomes – captive			8	8
Loss of control			8	8
Outsourcing outcomes – backsourcing			2	2
R&D spend		1		1
Outsourcing outcomes – switch providers			1	1
Loss of knowledge		1		1
Sourcing outcomes total	113	146	307	566
Sourcing decisions				
Outsourcing decision – make or buy	7	19	61	87
Outsourcing decision – offshore	14	34	26	74

(*continued*)

Table B.1 (continued)

Meta category/dependent variable	Frequency by type of service			
	Both	BP	IT	Total
Outsourcing decision – degree of outsourcing	3	27	42	72
Outsourcing decision – renewal	12	2	15	29
Outsourcing decision – shared services		18	7	25
Country selection	15	6		21
Outsourcing decision – backsourcing	4	7	4	15
Outsourcing decision – domestic		14	1	15
Outsourcing decision – switch providers	6		7	13
Outsourcing decision – multisourcing			7	7
Outsourcing decision – captive		7		7
Outsourcing decision – bundled services			4	4
Outsourcing decision – impact sourcing		3	1	4
Outsourcing decision – offshore – country	3			3
Outsourcing decision – rural			3	3
Outsourcing decision – degree of outsourcing – offshore	2			2
Outsourcing decision – provider selection			1	1
Outsourcing decision – commercial enterprise	1			1
Sourcing decisions total	65	140	178	383
Miscellaneous				
Adaptability		8	14	22
Provider employee turnover		7	7	14
Client power	11			11
Provider employee satisfaction		4	5	9
Transition management capability – client			9	9
Service integration		8		8
Absorptive capacity – client		1	6	7
Evaluation process – provider selection			7	7
Degree of internationalization – provider			6	6
Coopetition			6	6
Switching costs			6	6
Transaction costs	3		2	5

(*continued*)

Table B.1 (continued)

Meta category/dependent variable	Frequency by type of service			
	Both	BP	IT	Total
Corporate social responsibility capability – provider			5	5
Absorptive capacity – provider		1	4	5
Opportunism		4	1	5
Transition management capability – provider			4	4
Boundary spanning capability – provider			4	4
Organizational learning		4		4
Innovativeness – provider			4	4
Technical and methodological capability – client			3	3
CIO power			3	3
Knowledge formalization			3	3
Domain understanding			3	3
Provider employee performance		1	2	3
Technical and methodological capability – provider	1	1		2
Business service management capability – client		1	1	2
Provider employee – attitude			2	2
Measurement difficulty			2	2
Provider capabilities			2	2
Mutual dependency	1		1	2
Provider competition	1		1	2
Functional spend			2	2
Client management capability			2	2
Flexibility enablement			2	2
Human resource management capability – provider		1	1	2
Career development of employees			1	1
Centralization			1	1
Degree of internationalization – client			1	1
Change management capability – client			1	1
Client outsourcing readiness		1		1
Provider employee work life conflict			1	1
Client business change		1		1
Provider management capability			1	1

(*continued*)

Table B.1 (continued)

Meta category/dependent variable	Frequency by type of service			
	Both	BP	IT	Total
Provider dependency			1	1
Risk management capability – client			1	1
Department power		1		1
Security breach			1	1
External production cost advantage			1	1
Miscellaneous total	17	44	130	191
Relational governance				
Knowledge sharing		5	19	24
Relational governance		8	10	18
Trust		1	11	12
Commitment		3	8	11
Cooperation			10	10
Relationship quality	3		5	8
Mutual understanding			5	5
Mutual agreement			4	4
Social capital – relational dimension			2	2
Communication			2	2
Relationship-specific investment			2	2
Conflict resolution			1	1
Relational governance totall	3	17	79	99
Contractual governance				
Control mechanisms		9	8	17
Contract type	7	1	6	14
Contractual governance		8	3	11
Contract flexibility			10	10
Contract duration			6	6
Contract detail			4	4
Contract size	2			2
Organizational boundaries	1			1
Contractual governance total	10	18	37	65
Grand total	208	365	731	1304

Note: Total 105 unique variables appearing as dependent variables.

Appendix C

Table C.1 Frequency with which independent variables appear in this review by type of service

Meta category/dependent variable	Frequency by type of service			
	Both	BP	IT	Total
Transaction attributes				
Uncertainty	2	5	22	29
Transaction type	8	5	10	23
Critical role of business service – organization	6	2	9	17
Service interdependence	1	6	6	13
Measurement difficulty	3	3	7	13
Knowledge formalization	4	4	4	12
Service standardization	1	5	6	12
Service complexity	1	3	8	12
Asset specificity	2		9	11
Project size			11	11
Team size			10	10
Provider dependency	3	2	4	9
Risk		1	6	7
Client specific knowledge required	1	1	5	7
Transaction costs			6	6
Knowledge required	2	1	3	6
Project duration	1		5	6
External production cost advantage	1		4	5
Adaptability	1		4	5
Transaction size	1		4	5
Service integration		1	3	4
Asset specificity – human			4	4
Opportunism		2	1	3
Switching costs	2		1	3
Product quality	2	2		
Mutual dependency	1		1	2
Information quality	1		1	2
Task programmability		1	1	2
Information asymmetry			2	2
Asset specificity – physical			1	1
Training		1		1
Transaction frequency			1	1
Asset complementarity		1		1
Transaction attributes total	42	44	161	247

(continued)

Table C.1 (continued)

Meta category/dependent variable	Frequency by type of service			
	Both	BP	IT	Total
Relational governance				
Knowledge sharing	1	9	20	30
Communication	2	5	19	26
Relational governance	3	4	12	19
Trust	1	3	11	15
Client – provider interface design		3	9	12
Commitment	1	4	5	10
Social capital – relational dimension		3	5	8
Relationship-specific investment	2		5	7
Cooperation	1	2	3	6
Client – provider alignment	1	4	1	6
Client-provider coordination processes	2		3	5
Cultural distance management		2	2	4
Social capital – structural dimension		1	3	4
Conflict resolution		1	3	4
Mutual understanding		1	2	3
Partnership view		3		3
Culture		2	1	3
Social capital – cognitive dimension		1	1	2
Conflict resolution approach		2		2
Mutual agreement			2	2
Social norms		1		1
Team dispersion			1	1
Relational governance total	14	51	108	173
Client firm characteristics				
Client size	11	18	9	38
Industry	6	13	13	32
Client experience with outsourcing	3	5	3	11
Centralization		4	4	8
Client age	2	4	1	7
Degree of internationalization – client		7		7
Prior firm performance – client	1	1	3	5
Department performance		1	3	4
Functional spend		3	1	4
Innovativeness – client		4		4
Slack resources		2	1	3
CIO power			3	3
Culture			3	3
R&D spend	1	2		3

(*continued*)

Table C.1 (continued)

Meta category/dependent variable	Frequency by type of service			
	Both	BP	IT	Total
Department power		1	2	3
Business strategic type		2		2
Firm ownership structure – client		2		2
Department size			2	2
Client size – department			1	1
Client business change			1	1
Client prestige	1			1
Client firm characteristics total	25	69	49	143
Sourcing motivation				
Cost reduction	5	12	10	27
Access to expertise/skills	5	9	5	19
Quality improvement	3	9		12
Flexibility enablement	1	3	4	8
Concern for security/intellectual property		6	1	7
Strategic intent	2	2	3	7
Innovation	1	4	2	7
Focus on core capabilities	2	2	2	6
Rapid delivery	3		2	5
Access to global markets	2	1	2	5
Fear of losing control		1	4	5
Technology integration imperative		2	1	3
Scalability		2	1	3
Political reasons/influences			2	2
Technology upgrade			1	1
Convenience			1	1
Change catalyst		1		1
Compliance		1		1
Sourcing motivation total	24	55	41	120
Service sourcing decisions				
Outsourcing decision – make or buy	1	13	25	39
Outsourcing decision – degree of outsourcing	2	8	10	20
Outsourcing decision – offshore	4	4	7	15
Outsourcing decision – multisourcing		2	12	14
Outsourcing decision – bundled services			6	6
Outsourcing decision – shared services			6	6

(*continued*)

Table C.1 (continued)

Meta category/dependent variable	Frequency by type of service			
	Both	BP	IT	Total
Outsourcing decision – impact sourcing		3	1	4
Outsourcing decision – provider selection			2	2
Outsourcing decision – domestic	2			2
Configurational approach		2		2
Outsourcing decision – rural			1	1
Outsourcing decision – offshore – captive	1			1
Outsourcing decision – captive		1		1
Outsourcing decision – degree of outsourcing – offshore			1	1
Outsourcing decision – renewal	1			1
Service sourcing decisions total	11	33	71	115
Provider firm capabilities				
Human resource management capability – provider	2	9	12	23
Technical and methodological capability – provider	5	2	14	21
Domain understanding	1	2	9	12
Corporate social responsibility capability – provider			7	7
Client management capability	4		2	6
Absorptive capacity – provider		1	4	5
Contract management capability – provider	3	1		4
Provider breadth of service		1	2	3
Security, privacy, and confidentiality capability – provider			3	3
Business service management capability – provider	1	1	1	3
Project management capability – provider			3	3
Project scoping accuracy – provider		2	1	3
Delivery capability	2			2
Technology infrastructure quality – provider			2	2
Transition management capability – provider		1	1	2

(*continued*)

Table C.1 (continued)

Meta category/dependent variable	Frequency by type of service			
	Both	BP	IT	Total
Change management capability – provider		1	1	2
Quality management capability – provider		1		1
Provider capabilities			1	1
Boundary spanning capability – provider			1	1
Provider employee performance			1	1
Organizational learning		1		1
Provider firm capabilities total	18	23	65	106
Client firm capabilities				
Technical and methodological capability – client	2	9	15	26
Client outsourcing readiness	1	1	9	11
Absorptive capacity – client	1	6	4	11
Transition management capability – client		1	7	8
Human resource management capability – client	2	4	2	8
Corporate social responsibility capability – client			6	6
Contract management capability – client	1	1	3	5
Provider management capability	2		2	4
Business service management capability – client	2	1	1	4
Change management capability – client		3		3
Evaluation process – client assessment	1		1	2
Risk management capability – client			2	2
Boundary spanning capability – client			1	1
Project management capability – client			1	1
Client firm capabilities total	12	26	54	92
Contractual governance				
Contractual governance		4	15	19
Contract type	4		13	17
Contract detail	1	3	12	16
Control mechanisms	1	6	5	12

(*continued*)

Table C.1 (continued)

Meta category/dependent variable	Frequency by type of service			
	Both	BP	IT	Total
Contract size	4		4	8
Key performance indicators		5	1	6
Contract duration	2		3	5
Contract flexibility		1	3	4
Staff transfer			2	2
Organizational boundaries	2			2
Contractual governance total	14	19	58	91
Country characteristics				
Cultural distance	2	3	13	18
Country – financial attractiveness	4	1	2	7
Country – business attractiveness	4	1	2	7
Time zone differences			5	5
Culture	4			4
Geographic distance	2		2	4
Country – human resource attractiveness	2	1	1	4
Country	1	1	1	3
Legal and political uncertainties	1			1
Country size	1			1
Country characteristics total	21	7	26	54
Provider firm characteristics				
Provider size	2	4	8	14
Provider reputation	1	2	5	8
Provider firm age		3	1	4
Provider employee turnover		1	3	4
Firm ownership structure – provider	1	1	1	3
Senior leadership	1	2		3
Degree of internationalization – provider			1	1	2
Industry			2	2
Innovativeness – provider		1	1	2
Prior firm performance – provider			1	1
Adherence to environmental standards			1	1
Culture		1		1
Provider firm characteristics total	5	16	24	45
Relationship characteristics				
Prior client/provider working relationship			17	17

(*continued*)

Table C.1 (continued)

Meta category/dependent variable	Frequency by type of service			
	Both	BP	IT	Total
Length of relationship	3	1	4	8
Client power	1	1	2	4
Relationship quality	2		1	3
Team turnover			2	2
Provider power		1		1
Relationship characteristics total	6	3	26	35
Service sourcing outcomes				
Outsourcing outcomes – performance improvements	1	1	7	9
Service quality	1	1	4	6
Outsourcing outcomes – project performance	2		2	4
Loss of control	1	1	2	4
Innovation effects			3	3
Loss of knowledge		1	1	2
Outsourcing outcomes – success – offshore			2	2
Outsourcing outcomes – success – client	1			1
Outsourcing outcomes – organizational business performance – provider			1	1
Outsourcing outcomes – project performance – offshore			1	1
Service sourcing outcomes total	6	4	23	33
Environment				
Provider competition	3	4	8	15
Uncertainty		3		3
Public perceptions of outsourcing			3	3
Competition in client firm environment			2	2
Industry growth			1	1
Environment total	3	7	14	24
Influences				
Influences – mimetic	3	2		5
Influences – external and internal	1		3	4
Influences – coercive	1		1	2
Influences total	5	2	4	11

(*continued*)

Table C.1 (continued)

Meta category/dependent variable	Frequency by type of service			
	Both	BP	IT	Total
Decision characteristics				
Stakeholder buy-in		2	1	3
Top management commitment/ support		2	1	3
Evaluation process – provider selection			2	2
Middle management commitment/ support	2			2
Risk spread			1	1
Decision characteristics total	2	4	5	11
Employee level				
Practical intelligence			2	2
Provider employee satisfaction		1		1
Task variety		1		1
Employee level total		2	2	4
Grand total	208	365	731	1304

Note: Total 203 Unique Variables Appearing as Independent Variables. Three variables appear more than once under different meta categories.

Appendix D

Table D.1 Relationship Data for all Independent Variables and Five Categories of Dependent Variables

META CATEGORY / Independent Variable	Sourcing Outcomes					Sourcing Decisions					Miscellaneous Variables					Relational Governance					Contractual Governance					Grand Total
	+1	0	-1	M	Tot	+1	0	-1	M	Tot	+1	0	-1	M	Tot	+1	0	-1	M	Tot	+1	0	-1	M	Tot	
TRANSACTION ATTRIBUTES																										
Uncertainty	1	5	4		10	2	6	3	1	12	1	1			2						3	1		1	5(+)	29
Transaction Type		6		11	17(M)		3			3			1		1								2		2	23
Critical Role of Business Service-Organization	3		1		4	4	6	2		12											1				1	17
Service Interdependence	1	1	1		3		3			3	2				2	1				1	2	1	1		4	13
Measurement Difficulty	2	1	5		8(-)		1	1		2	2	1			3											13
Knowledge Formalization	2	2	1		5	4	1	1		6(++)	1				1											12
Service Standardization	2	1	1		4	1	5			6(+)	2				2											12
Service Complexity	1	2	1		4	1	1	4		6(-)	1				1	1				1						12
Asset Specificity	2				2	1	2			3	1				1	2				2	2		1		3	11
Project Size	3	1	3	1	8						1				1	1				1	1				1	11
Team Size	2	2	3		7						2				2			1			1				1	10
Provider Dependency	2		1		3		1			1	3	1			4		2			2	1				1	9
Risk	1		4		5(-)											2				2						7
Client Specific Knowledge Required	2	1			3		3	1		4																7
Transaction Costs	1				1	1	1	3		5(-)																6
Knowledge Required						3	2	1		6																6
Project Duration						4	1			5(+)		1			1											6
External Production Cost Advantage	2	1	1		4						1				1											5
Adaptability	1				1						1				1		3			3						5
Transaction Size	2		1		3											1				1		1			1	5

Table D. 1 (Continued)

META CATEGORY/ Independent Variable	Sourcing Outcomes					Sourcing Decisions					Miscellaneous Variables					Relational Governance					Contractual Governance					Grand Total
	+1	0	-1	M	Tot	+1	0	-1	M	Tot	+1	0	-1	M	Tot	+1	0	-1	M	Tot	+1	0	-1	M	Tot	
Service Integration	1				1			2		2											1				1	4
Asset Specificity - Human		1			1	1				1	1				1						1				1	4
Opportunism							1	1		2	1				1											3
Switching Costs						1		1		2			1		1											3
Product Quality	1				1			1		1																2
Mutual Dependency	1				1											1				1						2
Information Quality	1				1											1				1						2
Task Programmability	1				1																1				1	2
Information Asymmetry		2			2																					2
Asset Specificity - Physical											1				1											1
Training											1				1											1
Transaction Frequency								1		1																1
Asset Complementarity								1		1																1
Transaction Attributes Total	20	36	33	11	100	27	17	34	6	84	13	10	2	2	27	6	4	2		12	11	6	1	6	24	247
RELATIONAL GOVERNANCE																										
Knowledge Sharing	11	5	2		18(+)	1				1	6	2			8(+)	3				3						30
Communication	14	1			15(++)			1		1	4				4	5		1		6(++)						26
Relational Governance	13	2	1		16(++)						2		1		3											19
Trust	8	1	1		10(+)						2				2	3				3						15
Client - Provider Interface Design	2			3	5(M)						3			2	5(+)	1			1	2						12
Commitment	5				5(++)						2				2	3				3						10
Social Capital - Relational Dimension	1	1			2						4				4	2				2						8
Relationship Specific Investment	3	1			4	2				2	1				1											7
Cooperation	5				5(++)						1				1											6
Client - Provider Alignment	4	1			5(+)						1				1											6
Client - Provider Coordination Processes	2				2	1				1	1				1	1				1						5
Cultural Distance Management	3				3											1				1						4
Social Capital - Structural Dimension	1	1			2						2				2											4

Table D. 1 (Continued)

META CATEGORY/ Independent Variable	SO +1	SO 0	SO -1	SO M	SO Tot	SD +1	SD 0	SD -1	SD M	SD Tot	MV +1	MV 0	MV -1	MV M	MV Tot	RG +1	RG 0	RG -1	RG M	RG Tot	CG +1	CG 0	CG -1	CG M	CG Tot	Grand Total
Mutual Understanding	2				2											1				1						3
Partnership View	2				2											1				1						3
Culture				1	1								1		1	1				1						3
Social Capital - Cognitive Dimension	1				1						1				1											2
Conflict Resolution Approach																			2	2						2
Mutual Agreement																2			-	2						2
Social Norms			1		1								1													1
Team Dispersion																1				1						1
Relational Governance Total	77	14	5	4	100	4	2			6	30	6		2	38	19	5		5	29						173
CLIENT FIRM CHARACTERISTICS																										
Client Size	3	6		1	10(0)	6	9	4		19	1	2			3		1			1	1	3		1	5(0)	38
Industry		4	1	3	8		9		9	18	1				1	1	1			2		2		1	3	32
Client Experience with Outsourcing	1				3	5	2			7(+)							1			1	1	1			1	11
Centralization	3				3			4		5(-)																8
Client Age	2	1		1	4																2				2	7
Degree of Internationalization-Client						6		1		7(++)							1									7
Prior Firm Performance - Client	1				1	2		2		2	1					1										4
Department Performance						2	2			4																4
Functional Spend	1	1	1		2	1				1	1					1										4
Innovativeness - Client	1	1	1		2	1				1	1															4
Slack Resources	1	1			1						2															3
CIO Power	2				2	1				1	1															3
Culture				2	2						1															3
R&D Spend	1				1			1																		3
Department Power						2	1	1		2																3
Business Strategic Type									2	2																2
Firm Ownership Structure - Client	1				1		1																			2
Department Size	1				1		1																			2
Client Size - Department											1				1											1

Table D. 1 (Continued)

META CATEGORY/ Independent Variable	SO +1	SO 0	SO -1	SO M	SO Tot	SD +1	SD 0	SD -1	SD M	SD Tot	Misc +1	Misc 0	Misc -1	Misc M	Misc Tot	Rel +1	Rel 0	Rel -1	Rel M	Rel Tot	Contr +1	Contr 0	Contr -1	Contr M	Contr Tot	Grand Total
Client Business Change	1				1																					1
Client Prestige	1				1																					1
Client Firm Characteristics Total	16	18	3	6	43	23	29	13	12	77	5	3			8		3		1	4	1	8		2	11	143
SOURCING MOTIVATION																										
Cost Reduction	1				1	19	1	1	1	22(++)									1	1	2	1			3	27
Access to Expertise/Skills						17	1	1		19(++)												2			2	19
Quality Improvement						8		1		9(++)						1				1		2			2	12
Flexibility Enablement						8				8(++)																8
Concern for Security/Intellectual Property		1			1	1		1		2	1				1				1	1	2				2	7
Strategic Intent	3				3	2	1			3												1			1	7
Innovation	1				1	3				3						1				1	1		1		2	7
Focus on Core Capabilities						5		1		6(++)																6
Rapid Delivery						3				3													2		2	5
Access to Global Markets						5				5(++)																5
Fear of Losing Control						3			2	5(+)																5
Technology Integration Imperative						3				3																3
Scalability						3				3																3
Political Reasons/Influences						1	1			2																2
Technology Upgrade						1				1																1
Convenience						1				1																1
Change Catalyst						1				1																1
Compliance						1				1																1
Sourcing Motivation Total	5	1			6	85	4	5	3	97					1	2			2	4	5	4	3		12	120
SERVICE SOURCING DECISIONS																										
Outsourcing Decision - Make or Buy						16	7	10		**33**	4	2			**6(+)**											39
Outsourcing Decision - Degree of Outsourcing						4	5	5		**14(++)**	2	1			3						1				1	21
Outsourcing Decision - Offshore						7			1	**8(++)**	5				**5(++)**	1				1	1				1	15

META CATEGORY/ Independent Variable	Sourcing Outcomes					Sourcing Decisions					Miscellaneous Variables					Relational Governance					Contractual Governance					Grand Total
	+1	0	-1	M	Tot	+1	0	-1	M	Tot	+1	0	-1	M	Tot	+1	0	-1	M	Tot	+1	0	-1	M	Tot	
Outsourcing Decision - Bundled Services	2				2						3				3	3				3					3	6
Outsourcing Decision - Shared Services					1						3				3	3				3	1					6
Outsourcing Decision - Impact Sourcing	1				2						3				3					3						4
Outsourcing Decision - Provider Selection	1	1			2																					2
Outsourcing Decision - Domestic	1				1							1														2
Configurational Approach	1	1			2																					2
Outsourcing Decision - Rural	1				1																					1
Outsourcing Decision - Offshore - Captive			1		1																					1
Outsourcing Decision - Captive							1			1																1
Outsourcing Decision - Degree of Outsourcing - Offshore		1			1																					1
Outsourcing Decision - Renewal	1				1																					1
Service Sourcing Decisions Total	37	15	17	3	72	2	2			4	23	2	7	1	33	4				33	2				4	115
PROVIDER FIRM CAPABILITIES																										
Human Resource Management Capability - Provider	8		2		10(+)						6	7			13											23
Technical and Methodological Capability - Provider	9	1	1		11(++)					2	2	1				3	1			4						21
Domain Understanding	1	2			3	3	1			5(+)	2	1			3	1				1	1					12
Corporate Social Responsibility Capability - Provider					4					1	1				2	4				4						7
Client Management Capability	4				4						1					1				1						6
Absorptive Capacity - Provider	3				3						1					1				4						5
Contract Management Capability - Provider		1			2											1				1						4
Provider Breadth of Service			1		1		1				1	1														3
Security, Privacy, and Confidentiality Capability - Provider										2	1					1				2						3
Business Service Management Capability - Provider	3				3																					3
Project Management Capability - Provider	3				3																					3
Project Scoping Accuracy - Provider	2	1			3																					3
Delivery Capability	2				2																					2

Table D. 1 (Continued)

META CATEGORY/ Independent Variable	Sourcing Outcomes					Sourcing Decisions					Miscellaneous Variables					Relational Governance					Contractual Governance					Grand Total
	+1	0	-1	M	Tot	+1	0	-1	M	Tot	+1	0	-1	M	Tot	+1	0	-1	M	Tot	+1	0	-1	M	Tot	
Technology Infrastructure Quality - Provider																1				1						2
Transition Management Capability - Provider		1			1	1																				2
Change Management Capability - Provider	2				2																					2
Quality Management Capability - Provider											1				1											1
Provider Capabilities		1			1																					1
Boundary Spanning Capability - Provider		1			1																					1
Provider Employee Performance	1				1																					1
Organizational Learning	1				1																					1
Provider Firm Capabilities Total	38	4	8		50	8	1	2		11	16	2	9		27	16		2		18						106
CLIENT FIRM CAPABILITIES																										
Technical and Methodological Capability - Client	10	2			12(++)	7				11(+)	1				1	1				1	1				1	26
Client Outsourcing Readiness	10				10(++)	1				1																11
Absorptive Capacity - Client	4		1		5(+)	3				3	1				1	2				2						11
Transition Management Capability - Client	5				5(++)	2				2	1				1											8
Human Resource Management Capability - Client	4				4	1		1	1	3		1			1											8
Corporate Social Responsibility Capability - Client											1		1		2	4				4						6
Contract Management Capability - Client	4				4						1				1											5
Provider Management Capability - Client	4				4																					4
Business Service Management Capability - Client	3				3						1				1											4
Change Management Capability - Client	3				3																					3
Evaluation Process - Client Assessment		1			1						1				1											2
Risk Management Capability - Client	1				1						1				1											2
Boundary Spanning Capability - Client	1				1																					1
Project Management Capability - Client	1				1																					1
Client Firm Capabilities Total	50	4			54	17		5	1	23	5		1		7	7				7	1				1	92

META CATEGORY/ Independent Variable	Sourcing Outcomes +1	0	-1	M	Tot	Sourcing Decisions +1	0	-1	M	Tot	Miscellaneous Variables +1	0	-1	M	Tot	Relational Governance +1	0	-1	M	Tot	Contractual Governance +1	0	-1	M	Tot	Grand Total
Contractual Governance	5	5		1	11						2	1			3	1			4	5(M)						19
Contract Type		6		9	15(M)	2				2												1		1		17
Contract Detail	7	2	2		11(+)						1		1		2	1				1	1				1	16
Control Mechanisms	6	2		2	10(+)						1				1						1				1	12
Contract Size		3			3	1				1	2				2							2			2	8
Key Performance Indicators	6				6(++)																					6
Contract Duration		2			2		1			1		1			1								1		1	5
Contract Flexibility	1	1	1		3			1		1																4
Staff Transfer											2				2											2
Organizational Boundaries		1		1	2																					2
Contractual Governance Total	25	22	3	13	63	18	2	6	5	31	6	4	1		11	2			4	6	1	3	2		6	91
COUNTRY CHARACTERISTICS																										
Cultural Distance	1	1	3		5(-)	3				3	1	1	1		3	4	3			7						18
Country - Financial Attractiveness						7				7(++)																7
Country - Business Attractiveness						6		1		7(++)																7
Time Zone Differences	1				1			1		1	1				1			1		1						5
Culture								3		3	1				1											4
Geographic Distance	1				1			1		1	1				1			1		1						4
Country - Human Resource Attractiveness						4				4																4
Country								2		2			1		1											3
Legal and Political Uncertainties								1		1																1
Country Size						1				1																1
Outsourcing Outcomes - Success - Client								1		1																1
Country Characteristics Total	2	1	3		7	18	2	6	5	31					8	4				9						55
PROVIDER FIRM CHARACTERISTIC																										
Provide Size	1	4	1		6(0)	1	2	1													1			1		14
Provider Reputation	1	2	2		5	1	1															1		1		8
Provider Firm Age	3				3																					4
Provider Emplyee Turnover	1		2		3			1															1			4

Table D. 1 (Continued)

META CATEGORY / Independent Variable	Sourcing Outcomes					Sourcing Decisions					Miscellaneous Variables					Relational Governance					Contractual Governance					Grand Total
	+1	0	-1	M	Tot	+1	0	-1	M	Tot	+1	0	-1	M	Tot	+1	0	-1	M	Tot	+1	0	-1	M	Tot	
Firm Ownership Structure - Provider		2		1	3																					3
Senior Leadership	2			1	3																					3
Degree of Internationalization - Provider	1				1						1				1											2
Industry														2	2											2
Innovativeness - Provider	2				2																					2
Prior Firm Performance - Provider			1		1																					1
Adherence to Environmental Standards											1				1											1
Culture														1	1											1
Provider Characteristics Total	8	11	6	2	27	2		3		5	4	3		3	10						1	2			3	45
RELATIONSHIP CHARACTERISTICS																										
Prior Client / Provider Working Relationship	4	5			9					1	2	1		1	4						1	1	1		3	17
Length of Relationship	1	4			5(0)		1			1		1			1	1				1						8
Client Power	1		1		2											1				1		1			1	4
Relationship Quality	1				1									2	2											3
Team Turnover		1	1		2																					2
Provider Power												1			1											1
Relationship Characteristics Total	7	10	2		19		1			2	2	3		1	8	1	1			2	1	2	1		4	35
SERVICE SOURCING OUTCOMES																										
Outsourcing Outcomes - Performance Improvements	1				1					8																9
Service Quality	2	1			3		1			3																6
Outsourcing Outcomes - Project Performance	2				2															2						4
Loss of Control		1			1	2				2						1				1						4
Innovation Effects	1				1					2																3
Loss of Knowledge			1		1												1			1						2
Outsourcing Outcomes - Success - Offshore	1				1																1				1	2
Outsourcing Outcomes - Organizational Business														1	1											1

META CATEGORY / Independent Variable	Sourcing Outcomes					Sourcing Decisions					Miscellaneous Variables					Relational Governance					Contractual Governance					Grand Total
	+1	0	-1	M	Tot	+1	0	-1	M	Tot	+1	0	-1	M	Tot	+1	0	-1	M	Tot	+1	0	-1	M	Tot	
Service Sourcing Outcomes Total	7	1	2		10	6	2	8		16	1	1		2		2	1	1		4						32
ENVIRONMENT																										
Provider Competition	2		1		3	2	1	1		4	3	1	2		6			1		1	1		1		2	15
Uncertainty	1					1	2			3	3	1														3
Public Perceptions of Outsourcing								2		2	2	1		1												3
Competition in Client Firm Environment		1			1			1		1																2
Industry Growth						1				1																1
Environment Total	2	2			4	3	6			11	4	1	2		7			1		1	1		1		2	24
DECISION CHARACTERISTICS																										
Stakeholder Buy-in	3				3					1																3
Top Management Commitment / Support	2				2	1																				3
Evaluation Process - Provider Selection			1		1								1		1											2
Middle Management Commitment / Support	2				2																					2
Risk Spread						1				1																1
Decision Characteristics Total	7	1			8	2				2		1	1		1								1			11
INFLUENCES																										
Influences - Mimetic	1				1	2	1		1	4																5
Influences - External and Internal						3				4																4
Influences - Coercive								1		1	1				1											2
Influences Total	1				1	5	3		1	9	1				1											11
EMPLOYEE LEVEL																										
Practical Intelligence	2				2																					2
Provider Employee Satisfaction												1		1												1
Task Variety													1		1											1
Employee Level Total	2				2							1	1		2											4
Grand Total	303	138	85	40	566	202	78	76	27	383	117	30	33	11	191	59	22	8	10	99	23	26	2	14	65	1304

Notes: This appendix shows the relationships between independent variables and the five categories of dependent variables. For each relationship, Cells indicate the frequency with which a relationship was found to be a '+1' indicating a positive and significant relationship; '−1' indicating a negative and significant relationship; '0' indicating a not significant relationship; 'M' indicating the independent variable mattered when operationalized as a categorical variable (see Table 2 for detailed explanations). The relationships that were examined at least 5 times are boxed. The relationships that were examined at least 5 times and met the criteria for consistent results as described in the text are marked with (++), (+), 0, (−), (00), (0), (MM), (M). No such markings within a boxed cell indicate lack of consistent findings per our criteria.

References

Accenture (2012). *Exploring the Value Proposition from Impact Sourcing: The Buyer's Perspective* [www document] http://www.accenture.com/us-en/Pages/insight-exploring-value-proposition-impactsourcing.aspx, accessed 20 July 2015.

Agarwal, M., Kishore, R. and Rao, H.R (2006). Market Reactions to E-business Outsourcing Announcements, An event study, *Information & Management* **43**(7): 861–873.

Agrawal, P. and Haleem, A (2013). The Impact of the Outsourcing of IT on Firm Performance: An empirical study, *International Journal of Management* **30**(3): 121–139.

Agrawal, P. and Hall, S.C (2014). Using Accounting Metrics as Performance Measures to Assess the Impact of Information Technology Outsourcing on Manufacturing and Service Firms, *Journal of Applied Business Research* **30**(5): 1559–1568.

Agrawal, S., Goswami, K. and Chatterjee, B (2012). Factors Influencing Performance of ITES Firms in India, *Information Resources Management Journal* **25**(4): 46–64.

Ajzen, I. and Fishbein, M (1980). *Understanding Attitudes and Predicting Social Behavior*, Englewood Cliffs, NJ: Prentice-Hall.

Ali, S. and Green, P (2012). Effective Information Technology (IT) Governance Mechanisms: An IT outsourcing perspective, *Information Systems Frontiers* **14**(2): 179–193.

Alvarez-Suescun, E (2010). Combining Transaction Cost and Resource-Based Insights to Explain IT Implementation Outsourcing, *Information Systems Frontiers* **12**(5): 631–645.

Amiruddin, R., Aman, A., Auzair, S.M., Hamzah, N. and Maelah, R. (2013). Mitigating Risks in a Shared Service Relationship: The case of a Malaysian bank, *Qualitative Research in Accounting and Management* **10**(1): 78–93.

Andries, P. and Thorwarth, S (2014). Should Firms Outsource their Basic Research? The Impact of Firm Size on In-House versus Outsourced R&D Productivity, *Creativity and Innovation Management* **23**(3): 303–317.

Ang, S. and Cummings, L (1997). Strategic Response to Institutional Influences on Information Systems Outsourcing, *Organization Science* **8**(3): 235–256.

Angeli, F. and Grimaldi, R (2010). Leveraging Offshoring: The identification of new business opportunities in international settings, *Industry and Innovation* **17**(4): 393–413.

Argyres, N. and Zenger, T (2012). Capabilities, Transaction Costs, and Firm Boundaries, *Organization Science* **23**(6): 1643–1657.

Arnold, V., Benford, T., Hampton, C. and Sutton, S (2010). Competing Pressures of Risk and Absorptive Capacity Potential on Commitment and Information Sharing in Global Supply Chains, *European Journal of Information Systems* **19**(2): 134–152.

Aubert, B., Rivard, S. and Templier, M (2011). Information Technology and Distance-Induced Effort to Manage Offshore Activities, *IEEE Transactions on Engineering Management* **58**(4): 758–771.

Aubert,B.A., Houde, J.F., Patry, M. and Rivard, S (2012). A Multi-Level Investigation of Information Technology Outsourcing, *The Journal of Strategic Information Systems* **21**(3): 233–244.

Avasant/Rockefeller Foundation (2012). Incentives & Opportunities for Scaling the 'Impact Sourcing' Sector,2012. Corporate report by Avasant consultancy [WWW document] https://www.rockefellerfoundation.org/app/uploads/Incentives-Opportunities-for-Scaling-the-Impact-Sourcing-Sector.pdf, accessed 3 February 2016.

Babin, R (2008). Assessing the Role of CSR in Outsourcing Decisions, *Journal of Information Systems Applied Research* **1**(2): 1–14.

Babin, R., Briggs, S. and Nicholson, B (2011). Emerging Markets Corporate Social Responsibility and Global IT Outsourcing, *Communications of the ACM* **54**(9): 28–30.

Babin, R. and Nicholson, B (2009). Corporate Social and Environmental Responsibility in Global IT Outsourcing, *MIS Quarterly Executive* **8**(4): 123–132.

Babin, R. and Nicholson, B. (2011). How Green is My Outsourcer? Measuring Sustainability in Global IT Outsourcing, *Strategic Outsourcing: An International Journal* **4**(1): 47–66.

Babin, R. and Nicholson, B. (2012). *Sustainable Global Outsourcing: Achieving social and environmental responsibility in global IT and business process outsourcing*, London: Palgrave Macmillan.

Bachlechner, D., Thalmann, S. and Maier, R. (2014). Security and Compliance Challenges in Complex IT Outsourcing Arrangements: A multi-stakeholder perspective, *Computers & Security* **40**(2): 38–59.

Baldwin, L.P., Irani, Z. and Love, P.E.D (2001). Outsourcing Information Systems: Drawing lessons from a banking case study, *European Journal of Information Systems* **10**(1): 15–24.

Bandyopadhyay, J. and Hall, L (2009). Off-Shoring of Tax Preparation Services by US Accounting Firms: An empirical study, *Advances in Competitiveness Research* **17**(1&2): 72–90.

Baraldi, E., Proença, J.F., Proença, T. and De Castro, L.M. (2014). The Supplier's Side of Outsourcing: Taking over activities and blurring organizational boundaries, *Industrial Marketing Management* **43**(4): 553–563.

Bardhan, I., Mithas, S. and Lin, S (2007). Performance Impacts of Strategy, Information Technology Applications, and Business Process Outsourcing in US Manufacturing Plants, *Production and Operations Management* **16**(6): 747–762.

Barthélemy, J (2011). The Disney – Pixar Relationship Dynamics: Lessons for outsourcing vs. vertical integration, *Organizational Dynamics* **40**(1): 43–48.

Benamati, J. and Rajkumar, T.M (2002). The Application Development Outsourcing Decision: An application of the technology acceptance model, *The Journal of Computer, Information Systems* **42**(4): 35–43.

Betz, S., Oberweis, A. and Stephan, R (2014). Knowledge Transfer in Offshore Outsourcing Software Development Projects: An analysis of the challenges and solutions from German clients, *Expert Systems* **31**(3): 282–297.

Beulen, E., Tiwari, V. and Van Heck, E (2011). Understanding Transition Performance During Offshore IT Outsourcing, *Strategic Outsourcing: An International Journal* **4**(3): 204–227.

Bhagwatwar, A., Hackney, R. and Desouza, K.C. (2011). Considerations for Information Systems 'Backsourcing': A framework for knowledge re-integration, *Information Systems Management* **28**(2): 165–173.

Bharadwaj, S., Saxena, K. and Halemane, M (2010). Building a Successful Relationship in Business Process Outsourcing: An exploratory study, *European Journal of Information Systems* **19**(2): 168–180.

Bidwell, M (2010). Problems Deciding: How the structure of make-or-buy decisions leads to transaction misalignment, *Organization Science* **21**(2): 362–379.

Bidwell, M.J (2012). Politics and Firm Boundaries: How organizational structure, group interests, and resources affect outsourcing, *Organization Science* **23**(6): 1622–1642.

Bignoux, S (2011). Partnerships, Suppliers, and Coercive Influence, *Journal of Applied Business Research* **27**(3): 117–135.

Blaskovich, J. and Mintchik, N (2011). Accounting Executives and IT Outsourcing Recommendations: An experimental study of the effect of CIO skills and institutional isomorphism, *Journal of Information Technology* 26(2): 139–152.

Boell, S. and Cecez-Kecmanovic, D. (2015). On Being 'Systematic' in Literature Reviews in IS, *Journal of Information Technology* 30(2): 161–173.

Borman, M (2006). Applying Multiple Perspectives to the BPO Decision: A case study of call centers in Australia, *Journal of Information Technology* 21(2): 99–115.

Brcar, F. and Bukovec, B (2013). Analysis of Increased Information Technology Outsourcing Factors, *Organizacija* 46(1): 13–19.

Brewer, B., Wallin, C. and Ashenbaum, B (2014). Outsourcing the Procurement Function: Do actions and results align with theory?, *Journal of Purchasing and Supply Management* 20(3): 186–194.

Brown, D (2008). It is Good to Be Green: Environmentally friendly credentials are influencing business outsourcing decisions, *Strategic Outsourcing: An International Journal* 1(1): 87–95.

Budhwar, P., Luthar, H. and Bhatnagar, J (2006). The Dynamics of HRM Systems in Indian BPO Firms, *Journal of Labor Research* 27(3): 339–360.

Bustinza, O.F., Molina, L.M. and Gutierrez-Gutierrez, L.J (2010). Outsourcing as Seen From the Perspective of Knowledge Management, *Journal of Supply Chain Management* 46(3): 23–39.

Cable, D.M., Gino, F. and Staats, B.R (2013). Breaking Them in or Eliciting Their Best? Reframing Socialization around Newcomers' Authentic Self-Expression, *Administrative Science Quarterly* 58(1): 1–36.

Calantone, R. and Stanko, M (2007). Drivers of Outsourced Innovation: An exploratory study, *Journal of Product Innovation Management* 24(3): 230–241.

Cao, L., Mohan, K., Ramesh, B. and Sarkar, S. (2013). Evolution of Governance: Achieving ambidexterity in IT outsourcing, *Journal of Management Information Systems* 30(3): 115–140.

Carey, P., Subramanian, N. and Ching, K (2006). Internal Audit Outsourcing in Australia, *Accounting and Finance* 46(1): 11–30.

Carmel, E., Lacity, M. and Doty, A (2014). The Impact of Impact Sourcing: Framing a research agenda, R. Hirschheim, A. Heinzl and J. Dibbern (eds.) *Information Systems Outsourcing: Towards sustainable business value*, Heidelberg: Springer, pp. 397–430.

Ceci, F. and Masciarelli, F (2010). A Matter of Coherence: The effects of offshoring of intangibles on firm performance, *Industry & Innovation* **17**(4): 373–392.

Cezar, A., Cavusoglu, H. and Raghunathan, S (2014). Outsourcing Information Security: Contracting issues and security implications, *Management Science* **60**(3): 638–657.

Cha, H.S. and Quan, J. (2011). A Global Perspective on Information Systems Personnel Turnover, *Journal of Global Information Technology Management* **14**(4): 4–27.

Chakrabarty, S. and Whitten, D (2011). The Sidelining of Top IT Executives in the Governance of Outsourcing: Antecedents, power struggles, and consequences, *IEEE Transactions on Engineering Management* **58**(4): 799–814.

Chaudhuri, S. and Bartlett, K.R. (2014). The Relationship between Training Outsourcing and Employee Commitment to Organization, *Human Resource Development International* **17**(2): 145–163.

Ciravegna, L. and Maielli, G (2011). Outsourcing of New Product Development and the Opening of Innovation in Mature Industries: A longitudinal study of fiat during crisis and recovery, *International Journal of Innovation Management* **15**(1): 69–93.

Cordella, A. and Willcocks, L (2012). Government Policy, Public Value and IT Outsourcing: The strategic case of ASPIRE, *The Journal of Strategic Information Systems* **21**(4): 295–307.

Cullen, S., Seddon, P. and Willcocks, L (2005). Managing Outsourcing: The life cycle imperative, *MIS Quarterly Executive* **4**(1): 229–246.

Currie, W., Michell, V. and Abanishe, A (2008). Knowledge Process Outsourcing in Financial Services: The vendor perspective, *European Management Journal* **26**(2): 94–104.

Daityari, A., Saini, A. and Gupta, R (2008). Control of Business Process Outsourcing Relationships, *Journal of Management Research* **8**(1): 29–44.

Datta, P. and Bhattacharya, K. (2012). Innovation Returns and the Economics of Offshored IT R&D, *Strategic Outsourcing: An International Journal* **5**(1): 15–35.

Davenport, T. and Iyer, B. (2015). Bringing outsourcing back to machines *The Wall Street Journal* 1 July [WWW document] http://blogs.wsj.com/cio/2015/07/01/bringing-outsourcing-back-to-machines/, accessed 20 July 2015.

Davenport, T. and Kirby, J. (2015). Beyond Automation: Augmentation, *Harvard Business Review* **93**(6): 58–65.

De Toni, A., Fornasier, A., Montagner, M. and Nonino, F (2007). A Performance Measurement System for Facility Management, *International Journal of Productivity and Performance Management* **56**(5/6): 417–435.

Dedrick, J., Carmel, E. and Kraemer, K.L. (2011). A Dynamic Model of Offshore Software Development, *Journal of Information Technology* **26**(1): 1–15.

Dekker, H.C. and Van Den Abbeele, A. (2010). Organizational Learning and Interfirm Control: The effects of partner search and prior exchange experiences, *Organization Science* **21**(6): 1233–1250.

Delmotte, J. and Sels, L. (2008). HR Outsourcing: Threat or opportunity, *Personnel Review* **37**(5): 543–563.

Deng, C., Mao, J. and Wang, G (2013). An Empirical Study on the Source of Vendors' Relational Performance in Offshore Information Systems Outsourcing, *International Journal of Information Management* **33**(1): 10–19.

Devos, J., Van Landeghem, H. and Deschoolmeester, D (2012). Rethinking IT Governance for SMEs, *Industrial Management & Data Systems* **112**(2): 206–223.

Dey, D., Fan, M. and Zhang, C (2010). Design and Analysis of Contracts for Software Outsourcing, *Information Systems Research* **21**(1): 93–114.

Dibbern, J., Chin, W. and Heinzl, A (2012). Systemic Determinants of the Information Systems Outsourcing Decision: A comparative study of German and United States firms, *Journal of the Association for Information Systems* **13**(6): 466–497.

Dibbern, J., Goles, T., Hirschheim, R. and Jayatilaka, B. (2004). Information Systems Outsourcing: A survey and analysis of the literature, *ACM SIGMIS Database* **35**(4): 6–102.

DiMaggio, P. and Powell, W. (eds.) (1991). The Iron Cage Revisited: Institutional isomorphism and collective rationality in organizational fields, in *The New Institutionalism in Organizational Analysis*, Chicago, IL: The University of Chicago Press, pp. 63–82.

DiRomualdo, A. and Gurbaxani, V (1998). Strategic Intent for IT Outsourcing, *Sloan Management Review* **39**(4): 67–80.

Doh, J., Bunyaratavej, K. and Hahn, E. (2009). Separable but Not Equal: The location determinants of discrete services offshoring activities, *Journal of International Business Studies* **40**(6): 926–943.

Doloreux, D. and Shearmur, R (2013). Innovation strategies: Are knowledge-intensive business services just another source of information?, *Industry & Innovation* **20**(8): 719–738.

Du, W. and Pan, S.L (2013). Boundary Spanning by Design: Toward aligning boundary-spanning capacity and strategy in it outsourcing, *IEEE Transactions On Engineering Management* 60(1): 59–76.

Dunbar, A. and Phillips, J. (2001). The Outsourcing of Corporate Tax Function Activities, *The Journal of the American Taxation Association* 23(2): 35–49.

Dutta, A. and Roy, R (2005). Offshore Outsourcing: A dynamic causal model of counteracting forces, *Journal of Management Information Systems* 22(2): 15–36.

Dutta, D., Gwebu, K. and Wang, J (2011). Strategy and Vendor Selection in IT Outsourcing: Is there a method in the madness?, *Journal of Global Information Technology Management* 14(2): 6–26.

Ee, O., Halim, H.A. and Ramayah, T (2013). The Effects of Partnership Quality on Business Process Outsourcing Success in Malaysia: Key users perspective, *Service Business* 7(2): 227–253.

Eisenhardt, K. (1989). Agency Theory: An assessment and review, *The Academy of Management Review* 14(1): 57–76.

Everest Group (2014). The Business Case for Impact Sourcing [WWW document]http://www.everestgrp.com/2014-09-the-business-case-for-impact-sourcingsherpas-in-blue-shirts-15662.html, accessed 20 July 2015.

Fersht, P., Herrera, E., Robinson, B., Filippone, T. and Willcocks, L. (2011). The State of Outsourcing in 2011, Horses for Sources and LSE Outsourcing Unit, London, May–July [WWW document] www.hfsresearch.com, accessed 20 July 2015.

Fielt, E., Bandara, W., Miskon, S. and Gable, G.G (2014). Exploring Shared Services from an IS Perspective: A literature review and research agenda, *Communications of the Association for Information Systems* 34(1): 1001–1040.

Fifarek, B., Veloso, F. and Davidson, C. (2008). Offshoring Technology Innovation: A case study of rare-earth technology, *Journal of Operations Management* 26(2): 222–238.

Fink, L (2010). Information Technology Outsourcing Through a Configurational Lens, *Journal of Strategic Information Systems* 19(2): 124–141.

Fjermestad, J. and Saitta, J. (2005). A Strategic Management Framework for IT Outsourcing: A review of the literature and the development of a success factors model, *Journal of Information Technology Case and Application Research* 7(3): 42–60.

Freytag, P., Clarke, A. and Evald, M (2012). Reconsidering Outsourcing Solutions, *European Management Journal* **30**(2): 99–110.

Frick, W (2015). When Your Boss Wears Metal Pants, *Harvard Business Review* **93**(6): 84–89.

Gainey, T. and Klaas, B (2003). The Outsourcing of Training and Development: Factors impacting client satisfaction, *Journal of Management* **29**(2): 207–229.

Gao, G., Gopal, A. and Agarwal, R (2010). Contingent Effects of Quality Signaling: Evidence from the Indian offshore IT services industry, *Management Science* **56**(6): 1012–1029.

García-Vega, M. and Huergo, E (2011). Determinants of International R&D Outsourcing: The role of trade, *Review of Development Economics* **15**(1): 93–107.

Gefen, D., Ragowsky, A., Licker, P. and Stern, M (2011). The Changing Role of the CIO in the World of Outsourcing: Lessons learned from a CIO roundtable, *Communications of the AIS* **28**(15): 233–242.

Gewald, H. and Dibbern, J. (2009). Risks and Benefits of Business Process Outsourcing: A study of transaction services in the German banking industry, *Information & Management* **46**(4): 249–257.

Gewald, H. and Gellrich, T (2007). The Impact of Perceived Risk on the Capital Market's Reaction to Outsourcing Announcements, *Information Technology and Management* **8**(4): 279–296.

Gholami, S (2012). Critical Risk Factors in Outsourced Support Projects of IT, *Journal of Management Research* **4**(1): 1–13.

Gilley, K., Greer, C. and Rasheed, A (2004). Human Resource Outsourcing and Organizational Performance in Manufacturing Firms, *Journal of Business Research* **57**(3): 232–240.

Gino, F. and Staats, B. (2012). The Microwork Solution, *Harvard Business Review* **90**(12): 92–96.

Glaister, A.J (2014). HR Outsourcing: The impact on HR role, competency development and relationships, *Human Resource Management Journal* **24**(2): 211–226.

Gonzalez, R., Gasco, J. and Llopis, J (2010a). Information Systems Outsourcing: An empirical study of success factors, *Human System Management* **29**(3): 139–151.

Gonzalez, R., Gasco, J. and Llopis, J (2010b). Information Systems Offshore Outsourcing: An exploratory study of motivations and risks in large Spanish firms, *Information Systems Management* **27**(4): 340–355.

Goo, J., Kishore, R., Rao, H.R. and Nam, K. (2009). The Role of Service Level Agreements in Relational Management of Information Technology Outsourcing: An empirical study, *MIS Quarterly* **33**(1): 1–28.

Gopal, A., Mukhopadhyay, T. and Krishnan, M (2002). The Role of Software Processes and Communication in Offshore Software Development, *Communications of the ACM* **45**(4): 193–200.

Gopal, A., Espinosa, A., Gosain, S. and Darcy, D (2011). Coordination and Performance in Global Software Service Delivery: The vendor's perspective, *IEEE Transactions on Engineering Management* **58**(4): 772–785.

Gopal, A. and Gosain, S (2010). The Role of Organizational Controls and Boundary Spanning in Software Development Outsourcing: Implications for project performance, *Information Systems Research* **21**(4): 960–982.

Gopal, A. and Koka, B (2010). The Role of Contracts on Quality and Returns to Quality, *Decision Sciences* **41**(3): 491–516.

Gopal, A. and Koka, B.R (2012). The Asymmetric Benefits of Relational Flexibility: Evidence from software development outsourcing, *MIS Quarterly* **36**(2): 553–576.

Gorla, N. and Lau, M (2010). Will Negative Experiences Impact Future IT Outsourcing?, *Journal of Computer Information Systems* **50**(3): 91–101.

Gorla, N. and Somers, T.M (2014). The Impact of IT Outsourcing on Information Systems Success, *Information & Management* **51**(3): 320–335.

Gorp, D.V., Jagersma, P.K. and Livshits, A (2007). Offshore Behavior of Service Firms: Policy implications for firms and nations, *Journal of Information Technology Case and Application Research* **9**(1): 7–19.

Gospel, H. and Sako, M. (2010). The Unbundling of Corporate Functions,' The Evolution of Shared Services and Outsourcing in Human Resource Management, *Industrial and Corporate Change* **19**(5): 1–30.

Grimpe, C. and Kaiser, U (2010). Balancing Internal and External Knowledge Acquisition: The gains and pains from R&D outsourcing, *Journal of Management Studies* **47**(8): 1483–1509.

Gwebu, K.L., Wang, J. and Wang, L (2010). Does IT Outsourcing Deliver Economic Value to Firms?, *The Journal of Strategic Information Systems* **19**(2): 109–123.

Hahn, E.D., Bunyaratavej, K. and Doh, J.P (2011). Impacts of Risk and Service Type on Nearshore and Offshore Investment Location Decisions, *Management International Review* **51**(3): 357–380.

Hahn, E.D. and Bunyaratavej, K (2010). Services Cultural Alignment in Offshoring: The impact of cultural dimensions on offshoring location choices, *Journal of Operations Management* **28**(3): 186–193.

Hall, J. and Liedtka, S (2005). Financial Performance, CEO Compensation, and Large-Scale Information Technology Outsourcing Decisions, *Journal of Management Information Systems* **22**(1): 193–222.

Han, K. and Mithas, S (2013). Information Technology Outsourcing and Non-IT Operating Costs: An empirical investigation, *MIS Quarterly* **37**(1): 315–331.

Han, K., Kauffman, R. and Nault, B (2011). Returns to Information Technology Outsourcing, *Information Systems Research* **22**(4): 824–840.

Handley, S. and Benton, W.C (2009). Unlocking the Business Outsourcing Process Model, *Journal of Operations Management* **27**(5): 344–361.

Handley, S.M. (2012). The Perilous Effects of Capability Loss on Outsourcing Management and Performance, *Journal of Operations Management* **30**(1): 152–165.

Handley, S.M. and Benton, W.C (2012). Mediated Power and Outsourcing Relationships, *Journal of Operations Management* **30**(3): 253–267.

Hätönen, J (2010). Outsourcing and Licensing Strategies in Small Software Firms: Evolution of strategies and implications for firm growth, internationalisation and innovation, *Technology Analysis & Strategic Management* **22**(5): 609–630.

Heeks, R. (2012). The Research Agenda for IT Impact Sourcing, blog. ICTs for Development [WWW document] http://ict4dblog.wordpress.com/2012/05/06/the-research-agenda-for-it-impact-sourcing/, accessed 20 July 2015.

Heeks, R. and Arun, S. (2010). Social Outsourcing as a Development Tool: The impact of outsourcing IT services to women's social enterprises in Kerala, *Journal of International Development* **22**(4): 441–454.

Hodosi, G. and Rusu, L. (2013). How Do Critical Success Factors Contribute to a Successful IT Outsourcing: A study of large multinational companies, *Journal of Information Technology Theory and Application* **14**(1): 17–42.

Hoffman, C., Khan, S.A. and Mirchandani, D (2015). Developing an Interdisciplinary Cybersecurity Program in the Business School: Reflections and a view to the future, *Regional Business Review* **34**: 51–55.

Howells, J., Gagliardi, D. and Malik, K. (2008). The Growth and Management of R&D Outsourcing: Evidence from UK pharmaceuticals, *R&D Management* **38**(2): 205–219.

Huber, T.L., Fischer, T.A., Dibbern, J. and Hirschheim, R. (2013). A Process Model of Complementarity and Substitution of Contractual and Relational Governance in IS Outsourcing, *Journal of Management Information Systems* **30**(3): 81–114.

IAOP (2009) Summary of Findings from the IAOP 2009 CSR Survey, an IAOP Research White Paper [WWW document] http://www.iaop.org/Content/23/126/1698/.

Ippolito, A. and Zoccoli, P (2010). How Knowledge and Technology Relate in Creating Value: An Italian case of technology outsourcing, *Strategic Outsourcing: An International Journal* **3**(2): 72–88.

Iveroth, E (2010). Inside Ericsson: A framework for the practice of leading global IT-enabled change, *California Management Review* **53**(1): 136–153.

Jain, A. and Thietart, R.A (2014). Capabilities as Shift Parameters for the Outsourcing Decision, *Strategic Management Journal* **35**(2): 1881–1890.

Jain, R., Poston, R. and Simon, J. (2011a). An Empirical Investigation of Client Managers' Responsibilities in Managing Offshore Outsourcing of Software-Testing Projects, *IEEE Transactions on Engineering Management* **58**(4): 743–757.

Jain, R., Simon, J. and Poston, R. (2011b). Mitigating Vendor Silence in Offshore Outsourcing: An empirical investigation, *Journal of Management Information Systems* **27**(4): 261–297.

Jarvenpaa, S. and Mao, J (2008). Operational Capabilities Development in Mediated Offshore Software Service Models, *Journal of Information Technology* **23**(1): 3–17.

Jayaraman, V., Narayanan, S., Luo, Y. and Swaminathan, J.M. (2013). Offshoring Business Process Services and Governance Control Mechanisms: An examination of service providers from India, *Production and Operations Management* **22**(2): 314–334.

Jean, R., Sinkovics, R. and Cavusgil, S. (2010). Enhancing International Customer – Supplier Relationships through IT Resources: A study of Taiwanese electronics suppliers, *Journal of International Business Studies* **41**(7): 1218–1239.

Jeyaraj, A., Rottman, J.W. and **Lacity, M.C**. (2006). A Review of the Predictors, Linkages, and Biases in IT Innovation Adoption Research, *Journal of Information Technology* **21**(1): 1–23.

Ji-FanRen, S., Ngai, E.W.T. and Cho, V. (2011). Managing Software Outsourcing Relationships in Emerging Economies: An empirical study of the Chinese small and medium-sized enterprises, *IEEE Transactions on Engineering Management* **58**(4): 730–742.

Jorgensen, C (2010). Offshore Supplier Relations: Knowledge integration among small businesses, *Strategic Outsourcing: An International Journal* **3**(3): 192–210.

Kang, M., Wu, X., Hong, P., Park, K. and Park, Y. (2014). The Role of Organizational Control in Outsourcing Practices: An empirical study, *Journal of Purchasing and Supply Management* **20**(3): 177–185.

Kannabiran, G. and Sankaran, K (2011). Determinants of Software Quality in Offshore Development – An Empirical Study of an Indian Vendor, *Information and Software Technology* **53**(11): 1199–1208.

Kenyon, G. and Meixell, M. (2011). Success Factors and Cost Management Strategies for Logistics Outsourcing, *Journal of Management and Marketing Research* **7**(1): 1–17.

Kern, T., Willcocks, L.P. and Van Heck, E (2002). The Winner's Curse in IT Outsourcing: Strategies for Avoiding Relational Trauma, *California Management Review* **44**(2): 47–69.

Khan, S.A. and Lacity, M (2012). Survey Results: Are client organizations responding to anti-offshoring pressures?, *Strategic Outsourcing: An International Journal* **5**(2): 166–179.

Khan, S.A. and **Lacity**, M.C. (2014). Organizational Responsiveness to Anti-Offshoring Institutional Pressures, *The Journal of Strategic Information Systems* **23**(3): 190–209.

Kien, S., Kiat, L. and Periasamy, K (2010). Switching IT Outsourcing Suppliers: Enhancing transition readiness, *MIS Quarterly Executive* **9**(1): 23–33.

Kim, G (2008). E-Business Strategy in Western Europe: Offshore BPO model perspective, *Business Process Management* **14**(6): 813–828.

Klaas, B., McClendon, J. and Gainey, T (2001). Outsourcing HR: The impact of organizational characteristics, *Human Resource Management* **40**(2): 125–138.

Kobelsky, K.W. and Robinson, M.A. (2010). The Impact of Outsourcing on Information Technology Spending, *International Journal of Accounting Information Systems* **11**(2): 105–119.

Koh, C., Ang, S. and Straub, D (2004). IT Outsourcing Success: A psychological contract perspective, *Information Systems Research* **15**(4): 356–373.

Kotlarsky, J. Scarbrough, H. and Oshri, I (2014). Coordinating Expertise Across Knowledge Boundaries in Offshore-Outsourcing Projects: The role of codification, *MIS Quarterly* **38**(2): 607–627.

Kroes, J.R. and Ghosh, S (2010). Outsourcing Congruence with Competitive Priorities: Impact on supply chain and firm performance, *Journal of Operations Management* **28**(2): 124–143.

Kuhn, T (1970). *The Structure of Scientific Revolutions*, Chicago: University of Chicago Press.

Kuruvilla, S. and Ranganathan, A. (2010). Globalisation and Outsourcing: Confronting new human resource challenges in India's business process outsourcing industry, *Industrial Relations Journal* **41**(2): 136–153.

Kuula, M., Putkiranta, A. and Tulokas, P (2013). Parameters in a Successful Process Outsourcing Project: A case from the ministry of foreign affairs, Finland, *International Journal of Public Administration* **36**(12): 857–864.

Lacity, M., Feeny, D. and Willcocks, L (2004). Commercializing the Back Office at Lloyds of London: Outsourcing and strategic partnerships revisited, *European Management Journal* **22**(2): 127–140.

Lacity, M., Rottman, J. and Khan, S. (2010). Field of Dreams: Building IT capabilities in rural America, *Strategic Outsourcing: An International Journal* **3**(3): 169–191.

Lacity, M., Rottman, J. and Carmel, E (2012). *Emerging ITO and BPO Markets: Rural sourcing and impact sourcing*, IEEE Readynotes, IEEE Computer Society: Los Alamitos, CA.

Lacity, M. and Willcocks, L. (2014). Business Process Outsourcing and Dynamic Innovation, *Strategic Outsourcing: An International Journal* **7**(1): 66–92.

Lacity, M.C., Khan, S., Yan, A. and Willcocks, L.P. (2010). A Review of the IT Outsourcing Empirical Literature and Future Research Directions, *Journal of Information Technology* **25**(4): 395–433.

Lacity, M.C., Solomon, S., Yan, A. and Willcocks, L.P. (2011). Business Process Outsourcing Studies: A critical review and research directions, *Journal of Information Technology* **26**(4): 221–258.

Lacity, M.C., Rottman, J.W. and Carmel, E. (2014). Impact Sourcing: Employing prison inmates to perform digitally-enabled business services, *Communications of the AIS* **34**(1): 913–932.

Lahiri, S. and Kedia, B (2009). The Effects of Internal Resources and Partnership Quality on Firm Performance: An examination of Indian BPO suppliers, *Journal of International Management* **15**(2): 209–224.

Lam, W. and Chua, A (2009). An Analysis of Knowledge Outsourcing at Eduware, *Aslib Proceedings New Information Perspectives* **61**(5): 424–435.

Langer, N., Slaughter, S.A. and Mukhopadhyay, T. (2014). Project Managers' Practical Intelligence and Project Performance in Software Offshore Outsourcing: A field study, *Information Systems Research* **25**(2): 364–384.

Lee, J., Miranda, S. and Kim, Y (2004). IT Outsourcing Strategies: Universalistic, contingency, and configurational explanations of success, *Information Systems Research* **15**(2): 110–131.

Lee, R. and Kim, D (2010). Implications of Service Processes Outsourcing on Firm Value, *Industrial Marketing Management* **39**(5): 853–861.

Levina, N. and Ross, J. (2003). From the Vendor's Perspective: Exploring the value proposition in IT outsourcing, *MIS Quarterly* **27**(3): 331–364.

Levina, N. and Su, N. (2008). Global Multisourcing Strategy: The emergence of a supplier portfolio in services offshoring, *Decision Sciences* **39**(3): 541–570.

Lewin, A. and Peeters, C. (2006). Offshoring Work: Business hype or the onset of fundamental transformation?, *Long Range Planning* **39**(3): 221–239.

Li, Y., Zhao, X., Shi, D. and Li, X (2014). Governance of Sustainable Supply Chains in the Fast Fashion Industry, *European Management Journal* **32**(5): 823–836.

Lioliou, E., Zimmermann, A., Willcocks, L. and Gao, L (2014). Formal and Relational Governance in IT Outsourcing: Substitution, complementarity and the role of the psychological contract, *Information Systems Journal* **24**(6): 503–535.

Liu, C (2012). Knowledge Mobility in Cross-Border Buyer-Supplier Relationships, *Management International Review* **52**(2): 275–291.

Loh, L. and Venkatraman, N. (1992). Diffusion of Information Technology Outsourcing: Influence sources and the Kodak effect, *Information Systems Research* **3**(4): 334–358.

Lucena, A. (2011). 'The Organizational Designs of R&D Activities and Their Performance Implications,' Empirical Evidence for Spain, *Industry and Innovation* **18**(2): 151–176.

Luo, Y., Zheng, Q. and Jayaraman, V (2010). Managing Business Process Outsourcing, *Organizational Dynamics* **39**(3): 205–217.

Luo, Y., Wang, S., Zheng, Q. and Jayaraman, V. (2012). Task Attributes and Process Integration in Business Process Offshoring: A perspective of service providers from India and China, *Journal of International Business Studies* **43**(5): 498–524.

Macneil, I.R (1980). *The New Social Contract: An inquiry into modern contractual relations*, New Haven, CT: Yale University Press.

Madon, S. and Sharanappa, S (2013). Social IT Outsourcing and Development: Theorising the linkage, *Information Systems Journal* **23**(5): 381–399.

Maelah, R., Aman, A., Hamzah, N., Amiruddin, R., Sofiah and Auzair, M. (2010). Accounting Outsourcing Turnback: Process and issues, *Strategic Outsourcing: An International Journal* 3(3): 226–245.

Mahmoodzadeh, E., Jalalinia, S. and Yazdi, F. (2009). A Business Process Outsourcing Framework Based on Business Process Management and Knowledge Management, *Business Process Management Journal* 15(6): 845–864.

Mahnke, V., Overby, M.L. and Vang, J (2005). Strategic Outsourcing of IT Services: Theoretical stocktaking and empirical challenges, *Industry and Innovation* 12(2): 205–253.

Malik, A (2009). Training Drivers, Competitive Strategy and Client Needs: Case studies of three business process outsourcing organizations, *Journal of European Industrial Training* 33(2): 160–177.

Malik, A., Sinha, A. and Blumenfeld, S. (2012). Role of Quality Management Capabilities in Developing Market-Based Organisational Learning Capabilities: Case study evidence from four Indian business process outsourcing firms, *Industrial Marketing Management* 41(4): 639–648.

Malos, S. (2010). Regulatory Effects and Strategic Global Staffing Profiles: Beyond cost concerns in evaluating offshore location attractiveness, *Employee Responsibilities and Rights Journal* 22(2): 113–131.

Mani, D., Barua, A. and Whinston, A. (2010). An Empirical Analysis of the Impact of Information Capabilities Design on Business Process Outsourcing Performance, *MIS Quarterly* 34(1): 39–62.

Mann, A., Kauffman, R., Han, K. and Nault, B. (2011). Are There Contagion Effects in Information Technology and Business Process Outsourcing?, *Decision Support Systems* 51(4): 864–874.

Manning, S., Ricart, J.E., Rique, M.S.R. and Lewin, A.Y. (2010). From Blind Spots to Hotspots: How knowledge services clusters develop and attract foreign investment, *Journal of International Management* 16(4): 369–382.

Manning, S (2014). Mitigate, Tolerate or Relocate? Offshoring Challenges, Strategic Imperatives and Resource Constraints, *Journal of World Business* 49(4): 522–535.

Manning, S., Lewin, A.Y. and Schuerch, M. (2011). The Stability of Offshore Outsourcing Relationships, *Management International Review* 51(3): 381–406.

Martinez-Noya, A., Garcia-Canal, E. and Guillen, M.F. (2012). International R&D Service Outsourcing by Technology-Intensive Firms: Whether and where?, *Journal of International Management* 18(1): 18–37.

Martins, V. and Martins, R (2012). Outsourcing Operations in Project Management Offices: The reality of Brazilian companies, *Project Management Journal* **43**(2): 68–83.

Massini, S., Perm-Ajchariyawong, N. and Lewin, A. (2010). Role of Corporate-Wide Offshoring Strategy on Offshoring Drivers, Risks and Performance, *Industry & Innovation* **17**(4): 337–371.

Mathew, S (2011). Mitigation of Risks Due to Service Provider Behavior in Offshore Software Development a Relationship Approach, *Strategic Outsourcing: An International Journal* **4**(2): 179–200.

Mathew, S. and Das Aundhe, M. (2011). Identifying Vendor Risks in Remote Infrastructure Management Services, *Journal of Information Technology Case and Application Research* **13**(4): 32–50.

Mauri, A.J. and De Figueiredo, J.N (2012). Strategic Patterns of Internationalization and Performance Variability: Effects of US-based MNC cross-border dispersion, integration, and outsourcing, *Journal of International Management* **18**(1): 38–51.

Mayer, K.J., Somaya, D. and Williamson, I.O (2012). Firm-Specific, Industry-Specific, and Occupational Human Capital and the Sourcing of Knowledge Work, *Organization Science* **23**(5): 1311–1329.

Mayer, K.J. and Salomon, R.M (2006). Capabilities, Contractual Hazards, and Governance: Integrating resource-based and transaction cost perspectives, *Academy of Management Journal* **49**(5): 942–959.

McFarlan, F.W. and Nolan, R. (1995). How to Manage an IT Outsourcing Alliance, *Sloan Management Review* **36**(2): 9–24.

McIvor, R., Humphreys, P., McKittrick, A. and Wall, T (2009). Performance Management and the Outsourcing Process: Lessons from a financial services organisation, *International Journal of Operations and Production Management* **29**(10): 1025–1047.

McIvor, R., McCracken, M. and McHugh, M (2011). Creating Outsourced Shared Services Arrangements: Lessons from the public sector, *European Management Journal* **29**(6): 448–461.

McKeen, J. and Smith, H. (2011). Creating IT Shared Services, *Communications of the AIS* **29**(34): 645–656.

McKenna, D. and Walker, D (2008). A Study of Out-Sourcing Versus In-Sourcing Tasks within a Project Value Chain, *International Journal of Managing Projects in Business* **1**(2): 216–232.

Mehta, A., Armenakis, A., Mehta, N. and Irani, F (2006). Challenges and Opportunities of Business Process Outsourcing, *Journal of Labor Research* **27**(3): 323–337.

Mihalache, O.R., Jansen, J.J., Van Den Bosch, F.A. and Volberda, H.W. (2012). Offshoring and Firm Innovation: The moderating role of top management team attributes, *Strategic Management Journal* **33**(13): 1480–1498.

Miles, R.E. and Snow, C.C. (1978). *Organizational Strategy, Structure, and Process*, New York: McGraw-Hill Book Company.

Miozzo, M. and Grimshaw, D. (2011). Capabilities of Large Services Outsourcing Firms: The 'outsourcing plus staff transfer model' in EDS and IBM, *Industrial & Corporate Change* **20**(3): 909–940.

Mithas, S., Tafti, A. and Mitchell, W. (2013). How A Firm's Competitive Environment and Digital Strategic Posture Influence Digital Business Strategy, *MIS Quarterly* **37**(2): 511–536.

Monitor Group/Rockefeller Foundation (2011). Job creation through building the field of impact sourcing. Corporate Report by Monitor Consultancy, retrieved from Monitor Group/Rockefeller Foundation [WWW document] http://www.deloitte.com/view/en_US/us/Services/consulting/Strategy-Operations/strategyconsulting/index.htmRootchange.org.

Mudambi, R. and Venzin, M (2010). The Strategic Nexus of Offshoring and Outsourcing Decisions, *Journal of Management Studies* **47**(8): 1510–1533.

Nadkarni, S. and Herrmann, P. (2010). CEO Personality, Strategic Flexibility, and Firm Performance: The case of Indian business process outsourcing industry, *Academy of Management Journal* **53**(5): 1050–1073.

Nagpal, P., Nicolaou, A.I. and Lyytinen, K. (2014). Outsourcing and Market Value of the Firm: Toward a comprehensive model, *Intelligent Systems in Accounting, Finance and Management* **21**(1): 19–38.

Nahapiet, J. and Ghoshal, S. (1998). Social Capital, Intellectual Capital, and the Organizational Advantage, *Academy of Management Review* **23**(2): 242–265.

Narayanan, S, Balasubramanian, S. and Jayashankar, M. (2011). Managing Outsourced Software Projects: An analysis of project performance and customer satisfaction, *Production and Operations Management* **20**(4): 508–521.

Narayanan, S. and Narasimhan, R. (2014). Governance Choice, Sourcing Relationship Characteristics, and Relationship Performance, *Decision Sciences* **45**(4): 717–751.

Ndubisi, N.O (2011). Conflict Handling, Trust and Commitment in Outsourcing Relationship: A Chinese and Indian study, *Industrial Marketing Management* **40**(1): 109–117.

Netemeyer, R.G., Brashear-Alejandro, T. and Boles, J.S. (2004). A Cross-National Model of Job-related Outcomes of Work Role and Family Role Variables: A retail sales context, *Journal of the Academy of marketing Science* **32**(1): 49–60.

Nieto, M. and Rodriguez, A (2011). Offshoring of R&D: Looking abroad to improve innovation performance, *Journal of International Business Studies* **42**(3): 345–361.

O'Regan, N. and Kling, G. (2011). Technology Outsourcing in Manufacturing Small-and Medium-Sized Firms: Another competitive resource?, *R&D Management* **41**(1): 92–105.

Oshri, I. and Van Uhm, B. (2012). A Historical Review of the Information Technology and Business Process Captive Centre Sector, *Journal of Information Technology* **27**(4): 270–284.

Palvia, P., King, R., Xia, W. and Jain Palvia, S (2010). Capability, Quality, and Performance of Offshore IS Vendors: A theoretical framework and empirical investigation, *Decision Sciences* **41**(2): 231–270.

Palvia, S.C., Palvia, P., Xia, W. and King, R. (2011). Critical Issues of IT Outsourcing Vendors in India, *Communications of the AIS* **29**(11): 203–220.

Park, J. and Kim, J.S (2005). The Impact of IS Outsourcing Type on Service Quality and Maintenance Efforts, *Information & Management* **42**(2): 261–274.

Patane, J.R. and Jurison, J. (1994). Is Global Outsourcing Diminishing the Prospects for American Programmers?, *Journal of Systems Management* **45**(6): 6–10.

Pearce, J.A (2014). Why Domestic Outsourcing is Leading America's Reemergence in Global Manufacturing, *Business Horizons* **57**(1): 27–36.

Penfold, C. (2009). Off-shored Services Workers: Labour law and practice in India, *The Economic and Labour Relations Review* **19**(2): 91–106.

Pinnington, A. and Woolcock, P (1995). How Far is IS/IT Outsourcing Enabling New Organizational Structure and Competences?, *International Journal of Information Management* **15**(5): 353–365.

Plugge, A., Bouwman, H. and Molina-Castillo, F.J (2013). Outsourcing Capabilities, Organizational Structure and Performance Quality Monitoring: Toward a fit model, *Information & Management* **50**(6): 275–284.

Poppo, L. and Lacity, M (2006). The Normative Value of Transaction Cost Economics: What managers have learned about TCE principles in the IT context, R. Hirschheim, A. Heinzl and J. Dibbern (eds.) *Information Systems Outsourcing: Enduring themes, new perspectives, and global challenges*, Berlin, Heidelberg, New York: Springer-Verlag, pp. 259–282.

Poppo, L. and Zenger, T (2002). Do Formal Contracts and Relational Governance Function as Substitutes or Complements?, *Strategic Management Journal* **23**(8): 707–725.

Porter, M. and Kramer, M (2006). Strategy and Society: The link between competitive advantage and corporate social responsibility, *Harvard Business Review* **84**(12): 78–92.

Porter, M. and Kramer, M. (2011). Creating Shared Value, *Harvard Business Review* **89**(1/2): 62–77.

Poston, R., Simon, J. and Jain, Radhika. (2010). Client Communication Practices in Managing Relationships with Offshore Vendors of Software Testing Services, *Communications of the AIS* **27**(9): 129–148.

Premuroso, R., Skantz, T. and Bhattacharya, S. (2012). Disclosure of Outsourcing in the Annual Report: Causes & market returns effects, *International Journal of Accounting Information Systems* **13**(4): 382–402.

Prikladnicki, R. and Audy, J.L.N (2012). Managing Global Software Engineering: A comparative analysis of offshore outsourcing and the internal offshoring of software development, *Information Systems Management* **29**(3): 216–232.

Qi, C. and Chau, P (2012). Relationship, Contract and IT Outsourcing Success: Evidence from two descriptive case studies, *Decision Support Systems* **53**(4): 859–869.

Qi, C. and Chau, P.Y. (2013). Investigating the Roles of Interpersonal and Interorganizational Trust in IT Outsourcing Success, *Information Technology & People* **26**(2): 120–145.

Qin, L., Wu, H., Zhang, N. and Li, X (2012). Risk Identification and Conduction Model for Financial Institution IT Outsourcing in China, *Information Technology and Management* **13**(4): 429–443.

Qu, W.G., Oh, W. and Pinsonneault, A. (2010). The Strategic Value of IT Insourcing: An IT-enabled business process perspective, *The Journal of Strategic Information Systems* **19**(2): 96–108.

Qu, W.G., Pinsonneault, A. and Oh, W. (2011). Influence of Industry Characteristics on Information Technology Outsourcing, *Journal of Management Information Systems* **27**(4): 99–128.

Quayle, A., Ashworth, D. and Gillies, A (2013). BS 11000 for Health Commissioning, *Clinical Governance* **18**(1): 18–29.

Rai, A., Keil, M., Hornyak, R. and Wüllenweber, K (2012). Hybrid Relational-Contractual Governance for Business Process Outsourcing, *Journal of Management Information Systems* **29**(2): 213–256.

Rajeev, M. and Vani, B (2009). India's Exports of BPO Services: Understanding strengths, weaknesses, and competitors, *Journal of Services Research* 9(1): 51–67.

Raman, S., Budhwar, P. and Balasubramanian, G. (2007). People Management Issues in Indian KPOs, *Employee Relations* 29(6): 696–710.

Ramchandran, V. and Gopal, A (2010). Managers' Judgments of Performance in IT Services Outsourcing, *Journal of Management Information Systems* 26(4): 181–218.

Redondo-Cano, A. and Canet-Giner, M.T. (2010). Outsourcing Agrochemical Services: Economic or strategic logic?, *Service Business* 4(3): 237–252.

Reeves, M., Zeng, M. and Venjara, V (2015). The Self-Tuning Enterprise: How Alibaba uses algorithmic thinking, *Harvard Business Review* 93(6): 66–75.

Reitzig, M. and Wagner, S. (2010). The Hidden Costs of Outsourcing: Evidence from patent data, *Strategic Management Journal* 31(11): 1183–1201.

Rosa, E., Diekmann, A., Dietz, T. and Jaeger, C. (2010). *Human Footprints on the Global Environment*, MIT Press, Cambridge [WWW document] https://mitpress.mit.edu/sites/default/files/titles/content/9780262512992_sch_0001.pdf, accessed 20 July 2015.

Roses, L.K (2013). Strategic Partnership Building in It Offshore Outsourcing: Institutional elements for a banking ERP system licensing, *Journal of Information Systems and Technology Management* 10(1): 61–80.

Ross, J. and Beath, C. (2006). Sustainable IT Outsourcing: Let enterprise architecture be your guide, *MIS Quarterly Executive* 5(4): 181–192.

Rottman, J. and Lacity, M (2006). Proven Practices for Effectively Offshoring IT Work, *Sloan Management Review* 47(3): 56–63.

Sabherwal, R. (1999). The Role of Trust in Outsourced IS Development Projects, *Communications of the ACM* 42(2): 80–86.

Sako, M (2010). Technology Strategy and Management Outsourcing versus Shared Services, *Communications of the ACM* 53(7): 126–129.

Sakolnakorn, T.P.N (2011). The Good Aspects of Managing an Organization with an Outsourcing and Subcontracting Strategy, *International Journal of Management & Information Systems* 15(3): 11–18.

Salimath, M., Cullen, J. and Umesh, U. (2008). Outsourcing and Performance in Entrepreneurial Firms: Contingent relationships with entrepreneurial configurations, *Decision Sciences* 39(3): 359–381.

Sanders, N., Locke, A., Moore, C. and Autry, C. (2007). A Multidimensional Framework for Understanding Outsourcing Arrangements, *Journal of Supply Chain Management* 43(4): 3–15.

Sarker, S., Sarker, S. and Jana, D. (2010). The Impact of the Nature of Globally Distributed Work Arrangement on Work-Life Conflict and Valence: The Indian GSD professionals' perspective, *European Journal of Information Systems* 19(2): 209–222.

Saunders, C., Gebelt, M. and Hu, Q (1997). Achieving Success in Information Systems Outsourcing, *California Management Review* 39(2): 63–80.

Saxena, K. and Bharadwaj, S (2009). Managing Business Processes Through Outsourcing: A strategic partnership perspective, *Business Process Management Journal* 15(5): 687–715.

Sen, F. and Shiel, M (2006). From Business Process Outsourcing to Knowledge Process Outsourcing: Some issues, *Human Systems Management* 25(2): 145–155.

Sengupta, S (2011). An Exploratory Study on Job and Demographic Attributes Affecting Employee Satisfaction in the Indian BPO Industry, *Strategic Outsourcing: An International Journal* 4(3): 248–273.

Sengupta, S. and Dev, S (2013). What Makes Employees Stay?, *Strategic Outsourcing: An International Journal* 6(3): 258–276.

Sengupta, S. and Gupta, A (2011). Exploring the Dimensions of Attrition in Indian BPOs, *International Journal of Human Resource Management* 23(6): 1259–1288.

Shah Bharadwaj S,. and Saxena, K.B.C (2009). Building Winning Relationships in Business Process Outsourcing Services, *Industrial Management & Data Systems* 109(7): 993–1011.

Sharma, A., Sengupta, S. and Gupta, A (2011). Exploring Risk Dimensions in the Indian Software Industry, *Project Management Journal* 42(5): 78–91.

Sharma, A. and Iyer, G. (2011). Are Pricing Policies an Impediment to the Success of Customer Solutions, *Industrial Marketing Management* 40(5): 723–729.

Shearmur, R. and Doloreux, D (2013). Innovation and Knowledge-Intensive Business Service: The contribution of knowledge-intensive business service to innovation in manufacturing establishments, *Economics of Innovation & New Technology* 22(8): 751–774.

Sheehan, C. and Cooper, B.K (2011). HRM Outsourcing: The impact of organisational size and HRM strategic involvement, *Personnel Review* 40(6): 742–760.

Shih, H., Chiang, Y. and Hsu, C. (2005). Exploring HR Outsourcing and Its Perceived Effectiveness, *International Journal of Business Performance Management* 7(4): 464–482.

Shih, Y. and Lin, W (2011). Effects of the Outsourcing of Information Systems on User Satisfaction: An empirical study among Taiwanese hospitals, *International Journal of Management* **28**(3): 704–715.

Sia, S., Koh, C. and Tan, C (2008). Strategic Maneuvers for Outsourcing Flexibility: An empirical assessment, *Decision Sciences* **39**(3): 407–443.

Sivalogathasan, V.V. and Hashim, A (2013). Changes in Employer-Employee Relationship: Impact of Perceived Organizational Support on Social Exchange of the Outsourcing Industry in Sri Lanka, *Skyline Business Journal* **9**(1): 43–49.

Spithoven, A. and Teirlinck, P. (2015). Internal Capabilities, Network Resources and Appropriation Mechanisms as Determinants of R&D Outsourcing, *Research Policy* **44**(3): 711–725.

Srikanth, K. and Puranam, P. (2011). Integrating Distributed Work: Comparing task design, communication, and tacit coordination mechanisms, *Strategic Management Journal* **32**(8): 849–875.

Srivastava, S.C. and Teo, T.S (2012). Contract Performance in Offshore Systems Development: Role of control mechanisms, *Journal of Management Information Systems* **29**(1): 115–158.

Strassmann, P. (1995). Outsourcing: A game for losers. *Computerworld* 21 August.

Su, N (2013). Internationalization Strategies of Chinese IT Service Suppliers, *MIS Quarterly* **37**(1): 175–200.

Su, N. and Levina, N (2011). Global Multisourcing Strategy: Integrating learning from manufacturing into IT service outsourcing, *IEEE Transactions on Engineering Management* **58**(4): 717–729.

Susarla, A., Barua, A. and Whinston, A (2010a). Multitask Agency, Modular Architecture, and Task Disaggregation in SaaS, *Journal of Management Information Systems* **26**(4): 87–117.

Susarla, A., Subramanyam, R. and Karhade, P (2010b). Contractual Provisions to Mitigate Holdup: Evidence from information technology outsourcing, *Information Systems Research* **21**(1): 37–55.

Svejvig, P (2011). A Successful Enterprise System Re-Implementation against All Odds – A Multisourcing Case Study, *Journal of Information Technology Case and Application Research* **13**(4): 3–31.

Swar, B., Moon, J., Oh, J. and Rhee, C (2012). Determinants of Relationship Quality for IS/IT Outsourcing Success in Public Sector, *Information Systems Frontiers* **14**(2): 457–475.

Tajdini, S. and Nazari, M. (2012). IS Outsourcing Decision: A quantitative approach, *International Journal of Business and Management* **7**(2): 113–129.

Tambe, P. and Hitt, L. (2010). How Offshoring Affects IT Workers, *Communications of the ACM* **53**(10): 62–70.

Tate, W., Ellram, L. and Brown, S (2009). Offshore Outsourcing of Services: A stakeholder perspective, *Journal of Service Research* **12**(1): 56–72.

Tate, W. and Ellram, L (2009). Offshore Outsourcing: A managerial framework, *Journal of Business and Industrial Management* **24**(3/4): 256–268.

Tate, W.L. and Ellram, L.M (2012). Service Supply Management Structure in Offshore Outsourcing, *Journal of Supply Chain Management* **48**(4): 8–29.

Teo, T.S. and Bhattacherjee, A (2014). Knowledge Transfer and Utilization in IT Outsourcing Partnerships: A preliminary model of antecedents and outcomes, *Information & Management* **51**(2): 177–186.

Thompson, D. (2015). A World Without Work, *The Atlantic Monthly* **316**(1): 51–61.

Tiwana, A (2010). Systems Development Ambidexterity: Explaining the complementary and substitutive roles of formal and informal controls, *Journal of Management Information Systems* **27**(2): 87–126.

Uriona-Maldonado, M., De Souza, L.L.C. and Varvakis, G. (2010). Focus on Practice Service Process Innovation in The Brazilian Electric Energy Sector, *Service Business* **4**(1): 77–88.

Veltri, N.F., Saunders, C.S. and Kavan, C.B (2008). Information Systems Backsourcing: Correcting problems and responding to opportunities, *California Management Review* **51**(1): 50–76.

Ventovuori, T. and Lehtonen, T (2006). Alternative Models for the Management of FM Services, *Journal of Corporate Real Estate* **8**(2): 73–90.

Verner, J.M. and Abdullah, L.M (2012). Exploratory Case Study Research: Outsourced project failure, *Information and Software Technology* **54**(8): 866–886.

Vitasek, K. and Manrodt, K (2012). Vested Outsourcing: A flexible framework for collaborative Outsourcing, *Strategic Outsourcing: An International Journal* **5**(1): 4–14.

Vivek, S., Banwet, D. and Shankar, R (2008). Analysis of Interactions Among Core, Transaction, and Relationship-Specific Investments: The case of offshoring, *Journal of Operations Management* **26**(2): 180–197.

Wahrenburg, M., Hackethal, A., Friedrich, L. and Gellrich, T (2006). Strategic Decisions Regarding the Vertical Integration of Human Resource Organizations: Evidence for an integrated HR model for the financial services and non-financial services industry in Germany, Austria and Switzerland, *International Journal of Human Resource Management* **17**(10): 1726–1771.

Weeks, M.R. and Thomason, S (2011). An Exploratory Assessment of the Linkages Between HRM Practices, Absorptive Capacity, and Innovation in Outsourcing Relationships, *International Journal of Innovation Management* **15**(2): 303–334.

Weigelt, C. and Sarkar, M (2012). Performance Implications of Outsourcing for Technological Innovations: Managing the efficiency and adaptability trade-off, *Strategic Management Journal* **33**(2): 189–216.

Whitaker, J., Mithas, S. and Krishnan, M.S (2010). Organizational Learning and Capabilities for Onshore and Offshore Business Process Outsourcing, *Journal of Management Information Systems* **27**(3): 11–42.

Whitley, E. and Willcocks, L. (2011). Achieving Step-Change in Outsourcing Maturity: Toward collaborative innovation, *MIS Quarterly Executive* **10**(3): 95–107.

Whitten, D. and Leidner, D (2006). Bringing IT Back: An analysis of the decision to backsource or switch vendors, *Decision Sciences* **37**(4): 605–621.

Wickramasinghe, V (2010). Impact of Time Demands of Work on Job Satisfaction and Turnover Intention, *Strategic Outsourcing: An International Journal* **3**(3): 246–255.

Wiener, M. and Saunders, C. (2014a). Forced Coopetition in IT Multi-Sourcing, *The Journal of Strategic Information Systems* **23**(3): 210–225.

Wiener, M. and Saunders, C.S (2014b). Who is the Favored Bride? Challenges in Switching to a Multi-vendor Offshoring Strategy, R. Hirschheim, A. Heinzl and J. Dibbern (eds.) *Information Systems Outsourcing*, Berlin, Heidelberg: Springer, pp. 289–312.

Willcocks, L., Hindle, J., Feeny, D. and Lacity, M (2004). Information Technology and Business Process Outsourcing: The knowledge potential, *Journal of Information Systems Management* **21**(3): 7–15.

Willcocks, L.P. and Griffiths, C (2010). The Crucial Role of Middle Management in Outsourcing, *MIS Quarterly Executive* **9**(3): 177–193.

Williamson, O (1975). *Markets and Hierarchies: Analysis and antitrust implications*, New York: Free Press.

Williamson, O (1976). Franchise Bidding for Natural Monopolies in General and with Resoect to CAVT, *Bell Journal of Economics*. **XXVI**(3): 497–540.

Williamson, O (1991). Comparative Economic Organization: The analysis of discrete structural alternatives, *Administrative Science Quarterly* **36**(2): 269–296.

Wullenweber, K., Beimborn, D., Weitzel, T. and Konig, W (2008). The Impact of Process Standardization on Business Process Outsourcing Success, *Information Systems Frontiers* **10**(2): 211–224.

Zimmermann, A. and Ravishankar, M.N (2014). Knowledge Transfer in IT Offshoring Relationships: The roles of social capital, efficacy and outcome expectations, *Information Systems Journal* **24**(2): 167–202.

Dr. Mary Lacity is a curators' professor of Information Systems and an International Business Fellow at the University of Missouri-St. Louis. She is a Senior Editor at *MIS Quarterly Executive*, coeditor of the *Palgrave Series: Work, Technology, and Globalization*, and on the Editorial Boards for *Journal of Information Technology*, *MIS Quarterly Executive*, *IEEE Transactions on Engineering Management*, *Journal of Strategic Information Systems*, and *Strategic Outsourcing: An International Journal*. She was inducted into the IAOP's Outsourcing Hall of Fame in 2014, one of only three academics to ever be inducted. She has published 24 books, including *Nine Keys to World-class Business Process Outsourcing* (Bloomsbury Publishing, London, 2015; coauthor Leslie Willcocks) and *The Rise of Legal Services Outsourcing* (Bloomsbury Publishing, London, 2014; coauthors Leslie Willcocks and Andrew Burgess). Her publications have appeared in the *Harvard Business Review, Sloan Management Review, MIS Quarterly, IEEE Computer, Communications of the ACM*, and many other academic and practitioner outlets. She was Program Cochair for ICIS, 2010.

Dr. Shaji A. Khan is an assistant professor of Information Systems, in the College of Business, University of Missouri-St. Louis. He has published in journals such as the *Journal of Business Research, Journal of Strategic Information Systems, Journal of Information Technology, Strategic Outsourcing an International Journal, International Journal of Entrepreneurship and Innovation, Journal of Developmental Entrepreneurship*, and *Journal of Small Business Management*. He has also presented papers at national academic conferences, authored book chapters, and produced practitioner-oriented research and industry reports. His research interests include offshoring of business services, innovation and entrepreneurship, and management of information technology and information security in high-reliability environments. He is currently developing cybersecurity programs at the University of Missouri-St. Louis and teaches in the areas of data networking and information security.

Dr. Aihua Yan is a visiting professor at City University of Hong Kong. She has published articles in *Journal of Information Technology, Information Systems Frontiers* and *International Conference of Information Systems*. She won Best Paper award in 2015 for 'How Capabilities and Governance Mechanisms Influence Outsourcing Performance' at The First Annual IAOP North American Outsourcing Research Workshop, Desert Ridge Arizona.

Printed in the United States
By Bookmasters